Buffalo Bill's Story of the Wild West

Buffalo Bill's Story of the Wild West

FALL RIVER PRESS

New York

FALL RIVER PRESS

New York

An Imprint of Sterling Publishing
387 Park Avenue South
New York, NY 10016

This 2013 edition published by Fall River Press.

Originally published by Historical Publishing Company in 1888 as
Story of the Wild West and Campfire Chats.

Cover image digital restoration by Paul Girard

ISBN 978-1-4351-4587-0

Distributed in Canada by Sterling Publishing
c/o Canadian Manda Group, 165 Dufferin Street
Toronto, Ontario, Canada M6K 3H6
Distributed in the United Kingdom by GMC Distribution Services
Castle Place, 166 High Street, Lewes, East Sussex, England BN7 1XU
Distributed in Australia by Capricorn Link (Australia) Pty. Ltd.
P.O. Box 704, Windsor, NSW 2756, Australia

For information about custom editions, special sales, and premium and corporate purchases,
please contact Sterling Special Sales at 800-805-5489 or specialsales@sterlingpublishing.com.

Manufactured in the United States of America

2 4 6 8 10 9 7 5 3 1

www.sterlingpublishing.com

PREFACE

The task of writing the lives of the three greatest pioneers of western settlement has been assumed by me with no little diffidence, surrounded as the work has been with many hard disadvantages, and obstacles of no ordinary character. Chief of these is the disadvantage of poor literary qualification, as the opportunities for acquiring an education were denied me, except such as I could obtain by unaided endeavors and a favorable association with refined persons in latter years. The obstacles of which I complain are found in the confusion of information growing out of the fact that the several biographers of Boone, Crockett and Carson have generally made quite as much use of fiction as of actual, verified incident in making up their history of these three prominent characters. The idle stories thus incorporated in their work being left so long uncontradicted have become an almost inseparable part of frontier history, since few records are accessible, or were ever made, from which a truthful account of the valorous deeds and eventful lives of these heroes may be obtained. The work thus submitted, however, has been conscientiously performed, and the care exercised, as well as the information I have collected in the course of many years, lead me to believe that the facts are here presented as nearly free from exaggeration as it is possible to give them, however great may be the study, investigation and care devoted to the work.

The life of Daniel Boone is a particularly difficult one to write. He lived at a time and in a community that permitted of little attention to the recording of events, and thus the date, and even place of his birth, is made a matter for controversy. Nor were really valorous deeds accounted as worthy of perpetuation, since the times were such as compelled every man to be a hero—a fighter ready to meet on even or uneven ground the wily savage that lurked about each frontier cabin seeking a vantage stroke to arrest the progress of settlement by merciless massacre. The modesty imbued in his nature in earlier years was little changed even by the plaudits of his admiring countrymen, when he was recognized as a leading instrument in the opening up and settlement of the Great West. The caution necessary when surrounded by savage foes made of Boone a curiously quiet man, little given to speech, and less inclined to speak of the incidents of his strangely eventful life. My chief reliance for information concerning him has, therefore, been authenticated State annals, verified by circumstances and incontestable statements of his descendants interested in preserving a truthful, though necessarily fragmentary, record of this distinguished man. It has been my good fortune, as a partial recompense for the time expended in running down idle stories concerning adventures he is said to have participated in, to meet some half a dozen pioneers of Missouri who had been intimate neighbors and friends of Boone, and to whom he related many incidents of great historical interest that I have been permitted to record for what I believe is the first time.

The life of Crockett is accessible in an elaborate work written by his own hand, though this autobiography has been furbished up and garnished with not a few unsubstantial tales that, despite their frequent exposure, still cling tenaciously to nearly all his biographies, but which I have eliminated, or repeated only to deny.

Carson's character was in more than one respect enigmatic, and many of the difficulties encountered in preparing an authentic life of Boone are found interposing between the biographer and Carson. Modesty is a becoming trait, except when it serves to obscure important incidents in the life of a justly historic personage, and in Carson this obstacle to a proper knowledge of his career is particularly conspicuous. It was my fortunate privilege to enjoy a personal acquaintance with Carson, but this intimacy gave me little advantage, for he seldom spoke of his own deeds, though I hardly think he was so different from other men as to be wholly indifferent to praise. Indeed, his desire for promotion, as explained in his biography, proves that he was susceptible of the pride that grows on exaltation.

A considerable part of Carson's life was spent in the service of the Government, and from the departmental records I have therefore extracted much of the information given herein concerning him, and which I find frequently conflicts with the statements of those who in writing his life have made facts subservient to wild exaggeration, just as many romancers have done while soberly pretending to record the incidents in my own life. Many of those who were Carson's intimates, and who were his comrades in service in the far West, were also friends of mine, and from them I gathered much reliable information concerning his adventures that I treasured up, so to speak, until this opportunity was afforded to give them currency.

While writing principally biographically, I have sought to describe that great general movement westward—that irresistible wave of emigration which, arrested for a time by the Alleghenies, rose until at last it broke over and spread away across mountain, stream and plain, leaving States in its wake, until stopped by the shores of the Pacific.

The evolution of government and of civilization, and the adaptation of one to the other, are interesting to the student of history; but particularly fascinating is the story of the reclamation of the Great West and the supplanting of the wild savages that from primeval days were lords of the country but are now become wards of the Government, whose guardianship they were forced to recognize. This story is one well calculated to inspire a feeling of pride even in the breasts of those whose sentimentality impels to commiserate the hard lot of the poor Indian; for, rising above the formerly neglected prairies of the West are innumerable monuments of thrift, industry, intelligence, and all the contributory comforts and luxuries of a peaceful and God-fearing civilization; those evidences that proclaim to a wondering world the march of the Anglo-Saxon race towards the attainment of perfect citizenship and liberal, free and stable government.

For the small part I have taken in redeeming the West from savagery, I am indebted to circumstances rather than to a natural, inborn inclination for the strifes inseparable from the life I was almost forced to choose. But to especially good fortune must I make my acknowledgments, which protected me or preserved my life a hundred times when the very hand of vengeful fate appeared to lower its grasp above my head, and hope seemed a mockery that I had turned my back upon. Good fortune has also stood ever responsive to my call since I first came before the public, and to the generous American and English peoples, as well as to kind fortune, I here pour out a full measure of profound thanks and hearty appreciation, and shall hold them gratefully in my memory as a remembrance of old friends, until the drum taps "lights out" at the close of the evening of my eventful life.

Sincerely yours,

W.H. CODY

Buffalo Bill

CONTENTS

LIFE OF DANIEL BOONE

LIFE OF DAVY CROCKETT

LIFE OF KIT CARSON

AUTOBIOGRAPHY OF BUFFALO BILL

LIST OF ILLUSTRATIONS

Life of
Daniel Boone

DANIEL BOONE
(from the Harding painting)

CHAPTER I

Less than one hundred and fifty years ago, and within the age of four generations, America was distinctively the home of the Indian; only a narrow strip of land bordering the Atlantic had been reclaimed to civilization, and even this small section possessed very few of the comforts of the period, as compared with the mother country and nations of Europe. Agriculture was little thought of, beyond the compass of a garden-patch; the trades were few, and carried on chiefly by itinerant jobbers, who went from house to house, carrying their kits of tools, to perform such work as might be offered. There was little incentive to the artisan, but less to the agriculturist. Prowling bands of hostile Indians were a constant menace to material accumulations, so that settlers were compelled, for mutual protection, to conduct their several enterprises conjointly and thus live in a condition of semi-communism, which prevented, in large measure, the extension of settlements and the redemption of territory from the savages. But this adverse influence was largely compensated for by the fact that while money was scarce, fur-bearing animals were plentiful, and while dangers and difficulties were very great, these very conditions excited that innate rugged nature which slumbers in the breasts of those peacefully situated, and made heroes out of what would have been otherwise an effeminate people. The common currency of the times was peltries and the almost invariable food of the early settlers was meat of wild animals, victims of the chase, rifle or trap. Association with dangerous surrounding soon destroyed all feelings of fear, as it invariably does. A soldier trembles more before the battle than when in the thickest of the fight; so is it only upon occasions of greatest peril that heroes have their birth. Necessity made these pioneers familiar with the rifle and familiarity with this best friend to the settler in a primeval wilderness made them reckless of whatever adventure might occur. The evolution, so to speak, of brave men in the wilds of the Atlantic slope was as natural as a metamorphosis in the insect world, but their valorous deeds excite our admiration none the less, and no patriot will ever tire of reading the wonderful stories and marvelous adventures of those strong-hearted men who blazed out the first highways in the reclamation and settlement of our own God blessed country; and in rehearsing the sacrifices which they made, every true American will feel for them the same pride as for the great soldiers whose victories have made our institutions imperishable.

Birth of Daniel Boone

Of the many heroes produced under the influences described, none are more deservedly popular than Daniel Boone. This really great man was a hero not only because of a reckless spirit cast upon the flood-tide of fortuitous circumstances, and borne to the goal of lucky results. Boone was not so reckless as many even well-read persons suppose; indeed, so far from being a Hotspur, he was brave only with calculating cautiousness, and this trait of his character is most praiseworthy, because it was by an exercise of this rare combination that he was able to accomplish so much for the good of his country, as we shall hereafter see.

The immediate ancestors of Daniel Boone formed a small settlement in England near Exeter, where they nearly all followed a pastoral life. George Boone emigrated to America with his wife, Mary, in 1717, bringing with them eleven children, but very few other goods, for the family was extremely poor. Of the nine sons of George Boone the names of only three are preserved in history, viz.: James, John and Squire, the latter of whom became the father of Daniel, our hero.

George Boone settled in what is now Berk's County, Pennsylvania, where he bartered for a tract of land and founded a small settlement which, in honor of his birthplace, he called Exeter. It is also related, though with no better authority than a hazy tradition, that he also pre-empted the ground on which Georgetown, in the District of Columbia, is situated, and that he located the town and gave to it his own name, all of which is extremely doubtful.

Squire Boone married, in Pennsylvania, though in what year no record has been found to show, Mary Morgan. It is known, however, that he had seven sons and four daughters, as follows: Daniel, James, Squire, Edward, Jonathan, George and Samuel, and Mary, Sarah, Hannah and Elizabeth. Squire Boone seems to have remained on the original estate at Exeter, in Pennsylvania, and it was here that Daniel was born, though the exact date is not definitely known. Daniel's uncle, James, who was a school-master, left a memorandum in a book to the effect that Daniel was born July 14th, 1732. There are three other authorities, however, that fix upon as many different dates, two claiming that his birth occurred in February, 1735, and another fixing the event some time in 1746. Considering the little learning, and especially the negligence in keeping family records in those early days, it is not surprising that the date of Daniel's birth is uncertain; besides, an approximate date is all that was expected to be known of a pioneer.

Daniel's First Adventure

Daniel grew to manhood's estate on the farm where he was born and received no more advantages than were accorded to other poor boys of his neighborhood. Exeter was a very small settlement at the time, on what was then the frontier. Philadelphia had been founded by William Penn in 1682, and at the time of Boone's birth was a city of nearly 10,000 souls, but it had no trade with the interior, and was sustained solely by its shipping interest, which was considerable. Exeter was about sixty miles from Philadelphia, in what is now Buck's County, but of so unimportant a character that the settlement had hardly been heard of by the people of Philadelphia, nor were the settlers of the Boone district wiser concerning the first city of their State, each remaining in comparatively blissful ignorance of the other, their interests being so distinct.

Of his youth we know very little, chiefly from the fact that his early life was punctuated with few startling periods that were worth preserving in local history or tradition. It is related of him, however, that on one occasion, during his boyhood, while out hunting with some of his youthful companions, he and his party came suddenly upon a panther that viciously disputed their way. Its growls and fierce demonstrations

YOUNG BOONE'S FIRST DANGEROUS ADVENTURE

put the other boys to a quick retreat, but Daniel, with rare courage, boldly stood his ground, and with that calm self-possession which ever after characterized him, he brought his small flint-lock squirrel rifle to his shoulder and sent a bullet through the heart of the animal. This adventure must have occurred at a time before he had reached his teens, because the fact of killing a panther in those days was an incident so commonplace that it would hardly have been preserved in tradition as evidence of Boone's valor had he been more than a youth.

The praise which he received for having slain a panther inspired Boone to loftier deeds. Henceforth we find him, youth as he was, pursuing the life of a hunter. His rifle becomes his constant companion, and generally his only one. He followed up the Schuylkill where ducks and better game were to be found in abundance. Along its course he soon began trapping with considerable success, and so fond of the sport was he that before he was fifteen years of age he abandoned his home entirely and made a permanent camp in the wilderness.

The same adventurous spirit has moved thousands of other boys, but to this love for wild life and sports young Boone added that extremely rare trait which may be denominated persistency of purpose, fortified with a willingness to suffer discomforts of body when it brought satisfaction of mind.

In a rugged fastness, remote from any house, Daniel chose to make his home, where the inclination of his fancy might revel undisturbed by association with any of his race. Accordingly, without revealing even to his mother or father his intention, he left home as if upon his regular daily hunt, and after a journey of three days along the Schuylkill he found a dense copse, where the surroundings were so wild that he reckoned the retreat secure from discovery, and here he set to work to prepare a shelter. With great diligence he gathered brush and piled it about a space between two large stones, and made a covering of turf and leaves, leaving a hole at the top for smoke to escape. In this rude place he lived for many days, subsisting off the game that he killed and, though isolated from companionship save of rifle and dog, was happier than a lord in his buttressed and well lardered castle. His absence from home for so long a time excited the fears of his father and neighbors, who set out in quest of him with many misgivings. It was a week before they happened upon the well covered retreat of the youthful hermit, nor would they have found it, perhaps, at all, had not the smoke from his rude hovel directed them in the search.

Daniel was forced, very much against his will, to return home with his father, and was soon afterwards placed under the tuition of an elderly Irish school-master. Peck, and other of Boone's biographers relate that Daniel had not attended school many days before an incident occurred that resulted in his expulsion. The story, which is no doubt apocryphal, is to the effect that the teacher had a very strong appetite for whisky, which he contrived to clandestinely gratify by keeping a bottle hidden in the adjoining woods and visiting it when the scholars were at their classes under the monitorship of an elder. By chance young Boone found the well filled bottle, and, in a spirit of mischievousness, procured some ipecac with which he seasoned the whisky so highly that the next draught the teacher took from it made him violently ill. Investigation followed, which led to Daniel's conviction and the verdict of a sound thrashing. When the teacher undertook to apply the punishment, however, young Boone objected and a fight was the result, in which the teacher received the butt end of the penalty. This story, which I prefer to give thus briefly, is most probably a pure creation of some writer who had run short of matter and needed the sauce of a joke to spice the dull detail of history. The character of Daniel Boone, as learned in the light of later events, was never that of a brawler, but on the other hand, in his youth he was diffident, peaceable and obedient, nor did he change greatly in after life. In desperate situations he was wonderfully courageous, but never boastful or a bully, as a belief in such a story would influence us to believe.

WESTWARD, THE MARCH
OF CIVILIZATION

The Boone Family Remove to North Carolina

Before Daniel had reached his majority, and probably about the year 1750 or '51, Squire Boone removed from Exeter to a spot on Yadkin River, North Carolina, about ten miles from the present town of Wilkesborough, in what is now Wilkes County, where he followed hunting, and farming on a small scale. His life in this new location was so uneventful that little is preserved concerning either himself or his son Daniel. From the circumstance of this removal, however, many historians have been led into the error of declaring that Daniel was born in the State of North Carolina, a mistake that has even been repeated by encyclopedia writers.

How long Daniel lived with his father on the Yadkin River it has not been given later generations to know, but history records the fact that it was in this new home he first met Rebecca Bryan, possibly a neighbor's daughter, whom he married and afterwards raised up nine children by her, viz.: James (who it is said was born in 1756), Israel, Nathan, Daniel and Jesse; and Rebecca, Susan, Lavinia and Jemima. Five years after his marriage Daniel was still living on the Yadkin, following the same pursuits as his father, hunting, trapping and cultivating a garden-patch. How much longer he remained in this peaceful home no record is left to show, but it was during the seven years following 1752 that the most stirring scenes ever witnessed in Virginia occurred, and of which it is hardly supposed that Daniel was an uninterested spectator. The strife to which I refer was the war between the English and French, which, though ostensibly waged over the possession of Canada, seriously affected all the English settlements along the coast, and notably those in Virginia. But more disturbing than this was what is known in history as the Cherokee War, which brought massacre and ruin into the homes of the Carolinians, and no doubt developed in Boone the energies and heroic qualities that had remained latent in him until the occasion was ripe for their manifestation. Henceforth we will have to deal with Boone as a central figure in the exploration of the great west, that began to open up to the whites while in pursuit of fleeing savages.

CHAPTER II

Explorations in the West

History is still very meager in its records of Boone's life for ten years after the close of the Cherokee War—1759. Several scraps, recovered from books and letters, lead to the inference that he began his journey westward in 1771; but Mr. Ramsey, who is an excellent authority, in his *Annals of Tennessee* fixes the date of Boone's first trip west of the Appalachian range at 1760, which, for more than one reason, appears rect. The defeat of the Cherokees, and their retreat westward, would natural, the hardy pioneer adventurers in that direction, especially as glowing accounts of wonderful fertility of the soil, abundance of game, and vast mineral wealth of that di trict lying beyond the mountains had been current in the sparse settlements of North Carolina and Virginia even before the uprising of the Cherokees. Before this time several bold spirits had penetrated the western wilderness and brought back to the east wonderful descriptions of the country they had visited. A trader from Virginia, named Dougherty, had been among the Cherokees as early as 1690, and spent several years trading with different tribes. Adair, of South Carolina, had made a considerable tour of the southwest in 1730, and upon returning to his home wrote a very flattering account of the country, which was afterwards published in England. In 1740 several traders made a journey, with a Mr. Vaughan as guide, as far west as northern Alabama, from whence they returned to Charleston with a large quantity of peltries which they sold at an immense profit. In 1748 Dr. Thomas Walker, of Virginia, with seven companions made a tour of exploration to the west. They passed through a depression in a range of mountains to which they gave the name of Cumberland Gap, and soon afterwards came to a stream of water which they called Cumberland River, all in honor of England's prime minister, then the Duke of Cumberland. As early as 1754 there were six families living on the banks of the upper Ohio River, which was then known as the Wabash, but very soon after a party of Indians made a sortie on the pioneers and massacred seven of the number while the remainder fled under cover of the night to the fastnesses of the mountains and afterwards made their way back to the interior of Virginia.

In 1760 Dr. Walker made a second journey, at the head of a well equipped company of men, and is supposed to have penetrated as far west as central Kentucky. He was followed a year later by a party of nineteen hunters and traders, under the leadership of a man named Wallen, who conducted them to what is now known as Carter's Valley, in Hawkins County, Tennessee. Says Mr. Ramsey: "At the head of one of the companies that visited the west this year (1761), came Daniel Boone, from the Yadkin, in North Carolina, and traded with them as low as the place where Abingdon now stands, and there left them.

"This is the first time the advent of Daniel Boone to the western wilds has been mentioned by historians, or by the several biographers of that distinguished pioneer and hunter. There is reason, however, to believe that he had hunted upon Watauga earlier."

Mr. Ramsey, in proof of his assertion regarding the time when Boone first visited Kentucky, copies the following inscription which a few years ago was still to be

ech tree that stood within sight of the present stage road between
ntsville, Tennessee:

to be cor-
attract
the

D. Boon

A. BAR   On

In   ThE   Tree

YEAR

1760

"Boone was eighty-six years old when he died, which was September, 1820. He
was thus twenty-six years old when the inscription was made. When he left the company of hunters in 1761, as mentioned above by Haywood, it is probable that he did
so revisit the theater of a former hunt upon the creek that still bears his name, and
where his camp is still pointed out near its banks. It is not improbable, indeed, that he
belonged to, or accompanied, the party of Doctor Walker, on his first, or certainly on
his second, tour of exploration in 1760. The inscription is sufficient authority, as this
writer conceives, to date the arrival of Boone in Tennessee as early as its date, 1760,
thus preceding the permanent settlement of the country nearly ten years."

In the autobiography of Boone, dictated to John Folsom, and published in 1784,
occurs the following: "It was on the first of May, in the year 1769, that I resigned
my domestic happiness for a time, and left my peaceable habitation on the Yadkin
River, in North Carolina, to wander through the wilderness of America, in quest of
the country of Kentucky, in company with John Finley, John Stuart, Joseph Holden,
James Monay, and William Cool," etc.

The date of his first visit to Kentucky, therefore, it is impossible to fix, but notwithstanding this explicit declaration of the time, apparently by Boone himself,
I believe the preponderance of evidence is in favor of the earlier date (1760).

The Happy Hunting Ground of Kentucky

The man Finley, mentioned above, was an ardent sportsman and a successful trader.
He had made two trips to the far west and came into Boone's settlement with such
thrilling and captivating descriptions of the beautiful country and abounding game in
the far west that he easily enlisted the interest of Boone and four others who accepted
him as guide, and together the six set out on their perilous journey. Through dense
coverts, where night never lifted her veil, and over giant hills where daylight perpetually
lingered, traveled the adventurous party. Game of great variety, on wing and feet, flitted

PERILS OF EARLY SETTLEMENT IN THE WEST

by, or paused at the rifle's crack, to provide an ever bounteous feast. Every tree might shield an enemy, every pathway might lead to ambush, but with strong hearts the six marched on, fording creeks and rafting over larger streams, until at last, gaining a peak on the Cumberland range, the first view of Kentucky burst upon the enraptured vision of Boone. There at their feet flowed the headwaters of the Kentucky River, through delightful vales and fertile valleys filled with grazing buffalo and deer, that scarcely

FINLEY IN THE FAR WEST

noticed this invasion of their domain, thinking, perhaps, of the prodigality of nature, and of the plenty there was to share with any other creature that might choose to dwell in so gorgeous a clime. The sound of a gun had not echoed through this fair section, nor had a hunter's knife drawn blood from the throat or heart of any animal upon this heaven-blessed vale. All was innocence, all was happiness in this realm of contentment.

In this beautiful locality the six hunters prepared a rude habitation by piling up logs to a height of ten feet about a space some fifteen feet square, and then making a roof of the bark stripped from linden trees, which afforded partial protection from rain and was a complete shelter from the heavy dews. Here the party lived and hunted until after Christmas, spending a most enjoyable time, since they were adapted by nature to an appreciation of this most free and pleasurable existence.

During the several months of their stay in this first chosen locality they saw no Indians, though the grounds were occasionally hunted over by the Shawnees, Chickasaws and Cherokees. The land at this time was a portion of Virginia, but was soon after, in 1770, acquired by treaty from the Indians. Two years previously the Iroquois had ceded to Great Britain all their claims to the land lying south of the Ohio, so that the portion on which Boone and his companions were hunting was a neutral ground, so to speak, since neither hut nor wigwam had been erected on it.

The very fact of the district being neutral led to its designation as the "dark and bloody ground," for many different tribes came here to hunt and frequently fell into collisions of the most desperate and bloody character. The Indians called the country *Kentucky*, which means "at the head of a river," because the greatest abundance of game was then found in the district between what is now known as Big Sandy river, and the headwaters of the Tennessee, which was east of the present eastern line of Kentucky.

Capture of Boone by the Indians

Towards the early part of 1761 Daniel Boone and John Stuart left the encampment for a hunt further up the country and with the intention of exploring the district towards the Ohio. They journeyed for several days until they reached the banks of the Kentucky River where they were suddenly set upon by a band of savages and disarmed before being able to raise a hand in defense. The surprise was complete, because up to this time no Indians had been seen nor had any signs been met with to excite suspicion that hostiles were in the neighborhood.

Though his captivity was Boone's first experience with Indians, he had learned enough of the character of his captors, by hearing stories of their ferocity related about the firesides of every pioneer family, to admonish him of the perilous position he now occupied. Instead, therefore, of giving way to depression, or of making any open demonstration to arouse the special vigilance or animosity of the Indians,

CAPTURE OF BOONE AND STUART

he philosophically adapted himself to his new condition by appearing indifferent to the fate that might be meted out to him. Nothing so quickly or surely wins the good opinion of an Indian as bravery, just as cowardice will certainly excite his hatred, and jeopardize the life of his captive. Boone was, therefore, held rather as a hostage than as a captive, and as he manifested a desire to participate in the sports and hunts of his enemies they soon held him in such regard that they relaxed much of their former restraint and thus prepared the way to his liberty.

Several days after his captivity Boone, with his fellow-prisoner, was taken to a thick cane brake and made to assist in preparing an encampment, in which work they diligently applied themselves. Toward the middle watch of the night Boone, who had scarcely closed his eyes for watching the first favorable means for escape, perceived that all his captors were soundly sleeping, and seizing the opportunity quickly aroused Stuart and bidding him follow stole out into the thicket with such silence that none of the Indians were awakened. The two traveled rapidly during the remainder of the night, and also the following day, retreating in the direction of where their camp lay until at length they reached the spot. But imagine their surprise when, instead of being met by their glad companions, they found the camp deserted and nothing to mark the place but a few smoldering logs. What had become of Finley, Holden, Monay and Cool? There were no signs of a struggle, nor evidence of either massacre or retreat, and yet there were burning logs which might have been the funeral pyre of the four brave men, who had thus disappeared. Singular to relate, nothing whatever was ever afterwards learned concerning the fate of the four. Had they abandoned the camp and returned to their homes in North Carolina some record would have been left to this effect; and had they been massacred the fact would doubtless have been circulated among the Indian tribes and thus finally have reached the ears of some white settler, as such atrocities almost invariably did, but true it is that the fate of the four men was never learned and remains a profound mystery to this day.

CHAPTER III

Alone in the Wilderness

Boone and Stuart were now alone in the dark and bloody wilderness, with only a small supply of ammunition and conscious of the great danger that beset them on every side. They built a log house, such as they could erect by the aid of two hatchets carried always with them, and protected it as best they could by packing the interstices between the logs with hoop-pole "chinken" plastered with mud, by which means the hut was fairly impervious to wind, snow and rain, while it served as an admirable defense in case of attack. Here they lived, subsisting on the game they killed, until some time in February when a delightful surprise was given them in the appearance of Squire Boone, one of Daniel's brothers, accompanied by another white man, whose name has not been preserved. The long absence, without tidings, of Daniel Boone had caused his family such alarm that they dispatched Squire in search of him, who, guided by good fortune came directly upon his long-lost brother after a journey of nearly one month. The meeting was a joyful one, as we may well believe, not only because the lost was found, and glad news from his family was thus brought to the great hunter, but also because Squire brought with him a goodly supply of ammunition, the value of which to Boone was positively inestimable. Thus encouraged and provided the party made some improvement to their winter quarters, which greatly increased its comforts, and then began hunting as a business, intending to collect a large number of peltries for marketing in the following spring.

Death of Stuart at the Hands of the Indians

Scarcely a week had passed after the joyful meeting described when a distressing misfortune befell the party, which materially altered its plans and changed rejoicings to deepest mourning. Daniel Boone and Stuart were out on a hunt together, leaving

ESCAPE OF BOONE AND DEATH OF STUART
(from the Harding painting)

Squire and his companion at the camp dressing skins, least suspecting the proximity of hostile Indians, for no evidence of any had been seen for more than a month, besides Boone knew that it was a very unusual thing for Indians to either hunt or forage during winter time. But his fancied security was delusive, for, without warning, suddenly a volley of shots poured out of a thick copse of cane and Stuart fell mortally wounded only to be scalped a moment afterward. Boone, more fortunate than his companion, escaped the fire of the Indians, and being favored by a dense brake on his right plunged into it and contrived to make good his escape by fleeing back to the camp, where the Indians were afraid to attack him. Three days after this tragic incident, the man who had accompanied Squire Boone from North Carolina went out of camp early in the morning, for what purpose is not known, and was never afterwards seen again, though a skeleton was found some months afterwards in a swamp a few miles from the camp that was supposed to be his. The poor fellow had doubtless become deranged by the horrible death of Stuart, and reflecting on the perils that surrounded him, probably wandered away only to fall a victim to the Indians or some wild animal.

Boone Left Alone in the Wilderness

Two of their number having been rudely snatched away by a cruel fate, and the party thus reduced to the two brothers, Daniel and Squire Boone, the plans which had been adopted with so much expectation were necessarily abandoned, and the two were for a time oppressed with a sense of their great misfortune and utter loneliness. The remainder of the winter was spent without further interruption from the Indians, but with feelings of more or less despondency. When spring arrived very few peltries had been collected, certainly not enough to justify a special trip to the nearest market, five hundred miles distant, but the store of ammunition had again run so low that a new supply must be obtained, as their very lives depended upon it. After many suggestions it was at length determined between the two that Squire should return to North Carolina for supplies while Daniel would remain at the cabin to defend the place during his brother's absence. Accordingly, Squire bade Daniel good-bye on the 1st day of May 1761, and set out for home, which he reached without serious adventure early in June.

In this period of utter isolation Daniel endeavored to relieve the loneliness from which he suffered by exploring the country between the Kentucky and Green Rivers. He was absent from the camp more than a month, and when he at length returned it was to find that the cabin and its contents had been burned. It would appear, therefore, that the desire which prompted him to make a journey to the southwest was a providential incentive to save his life, for had he been attacked in the cabin by a band of Indians he must certainly have perished at their hands.

Daniel Boone remained in the vicinity of his old camp until the 27th of July when his brother Squire returned with two horses and a large supply of ammunition, cooking utensils and other needful articles, and also with the pleasing news that Daniel's family was in good health and easy circumstances. The burned cabin and evidences of hostile Indians induced the brothers to abandon their old camping ground and take up new quarters on the Kentucky River, at a spot Boone had selected some time before as an admirable place for a settlement. Here the two constructed another cabin, and then began hunting and collecting peltries, which they followed with success until the spring of the following year, when having all that their two horses could carry they returned to their old home on the Yadkin River and disposed of their furs and peltries at excellent prices. Daniel Boone had been absent from his family, in the wilderness of the unexplored country, for a period of two years, and the joy of his

GLAD MEETING OF BOONE AND HIS BROTHER

return may be imagined. In all this time he had seen no other white men than those who had been his companions, five of whom had met their death in a mysterious way, and another killed and scalped by Indians. This awful experience, however, did not repress his love for adventure, nor the ambition, which ever actuated him, to open a pathway through the west for settlement and civilization.

CHAPTER IV

Boone Moves His Family to the Wilderness

For some considerable length of time Boone busied himself with the affairs of his North Carolina home. He had resolved, before leaving Kentucky River, that ultimately he would found a settlement upon its banks and remove his family there, but this could not be done hurriedly. He had acquired some property on the Yadkin and this had first to be disposed of; other preliminaries were also necessary, not the least of which was gaining his wife's consent to the change, and the conversion of such effects as he had no special need for into money. All this required much time, and years had elapsed before he was prepared to move. At this point in Boone's life the dates are very much confused, as indeed they are in his entire history, as already explained. Nearly all his biographers hold to the dates as given by Boone's autobiography, as it was dictated to John Folsom, in which appears the statement that he first left North Carolina for the region of Kentucky May 1st, 1769. That this is an error, and also that Boone was in Kentucky nearly ten years earlier than this is almost positively certain, as Mr. Ramsey and others have conclusively shown. But in the confusion of dates, which no future historian may ever hope now to correct, I am compelled to adopt even with their manifest errors those most generally given.

I may therefore say that on September 25th, 1773, Daniel and Squire Boone, accompanied by their families, set out with six pack horses and three milch cows for the land of their last adoption. At Powell's Valley, nearly one hundred miles from the Yadkin, the Boones were re-enforced by five other families and forty men, the latter being well armed. With this large force the party felt secure from attack, or, if attacked, they believed themselves able to repel any force of Indians that was likely to be met with.

Attack of the Indians

The cavalcade of emigrants continued their journey without molestation or incident until they reached Cumberland Gap, through which the party was upon the point of passing when seven young men who were bringing up the rear, driving the cattle, were set upon by a band of nearly one hundred Indians. So sudden was the attack that six were slain before the alarm could be given. The remaining young man escaped as by a miracle, but was pursued to the very front of the armed men who were in the lead. A desperate battle now took place. There was no time for corralling the wagons, as the enemy was upon them. The women and children began screaming, but their cries were soon hushed in the louder rattle of fire-arms. After a few volleys the Indians were driven off with the loss of several of their number, but the cattle had been stampeded and none of them were afterwards recovered. Among the emigrants that were killed in this battle was James, the eldest son of Daniel Boone, a bright and fearless young man, whose love for adventure was quite as strong as that of his father's.

The party was so alarmed and disheartened by the loss of six of their number that they abandoned the effort to reach the Kentucky River, and changing their course they went southward to a settlement established two years previously on Clinch River in southwest Virginia, forty miles from the scene of their battle. Boone remained here with his family until the June following when, in response to a request made by Governor Dunmore, of Virginia, of which State Kentucky at that time constituted

THE ATTACK AT CUMBERLAND GAP

a part, he took with him a man named Michael Stoner, and returned to Kentucky to assist the escape of several surveyors who were in that region and supposed to be besieged by Indians. The object of this journey was accomplished without special incident, for the surveyors were found without difficulty, peacefully pursuing their duties, with no Indians near them, but they were nevertheless glad to accept Boone as their guide and to return to the settlements in Virginia. This journey, which covered eight hundred miles, Boone accomplished on foot in sixty-two days.

Earliest Efforts at Settlement

It must not be supposed that up to this time no efforts had been made to settle the region west of the Cumberland Mountains. As early as 1770 George Washington had himself penetrated as far as the Kanawha River and surveyed a considerable portion of the lands in that section, to which he laid claim. In the same year a party of forty men under Colonel James Knox had crossed the Cumberland range and explored many miles of territory between Kentucky and Tennessee. They were absent from the Clinch River country, from whence they started, for such a length of time that the party afterwards became known in the traditions of the west as the "Long Hunters."

In the summer of 1773 Thomas Bullitt and ten men descended the Ohio River, while another party that had started with him followed up the Kentucky River as far as the spot where Frankfort now stands, and the valley of which they surveyed. Bullitt went down the Ohio to the falls where, in connection with John Campbell and John Connelly, he laid out the town of Louisville. In the same year General Lyman and several other adventurers floated down the Ohio and Mississippi Rivers as far as the place where Natchez was afterwards located, and were followed shortly after by no less than four hundred families, who settled along the banks of the two rivers.

All these facts, which are well attested, furnish so many proofs that Boone's first visit to the regions of Kentucky was made many years before the time stated in his autobiography, for, if it is true that he first started west in 1769, and that no other white man had ever been west of the Cumberland range, it is impossible to believe that the region was so well known in 1770, only a year later.

The War Against the Shawanese

During the absence of Boone, in search of the surveyors in Kentucky, the Shawanese Indians in the northwest began to murder the settlers in that region and rendered life so insecure on the border that Governor Dunmore appealed to the legislature, then in session, which was responded to by a call for three thousand men to be raised in

THE BATTLE AT POINT PLEASANT

Virginia. Immediately upon Boone's return the governor appointed him to the command of three contiguous garrisons, but he was not called on to do any fighting. The Shawanese were joined by the Delawares, Mingos, Wyandottes and Cayugas under such well-known chiefs as Logan, Cornstalk and Red Eagle. The final battle of this war was fought in the neighborhood of Point Pleasant, at the junction of the Ohio and Kanawha, where, after one of the bloodiest contests ever waged in any Indian war, the savages were beaten by fifteen hundred Virginians commanded by General Andrew Lewis. They soon after sued for peace and a treaty was made by which the

Indians surrendered all claims to Kentucky. The six nations had already resigned their claims to the region by the treaty of 1768, and the Cherokees had sold their rights to the territory to Colonel Richard Henderson, who founded what was known as the Transylvania Company.

Thus we see that at the time Daniel Boone was trying to settle in Kentucky with his family the territory was free of Indian titles, though for many years afterwards several tribes continued to use it as a hunting ground and, as we shall see, treacherously waylaid and massacred the settlers as if they considered every white person who came within the region an invader.

Another Exploration of Kentucky

Almost immediately after the conclusion of peace with the Shawanese and their allies, Boone was employed by the Transylvania Company, organized for the purpose of exploring, surveying and speculating in western lands, to guide a party of surveyors who were sent out to open a road from the settlements on the Holsten to the Kentucky River, and to establish a station at the mouth of Otter Creek, on the latter. At the head of a considerable party Boone started on a hazardous march to the scene of his future and most important labors. Concerning this journey Boone himself has written: "We proceeded with all possible expedition until we came within fifteen miles of where Boonesborough now stands, and where we were fired upon by a party of

PERILS ENCOUNTERED BY THE EARLY SETTLERS OF KENTUCKY

Indians that killed two and wounded two more of our number; yet, although surprised and taken at a disadvantage, we stood our ground. This was on the 20th of March, 1775. Three days after we were fired upon again, and had two men killed and three wounded. Afterward we proceeded on to Kentucky River without opposition, and on the first day of April began to erect the fort of Boonesborough at a salt lick, about sixty yards from the river, on the south side.

"On the fourth day, the Indians killed one of our men. We were busily employed in building this fort until the fourteenth day of June following, without any further opposition from the Indians; and having finished the works, I returned to my family on the Clinch.

"In a short time I proceeded to move my family from Clinch to this garrison, where we arrived safe, without any other difficulties than such as are common to this passage; my wife and daughter being the first white women that ever stood on the banks of Kentucky River."

CHAPTER V

The Fort at Boonesborough

The fort at Boonesborough, by which the settlement was to be protected, was completed in June, 1775, or within two months after it was begun. A description of this celebrated fort has been given in Collins' *Historical Sketches of Kentucky*, and there is also in existence a print made from a drawing by Colonel Henderson himself. From the former I extract the following: "It was situated adjacent to the river, with one of the angles resting on its bank near the water, and extending from it in the form of a parallelogram. The length of the fort, allowing twenty feet for each cabin and opening, must have been about two hundred and sixty, and the breadth one hundred and fifty feet. In a few days after the work was commenced, one of the men was killed by the Indians." The houses, being built of hewn logs, were bullet proof. They were of a square form, and one of them projected from each corner, being connected by stockades. The remaining space on the four sides, as will be seen by the engraving, was filled up with cabins erected of rough logs, placed close together. The gates were on opposite sides, made of thick slabs of timber, and hung on wooden hinges. This was in accordance with the fashion of the day.

"A fort, in those rude military times," says Butler, "consisted of pieces of timber sharpened at the end and firmly lodged in the ground; rows of these pickets enclosed the desired space, which embraced the cabins of the inhabitants. A block-house or more, of superior care and strength, commanding the sides of the fort, with or without a ditch, completed the fortifications or stations, as they were called. Generally the sides of the interior cabins formed the sides of the fort. Slight as this advance was in the art of war, it was more than sufficient against attacks of small arms in the hands of such desultory warriors, as their irregular supply of provisions necessarily rendered the Indians. Such was the nature of the military structures of the provision against their enemies. They were ever more formidable in the canebrakes and in the woods than before even these imperfect fortifications."

Upon completion of the fort it was called Boonesborough, in honor of its intrepid founder, and very soon after assumed considerable importance as a settlement. Before fall, Col. Henderson, Nathan Hart and John Luttrell, who were interested in the Transylvania Company, came out to the fort with nearly forty men, and pack-horses loaded with necessary supplies for the new colony, that had already begun to grow rapidly. Boone also returned to Clinch River and brought out his family, as previously related, but he did not come alone, for in passing through Powell's Valley he was joined by Hugh McGary, Richard Hogan and Thomas Denton and their families, and twenty other adventurers, chiefly young unmarried men. Upon reaching the confluence of the Monongahela and Ohio however, McGary, Hogan and Denton separated from Boone and went on to a settlement founded the year before by Harrod and called in his honor Harrodsburg. In the same fall Logan's Fort and Bryan Station were also established, the four settlements, however, being in close proximity to each other and thus capable of affording a measure of mutual protection.

The Founding of Lexington

The year 1775 was one of unusual activity as it was crowded with extraordinary and momentous events. The founding of Boonesborough was the opening of a gateway to the settlement of all Kentucky. Previous to this every effort to open up the country and make productive its almost incomparably fertile soil had been frustrated by the perils that menaced its peaceful invaders. It was therefore like some marvelously rich treasure guarded by an invulnerable or fright-inspiring monster until Boone, as the modern St. George, Hercules or Perseus offered combat with the hard-visaged creature of savagery and overcame it, and gave the fruits of his victory to those who would enjoy it.

While the bustle and promise of Boonesborough was attracting hardy adventurers from the east the report came by some of these of the first gun fired in the battle for freedom on the field of Lexington. The stirring news was first received within the territory of Kentucky by a party of hunters encamped at a beautiful spot in the center

FIRST HOUSE IN LEXINGTON

of what is now known as Fayette County, about thirty miles from Boonesborough. Stimulated by a spirit of intense patriotism the hunters, whose names have unfortunately perished, resolved to dedicate the ground of their encampment by founding thereon a settlement to be called in honor of the first battle-field for American independence, *Lexington*. The honor and glory of that sacred dedication still remains in the beautiful city that is now not only the capital of Fayette County, but the metropolis of that fairest section of all Kentucky, the justly celebrated "Blue Glass Region," where grows the most bounteous crops, finest horses and loveliest women in all the world.

Capture of Three White Girls by Indians

Affairs at Boonesborough continued prosperous and the settlement increased so rapidly that towards the middle of 1776 the colony numbered nearly three hundred souls. Nothing specially alarming had occurred to disturb the serene and prosperous condition of the settlers, though a vigilant watch was maintained against the Indians who continued to hover about and menace the place. Considerable progress had now been made in clearing away the surrounding forest, and in the cultivation of corn, wheat and tobacco, which promised a goodly yield. This quiet and peaceful condition of the settlement was, however, suddenly and rudely violated on the fourteenth of July, by the capture of three girls from the fort, one of whom, Jemima, was the daughter of Daniel Boone, and the other two, Betsy and Frances, were the daughters of Richard Callaway, who had moved to Boonesborough from North Carolina the preceding spring.

CAPTURE OF MISS BOONE AND THE MISSES CALLAWAY

The girls were about fourteen years of age, were devoted friends, and spent most of their time together. The friendship of the three was cemented more closely by the fact that they each had young lovers among the settlers, and in their love-making shared each other's confidences. On the evening of their capture they were amusing themselves by rowing along the river in a canoe, which they handled with great dexterity. Anticipating no danger, and, being governed by the desire that possesses all human beings to know what lies beyond them, they crossed over to the opposite shore. Here the attention of the girls was caught by a cluster of wild flowers, and desiring to possess them, they turned the prow of the canoe toward the shore. The trees and shrubs were thick, and extended down to the water's edge, affording a safe shelter for a band of Indians who lay concealed there. Just as one of the girls was in the act of grasping the flowers an Indian slid stealthily down the bank into the water, and seizing the rope that hung at the bow of the canoe, turned its course up stream, in a direction to be hidden from a view of the fort by a projecting point. At the same time four other Indians appeared with drawn tomahawks and knives, and intimated to the girls by signs and motions that if they caused any alarm they would be killed on the spot. Yet, terrified at their sudden and unexpected capture, the girls shrieked for help. Their cries were heard at the fort, but too late for their rescue. The canoe was the only means the garrison had of crossing the river, and that was now on the opposite side and in possession of the enemy. None dared to swim the stream, fearing that a large body of Indians were concealed in the woods on the opposite bank.

Boone and Callaway were both absent, and night set in before their return and arrangements could be made for pursuit. The following account of the recapture of the girls is given by Colonel Floyd, who was one of the pursuing party of eight, three others of whom were the girls' lovers:

"The affair happened late in the afternoon, and the spoilers left the canoe on the opposite side of the river from us, which prevented our getting over for some time to pursue them. Next morning by daylight we were on the track, but found they had totally prevented our following them by walking some distance apart through the thickest cane they could find. We observed their course, however, and on which side they had left their sign, and traveled upward of thirty miles. We then imagined that they would be less cautious in traveling, and made a turn in order to cross their trace, and had gone but a few miles before we found their tracks in a buffalo-path.

"Pursuing this for the distance of about ten miles, we overtook them just as they were kindling a fire to cook. Our study had been more to get the prisoners without giving their captors time to murder them after they should discover us, than to kill the Indians.

"We discovered each other nearly at the same time. Four of our party fired, and then all rushed upon them, which prevented their carrying anything away except one shot-gun without any ammunition. Mr. Boone and myself had a pretty fair shot, just as they began to move off. I am well convinced I shot one through; the one he shot dropped his gun, mine had none. The place was very thick with canes, and being so much elated on recovering the three little broken-hearted girls, prevented our making further search. We sent the Indians off without their moccasins, and not one of them with so much as a knife or tomahawk."

The return with the rescued girls was the occasion for great rejoicing. To crown their satisfaction the young lovers had proved their prowess, and under the eye of the greatest of all woodsmen had shown their skill and courage. They had fairly won the girls they loved. Two weeks later a general summons went throughout the little settlements to attend the first wedding ever solemnized on Kentucky soil. Samuel Henderson and Betsey Callaway were married in the presence of an approving company that celebrated the event with dancing and feasting. The formal license from the county court was not waited for, as the court-house of Fincastle, of which county Kentucky was part, was distant more than six hundred miles. The ceremony consisted of a contract with witnesses, and religious vows administered by Boone's brother, who was an occasional preacher of the persuasion popularly known as Hardshell Baptists. Frances Callaway became within a year the wife of the gallant Captain John Holder, afterward greatly distinguished in the pioneer annals; and Boone's daughter married the son of his friend Callaway.

CHAPTER VI

Troubles Begin to Multiply

Of the first ten years of the existence of Boonesborough, the year of its founding, though perhaps not the most prosperous, was certainly the most peaceful the place had. After the capture of the girls, as just related, other harassing incidents occurred, to be followed soon after by a terrible warfare with the Indians, and an obstinate attack on the fort, as will be presently described.

When Boone went to Kentucky, under the employment of Colonel Henderson, in 1773, it was as an agent, so to speak, to examine, explore and open up that section of the country that the Transylvania Company had obtained as already explained. The lands acquired by purchase from the Cherokees constituted an area equal to that of the present commonwealth of Kentucky, though the boundary lines were not fully made, nor were the limits circumscribed by the State lines as they now exist. It is impossible at this day to definitely define the extent of that purchase because the surveys were never completed, but the tract included a considerable portion of what is now West Virginia, western Tennessee and nearly the western two-thirds of Kentucky. It was within these limits that Colonel Henderson designed the establishment of an independent republic, the right of which was not disputed until about the year 1778. The settlers took leases of lands within the Transylvania district from

HARRASSMENTS
OF EARLY SETTLERS

the company, and the independent character of the governmental organization was further recognized by the assembling of a convention at Boonesborough, which was attended by eighteen delegates, at which the company was declared the government. At this convention courts of justice were established and the rules for all proceedings therein. A militia law was also enacted, by which all persons subject to military service were required to be enrolled and to perform a certain amount of drilling and active duty. Singularly enough, at this same assembling a law was passed for the preservation of game. "This was," as Peck says, "the first political convention ever held in the western valley (west of the Cumberland range) for the formation of a free government."

Annoyed by the Indians

Hostilities between Great Britain and the American colonies were not confined wholly to the New England, Middle and Southern States, for the influence of the English extended to what was then the far west, where they secured the services of several tribes of Indians that made attacks upon the settlers, which led finally to a regular Indian war, in which Boonesborough and the surrounding settlements suffered greatly. It was at first believed that the independent republic would be exempt from Indian molestation, but England refused to consider Transylvania as other than an appanage of the colonies, and therefore the Kentucky settlers were subjected to all the injuries that a savage foe, acting as allies of the crown, could inflict. The result of this, eventually, was an overthrow of the British posts in Illinois and Indiana, in 1778, and the transfer of the west, ultimately, to the American Union.

Alarm of the Settlers

The capture of the Boone and Callaway girls, though attended, fortunately, by no tragic consequences, served, nevertheless, to spread great alarm among the settlers, who were thus made to realize the constant peril of their surroundings. Many entertained a sanguine belief in the final triumphs of English arms, and learning that the Indians were now in open hostility against the whites, as allies of the British, created such consternation that no less than three hundred surveyors, hunters and land speculators that had come to Kentucky for permanent settlement, hastily packed up their movable possessions and returned to their several old homes in the east. For a time it appeared as if the entire country of Kentucky would be abandoned, so general was the alarm of the people, and no doubt would have been but for the influence of Boone and other courageous spirits that had united their fortunes with his. Among these bold adventurers who helped Boone save Kentucky, whose names have passed into history, were Simon Kenton, John Floyd, and the four McAfee brothers. The former had settled in Kentucky in the spring of '75, and at once became, in connection with Boone, a governing spirit in the settlements.

The Attack on Boonesborough

Notwithstanding the grave alarm that possessed the people after the capture of the Boone and Callaway girls, the settlers enjoyed a period of immunity from further Indian outrages for nearly one year. The settlements, however, received very few new members until July of 1777, when a party of forty-five men from North Carolina came into the territory and made their camp in the vicinity of Boonesborough. Their coming caused much rejoicing to the settlers, who had lived so long in constant fear of an attack from the Indians; and particularly glad were the people of Boonesborough, who had sustained, though with little loss, a fierce attack made upon them by a band of one hundred Indians the preceding April.

It was less than one month after the arrival of the new party that another attack was made on Boonesborough, this time by a band of Cherokees numbering more than two hundred. These Indians had the aid of several others from neighboring tribes who were sent simultaneously against the white settlements about Bryan Station, Harrodsburg and Lexington, more to harass the people of those places and hold them in a state of alarm so as to prevent the reinforcement of Boonesborough. Thus having placed the other stations in a state of siege by their allies, the Cherokees invested Boonesborough and attempted its reduction by starving out the garrison. Perceiving their tactics, Boone invited the Indians to a combat by deploying some of his men and opening a fire on the besiegers from the adjacent woods and covering his retreat into

THE BATTLE OF BOONESBOROUGH

the fort again. By this means several men would sally out and deliver their fire, taking the chances of getting back into the fort and luring the Indians after them. Two days and nights were spent in this daring invitation to battle, until at length the Indians opened the attack in earnest, but were met with a resistance so heroic that they retired after losing seven of their warriors and twice as many wounded.

This battle is declared by some of Boone's biographers to have occurred only a few days previous to the arrival of the party of forty-five hunters, and it is so made to appear in Boone's autobiography, but in the sequence of his narrative it is placed after and circumstances clearly indicate that the attack was made at a time when the garrison was strongest. In this connection I may add that nearly all the writers on the history of Kentucky fix the date of the Indian attack on Logan's Fort and Harrodsburg in May, 1777; whereas, Boone states that the two attacks were made on the nineteenth of July, subsequent to that on Boonesborough, which is unquestionably an error. We also know, by Boone's admissions, that after the attack on Boonesborough the settlers of that section were not again seriously molested by Indians until some time in February of the following year. In a spirit of self-gratulation Boone thus writes of the results of the attack on the fort:

"The savages now learned the superiority of the Long Knife, as they called the Virginians, by experience; being out-generaled in almost every battle. Our affairs began to wear a new aspect, and the enemy, not daring to venture an open war, practiced secret mischief at times."

CHAPTER VII

Boone Is Again Made Prisoner by the Indians

During the winter of 1777–78, the people began to suffer greatly for salt, the cost of bringing so heavy an article across the mountains on horseback being so great that but few of them could afford to use it. Therefore, after considering the matter, it was decided that thirty men, headed by Boone, should take such kettles as could be spared, and proceed to the Lower Blue Licks, on Licking River, and there manufacture salt. They commenced operations on New Year's Day, 1778.

In this expedition Boone served in the several positions of captain, hunter and scout, his chief duties being to provide meat for the men and guard against surprise. The party proceeded with their work without molestation until the seventh of February when Boone, while hunting some distance from the lick, was surprised by a party of two hundred Indians and made captive. The danger of his own situation, though in the hands of inveterate foes, gave Boone less concern than his anxiety for the safety of those working at the lick. Understanding the Indian character thoroughly Boone put his knowledge to excellent use now. Knowing that the party of salt makers were practically defenseless against so large a force, and that the Indians would certainly attack them unless some strategy were devised to prevent such a calamity, Boone adopted the tactics that once before served him so admirably: instead of appearing depressed or sullen, he accepted his fate with apparent satisfaction and so conducted himself as to win the admiration of his captors. His next step was to make favorable terms with the Indians for the surrender of his friends at the lick, in which he was so far successful as to secure a promise that in the event of their quiet surrender his party should receive honorable treatment. A submission of the salt makers having thus been provided for, Boone led the Indians into the presence of his party and advised a peaceable capitulation, which was immediately obeyed, and thus without the firing of a gun, or injury of a single one of the really defenseless party, the Indians took their captives away to old Chillicothe, the principal town on Little Miami, and on the eighteenth of February turned over their charge to the British authorities there. This admirable strategy of Boone's not only saved himself and party from massacre, but prevented an attack on Boonesborough also. The men captured at Blue Licks were paroled in a few days and returned to their friends, but nevertheless, Boone was subsequently tried by a court-martial for his conduct in advising the surrender of his party, which resulted, however, not only in his honorable discharge, but also a special approval by the court of his wisdom and service.

Boone Is Adopted by the Shawanese

Though the party captured at the lick were paroled by the British and permitted to quietly return to Boonesborough, another fate was reserved for Boone himself, for his reputation, so well established among the Indians, was now to lead him into new trials. The British desired to include him in the parole to which, however, the Indians objected, nor would they restore him to liberty, though a ransom of one hundred pounds was offered them by the governor, their desire being to adopt him into their tribe, reckoning the value of his services to them very highly and hoping to gain his confidence by a course of generous treatment, which they began forthwith to show him.

This determination of the Indians greatly distressed Boone, who now foresaw a long and doubtful interval between his separation from his family and a return to them again, but he was too wise to manifest any disappointment or vexation in the presence of the Indians, which must have excited greater vigilance in their guard over him and

BOONE UNDERGOING THE CEREMONY OF ADOPTION BY THE TRIBE

thereby lessened the possibility of escape. On the other hand, he expressed much pleasure with their company and a desire to become a faithful companion and follower of the band. Thus deceived by his conduct, Blackfish, chief of the Shawanese, adopted Boone, with much ceremonial display, as his son, to supply the place of a favorite son who had fallen in a battle with the white settlers sometime in the preceding year.

After his adoption Boone was regarded with great affection by his Indian father and mother, and was treated on all occasions with marked attention as a distinguished hunter and mighty brave. He took care to encourage this affection for him, and treated all his fellow-warriors in the most familiar and friendly manner. He joined them in their rifle and musket shooting contests, and gained great applause by his skill as a marksman; but was careful not to excel them too frequently, as nothing will so soon excite the envy and hatred of an Indian as to be beaten at anything in which he takes pride.

After he had been with them some time he was permitted to go alone into the woods in quest of game, but his powder was always measured to him and his balls counted, and when he returned he was required to account in game for all the ammunition he could not produce. But by using small charges of powder, and cutting balls in halves, with which he could kill squirrels and other small game, he managed to save a few charges of powder and ball for use in case he should find an opportunity to escape.

Wonderful Escape of Boone

Early one afternoon, in the June following his capture, Boone was much distressed, upon returning from a customary hunt, to find nearly five hundred Indians collected in Chillicothe, fitted out with war-paint and weapons, contemplating a descent upon the settlement at Boonesborough. He at once decided to lose no more time, but make his escape immediately, and proceed as rapidly as possible to the settlements in Kentucky, and alarm the people in time to save them from a general massacre.

That night he secreted about his person some jerked venison, to sustain him during his long journey, and early the next morning he left the Indian village, with his gun on his shoulder, as if he were going into the woods for his usual day's hunt. But after wandering about for some time, as if in quest of game, in order to allay the suspicions of any spies that might follow him, and having placed several miles between himself and the town, he suddenly changed his course in the direction of Boonesborough, and set off with all his might for his beloved home. The distance exceeded one hundred and sixty miles, which he traveled in less than five days, eating but one regular meal, which was a turkey that he shot after crossing the Ohio River.

Until he left that stream behind him, his anxiety was very great, for he knew that he would be followed, and being but an indifferent swimmer he anticipated trouble in crossing the river. But he was rejoiced upon reaching its banks to find an old canoe that had floated into the brush and lodged. There was a hole in one end of it, but this he contrived to stop, and the frail vessel bore him safely to the Kentucky shore.

His appearance at Boonesborough was almost like one risen from the dead, and he was received by the garrison with joyful shouts of welcome. His capture and journey to Detroit were known by reports of prisoners who had escaped, but his friends did not expect ever to see him again. His wife, despairing of his return, had conveyed herself and some of the children, on pack-horses, to her father's home in North Carolina, and he keenly felt the disappointment at not meeting her. The tongue of calumny, too, ever ready to stir up strife, endeavored to bring about a permanent separation of these two devoted people, but without success, though it cost them both much trouble and anguish. This is a period of Boone's life that he never mentioned to his most intimate friends, and justice to a noble reputation demands that the historian should also cover it with the mantle of silence.

A Brush with the Indians

As he had expected, upon Boone's arrival at the fort he found it in a sorry state of defense. The long period of quiet that had succeeded the attack on Boonesborough, and the lack of a leader, caused the garrison to relapse into a state of negligence which, had the Indians taken advantage of, must have resulted in the capture of the fort and probable massacre of those within it. Boone, therefore, aroused the people from their lethargy and set about at once making the fort secure against attack.

ADVANCE OF THE INDIANS UNDER BLACKFISH

His energy was not immediately necessary, however, since his escape had caused the Indians to forego their intention of making a descent on the garrison, but they made their camps in the vicinity and threatened the several settlements in that section.

After a month of expectancy more harassing, possibly, than an open attack, Boone decided to make a foray with the view of feeling the strength and position of the enemy. Accordingly, taking thirty well-armed men, he marched by night as far as the banks of the Scioto, where he surprised a camp of fifty Indians and fell upon them with such impetuosity that they retreated precipitately after firing a single volley, leaving two of their dead in the hands of Boone. Immediately after this attack Boone learned that the Indians he had fired upon was a detachment from a large party under Blackfish and eight Canadian officers, on their way to Boonesborough. Following fast on their trail, Boone overtook and stealthily passed the main body of Indians, nearly five hundred strong, and by rapid traveling day and night he reached the fort nearly one day in advance of the enemy, thus having time to arouse the garrison to their danger and prepare for the threatened attack.

The Siege of Boonesborough

The Indians, who were commanded by Captain Duquesne, acting under orders of Hamilton, British governor of the northwest, appeared before the fort on the eighth of July. Displaying the British flag, Duquesne demanded an immediate surrender of the garrison, coupling the demand with a threat of massacre in the event of a refusal.

Boone asked time to consult with his comrades and employed the delay thus secured in preparing for the siege. The pioneers resolved unanimously to fight to the death. Captain Duquesne, disappointed in his hopes of surprise or surrender, next asked a conference with nine of the pioneers. Strange as it may appear, Boone, for the only time in all his frontier experience, was deluded by the shallow artifice. Accompanied by eight others, among whom were Flanders Callaway, Stephen Hancock, William Hancock and Squire Boone, he went out of the stockade to treat with the enemy. A crowd of Indians immediately surrounded the little party, while Duquesne attempted to engage their attention in a talk about the surrender of the post. At length it was suggested that a solemn custom of the Indians should be observed—that the hands of each white man should be grasped by two warriors in a token of permanent friendship. Boone acquiesced, and the warriors approached and seizing the hands of the whites tried to make them prisoners. Those from the fort seeing the treachery, fired upon the Indians and covered the retreat of the party as they fled back into the stockade. In this melee Squire Boone was wounded quite seriously. The incident brought upon Boone for a time a suspicion with some that he was not at heart true to his fellow pioneers.

THE INVESTMENT OF BOONESBOROUGH—LURKING BESIEGERS

But the injurious thought was soon dismissed, and Boone's frank explanation "that he didn't know how it happened, but he had played the great fool," was accepted as true. It was the first and only time that the old pioneer lost even for a moment his sagacity and self-possession. He had the singular gift of becoming more discreet and resourceful, and at the same time more daring, as danger became more pressing.

The main body of Indians, who were prepared for the turn affairs had taken, now rushed forward and made a furious assault upon the fort. But they met with a warm reception, and were soon glad to withdraw to the cover of the woods again.

After the first assault they remained at a respectful distance, for they had a whole-some dread of the rifles of the Kentuckians, which would shoot further and with much greater accuracy than their old smooth-bore muskets. Most of their balls were spent before they reached the fort, and fell harmlessly back from the tough oaken palisades.

Finding they could not carry the fort by assault, they attempted to set it on fire, by throwing combustibles on the roofs; and for a time this new mode of attack seemed about to prove successful. But a daring young man climbed to the roof in the midst of a shower of balls, and remained there with buckets of water until the fire was extinguished.

Failing in this attempt, the Indians, under directions from the Canadians, resorted to another experiment, and tried to enter the fort by means of a mine. The fort stood about sixty yards from the river, and they began an excavation under the bank, which concealed them from view. But their project was detected by the muddy water seen at a little distance below, and it was defeated by the Kentuckians, who began a coun-termine within the fort, and threw the dirt over the palisades. While the men were engaged in digging this mine, Captain Boone constructed a wooden cannon, which was loaded with powder, balls, old nails, pieces of iron, etc. It was his intention to place this instrument at the head of the mine, and as the Indians entered, fire it into their midst. But on the 20th of the month they raised the siege and departed for their own country, having lost thirty-seven warriors killed, and many more wounded. The Kentuckians had two men killed, and four wounded.

During the siege, which lasted nine days, the women and girls molded bullets, loaded the rifles, and carried ammunition to their husbands, fathers and brothers; besides preparing refreshments, nursing the wounded and assisting in various other ways. Jemima Boone, while carrying ammunition to her father, received a contusion in her hip from a spent musket ball, which caused a painful, though fortunately not a dangerous wound.

While the parley was in progress between Boone and the Indians, previous to the first attack, a negro, who had been whipped a few days before by his master in the fort, deserted, and went over to the enemy, carrying with him a large, long-range rifle. He crossed the river, and stationed himself in a tree, so that by raising his head above a fork, he could fire directly down into the fort. He had killed one man and wounded another, when Boone discovered his head peering above the fork for another shot. "You black scoundrel!" said the old pioneer, as he raised his rifle to his shoulder, "I'll fix *your* flint for you," and quickly running his eye along the bright barrel of his rifle, he fired. The negro fell, and at the close of the battle was found at the roots of the tree with a bullet hole in the center of his forehead. The distance was one hundred and seventy-five yards.

Boone states that during the siege the garrison sustained a loss of only two men killed and four wounded, while the loss of the enemy was certainly thirty-seven, and probably many more. After the battle one hundred and twenty-five pounds weight of bullets were picked out from the logs of the fort, fired into it by the Indians.

CHAPTER VIII

Boone Is Ambushed and Robbed of a Large Sum of Money

After the successful repulse of the Indians from before Boonesborough, which proved to be, as Marshall observes, the most formidable siege that ever took place in Kentucky during any of the Indian wars, Boone returned to North Carolina, whither his wife had gone two months before. He remained with his family on the Yadkin River until the summer of 1780, when he returned again to Kentucky with his wife and a large supply of things specially useful to the early settlers. Among other valuables which he brought away with him was a sum of $20,000, entrusted to him by persons in North Carolina to take to their friends in Kentucky. At this time a rapid settlement of the territory was being made and the pioneers were entering homesteads and taking pre-emptions which required money to hold and perfect the titles. The funds therefore entrusted to Boone were contributed by friends and relatives of those in North Carolina for this purpose. While on the route Boone was set upon by a large party of Indians and white renegades who, no doubt had, in some way, received information that a large treasure was in his possession, and after an unequal struggle he was overpowered and the money taken from him. This stroke of misfortune fell with terrible effect upon Boone, for not only was a large portion of the total sum his own, for which he felt the least concern, but the principal part belonged to his intimate and very poor friends, who could least afford its loss.

But in addition to this sorrowful fact many reflections were cast, though without a scintilla of reason, upon his honesty by those who had known him longest and best. This imputation caused him the keenest anguish, and so depressed him that Colonel Thomas Hart addressed the following letter under date of August 3, 1780, to his brother, Captain Nathan Hart, with instruction that the confidence therein expressed be communicated to Boone. Both of the Harts were large losers by the robbery:

"I observe what you say respecting our losses by Daniel Boone. I had heard of the misfortune soon after it happened, but not of my being partaker before now. I feel for the poor people who, perhaps, are to lose even their pre-emptions; but I must say, I feel more for Boone, whose character, I am told, suffers by it. Much degenerated

ATTACK ON THE EMIGRANTS AND THE ROBBING OF BOONE

must the people of this age be, when amongst them are to be found men to censure and blast the reputation of a person so just and upright, and in whose breast is a seat of virtue too pure to admit of a thought so base and dishonorable. I have known Boone in times of old, when poverty and distress had him fast by the hand; and in these wretched circumstances, I have ever found him a noble and generous soul, despising every thing mean; and therefore I will freely grant him a discharge for whatever sums of mine he might have been possessed of at the time."

Killing of Boone's Brother

Soon after Boone's return to Kentucky with his family, or some time in the October following, he went to the Blue Licks with his brother Squire, on the double mission of hunting and examining the salt works that had been erected there. The two remained in the vicinity of the licks for two days without encountering any Indians or discovering signs that the neighborhood had been visited by enemies for several months past. When on the point of returning to Boonesborough, however, they were fired upon by

THE KILLING AND SCALPING OF BOONE'S BROTHER

RENDEZVOUS OF THE KENTUCKY MILITIA

a party of Indians in ambush and the gallant Squire Boone was instantly killed, but Daniel was so fortunate as to escape injury. As he darted into the bushes he saw a dozen or more Indians rush upon his dead brother and cut the scalp from his head. This delay gave Boone a good start of his foes which he maintained until night set in and he felt he had baffled all pursuit. His fancied security was soon after dissipated by the appearance of a large dog hard on his trail, giving voice at every bound like a hound on the track of a deer. Boone now knew that he was being hotly pursued and his spirits fell rapidly, but he immediately decided upon his action. Throwing his gun to his shoulder he shot the dog when it was almost in the act of springing upon him, then doubling back to confuse his trail he ran off at an angle from his former course and easily threw the Indians off his track. After a hard run of nearly two days he reached the fort in safety, but was almost spent with fatigue.

The loss of his favorite brother, following so soon after the misfortune which befell him on the route to Kentucky, and the loss of confidence of some of his friends, as already described, threw Boone into a state of melancholia from which he would have hardly recovered, but for the stirring events which speedily succeeded. The Indians had again invaded the territory and began a massacre of the settlers, besides threatening every garrison, several of which had been invested and two, Ruddle's

Station and Martin's Fort, captured. The time for energetic action by every pioneer was at hand. The day had arrived when the dead must bury their dead and the living must perform their duty.

In the latter part of October, the territory of Kentucky was divided into three counties by the legislature of Virginia, and a military and civil organization was perfected. Each county formed a regiment, of which that in Lincoln was headed by Boone as lieutenant-colonel. Colonel Clark assumed command of the three regiments, and placed himself immediately at the head for active operations. This show of a strong military force had the good effect of overawing the Indians for more than a year, during which time the settlements enjoyed peace and great prosperity. In fact, 1781 was the most prosperous year ever passed by the settlers up to the time of the admission of Kentucky to the Union in 1792.

Rescue of Boone by Simon Kenton

One incident alone is recorded of any molestation of the settlers or posts during the favorite year of '81, and some historians have even made bold to dispute the report in this particular instance. Without vouching for its authenticity, or throwing any discredit upon the popular version of the event, if it occurred, I will content myself with describing the incident as previous biographers of Boone have done: It is related that when Gen. Clark became invested with the military leadership of the west, by Gov. Patrick Henry, he placed great reliance on Daniel Boone as his coadjutor in Kentucky in defending the frontier stations against the Indians.

General Clark assumed the general superintendence of the border settlements and organized a company of spies, for the payment of whom the General pledged the faith of Virginia. This body of spies was charged with the duty of scouting up and down the Ohio River, watching the signs of Indian approach and reporting to Colonel Boone, who appointed two of these spies, one of whom was the renowned Simon Kenton. In selecting Kenton, Boone brought into service a man who has since been cherished in Kentucky for heroic bravery as second only to himself.

SIMON KENTON

KENTON'S HEROIC RESCUE OF BOONE

The Indians, no doubt spurred on by the British commanders at Detroit and Vincennes, were intent on destroying the stations in Kentucky, particularly Boonesborough, which place was to them the one most dreaded because it held in safety the man whose skill and boldness was proof against the terrors of solitude and the wiles of a savage, cunning and relentless foe.

During Boone's command of the fort he was frequently indebted to this roving body of spies for early information of the enemy's design, and for efficient service in the hour of attack. He knew his enemy and felt that with such a lurking foe there was no hour for quiet.

On one occasion, Kenton, while still engaged in the spy service, and having his headquarters at the fort, took up his gun early one morning and went out in quest of game. Just before leaving the gate of the fort, however, he saw two of his own men at some distance in a cleared field fired upon by several Indians. The men not being hit, ran with all their speed, followed by the savages in pursuit, who overtook one of the poor fellows and tomahawked and scalped him within a few hundred yards of the fort. Kenton drew a bead with his trusty rifle on the savage perpetrator of the deed and shot him dead on the spot. He then gave chase to the others. Colonel Boone, hearing the alarm in the fort, rushed out with ten men to the assistance of Kenton. The Indians did not retreat without a fight, Kenton killing one of them in the act of firing on Boone's party. Warmed up by the skirmish, Boone did not recognize in how large force the Indians had collected until he found himself unexpectedly cut off from the fort by a body of savages who had got in his rear. The crisis called for a bold movement. Boone gave the signal to fire and charge, which order was promptly obeyed by his men, but they were met by a withering volley from the Indians, so effectively delivered that six of the ten men were badly wounded, and Boone himself fell with a broken leg, and in the next moment seemed to be at the mercy of the Indians. One of the savages rushed upon him with uplifted tomahawk to cleave Boone's skull, but fortunately Kenton saw the danger that threatened and before the fatal stroke could be given he shot the Indian dead. Kenton and his men then rushed up to the rescue of the wounded party, and seizing Boone and raising him on his shoulders, carried him back into the fort, while the Indians were kept at bay by the men that had escaped injury. Boone was ever afterwards warm in the expressions of his gratitude to Kenton. At this time it is a sort of poetical justice to reflect, that the remains of Simon Kenton, who died in 1836, repose in the same cemetery at Frankfort, Kentucky, with those of Daniel Boone, his early companion of pioneer days.

The year 1782 was as eventful for its calamities as was '81 distinguished for peaceful and uninterrupted prosperity, and may be reckoned as the most trying and disastrous year in all the annals of Kentucky, though more than one-half the year had passed before any trouble with the Indians occurred.

The Siege of Bryan Station

On the fourteenth of August one of the principal posts in the territory, that had been settled by three brothers of Boone's wife, James, William and Daniel Bryan, and named in their honor Bryan Station, situated five miles northeast of Lexington, was attacked by a force of five hundred Indians under the notorious white renegade, Simon Girty, a man as much dreaded among Kentucky settlers as was Quantrill during the guerrilla warfare on the Kansas and Missouri borders.

The garrison at Bryan numbered scarcely fifty men, and even this small force was illy prepared for the attack, which came as a surprise, at a time when the defenses of the fort were in poor condition. But though few in number, and disadvantaged in other ways, every man within the stockades was a hero who had met odds before, and they were none the less willing to hazard a battle under unequal conditions now.

The attack was begun by an advance body of twenty Indians, who came close to the fort and delivered their fire, retreating quickly again to the cover of the adjacent

PRESENT SITE OF BRYAN STATION

woods. This was no doubt a ruse to entice the garrison from the fort into a pursuit, as the main party had not as yet shown themselves and were concealed in a place from whence they could most readily cut off retreat should the garrison sally out. But there were several within the fort who were old Indian fighters and knew the tactics of their cunning foe. Runners were quietly dispatched from the fort for assistance, who crept out so secretly that they were not detected by the Indians, while the garrison maintained a stolid and fearless silence, awaiting an onslaught which they had every reason to believe would soon be made.

But while the Indians continued to show themselves in small parties, they made no further demonstration than firing an occasional shot, evidently still expecting that the defenders of the fort would make a sortie and leave the entrances to the stockade exposed.

The Brave Water-Carriers

It unfortunately and unwisely happened that Bryan Station had been selected and built without regard to a water supply. Not only was there no well or spring within the walls, but the nearest source was quite a quarter of a mile distant. The garrison, fearing a siege, and distress for want of water, which seemed now to threaten, debated for some time the question of how this approaching need could be supplied, finally deciding that women from the fort should be sent with buckets to bring in such quantity as might suffice for two days. It was wisdom that dictated this course, for women

THE DEFENSE OF BRYAN STATION

had invariably performed this duty for the garrison and to send them now would serve to allay any suspicion that the Indians might have, and lead to the impression among them that the garrison was resting under the belief that the enemy had either drawn off, or were in no considerable number about the fort.

When the decision was communicated to the women nearly all of them refused to undertake the perilous duty, but after the situation was fully explained, a resolute old lady offered to go alone to the spring, at the same time saying that, being so aged, her services were of little use, and that should she be killed her loss would be felt much less than if one of the men were slain. This spirited and patriotic declaration had such an effect upon the other women present that more than twenty now volunteered to undertake the hazardous duty. Accordingly, seizing buckets, they marched boldly out and to the spring, singing and laughing on the way in order to better deceive the Indians. They each filled their buckets in turn without betraying the least alarm, although they felt certain that within a few yards several hundred Indians were lying concealed, awaiting the first favorable opportunity to make a strategic entry into the fort. The women returned with their buckets filled with water, to the great relief of the garrison, without drawing the fire of a single Indian.

Bringing on the Engagement

A supply of water having now been provided, it was decided to bring on an engagement by a cunning move upon the enemy which would bring them within range of the deadly rifles from the fort. Thirteen men were accordingly sent out to attack the small party of Indians that continued to make a demonstration, and, as had been anticipated, the Indians retreated at the first fire in such a manner, too, as to invite pursuit. When the thirteen had chased the fleeing savages a short distance the main body of Indians, who were concealed on the opposite side of the fort, as was well known to the garrison, rushed out from their place of hiding, headed by Girty, to cut off the retreat of the pursuing party, believing that the entire garrison had been decoyed out of their defenses. But the Indians speedily learned their fatal mistake by being met with a galling fire from the thirty-five rifles yet within the fort, which sent those that escaped the rain of bullets pell-mell back again to cover. The thirteen that had first gone out to bring on the battle returned now to the fort without one of them receiving so much as a wound, though they had killed three of the enemy.

After retiring to hold a consultation the Indians, in combined force, made a second charge, headed by Girty himself, but they were received with such a murderous fire that again they fled in consternation. Perceiving now the futility of attempting to take the fort by assault, Girty disposed the Indians about the garrison to cut off all possibility of escape and then settled down to a siege, keeping up in the meantime a desultory fire as a warning of his presence.

Ambush of a Relief Party

Towards two o'clock in the afternoon a relief party from Lexington, numbering fifty men, on horseback and afoot, arrived before the fort in response to the call made upon them by messengers sent out in the morning. Their approach had been discovered by the Indians who laid in ambush, from which they poured a heavy fire but without great execution. The horsemen plunged through without losing a man, and the footmen would have been equally fortunate but for an exhibition of imprudent daring. Supposing the enemy to be in small force on account of the ineffectual attack on the horsemen, the footmen left a cornfield, through which they were passing in concealment from the Indians, and dashing out into the clearing in search of the enemy they were received by a volley that killed six of their number. Their loss would have been much greater but for the fact that the boldness with which the attack was made led the Indians to believe that a larger re-enforcement was at hand, and therefore after firing a single volley they fled to cover and were in favor of retreating back to Chillicothe.

Girty was furious at being foiled in his attempt to subdue the station by force, and smarting from a slight wound received in the morning, resorted to stratagem with the hope of gaining his purpose. He crawled to a stump, near one of the bastions, and demanded a parley. Commending their manly defense and bravery, he urged that further resistance was useless, alluded to the large number and fierceness of his followers, and asserted that he had a large re-enforcement near at hand, with several pieces of artillery. He warned them that if they continued to resist, and were finally captured by force, they would all be massacred; but assured them, "upon his honor," that if they would surrender then, they should be treated as prisoners of war. The commander of the station would not deign to pay the least attention to him, but he was answered in a taunting and pungent manner by a young man named Reynolds, who told him that he had a worthless dog, to which he had given the name of Simon Girty, in consequence of his striking resemblance to the man who bore that name; that if he had artillery and re-enforcements he might bring them on, but if he or any of the naked rascals with him found their way into the fort, they would disdain to use their guns against them, but would drive them out with whips, of which they had collected a large number for that purpose. When he ceased speaking, some of the young men began to call out, "Shoot the scoundrel!" "Kill the renegade!" etc., and Girty, seeing that his position was no longer safe, crawled back, crestfallen, to the camp of his followers, and next morning they had disappeared.

ARRIVAL OF RE-ENFORCEMENTS AT BRYAN STATION

CHAPTER IX

Pursuit of the Indians

Successful and decisive as had been the defense of Bryan Station, with a complete rout of the Indians, yet it was not to conclude hostilities, nor was it to be the most serious battle in which the early settlers had to engage. The news of the investment of the station had spread with almost inconceivable rapidity, and an equally quick response was made to the cry of distress. On the morning following the retreat of the Indians assistance arrived in the shape of militia bodies from all the neighboring forts and stations, until a party of one hundred and eighty well armed men was gathered together, most of them from Boonesborough, Harrodsburg and Lexington. Among those who had thus hastened to Bryan were Daniel Boone, his son Israel, and his brother Samuel, besides many other brave spirits whose names have become imperishable in Kentucky history.

Within a few hours after the re-enforcements arrived, a consultation had been held, at which it was decided to begin at once a pursuit of the fleeing Indians, whose trail was plainly visible leading by way of the Lower Blue Licks. Boone alone opposed this hasty action, but with such reasons as must have prevailed among less hot-headed and over-courageous militia. He admonished the men that a pursuit in their unprepared condition must certainly lead them into an ambush. He called their attention to the prominent trail which the Indians had left, the cast off garments and utensils which were strewn along the path, and particularly the marks upon the trees on the line of retreat, which were evidently made to insure and enable the pursuit to be pushed rapidly, and thus the more surely lead the pursuers into an ambush.

Boone urged that Colonel Logan was then on the way to the station with a considerable body of men, and that it were the part of wisdom to await his arrival so that the forces could be consolidated and afterwards divided, as precaution might dictate, and the Indians surrounded, or be brought between two fires, which could have been done by a proper distribution of the force available after forming a junction with Logan.

But Boone's counsel was opposed by words of bravado, and the pursuit was begun almost regardless of every tactic known to those experienced in fighting the Indians.

A Critical Situation

The march was quite rapid for several miles and until Blue Licks was reached. No Indians had as yet been seen, but the trail was growing fresher and some little precaution was now observed, as even those most anxious for a fight began to seriously reflect on Boone's advice. Upon the arrival of the militia at Licking River, a few Indians were noticed skulking among the brush on the opposite side, but betraying little anxiety to conceal themselves or to throw off pursuit. This discovery led Major McGary, who was in command, to call a halt for consultation. A sight of the enemy had suddenly cooled the eager desire before manifested and a disposition was now shown to consider the position, which appeared to be one of grave danger. Boone was accordingly appealed to for that advice which had only a few hours before been scorned, with an imputation of cowardice; but like the really brave always are, Boone harbored no animosities for the treatment accorded his former counsel, but willingly lent his advice, which was to the following effect: He declared that their situation was critical in the extreme; that the force opposed to them was undoubtedly very large and ready if not eager for battle, as might be readily judged from the leisurely retreat of the few Indians who had appeared upon the crest of the hill; that he was well acquainted with the ground in the neighborhood of the Licks, and was apprehensive that an ambuscade was formed at the distance of a mile in advance, where two ravines, one upon each side of the ridge, ran in such a manner that a concealed enemy might assail them at once both in front and flank before they were apprised of the

THE BATTLE ON
LICKING RIVER

THE FIGHT AT BLUE LICKS CROSSING

danger. Under the circumstances, therefore, Boone urged that one of two things be at once resolved upon, viz., either to await the arrival of Logan, who was now undoubtedly on his march to join them; or, to make an immediate attack by disposing the force as follows: one-half their number should be sent up the river to the rapids, and there to cross and fall upon the enemy's rear, while the other division would begin a simultaneous attack in the front. But whatever course might be resolved upon Boone cautioned his associates against uncovering their position by crossing the river until the ground was first thoroughly reconnoitered.

The Attack

McGary listened with some impatience to Boone's counsel, and being a man of sudden impulses, he abruptly left Boone, and mounting his horse dashed down the bank and into the shallow river, at the same time giving the challenge, "All who are not cowards will follow me!" In another moment the whole party plunged into the stream and rapidly crossing, rode in a swift gallop towards the spot where the last Indians had been seen. As they reached the junction of two well wooded ravines, where a high ridge headed, that was almost bare of growth, a murderous fire blazed forth as if from the very ground, that sent the van in wild disorder, for the Indians were in such a dense cover that they did not show themselves. The rear closed up rapidly to the assistance of their comrades, but only to fall into the ambush that the Indians had so skillfully laid. The whole party was now flanked and enclosed as if in the wings of a net, and exposed to a galling fire. The destruction was terrible. Young Israel Boone, Daniel's youngest son, was among the first to fall, for he rode directly in the front and sought the most dangerous position. Officers Harland, McBride, Todd and Trigg, one after the other fell before the dreadful blast of death; but notwithstanding their disadvantages the whites fought with desperate bravery. Daniel Boone proved himself a hero here again by forging to the front and baring himself to the blaze of the Indians' guns and arrows over the body of his fallen son.

The Slaughter

But despite the valor of the whites their unequal force was at last compelled to give way before the consuming fire that was poured upon them. The Indians extended their lines until the whites were entirely surrounded, and the rapidly melting band was thrown into disorder that was soon after followed by a rout and terrific slaughter. The whites broke through the line and fled towards the river pursued by the Indians, who, with tomahawks, hewed down scores and left a trail of mutilated men from the ridge back and across the stream. The whites that were mounted generally escaped, but those on foot made no further resistance, throwing away their arms and trusting to fleetness alone for safety. At the crossing the slaughter was even more terrible, for many of the men could not swim and even those that could, being retarded by the stream gave time for the entire body of Indians to come upon them and with arrows, rifles, stones and tomahawks they shot many and dashed the brains out of others while a number was drowned in a vain effort to cross, until the river was almost choked with the dead.

Boone was among those on foot, but when the rout began, instead of fleeing with the main body of his comrades, he, with twelve others, made off down the ravine which had just been abandoned by the Indians, and making his way down the stream to a ford, he finally crossed and returned to Bryan Station. Scarcely had he reached the post, however, when he met Colonel Logan advancing, who, up to this time, was ignorant of the movement made by McGary. Upon learning from Boone the particulars of the disaster at Licking River, he made a forced march to the scene, guided by Boone, but arrived too late to be of any assistance, as the Indians had drawn off from the pursuit in anticipation of the arrival of re-enforcements, and went on to Old Chillicothe. They rendered a useful service, however, in giving burial to the dead, after which Boone returned to Boonesborough and there made out a

BOONE FIGHTING OVER THE BODY OF HIS DEAD SON

report of the battle, which he transmitted to the governor of Virginia, Benjamin Harrison, as follows:

BOONE'S STATION, FAYETTE COUNTY, AUGUST 30TH, 1782.

Sir: Present circumstances of affairs cause me to write to your Excellency as follows: On the 16th instant, a large number of Indians, with some white men, attacked one of our frontier stations, known by the name of Bryans' Station. The siege continued from about sunrise till about ten o'clock the next day, when they marched off. Notice being given to the neighboring stations, we immediately raised one hundred and eighty-one horse, commanded by Colonel John Todd, including some of the Lincoln county militia, commanded by Colonel Trigg, and pursued about forty miles.

On the 19th instant, we discovered the enemy lying in wait for us. On this discovery, we formed our columns into one single line, and marched up in their front within about forty yards before there was a gun fired. Colonel Trigg commanded on the right, myself on the left, and Major McGary in the center, and Major Harland the advanced party in front. From the manner in which we had formed, it fell to my lot to bring on the attack. This was done with a very heavy fire on both sides, and extended back of the line to Colonel Trigg, where the enemy was so strong they rushed up and broke the right wing at the first fire. Thus the enemy got in our rear, with the loss of seventy-seven of our men, and twelve wounded. Afterwards we were re-enforced by Colonel Logan, which made our force four hundred and sixty men. We marched again to the battle ground; but, finding the enemy had gone, we proceeded to bury the dead.

We found forty-three on the ground, and many lay about, which we could not stay to find, hungry and weary as we were, and somewhat dubious that the enemy might not have gone off quite. By the sign, we thought that the Indians had exceeded four hundred; while the whole of the militia of this county does not amount to more than one hundred and thirty. From these facts your Excellency may form an idea of our situation.

I know that your own circumstances are critical; but are we to be wholly forgotten? I hope not. I trust about five hundred men may be sent to our assistance immediately. If these shall be stationed as our county lieutenants shall deem necessary, it may be the means of saving our part of the country; but if they are placed under the direction of General Clark, they will be of little or no service to our settlement. The falls lie one hundred miles west of us, and the Indians northeast; while our men are frequently called to protect them. I have encouraged the people of this county all that I could; but I can no longer justify them or myself to risk our lives here under such extraordinary hazards. The inhabitants of this county are very much alarmed at the thoughts of the Indians bringing another campaign into our country this fall. If this should be the case, it will break up these settlements. I hope, therefore, your Excellency will take this matter into your consideration, and send us some relief as quick as possible.

These are my sentiments, without consulting any person. Colonel Logan will, I expect, immediately send you an express, by whom I humbly request your Excellency's answer. In the meanwhile, I remain, &c.

DANIEL BOONE

FORD AT BLUE LICKS, SCENE OF THE MASSACRE, AS IT NOW APPEARS

CHAPTER X

A Retaliatory Expedition

The troubles of 1782 did not end with the disaster at Blue Licks, though it was now that the Kentuckians became the aggressors and carried the war into the heart of the Indian settlements.

A retaliatory expedition was immediately proposed by Gen. Clark, who, first calling a council of his officers, formulated a plan for devastating that portion of Kentucky where the Indians had established permanent homes and were carrying on a commerce with the British besides paying some attention to agriculture. It was first thought to be necessary to issue a draft for the requisite number of troops, but at the earliest intimation of Gen. Clark's wishes enough volunteers and supplies were offered to more than meet the requirement, and an assembling soon took place at Bryan Station, where one thousand well armed and mounted men proffered their services. The organization being completed at this post the force was divided into two detachments, under the respective leaderships of Colonels Logan and Floyd, and then marched to Licking, where Gen. Clark assumed command. Daniel Boone participated in the expedition, but not as an officer, presumably on account of the unjust reports then being circulated regarding his conduct at the battle of Blue Licks; for, though his counsel, and action as well, on that occasion, was that of a brave and sagacious soldier, yet the original charge made against him by McGary—or rather implied by the challenge which that impulsive officer gave when leading his men into the fight—had still some circulation, if not influence. Whatever may have been the cause, Boone served as a volunteer in the Clark expedition, on which account little is known of his acts, but that he demeaned himself with bravery and good judgment may confidently be assumed.

Although the expedition was planned with great care, and was composed of the best material for rapid marching and effective fighting, it failed to accomplish any decisive results, beyond the destruction of considerable property and the dispersion of the Indians from their ancient settlements. Several skirmishes were had with prowling bands, in one of which seven Indians were taken prisoners and four killed, with a loss of two of the Kentuckians, but beyond this no other fatalities occurred, and after several fatiguing marches with invariably barren results the expedition returned to Bryan Station where the force was disbanded.

Atrocities Perpetrated by the Indians

The failure of the expedition seems to have served the opposite purpose for which it was organized. Gen. Clark believed that with a properly equipped body of men, and in such force as to render resistance by the enemy ineffectual and useless, he could lay waste the Indian villages and inspire such terror that the settlers would thereafter be exempt from further depredation by the savages. No doubt he might have accomplished this object had it been possible for him to meet the Indians in large force and defeat them in a decisive battle, but this he was unable to do; for, instead of massing, to resist the invasion of their settlements, the Indians scattered, and in small bands turned back upon the unprotected settlers and began their murderous work among the defenseless homes, braining women and children, shooting down unsuspecting farmers, stealing stock, and committing every conceivable atrocity.

In this devilish and savage riot the squaws performed an equal part, for to them was frequently delegated the bloody work of scalping after a murder in the field or

BLOODY WORK OF SQUAWS

on the highway had been committed, and in a hundred well authenticated instances, as recorded in the history of Kentucky, squaws perpetrated acts that would almost mantle the cheeks of the warriors with shame.

The frequency of these massacres, as well as the boldness with which they were done, reduced the settlers in middle and northern Kentucky to the greatest extremity, and checked immigration entirely. But amid all the gloom that pervaded this savage-cursed section there were still occasional manifestations of fortune that inspired hope where despair would otherwise have entered every home in the Dark and Bloody Ground. The Indians sought the most helpless, forming their ambush beside culti-vated fields, or stealthily descended upon cabins under cover of the night to apply a torch and afterwards hew down with knife and tomahawk the fleeing inmates. But it sometimes happened that the families thus attacked were not so helpless as they appeared, and there has been left us the record of many a brave and desperate battle fought by courageous settlers with his savage foe, in which even against the greatest disadvantages he has won victories worthy of enduring fame.

Major Ballard's Great Fight

Bland Ballard, afterwards known as Major Ballard, was one of the brave settlers of Kentucky who met the Indians on unequal ground and defended his home success-fully against a score of savages, thus linking his name with a history that is at once sad but fascinating. Mr. Ballard removed with his family from Virginia in 1780, and after two short stops on the way came to Boonesborough and there settled, becoming a very intimate companion of Daniel Boone, who secured for him an official appointment in what was known as the *spy-guard*. Just what this organization was, we are left to conjecture, nor is it related what office Mr. Ballard filled, but most probably it was that of lieutenant. There is also some confusion in the history as to whether it was the father or son who participated in the incident about to be related. In one account before me there is no mention of a son, while in another it is specially stated that the hero was "Bland Ballard, the son of Major Ballard."

In 1782 the Ballards removed from Boonesborough to a place some fifty miles distant, known as Tyler's Station. There was a small settlement at Tyler, composed exclusively of Virginians, among the families being that of Captain Williamson's, a gentleman frequently mentioned in Kentucky history. He had a daughter, Elizabeth, famed throughout the district for her beauty, but no less for her heroic disposition, displayed on more than one occasion, when an attack was threatened by the Indians. Young Ballard fell in love with Miss Williamson, directly after his settlement at Tyler, and after a brief courtship the two were married. Soon after this happy consummation of their loves, young Ballard erected a log cabin about half a mile from the stockade that surrounded Tyler and here he settled with his pretty bride, where they lived without molestation for nearly one month. On account of the somewhat crowded condition of Tyler, the elder Ballard followed the example of his son by also building

INVASION OF THE PEACEFUL HOME

a cabin beyond the defenses of the settlement, into which he immediately moved with his considerable family. The two houses were located within two hundred yards of each other, and in full view, but owing to intervening woods Tyler Station was not visible from either.

Massacre of the Ballard Family

The elder Ballard had not been settled in his new quarters more than a week when one morning about daybreak his cabin was furiously assaulted by a band of twenty Cherokee Indians, who burst in the door before their presence became known to the inmates, and proceeded to do their bloody work. Mr. Ballard seized the only weapon at hand, and attempted to defend himself, but after striking down one of his foes, he was struck on the head with a tomahawk and at the same instant stabbed to the heart, before he could make any further resistance. The children, six in number, two boys and four girls, quickly met a similar fate, but Mrs. Ballard managed to escape through a rear window, and fled towards her son's cabin for protection. She was discovered by the Indians when midway between the two cabins and three of the savages fired at her, a ball from one of the rifles striking her in the side and knocking her down. She struggled to her feet, however, and ran on until she reached the door of her son's

HEROIC DEATH OF MR. BALLARD

cabin, where she fell, covered with blood, and expired just as young Ballard—whom we will call Major, by which title he is best known—awakened by the firing, rushed out to ascertain the cause.

In a moment he comprehended the dreadful situation and like the brave man he was, prepared to give battle notwithstanding the heavy odds against him. Grasping his rifle and ammunition pouch, he boldly sallied out and made a rush for the woods that were near at hand, bidding his wife to remain in the cabin and to signal to him, as occasion offered, the position of the Indians. By these tactics he was enabled to keep the savages at bay, for though strong in numbers they were cowardly, and entertained great dread of the Kentuckians whose rifles, they had learned before, were certain instruments of death.

Gaining the shelter of a neighboring tree, as the Indians advanced towards the cabin Major Ballard shot the chief of the party, which caused them to withdraw to shelter also. He moved from tree to tree, always keeping the Indians at such a distance that they could not rush upon him before he could reload his gun after firing, and being an excellent marksman he kept up a kind of running fight around his cabin until he had killed seven of the Indians without receiving any injury himself. During all this time Mrs. Ballard showed the greatest coolness, appearing at the door or window time and again to signal the position of the enemy, and occasionally to speak to her husband as he came within the sound of her voice.

The frequent firing of guns at length aroused the people at Tyler's Station, and a dozen men came out of the stockade to ascertain the cause, but armed for any emergency. When this armed force came into view the Indians beat a precipitate retreat, leaving their dead in the hands of the brave Ballard to expose to any indignity he might choose to inflict.

This fight, the particulars of which are so well authenticated, was one of the most remarkable and memorable that ever took place in the warfare between Indians and whites for possession of the western territory and, to the credit of Kentucky, it has been appropriately commemorated by legislative action.

For many years Major Ballard and his heroic wife continued to live in the quiet house so bravely defended by them. He died on his farm in Shelby County on the fifth of September, 1853, at the advanced age of ninety-three years, and was buried on the old homestead beside his wife, who had preceded him to the grave many years before. The legislature of Kentucky, in the winter of 1853–54, passed an act to honor the bodies of Major Ballard and his wife, in pursuance of which in the following summer they were taken up and re-interred at a public funeral attended by the members of the legislature and many other prominent persons, in the State cemetery at Frankfort, where they repose beside those of Daniel Boone.

A Negro Defends a Family

The attack on the Ballard family was but one of a hundred others of a similar nature, made upon defenseless homes in the neighborhood of Boonesborough, Bryan, Lexington and Tyler, and the whole territory was thrown into a state of the wildest alarm. In the vicinity of Crab Orchard settlement an attack was made upon a cabin sheltering a woman and three children. It chanced at the time of the attack the husband was absent, but a negro man, a neighbor, was in the cabin, having come upon a business errand. The assailing party consisted of six Indians who were bent upon the double purpose of massacre and pillage. As they approached within sight of the cabin one of the Indians was sent forward to reconnoiter, to ascertain if any men were

A BRAVE WOMAN'S DEFENSE OF HER HOME

FLAT-BOAT EMIGRATION

present to defend the home, and as this Indian saw only a woman and her children, he believed them to be defenseless and pushed open the door and entered. But his reception was a warm one. The negro boldly grappled with the savage and in a trice threw him upon the floor and held him there until the woman could seize an ax and brain him, which she did with such promptness that the Indian was dead before his comrades could come to his aid. The other Indians rushed forward, but the door was shut and barred in their faces. With great presence of mind the woman grabbed down from its rack an old rusty musket, and thrusting the muzzle through a crack gave such an appearance of valorous resistance that the five Indians beat a hasty retreat.

Flat-Boat Emigration

As previously mentioned, emigration to Kentucky had almost entirely ceased on account of the depredations committed by Indians, which, after the Clark expedition, became more numerous and of a more terrible character than ever before in the history of Kentucky. But the great flow of emigration westward continued over the route opened by Boone through Cumberland Gap and Powell's Valley. Instead of following that course into Kentucky, however, the travel was northward through the extreme eastern part of the territory and to the Ohio River, down which the tide now poured. Flat-boat building became a great industry, hundreds being constructed near the headwaters, in which families floated with all their possessions to lower Louisiana, where settlements began to spring up rapidly along the Mississippi banks. This mode of travel continued to be popular with emigrants for nearly fifty years, and until John A. Murrell's band of river pirates rendered it more perilous than overland routes.

It has been estimated that during the months of August, September and October of 1782, no fewer than five hundred families floated down the Ohio River in flat-boats, seeking homes in the newly opened up territory of western Tennessee and in Arkansas, Mississippi and Louisiana. This cavalcade, so to speak, of water craft, freighted as they were with horses, cattle, provisions, etc., excited the cupidity of Indians living along the north shore of Kentucky, and this new path of safety soon became a route of great peril. On account of the numerous attacks made nearly every day on the occupants of these boats Daniel Boone, acting under authority of Governor Harrison, appointed a force of forty spies to patrol the river banks for the double purpose of watching and reporting the movements of Indians, and to furnish assistance, whenever possible, to endangered emigrants.

Massacre of a Family and Capture of Two Girls

At the head of the spies thus appointed were Major Ballard—whose brave fight with twenty Indians at Tyler's Station has just been described, and which made him at once a noted frontiersman—and Captain McClanahan, another hero whose dust consecrates Kentucky soil.

While the spies were reconnoitering in the Miami Valley, they found in the lonely forest a young man in tatters, bewildered, and almost famished from hunger, who had effected an almost miraculous escape from a party of Indians, the particulars of which he related to the following effect: His father, mother and their family of five children were emigrating to West Tennessee by the common means of transportation, a flat-boat, well provisioned with necessaries for establishing themselves in a new home, when they were attacked by fifty Mississinawa and Pottawatami Indians, who approached the boat in canoes and massacred the entire family save himself and a sister named Harriet, and another young lady, a relative, named Lucy Smith. He effected his escape by leaping overboard and swimming to the shore unperceived, where he secreted himself in the hollow of a large sycamore tree until the boats had floated by. He gave his name as Henry Lane and stated that his former home was in Virginia, but what place has been forgotten.

Pursuit of the Savages

The immediate wants of young Lane were attended to and Major Ballard proposed at once to go in pursuit of the savages, whose trail the youth had discovered not far from the place where he was found. Every man in the company was equally eager for an affray with the murderous Indians, and a systematic hunt for the trail was soon begun. Towards evening of the same day a fresh heap of ashes was found near the river shore, and unmistakable evidences of a camp having been made at the spot not more than twenty-four hours before. This was regarded as a very fortunate discovery, since no one doubted that it had been the camp of the savages and that they were making no effort to hide the trail, but were doubtless still in the vicinity. Further on the party found the half of a broken tray, which young Lane recognized as one that his mother had used for kneading dough. They were now unmistakably on the trail, that led northward and which, being followed two miles further, revealed another evidence of the Indians' march in the finding of a garter that had belonged to Miss Lane.

AN INCIDENT OF THE BLOODY YEAR OF '82

It was now sun-down and the spies resolved to go into camp, as they were very tired, and to follow further at night might bring them into an ambush, for it was evident that the Indians were not far in advance.

Rescue of the Girls

Early on the following morning the pursuit was renewed and was continued all day on a hot trail, until darkness again compelled a halt. Wood was gathered for fire and everything made ready for camp, but before the match was applied a rifle shot was heard not more than a quarter of a mile distant, and on the bank of the river which the party had been following down. In a wilderness such as they were now traversing the report of a gun was the harbinger of danger, and the spies immediately held a council to decide what movement should be made. In pursuance of the result of the council's hasty deliberation, Maj. Ballard and a man named Basey went forward to reconnoiter, and after an absence of an hour returned and reported their discovery of a band of nearly fifty Indians under the river bank, who were then making camp, but had not yet lighted their fire. Every man seemed now eager to engage the savages, but they resolved to wait until the Indians had kindled their fire, by the light of which the attack could be made with better execution; besides, it was important to first know if the white girls were still with their captors, and also their position in the camp, lest in firing upon the Indians the girls might be killed.

The spies, well prepared for making the attack, advanced towards the Indians after another hour had elapsed and found them seated about a large fire holding a council. At the same time the two girls were discovered seated on the outskirts of the camp with their hand bounds together and their feet tied to a tree, and in a position between the spies and the savages, which would expose them if the attack were now made. It therefore became necessary for the spies to move further down and closer to the enemy, which they did without betraying their presence. At the word of Maj. Ballard the spies now poured a volley into the completely surprised savages with such deadly effect that twelve Indiana were instantly killed and nearly as many more were wounded. The greatest confusion now prevailed among the Indians, but those not injured seized their guns and began firing in the direction from whence the shots first came, but without doing any damage, on account of the darkness which completely concealed the spies. The Indians then scattered and a lively but random fusillade was kept up between the two parties for a few minutes until the savages got a chance to break through the lines of their foes and escaped, leaving their dead and wounded on the ground. With tomahawk and knife the latter were dispatched with as little mercy as the Indians themselves had shown in massacring the defenseless people on the

THE SAVAGE CAPTORS IN COUNCIL

flat-boat, and when the action was over twenty-one dead Indians lay in promiscuous heaps about the bloody camp-fire; but sad to relate, among the slaughtered savages was found the body of a white woman who had not been seen by the spies when the attack was made. She had been captured by the Indians some time before the massacre of the Lanes, but it was never ascertained where or under what circumstances, as she had not been allowed to converse with the two girls. It was supposed, however, that she was a French lady, made prisoner at the pillage and massacre of Heckerwelder, a Moravian town near the Muskingum River, that was laid waste by the Pottawatamies a month before.

The First Marriage in Cincinnati

The two girls were so transported with joy at their deliverance that for a time they were hysterical, and fears were entertained that they had become insane; but kind treatment restored their reason on the following day, though they were never able to give any rational account of the indignities they had been subjected to at the hands of their captors. They were conveyed to the nearest post, which was Fort

CRAWFORD'S FIGHT WITH THE WYANDOTTES

Washington (now Cincinnati), and turned over to the care of Governor St. Clair and his wife. A happy sequel terminated this singular and bloody adventure. Miss Lucy Smith was a very beautiful girl and the strange manner and romance of her rescue, added to the attractions of her form and face, won the love of Charles Wilson, one of the spies. He gave her every possible attention on the route to Fort Washington and on the day of their arrival at the post he made an offer of marriage to Miss Smith, which was accepted. Three weeks afterwards the two were quietly married by Gov. St. Clair, being the first couple joined in matrimony within the limits of what is now Cincinnati.

The Crawford Expedition

The whites did not always meet with such success as that which attended the pursuit just described; in fact, during the whole of 1782 the Indians held the advantage, and gained several battles, one of which was quite as disastrous to the whites as the fight at Blue Licks. From every post came news of invasions and massacres; men were shot down in the fields, women and children were brained in their cabins, small parties were captured, and torture was inflicted upon not a few. It was, indeed, a terribly bloody year. The western frontiers of Pennsylvania and Virginia were not exempt from these outrages, and their frequent perpetration aroused the people of those two States as well as those of Kentucky. An expedition, consisting of four hundred men, was planned against the Wyandotte Indians, who had been scourging Virginia for a year past. The command of this force was given to Colonel William Crawford, who set out through the wilderness northwest of the Ohio River for the Wyandotte towns on the Sandusky, intending to beard the enemy in their own territory and, if possible, to devastate their lands and to break their power for evil.

There was, unfortunately, a spirit of insubordination manifested in the expedition directly after it was organized, that resulted finally in the desertion of fifty men. The others continued on, however, until the enemy's country was reached, but at no time was there any heroic resolve exhibited by the force to engage the Indians, but on the contrary a lukewarmness that constantly threatened the party with grave danger.

When the expedition at length, after a tedious march and numerous complaints, reached the Sandusky, Colonel Crawford received reports from his scouts that the Indians were in force within less than three miles distant and marching to meet the whites, whose approach had evidently been discovered. Immediate preparations were made for a fight, which began about three o'clock and continued briskly, though without material results to either side, until dark. The Indians now drew off while the whites held the ground and slept on their arms. The engagement opened early the following morning, but it was evident from the maneuvering of the enemy that they were waiting re-enforcements. Colonel Crawford accordingly pushed his advantage, with the hope of crushing the Indians before other bodies could come up, but he was not able to accomplish his object, the savages adopting their customary tactics of scattering so as to avoid a general conflict.

A second time darkness put an end to the battle, and when firing ceased Crawford held a council with his men to decide their action on the morrow. He was somewhat surprised to learn that the universal sentiment was in a favor of a retreat, though the decision was in accordance with his own opinion, for he now saw that his force was inadequate to meet so large a body of Indians as could be brought against him; and that too, in a country which was a perfect wilderness, unknown to any in his command.

A Disastrous Retreat

It having been resolved to retreat, time was precious, and orders were immediately given to prepare to break camp. A great bustle at once began, and no little confusion, as fear seemed to suddenly take possession of every man. By nine o'clock the retreat commenced which was so far from being orderly that the men acted like startled quails, each one looking to his own safety, by which the peril of all was vastly increased. The noise caused by the stampede aroused the Indians who, appreciating the situation,

THE HORRIBLE PUNISHMENT OF COL. CRAWFORD

charged upon the discomfited troops that were now incapable of defense, and a carnage began that was simply terrible. Notwithstanding the darkness scores were shot down or tomahawked while others were taken prisoners, not out of mercy but to be reserved for a worse fate.

Among the captives taken in this awful rout was Colonel Crawford himself, who was knocked down and bound and then taken to a position where he could see, though imperfectly, by reason of the darkness, the slaughter of his wounded comrades.

Only a few of the original three hundred and fifty volunteers who went into the battle escaped. On the following morning the scene that was presented was sickening in the extreme. Not yet satisfied with their victory the Indians went among the slain whites and committed such indignities upon the bodies as beggars description. Wherever one was found in which the spark of life still lingered the torch of torture was applied, while the dead were stripped and mutilated until they resembled a vultures' feast.

Among the fiends engaged in this dread sacrilege the captive Colonel recognized his old enemy, the border Nemesis, Simon Girty, and though the scenes enacted before his eyes prefigured what his own fate must be, he now knew that escape from a more dreadful death than he had yet witnessed was impossible.

The Burning of Colonel Crawford

Preparation for the holocaust was soon begun. A large fire was built, around which gathered nearly fifty squaws, each provided with a cudgel. Colonel Crawford was next brought within this circle, and being divested of all his clothes his body was blackened with charcoal, after which the squaws set upon him with their sticks and beat him into

THE BURNING OF CRAWFORD

insensibility. While this torture was being inflicted several other Indians were engaged gathering a quantity of dry brush and piling it in a circle around a tree that stood within sight of the victim.

The sufferer was permitted to lie for a time unmolested, and until he had recovered consciousness, when he was taken and bound to the tree to undergo a yet more terrible ordeal. Comprehending the horror of his situation, Crawford appealed to Girty for compassion, but his supplications were of no more avail than the bleat of a lamb in the jaws of a wolf, the malignant renegade giving no other reply than a mocking laugh. In another moment the circle of brush was fired and amid the yells of the savages, to drown the cries of the victim, the sacrifice was begun. The small mercy of applying the fire directly and consuming his body was denied him, the circle of flame being just large enough to blister the flesh, in which position he was kept until his body was roasted, and yet life remained. Thus was his agony protracted for nearly an hour, and until he became unconscious, when the brands were kicked under him and heaped up anew, until his body was completely consumed.

The torture and agonizing death suffered by Crawford was witnessed by Dr. Knight, who was captured at the same time with his more unfortunate companion, but the fates were more merciful to him. Instead of submitting him to the stake the Indians carried the doctor back with them to Chillicothe, where it was proposed to burn him, in which resolution they were foiled, however, by the doctor effecting his escape, through the aid of a Shawanee Indian whom he had cured of a fever. The doctor afterwards wrote and published an account of the disasters that overtook the expedition, and a description of the tortures inflicted on Colonel Crawford, from which the facts, as given above, were obtained.

It is some consolation to know that justice, though long delayed, finally overtook the miscreant through whose influence, there is no doubt, Crawford was brought to the stake. Girty continued his criminal career among the Indians until the year 1814, when he was with Proctor at the battle of the Thames, and there met his doom at the hands of the Kentuckians, who were led to victory by the gallant Colonel Johnson.

CHAPTER XI

Cessation of Hostilities and a Period of Prosperity

With the close of 1782 there came a period of inviting peace, dearly purchased and therefore all the more highly prized. The Kentuckians had fought with the pride of a true knight who finds honor only on a bloody field, but incessant warfare or watchfulness, with almost daily reports of outrage, massacre or torture, had taught them the value of peace, for which they now sincerely longed.

The fortune of Kentucky began under new auspices in 1783, when hostilities between the United States and Great Britain were concluded. A fortunate termination of the war gave promise of a speedy cession of all British posts on the northwestern frontier, which so discouraged the Indians, whose powerful allies were thus withdrawn from them, that they ceased their incursions into Kentucky and gave the settlers opportunity to acquire and cultivate new tracts of land.

Up to this time Boone had, in common with all other Kentuckians, devoted his attention to devising measures of defense and giving both his counsel and help in repelling the savage invaders. A period of quiet having now come, he turned his energies in a new direction and became an excellent example to his associate pioneers. For his services as an officer in the militia and volunteer forces, as well as for other and special aid extended to the government of Virginia, under appointment of the governor, he was paid a sum equal to one thousand dollars, which he used in making purchases of several desirable bodies of land and in surveying others that he expected to acquire later. Upon one of these locations he erected a substantial log house, into which he moved, and after clearing several acres began farming in a primitive way common to the times.

It was in 1783 that the three counties organized in 1780 were united in one district, with the establishment of a court of common law for the whole territory that now constitutes the entire State. Harrodsburg was at first selected as the capital, but on account of its inconvenient situation, the seat was established at Danville, which was nearer the center of population. This action, which was equivalent to a territorial organization and the fore-runner of Statehood, gave an immense impetus to immigration, that soon began to pour into Kentucky from Virginia proper, North Carolina and Pennsylvania. Land was rapidly taken up by new settlers, and Boone soon found his hands full acting as a surveyor, to which position he had been appointed two years before.

Boone Discomfits Four Indians

There was uninterrupted prosperity in the Kentucky settlements until 1784, when a few bands of thieving Indians made incursions into the territory and created considerable alarm, though their depredations consisted chiefly in running off stock, and occasional outrages on isolated families. During this period of renewed alarms a curious adventure befell Daniel Boone, which at once serves to illustrate his bravery and cunning: In addition to a considerable field planted with corn, Boone cultivated a small patch of tobacco, not for his own use, however, as nearly all his neighbors did, for he was free from the habit of either chewing or smoking so prevalent among early

BOLD STRATAGEM OF BOONE

settlers and especially hunters. At the time referred to Boone had gathered his crop and housed it in a rude kind of barn for curing. This shelter was built of rails raised to a height of nearly fifteen feet and covered with grass which was twisted and wrought into a thatch. In the curing of tobacco the stalks are split and strung on sticks some four feet in length. The ends of these sticks are laid on poles that extend across the barn, and arranged in slanting tiers parallel with the sloping roof. Boone was engaged in disposing his tobacco in this manner, and in shifting the lower tier, which dries quicker than the upper ones. While thus employed least suspecting any danger, and therefore not prepared for resistance, four Shawanese Indians, armed with guns, entered the low door of the shelter and drew a bead upon him, at the same time challenging him to come down, that his fate was now sealed. With wonderful self-possession Boone pleasantly hailed his enemies with assurances that he was glad to see them, and that he was curing some tobacco which he had intended for their use; he therefore asked that he might be allowed to change the tiers which would require but a short while, when he promised to willingly accompany them whither they had a mind to take him. Their advantage being so great, the Indians acceded to his request, and lowering their guns stood patiently beneath their prisoner until the adroit Boone had collected an armful of the very driest tobacco, with which he jumped down upon the heads of his astounded captors, at the same time crushing and scattering it so that the pungent dust arose in a cloud, filling the eyes, mouths and noses of the Indians, and so discomfiting them that he easily contrived to run out of the shelter and gain his cabin. The savages were so nearly blinded and choked by the tobacco dust, that it was several minutes before they were able to find their way out of the rude barn, and now expecting to be in turn attacked by Boone, they fled to the woods and were not again seen.

Another Threatened Invasion by the Indians

During the year 1784 a census was taken of the people within the borders of Kentucky proper—though how it was done, if at all, is not recorded—which showed a population of thirty thousand whites. A store had been opened at Louisville by Daniel Broadhead, and a large commercial company, with James Wilkinson at the head, was planted at Lexington, which opened a traffic with the settlers whereby all kinds of provisions calculated to increase the comforts of the pioneers were exchanged for peltries, tobacco and corn, which latter began now to be considerably cultivated.

INDIANS KILLING AND RUNNING OFF STOCK

But in the midst of the fullest promise and prosperity that Kentucky had ever experienced report came of another Indian invasion. The posts of the Northwest had not been surrendered at the close of hostilities with Great Britain, contrary to general anticipation, and a destruction of several wigwams in upper Ohio by an expedition headed by General Clark again aroused the Indians, who resolved upon wreaking retribution upon the Kentuckians, who chiefly composed the expedition.

The alarm which this report occasioned was very great and a meeting was immediately called at Danville, which Boone attended as a counselor, to consider measures for the public defense. It fortunately transpired that the Indians were deterred from their purpose by some reverses in minor engagements with bands of militia sent out to intercept them, and the threatened invasion was happily averted. But the need of organizing a military force for defense in any emergency was recognized as being still imperative, and in pursuance of this general opinion a convention of settlers met at Danville, December 27th. At this assembling the belief was expressed that Kentucky ought to seek a severance from Virginia which, considering the extent of territory, was unable to afford protection, and that in such a division only could Kentucky find security, by a reliance upon her own resources.

Though there was great unanimity among the settlers upon the question of separating from Virginia, no decisive action was taken; several other conventions were held in the following year, at which the same question was debated affirmatively, and the agitation was so persistent that in 1786 the legislature of Virginia passed a bill providing for the separation of Kentucky and its erection into a separate State, when it should possess the required population, but it was not until 1792 that it was finally adopted into the Union.

Trouble with the Indians Renewed

Though the threatened invasion of 1786 was not made in force, yet several roving bands of Indians crossed into Kentucky from the Indian territory of Ohio and committed many depredations, principally in stealing stock. In April of that year a party of a dozen made a raid on the Bear Grass settlement and succeeded in getting away with seven horses belonging to the settlers.

Colonel Christian, who was one of the sufferers, called together a score of his neighbors as hastily as possible and went in pursuit. The Indians were overtaken shortly after they had crossed the Ohio and so completely surprised that every one was destroyed, but not until two or three of them returned the fire, by which Colonel Christian and one of his followers were killed. His loss was severely felt by the Kentuckians, who held him in great favor for his bravery, good judgment, and excellent citizenship.

DEATH OF COL. CHRISTIAN

Following on the affair just described came an attack on Higgin's Fort which was a stockade protecting six or seven cabins, built on the bank of the Licking River. There were perhaps twenty Indians in the attacking party, but after firing a single volley they retired, but only as a ruse to draw the settlers out of their defenses. Those within the stockade were too well versed in Indian tactics to be thus deceived, and instead of sallying out began to prepare for a siege. Perceiving that their plans were of no avail the Indians made a descent on the cabin of William McCombs which occupied a site on the river bank a quarter of a mile below the fort. The old gentleman was not at home at the time, but his son Andrew and a hired man named Joseph McFall, besides the female members of the family, were in the cabin, having just risen, it being so early in the morning as to be hardly daylight. The two men were first apprised of their danger when upon coming outside to wash themselves they were both shot down, McCombs receiving a bullet in the knee and McFall one in the pit of the stomach. The former was dragged back into the cabin by his sisters, but though desperately wounded McFall regained his feet and ran with great speed toward the stockade which he gained without further injury, though what he had received was sufficient for he died on the following day. Ten men within the stockade, learning of the peril of the McCombs family, mounted their horses and with ready rifles went to the relief. The Indians seeing advancing horsemen, and not being able to discover the number, broke and fled, not even taking time to deliver a single volley.

ATTACK ON THE PENNSYLVANIA EMIGRANTS

In October following a number of emigrant families from Pennsylvania were surprised in camp, by a band of Indians on Little Laurel River, and twenty-one persons,
including men, women and children, were massacred, and ten others were taken captive, but what fate ultimately befell them was never known by their friends.

Two months later Colonel Hargrave, with a party of thirty spies were attacked
at night at the mouth of Buck Creek, on the Cumberland River and routed, but with
the loss of only a single man. Hargrave was himself wounded and became engaged
in a hand-to-hand encounter with one of the savages. The fight lasted only for a
moment when Hargrave wrested the Indian's tomahawk from his grasp and would
have brained him had not the savage foe retreated at an opportune moment. The
Indians were so cowardly that they refused to follow up the advantage, but drew off
after discharging their guns and throwing the camp into disorder.

A Horrible Story of a Massacre

The year 1787 began less auspiciously than any preceding period, for the Indians
were increasing in number in Kentucky, and their outrages were constantly more
daring and numerous, until the entire territory was in a state of intense excitement
and alarm.

Early in April the house of a widow named Rankin, in Bourbon County, became the scene of a desperate adventure. The house was a double cabin one end of which was occupied by the old lady, two grown sons, and a married daughter, who had an infant. The other end of the dwelling was a sleeping room for three daughters aged, respectively, eighteen, fifteen and ten years.

On the night in question, about eleven o'clock, when all of the family was in bed with the exception of the elder girl, who was engaged at the loom, and her older brother, some singular noises were heard that put them immediately in a state of grave anxiety. A frequent hooting, in imitation of owls, was heard in the neighboring wood, and as this was known to be a common signal among Indians, a suspicion was at once excited that enemies were about.

Soon afterwards a step was heard in the yard, followed quickly by a knock on the door of the cabin occupied by the widow and two sons and a voice that asked in good English, "Who keeps house?" The young man, who had first heard the unusual noises was deceived by the inquiry, believing that some belated traveler was without who sought shelter. He was accordingly upon the point of opening the door when his mother sprang out of bed and arrested his hand, declaring at the same time that it was Indians who desired admittance.

The mother quickly awakened the other son, and the two young men seized their guns and prepared to receive the enemy with becoming heroism. The Indians, finding that they could not deceive the family, began to batter the door with the butts of their rifles, when a shot from a loophole admonished them to seek a less exposed point from which to make the attack, and in making a circuit of the dwelling they unfortunately discovered the door of the other cabin which sheltered the three daughters. The brothers could not defend this point without exposing their persons, and the Indians were thus secure in perpetrating their fiendish atrocities on the defenseless girls. With rails they quickly broke the door from its hinges, and rushing in, grabbed one of the daughters, but the eldest defended herself with a knife, which she used to cut the thread of her loom, and stabbed one of the villains to the heart before her brains were dashed out with a tomahawk.

In the meantime the little girl, who had been overlooked by the enemy in their eagerness to secure the others, ran out into the yard, and might have effected her escape, had she taken advantage of the darkness and fled; but instead of that, the terrified little creature ran around the house wringing her hands, and crying out that her sisters were killed. The brothers, unable to hear her cries without risking everything for her rescue, rushed to the door and were preparing to sally out to her assistance, when their mother threw herself before them and calmly declared that the child must be abandoned to its fate; that the sally would sacrifice the lives of all the rest, without

ATTACK ON THE CABIN

the slightest benefit to the fated child. Just then the little girl uttered a loud scream, followed by a few faint moans, and all was again silent. Presently the crackling of flames was heard, accompanied by a triumphant yell from the Indians, announcing that they had set fire to that division of the house which had been occupied by the daughters, and of which they held undisputed possession.

The fire was quickly communicated to the rest of the building, and it became necessary to abandon it or perish in the flames. In the one case there was a possibility that one more of the family might escape; in the other their fate would be equally certain and terrible. The rapid approach of the flames cut short their momentary suspense. The door was thrown open, and the old lady, supported by her eldest son, attempted to cross the fence at one point while her daughter, carrying her child in her arms, and attended by the younger of the brothers, ran in a different direction. The blazing roof shed a light over the yard but little inferior to that of day, and the savages were distinctly seen awaiting the approach of their victims. The old lady was permitted to reach the stile unmolested, but in the act of crossing received several balls in her breast and fell dead. Her son, providentially, remained unhurt, and by extraordinary agility effected his escape.

The daughter and son succeeded also in reaching the fence unhurt, but here they were vigorously assailed by several Indians, who, throwing down their guns, rushed upon the two with their tomahawks. The young man defended his sister gallantly, firing upon the enemy as they approached, and then wielding the butt of his rifle with a fury that drew their whole attention upon himself, and gave his sister an opportunity of effecting her escape. He soon fell, however, under the tomahawks of his enemies, and was found at daylight scalped and mutilated in a shocking manner. Of the entire family, consisting of eight persons at the time of the attack, only three escaped. Four were killed upon the spot, and the second daughter was carried off a prisoner, but only to soon meet a fate as horrible as that which befell her gallant brother.

Killing of the Captive Girl

News of the dreadful massacre spread with such rapidity through the neighborhood that before noon a party of thirty brave men had gathered together and, under the leadership of Captain Edwards, set out in pursuit. A light snow had fallen during the night which made the Indian trail so plain that it could be followed at a swift gallop. It led directly into the mountains bordering the Licking, and showed great haste on the part of the fugitives, but it was manifest that they could not travel so rapidly as the well-mounted pursuers, who were burdened with no baggage and had perfectly fresh horses.

Unfortunately, a hound had been permitted to accompany the whites, and as the trail became fresher the dog naturally enough gave voice and rushed on ahead, until

MURDER OF THE YOUNG GIRL

the Indians were apprised, by the loud baying, of the proximity of the pursuing party. The enemy thus finding themselves so nearly overtaken and the strength of their prisoner failing, to relieve themselves of the burden, they sank a tomahawk into the poor girl's head and left her dying upon the snow.

When the whites came up they found the girl gasping, but she had not yet lost consciousness; the brother, who had joined in the pursuit, leaped from his horse and took her outstretched hand in his, but in another moment she was dead. He remained beside her body, however, while his comrades pushed on in rapid pursuit until within another hour they had run the Indians to cover, and a desultory fight began. The enemy masked their movements so thoroughly that the main body made good their escape by leaving two of their number to cover the retreat. These two kept up their fire and succeeded in completely deceiving the whites, who believed the whole force was still engaged, while in fact they had drawn off and were then in the fastnesses of the mountain and scattered, so that the trail could not be followed. The two Indians who had thus apparently offered themselves as a sacrifice to secure the safety of their comrades, were killed, but no other casualties attended the fight.

Finding that the enemy had escaped them, the party of whites returned to the spot where Miss Rankin had been murdered and carried the body back to the ruins of the cabin. The other bodies were then recovered and all were buried in one grave, at which a headboard was erected on which was briefly inscribed a record of the terrible massacre.

Capture of Simon Kenton and His Punishment

The settlements throughout Kentucky were thrown into the greatest disorder by the harrowing outrages that continued to be reported, and several measures were proposed to repel the invaders, but there was lacking a unanimity of action which gave little hope of security from the Indians. At length, Boone sent Simon Kenton out at the head of fifty men to patrol the settlements and to act as a band of succor to those residing within the district that was suffering most. This distinguished leader was not long in finding the savages, but his gallantry was ill requited, for in his first encounter with the enemy his comrades deserted him at the sight of a force of nearly two hundred Indians, but which Kenton did not hesitate to attack. The result was disastrous, for Kenton was made prisoner while fighting against an overwhelming number and was carried away to Chillicothe to undergo a torture like that to which other brave but unfortunate pioneers had been subjected.

Directly upon arriving at Chillicothe the Indians assembled on a common in the suburbs of their village, and here stripping Kenton, they formed a double line and compelled him to run the gauntlet. Each Indian in the two lines was armed with a stout cudgel, and as the prisoner ran down between them they showered blows upon his bared back which must have killed an ordinary man, but his endurance was so great that he passed through the ordeal without serious injury. In some accounts of

KENTON PASSING THE GAUNTLET

this event it is reported that Kenton conducted himself with such an exhibition of nerve and bravery that the Indians permitted him to walk down their two files without administering a single blow; but whichever version of the incident be true, it is certain that he was subjected to a yet more terrible trial.

When the amusement of having Kenton run the gauntlet was concluded the Indians prepared to burn him at the stake. Brushwood was gathered and piled in heaps about a tree to which it was intended to bind the prisoner for the sacrifice. When these preparations were completed Kenton was led forth, still bound, but before the fire was lighted he recognized among his captors the grizzly form and face of the wolfish Girty, whom he had known intimately in earlier years, before the renegade had been adopted into the brotherhood of savages.

To this scourge and disgrace of his race Kenton now made an appeal which, singularly enough, was not without avail, to the surprise of even Kenton himself. Until now Girty had not recognized in the troubled features of the prisoner the face of his old comrade with whom he had often hunted in their native haunts of Virginia and who had been the associate of his boyhood. However, the recognition being now complete, Girty immediately became the champion of his friend, and pleaded for his life with all the power and influence that he could command. While Girty had never acted as a chief among the Indians, he was held in such great esteem by them that his counsel had almost the weight of the most important men of the several tribes, and in special instances he had exercised a complete control, amounting to virtual supremacy. The fullest power of his influence was now exerted on behalf of Kenton, and with such effect that the Indians abandoned their intention of burning him, but could not be induced to liberate him without some farther punishment.

A Mazeppa Ride

After debating for a while among themselves, from which counsel Girty himself was excluded, the Indians decided to submit Kenton, bound and helpless, to the back of a fiery horse and trust the result to fortune. It was a novel mode of punishment, and promised to the savages an enjoyment greater than even the gauntlet or the stake afforded. Accordingly a very wild, and as yet unbroken, horse was brought out and held by a dozen Indians while Kenton, whose back still remained stripped of clothing, was placed astride the struggling animal and his feet tied fast under its belly. At a word the horse was now liberated and with several severe lashes from those who stood near, to make him start the more suddenly, the animal bounded off and through the woods at a wonderful speed, followed by a dozen mounted savages anxious to enjoy the sport as long as possible. The horse ran in a direct line for nearly a dozen miles,

GIRTY, THE RENEGADE

over hills, through valleys, across brooks, down declivities and into thick primeval forests until at last his strength was spent and he stopped from sheer exhaustion. The Indians, who had at first followed the mad steed, were soon left behind in the race, for they were unwilling to stake such desperate chances, at a break-neck speed, as would be necessary to keep up with the scared animal, that had been thus strangely released of all restraint.

For two days the horse wandered about the broken country, somewhat reconciled to the helpless rider, who maintained his seat despite all efforts to throw him off, and notwithstanding the suffering he endured from branches striking him in the face, and the pain caused by the cords with which he was bound. At length the horse, in grazing about, strayed back to the place from which he was started and the Indians, through Girty's influence, now had such compassion upon the bleeding and almost unconscious rider that they released him, and a few days afterwards permitted him to return to Kentucky and his friends.

This wonderful ride of Kenton's will constitute forever one of the most interesting chapters in the annals of Kentucky, but it is not alone celebrated in the history of the pioneers, for the tale has been immortalized by one of the world's greatest poets, Byron, whose story of Mazeppa, it is claimed, was inspired by the incident. In his advertisement of the story, Byron quotes from Voltaire's *History of Charles XII* (of Sweden) in which he gives the idea that the facts for his verse were taken from an incident that transpired during the war between Russia and Sweden; but there is better evidence for believing that the poem was prompted by Kenton's ride, based chiefly on the knowledge that Byron delighted in reading tales of adventure between the Indians and white men and used many such incidents in his verse, his poem on Daniel Boone being particularly favorable to the argument.

A Treaty of Peace That Brought No Security

The harsh experience through which Kenton had passed instead of abating his fighting ardor aroused him the more and thenceforth for several years he hunted Indians as he would hunt game, and scores fell before his rifle. He became, therefore, to the Indians, and particularly to the Wyandottes, who had subjected him to such hard punishment, what Girty was to the whites, a cunning, dangerous and implacable foe, seeking an extermination of his enemies.

A desultory warfare was carried on, in which defenseless families were the chief sufferers, until 1789, when a conference was held with a majority of the northwestern

A SAMPLE OF SHAWANESE ATROCITY

tribes at one of their villages on the Muskingum, which resulted in the adoption of a treaty of peace, and on such favorable terms and with such assurances of public security that the settlers entertained hopes that their troubles with the Indians were at an end.

The Shawanese tribe had refused, or neglected, to attend the conference, but though they had committed more outrages than any other of the confederated tribes, their numbers were comparatively small and it was therefore believed that they would cease their depredations with the others. In this opinion, however, the settlers were deceived, for the Shawanese continued to infest the settlements and to pillage, outrage and massacre wherever they could find unprotected cabins, or opportunity to exercise their fiendish propensities. The whites were therefore aroused to action and as it was difficult for them to distinguish between hostile and friendly Indians, in their determination to avenge injuries they soon became involved with the tribes that had subscribed to the treaty. Thus the old trouble broke out afresh and with great virulence, and during the next two years it is said that nearly fifteen hundred white people were killed on Kentucky soil. It was a dreary and horrible repetition of every species of vandalism, reported nearly every day, until 1794, when the Indians were finally subjugated by Wayne's decisive victory. A treaty was soon afterwards signed at Greenville, and peace was restored, the first substantial fruits reaped by Kentucky in the efforts of pioneers to reclaim her territory to civilization.

CHAPTER XII

The Last Days of Boone

During the long period of a continuous and bloody struggle, through which Kentucky passed, until the Indian power for evil was broken in 1794, Boone conducted himself as a true hero, but with genuine regret must it be said that a record of his services after 1784 is entirely wanting. In this year he related some of the more important incidents of his life to a young man named John Folsom, who wrote and published a brief account of the great hunter, but which makes no mention of any act of his life subsequent to 1794. Even this account, which professes to have been written at the dictation of Boone, contains many erroneous statements, manifest even to the casual reader. Why they were suffered to remain uncorrected we are not permitted to know.

Occasional references to Boone, in the history of the commonwealth, afford us a mere indication of the part he played and the influence he exerted in the campaigns against the Indians. These brief references have justified the descriptions of incidents which appear foreign to the subject of Boone's biography; their importance and connection with the life of our hero will be seen in the necessity for showing the progress of settlement in Kentucky, and the probable part he continued to play, in which the record is wanting.

From contemporaneous pioneers, more careful to preserve to history the incidents of their lives and of their prominent associates, are we indebted for what we know of Boone after 1794 and until his death, the latter years of his life being particularly described by several writers who visited him, and by his neighbors.

As stated in a previous chapter, Boone invested the money which he received from the State of Virginia for services rendered the State in acquiring lands, large bodies of which he owned at the conclusion of the treaty of 1794, considerable tracts being brought under cultivation, while he held others for investment. But a series of misfortunes now overtook him, by which the accumulations of years were ultimately entirely swept away.

Boone Is Impoverished and Removes from Kentucky

In 1792 Kentucky was admitted into the Union as a State. As courts of justice were established in every community, litigation increased, and was carried to a distressing extent. Many of the old pioneers, who had cleared farms in the midst of the wilderness, and were prepared to spend the remainder of their days surrounded by peace and plenty, had their homes wrested from them, through lack of legal titles, by greedy and avaricious speculators, and were cast adrift in their old age, to again fight the battle of existence. Colonel Boone was among the sufferers. Every foot of his land was taken from him, and he was left penniless. His recorded descriptions of location and boundary were defective, and shrewd speculators had the adroitness to secure legal titles by more accurate and better defined entries.

Disgusted and heart-sick over the difficulties that beset him, he removed to Point Pleasant, in the Kenawha Valley in Virginia, where he remained only a short time, when he decided to once more seek a home in the western wilderness, in some place where he might hope to live free from oppressions such as the law, or ignorance of it, sometimes impose. In 1792, his son, Daniel M., had removed from Boonesborough and settled in Missouri, which was then called Upper Louisiana. The letters which he sent back to his father were filled with praises for the new country; its soil was alluvial and rich beyond any that could be found in the east, the game was so plentiful as to furnish a variety of meats for a king's table, deer, buffalo, bear, turkey, chickens, quail, etc., in picturesque profusion, while the climate was like that of paradise. These descriptions fascinated Boone, and he resolved to seek this new and marvelous country which promised so

ON THE HAPPY HUNTING GROUNDS OF MISSOURI

much in exchange for the sufferings and privations he was then enduring. About the same time that he had formed this resolution, he received a letter from the lieutenant-governor of Upper Louisiana, Zenon Trudeau, inviting him to make his home in the territory and offering him, as an inducement, the grant of a large tract of land.

Boone was greatly affected by this generous offer, which proved a balm to the indignities and wrongs he had suffered in Kentucky, and in the spring of 1795, he gathered up his few possessions, which he put upon the backs of three pack-horses, and started on his long journey for the home of the son who had preceded him.

A part of his family was left behind, his two daughters, Lavinia and Rebecca, having married in Kentucky, remained there until their death, while Jesse settled down on a farm in the Kenawha Valley, married, and continued farming on his original homestead until 1819, when he, too, removed to Missouri.

Acquiring Land from the Spanish Government and His Troubles

For several years after Colonel Boone's removal, Upper Louisiana remained under Spanish rule, and the promise of the lieutenant-governor was faithfully fulfilled. On the 24th of January 1798, he received a concession of 1,000 arpents of land, situated in Femme Osage district. He afterward made an agreement with the Spanish

INDIANS IN MOCK COMBAT

authorities to bring one hundred families from Kentucky and Virginia to Upper Louisiana, for which he was to receive 10,000 arpents of land. The agreement was fulfilled on both sides; but in order to confirm his title to this grant it was necessary to obtain the signature of the direct representative of the crown, who resided in New Orleans. Colonel Boone neglected this requirement, and his title was therefore declared invalid when the country came into possession of the United States by Jefferson's purchase.

Boone's title to the first grant of 1,000 arpents was also declared void, but was subsequently confirmed by special act of Congress. Both the American and Spanish governments, as a condition precedent to the confirmation of titles to lands, required actual settlements, but in 1800 Boone received the appointment of commandant of Femme Osage district, and was informed by Don Charles De Lassus, who had succeeded Don Zenon Trudeau as lieutenant-governor, that as his duties as commandant would require a considerable portion of his time, the Spanish government would confirm his title without requiring actual settlement. Relying upon this promise, Boone neglected to have the proper entries made upon the records, and when

Upper Louisiana was transferred to the United States, there was nothing to support his claim to a title for the lands. He subsequently petitioned Congress to confirm his title, which request, we are glad to know, was some years after granted.

Boone's Autograph Letter

It is not to be supposed that during this interval Boone made no personal effort to secure justice at the hands of the government, though his diffidence and quiet submission to the wrongs which he suffered in having his Kentucky lands wrested from him, would give color to such a presumption if evidence to the contrary were not supplied in the form of an autograph letter which is herewith printed in facsimile. So far as I have been able to learn, after a somewhat diligent inquiry, this is the only writing that is now preserved and known positively to have been by the pen of Boone. It is therefore a valuable curiosity, as indicating the measure of his schooling and his character of expression, as well as for its importance as a memento of a great man.

It will be observed in the letter that he uses the word "markery" for mercury, or calomel, a remedy in very general use fifty years ago, and particularly among pioneers, whose "homemade" practice was confined to two remedies, blisters and a cathartic. But what appears as a mistake in the spelling of the word is really only a localism, for in early days in Kentucky mercury was invariably called *markery*.

Judge John Coburn, the party to whom the letter was addressed, was a warm personal friend of Boone, whose acquaintance he had made at Boonesborough. He emigrated to Kentucky in 1784, and engaged in business at Lexington where he remained until the purchase of Louisiana when he settled in Missouri in the neighborhood of Ste. Genevieve. He afterward became a member of the territorial committee and was a colleague of Hon. Frederick Bates, subsequently acting governor, and also of Jno. B. C. Lucas and Otis Shrader, with whom he was associated in legislative duties.

In about the year 1807 Boone appealed to the legislature of Kentucky through Judge Coburn, who acted as his attorney, for a restoration of the lands that had been taken from him by reason of his failure to comply with technical requirements of the law. His petition was received with favor and a committee proposed a preamble to their report in which the following language was used.

"Taking into view the many eminent services rendered by Colonel Boone, in exploring and settling the western country, from which great advantages have resulted, not only to this State, but to this country in general, and that from circumstances over which he had no control he is now reduced to poverty, not having, so far as appears, an acre of land out of the vast territory originally granted to him and which he has been a great instrument in peopling. Believing, also, that it is as unjust as impolitic that

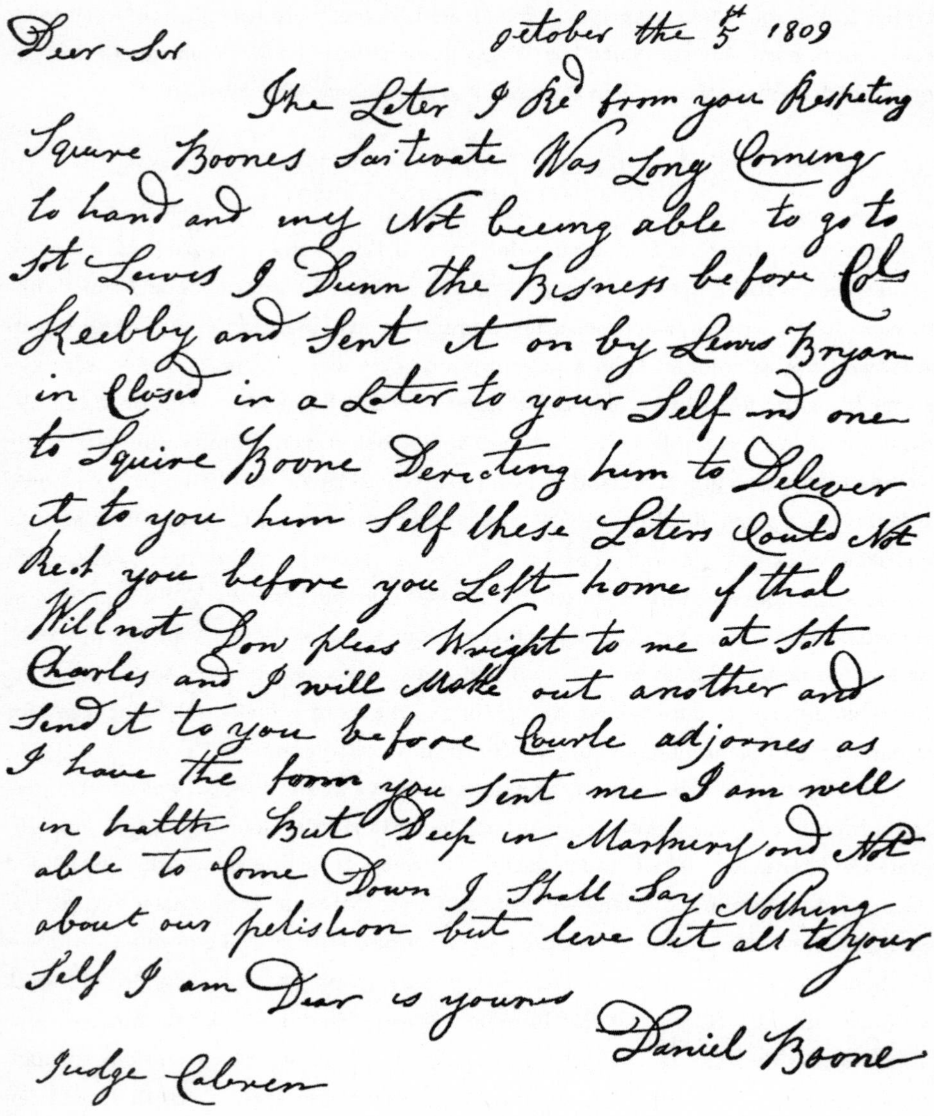

Dear Sir   october the 5th 1809

The Leter I Re'd from you Respeting Squire Boones Saitivate Was Long Coming to hand and my Not beeing able to go to St Lewis I Dunn the Bisness before Col Keebby and Sent it on by Lewis Bryan in Closed in a Leter to your Self and one to Squire Boone Derecting him to Deliver it to you him Self these Leters Could Not Rech you before you Left home if that Will not Do pleas Wright to me at St Charles and I will Make out another and Send it to you before Courte adjornes as I have the foom you sent me I am well in hatth But Deep in Marbury and Not able to Come Down I Shall Say Nothing about our petishon but leve it all to your Self I am Dear is yours

                              Daniel Boone

Judge Colvren

BOONE'S AUTOGRAPH LETTER

useful enterprise and eminent services should go unrewarded by a government where merit confers the only distinction; and having sufficient reason to believe that a grant of ten thousand acres of land, which he claims in Upper Louisiana, would have been confirmed by the Spanish Government had not said territory passed, by cession, into the hands of the general government; wherefore it is resolved, etc., that our senators in congress be requested to make use of their exertions to procure a grant of land in said territory to Boone; either the ten thousand acres, to which he appears to have an equitable claim, from the grounds set forth to this legislature, by way of confirmation, or to such quantity in such place as shall be deemed most advisable by way of donation."

This preamble it is believed was drafted, or at least supplied, from the facts and representations made by Judge Coburn, for which Boone was most grateful.

Boone's memorial to Congress was ably supported by the exertions of Judge Coburn, who greatly interested himself in his behalf.

Joseph Vance, then a member of Congress and afterwards governor of Ohio, and Judge Burnett, the efficient friend of General Morrison, both likewise called the attention of Congress "to the condition of the man who had been the foremost man of the west—a name (section) that even then influenced Congress, as it soon will rule it." Congress in December, 1813, then preoccupied by the attack of Canadians and Indians on our northern frontier, awarded to Boone the lesser donation of eight hundred and fifty acres out of the untold millions of the public domain, which the United States could so well spare. It made no reference to the 10,000 arpents (equivalent to nearly eight thousand five hundred acres) which the Spanish commandant had donated to him, and which decent gift for services rendered to the Spanish authorities Judge Coburn attempted to obtain for Boone, as explained.

It is matter for small wonder, in view of the facts as described, that it was only by the expenditure of great effort and persistency that Boone secured a title to even a small portion of the lands which he justly owned. More than one-half the applications for titles made at that period were rejected, and opposite the names of a majority of the claimants was written on the records the significant words, "forgery," "perjury," etc.

Colonel Boone and members of his family were the first actual American citizens to settle within the present limits of Missouri. The French had established trading posts at several points, and had founded a village at St. Louis which, at the time of Boone's coming, contained a population of about four hundred, but no regular settlements were made beyond these.

Louisiana was settled and remained in possession of the French until 1762, when, by a secret treaty, it was transferred to Spain. It thereafter became the policy of Spanish authorities to encourage immigration from the United States. Fears were entertained that an invasion of the country would be made by the British or Indians from Canada, and the Americans being regarded as the natural adversaries of the British, it was natural to suppose that they would the more readily fight to repel an invasion. The confidence thus imposed, as well as the fears entertained, was soon after verified. In 1781 St. Louis was attacked by a small army of confederated British and Indians, ostensibly in retaliation for the part the King of Spain had taken in favor of the independence of the United States.

ATTACK ON THE POST AT ST. LOUIS

Fifteen hundred Indians, and a small party of British soldiers, constituted the invading force, which came down the Mississippi. In the battle that ensued, more than sixty of the inhabitants were killed, and about thirty taken prisoners. At this crisis, Gen. George R. Clark, who was at Kaskaskia with several hundred men, besides the Illinois militia, appeared on the opposite side of the river. The British immediately raised the siege and retreated, and the Indians, declaring that they had no hostile intentions against the Spanish government, but had been deceived by the British, dispersed to their villages.

This event caused the Spanish authorities to increase their efforts for the encouragement of American immigration, and the most liberal offers were made and disseminated throughout the western settlements. The result was that the American population increased rapidly, and when the country was transferred to the United States in 1804 more than three-fifths of the population were Americans.

Restrictions on Religious Worship

During the Spanish administration, no religious sect was tolerated except the Roman Catholic. Each emigrant was required to be a Catholic, but this requirement was evaded by a pious fiction in the examination of the Americans; and Protestant families of all denominations settled in the province, obtained land grants, and were undisturbed in their religious beliefs. Protestant ministers came over from Illinois and preached in the cabins of the settlers, unmolested by the Spanish officers; although for the sake of keeping up a show of authority, they were occasionally threatened with imprisonment in the *calabozo* at St. Louis.

The late Reverend John Clark, a devoutly pious, but rather eccentric preacher, whose residence was in Illinois, made monthly excursions to the Spanish territory, and preached in the houses of the religious emigrants. He was a man of great simplicity of character, and much respected and beloved by all who knew him, amongst whom was M. Trudeau, the gentlemanly commandant at St. Louis. M. Trudeau would delay until he knew Mr. Clark's tour for that occasion was nearly finished, and then send a threatening message, that if Monsieur Clark did not leave the Spanish country in three days, he would put him in prison. This was repeated so often, as to furnish a pleasant joke with the preacher and his friends.

During these times, Mr. Abraham Music, who was a Baptist, and well acquainted with the commandant, and who likewise knew his religious principles, presented a petition for leave to hold meetings at his house, and for permission for Mr. Clark to preach there. The commandant, inclined to favor the American settlers secretly, yet compelled to reject all such petitions officially, replied promptly that such a petition could not be granted. It was in violation of the laws of the country. "I mean," said the accommodating officer, "you must not put a bell on your house, and call it a *church* nor suffer any person to christen your children but the parish priest. But if any of your friends choose to meet at your house, sing, pray, and talk about religion, you will not be molested, provided you continue, as I suppose you are, *un bon Catholique*." He well knew, that as Baptists they could dispense with the rite of infant baptism, and that plain, frontier people, as they were, could find the way to their meetings without the sound of the "church-going bell."

As early as the year 1800, the population of Femme Osage district had increased so much that some sort of a local government was required, and on the 11th of June of that year Colonel Boone, as before stated, was appointed commandant of the district. The powers of his office were both civil and military, and were almost absolute, if he had possessed either the means or the desire to make them so. His decision of all questions was final, except those in regard to land titles, which could only be decided by the crown or its direct representative.

But few crimes or misdemeanors were committed, and for these summary justice was dealt out to the offender. Whipping on the bare back was generally the punishment, and so just and equitable were Boone's sentences that the most abandoned characters never thought of raising objections to them or harboring resentment afterward.

In 1801 the territory of Upper Louisiana was ceded back to France by Spain, and in 1803 the country was purchased from France by the United States. During that interval the French did not again assume the government of the province, but the Spanish laws remained in force. The formal transfer of the country to the United States was made in March, 1804, and one year later the territory of Louisiana was regularly organized by act of Congress. As a temporary arrangement, the Spanish laws remained in force for a short time, and Colonel Boone continued to exercise the authority of his office. In fact, during the remainder of his life he had more to do with the government of his settlement than the laws, or the officers elected and appointed under them. The people had such unbounded confidence in his wisdom and justice that they preferred to submit their disputed questions to his arbitration, rather than to the uncertain issues of law.

How Boone Paid His Debts

During the first few years of their residence in Upper Louisiana Colonel Boone and his wife lived with their son, Daniel M., who had built a house in Darst's Bottom, adjoining the tract of 1,000 arpents of land granted to his father by the Spanish government. This entire tract, with the exception of 181 acres, was sold by Daniel M. Boone, who had charge of his father's business, to pay the old Colonel's debts in Kentucky, of which he had left quite a number upon his removal to the Spanish dominions, and although his creditors never would have made any demands upon him, yet he could not rest easy until they were paid. All his earnings, which he derived from peltries obtained in his hunting excursions, were carefully saved, and at length having made a successful hunt and obtained a valuable supply of peltries, he turned it all into cash, and visited Kentucky for the purpose of paying his debts. He had kept no book accounts, and knew not how much he owed, nor to whom he was indebted, but in the honest simplicity of his nature, he went to all with whom he had had dealings, and paid whatever was demanded. When he returned to his family he had half a dollar left. "But," said he to his family and a circle of friends who had called to see him, "now I am ready and willing to die. I have paid all my debts, and nobody can say, when I am gone, 'Boone was a dishonest man.'"

There is only one deed on the records in St. Charles signed by Daniel Boone, and that is for 181 acres of land (being a portion of the 1,000 arpents) sold to Wm. Coshow, August 6, 1813, for $315. The witnesses were D. M. Boone and John B. Callaway.

Colonel Boone and his son laid off a town on the Missouri River and called it Missouriton, in honor of the then territory of Missouri. They built a horse mill there, which was a great thing in those early days, and for a while the town flourished and promised well. At one time an effort was made to locate the capital of the territory there, but it failed, and the town soon declined. The place where it stood has since been washed away by the river, and no trace of it now remains. There is still a post-office in the neighborhood, called Missouriton, but the town no longer exists.

The settlers did not experience much trouble with the Indians until after the commencement of the war of 1812, and the settlements rapidly extended over a portion of the present counties of St. Charles, Lincoln, Warren, Montgomery, and Callaway; and in 1808, a settlement was formed in (now) Howard County, near the salt springs, called Boone's Lick.

Salt was very scarce among the first settlers, and it was so expensive that but little was used. It had to be transported on horseback from Kentucky, or shipped in keel-boats and barges from New Orleans up the Mississippi River to St. Louis, from whence it was distributed through the settlements by traders, who charged enormous profits.

Sometime early in the commencement of the present century, Colonel Boone, while on a hunting expedition, discovered the salt springs in Howard county; and during the summer of 1807 his sons, Daniel M. and Nathan, with Messrs. Baldridge and Manly, transported kettles there and made salt, which they floated down the river that fall in canoes made of hollow sycamore logs, daubed at the ends with clay.

The making of salt at these springs subsequently became a regular and paying business, and, assisted by the tide of immigration that began to flow there, led to the opening of the Booneslick road, which for years afterward was the great thoroughfare of western emigration.

The remaining incidents of Colonel Boone's life, of interest to the public, are so closely connected with the events of the Indian war of 1812–15, that we cannot give them without going into a history of those times, and as that would interfere with the arrangement of this work, we must now bring this sketch to a close.

Death of Mrs. Boone

On the 18th of March, 1813, Colonel Boone experienced the saddest affliction of his life, in the death of his aged and beloved wife. She had been the companion of his toils, dangers, sorrows and pleasures for more than half a century, participating in the same generous and heroic sacrifices as himself. He loved her devotedly, and their long and intimate association had so closely knitted their hearts together that he seemed hardly able to exist without her, and her death to him was an irreparable loss.

She was buried on the summit of a beautiful knoll, in the southern part of (now) Warren County, about one mile southeast of the little town of Marthasville. A small stream, called Teuque Creek, flows by the foot of this knoll, and pursues its tortuous course to where it empties into the Missouri River, a few miles to the southeast. Her grave overlooked the Missouri bottoms, which are here about two miles in width, and now, since the timber has been cleared away, a fine view of the river can be obtained from that spot.

Soon after the death of his wife, the old pioneer marked a place by her side for his own grave, and had a coffin made of black walnut for himself. He kept this coffin under his bed for several years, and would often draw it out and lie down in it, "just to see how it would fit." But finally a stranger died in the community, and the old man, governed by the same liberal motives that had been his guide through life, gave his coffin to the stranger. He afterward had another made of cherry, which was also placed under his bed, and remained there until it received his body for burial.

The closing years of his life were devoted to the society of his neighbors, and his children and grandchildren, of whom he was very fond. After the death of his wife, wishing to be near her grave, he removed from his son Nathan's, on Femme Osage Creek, where they had lived for several years previously, and made his home with his eldest daughter, Mrs. Flanders Callaway, who lived with her husband and family on Teuque Creek, near the place where Mrs. Boone was buried. Flanders Callaway removed from Kentucky to Missouri shortly before purchase of the territory by the United States, and received a grant of land from the Spanish government.

Frequent visits were made by the old pioneer to the homes of his other children, and his coming was always made the occasion of an ovation to "grandfather Boone," as he was affectionately called. Wherever he was, his time was always employed at some useful occupation. He made powder-horns for his grandchildren and neighbors, carving and ornamenting many of them with much taste. He repaired rifles, and performed various descriptions of handicraft with neatness and finish.

Twice a year he would make an excursion to some remote hunting ground, accompanied by a negro boy, who attended to the camp, skinned and cleaned the game, and took care of his aged master. While on one of these expeditions, the Osage Indians attempted to rob him, but they met with such prompt and determined resistance from Boone and his negro boy, that they fled in haste, and molested him no more.

One winter he went on a hunting and trapping excursion up the Grand River, a stream that rises in the southern part of Iowa and empties into the Missouri River between Carroll and Ray Counties. He was alone this time. He paddled his canoe up the Missouri and then up the Grand River, until he found a retired place for his camp in a cave among the bluffs. He then proceeded to make the necessary preparations for trapping beaver, after which he laid in his winter's supply of venison, turkey, and bear's meat.

BOONE BEATING OFF THE INDIANS

Each morning he visited his traps to secure his prey, returning to his camp in such a manner as to avoid discovery by any prowling bands of Indians that might be in the vicinity. But one morning he had the mortification to discover a large encampment of Indians near his traps, engaged in hunting. He retreated to his camp and remained there all day, and fortunately that night a deep snow fell and securely covered his traps. He continued in his camp for twenty days, until the Indians departed; and during that time he had no fire except in the middle of the night, when he cooked his food. He was afraid to kindle a fire at any other time, lest the smoke or light should discover his hiding place to the savages. When the snow melted away, the Indians departed and left him to himself.

Boone Marks the Site for His Grave

On another occasion he took pack-horses and went to the country on the Osage River, accompanied by his negro boy. Soon after he had prepared his camp he was taken sick, and lay for a long time in a dangerous condition. The weather was stormy and disagreeable, which had a depressing effect upon the old colonel and his servant boy. Finally the weather cleared up, and there came a pleasant and delightful day. Boone felt that it would do him good to walk out, and, with the assistance of his staff and the boy, he made his way to the summit of a small eminence. Here he marked out the ground in the shape and size of a grave, and told the boy that in case he should die he wanted to be buried there, at the same time giving full instructions as to the manner of his burial. He directed the boy, in case of his death, to wash and lay his body straight, wrapped in one of the cleanest blankets. He was then to construct a kind of shovel, and with that instrument and the hatchet, to dig a grave, exactly as he had marked out. Then he was to drag the body to the spot and push it in the grave, after which he was to cover it, placing posts at the head and foot. Poles were to be placed around and over the surface, to prevent the grave from being opened by wild beasts; the trees were to be marked, so the place, could be found by his friends, and then the boy was to get the horses, pack up the skins, guns, camp utensils, etc., and return home, where he was to deliver certain messages to the family. All these instructions were given with entire calmness, as if he were directing his ordinary business affairs.

In December, 1818, Boone was visited by the historian, Rev. John M. Peck, who was deeply and favorably impressed by the venerable appearance of the aged pioneer. Mr. Peck had written his biography, and expected to obtain some additional notes from him, but was so overcome by veneration and wonder, that he asked only a few questions. If he had carried out his first intention he would no doubt have given us a perfectly correct account of the life of this remarkable man, but as it was, a number of mistakes crept into his work, and many events of interest that occurred during the last few years of Boone's life were lost forever.

The Painting of Boone's Portrait

In the year following, 1819, the distinguished American artist of Boston, Mr. Chester Harding, paid a visit to Boone for the express purpose of painting his picture, to be placed in the gallery of prominent American portraits. After executing the work to the great satisfaction of Boone and of himself as well, Mr. Harding wrote a little book which he curiously titled his *Egotistigraphy*, in which he gave an account of his visit to Boone. Mr. Harding states that he had great trouble in locating the habitation of his distinguished subject, which was several miles off the old State road leading out from St. Charles, and in a very sparsely settled country. Enquiries among those in the nearest neighborhood failed to locate him, as few seemed to know who Colonel Boone was. This ignorance of his residence was due to the fact that for ten years previous to his death Boone had suffered so much from rheumatism and the weaknesses incident to old age that he had kept closely confined to the house, and was so taciturn that very few persons visited him, in consequence of which he almost dropped out of notice.

Mr. Harding writes: "I found the object of my search engaged in cooking dinner. He was half-reclining on the bunk, near the fire, and had a long strip of venison spitted on a ramrod, and while turning it before a hot blaze he used considerable pepper and salt to season it. I at once explained to him the object of my visit, but it was with some difficulty I could make him understand. When, at length, he comprehended my purpose he agreed to sit, and also to dress himself in a buckskin suit in order to make the portrait more characteristic. He was quite infirm and his memory much impaired, yet he amused and interested me much with recitals, often humorous, of his adventures in earlier years, and made the several days of my visit with him extremely pleasant."

It was from this celebrated portrait painted by Mr. Harding, and the only picture of Boone in existence, that the engraving in this work was made. The original is owned by a private gentleman residing in Boston, who refused a liberal offer made him for the picture by General James Harding, who tried to secure it with the view of placing it in the State capitol of Missouri.

Death of Daniel Boone

In the latter part of the summer of 1820, Boone had a severe attack of fever, which confined him to his bed for some time at Flanders Callaway's, but he rallied and was able to visit his son, Major Nathan Boone, who lived on Femme Osage Creek. The children were greatly delighted to see their grandfather again and everything was done to render him comfortable. For a few days he was happy in their society, and by his genial disposition and pleasant manners diffused joy and gladness throughout the entire household. His true character was never manifested in the presence of strangers, before whom he always appeared somewhat diffident, if not morose; but in the company of his relatives or intimate acquaintances he was the soul of good humor and geniality.

One day a dish of baked sweet-potatoes—of which he was extremely fond—was prepared for him. He ate heartily and soon after had an attack from which he never recovered. He grew rapidly worse and after three days' illness expired, on the 26th of September, 1820, in the 86th year of his age. He died peacefully, without a single fear of death or misgivings about a future existence. He had never made any profession of religion, or united with any church, but his entire life was a beautiful example of the golden rule—"do unto others as you would that they should do unto you." In a letter to one of his sisters, written a short time before his death, he said that he had always tried to live as an honest and conscientious man should, and was perfectly willing to surrender his soul to the discretion of a just God. His mind was not such as could lean upon simple faith or mere belief, but it required a well considered reason for everything, and he died the death of a philosopher rather than that of a Christian. His

BOONE'S HOME

death was like the sleep of an infant—quiet, peaceful and serene. We present on this page a picture of the house in which Daniel Boone died. At the time of his death he occupied the front room on the first floor, to the right of the hall as you enter.

It has been stated in many of his "lives" that he died at a deer "lick," with his gun in his hands, watching for deer. In others, that he died, as he had lived, in a log cabin. But on the contrary, the house was, and is—for it is still standing, just as represented in the picture—a neat, substantial, and comfortable stone building.

The remains of the departed pioneer were sorrowfully placed in the coffin he had prepared, and conveyed, the next day, to the home of Mr. Flanders Callaway. The news of his decease had spread rapidly, and a vast concourse of people collected on the day of the funeral to pay their last respects to the distinguished and beloved dead.

The funeral sermon was preached by Rev. James Craig, a son-in-law of Major Nathan Boone; and the house being too small to accommodate the immense concourse of people, the remains were carried to the large barn near the house, into which the people crowded to listen to the funeral services. At their close the body was borne to the cemetery and sadly deposited in the grave that had been prepared for it, close by the side of Mrs. Boone.

At the time of Boone's death the Constitutional Convention of Missouri was in session at St. Louis, and upon receipt of the intelligence a resolution was offered by Hon. Benjamin Emmons, of St. Charles, that the members wear the usual badge of mourning for thirty days, in respect to the memory of the deceased and adjourn for one day. The resolution was unanimously adopted.

The Boone family was noted for longevity. George Boone, a brother of Daniel, died in Shelby County, Ky., in November, 1820, at the age of eighty-three; Samuel, another brother, died at the age of eighty-eight; Jonathan at eighty-six; Mrs. Wilcox, a sister, at ninety-one; Mrs. Grant, another sister, at eighty-four; and Mrs. Smith, a third sister, at eighty-four. There is no record of the deaths of the rest of Boone's brothers and sisters, except those given heretofore, but they all lived to be old men and women.

The Remains Honored by Kentucky

When Colonel Boone made choice of a place of burial for himself and family, and was so particular to enjoin his friends, if he died from home, to remove his remains to the hill near Teuque, he did not anticipate an event which occurred a quarter of a century after his death, and which resulted in the remains of himself and wife finding their last resting place on the banks of the Kentucky River in the land he loved so well.

In 1845 a new cemetery was dedicated by the citizens of Frankfort, Kentucky, and it was proposed to consecrate the ground by interring therein the bodies of Daniel Boone and his devoted wife, that had slumbered together in a sacred spot prepared by loving hands, on the banks of the Missouri, for a quarter of a century. When the proposal was suggested the legislature of Kentucky was in session, and one of its leading members, Mr. Collins, arose and eloquently favored the proposition in the following language: "There seems to be a peculiar propriety in this testimonial of the veneration borne by the Commonwealth for the memory of its illustrious dead; and it is fitting that the soil of Kentucky should afford the final resting place for *his* remains, whose blood in life was so often shed to protect it from the fury of savage hostility. It is a beautiful and touching manifestation of filial affection shown by children for a beloved parent. It is right that the generation that is reaping in peace the fruits of his toils and dangers, should desire to have in their midst, and decorate with the tokens of their love, the sepulcher of this Primeval Patriarch, whose stout heart watched by the cradle of this now powerful Commonwealth."

The legislature appointed a committee, consisting of Hon. John J. Crittenden, William Boone, a distant relative, and Mr. Swaggart, to superintend the removal of the remains to the Frankfort cemetery. In the succeeding summer the committee

BOONE'S MONUMENT IN THE FRANKFORT CEMETERY

went to Missouri, taking passage, by water, at Louisville, on the steamer *Daniel Boone*, and were received at St. Louis by a delegation of citizens, and by them conducted to the site of the interment.

The graves were situated on land belonging to Mr. Harvey Griswold, who at first objected to the removal, as he intended to build a monument over them, and beautify the place. Mr. Griswold was supported in his objections by a number of influential citizens, who claimed that Missouri had as much right to the remains of Daniel Boone as Kentucky, especially as the old pioneer had selected the location of his grave, and had given such particular instructions in regard to his being buried there.

The gentlemen from Kentucky finally carried their point, however, and on the 17th of July, 1845, the remains of Daniel Boone and his wife were removed from their graves. The work was done by King Bryant, Henry Augbert and Jeff. Callaway, colored. Mrs. Boone's coffin was found to be perfectly sound, and the workmen had but little difficulty in removing it; but Colonel Boone's coffin was entirely decayed, and the remains had to be picked out of the dirt by which they were surrounded. One or two of the smaller bones were found afterward, and kept by Mr. Griswold as relics.

The remains were placed in new coffins prepared for their reception, and conveyed to Kentucky, where they were re-interred, with appropriate ceremonies, in the cemetery at Frankfort, on the 20th of August, 1845. A vast concourse of people from all parts of the State had collected to witness the ceremonies. An oration was delivered by Hon. John J. Crittenden, and Mr. Joseph B. Wells, of Missouri, made an appropriate address.

The graves on the hill near Teuque Creek were never refilled, but remain to-day as they were left by the workmen, except that the rains have partly filled them with dirt, and they are overgrown with weeds and briars. Rough head stones had been carved by Mr. Jonathan Bryan, and placed at the heads of the graves. These were thrown back on the ground, and are still lying there. Recently, pieces of these stones have been chipped off and sent to Kentucky as mementoes.

A beautiful monument was erected over the graves of Boone and his wife in the Frankfort cemetery, a few years after the re-interment of the bodies, on the four squares of which were carved scenes representing his conflicts with the Indians. The site selected is a fit resting place for the noble hero of the "dark and bloody ground."

Life of
Davy Crockett

DAVY CROCKETT

CHAPTER I

A Unique Character in American History

If I were asked to name the most singular, and in many respects the most remarkable, man in the history of pioneer settlement in the great west I should, without a moment's consideration of others, say: "Davy Crockett." He possessed a rare combination of astonishing traits of character that marked him for a prominent place among western men, and that he attained to considerable prominence in American politics was, like the operation of the law of gravity, because his specific weight, so to speak, brought him naturally to that position. Few men could tell a story better, and none had a more abundant supply of motherwit at his fingers' ends, than Davy Crockett. He could play the fiddle too, dance a jig, and shoot with the best riflemen of the times. These were accomplishments that went very far in recommending him to public favor, but they were the least of his powers of attraction. He possessed those bolder traits and faculties of pride and ambition, a heart that was absolutely fearless as it was honest, open, generous and sympathetic. Bravery and generosity had a perpetual home in his bosom, and he may be said to have carried his character on his sleeve, so easy was it to read and understand. Davy Crockett lived in a day when an honest declaration of policy and intention counted for something, when even politics was leavened with principle, and a promise was worth its face value.

He came upon the stage of action as a hewer and fashioner of the wilderness into homes for civilization just as Boone was retiring, a prototype of the Kentucky hunter, improved by the advantages of example, and the opportunities of the age.

Accomplishing results similar to those wrought out by Boone, yet Crockett was as unlike the great Kentucky hunter as torrents are unlike the perennial brook. Instead of that quiet modesty which was characteristic of Boone in his intercourse with the people, and which was the cause of much that was interesting in his life being lost to history, Crockett was full of self-complacency and pushed himself forward, though never in a vainglorious or offensive manner. But he knew how to measure his own merit, and has done the public a service, while gratifying an excusable pride, by leaving us an autobiography that has carried delight into thousands of homes. From this book, abounding with so much original humor and thrilling adventure, I have taken most of the facts concerning his career, though other sources of information have not been neglected, which have yielded some very interesting returns.

Murder of Crockett's Grandparents

According to his own statement, Davy Crockett was born on the 17th of August, 1786, in a small cabin located in the wilderness of East Tennessee, then a part of Virginia, at the mouth of Lime Creek, where it debouches into the Nolachucky River and in what is now Washington County. His father, John Crockett, was an Irishman, but his mother, *née* Rebecca Hawkins, was a native of Maryland. Davy knew very little about the history of his parents, as genealogical information was not regarded as having much value in that day among pioneers; the most that he learned concerning them was that his father fought at King's Mountain, in the Revolutionary War, and that his grandparents were killed by the Indians on the very ground where Rogersville, in Hawkins County, Tennessee, now stands. At the time of the murder of his grandparents his uncle James, a deaf mute, was captured by the Indians with whom he remained nearly eighteen years and until recovered, by ransoming, by his elder brother, William.

The family of John Crockett comprised nine children, six sons and three daughters, and as he was a very poor man there was little opportunity for the numerous progeny beyond hard work and abundant privations. After trying to improve a really miserable existence on the Nolachucky for some years without avail, the elder Crockett moved to Cove Creek where, in connection with a man named Galbreath, he erected a water-mill, but without mending his fortune, for a freshet swept away every vestige of the building and came near drowning the family also, as all were compelled to wade through the rushing waters to dry ground. His next removal was to what is now Jefferson County, Tennessee, where he opened a tavern on the road from Abbingdon to Knoxville.

Young Crockett's Graduation

At the age of twelve years young Davy was hired by his father to a German cattle dealer named Siler, who treated him with some kindness, and with whom he remained for six weeks, when he ran away and joined a teamster who was *en route* to Knoxville. After a week of hardships he abandoned the second service in which he had engaged and returned home, where he remained until the succeeding fall. There being no special work for him to do his father sent him to a country school kept by a typical backwoods schoolmaster, who knew better how to wield the birch than to impart instruction. On the fourth day of his attendance, when he had just begun to learn his letters, Davy had a misunderstanding with one of his fellow-pupils, whom he waylaid and severely flogged. Fearful of the punishment that awaited him for this arbitrary assumption of the privilege which the schoolmaster jealously reserved to himself, Davy kept clear of the teacher for a week and until his truancy was reported to his father. The old man was given to the habit of taking a drink and then of swallowing several more to keep the first one company, which generally served to excite a temper that was at no time very amiable. Gathering three heavy switches, as a preparatory measure, the elder Crockett called Davy to him with ill-disguised purpose in his expression and a manifest avowal in his brawny right hand. But Davy was so averse to submitting himself to the discipline that was threatened, that he turned his back upon the irate old man and broke for liberty. A lively chase ensued, in which Davy maintained a good lead until his father was blowed and distanced. The die was now cast, and young as he was, Davy thought only of a final dissolution of partnership with the family.

Being a likely boy, with plenty of pluck and resolution, on the same day he found employment with a drover named Cheek, with whom he traveled to Front Royal, in North Carolina. Receiving about seven dollars for his services with the drover, Davy drifted about in the east for some time, working at odd jobs, until at last he found himself in Baltimore. Here he engaged to make a voyage to London on a sailing vessel, but was prevented by a wagoner, who had his clothes, and who wanted him to drive a load of flour to Winchester. The result of this restraint over Davy was, that he gave the wagoner the slip and started west on foot, but soon meeting with another teamster, named Myers, he put himself upon such good terms with the stranger that he secured a ride as far as Montgomery Court House in Virginia. Here he set in to work for a farmer at five dollars per month, but at the end of the first month quit, and

DAVY AS A DROVER BOY

bound himself as an apprentice to a hatter named Griffith, with whom he continued for eighteen months, when the hatter became so involved in debt that he broke up and left the country, leaving Davy without so much as a shilling or a good suit of clothes.

Discouraged and desperately homesick, the poor boy resolved to seek his parents from whom he had not heard a word since his sudden departure more than two years before. To procure the means for traveling through the country he worked at odd employments, sometimes sawing wood for his supper, and again doing the evening chores of a farm house for lodging. Occasionally riding a short way on some passing wagon, but more often trudging along on foot, after several weeks of toilsome but patient travel he at length reached home so changed in appearance that none of the family recognized him. At this time Davy was nearly fifteen years of age, and, as he says, was so ignorant that he did not know a single letter of the alphabet.

Davy Earns His Freedom but Meets with Disappointment in His Love-Making

After remaining at home a few weeks Davy accepted a proposition made to him by his father, whereby the latter agreed that if Davy would engage to work out a debt of thirty-six dollars, which Mr. Crockett owed to a man named Wilson, a neighbor, he would set him free, which offer was immediately accepted, and Davy entered upon a service of six months to discharge the debt. Having won his freedom, the industrious youth, of his own volition, worked six months for another of his father's creditors, named Kenedy, to whom Mr. Crockett owed forty dollars, in which service he discharged his duties so well that he was employed for another term of six months by the same gentleman.

During this latter engagement Davy fell violently in love with a lass of the neighborhood, to whom he paid assiduous court, and made such excellent progress in his suit that, at his request, she promised to marry him. The wedding day was fixed, but almost at the last moment the fickle girl changed her mind so radically that she married another fellow who had long been her suitor, and was not even so courteous as to invite Davy to the wedding.

After hugging this disappointment to his badly wounded heart for several weeks, Davy concluded that he must prepare himself for future exigencies by acquiring at least a limited education. With this resolve he engaged to work two days of each week for a Quaker schoolmaster as payment for instruction during the other four, and under this arrangement he continued for a period of six months, by which he learned to read in a primer, to write his name, and, as he says, "to cypher some in the first three rules of figures," whatever this may mean. At the end of this time he quit school to devote his energies to searching for a wife. Being a natural born hunter, he was not long in finding a repository for his affections in a niece of the Quaker schoolmaster, and became a second time engaged, but sad to relate, with no better results than attended his first courtship, for he was again jilted at the very hour he reckoned his happiness nearly complete, which threw him into a melancholy that he did not recover from for a long time.

Courting under Difficulties, but Married at Last

As all things have an ending so did that of Davy's grief, which terminated quickly by a fortunate meeting with a pretty little Irish girl who, in addition to being handsome and interesting, encouraged his suit and thus relieved the sickness of his heart like an instantaneous panacea. He first met her at a reaping, where a goodly company of neighbors had assembled who, after their labor was done, fell to with joyful zest in a country dance, in which Davy participated. The night was thus spent all too quickly, as pleasure travels with a light step, but Davy had made the most of his opportunity, and was invited by the little Irish girl to call on her. The following Sunday he availed himself of this invitation, but was much chagrined to find that the girl already had company, and that too, in the person of a likely appearing young man, whose motives in making the visit was only too apparent. Davy again felt the pricking of bitter disappointment, but with characteristic pertinacity he remained at the house until the girl gave him some attention, and this, too, of an encouraging character. He soon learned, however, that while favoring his suit the girl was compelled to forego her own desires by reason of the determination of her mother that she should marry the likely young man. Here was opposition which Davy had not before encountered, but which threatened no less painful results.

The visits of Davy to his inamorata being displeasing to her parents he was forced to other expedients for gaining interviews which were not always agreeable nor successful, but at length good fortune came to his aid in a singular way, as the mysterious dame usually employs to bring troubled lovers together.

Wolves were very numerous in eastern Tennessee at this time and farmers suffered greatly from their depredations. To rid themselves of these voracious pests of the sheep-fold, the farmers frequently organized wolf-hunts, at which every man of the neighborhood capable of bearing a rifle met at an appointed rendezvous and there made plans for the hunt. Pursuant to these plans the hunters were sent out in appointed directions a considerable distance and then hunted towards a common center until on the incoming, a circle was formed in which large numbers of wolves were invariably driven together when the slaughter would begin.

THE WOLF HUNTERS

Davy attended one of these famous hunts, which was arranged to take place in a section of country very thinly settled, and which was totally unknown to him. It happened, therefore, that being sent out some distance from any others of the party he found himself bewildered when hunting back, and as it suddenly grew quite dark, by reason of the passage of a dense, black cloud portending a storm, he became lost. For a considerable time he rode about the country in a vain search for some habitation until he saw ahead of him the figure of a female who appeared as distracted as himself. What was his amazement upon coming within hailing distance, to find that it was the pretty little Irish girl who, being out in quest of her father's horses that had strayed from their usual grazing grounds, had lost her way and was now like himself in search of shelter, or some one who could direct her home. Their fortunate meeting reconciled them both to the mischance of being lost, since it afforded an opportunity for frank speech regarding the subject of matrimony, which they had not before had. So well did they embrace it, too, that before nightfall they came upon a house in the wood where a hospitable family lived that gave them accommodations, but instead of retiring at a proper hour Davy and his girl sat up all night love-making and planning for going to housekeeping within the next few days, and, if necessary how they might make an elopement successful.

The result of the wolf hunt was, that on the following Thursday, despite the protests of the mother, whose opposition was almost venomous with passionate resistance, Davy secured his girl and together they went off in triumph and were married by a justice of the peace. At the last moment, however, the old lady relented and gave the happy twain her blessing, which was about all that she was able to bestow.

Davy having at length, by the expenditure of much effort and the experience of no little suffering, become a married man, he set in to earn a home. He engaged to work for a neighbor six months for a very poor and aged horse, while his wife sat hard by the spinning wheel and made it profitable. Thus working together, before the first year of their married life had passed, they owned a horse, some few household effects, a cabin in a one-acre clearing and—one baby. To this was added, also, two cows and a calf as a marriage portion, so that there were families in Tennessee, and in trumpet call, too, not so well off in worldly goods as was Davy's, which excited a pride he had never felt before. He continued farming during the years 1809-10, when, having heard much concerning the fertility of the Duck and Elk River country, which was then just beginning to be settled, he determined to remove thither. His possessions were not so large or the distance so great but that this removal was made with little difficulty and he settled on Beans Creek, in Franklin County, near Winchester. Here his life took on the glamour of that excitement for which his nature longed, and brought out points of character that might have remained passive but for the stirring events that called them into action.

CHAPTER II

The Creek War

Among the farmer folk with whom he had been raised, Davy Crockett was only a plain, plodding, unambitious man, with little even of the humor that afterwards made him so famous, and no revealed traits that set him above the humblest of his neighbors. That circumstances, quite as much as condition, develop genius, finds remarkable illustration in the life of this great pioneer, and it was to contrast the character of Davy the farmer boy, with that of Davy the renowned hunter, congressman and heroic defender, that I have given so much, which appears unimportant, of his early life. Henceforth we are to see him in more exciting positions, and behold the unfolding of a character that originally promised so little, but which developed so much, and gave his name to history.

The Creek War began with the soul harrowing massacre at Fort Mimms, August 30, 1813, and as Crockett participated as a volunteer in the sanguinary struggle that followed, the circumstances precipitating it, should be given here.

Fort Mimms was built of logs, in the frontier style, in the center of a fallow field, near the junction of the Tom Bigby and Alabama Rivers. It had no special garrison, but afforded protection to nearly a dozen families, and consequently as many men. No Indians had shown themselves in the vicinity of the fort for a long time, nor had there been any depredations committed by them in East Tennessee or Northern Alabama for so many years that an Indian outbreak was not thought of. But in this hour of peace and fancied security danger was hovering about the little fort with bloody eye and merciless hands. Towards evening on the fateful day a little negro boy belonging to a family residing within the stockades was sent out to drive in the cows. Going some distance into the woods, where the animals were accustomed to range, he was startled from a dreamy reverie by the appearance of three Indians, who dodged behind trees to hide themselves from view. But the little negro had seen enough, and broke through the woods at his best pace, and not being pursued he gained the fort without other injury than a severe fright. He quickly related to those within what he had seen, but they received his declarations with such incredulity that he was sent again for the cows under a penalty of a flogging if he did not bring them in speedily.

A second time, but now with great alarm, the boy left the fort and warily felt his way until he again reached the woods, when before his startled gaze burst the forms of a hundred or more Indians, who were evidently approaching the fort stealthily with the view of making an attack. As before, the little negro ran with all possible fleetness back to the stockade, crying out as he entered: "Indians! Indians! the woods are full of them!"

OLD FORT MIMMS

Instead of making an investigation, the master seized the terror-stricken boy and began punishing him, when another cry arrested his attention, but this time it was a woman's screams, who had discovered the enemy only when it was too late to provide a defense.

The Massacre

The Indians managed to crawl up in a body under the very port-holes of the fort before their presence was detected, and but for an accidental closing of the gate they would have gained access to the enclosure. As it was they rushed up with rails and pushed the ends into every port-hole on one side except those in the bastion, which was so high as to be out of their reach. Having thus protected themselves from possible attack on one side, the Indians fell to with their tomahawks and cut down several piles composing the stockade. The men rushed between two bastions where the principal arms were stored, and opened fire upon the Indians with telling effect, but while chopping at the stockade though many fell, others stood ready to take the place of the fallen until a breach was effected that admitted the entire assailing body. A frightful scene now followed. The Indians, fully one hundred in number, rushed first upon the women and children, who had not gained protection in the bastions, and with knives and tomahawks glutted their savage ambitions, sparing neither sex nor age until the ground was bloody with lifeless bodies. When the defenseless ones were thus butchered, the Indians turned their attention to those in the bastions. Stacks of straw, gathered from the cow-sheds, were piled up under the well seasoned woodwork and then set on fire, while the Indians stood about with rifles and tomahawks ready to slay any that sought escape. The men within their fatal prisons fought with desperation, firing whenever opportunity offered, but seldom with any effect, as the bastions had no openings looking out upon the enclosure, except a door, which was so well guarded that whenever an effort was made to shoot from it, an Indian was certain to kill the person who made the attempt. The fire was not long in doing its deadly work. Those who entrusted themselves to the chance of escape by boldly breaking for liberty were quickly dispatched, and three were burned to death with the consumed bastions.

Of the thirty-seven persons within the fort when the attack was made only one escaped, and this was a boy sixteen years old, who contrived to climb to the top of a bastion and jump off on the outside without being observed, and to gain a distance of quite three hundred yards before he was discovered. When the Indians at length descried him two of them went in pursuit, but the boy made directly for a large hollow tree that had fallen across a small brook, one end of which projected under a steep, shelving bank. Having so much the start of his pursuers, the boy leaped over the bank and ran along in the water, to hide his tracks, some little distance, until he came to the fallen tree, the hollow of which was large enough to admit his body, though the entrance, which was at the butt, was not easily discovered. Here he took refuge, and remained for twelve hours without detection, though he heard the Indians cross the brook upon the very tree that concealed him. Almost paralyzed by his cramped position so long maintained, it was only by the greatest exertion that he was able to crawl out. When, at length, he gained his liberty he looked towards the fort and saw that it had given place to smoldering ruins, which told to him what had been the ending of the attack he had not remained to see concluded. He wandered about for a time, fearing to seek any neighbor's house lest he might come upon the Indians, who, he supposed, would lay waste every field and burn every cabin in the settlement. On the second day after his escape, however, he met a man who was then on his way to the fort, not having heard of the massacre. To this man the boy told his story and very soon thereafter the news was spread over all Eastern Tennessee and Northern Alabama.

Crockett Enlists as a Volunteer

Within less than a week after the slaughter and burning of Fort Mimms, it was ascertained definitely that the savage depredators had been Creek Indians, and a meeting of militia was called which was promptly responded to by nearly every man living within a hundred miles of where the butchery had taken place. Crockett was among the first to volunteer for a war against the Indians, and was one of the earliest at the place of rendezvous, notwithstanding the pleadings of his wife, who used all her influ-

SPREADING NEWS OF THE MASSACRE

ence in a vain effort to persuade him to remain at home and defend it against possible, and even probable, attack. Nor is such an argument easy to overcome, for Crockett, like other settlers of his neighborhood, lived in a small cabin that might any time be set upon by prowling bands of Indians, in which event his wife and children would certainly fall victims, having no one to defend them. It was, therefore, with many misgivings that Crockett took leave of his family, which he was able only to do by a heroic consideration of his duty and a reflection upon the necessity of every man giving his services in such an hour of peril, by which action alone could means for a general defense be provided. It was the application of that principle which promises the greatest good to the greatest number.

Winchester was the appointed place of muster, which was quite ten miles from Crockett's cabin, but it was scarcely more than daylight when he reached the rendez-vous, having started shortly after three o'clock A.M. with a resolve to be among the first to volunteer. He found only two men ahead of him, but by nine o'clock a considerable number had arrived, and at high noon a Mr. Jones, who afterwards represented the district in Congress, addressed the assemblage on the purposes for which they had gathered, and then requested those who desired to enlist for a sixty days' service to subscribe their names. A company of ninety men was thus speedily raised, of which Jones was elected captain.

The men were then instructed to repair to their several homes and make preparations for joining their company again on the following Monday, which day was appointed for entering upon active service. This interval Crockett employed in laying in provisions for his family and arranging for their comfort during his contemplated absence, as well as providing himself with a few articles that might be serviceable in camp and on the march.

Crockett in Peril

On the day appointed for the reassembling every man was prompt at roll-call, and the company at once took up their march for Beaty's Spring, which was reached in due season. Here they remained for two days awaiting the arrival of other volunteers, twelve hundred of whom soon collected and were formed into two regiments. While encamped here awaiting orders from General Jackson, who was at Nashville, a Major Gibson approached Captain Jones with a request for a detail of two men to accompany him across the Tennessee River and act as scouts, and also as spies, to discover the position and intentions of the Creek Indians. As the Major wanted men expert in woodscraft and with the rifle, Captain Jones pointed out Crockett as the man preeminently qualified for such service. Major Gibson made some objections to his youthful appearance, but finally accepted Crockett and also left it to him to select his companion, and another young man, named George Russell, was accordingly chosen.

On the following morning the company of spies, twelve in number, started out on their perilous mission headed by Major Gibson. They crossed the Tennessee at Ditt's Landing, and made a march of nearly fifty miles before going into camp, and which brought them into the enemy's country. This short journey of a single day's ride served to inspire the company with such confidence in the judgment, bravery and woodscraft of Crockett that Major Gibson divided his small force into two parties, one of which he gave in charge of Crockett, and retained command of the other himself. The two parties now separated in order to make a circuit of a dangerous piece of ground, with an understanding that they should meet again at night at an appointed place. Accordingly, Crockett set out with four men and passed through the section he was ordered to examine, but found no traces of any Indians. He reached the place chosen for meeting Major Gibson shortly after nightfall and went into camp, but the Major did not arrive, nor was any word received from him next morning. Concluding that some disaster had overtaken the other party Crockett set out for a Cherokee town twenty miles distant and from thence to a place where he learned ten Creek Indians had made their camp. On the way he met two negroes, who were riding at great speed, evidently alarmed at some imminent danger. Crockett stopped them, and asking the cause of their haste, was informed that nearly two thousand Creeks were then crossing the Coosa River at the Ten Islands to attack Gen. Jackson. No time was to be wasted now, and it became a question whether Crockett would be able to pass the flank of this large army and get back to the camp at Beaty's Spring to apprise the troops there of their danger. His men were panic stricken at this news, as well they might be, for they were fully sixty-five miles from the general camp, with the intervening woods fairly filled with Indians. Besides this, no news had been received from Major Gibson, and they naturally supposed he had been met and his party massacred, as they themselves must soon be.

Crockett showed no signs of fear, however, and encouraging his men in every possible way, he set out and traveled all night, passing several Indian fires, but fortunately meeting none of the enemy. By desperate riding he reached camp at ten o'clock and immediately reported the force and design of the Indians to Colonel Coffee, who was commanding. The Colonel, however, treated his report with great indifference and made no preparations to receive the enemy. Two hours later, Major Gibson returned with his party and made a report similar to that of Crockett's, whereupon the Colonel instantly ordered the construction of breastworks, and sent an express with all possible expedition to General Jackson, who was now at Fayetteville, urging him to come to his relief at once. The attention which Colonel Coffee paid to Major Gibson's report, while ignoring that of Crockett's, because one was made by an officer and the other by a private, sorely nettled the latter, who accepted it as an affront too great to ever be pardoned. However, General Jackson responded promptly to the call, and by a forced march through the night arrived at the camp the next day, but his men were in a terrible condition, their feet being so badly blistered that for a week they were incapable of active service.

It fortunately happened that instead of pushing forward and making a swift attack on the volunteers' camp at Beaty's Spring, as had been their intention, the Indians stopped for a day on the way to commit petty pillage, which gave time for Jackson's re-enforcements to arrive, and also for Coffee to throw up such entrenchments as would have made even his original force of thirteen hundred men invincible before the number of Indians that had set out to attack him. Seeing the preparations made to receive them, the Indians drew off and penetrated the wilderness of Alabama.

Crockett Becomes Hunter for the Army

Finding that the Indians had retreated Col. Coffee placed himself at the head of eight hundred volunteers and started in pursuit, hoping to fall in with one or more of the smaller bands which he knew the original force of two thousand would be divided into. They crossed the Tennessee at Muscle Shoals and prepared to attack Black Warrior's town, an Indian village that occupied the site where Tuscaloosa now stands. But the scouts found the place deserted, its inhabitants having evidently made a hurried retreat, as there were several fires still burning within the village limits, and a large field of ripe corn was left ungathered while several cribs contained a goodly store. The corn was quickly appropriated, the cabins pillaged of what few things had been left behind, and then fire was set to every cabin within the place.

Having accomplished this much by way of retaliation for the destruction of Fort Mimms, the expedition turned northward again. Though grain was fairly plentiful, especially after the supply gathered at Black Warrior, meat was extremely scarce, the want of which induced Crockett to request permission of Col. Coffee to hunt while on the march. The application was readily granted, under an implied expectation of sharing whatever game might fall before his rifle, and Crockett set out alone, though keeping a sharp eye wide open for lurking savages who infested the woods. He had proceeded scarcely a mile when he found the body of a deer partly skinned, but so recently killed that it was not yet cold. Evidently an Indian had been the slayer and that he was not far off, but Crockett took chances of discovery and hastily flinging the carcass upon his horse, galloped back to the army and shared the spoils with his comrades.

Crockett's First Battle

The expedition marched back to the Coosa River and established a fort at Ten Islands, from whence excursions were made, and occasional descents upon the Indians as opportunity offered. Scouting parties were kept out constantly and the appearance of Indians was immediately reported. Several Cherokees, who continued friendly to the whites, were engaged to act as spies and guides and rendered valuable services. One of these spies reported the return of a party of Creeks to a village about eight miles from Ten Islands, which they were then fortifying. Five hundred volunteers were dispatched against the place, commanded by a Colonel Cannon, who had only a few days before been promoted from captain at the same time that Colonel Coffee was advanced to the position of general.

Upon nearing the village the force was divided so as to pass simultaneously on both sides of the town and thus make its investiture complete. Having surrounded the

THE SCALP DANCE

place the lines were gradually contracted while a company of rangers under Captain Hammond was thrown out in front to bring on the attack. As he swung his men into full view the Indians rushed out and delivered their fire with some effect, but immediately seeing the circle that had been formed around them they ran as quickly back to the cover of their cabins. The lines continued to close up without a shot being fired, which so alarmed the Indians that many of them, and especially the squaws, cried out for quarter and desired to surrender themselves. In fact, Crockett states that he saw as many as seven Indian women clinging to the hunting-shirt of a single volunteer at one time. Those that thus freely gave themselves up were given protection and sent back to the rear under close guard; but Crockett noticed a party of forty-six warriors taking refuge in a strong and large log house admirably constructed for defense, and so reported to his commanding officer and an attack was ordered to be made upon the building. As they came within range of the cabin a volley greeted them but without casualty, at the same time a squaw ran to the threshold of the closed door where, with much deliberation she sat down, and by the aid of her feet drew a strong bow and sent an arrow whizzing into the ranks of the volunteers. It struck a lieutenant named

Moore with such force as to pierce entirely through his body, killing him almost instantly. The act was such a brave one that for a moment the entire attacking force of whites was rendered inactive by their surprise, but soon rallying, the daring squaw fell dead with twenty-three bullet wounds in her body. She had courted and received such death marks as only heroes may wear.

So bitter was the revenge felt for Moore's death that a terrible fate was prepared for those within the cabin. Gradual approaches were made behind portable barriers until the house was reached when the door was barred against possibility of escape and the building then fired. The screams of those within were frightful to hear, and well might soften a hard heart, but the volunteers were steeled against mercy by remembrance of atrocious acts so frequently committed by the Indians, and the entire forty-six were suffered to burn to death. While the building was burning many squaws and their children were shot down. Of this holocaust and massacre Crockett himself wrote as follows: "We now shot them down like dogs; and then set the house on fire and burned it up with the forty-six warriors in it. I recollect seeing a boy who was shot down near the house. His arm and thigh was broken, and he was so near the burning house that the grease was stewing out of him. In this situation he was still trying to crawl along; but not a murmur escaped him, though he was only about twelve years old. So sullen is the Indian, when his dander is up, that he had sooner die than make a noise, or ask for quarters.

"The number that we took prisoners, being added to the number we killed, amounted to one hundred and eighty-six; though I don't remember the exact number of either. We had five of our men killed. We then returned to our camp, at which our fort was erected, and known by the name of Fort Strother."

This first engagement in which Crockett ever engaged, was called the battle of Tallushatchie, and was fought some time in November following his enlistment.

The Battle of Talladega

The enlistment of volunteers for the Creek War was for sixty days, but at the end of that time there were no signs apparent of an early termination of hostilities and another call for volunteers was therefore made, while nearly all of those who first entered the service promptly re-enlisted. The battle of Tallushatchie, though fought more than two months after the muster at Winchester, was really the beginning of serious fighting; for while the massacre at Fort Mimms had thoroughly aroused the whites to vengeance, the Creeks had evaded measuring their strength with the settlers until goaded into action by the slaughter as just described. They now thirsted for a bloody retaliation and soon precipitated the famous battle of Talladega, as we shall see.

After their signal victory, the volunteers returned to Fort Strother where they remained inactive, and in a fairly starving condition, for several days. So great, indeed, was their extremity that the men were forced to exist for a while on beef-hides which had been taken some time before from cattle slaughtered for their subsistence. While in this desperate situation, and with little expectation for an early relief from pressing hunger, a friendly Indian approached the guard one night and expressed a wish to see the commandant. He was conducted to General Jackson's tent where he remained above an hour, at the end of which time he came out and disappeared. Following his departure orders were issued to prepare for an immediate march. Within a short while the army of nearly eight hundred men was put in motion towards Fort Talladega which was garrisoned by a hundred or more Cherokee and a few friendly Creek Indians.

Upon arriving before the fort it was found invested by a force of eleven hundred Creeks who had been conducting negotiations with those within, trying to induce them to join in the war against the whites, and threatening extermination in case they refused. The force of Indians friendly to the whites had asked for a three days' truce in which to consider the proposition, which being granted, they dispatched a runner to General Jackson to acquaint him with their situation, having no disposition to accept the terms, or to break friendly relations with the whites. This was the import of the news imparted to General Coffee by the Indian who had sought the interview.

It was nearly an hour before sunrise when the volunteers came within sight of Fort Talladega, but their approach had been discovered by Creek scouts who hastened

BATTLE OF TALLADEGA

back and gave the alarm. The Indians were in such force, however, and so confidently expected aid from those within the fort, that instead of retiring they fell back to the stockades, and under cover of the loop-holes from the cabins.

As the volunteers drew near, several Cherokees mounted to the top of the fort and made signs against a further advance, but their movements not being understood, two of the bolder ones leaped down and ran from the advancing party as if to retreat, but made a circuit out of sight of the Creeks, and contrived to reach Major Russell who was leading the van, and apprised him of the position of the enemy.

Terrible Slaughter of the Indians

This information was not imparted until Russell had proceeded almost abreast of a party of Creeks that had formed an ambush under the slope of a bank covered with a dense growth. These now rose up and delivered a volley from muskets and bows that killed five of Russell's men, but instead of following the advantage which this movement gave them, by charging, the cowardly Creeks fled to their companions who were massed about the fort. General Jackson, who had command of the troops, seeing the position of the Creeks, and learning how completely the Cherokees had deceived them, now adopted the tactics that had succeeded so well at Tallushatchie. Masking his design by falling back out of sight of the fort, he divided his force and sent the two divisions towards the right and left flanks, with orders to converge on the lower side of the fort that a circle, or hollow square, might be formed about it. This movement was accomplished so expeditiously that the Indians did not discover Jackson's design until they found themselves completely surrounded. The troops now charged towards the center and massed their lines so solidly and quickly that the first efforts of the Creeks to break through were defeated, more than fifty of their number falling dead at the first fire of the volunteers. As the Indians were repulsed on one side they rushed back towards the other, but only to be received by the same withering fire.

A panic now seized them, and they ran distractedly from one part of the circle to another, making no defense, but falling like leaves in autumn. This slaughter was continued until four hundred of the enemy lay dead upon the field, when the confusion became so great that the Indians massed together like cattle stampeding in a pen, and pushing their way through the death-dealing pile by sheer force of numbers escaped to the woods.

The volunteers lost only seventeen men, the bodies of whom were buried in one grave just outside the fort.

This battle was fought December 7th, 1813.

After this fight the volunteers remained at the fort for several days, when the weather being very cold and provisions so scarce that starvation still threatened, it was proposed that a disbandment be ordered but with instructions to reassemble within thirty days. This proposition was a novel one for soldiers to make, but at most these volunteers were only irregulars, considering the fact that the time of their enlistment had expired more than two months before, and that at no time was severe military discipline enforced.

General Jackson received the request for a temporary disbandment with such disfavor that he declared the men should serve six months, if necessary, notwithstanding that the term for which they engaged had expired; and further, he denied the privilege of even a furlough to any man in the command. This so angered the men, suffering as they were for the necessaries of life, that two-thirds of the entire force resolved to go home regardless of their General's prohibition. To enforce compliance with his orders, against the threat of desertion, he stationed a company of artillery on a bridge over which the men, if they deserted, would be compelled to pass, with orders to fire on them if they should attempt to carry out their resolve. But this movement did not intimidate them, for with muskets loaded and at "a ready," the deserters, numbering about eight hundred, took up their march, resolved to fight if the artillery opened on them. For a time it looked as if a sanguinary encounter must take place, but seeing the determination of the deserters the artillerists gave way, being in fact as anxious to return home as any of their comrades. General Jackson was furious at the disobedience of his soldiers, and in an outburst of passion declared that they were the d——nst volunteers he had ever seen; that they would volunteer to go and fight and then at their own pleasure would *volunteer* to go home again in spite of the devil.

CHAPTER III

Resumption of Hostilities

Various reasons have been assigned for the insubordination just described, but whatever may have been the true cause—and it is more than probable that Crockett's explanation is correct—the volunteers were not disposed to shirk their duty because of the dangers that threatened. This is proved by the fact that after the deserters—for such they must be called—had spent two weeks at their several homes, they voluntarily returned for re-enlistment to Fort Deposit, where a reorganization was quickly effected. Immediately prior to the second muster General Jackson told his men that if any of them desired to quit the service, they had liberty to do so, but those who wished to continue would be re-enlisted for a term of three months more. In proof of the valor and self-sacrificing disposition of those who had returned to the fort, it is said that less than a dozen dropped out of ranks to avail themselves of the opportunity to shirk further service.

Crockett, after the reorganization, was attached to Major Russell's company of spies, but was in the engagement fought on January 23, 1814, known as the battle of Enstichopco, where Jackson sustained his first and only defeat.

After this fight the whites remained inactive for a considerable time, and a disbandment was ordered, the term of the second enlistment having expired, nor was their service longer required, for though the Indians had won a victory at Enstichopco, it was a barren one, and they retired to Georgia and Florida.

Crockett returned home and began farming, but he followed this peaceful pursuit only a short while when the British threatened the coast towns, and it was resolved to send an army to the relief of Pensacola, and to defend other places along the gulf that were in jeopardy. To raise the necessary force a draft was ordered, and one of Crockett's neighbors was drawn for this enforced service. Being averse to war, upon the grounds that it involved too much personal risk, he offered Crockett one hundred dollars to go as his substitute. This offer was brusquely refused with some pointed advice on the duty which every man owed to his country. But though Crockett refused to go as a substitute, he promptly enrolled himself as a volunteer and was attached to Major Russell's company of spies.

A CREEK FEAST

A Ground-Hog Case

The company that Crockett joined consisted of one hundred and thirty men, and being in special service, did not start with the main army on the march to Pensacola, but made a detour around through Alabama, by way of old Fort Mimms, and thence through western Georgia for the purpose of ascertaining what the Creeks were doing in those sections. It thus happened that Jackson's army reached Pensacola and took possession of the town two days before Major Russell's company reached there. Everything being quiet along the Florida coast, and the fear of an attack from the British having abated, General Jackson divided his force into two divisions with one of which he set out for New Orleans, while the others, comprising two battalions under Majors Russell and Childs, and with Colonel Blue in chief command, was sent back through Georgia and Alabama to the Scamby River valley, where it was reported large parties of Creeks were massing. Crockett was with this latter division of the army and continued to act as a spy.

When Colonel Blue reached the Scamby River his force numbered one thousand men, including one hundred and eighty Choctaws and Chickasaw Indians who were employed principally as guides. To feed so large an army in an unsettled country became a serious matter, which increased in gravity as the Indian villages along the way had been deserted, and what they had been unable to remove was burned. A foraging party of sixteen men, headed by Major Russell, with Crockett among the number, was sent out with the hope that they might find an Indian camp. After traveling nearly a score of miles they discovered two Indians that were out hunting their horses. These they promptly killed and cut off their heads. Soon after a small Indian camp was found on an island, but after capturing it, all the booty it yielded was two squaws and ten children.

Crockett and his party continued wandering about in the wilderness of Northern Alabama, fighting occasionally, but always suffering for food, and subsisting much of the time on roots, or such small game as birds and squirrels, and even these were extremely scarce. Of the desperate extremity of himself and men at this time and the means taken to avoid starvation, Crockett thus writes:

"And now, seeing that every fellow must shift for himself, I determined that in the morning I would come up missing; so I took my mess, and cut out to go ahead of the army. We know'd that nothing more could happen to us if we went than if we staid, for it looked like it was to be starvation any way; we therefore determined to go on the old saying, root hog or die. We passed two camps, at which our men, that had gone on before us, had killed Indians. At one they had killed nine, and at the other three. About daylight we came to a small river, which I thought was the Scamby; but we continued on for three days, killing little or nothing to eat; till, at last, we all began to get nearly ready to give up the ghost, and lie down and die; for we had no prospect of provision, and we knew we couldn't go much further without it.

"We came to a large prairie, that was about six miles across it, and in this I saw a trail which I knowed was made by bear, deer, and turkeys. We went on through it till we came to a large creek, and the low grounds were all set over with wild rye, looking as green as a wheat field. We here made a halt, unsaddled our horses, and turned them loose to graze.

"One of my companions, a Mr. Vanzant, and myself, then went up the low grounds to hunt. We had gone some distance, finding nothing, when, at last, I found a squirrel, which I shot, but he got into a hole in the tree. The game was small, but necessity is not very particular; so I thought I must have him, and I climbed that tree thirty feet high, without a limb, and pulled him out of his hole. I shouldn't relate such small matters, only to show what lengths a hungry man will go to to get something to eat. I soon killed two other squirrels and fired at a large hawk. At this a gang of turkeys rose from the cane-brake, and flew across the creek to where my friend was, who had just before crossed it. He soon fired on a large gobbler and I heard it fall. By this time my gun was loaded again, and I saw one sitting on my side of the creek, so I blazed away and brought him down, and a fine turkey he

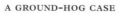

A GROUND-HOG CASE

was. I now began to think we had struck a breeze of luck, and almost forgot our past sufferings in the prospect of once more having something to eat. I raised a shout and my comrade came to me, and we went on to the camp with the game we had killed."

For above a month the army under Colonel Blue did nothing but beat about the country, rarely finding any Indians, but nearly always on the point of starvation. In the entire campaign less than twenty Indians had been killed and little damage of any kind inflicted on the enemy. Nor, in the meantime, were the Indians doing any serious harm, though they continued to menace the forts and settlers. The only damage wrought by the Creeks, that Crockett observed on the return march and scout from Pensacola, was inflicted on the family of an Irishman who had erected a cabin on the Scamby River, not many miles from Mimms.

He had been attacked by the Indians and himself, wife and three children killed, all of whom had been scalped, and their bodies stripped and then left on the ground before the cabin door, where Crockett's party found and buried them.

The command gradually worked its way back to Fort Strother and went into quarters. News of Jackson's victory at New Orleans soon reached them here, and also the report of a treaty of peace with Great Britain. General Jackson then met the Indians at what is called Hickory Ground, fifty miles from Fort Williams, and concluded a treaty with them. It was thus the war ended, and Crockett returned home to pursue the peaceful tenor of domestic ways, delighted to escape further privation, especially when that which he had endured brought him so little glory.

CHAPTER IV

A Philosopher in Affliction

During the time that Crockett was serving as a volunteer his wife managed, with the best of her ability, to keep the farm-place in order and at the same time care for her dependent family of three children, the eldest of whom was less than five years of age. The hard work, exposure and worry she was compelled to endure made serious inroad upon her once rugged constitution, and when Crockett at length returned, his wife was as the shadow of her former self. Nor did her health improve under the good care of her husband, but continued to grow worse, and Crockett saw that the finger of death had touched her brow. Everything possible, in a section of country where so few comforts were procurable, was done to relieve her sufferings and prolong her life, but without avail, for within less than two months after Crockett's return she died, leaving him a heritage of profound grief and the responsibility of three children too small to appreciate the loss of a mother. In this hour of bitter tribulation, when the world appeared to frown upon his efforts, and fortune had turned her back, Crockett paused to reflect upon what fate had bequeathed him. At first, utterly inconsolable and therefore incapacitated for the duty which had now been thrust upon him, he soon perceived the helplessness of his condition while nursing his grief, and boldly facing misfortune acted the part of a philosopher by resolving to make the best of every circumstance. One of his brothers was married, but as yet childless, and Crockett engaged him to make his home with him and to take charge of the three orphans.

Crockett's Second Marriage

For some time—though how long he does not say—Crockett remained a widower, but it was manifest from the manner in which he describes his situation, that he was anxious to marry again within a short while after his wife's death. He excuses his longing, however, by saying that while his brother and sister-in-law acted a goodly part by his children, yet their care fell short of that of a wife, and for this reason he resolved to marry again.

There was a widow residing in the neighborhood, who had lost her husband in the Creek War, and who had a fair patrimony, including a farm and considerable stock; she also had two small children, that Crockett thought might make excellent playmates for his own, and these several advantages led our hero to aspire to winning the widow and thus possess himself, at one master stroke, of them all. But Crockett was much like Miles Standish, good at fighting, but a coward at love-making. When he first set out to see the widow he acted, as he frankly admits, like a fox preparing to rob a hen-roost, and was so sly and scared that a pooh! would have sent him scampering away into the bushes. With the widow's help, however, he managed to get on finally, and in due time married her.

Though his second marriage secured for him a good home and well-stocked farm, this fact did not change his disposition for roving, and in the following fall Crockett set out with three of his neighbors to examine a section of the Creek country, in northern Georgia, with a view to settling there. He had not proceeded far, however, when one of his companions was bitten by a poisonous snake, and was left at a wayside cabin to the care of an Indian family. Three days later Crockett, while in pursuit of his horses that had broken loose and taken a back track home, fell very ill, and but for the kind attention of two Indians must certainly have died. For several weeks his life seemed to hang by a thread, and report went back to his wife that he was dead. Indeed, one man affirmed that he had helped to bury him. But Crockett recovered, despite these rueful reports, and after an absence of five weeks returned home to the wondering surprise of his wife, who at first sight believed it to be his ghost.

Crockett as a Magistrate

Though his efforts to reach the Creek country had been futile, and came near costing him his life, his ambition for removal had not been quenched, and a year later he set out for the Chickasaw country, in northern Alabama, this time taking his family with him. Upon reaching Muscle Shoals he was taken with chills and fever and compelled to make a stop, as his system appeared to be so saturated with malarial poison that he despaired of rallying, and gave himself over to die. For several weeks he continued very ill and when, at length, he recovered he was so well satisfied with the country, considering himself as now being acclimated, that he was resolved to remain in the vicinity of Muscle Shoals, which was just within the border of the district purchased from the Chickasaw tribe. He accordingly built a cabin on Shoal Creek and there lived in contentment for a period of three years. By this time the country gained a reputation for great fertility and salubrity, which attracted so many settlers that a temporary government had to be established. Among the settlers was a large number of disorderly characters, and punishment of offenders could only be provided by the adoption of arbitrary measures among the settlers themselves, for there were neither courts nor law officers within two hundred miles of the section.

To provide for the public peace a meeting of settlers was called at which magistrates and constables were appointed, with powers delegated, by the passage of resolutions and a vote by the assemblage, to make arrests and award punishments. There was neither statute-book nor special law, the magistrates being both court and jury, from whose decisions no appeal would lie. Nor did these original settlers bother with writs and warrants, nor keep so much as a court record, all of which appeared superfluous and as weights on the nimble heels of justice.

Crockett was chosen a magistrate and right well did he fill the office, with satisfaction if not with dignity. He had a constable that was competent to enforce the orders of the court, and thus together they became a terror to evil doers and lax debtors a well. Crockett held his court in one room of his double cabin and charged the State neither rent nor fuel; but his economical administration did not stop here, for costs were never taxed up from one term to another, nor was any expense incurred by the State in prosecutions. In other words, when complaint was made against one settler by another, Crockett would send his constable to bring in the offender, issuing his mandates in the form of what he called "verbal writings." In serving summons of this character it very frequently happened that the constable was compelled to use force and unless, after an arbitrament of muscle, he proved himself the better man, the return was something to this effect: "I found John Jones (the delinquent) and ordered him to come with me and be tried before your honor, but to this order he demurred, whereupon, I seized him by the collar and proceeded to enforce the order, but was viciously and unfairly attacked, bruised, beaten and compelled to see the dignity of this court insulted, and your orders, as well as my own, set at defiance."

It was very seldom that such a return had to be made, and in all cases where it was necessary, Crockett took it upon himself to bring the defendant to court, which it was convenient to do, for wherever Crockett appeared there was the court also. It was all one to him whether the defendant submitted to a fine or a thrashing, either of which penalties Crockett always felt himself able to impose. Generally, the constable, who was a powerful fellow, brought the offender before the court, sometimes in a peaceable, submissive way, but often in such a dilapidated condition that further punishment would appear like persecution.

Describing these curious processes of his court, Crockett thus writes: "At first, whenever I told my constable, says I—'Catch that fellow and bring him up for trial'— away he went, and the fellow must come, dead or alive; for this we considered a good warrant, though it was only in verbal writing. But after I was appointed by the assembly, they told me my warrants must be in real writing, and signed; and that I must keep a book, and write my proceedings in it. This was a hard business on me, for I could just barely write my own name; but to do this, and write the warrants too, was at least a huckleberry over my persimmon. I had a pretty well informed constable, however, and he aided me very much in this business. Indeed, I had so much confidence in him, that I told him, when he should happen to be out anywhere, and see that a warrant was necessary, and would have a good effect, he needn't take the trouble to come all the way to me to get one, but he could just fill out one; and then on the trial I could correct the whole business if he had committed any error."

ENFORCING ORDERS OF THE COURT

Crockett Is Elected to the Legislature

Within five years after Crockett had settled on Shoal Creek, and had reformed the abuses so common in frontier settlements, where might and right are often used as synonymous terms, his reputation had extended so far and favorably that he was elected colonel of a militia regiment formed for protection against the Indians. This success so increased his ambition that soon after, which was the year 1821, he offered himself as a candidate for the legislature, to represent the counties of Lawrence and Hickman. At this time Crockett, as he frankly admits, scarcely knew what the word *legislature* meant, nor did he have the slightest suspicion of what a member of that body was elected to do. In his profound ignorance he would have made a sorry candidate but for the natural wit and good judgment with which he was so abundantly endowed. To escape criticism he wisely adopted the policy of, what he calls, *non-committal*, which enabled him to look wise while feeling very ignorant.

Crockett's opponent was really a very able fellow, who had studied law, preached a little, and was a fairly good fiddler, but he was a poor hunter and worse than all, couldn't tell a story, and was too stingy to buy whisky for the crowd that gathered at the political meetings. Crockett soon learned his weak points and prepared to take advantage of them. A big hunt and frolic was therefore proposed, upon the condition that the two parties, one representing Crockett and the other his opponent, be chosen to hunt two days, at the end of which time the side showing the fewer number of squirrel scalps should pay all expense of a dinner and country frolic. As the principals headed the respective parties, Crockett easily won and had the pleasure which such a victory gave, in addition to escaping the expense of a grand barbecue.

Crockett's opponent, however, thought he discovered a means for turning the frolic to his own advantage and with this end in view, after the dinner was over, proposed to debate certain public questions with his opponent, leading off first himself in a one hour's speech that was no mean effort, considering his surroundings.

Crockett was, for a while, completely discomfited, but gathering courage after a time, mounted a stump that stood before a saloon, where the people had assembled, and told his audience that he was like a fellow whom he met some weeks before belaboring an empty barrel which had been dropped from some passing wagon by the wayside. Upon being asked what he was doing, the fellow replied that the breath of the bung-hole convinced him that there had been cider in that barrel some time before, and he was then trying to ascertain if some did not still remain. Crockett likened himself to the empty cider barrel, telling his audience that he contained a speech a short time before, but now only the odor of one remained, so he invited all his auditors to join him in a drink.

This story, though as poor as the horse that could be put to no better service than a fodder-rack, served its purpose admirably, and brought vociferous applause from the crowd, the majority of whom were even more ignorant than Crockett, but who could appreciate an invitation to drink with an accomplishment worthy of a more refined taste.

Crockett adopted the same tactics wherever he was called upon to speak, always carefully avoiding expressions that might betray his ignorance, and filling in the spaces between what he did know and what he only surmised with witty stories, and winding up with that grand peroration, "Let's all take a drink." Fortunately for him cold water campaigns were not known in his day. When the result of the election was finally announced it was found that Crockett had beaten his competitor more than two to one. Shortly after the election Crockett made a visit on some business to Pulaski, where he met Colonel James K. Polk, who had also been elected to the same legislature. It unfortunately happened that the two were introduced in a large crowd of admiring constituents, and both were expected to say something in acknowledgment of the cheers that were given them. But confusion was precipitated by Polk thus addressing Crockett immediately after the introduction, "Well, Colonel, I suppose we shall have a radical change of the judiciary at the next session of the legislature?" "Very likely, sir," Crockett replied, and then shot out of the room as if urgent business, just called to mind, had demanded instantaneous attention. He explains this singular conduct in his autobiography, as follows:

"I put out quicker, for I was afraid some one would ask me what the judiciary was; and if I knowed I wish I may be shot. I don't indeed believe I had ever before heard that there was any such thing in all nature; but still I was not willing that the people there should know how ignorant I was about it."

Crockett's services, as a member of the legislature, were distinguished chiefly for the amusement they created among the other members, though his good judgment in the consideration of proposed bills was generally commended, and no one was held in higher esteem for social qualifications.

Though never essaying the role of an orator, in which he would have immediately appeared glaringly deficient, it must not be supposed that he took no part in the debates, for so far from this being the case he made himself a factor, so to speak, in nearly every question that was brought to the consideration of the House.

Crockett was an inimitable story-teller, and had always at hand, like Lincoln, a good story to illustrate any particular point he desired to make. Whenever he arose to speak he was certain to receive great attention, as the members knew that they would be regaled with some amusing anecdote. It is much to be regretted that his stories have not been preserved, for though, unfortunately, they were most often punctuated, or rather accentuated, with profane expressions characteristic of the frontier, these objectionable sayings might be omitted without seriously impairing the effectiveness and laughable features of the comic illustration. But with very few exceptions the stories have been forgotten, though many of his quaint maxims are still current and so appropriate that many learned men do not disdain to quote and apply them.

I recall to mind having seen in print two anecdotes related by Crockett during the time he was a member of the legislature, which are worth repeating, though no one can hope to tell them with the effect produced by Crockett's own recital.

The Story of the Three Millers

I do not remember the connection or the question in debate that brought forth these anecdotes, so that the application, which is the point and substance of the story, is lost. Said he: "There were three Dutch millers who had erected as many mills in close proximity, on a stream in Virginia. Two of the men were brothers named George and Jake Fulwiler, and the other, who was mean, close and eccentric, and withal a mono-maniac on the subject of religion, was named Henry Snyder. This latter, who was a curious character in many ways, occasionally imagined himself to be Jehovah, during which intervals he sometimes held an imaginary court and summoned before him for judgment all his enemies. It was but natural that there should be a lively rivalry between the three millers and that Snyder should hold the two Fulwilers in contempt, and thus regarding them as his worst enemies he did not fail to bring them to account whenever he chose to sit in judgment as Jehovah.

"Giving full play to his imagination, Snyder called his court one day, and assuming that his two enemies were before him, began to try them for their offenses in this wise:

"'Shorge Fulwiler, come forward und tell what you haf been doing in te lower worldt since you built tat mill?'

"'Oh, Lort, I cannot tolt you all.'

"'Vell, Shorge Fulwiler, I like to know if you never took more toll like you had a rite to somedimes?'

"'Yes, Lort; somedimes, vhen der vater vas low und mein stones vas dull, I take a leetle too much toll.'

"'Vell, den, Shorge Fulwiler, you must go to der left mit der goats.'

"'Now, Shake Fulwiler, vill you please coom up und told der coort what you been doing in der lower worldt?'

"'Oh, Lort, I cannot tolt you all.'

"'Vell, Shake Fulwiler, I like to know if you never took more toll like you had a rite to somedimes?'

"'Yes, Lort; somedimes, vhen der vater vas low und mein stones vas dull, I take a leetle too much toll.'

"'Vell, den, Shake Fulwiler, you must go by der left mid dem goats.'

"'Now, den, I vill try Henry Snyder (himself).'

"'Vell, Henry Snyder, please tolt me what you been doing in der lower worldt?'

"'Oh, Lort, I cannot tolt you all.'

"'Vell, Henry Snyder, I like to know if you never took more toll like you had a rite to somedimes?'

"'Yes, Lort; somedimes, vhen der vater vas low und mein stones vas dull, I take a leetle too much toll.'

"'But, Henry Snyder, vat did you do mit der toll?'

"'Oh, Lort, I gives it to der poor.'

"After a long pause, passed in solemn meditation, the judge said:

"'Vell, Henry Snyder, you may go to der right mit der sheep, but it is a mighty tight squeeze.'"

The Iron Hot Is Different from the Iron Cold

Another story related by Crockett was intended to illustrate the cupidity of a fellow legislator, who had introduced a bill for the formation of a new county and had fixed the boundary lines so as to promote his private interests. Preserving his exact language, as nearly as possible, the story is as follows:

"Mr. Speaker: Do you know what that man's bill reminds me of? Well, I s'pose you don't, so I'll tell you. Well, Mr. Speaker, when I first came to this country a blacksmith was a rare thing. But there happened to be one in my neighborhood. He had no striker; and whenever one of the neighbors wanted any work done, he had to go over and strike until his work was finished. These were hard times, Mr. Speaker, but we had to do the best we could.

"It happened that one of my neighbors wanted an axe. So he took along with him a piece of iron, and went over to the blacksmith's to strike till his axe was done. The iron was heated, and my neighbor fell to work, and was striking there nearly all day, when the blacksmith concluded that the iron wouldn't make an axe, but 'twould make a fine mattock.

"So my neighbor, wanting a mattock, concluded that he would go over and strike till the mattock was done. Accordingly he went over the next day, and worked faithfully. But toward night the blacksmith concluded his iron wouldn't make a mattock but 'twould make a fine ploughshare.

"So my neighbor, wanting a ploughshare, agreed that he would go over next day and strike until that was done. Accordingly, he went over and fell hard to work. But towards night the blacksmith concluded that his iron wouldn't make a ploughshare, but 'twould make a fine *skeow*. So my neighbor, tired of working, with some impatience said: 'Well, then a *skeow* let it be,' and the blacksmith, taking up the red-hot iron, threw it into a tub of cold water near him, and as it fell in the iron cried out *skeow*.

"And this, Mr. Speaker, will be the way of that man's bill for a new county. He'll keep us all here working his schemes over, and finally his bill will turn up a *skeow*; now mind if it don't."

Crockett Bankrupted

During Crockett's attendance at the legislature a misfortune befell him by which he lost all his possessions, including the means acquired by his marriage. He built a large grist mill, that was run by water power, and subsequently added to it a distillery and powder mill, which for a time proved very profitable, being the only mill of the kind within a radius of more than one hundred miles, and thus having a monopoly of an immense trade. An early spring freshet, however, caused Shoal Creek to rise so rapidly that the stream became a roaring river and swept down with such impetuous force that the mill and all its contents was dashed into pieces almost in an instant, and carried away so completely that after the flood subsided there was not left a sign to show where it had stood. Crockett had exhausted his credit in building the mill and its destruction left him burdened with debts which would bring him to the limit of poverty to pay. Nevertheless, he did not hesitate to sacrifice everything that remained to him to discharge his obligations, parting even with his household effects and reserving not so mach as the little cabin that gave shelter to his family.

Upon adjournment of the legislature Crockett moved his family into a small house, which he rented from one of his creditors, and taking his eldest son and a borrowed horse, he set out in search of a desirable place in which to settle. He went on to Obion River and chose a spot on its bank to erect another cabin. The place was a more complete wilderness than any he had before settled in, but this fact he considered to his advantage, for the country abounded with game, which afforded a means for subsistence that he would not have possessed had he remained at Shoal Creek. Indians, too, were numerous, but they were friendly and willing to extend a helping hand.

It fortunately happened that a boat came by on its passage up the river, the first, too, that had succeeded in advancing so far, as it was a trip made with the view of determining how far the stream was navigable. The boat landed to await a rise in the river and as help was scarce, the captain engaged Crockett and his son to ship with him as roustabouts to unload the cargo he had undertaken to transport to a place called McLemore's Bluff. In payment for this service the captain and the men that were with him helped Crockett put up a cabin, and also gave him some flour and other provisions so as to enable him to begin housekeeping in a respectable and comfortable manner.

The boat was delayed at Crockett's Landing several days before the expected rise came, which time Crockett employed in hunting and killed such a number of elk as supplied meat for the crew during the remainder of the trip.

Crockett served the captain faithfully and on returning from McLemore's Bluff, where the cargo had been safely landed, he made a small clearing and planted a little patch of corn, after which he went back to Shoal Creek for his family. Upon arriving there he received notice of a called session of the legislature, which he attended and then gathering the few things he had together set out for his new home on the Obion, one hundred and fifty miles distant.

Nothing had been disturbed during his absence and though the corn had received no attention it yielded a surprisingly large crop. This being gathered Crockett resolved to go on a hunt to lay in a supply of meat for the winter. It was about Christmas when he formed this resolution, but before putting his resolve into execution he discovered that his supply of powder was so nearly exhausted that to begin a hunt so poorly provided for must end in failure. His brother-in-law had settled, a few months before, at a place six miles west of where Crockett lived, and had brought a keg of powder with him for Crockett which had not yet been delivered; recalling to mind this fact the latter now determined to bring the powder home though a journey to his brother-in-law would necessitate the crossing of two streams not yet sufficiently bridged with ice to admit of a safe passage. Crockett thus describes this remarkable trip, which I quote because it serves to show the extraordinary nerve and resolution of the man, and enables us to discover how he won his way from a position most lowly, to that which elicited the admiration of all his countrymen:

A Journey of Extraordinary Hardships

"The snow was about four inches deep when I started; and when I got to the water, which was only about a quarter of a mile off, it looked like an ocean. I put in, and waded on till I come to the channel, when I crossed that on a high log. I then took water again, having my gun and all my hunting tools along, and waded till I came to a deep slough, that was wider than the river itself. I had crossed it often on a log; but behold, when I got there, no log was to be seen. I knowed of an island in the slough, and a sapling stood on it close to the side of that log, which was now entirely under water. I knowed further, that the water was about eight or ten feet deep under the log, and I judged it to be about three feet deep over it. After studying a little what I should do, I determined to cut a forked sapling, which stood near me, so as to lodge it against the one that stood on the island, in which I succeeded very well. I then cut me a pole, and then crawled along on my sapling till I got to the one it was lodged against, which was about six feet above the water. I then felt about with my pole till I found the log, which was just about as deep under the water as I had judged. I now crawled back and got my gun, which I had left at the stump of the sapling I had cut, and again made my way to the place of lodgment, and then climbed down the other sapling so as to get on the log. I next felt my way along with my feet, in the water, about waist deep, but it was a mighty ticklish business. However, I got over, and by this time I had very little feeling in my feet and legs, as I had been all the time in the water, except what time I was crossing the high log over the river, and climbing my lodged sapling.

"I went but a short distance before I came to another slough, over which there was a log, but it was floating on the water. I thought I could walk it, and so I mounted on it; but when I had got about the middle of the deep water, somehow or somehow-else, it turned over, and in I went up to my head. I waded out of this deep water, and went ahead till I came to the highland where I stopp'd to pull off my wet clothes, and put on the others, which I had held up with my gun, above the water, when I fell in. I got them on, but my flesh had no feeling in it, I was so cold. I tied up the wet ones, and hung them up in a bush. I now thought I would run, so as to warm myself a little, but I couldn't raise a trot for some time; indeed, I couldn't step more than half the length of my foot. After a while I got better, and went on five miles to the house of my

CROCKETT BREAKING HIS WAY THROUGH THE ICE

brother-in-law, having not even smelt fire from the time I started. I got there late in the evening, and he was much astonished at seeing me at such a time. I staid all night, and the next morning was most piercing cold, and so they persuaded me not to go home that day. I agreed, and turned out and killed him two deer; but the weather still got worse and colder, instead of better. I staid that night, and in the morning they still insisted I couldn't get home. I knowed the water would be frozen over, but not hard enough to bear me, and so I agreed to stay that day. I went out hunting again, and pursued a big *he-bear* all day, but didn't kill him. The next morning was bitter cold, but I knowed my family was without meat, and I determined to get home to them, or die a-trying.

"I took my keg of powder and all my hunting tools, and cut out. When I got to the water, it was a sheet of ice as far as I could see. I put on to it, but hadn't got far before it broke through with me; and so I took out my tomahawk, and broke my way along before me for a considerable distance. At last I got to where the ice would bear me for a short distance, and I mounted on it, and went ahead; but it soon broke in again, and I had to wade on till I came to my floating log. I found it so tight this time, that I know'd it couldn't give me another fall, as it was frozen in with the ice. I crossed over it without much difficulty, and worked along till I got to my lodged sapling, and my log under the water. The swiftness of the current prevented the water from freezing over it, and so I had to wade, just as I did when I crossed it before. When I got to my sapling, I left my gun, and climbed out with my powder-keg first, and then went back and got my gun. By this time I was nearly frozen to death, but I saw all along before me, where the ice had been fresh broke, and I thought it must be a bear straggling about in the water. I therefore fresh primed my gun, and, cold as I was, I was determined to make war on him, if we met. But I followed the trail till it led me home, and I then found it had been made by my young man that lived with me, who had been sent by my distressed wife to see, if he could, what had become of me, for they all believed that I was dead. When I got home, I wasn't quite dead, but mighty nigh it; but had my powder, and that was what I went for."

CHAPTER V

A Great Bear Hunt

Having first provided his family with such necessaries as they might need during his absence, which he supposed would be for several days, Crockett set out with his trusty rifle and three equally trusty dogs for a hunt. Two young men started out with him, but they sought no larger game than turkeys, while Crockett would not be satisfied with anything less than bear, hence they soon separated, but not until they had agreed upon certain signals that might be used to summon each other together in case assistance was needed.

A very heavy rain had fallen during the preceding night which afterwards turned to sleet and covered the ground with ice that made traveling on foot precarious; but notwithstanding this Crockett pushed on alone and followed along the Obion banks for a distance of six miles before discovering any traces of game. The first living thing that greeted his sight was a large flock of turkeys, two of which he shot, but he had proceeded only a short distance further when his dogs threw their heads into the air and, after sniffing a moment, broke away evidently on the scent of some large game. Crockett followed after as rapidly as his now fatigued condition would allow, until he found the dogs barking up a tree in which some kind of game had undoubtedly taken refuge a short time before, but had now moved to other quarters. The dogs tarried only a moment, when they ran on and barked up another tree which the game had also abandoned, and thus continued their false alarms at half a dozen trees until Crockett's patience was quite exhausted, as his dogs appeared to be indulging a habit no less reprehensible in dogs than in men, that of lying. But as they changed positions rapidly and kept sniffing the air, Crockett still had a suspicion, though a faint one, that the dogs had been unable to keep the scent on account of the fall of sleet, and so kept on after them until he came to the edge of a prairie, when upon his astonished gaze burst a vision that caused him to halt with a feeling of trepidation. Right before the

"I GOT BACK IN ALL SORTS OF A HURRY"

dogs, that had now caught sight of the game, but were afraid to attack it, was a bear of ponderous proportions, larger than any the courageous hunter had ever before seen.

Hanging his two turkeys upon a sapling, Crockett looked to the priming of his gun, and then dashed after the bear that was now approaching the skirts of the prairie, which was lined with a dense thicket, and into which the game disappeared before Crockett could get within gun-shot. Of the adventure that followed he thus writes:

"In a little time I saw the bear climbing up a large black oak tree, and I crawled on until I got within about eighty yards of him. He was setting with his breast to me, and so I put fresh priming in my gun and fired at him. At this he raised one of his paws and snorted loudly. I loaded again as quick as I could, and fired as near the same place in his breast as possible. At the crack of my gun here he came tumbling down; and the moment he touched the ground, I heard one of my best dogs cry out. I took my tomahawk in one hand, and my big butcher-knife in the other, and ran up within four or five paces of him, at which he let my dog go and fixed his eyes on me. I got back in all sorts of a hurry, for I knowed if he got hold of me he would hug me altogether too close for comfort. I went to my gun and hastily loaded her again, and shot him the third time, which killed him good."

Again a Candidate for the Legislature

Game was so abundant that from natural inclination Crockett continued to hunt, and by killing coons, elk, deer and bear that winter he collected a large number of peltries which in February he carried to a little town that had sprung up in the year Crockett settled on the Obion, forty miles east of his cabin, called Jackson. Here he disposed of his peltries in exchange for coffee, sugar, powder, lead and salt.

While at Jackson he met some of his old comrades with whom he had served in the Creek War; he was also presented to three candidates for the legislature, one of whom, Dr. Butler, was a nephew of General Jackson. As was the custom among frontiersmen who thus casually met, the party drank several rounds to the health of each other, and in the course of their convivial entertainment some one suggested that Crockett should also offer himself as a candidate for the legislature, but to this proposal he objected, upon the grounds that he had no further desire for office, besides he lived forty miles from the nearest settlement and could not, therefore, conduct a canvass.

Crockett thought no more about the proposition to run him for the legislature and returned home to renew his hunt for peltries. However, two weeks after the meeting at Jackson, a gentleman came by Crockett's house and lodged there over night. Sometime during the evening he drew a newspaper from his pocket and began reading, when to his surprise he saw an announcement of Crockett's candidacy and in such language too that it would have been more difficult to explain the mistake than to make the canvass, so Crockett resolved to offer himself at the next fall election. Accordingly, he hired a man to work the farm in his place and started out electioneering.

The Bear Hunter to the Front

So rapidly had Crockett's reputation spread even among the sparse settlements, that he had not lived six months on the Obion before every one within a hundred miles were familiar with his name and had heard what a capital story-teller and bear-hunter he was. This was so much in his favor that he only needed to make a show of himself to secure votes. The three who had previously announced themselves as candidates, upon hearing that Crockett was in the field, met at Jackson and cast lots to decide who should withdraw from the race and which one remain to contest the election with Crockett. The choice fell on Dr. Butler, who was by far the ablest and most popular of the three, besides, his connection with Jackson gave him no small prestige. Realizing this, and supposing that the opposition he now had to contend with was of the feeblest character, he made many contemptuous allusions to Crockett, calling him the "bear hunter" and "the man from the cane."

Crockett thus describes the manner in which he conducted his electioneering, which is original enough to well merit preserving:

"At this time Colonel Alexander was a candidate for Congress, and attending one of his public meetings one day, I walked to where he was treating the people, and he gave me an introduction to several of his acquaintances, and informed them that I was out electioneering. In a little time, my competitor, Doctor Butler, came along; he passed by without noticing me, and I supposed he did not recognize me. But I hailed him, as I was for all sorts of fun; and when he turned to me, I said to him, 'Well, doctor, I suppose they have weighed you out to me; but I should like to know why they fixed your election for *March* instead of *August*? This is,' said I, 'a branfire new way of doing business, if a caucus is to make a representative for the people!' He now discovered who I was, and cried out, 'D——n it, Crockett, is that you?' 'Be sure it is,' said I, 'but I don't want it understood that I have come electioneering. I have just crept out of the cane, to see what discoveries I could make among the white folks.' I told him that when I set out electioneering, I would go prepared to put every man on as good a footing when I left him as I found him on. I would therefore have me a large buckskin hunting-shirt made, with a couple of pockets holding about a peck each; and that in one I would carry a great big twist of tobacco, and in the other my bottle of liquor; for I knowed when I met a man and offered him a dram, he would throw out his quid of tobacco to take one, and after he had taken his horn, I would out with my twist, and give him another chew. And in this way he would not be worse off than when I found him; and I would be sure to leave him in a first rate good humor. He said I could beat him electioneering all hollow. I told him I would give him better evidence of that before August, notwithstanding he had many advantages over me, and particularly in the way of money; but I told him I would go on the products of the country; that I had industrious children, and the best of coon-dogs; and they would hunt every night till midnight to support my election; and when the coon fur wasn't good, I would myself go a wolfing, and shoot down a wolf and skin his head and his scalp would be good to me for three dollars, in our State treasury money; and in this way I would get along on the big string. He stood like he was both amused and astonished, and the whole crowd was in a roar of laughter. From this place I returned home, leaving the people in a first-rate way, and I was sure I would do a good business among them. At any rate, I was determined to stand up to my lick-log, salt or no salt.

"In a short time there came out two other candidates, a Mr. Shaw and a Mr. Brown. We all ran the race through; and when the election was over, it turned out that I beat them all by a majority of two hundred and forty-seven votes, and was again returned as a member of the legislature from a new region of the country, without losing a session. This reminded me of the old saw—'A fool for luck, and a poor man for children.'"

Becomes a Candidate for Congress

Crockett served in the legislature of 1823-24, making his second term. It was during this term that Jackson was a candidate for the Senate, and being the idol of his people was, of course, elected, but it was not by Crockett's vote, and in fact despite his active opposition, for, though the reason has never been explained, to my knowledge, Crockett always bore a hatred towards Jackson, probably caused by some act of the latter during the Creek War.

In 1824 the tariff question was a paramount issue in Congress, of especial importance to the Southern States, as it promised to largely increase the price of cotton; but the proposition to increase the tariff did not apply to cotton only, but to hundreds of household necessaries as well, on which account the law was generally opposed. Col. Alexander represented Crockett's district in Congress, and had voted for the new tariff bill, which affected his popularity so much that the opposition had excellent hopes for defeating him at the next election. They cast about for a man to set up against him, and at length united upon Crockett who, at first, positively refused to run, on account of his ignorance of matters that every representative in Congress ought to be familiar with. But persuasion altered his determination and he entered into the race with energy. Alexander's sudden loss of popularity, on account of his vote on the new tariff bill, was offset by Crockett's decline in public favor because of his opposition to Jackson. But Alexander could plead that the tariff bill advanced the price of cotton, which was some extenuation of his fault in the eyes of his constituents, while Crockett, as he maintains, might as well have sung psalms over a dead horse, as to try to convince the people that he had done his duty in voting against Jackson. He was thus put to disadvantage that showed clearly in the election result, for Crockett was defeated, though by the narrow majority of only *two votes*. In other words, to use Crockett's illustration, Alexander had crawled into Congress by as tight a squeeze as Henry Snyder had got into heaven.

An Extraordinary Bear Hunt

Crockett accepted his defeat with good grace and immediately set about to improve his fortune, but in a way entirely new to him, and, like a majority of new ways, the experiment proved a disastrous failure. Having acquired, by entry, considerable land that was well timbered, he undertook to make it available by converting a large amount of the timber into pipe-staves, which were in good demand in New Orleans. Ha accordingly hired a dozen men, some of whom he put to work cutting staves, and others to building boats in which to float them to market. He continued at this employment until the spring of 1826, when the bear season having opened—that is to say, the time when bears crawl out of their winter quarters, which is usually about April 1st—he gave over work in order to enjoy a grand hunt for his favorite game and lay in a supply of meat.

Within a few days after going upon the hunt he had killed and salted down as many bear as his family could consume in a year, and was upon the point of resuming the cutting of staves, when a settler, whose ranch was twenty-five miles west of Crockett, came and requested him to continue the hunt in his section, where bears had become so numerous that he could keep neither pigs, sheep nor calves for their depredations. To accommodate this neighbor Crockett accompanied him home, and with his pack of eight dogs went in pursuit of the game, and continued the hunt for two weeks, during which time he killed *fifteen bears*.

As much of Crockett's fame rests upon his quaint bear-stories, I will let him relate in his own language the adventures that befell him in his next hunt:

"Having now supplied my friend with plenty of meat, I engaged occasionally again with my hands in our boat building, and getting staves. But I at length couldn't stand it any longer without another hunt. So I concluded to take my little son and cross over the lake, and take a hunt there. We got over, and that evening turned out and killed three bears in little or no time. The next morning we drove up four forks, and made a sort of scaffold, on which we salted up our meat, so as to have it out of reach of the wolves, for as soon as we would leave our camp, they would take possession. We had just eat our breakfast, when a company of hunters came to our camp who had fourteen dogs, but all so poor, that when they would bark they would almost have to lean up against a tree and take a rest. I told them their dogs couldn't run in smell of a bear, and they had better stay at my camp and feed them on the bones I had cut out of my meat. I left them there and cut out; but I hadn't gone far, when my dogs took a first rate start after a very large fat old he-bear, which run right plump toward my camp. I pursued on, but my other hunters had heard my dogs coming, and met them and killed the bear before I got up with him. I gave him to them, and cut out again for a creek called Big Clover which wasn't very far off. Just as I got there, and was entering a cane-brake, my dogs all broke and went ahead, and in a little time they raised a fuss in the cane, and seemed to be going every way. I listened a while, and found my dogs was in two companies, and that both was in a snorting fight. I sent my little son to one and I broke for t'other. I got to mine first, and found my dogs had a two-year old bear down a-wooling away on him, so I just took out my big butcher, and went up and slapped it into him, and killed him without shooting. There was five of the dogs in my company. In a short time I heard my little son fire at his bear; when I went to him he had killed it too. He had two dogs in his team. Just at this moment we heard my other dog barking a short distance off, and all the rest immediately broke to him. We pushed on too, and when we got there, we found that he had still a larger bear than either of them we had killed, treed by himself. We killed that one also, which made three we had killed in less than half an hour. We turned in and butchered them, and then started to hunt for water and a good place to camp. But we had no sooner started, than our dogs took another start after another one, and away they went like a thundergust and was out of hearing in a minute. We followed the way they had gone for some time, but at length we gave up the hope of finding them, and turned back. As we were going back, I came to where a poor fellow was grubbing, and he looked like the very picture of hard times. I asked him what he was doing away there in the woods by himself? He said he was grubbing for a man who intended to settle there; and the reason why he did it was, that he had no meat for his family, and he was working for a little.

"I was mighty sorry for the poor fellow, for it was not only a hard but a very slow way to get meat for a hungry family; so I told him if he would go with me, I would give him more meat than he could get by grubbing in a month. I intended to supply him with meat, and also to get him to assist my little boy in packing and salting up my bears. He had never seen a bear killed in his life. I told him I had six killed then, and

AN EXCITING BATTLE

my dogs were hard after another. He went off to his little cabin, which was a short distance in the brush, and his wife was very anxious he should go with me. So we started and went to where I had left my three bears, and made a camp. We then gathered my meat, and salted and scaffolded it, as I had done the other. Night now came on, but no word from my dogs yet. I afterwards found they had treed the bear about five miles off near to a man's house, and had barked at it the whole enduring night. Poor fellows! many a time they looked for me, and wondered why I didn't come, for they know'd there was no mistake in me, and I know'd they were as good as ever fluttered. In the morning, as soon as it was light enough to see, the man took his gun and went to them, and shot the bear and killed it. My dogs, however, wouldn't have anything to say to this stranger; so they left him, and came early in the morning back to me.

"We got our breakfast and cut out again, and we killed four large and very fat bears that day. We hunted out the week, and in that time we killed seventeen, all of them first-rate. When we closed our hunt, I gave the man over a thousand weight of fine, fat bear-meat, which pleased him mightily, and made him feel as rich as a Jew. I saw him the next fall, and he told me he had plenty of meat to do him the whole year, from his week's hunt. My son and me now went home. This was the week between Christmas and New Year, that we made this hunt.

A Curious Habit and Singular Results

"When I got home, one of my neighbors was out of meat, and wanted me to go back, and let him go with me to take another hunt. I couldn't refuse; but I told him I was afraid the bear had taken to house by that time, for after they get very fat in the fall and early part of the winter, they go into their holes in large hollow trees, or into hollow logs, or their cane-houses, or the harricanes, and lie there till spring, like frozen snakes. And one thing about this will seem mighty strange to many people: From about the first of January to about the last of April, these varments lie in their holes altogether. In all that time they have no food to eat; and yet when they come out they are not an ounce lighter than when they went to house. I don't know the cause of this, and still I know it is a fact; and I leave it for others who have more learning than myself to account for it. They have not a particle of food with them, but they just lie and suck the bottom of their paw all the time. I have killed many of them in their trees, which enables me to speak positively on this subject. However, my neighbor, whose name was McDaniel, and my little son and me, went on down to the lake to my second camp, where I had killed my seventeen bears the week before, and turned out to hunting. But we hunted hard all day without getting a single start. We had carried but little provisions with us, and the next morning was entirely out of meat. I sent my son about three miles off to the house of an old friend to get some. The old gentleman was much pleased to hear I was hunting in those parts, for the year before the bears had killed a great many of his hogs. He was that day killing his bacon hogs, and so he gave my son some meat, and sent word to me that I must come to his house that evening, that he would have plenty of feed for my dogs, and some accommodations for ourselves; but before my son got back, we had gone out hunting, and in a large canebrake my dogs found a big bear in a cane-house, which he had fixed for his winter-quarters, as they sometimes do.

"When my lead dog found him, and raised the yell, all the rest broke to him, but none of them entered his house until we got up. I encouraged my dogs, and they knowed me so well, that I could have made them seize the old serpent himself, with all his horns and heads, and cloven foot and ugliness into the bargain, if he would only have come to light, so that they could have seen him. They bulged in, and in an instant the bear followed them out, and I told my friend to shoot him, as he was mighty wrathy to kill a bear. He did so, and killed him prime. We carried him to our camp, by which time my son had returned; and after we got our dinners we packed up, and cut for the house of my old friend, whose name was Davidson.

Look Out for the Bear

"We got there and staid with him that night; and the next morning, having salted up our meat, we left it with him, and started to take a hunt between the Obion Lake and the Red Foot Lake, as there had been a dreadful hurricane, which passed between them, and I was sure there must be a heap of bears in the fallen timber. We had gone about five miles without seeing any sign at all; but at length we got on some high cany ridges, and as we rode along, I saw a hole in a large black-oak, and on examining more closely, I discovered that a bear had clomb the tree. I could see his tracks going up, but none coming down, and so I was sure he was in there. A person who is acquainted with bear-hunting, can tell easy enough when the varment is in the hollow; for as they go up they don't slip a bit, but as they come down they make long scratches with their nails.

"My friend was a little ahead of me, but I called him back, and told him there was a bear in that tree, and I must have him out. So we lit from our horses; and I found a small tree which I thought I could fall so as to lodge against my bear tree, and we fell to work chopping it with our tomahawks. I intended, when we lodged the tree against the other, to let my little son go up, and look into the hole, for he could climb like a squirrel. We had chopp'd on a little time and stopped to rest, when I heard my dogs barking mighty severe at a distance from us, and I told my friend I knowed they had a bear; for it is the nature of a dog, when he finds you are hunting bears, to hunt for nothing else; he becomes fond of the meat, and considers other game as 'not worth a notice,' as old Johnson said of the devil.

"We concluded to leave our tree a bit, and went to my dogs, and when we got there, sure enough they had an eternal great big fat bear up a tree, just ready for shooting. My friend again petitioned me for liberty to shoot this one also. I had a little rather not, as the bear was so big, but I couldn't refuse; so he blazed away, and down

ALMOST TOO MUCH FOR THE CROWD

came the old fellow like some great log had fell. I now missed one of my dogs, the same that I before spoke of as having treed the bear by himself sometime before, when I had started the three in the cane-brake. I told my friend that my missing dog had a bear somewhere, just as sure as fate; so I left them to butcher the one we had just killed, and I went up on a piece of high ground to listen for my dog. I heard him barking with all his might some distance off, and I pushed ahead for him. My other dogs hearing him broke to him, and when I got there, sure enough again he had another bear ready treed; if he hadn't, I wish I may be shot. I fired on him, and brought him down; and then went back, and help'd finish butchering the one at which I had left my friend. We then packed both to our tree where we had left my boy. By this time, the little fellow had cut the tree down that we intended to lodge, but it fell the wrong way; he had then feather'd in on the big tree, to cut that, and had found that it was nothing but a shell on the outside, and all doted in the middle, as too many of our big men are in these days having only an outside appearance. My friend and my son cut away on it, and I went off about a hundred yards with my dogs to keep them from running under the tree when it should fall.

A Rough-and-Tumble Fight

"On looking back at the hole, I saw the bear's head out of it, looking down at them as they were cutting. I hollered to them to look up, and they did so; and McDaniel catched up his gun, but by this time the bear was out and coming down the tree. He fired at it, and as soon as he touched the ground the dogs were all around it, and they had a roll-and-tumble fight to the foot of the hill, where they stopp'd him. I ran up and putting my gun against the bear, fired and killed him. We had now three, and so we made our scaffold and salted them up.

"In the morning I left my son at the camp, and we started on towards the harricane; and when we had went about a mile, we started a very large bear, but we got along mighty slow on account of the cracks in the earth occasioned by earthquakes. We however made out to keep in hearing of the dogs for about three miles, and then we come to the harricane. Here we had to quit our horses, as old Nick himself couldn't have got through it without sneaking along in the form that he put on to make a fool of our old grandmother Eve. By this time several of my dogs had got tired and come back; but we went ahead on foot for some little time in the harricane, when we met a bear coming straight to us, and not more than twenty or thirty yards off. I started my tired dogs after him, and McDaniel pursued them, and I went on to where my other dogs were. I had seen the track of the bear they were after, and I knowed he was a screamer. I followed on to about the middle of the harricane, but my dogs pursued him so close that they made him climb an old stump about twenty feet high. I got in shooting distance of him and fired, but I was all over in such a flutter from fatigue and running, that I couldn't hold steady; but, however, I broke his shoulder, and he fell. I run up and loaded my gun as quick as possible, and shot him again and killed him. When I went to take out my knife to butcher him, I found I had lost it in coming through the harricane. The vines and briers was so thick that I would sometimes have to get down and crawl like a varment to get through at all; and a vine had, as I supposed, caught in the handle and pulled it out. While I was standing and studying what to do, my friend came to me. He had followed my trail through the harricane, and had found my knife, which was mighty good news to me; as a hunter hates the worst in the world to lose a good dog, or any part of his hunting tools. I now left McDaniel to butcher the bear, and I went after our horses, and brought them as near as the nature of the case would allow. I then took our bags, and went back to where he was; and when we had skinned the bear, we fleeced off the fat and carried it to our horses at several loads. We then packed it up on our horses, and had a heavy pack of it on each one. We now started and went on till about sunset, when I concluded we must be near our camp; so I hollered and my son answered me, and we moved on in the direction to the camp. We had gone but a little way when I heard my dogs make a warm start again; and I jumped down from my horse and gave him up to my friend, and told him I would follow them. He went on to the camp, and I went ahead after my dogs with all my might for a considerable distance, till at last night came on. The woods were very rough and hilly, and all covered over with cane.

Crockett Beards a Bear in His Den

"I now was compelled to move on more slowly; and was frequently falling over logs, and into the cracks made by the earthquakes, so that I was very much afraid I would break my gun. However, I went on about three miles, when I came to a good big creek, which I waded. It was very cold, and the creek was about knee-deep; but I felt no great inconvenience from it just then, as I was all over wet with sweat from running, and I felt hot enough. After I got over this creek and out of the cane, which was very thick on all our creeks, I listened for my dogs. I found they had either treed or brought the bear to a stop, as they continued barking in the same place. I pushed on as near in the direction of the noise as I could, till I found the hill was too steep for me to climb, and so I backed and went down the creek some distance, till I came

A FIGHT AT CLOSE QUARTERS

to a hollow, and then took up that, till I came to a place where I could climb up the hill. It was mighty dark, and was difficult to see my way, or anything else. When I got up the hill, I found I had passed the dogs; and so I turned and went to them. I found, when I got there, they had treed the bear in a large forked poplar, and it was setting in the fork.

"I could see the lump, but not plain enough to shoot with any certainty, as there was no moonlight; and so I set in to hunting for some dry brush to make me a light; but I could find none, though I could find that the ground was torn mightily to pieces by the cracks.

"At last I thought I could shoot by guess, and kill him; so I pointed as near the lump as I could, and fired away. But the bear didn't come, he only clumb up higher, and got out on a limb, which helped me to see him better. I now loaded up again and fired, but this time he didn't move at all. I commenced loading for a third fire, but the first thing I knowed, the bear was down among my dogs, and they were fighting all around me. I had my big butcher in my belt, and I had a pair of dressed buckskin breeches on. So I took out my knife, and stood determined, if he should get hold of me, to defend myself in the best way I could. I stood there for some time, and could now and then see a white dog I had, but the rest of them, and the bear, which were dark colored, I couldn't see at all, it was so miserable dark. They still fought around me, and sometimes within three feet of me, but at last the bear got down into one of the cracks that the earthquakes had made in the ground, about four feet deep, and I could tell the biting end of him by the hollering of my dogs. So I took my gun and pushed the muzzle of it about, till I thought I had it against the main part of his body, and fired; but it happened to be only the fleshy part of his foreleg. With this he jumped out of the crack, and he and the dogs had another hard fight around me, as before. At last, however, they forced him back into the crack again, as he was when I had shot.

"I had laid down my gun in the dark, and I now began to hunt for it; and while hunting I got hold of a pole, and I concluded I would punch him awhile with that. I did so, and when I would punch him, the dogs would jump in on him, when he would bite them badly, and they would jump out again. I concluded, as he would take punching so patiently, it might be that he would lie still enough for me to get down in the crack, and feel slowly along till I could find the right place to give him a dig with my butcher. So I got down, and my dogs got in before him and kept his head towards them, till I got along easily up to him; and placing my hand on his rump, felt for his shoulder, just behind which I intended to stick him. I made a lunge with my long knife, and fortunately stuck him right through the heart, at which he just sunk down, and I crawled out in a hurry. In a little time my dogs all come out too, and seemed satisfied, which was a way they always had of telling me that they had finished him.

A Funny Exercise to Keep Warm

"I suffered very much that night with cold, as my leather breeches, and everything else I had on was wet and frozen. But I managed to get my bear out of this crack after several hard trials, and so I butchered him and laid down to try to sleep. But my fire was very bad, and I couldn't find anything that would burn well to make it any better; and so I concluded I should freeze if I didn't warm myself in some way by exercise. So I grot up and hollered awhile, and then I would just jump up and down with all my might, and throw myself into all sorts of motions. But all this wouldn't do; for my blood was now getting cold, and the chills coming all over me. I was so tired, too, that I could hardly walk; but I thought I would do the best I could to save my life and then, if I died, nobody would be to blame. So I went to a tree about two feet through, and not a limb on it for thirty feet, and I would climb up to the limbs, and then lock my arms together around it, and slide down to the bottom again. This would make the insides of my legs and arms feel mighty warm and good. I continued this till daylight in the morning, and how often I clumb up my tree and slid down I don't know, but I reckon at least a hundred times.

"In the morning I got my bear hung up so as to be safe, and then set out to hunt for my camp. I found it after awhile, and McDaniel and my son were very much rejoiced to see me get back, for they were about to give me up for lost. We got our breakfasts, and then secured our meat by building a high scaffold, and covering it over. We had no fear of its spoiling, for the weather was so cold that it couldn't.

"We now started after my other bear, which had caused me so much trouble and suffering; and before we got him, we got a start after another, and took him also. We went on to the creek I had crossed the night before, and camped, and then went to where my bear was that I had killed in the crack. When we examined the place, McDaniel said he wouldn't have gone into it, as I did, for all the bears in the woods.

"We then took the meat down to our camp and salted it, and also the last one we had killed; intending in the morning, to make a hunt in the harricane again.

An Earthquake

"We prepared for resting that night, and I can assure the reader I was in need of it. We had laid down by our fire, and about ten o'clock there came a most terrible earthquake, which shook the earth so that we were rocked about like we had been in a cradle. We were very much alarmed; for though we were accustomed to feel earthquakes, we were now right in the region which had been torn to pieces by them in 1812, and we thought it might take a notion and swallow us up, like the big fish did Jonah.

"In the morning we packed up and moved to the harricane, where we made another camp, and turned out that evening and killed a very large bear, which made eight we had now killed in this hunt.

"The next morning we entered the harricane again, and in a little or no time my dogs were in full cry. We pursued them, and soon came to a thick cane-brake, in which they had stopp'd their bear. We got up close to him, but the cane was so thick that we couldn't see more than a few feet. Here I made my friend hold the cane a little open with his gun till I shot the bear, which was a mighty large one. I killed him dead in his tracks. We got him out and butchered him, and in a little time started another and killed him, which now made ten we had killed; and we knowed we couldn't pack any more home, as we had only five horses along; therefore we returned to the camp and salted up all our meat, to be ready for a start homeward next morning.

Wonderful Result of the Hunt

"The morning came, and we packed our horses with the meat, and had as much as they could possibly carry, and sure enough cut out for home. It was about thirty miles, and we reached home the second day. I had now accommodated my neighbor with meat enough to do him, and had killed in all, up to that time, fifty-eight bears, during the fall and winter.

"As soon as the time arrived for them to quit their houses and come out again in the spring, I took a notion to hunt a little more, and in about one month I killed forty-seven more, which made one hundred and five bears which I had killed in less than one year."*

CHAPTER VI

Crockett's Disastrous Flat-Boat Experience

Life in the lonely wilderness of early Tennessee was a strange compound of excitement and contemplation; there was no medium ground for mind employment, or social amusement, as even neighborly interchange of thought was impossible in that

---

*These bear hunts of the Colonel entirely surpass anything on record. Mr. Gordon Cumming's record of his fights with lions, elephants, giraffes, hippopotamuses and African buffaloes, is full of excitement and interest; but in real peril and adventure, they by no means surpass Colonel Crockett's bear fights.

vast solitude. The dull monotony of isolation could only be relieved by plunging into the excitement of a hunt for wild animals, or by a visit to some cross-roads saloon, perhaps fifty miles distant, where congregated the boisterous element of a sparse settlement to drink liquor, shoot matches and carouse without fear of disturbing the public peace, because there was no public peace.

While Crockett delighted in adventure, he also loved the quiet that his seclusion from busy life afforded, and nature became to him a school wherein were taught those severe lessons of discipline which, learned from such a master, are never forgotten. His mind was never groveling, but always soaring; hence, though wholly unlettered in the learning of books, he inherited a quick perception and excellent mind, which enabled him to absorb from his good teacher the fundamental principles of knowledge and its application to human affairs. Thus he developed from the pupil to the philosopher of nature, and became an adept in the art of apt illustration, with which he painted his anecdotes so felicitously. But this process of enlargement of his understanding, instead of satisfying his appetite, grew with what it fed on and made him long for other spheres, to increase the domain in which he had so long moved, but which now appeared too small for free action.

His failure to realize those congressional aspirations that had received undue stimulation from assurances of his friends, as well as from his own ambition, undoubtedly caused him intense mortification, though outwardly he maintained a stolid composure that reflected none of his real feelings.

Finding no other avenue open for retreat from the scene of his defeat, and actuated largely by a desire to see something more of the world, he began the loading of two flat-boats with pipe-staves, as already explained, with the view of making a profitable trip to New Orleans, and thence—to whatever country fate or impulse might carry him.

The boats were at length loaded, in the summer of 1827, with thirty thousand staves, and on a beautiful afternoon he pushed away from the shore, and floated out on the Obion and away to the Mississippi. No man had less experience than he in the management of flat-boats, for these that he built were the first he had ever seen, while his crew of six men was no better qualified for the trip; even the pilot was a landsman whose knowledge of boating had been acquired entirely in the management of a canoe. Notwithstanding the almost criminal ignorance of both officers and crew the boats floated two days before any trouble was encountered, though at no time did Crockett feel so secure as he would in a rough-and-tumble fight with a bear, when he could bring his experience into use. The boats were unwieldy, as flat-boats always are, and the crew could not control them. Time and again they tried to land, but threatening storms, dark nights, treacherous cut-offs, dangerous crevasses, inviting sandbars, and frowning sawyers, had to be braved, with hope the only pilot and trust to providence acting as gouger (the bow steering oar) watch. It would be expecting too much of fortune to suppose the boats could escape disaster and reach their destination under such circumstances, nor did they, as we shall soon see.

A Hair-Breadth Escape

The story of the wreck that came at last is thus related by Crockett:

"In a short distance we got into what is called the *Devil's Elbow*; and if any place in the wide creation has its own proper name I thought it was this. Here we had about the hardest work that I ever was engaged in in my life to keep out of danger; and even then we were in it all the while. We twice attempted to land at wood-yards, which we could see, but couldn't reach.

"The people would run out with lights, and try to instruct us how to get to shore, but all in vain. Our boats were so heavy that we couldn't take them much any way, except the way they wanted to go, and just the way the current would carry them. At last we quit trying to land, and concluded just to go ahead as well as we could, for we found that we couldn't do any better. Some time in the night I was down in the cabin of one of the boats, sitting by the fire, thinking on what a hobble we had got into, and how much better bear-hunting was on hard land, than floating along on the water, when a fellow had to go ahead whether he was exactly willing or not.

"The hatchway into the cabin came slap down, right through the top of the boat; and it was the only way out except a small hole in the side, which we had used for putting our arms through to dip up water before we lashed the boats together.

"We were now floating sideways, and the boat I was in was the hindmost as we went. All at once I heard the hands begin to run over the top of the boat in great confusion, and pull with all their might; and the first thing I know'd after this we went broadside full-tilt against the head of an island where a large raft of drift-timber had lodged. The nature of such a place would be, as everybody knows, to suck the boats down, and turn them right under this raft; and the uppermost boat would, of course, be suck'd down and go under first. As soon as we struck, I bulged for my hatchway, as the boat was turning under sure enough. But when I got to it, the water was pouring through in a current as large as the hole would let it, and as strong as the weight of the river would force it. I found I couldn't get out here, for the boat was now turned down in such a way that it was steeper than a house-top. I now thought of the hole in the side, and made my way in a hurry for that. With difficulty I got to it, and when I got there I found it was too small for me to get out by my own power, and I began to think that I was in a worse box than ever. But I put my arms through and hollered as

AN ESCAPE AT THE SACRIFICE OF SHIRT AND HIDE

loud as I could roar, as the boat I was in hadn't yet quite filled with water up to my head, and the hands who were next to the raft, seeing my arms out and hearing me holler, seized them and began to pull. I told them I was sinking, and to pull my arms off, or force me through, for now I know'd well enough it was neck or nothing, come out or sink.

"By a violent effort they jerked me through; but I was in a pretty pickle when I got through. I had been sitting without any clothing over my shirt; this was torn off and I was literally skin'd like a rabbit. I was, however, well pleased to get out in any way, even without shirt or hide, as before I could straighten myself on the boat next to the raft the one they pulled me out of went entirely under, and I have never seen it any more to this day. We all escaped on to the raft where we were compelled to sit all night about a mile from land on either side. Four of my company were bareheaded, and three barefooted; and of that number I was one. I reckon I looked like a pretty cracklin ever to get to Congress!!

"We had now lost all our loading, and every particle of our clothing, except what little we had on; but over all this, while I was setting there, in the night, floating about on the drift, I felt happier and better off than I ever had in my life before, for I had just made such a marvelous escape that I had forgot almost everything else in that; and so I felt prime."

Crockett Is Elected to Congress

For a second time all of Crockett's possessions were swept away by water and the world was before him again. Though the loss of his boats cost him the little that he had accumulated while living on the Obion, yet it did not alienate his friends or lessen his popularity. Almost immediately upon his return home he was solicited by a large number of his neighbors to stand again for Congress, though the election was only two months off. There were two candidates already announced, viz.: Colonel Alexander, his former competitor, and General William Arnold, both men of considerable property and highly educated. Crockett was quite willing to undertake the race, having nothing then in view at which to turn his hand for a living, but being penniless he could conceive of no way to raise the necessary funds for conducting a campaign. His embarrassment, however, was speedily relieved by a neighbor, who advanced him one hundred and fifty dollars, and offered to furnish him more if he should require it. Thus armed for the contest Crockett entered it with a determination to succeed.

A week after announcing his candidacy Crockett attended a mass meeting at which Alexander and Arnold were advertised to speak, and was there introduced to the latter. Though he had not expected to deliver an address, after the introduction Crockett was invited, rather out of courtesy, by Arnold to make the opening speech which was made so publicly that he could not decline. Being thus pushed into a position always embarrassing to Crockett he arose and told a few jokes, but failed to make any apparent impression upon his auditors. When he descended from the platform he was succeeded by Alexander, who made a speech of an hour's length to which Arnold replied in the fashion of political debate. The latter had considered Crockett as only a mere pretender, without either sagacity or popularity, and refused to consider him as a competitor worthy of notice, so that in all his speech he did not once so much as make a reference to Crockett. His remarks were generally well received and he would, no doubt, have reaped considerable benefit from the meeting, but for an incident that Crockett, by his cunning humor, turned against his antagonist and to his own credit. While Arnold was closing in a special effort wreathed with the flowers of eloquent speech, a flock of guinea-hens appeared just behind the platform and set up such a "put-racking" that the speaker could scarcely make himself heard, which so annoyed him that he requested some one of his hearers to drive them away. At this juncture Crockett arose and with a merry twinkle in his eyes said, "Well, Colonel, you are the only man I ever met who could understand fowl-language. You had not the small

CROCKETT ON THE STUMP

courtesy to even mention me in your speech, and when my little speckled friends, the guinea-fowls, came up to protest, with their cry of 'Crockett, Crockett, Crockett,' you are so uncivil as to order them away." This felicitous joke fell with such pointed force that the crowd roared with laughter and so disconcerted Arnold that he abruptly left the stand and in so doing surrendered the honors of the day to Crockett.

The election followed soon after and resulted in favor of Crockett by a majority of twenty-seven hundred and forty-eight votes. His total constituency was one hundred thousand, which indicates that the polling strength of his district was about twenty thousand.

Crockett's Dinner with President Adams

Although now a member of Congress, which in his time was a mark of great distinction and honor, Crockett was entirely destitute of money, having spent the one hundred and fifty dollars he had borrowed in the canvass. It now became a question how he should be able to get to Washington, but this perplexity was soon relieved by his friend coming to his rescue a second time and making him another loan of one hundred dollars. With this Crockett set out for the capital, and upon arriving there he immediately obtained an advance from the government treasurer of the two hundred and fifty dollars borrowed and sent the sum to his friend with expressions of thanks, as became an honest man fully appreciating the favor that had been extended to him.

Soon after his arrival at Washington he was invited to dine with President Adams, a man of the highest culture, whose manners had been formed in the courts of Europe. Crockett, totally unacquainted with the usages of society, did not know what the note of invitation meant, and immediately sought his friend, the Hon. Mr. Verplanck for an explanation. Concerning this incident Crockett says:

"I was wild from the backwoods, and didn't know nothing about eating dinner with the big folks of our country. And how should I, having been a hunter all my life? I had eat most of my dinners on a log in the woods, and sometimes no dinner at all. I knew, whether I ate dinner with the President or not was a matter of no importance, for my constituents were not to be benefited by it. I did not go to court the President, for I was opposed to him in principle, and had no favors to ask at his hands. I was afraid, however, I should be awkward, as I was so entirely a stranger to fashion; and in going along, I resolved to observe the conduct of my friend Mr. Verplanck, and to do as he did. And I know that I did behave myself right well."

Some cruel wag wrote the following ludicrous account of this dinner-party, which went the round of all the papers as veritable history. The writer pretended to quote Crockett's own account of the dinner:

CROCKETT CALLING FOR HIS GOOSE

"The first thing I did," said Davy, "after I got to Washington, was to go to the President's. I stepped into the President's house. Thinks I, who's afeard. If I didn't, I wish I may be shot. Says I, 'Mr. Adams, I am Mr. Crockett, from Tennessee.' So, says he, 'How d'ye do, Mr. Crockett?' And he shook me by the hand, although he know'd I went the whole hog for Jackson. If he didn't, I wish I may be shot.

"Not only that, but he sent me a printed ticket to dine with him. I've got it in my pocket yet. I went to dinner, and I walked all around the long table, looking for something that I liked. At last I took my seat beside a fat goose, and I helped myself to as much of it as I wanted. But I hadn't took three bites, when I looked away up the table at a man they called *Tash* (attaché). He was talking French to a woman on t'other side of the table. He dodged his head and she dodged hers, and then they got to drinking wine across the table.

"But when I looked back again my plate was gone, goose and all. So I jist cast my eyes down to t'other end of the table, and sure enough I seed a black man walking off with my plate. I says, 'Hello, Mister, bring back my plate.' He fetched it back in a hurry, as you may think. And when he set it down before me, how do you think it was? Licked as clean as my hand. If it wasn't, I wish I may be shot!

"Says he, 'What will you have sir?' And says I, 'You may well say that, after stealing my goose.' And he began to laugh. Then says I, 'Mister, laugh if you please; but I don't half-like sich tricks upon travelers.' I then filled my plate with bacon and greens. And whenever I looked up or down the table, I held on to my plate with my left hand.

"When we were all done eating, they cleared everything off the table, and took away the table-cloth. And what do you think? There was another cloth under it. If there wasn't, I wish I may be shot! Then I saw a man coming along carrying a great glass thing, with a glass handle below, something like a candlestick. It was stuck full of little glass cups, with something in them that looked good to eat. Says I, 'Mister, bring that thing here.' Thinks I, let's taste them first. They were mighty sweet and good, so I took six of them. If I didn't, I wish I may be shot."

The story was copied into nearly every newspaper then published, and caused Crockett so much annoyance that he procured the statements of several persons who were guests of the President at the dinner, in denial of the report, and in certification of his proper conduct at the banquet. But the bad effects were never fully removed, and to the day of his death he was haunted by constant repetitions of the story, told with occasional variations, but always to his discredit and chagrin.

Crockett Re-Elected and Opposes Jackson

In 1829 Crockett was a candidate for re-election, in which his hopes were not disappointed. He had so conducted himself in Congress as to win the praise of the whole country and so increased in popular favor at home that he was again chosen by an overwhelming majority.

During his first term he generally affiliated with what was known as the Jackson party. At this time, however, Jackson was in the Senate, but while a leader in that body, a large party had organized to make him President, and everywhere the live issue was presented of *pro* and *anti* Jackson, which culminated in his election to the presidency in the fall of 1828.

"It may be doubted," as Abbott, the historian says, "whether there ever was a more honest, conscientious man in Congress than David Crockett. His celebrated motto, 'Be sure that you are right, and then go ahead,' seemed ever to animate him. He could neither be menaced or bribed to support any measure which he thought to be wrong. Ere long he found it necessary to oppose some of Jackson's measures. We will let him tell the story in his own truthful words":

"Soon after the commencement of this second term, I saw, or thought I did, that it was expected of me that I would bow to the name of Andrew Jackson, and follow him in all his motions, and windings, and turnings, even at the expense of my conscience and judgment. Such a thing was new to me and a total stranger to my principles. I knowed well enough, though, that if I didn't 'hurrah' for his name, the hue and cry was to be raised against me, and I was to be sacrificed, if possible. His famous, or rather I should say his *infamous* Indian bill was brought forward, and I opposed it from the purest motives in the world. Several of my colleagues got around me, and told me how well they loved me, and that I was ruining myself. They said this was a favorite measure of the President and I ought to go for it. I told them I believed it was a wicked, unjust measure, and that I should go against it, let the cost to myself be what it might; that I was willing to go with General Jackson in everything that I believed was honest and right; but, further than this, I wouldn't go for him or any other man in the whole creation.

"I had been elected by a majority of three thousand five hundred and eighty-five votes, and I believed they were honest men, and wouldn't want me to vote for any unjust notion, to please Jackson or any one else: at any rate, I was of age, and determined to trust them. I voted against this Indian bill, and my conscience yet tells me that I gave a good, honest vote, and one that I believe will not make me ashamed in the day of judgment. I served out my term, and though many amusing things happened, I am not disposed to swell my narrative by inserting them.

"When it closed, and I returned home, I found the storm had raised against me sure enough; and it was echoed from side to side, and from end to end of my district that I had turned against Jackson. This was considered the unpardonable sin. I was hunted down like a wild varment, and in this hunt every little newspaper in the district, and every little pin-hook lawyer was engaged. Indeed, they were ready to print anything and everything that the ingenuity of man could invent against me."

In consequence of this opposition, Crockett lost his next election, and yet by a majority of but seventy votes. For two years he remained at home hunting bears. But having once tasted the pleasures of political life, and the excitements of Washington, his silent rambles in the woods had lost much of their former charms. He was again a candidate at the ensuing election, and, after a very warm contest, gained the day by a majority of two hundred and two votes.

CHAPTER VII

Grand Ovations Tendered Crockett

"Be sure you're right, then go ahead." This saying of Crockett's, repeated often for his own encouragement, became a maxim as celebrated as any of Poor Richard's proverbs, and was heard fifty years ago, as it is to-day, in every village of America. His droll stories made him an interesting character, but his philosophy was a no less distinguishing trait, and served to bring him into public notoriety and to perpetuate his fame. Though without education, or the polish that contact with persons of refinement gives; cast as he was in a rugged mold and spending his life among surroundings unfavorable to courtly manners and social accomplishments, yet these disadvantages, used as a background to his unaffected style, scintillating witticisms, and wonderful magnetism, made of his life a pleasing mosaic, doubly picturesque because of its contrasts. The wonderful popularity of the man is evidenced by what followed directly after his return to Congress, as we shall now see.

Shortly after his arrival in Washington Crockett was advised by his physicians that a trip through the North would be of great benefit to his health, which had become much impaired by exposure and hard work in the preceding campaign. This advice was not entirely disagreeable to the patient, for he had long wished for an excuse to make a journey to some of the Eastern and New England cities in order that he might become acquainted with the people, and needs of that industrious and wealthy section. Accordingly on April 25th, 1834, he started on a tour that has ever since been memorable because of the excitement created in all the cities he visited, and the droll speeches and interesting events that characterized it.

Crockett proceeded to Baltimore, where he was entertained by the city officials and given a grand supper, that was attended by many distinguished guests. Leaving Baltimore on the following afternoon he started down the bay en route for Philadelphia, at which place great preparations had been made to receive him. His descriptions of the novel sights that met his gaze on this trip are characteristic and highly amusing. He says:

"Our passage down the Chesapeake Bay was very pleasant; and in a very short run we came to the place where we were to get on board of the railroad cars.

"This was a clean new sight to me; about a dozen big stages hung on to one machine, and to start up hill. After a good deal of fuss, we all got seated and moved slowly off, the engine wheezing as if she had the tizzick. By-and-by she began to take short breaths, and away we went with a blue streak after us. The whole distance in seventeen miles, and it was run in fifty-five minutes.

"While I was whizzing along, I burst out a laughing. One of the passengers asked me what it was at. 'Why,' says I, 'it's no wonder the fellow's horses run off.' A Carolina wagoner had just crossed the railroad, from Charleston to Augusta, when the engine hove in sight with the cars attached. It was growing dark, and the sparks were flying in all directions. His horses ran off, broke his wagon, and smashed his combustibles into items. He ran to a house for help, and when they asked him what scared his horses, he said he did not jist know, but it must be hell in harness."

Crockett debarked from the train at Delaware City and resumed his journey by the *Charles Carroll*, a fine steamer plying between that point and Philadelphia. The boat was gaily decorated with bunting in honor of his passage, and as she went up the Delaware River three large flags were hoisted as the signal previously agreed upon to inform the people that Crockett was on board.

Crockett's First Visit to a Big City

He thus describes his reception by the Philadelphians:

"We went on till we came in sight of the city and as we advanced towards the wharf, I saw the whole face of the earth covered with people, all anxiously looking on towards the boat. The captain and myself were standing on the bow-deck; he pointed his finger at me, and people slung their hats, and huzzaed for Colonel Crockett. It struck me with astonishment to hear a strange people huzzaing for me, and made me feel sort of queer. It took me so uncommon unexpected, as I had no idea of attracting attention. But I had to meet it, and so I stepped on to the wharf, where the folks came crowding around me, saying, 'Give me the hand of an honest man.' I did not know what all this meant; but some gentleman took hold of me, and pressing through the crowd, put me into an elegant barouche, drawn by four fine horses; they then told me to bow to the people; I did so, and with much difficulty we moved off. The streets were crowded to a great distance, and the windows full of people, looking out, I suppose, to see the wild man. I thought I had rather be in the wilderness with my gun and dogs, than to be attracting all that fuss. I had never seen the like before, and did not know exactly what to say or do. After some time we reached the United States Hotel, on Chestnut street.

"The crowd had followed me filling up the street, and pressing into the house to shake hands. I was conducted up stairs, and walking out on a platform, drew off my hat, and bowed around to the people. They cried out from all quarters, 'A speech, a speech, Colonel Crockett.'

"After the noise had quit, so I could be heard, I said to them the following words:—

"'GENTLEMEN OF PHILADELPHIA:

"'My visit to your city is rather accidental. I had no expectation of attracting any uncommon attention. I am traveling for my health, without the least wish of exciting the people in such times of high political feeling. I do not wish to encourage it. I am unable at this time to find language suitable to return my gratitude to the citizens of Philadelphia. However, I am almost induced to believe it flattery—perhaps a burlesque. This is new to me, yet I see nothing but friendship in your faces; and if your curiosity is to hear the backwoodsman, I will assure you I am illy prepared to address this most enlightened people. However, gentlemen, if this is a curiosity to you, if you will meet me to-morrow at one o'clock, I will endeavor to address you, in my plain manner.'"

Crockett's Original Observations

The following day Crockett devoted to sight-seeing, under conduct of the mayor and other leading citizens. He went out to see the great Fairmount waterworks and was so astonished at the sight that he writes: "Just think of a few wheels throwing up more water than five hundred thousand people can use; yes, and waste, too: for such scrubbing of steps, and even the very pavements under your feet, I never saw. Indeed, I looked close to see if the housemaids had not web-feet, they walked so well in water; and as for fire, it has no chance at all; they just screw on a long hollow leather with a brass nose on it, dash up stairs, and seem to draw on Noah's flood."

He was next shown the mint, where his surprise was greater than before and his remarks equally droll. He was astounded at the sight of such large piles of freshly coined dollars and wondered how the employees could withstand the temptation to fill their pockets every evening before going home. So impressed was he with the belief that only a novel device could prevent such an appropriation of the nation's money, that he made bold to offer a suggestion: He told the manager of the mint that down in Tennessee lived an old fellow who made his negroes whistle while they were picking cherries, for fear they should eat some, and that as this plan worked well, it might be possible to devise one on the same principle that would make the mint employees honest.

He went from one place of interest to another, until in the afternoon he was conducted to the house of Mr. Neil where a collation was served and good liquor was not used sparingly. Crockett says: "And I observed the man of the house, when he asked me to take a drink, didn't stand by to see how much I took, but turned away, and told me to help myself. That's what I call genteel."

Crockett at the Theater

In the evening he repaired to the Exchange and addressed a crowd of fully five thousand people, who were so enthusiastic that but little of his speech could be heard for their almost continuous applause. He managed to tear himself away from the crowd at length and, chaperoned by the mayor, he attended a variety theater. Of the sight he here witnessed Crockett makes some observations that are as pertinent and valuable now as they were then, for the variety stage is not, perhaps, as chaste as members in the higher branches of the profession would like to have it:

"What a pity it is that these theaters are not contrived that everybody could go; but the fact is, backwoodsman as I am, I have heard some things in them that was a leetle too tough for good women and modest men; and that's a great pity, because there are thousands of scenes of real life that might be exhibited, both for amusement and edification, without offending. Folks pretend to say that high people don't mind these things. Well, it may be that they are better acquainted with vice than we plain folks; but I am yet to live and see a woman polished out of the natural feelings, or too high not to do things that ain't quite reputable in those of low degree.

"Their fiddling was pretty good, considering every fellow played his own piece; and I would have known more about it if they had played a tune, but it was all twee-wee-tadlum-tadlum-tum-tum, tadle-leedle-tadle-leedle-lee. The 'Twenty-second of February,' or 'The Cuckoo's Nest,' would have been a treat.

"I do not think, however, from all I saw, that the people enjoyed themselves better than we do at a country frolic, where we dance till daylight, and pay off the score by giving one in our turn. It would do you good to see our boys and girls dancing. None of your straddling, mincing, sadying; but a regular sifter, cut-the-buckle, chicken-flutter set-to. It is good wholesome exercise; and when one of our boys puts his arm round his partner, it is a good hug, and no harm in it."

Crockett in New York

Having been entertained like a prince for three days, Crockett left Philadelphia thinking there could be no larger city in the world, and went over to New York. He made this latter journey by the train which he had heard ran at the rate of twenty-five miles an hour, a speed which he thought could not possibly be attained until, as he says, "I put my head out of the window to spit out my tobacco, when we overtook it so quick that it hit me smack in the face and filled my left eye. The pain I suffered for the next several minutes made me ready to believe anything."

Crockett left the train at Amboy and was taken to New York by boat. At the wharf he was met by a committee of young Whigs, who conducted him to the American Hotel, where he was introduced to a large party of prominent gentlemen who had been waiting his arrival. At night he attended a first-class theater and was delighted to such an extent that he never afterwards ceased praising the legitimate drama.

His time in New York was well occupied, for there was not an hour, save after midnight, that he could call his own. Committee after committee, and one distinguished man after another, was always pushing him to accept invitations. Among the many that he accepted was one extended by a Colonel Draper, who had also invited more than a hundred others, to meet him at a supper to be given in Crockett's honor, and which promised, as it proved, a grand affair. But though he did not get away from the Colonel's jolly party until the night was far advanced, upon his return to the hotel he was confronted with another invitation to banquet that night with the young Whigs. Though "full as a stuffed cub," as he declared, Crockett could not refuse to grace the banquet with his presence. Upon entering the hall a toast was proposed, "To Crockett, the undeviating supporter of the constitution and laws." To this Judge Clayton responded, but Crockett was also called to say something in reply. He says: "I made a short speech, and concluded with the story of the 'Red Cow,' which was, that as long as General Jackson went straight, I followed him; but when he began to go this way, and that way, and every way, I wouldn't go after him; like the boy whose master ordered him to plough across the field to the red cow. Well, he began to plough and she began to walk; and he ploughed all forenoon after her. So when the master came, he swore at him for going so crooked. 'Why, sir,' said the boy, 'you told me to plough to the red cow, and I kept after her, but she always kept moving.'"

Crockett concluded his visit to New York after three days of almost ceaseless divertissement, and took the steamer for Boston, where his reception was no less hearty and his stay of two days equally enjoyable. From Boston he went to Lowell, and then back to New York, where he was again received by a committee and then escorted to Camden, where a large banquet was given in his honor by a Mr. Hoy. Though his host was a very clever and honest gentleman, some of the guests were evidently of a different character, for while feasting at the sumptuous board Crockett had his pocket picked of one hundred and sixty-eight dollars, and two other guests were victims of the same nimble-fingered gentry. This misfortune would have stranded him but for the kindly aid that was at once proffered, and which he was extremely glad to accept.

Presented with a Rifle by Philadelphia Admirers

Crockett returned to Washington barely in time to participate in the closing scenes of Congress, having been absent during the entire session, on which account he was severely criticized by his constituents.

Upon the adjournment of Congress Crockett started for home, going by way of Philadelphia in response to an invitation by the young Whigs of that city, who had prepared a pleasant surprise for the celebrated hunter. He put up at the United States Hotel, and on the evening following his arrival a committee called and conducted him to a public hall opposite the old State House, which was filled to its utmost capacity with an admiring crowd. When he entered, his gaze fell at once upon a table that was set in the center of the room, upon which lay a magnificent rifle, powder-horn, a tomahawk and butcher-knife, all of which had been made specially to order from the finest material and by the best workmen in Philadelphia. When the cheers of greeting finally subsided Crockett was conducted to a position beside the table, and John M. Sanderson made an admirable presentation speech, reciting the circumstances under which the articles had been made; expressing the desire felt by his associates to manifest their regard for the great hunter and constitution defender, he asked Crockett to accept the presents before him as a mark of the high appreciation felt for his services by the people.

Crockett was so nearly overcome with surprise and embarrassment that several minutes elapsed before he could collect his thoughts and make a reply. When somewhat composed, he made his acknowledgments as follows:

"Gentlemen: I receive this rifle from the young men of Philadelphia as a testimony of friendship, which I hope never to live to forget. This is a favorite article with me, and would have been my choice above all presents that could have been selected. I love a good gun, for it makes a man feel independent, and prepared either for war or peace.

"This rifle does honor to the gentleman that made it. I must say, long as I have been accustomed to handle a gun, I have never seen anything that could come near a comparison to her in beauty. I did not think that ever such a rifle was made, either in this, or any other country; and how, gentlemen, to express my gratitude to you for your splendid present, I am at loss. This much, however, I will say, that myself and my sons will not forget you while we use this token of your kindness for our amusement. If it should become necessary to use her in defense of the liberty of our country, in my time, I will do as I have done before; and if the struggle should come when I am buried in the dust, I will leave her in the hands of some who will honor your present, in company with your sons, in standing for our country's rights.

"Accept my sincere thanks, therefore, gentlemen, for your valuable present, which I will keep as a testimony of your friendship, so long as I am in existence."

After the ceremony of presenting the rifle was concluded, the large company assembled fell to enjoying several good things that had been provided, not the least abundant being several brands of wines and liquors, which everybody appreciated in those days and which have preserved their popularity even to our own times. Drinking and eating was interlarded with toasts and anecdotes, and of course Crockett was called on to tell a story, with which request he complied in his own inimitable way by relating the following:

Crockett's Story of How He Got Out of a Quandary

"While in a brown study trying to conceive of some plan to outstrip my opponent, who was not so unpopular as I was trying to make myself believe, my train of thoughts was brought up as suddenly as though they had come into collision with another train on the same track, by a low whining noise that at first I could not locate. After listening awhile I knew that young bears were somewhere about, but it was several minutes before I discovered their lair; when at length I looked up towards the top of a big dead tree near which I was standing I saw a hole in the end of the trunk that had been broken off by lightning or some of Jackson's cuss-words during the Creek War. I now knew that there was a bear's nest in the vicinity, and that the vicinity was the hollow of that tree, and as I never allowed an opportunity to kill a bear slip me, I took up an extra reef in my belt and shinned up the tree to the hole, which "was full fifty feet from the ground. It was a long climb, but I got there in due season and reached my hand down to draw out the cubs, for the noise of their whining sounded as if they were within a foot or two of the opening. But finding that I could not reach them with my hands, I pulled off my shoes and let myself into the hole feet foremost to see if I couldn't draw them out with my toes. I hung on to the edge of the hole, gradually letting myself down further and further, thinking all the while that another inch would reach them, until at last I was in full length and still a straining to let out one more reef in my body, when I wish I may be shot if I didn't lose my hold, and down I went ker-slap full twenty feet among a promising family of young bears not yet old enough to have their claws on. I soon found I might as well undertake to climb the greased end of a rainbow as to get back, the tree being so large and smooth. *Now this was a real quandary.* If I was to shout it would have been doubtful if they heard me from the settlement, and if they did, the story told by my opponents would ruin my election. They would not vote for a man that ventured into a place that he could not get out of himself. While considering whether it was best to call for help, or wait there till after the election, I heard a kind of scratching and

HERE IS THE FAMILY

growling above me, and looking up, I saw the old bear coming stern foremost upon me. My motto is, 'Go ahead.' As soon as she came within my reach, I seized her tail with my left hand, and with a small pen-knife in the other, I commenced spurring her forward. I'll be shot if ever a member of Congress raised quicker in the world than I did. She took me out in the shake of a lamb's tail."

This story has since found its way into school readers, where I remember to have seen it when I was a boy, though the credit was not given to Crockett, some other person having filched the honor from him.

Crockett was detained in Philadelphia nearly a week by invitations, which were of such a character that he could not refuse. The people were much more enthusiastic over him during this second visit than before, and judging by the numerous demonstrations of their regard, he appeared to be the most popular man that had ever been in their midst. When at length he left Philadelphia, he started again for home, going by way of Pittsburg, where his reception was very cordial, and where invitations poured in on him necessitating a stay of two days. Along the route over which he traveled the people made great demonstrations, the depots being thronged and flags displayed, while at every point he was called on to speak, so that the ovations he received were continuous.

Reaching Cincinnati, the citizens of that place turned out en masse to receive him, and here he was fairly forced to stay two days, during which time he was banqueted five times and scarcely allowed an hour for sleep. At Louisville the same

CROCKETT'S RECEPTION AT LOUISVILLE

manifestations of cordial feeling and profound regard were repeated. So eager were the people of Louisville to see and hear Crockett that provision was made to receive him in the public square. A stand was erected and covered with flags which, at the appointed time, Crockett ascended and saw upturned before him the largest gathering of faces that had ever before assembled in the city. The meeting was very much greater, it is stated, than that which met to do honor to Lafayette, and equally demonstrative.

The triumphal tour was ended at Louisville, for he made no more stops until he reached the shore of Tennessee, at Mill's Point, where he was met by his son William, and in a wagon started for his home, thirty-five miles distant. In concluding an account of his tour he writes:

"In a short time I set out for my own home; yes, my own home, my own soil, my own humble dwelling, my own family, my own hearts, my ocean of love and affection which neither circumstances nor time can dry up. Here, like the wearied bird, let me settle down for awhile, and shut out the world."

CHAPTER VIII

Crockett Again on the Stump

Energy such as Crockett's, abnormally stimulated, as it had been by the position of political preferment he had attained, and the outbursts of popular applause and hearty commendation of his course in Congress by vast crowds of people wherever he went, could not long remain pent up, or be confined to the now dreary pastime of what was once his greatest pleasure. Lonely, miserable in the wilderness of his home, he again sought excitement in the hunt. The new rifle and its beautiful accoutrements were brought into service, but he used it only long enough to prove how accurately it threw a ball, and how much superior it was to the old flint-lock that had served him faithfully in many a contest with the lordly bears of his forest home. Then he turned back again to his cabin, hung the rifle in a rack of buck-horn above his door, to gather the dust of time, and sought for other scenes to relieve the tedious time that hung upon his hands.

But Crockett was not only oppressed with the extreme quiet of his surround-ings—the sudden transition by which he was snatched, as it were, from a swirl of pleasurable excitement and dropped into the wilderness where even his home and family could not charm away the glamour of public life that, like an *ignis fatuus*, still lured him towards Washington; his restlessness was caused by a thirst for ambition, the attainment of a position far above that he had yet occupied. In short, Crockett was an aspirant for the Presidency. Ignorant, in book learning, though he knew himself to be, and wholly destitute of the refinements which the chief of the nation should possess, yet so great had been the manifestations in his favor, that with all his shortcomings he still believed himself available, if not thoroughly competent, to fill the Presidential chair.

The following year (1835) saw Crockett again in the field for the fourth time as a congressional candidate, his opponent being a one-legged man named Adam Huntsman, who had lost his limb in a battle with the Indians ten years before. Under ordinary circumstances Crockett could easily have defeated his antagonist, but unfortunately he lived in a section where the pro-Jackson sentiment was overwhelmingly dominant; and as he had fought Jackson in public and private and with a vindictiveness that subordinated all public questions, a feeling was excited against him, intensified as the canvass proceeded, that gave him unmistakable promise of his defeat. To arrest the moving tide of popular disfavor Crockett resorted to every expedient that suggested itself, to regain his waning popularity. He went about in his district clothed in buckskin, and with a flint-lock rifle on his shoulder. Every saloon became his headquarters and every joke that came into his mind was hauled out, burnished up with new regimentals and put on detached service. He made much sport of his opponent, whom he dubbed the "Flying Dutchman," and spoke many a gibe and perpetrated scores of puns on Adam, whom he declared was "on the eve of an almighty thrashing." These jokes made the people laugh, but they failed of their better purpose, to make them forget his antagonism to Jackson, particularly as he lost no occasion to attack the administration.

Crockett's Great Coon-Skin Trick

The canvass was a red-hot one, to use a Western expression, and was not without humorous incidents that helped much to sustain the interest that had been excited. Money was extremely scarce, on which account little was spent, but coon-skins, which were its equivalent, and the standard medium of exchange, were put into rapid circulation and made every saloon look like a tannery, for here they came as naturally as our paper currency of to-day finds its way back to the national treasury for redemption.

Crockett thus describes a laughable incident, characteristic of his resource and cunning, that occurred during the canvass:

"But I am losing sight of my story. Well, I started off to the Cross Roads, dressed in my hunting shirt, and my rifle on my shoulder. Many of our constituents had assembled there to get a taste of the quality of the candidate at orating. Job Snelling, a grinder-shanked Yankee, who had been caught somewhere about Plymouth Bay, and been shipped to the West with a cargo of codfish and rum, erected a large shantee, and set up shop for the occasion. A large posse of the voters had assembled before I arrived, and my opponent had already made considerable headway with his speechifying and his treating, when they spied me about a rifle shot from the camp, sauntering along as if I was not a party in business. 'There comes Crockett,' cried one. 'Let us hear the Colonel,' cried another, and so I mounted the stump that had been cut down for the occasion, and began to bushwhack in the most approved style.

"I had not been up long before there was such an uproar in the crowd that I could not hear my own voice, and some of my constituents let me know that they could not listen to me on such a dry subject as the welfare of the nation, until they had something to drink, and that I must treat them. Accordingly I jumped down from the rostrum, and led the way to the shantee, followed by my constituents, shouting, 'Huzza for Crockett,' and 'Crockett for ever!'

"When we entered the shantee, Job was busy dealing out his rum in a style that showed he was making a good day's work of it, and I called for a quart of the best, but the crooked critur returned no other answer than by pointing to a board over the bar, on which he had chalked in large letters, '*Pay to-day and trust to-morrow.*' Now that idea brought me up all standing; it was a sort of cornering in which there was no back

CROCKETT MAKING A CHARACTERISTIC CANVASS

out, for ready money in the West in those times was the shyest thing in all natur, and it was most particularly shy with me on that occasion.

"The voters seeing my predicament, fell off to the other side, and I was left deserted and alone, as the government will be, when he no longer has any offices to bestow. I saw as plain as day that the tide of popular opinion was against me, and that unless I got some rum speedily I should lose my election as sure as there are snakes in Virginny—and it must be done soon, or even burnt brandy wouldn't save me. So I walked away from the shantee, for popularity sometimes depends on a very small matter indeed; in this particular it was worth a quart of New England rum, and no more.

"Well, knowing that a crisis was at hand, I struck into the woods with my rifle on my shoulder, my best friend in time of need, and as good fortune would have it, I had not been out more than a quarter of an hour before I treed a fat coon, and in the pulling of a trigger, he lay dead at the root of the tree. I soon whipped his hairy jacket off his back, and again bent my steps towards the shantee, and walked up to the bar, but not alone, for this time I had half a dozen of my constituents at my heels. I threw down the coon skin upon the counter, and called for a quart, and Job, though busy in dealing out rum, forgot to point at his chalked rules and regulations, for he knew that a coon was as good a legal tender for a quart, in the West, as a New York shilling, any day in the year.

"My constituents now flocked about me, and cried, 'Huzza for Crockett,' 'Crockett for ever,' and finding the tide had taken a turn, I told them several yarns, to get them in a good humor, and having soon dispatched the value of the coon, I went out and mounted the stump, without opposition, and a clear majority of the voters followed me to hear what I had to offer for the good of the nation. Before I was half through, one of my constituents moved that they would hear the balance of my speech after they had washed down the first part with some more of Job Snelling's extract of cornstalk and molasses, and the question being put, it was carried unanimously. It wasn't considered necessary to call the yeas and nays, so we adjourned to the shantee, and on the way I began to reckon that the fate of the nation pretty much depended upon my shooting another coon.

"While standing at the bar, feeling sort of bashful while Job's rules and regulations stared me in the face, I cast down my eyes, and discovered one end of the coon skin sticking between the logs that supported the bar. Job had slung it there in the hurry of business. I gave it a sort of quick jerk, and it followed my hand as natural as if I had been the rightful owner. I slapped it on the counter, and Job, little dreaming that he was barking up the wrong tree, shoved along another bottle, which my constituents quickly disposed of with great good humor, for some of them saw the trick, and then we withdrew to the rostrum to discuss the affairs of the nation.

"I don't know how it was, but the voters soon became dry again, and nothing would do, but we must adjourn to the shantee, and as luck would have it, the coon skin was still sticking between the logs, as if Job had flung it there on purpose to tempt me. I was not slow in raising it to the counter, the rum followed of course, and I wish I may be shot, if I didn't, before the day was over, get ten quarts for the same identical skin, and from a fellow, too, who in those parts was considered as sharp as a steel trap and as bright as a pewter button."

Crockett Overwhelmed by His Defeat

Crockett's speeches in this campaign were the most interesting he had ever delivered. His wit as well as his manners had received no little polish during the two terms he had served in Congress, while his ambition lent wings to his fancy and permitted him to soar to the heights of eloquence. But all his jokes, philosophy, reasoning and eloquence availed him nothing, for he was defeated by a majority of two hundred and thirty votes. The returns were such a surprise and disappointment that he was quite overwhelmed, and his chagrin knew no bounds. Like most men suffering under the poignant smart of cruel defeat, Crockett lay all his misfortunes at the door of an unfair election and the dishonorable, knavish acts of his opponents. With a fairly breaking heart he bewailed the prospects of his country's future, that to him now appeared as if enveloped in the deep pall of eternal night. An enemy of Jackson before, he was now vengeful in his hatred and did not stop short of charging the President with using the government's money in buying up votes, at the rate of twenty-five dollars each, against him. He declared, too, that the judges were bought up, and took their places at the polls with pockets filled with Huntsman tickets, which were counted in the result after the polls were closed.

Crockett concludes his tirade against Jackson and his enemies as follows:

"As my country no longer requires my services, I have made up my mind to go to Texas. My life has been one of danger, toil, and privation, but these difficulties I had to encounter at a time when I considered it nothing more than right good sport to surmount them; but now I start anew upon my own hook, and God only grant that it may be strong enough to support the weight that may be hung upon it. I have a new row to hoe, a long and rough one, but come what will I'll go ahead. . . . I am done with politics and you may all go to hell, and I'll go to Texas."

But though these were his public utterances, and the last he made to his constituents, he could not forego the application of a poetic balm to his deeply wounded feelings, and accordingly composed the following lines, which he sent to the Nashville *Banner* for publication. It is rather bad poetry, but splendid sentiment:

Farewell to the mountains whose mazes to me
Were more beautiful far than Eden could be;
No fruit was forbidden, but nature had spread
Her bountiful board, and her children were fed.
The hills were our garners—our herds wildly grew,
And Nature was shepherd and husbandman too,
I felt like a monarch, yet thought like a man,
As I thanked the Great Giver, and worshiped his plan.

The home I forsake where my offspring arose;
The graves I forsake where my children repose.
The home I redeemed from the savage and wild:
The home I have loved as a father his child;
The corn that I planted, the fields that I cleared,
The flocks that I raised, and the cabin I reared;
The wife of my bosom—Farewell to ye all!
In the land of the stranger I rise or I fall.

Farewell to my country!—I fought for thee well,
When the savage rushed forth like the demons from hell.
In peace or in war I have stood by thy side—
My country, for thee I have lived—would have died!
But I am cast off—my career now is run
And I wander abroad like the prodigal son—
Where the wild savage roves, and the broad prairies spread,
The fallen—despised—will again go ahead!

CHAPTER IX

Crockett Enters the War for Texas Independence

"My thermometer stood somewhat below the freezing point as I left my wife and children; still there was some thawing about the eyelids, a thing that had not taken place since I first ran away from my father's house when a thoughtless vagabond boy. I dressed myself in a clean hunting shirt, put on a new fox-skin cap with the tail hanging behind, took hold of my rifle Betsey, which all the world knows was presented to me by the patriotic citizens of Philadelphia, as a compliment for my unflinching opposition to the tyrannic measures of 'the Government,' and thus equipped, I started off with a heavy heart for Mill's Point, to take steamboat down the Mississippi, and go ahead in a new world."

In this language Crockett describes his departure from home, and in search of excitement, if not consolation, in the wilds and wars of Texas, where courage might win for him public favors that were denied him by the Jacksonians of Tennessee.

He took passage for Little Bock, where he arrived without adventure in three days and sought for accommodations at the best hotel in the place, which was poor even for a far west town. Going up the street, he was surprised to see a large crowd congregated in front of the hotel, evidently waiting for some one, which, by reason of his experience in Philadelphia, Boston and other Eastern cities, led him to believe that the people of Little Rock had information of his coming and had assembled to extend him a hearty welcome. He therefore began to collect his thoughts for a speech and was full primed for the occasion when he reached the hotel. But here he was surprised for a second time, because the people gave him no attention whatever, as if unconscious of the existence of such a man as Davy Crockett.

The Punch and Judy Exhibition

Men are often brought to a realizing sense of the true measure of their importance by common-place incidents, and when lowered to their real level are sometimes like a large bubble floating down a stream that bursts when it strikes an obstruction. They still float on, but have lost their identity. Though Crockett may not be likened to the emptiness of a bubble, he felt quite as unsubstantial upon discovering that the crowd had gathered to welcome a juggler who had come to regale them with some small tricks and a Punch and Judy exhibition. Thus does greatness sometimes stumble upon its counterpart.

It happened that in the afternoon, when the performance was announced to take place, that the orchestral portion of the company—which was composed exclusively of a one-legged fiddler—was too drunk for service, and had crawled into a neighboring hay-loft to rest. Without a fiddler it was impossible to go on with the show, and as several tickets of admission had already been disposed of, there was a lively threatening by those who had paid their money, and a confiscation of the paraphernalia used in the performance was imminent, and which was only prevented by a fortunate arrival, in the person of an original Arkansas character. This man was the long, lank, frizzled-featured specimen of individual "from away back." His pants were yellow and his coat was long, while his hat had seen better days, but it was evidently a long time ago; so was it a dreary time since last his locks were combed and his saffron face washed. But if his toilet was somewhat melancholy, his countenance was mild and his tones full of sympathy. He drove up in a mud-bespattered sulky, with three spokes out of each wheel, but there were no ribs missing in his horse, for they were all plain to be seen. In his way-worn vehicle he carried many pamphlets of his own composition, while over the back of it was thrown a crazy flannel undershirt that he had washed at the last brook passed and hung there to dry. His profession was a composite one; that is to say, it was a blending of preacher, lecturer, author, bookseller, fiddler and missionary generally. When preaching was poor he often turned a penny at lecturing and when neither accomplishment could be turned to account he would dispose of a book, whenever fortune assisted him to make a sale; but should all of these fail him he had recourse to his fiddle, his great soul-harmonizer which, however, he kept carefully secreted in a box under the bed of his vehicle, lest a sight of it at an inopportune time might interfere with the success of his other professions.

Crockett describes what followed the arrival of the moral lecturer in his own inimitable way:

"The landlord now made his appearance, and gave a hearty welcome to the reverend traveler, and shaking him by the hand added, that he never came more opportunely in all his life.

"'Opportunely!' exclaimed the philosopher.

"'Yes,' rejoined the other; 'you have a heart and head that labor for the benefit of us poor mortals.'

"'Oh! true, an excellent market for my pamphlets,' replied the other, at the same time beginning to open the trunk that lay before him.

"'You misunderstand me,' added the landlord. 'A poor showman with a sick wife and five children has arrived from New Orleans—'

"'I will sell my pamphlets to relieve their wants, and endeavor to teach them resignation.'

"'He exhibits to-night in my large room; you know the room, sir—I let him have it gratis.'

"'You are an honest fellow. I will witness his show, and add my mite to his assistance.'

"'But,' replied the innkeeper, 'the lame fiddler is fond of the bottle, and is now snoring in the hayloft.'

"'Degrading vice!' exclaimed the old man, and taking 'God's Revenge against Drunkenness' from the trunk, and standing erect in the sulky, he commenced reading to his astonished audience. The innkeeper interrupted him by observing that the homily would not fill the empty purse of the poor showman and unless a fiddler could be obtained, he must depend on charity, or go supperless to bed. And moreover, the people, irritated at their disappointment, had threatened to tear the show to pieces.

"'But what's to be done?' demanded the parson.

"'Your reverence shakes an excellent bow,' added the innkeeper, in an insinuating tone.

"'I!' exclaimed the parson; 'I fiddle for a puppet show!'

"'Not for the puppet show, but for the sick wife and five hungry children.'

"A tear started into the eyes of the old man, as he added in an under tone, 'If I could be concealed from the audience—'

"'Nothing easier,' cried the other; 'we will place you behind the scenes, and no one will ever dream that you fiddled at a puppet show.'

"The matter being thus settled they entered the house, and shortly after the sound of a fiddle, squeaking like a giggling girl tickled into ecstasies, restored mirth and good humor to the disappointed assemblage, who rushed in, helter-skelter, to enjoy the exhibition.

"All being seated, and silence restored, they waited in breathless expectation for the rising of the curtain. At length Harlequin made his appearance, and performed astonishing feats of activity on the slack-rope; turning somersets backward and forward, first on this side, and then on that, with as much ease as if he had been a politician all his life—the parson sawed vigorously on his fiddle all the time. Punch followed, and set the audience in a roar with his antic tricks and jests; but when Judy entered with her broomstick the burst of applause was as great as ever I heard bestowed upon one of Benton's slang-whang speeches in Congress, and I rather think quite as well merited.

"As the plot thickened, the music of the parson became more animated; but unluckily in the warmth of his zeal to do justice to his station, his elbow touched the side scene, which fell to the floor, and exposed him, working away in all the ecstasies of little Isaac Hill, while reading one of his long orations about things in general to empty benches. No ways disconcerted by the accident, the parson seized upon it as a fine opportunity of conveying a lesson to those around him, at the same time that he might benefit a fellow mortal. He immediately mounted the chair upon which he was seated, and addressed the audience to the following effect:

"'Many of you have come here for amusement, and others no doubt to assist the poor man, who is thus struggling to obtain a subsistence for his sick wife and children. Lo! the moral of a puppet show! But is this all? Has he not rendered unto you your money's worth? This is not charity. If you are charitably inclined, here is an object fully deserving of it.'

"He preached upon this text for full half an hour, and concluded with taking his hat to collect assistance from his hearers for the friendless showman and his family.

THE PHILANTHROPIST IN AN EMBARRASSING SITUATION

"The next morning, when his sulky was brought to the door, the showman and his wife came out to thank their benefactor. The old man placed his trunk of pamphlets before him, and proceeded on his pilgrimage, the little children following him through the village with bursts of gratitude."

Crockett Is Banqueted—The Bass-Drum and Fife Orchestra

On the day after Crockett's arrival in Little Rock his identity was discovered, and immediately preparations were made by the leading citizens to formally "recognize" him. He had been banqueted a hundred times in the North, and it occurred to the citizens that similar treatment would not be offensive, especially if due care were taken that the liquor didn't give out. To provide for this affair a big fat bear, a deer, wild turkeys and small game in abundance, were purchased and given over to the hotel landlord to prepare for the table. The only thing now wanting to make the occasion complete was a band of music, but unfortunately this was an article not purchasable at Little Rock, but by persistent foraging a bass-drum and a beater, and a fife and fifer, were brought into service that answered well enough under the circumstances. When the banquet was ready, the guests arranged themselves in double file with Crockett and the mayor at the head, and marched into the dining-room. As they entered the orchestra set up, playing, "See the Conquering Hero Comes."

Crockett thus describes the exercises that followed the feasting:

"The fragments of the meats being cleared off, we went through the customary evolution of drinking thirteen regular toasts, after every one of which our drum with the loose skin grumbled like an old horse with an empty stomach; and our asthmatic fife squeaked like a stuck pig, a spirit-stirring tune, which we put off christening until we should come to prepare our proceedings for posterity. The fife appeared to have but one tune in it; possibly it might have had more, but the poor fifer, with all his puffing and blowing, his too-too-tooing, and shaking his head and elbow, could not, for the body and soul of him, get more than one out of it. If the fife had had an extra tune to its name, sartin it wouldn't have been quite so hide-bound on such an occasion, but let us have it, good, bad, or indifferent. We warn't particular by no means."

Crockett Again Meets the Fiddling Parson

Crockett's stay of three days in Little Rock was made pleasant by every attention the citizens could show him, their desire to accord him the fullest hospitality extending so far that they got up a shooting match to which the best marksmen in the vicinity were invited, all of whom, with true Southern courtesy, permitted themselves to be beaten by their guest.

He tried to induce several gentlemen of the place to join him in an expedition to Texas, but though they were in full sympathy with the movement to establish the independence of the Lone Star State, they pleaded many excuses for not joining in the struggle, but five of them consented to accompany him, as a kind of escort, on his journey as far as the Ouachita River, fifty miles from Little Rock.

The party was a gay one, their natural good spirits being increased by several friendly bottles that kissed their lips with great frequency, and put them on good terms with all of the world. They pushed on with fair speed and towards evening approached the fording place of the river, but when about to descend the bank there fell upon their ears a sound of music, faint but exquisitely sweet. The party stopped and listened in a kind of mysterious awe, and heard floating down the blue waters that inspiring patriotic air, "Hail Columbia." What could it mean? Suddenly the tune was changed, and there came the sweet, clear and brisk notes of "Over the Water to Charley." This tune never failed to awaken an echo in the hearts of pioneers in the early days, and Crockett dashed forward under the thrilling impulse to discover from whence the dulcet sounds proceeded. Reaching the crossing what was his astonishment to discover a man seated in a sulky in the middle of the shallow stream, playing for dear life on a fiddle. The horse was standing as if in deep reverie half covered with water, while the flimsy vehicle appeared to be on the point of going to pieces. "Still the man fiddled on composedly, as if his life had been insured, and he was nothing more than a passenger. We thought," said Crockett, "he was mad and shouted to him. He heard us, and stopped his music. 'You have missed the crossing,' shouted one of the men from the clearing. 'I know I have,' returned the fiddler. 'If you go ten feet farther you will be drowned.' 'I know I shall,' returned the fiddler. 'Turn back,' said the man. 'I can't,' said the other. 'Then how the devil will you get out?' 'I'm sure I don't know: come you and help me.'

"The men from the clearing, who understood the river, took our horses and rode up to the sulky, and after some difficulty succeeded in bringing the traveler safe to

THE FIDDLING PARSON ATTRACTING UNIVERSAL NATUR

shore, when we recognized the worthy parson who had fiddled for us at the puppet show at Little Rock. They told him that he had had a narrow escape and he replied that he had found that out an hour ago. He said he had been fiddling to the fishes for a full hour, and had exhausted all the tunes that he could play without notes. We then asked him what could have induced him to think of fiddling at a time of such peril; and he replied, that he had remarked in his progress through life, that there was nothing in universal natur so well calculated to draw people together as the sound of a fiddle; and he knew that he might bawl until he was hoarse for assistance, and no one would stir a peg; but they would no sooner hear the scraping of his catgut than they would quit all other business, and come to the spot in flocks."

A Stag Dance in the Lonely Woods

The parson had interpreted the hearts of Arkansas gentlemen with extraordinary fidelity, for the fiddle's appeal was as effective in that section in those days, as the voice of an angel. Its notes were the links that composed the cord binding all nature together in one universal soul, the essence of poetry, patriotism, frolic and sentiment.

Though in the lonely woods and remote from any house or indication of civilization the parson's fiddle had so cheered Crockett and his companions that a dance was proposed, in which all heartily participated on the green sward until the musician's store of tunes was exhausted. After this exhibition of hilarious delight was concluded, Crockett's companions bade him adieu and returned to Little Bock, while he journeyed on with the parson, whom he found so agreeable that he pays the following eloquent tribute to his goodly influence:

"I kept in company with the parson until we arrived at Greenville, and I do say, he was just about as pleasant an old gentleman to travel with as any man who wasn't too darned particular could ask for. We talked about politics, religion, and nature, farming, and bear hunting, and the many blessings that an all bountiful providence has bestowed upon our happy country. He continued to talk upon this subject, traveling over the whole ground as it were, until his imagination glowed, and his soul became full to overflowing; and he checked his horse, and I stopped mine also, and a stream of eloquence burst forth from his aged lips, such as I have seldom listened to: it came from the overflowing fountain of a pure and grateful heart. We were alone in the wilderness, but as he proceeded, it seemed to me as if the tall trees bent their tops to listen—that the mountain stream laughed out joyfully as it bounded on like some living thing; that the faded flowers of autumn smiled, and sent forth fresher fragrance, as if conscious that they would revive in spring, and even the sterile rocks seemed to be endowed with some mysterious influence. We were alone in the wilderness, but all things told me that God was there. The thought renewed my strength and courage. I had left my country, felt somewhat like an outcast, believed that I had been neglected and lost sight of; but I was now conscious that there was still one watchful Eye over me no matter whether I dwelt in the populous cities, or threaded the pathless forest alone; no matter whether I stood in the high places among men, or made my solitary lair in the untrodden wild, that Eye was still upon me. My very soul leaped joyfully at the thought; I never felt so grateful in all my life. I never loved my God so sincerely in all my life. I felt that I still had a friend.

"When the old man finished, I found that my eyes were wet with tears. I approached and pressed his hand, and thanked him, and says I, 'Now let us take a drink.' I set him the example, and he followed it, and in a style too that satisfied me, that if he had ever belonged to a temperance society, he had either renounced membership or obtained a dispensation."

The two journeyed together as far as Greenville, where Crockett bade the parson an affectionate good-bye and then pushed on alone for Fulton, at which place he arrived in due season and was received in a most hospitable manner by gentlemen to whom he presented letters of introduction. Here he embarked on a steamer for Natchitoches that was well loaded with a heterogeneous cargo of passengers: white and black, sober and drunk, vulgar and saintly, thieves and honest men, sharpers and gullibles.

Crockett Exposes the Gambler

The boat had hardly gotten well under way before a gambling juggler set up his devices for fleecing such dupes as might be allured into his game. A table was set in the forward cabin upon which he placed his hat and three thimbles, under one of which he deposited a pea. Having made these preliminaries in plain view of the crowd that gathered about him, he made his offers to bet that no one could guess under which thimble the pea would be found. This he called the game of "thimblerig," and so well did he play it, and so numerous were the fools about him, that for several minutes he was reaping a golden harvest of such grain as would not require thrashing before using.

Crockett moved over from a seat he had occupied on the forecastle to the crowd of greedy speculators and amused himself for a time watching the game and studying the greenhorns. Seeing that he was much interested, the gambler at length asked Crockett to try his skill at guessing, offering to wager a round sum that he could not locate the pea. But Crockett declined the invitation by declaring that he never gambled, and was opposed to the practice on principle. This confession of virtue did not discourage the gambler, who insisted that his game was only one of innocent amusement, with a small stake only to make it a little more interesting.

CROCKETT DISCOMFITS THE GAMBLER

Having observed that the gambler invariably permitted his victim to win the first bets in order to establish confidence and increase the stakes, and being persistently begged to hazard a small sum, at least, on his skill as a guesser, Crockett at length offered to bet the drinks for the crowd that he could lift the thimble which covered the pea. Though the wager was not a profitable one to the gambler even should he win it, yet with the hope that it might encourage Crockett to make a larger bet, he accepted it and began juggling with the thimbles and pea, but with no intention of deceiving Crockett, whom he believed must soon be another of his victims. At length he placed the thimbles in a row and asked which one covered the pea; Crockett promptly lifted the middle thimble and, sure enough, there lay the pea, and the gambler with equal promptness acknowledged that he had fairly lost.

But having lost, he praised Crockett's quick eye and offered to make another bet of a sum of money that he could not make a second successful guess; this, however, Crockett obstinately declined, and insisted on the payment of the wager he had won, at the same time taunting the gambler in such facetious manner that the crowd roared with laughter. The discomfited gamester soon saw that he had caught a Tartar and was glad enough to stop the waggish raillery of Crockett by ordering the bar-keeper to set out liquor for everybody. While the crowd was preparing to drink some one proposed a toast to the man who could beat a gambler at his own game, to which Crockett replied in a humorous speech that betrayed his identity. When it was learned that Davy Crockett was their fellow-passenger, every one on board forgot all about the gambler and gave him their individual attention, which he repaid with many a pleasing joke and laughable anecdote as well as political diatribes that expressed his feelings against Jackson and his enemies back in Tennessee. The gamester himself became merry under Crockett's humorous sayings, and at length sought him in quiet and gave him such an account of his own wanderings that the two became very intimate before the trip was concluded.

The Juggler Follows Crockett to Texas

Finding the juggler a well-meaning man, outside his profession, Crockett undertook to convert him into ways of rectitude by appealing to his better nature. Said he: "It is a burlesque on human nature, that an able-bodied man possessed of your share of good sense, should voluntarily debase himself, and be indebted for subsistence to such a pitiful artifice."

"But what's to be done, Colonel?" he replied. "I'm in the slough of despond, up to the very chin. A miry and slippery path to travel."

"Then hold your head up before the slough reaches your lips," retorted Crockett.

"But what's the use?" said he: "it's utterly impossible for me to wade through; and even if I could, I should be in such a dirty plight that it would defy all the waters in the Mississippi to wash me clean again. No," he added in a desponding tone, "I should be like a live eel in a frying-pan, Colonel, sort of out of my element, if I attempted to live like an honest man at this time o' day."

"That I deny," replied Crockett. "It is never too late to become honest. But even admit what you say to be true—that you cannot live like an honest man—you have at least the next best thing in your power, and no one can say nay to it."

"And what is that?"

"Die like a brave one. And I know not whether, in the eyes of the world, a brilliant death is not preferable to an obscure life of rectitude. Most men are remembered as they died, and not as they lived. We gaze with admiration upon the glories of the setting sun, yet scarcely bestow a passing glance upon its noonday splendor."

"You are right; but how is this to be done?"

"Accompany me to Texas," was the reply. "Cut aloof from your degrading habits and associates here, and, in fighting for the freedom of the Texans, regain your own."

The man seemed much moved. He caught up his gambling instruments, thrust them into his pocket, with hasty strides traversed the floor two or three times, and then exclaimed:

"By heaven, I will try to be a man again. I will live honestly, or die bravely. I will go with you to Texas."

The Bee-Hunter and His Nerve

At Natchitoches, Crockett encountered another very singular character. He was a remarkably handsome young man, of poetic imagination, a sweet singer, and with innumerable scraps of poetry and of song ever at his tongue's end. Honey-trees, as they were called, were very abundant in Texas. The prairies were almost boundless parterres of the richest flowers, from which the bees made large quantities of the most delicious honey. This they deposited in the hollows of trees. Not only was the honey valuable, but the wax constituted a very important article of commerce in Mexico, and brought a high price, being used for immense candles which are burned in the churches. The bee-hunter, finding his profession very profitable, followed it until he became wonderfully adept in finding bees and following them to their hives.

The meeting of Crockett and the bee-hunter was under rather romantic circumstances. Natchitoches was a small river town, consisting of a single dirty street and a dozen saloons. It was nearly identical in character with Natchez-under-the-hill, a famous headquarters for gamblers and debased specimens of humanity fifty years ago. Though his surroundings were extremely repulsive, the heart of the bee-hunter was cheerful as a bird in mating-time. Crockett was first attracted to him by his sweet songs, which he was singing early on the morning following Crockett's arrival in the place. The man was leaning up against a sign-post, apparently in a deep reverie, and singing as if trying to forget some secret sorrow. He was light and graceful in figure, and his trim form was set off exceedingly well by the fringed hunting-shirt and buckskin pants that he wore. In his hands he held a polished rifle, while across his shoulders was slung a hunting-pouch and powder-horn embellished with Indian ornaments.

Crockett had been aroused at an unusually early hour by an interminable din which, upon investigation, he learned proceeded from an irate local politician, who had just discovered that his horse had been stolen, and was berating everybody because of his misfortune. As Crockett came out of the tavern he saw the enraged citizen flourishing a whip, followed by a dozen men who were trying to console him, but disdaining their sympathy and cursing them soundly on general principles, he went on until he perceived the bee-hunter, whose songs and placid temper appeared to increase his excitement to the point of explosion. Crockett thus describes the encounter: The politician, assuming a threatening attitude, exclaimed fiercely:

"'You're an infernal scoundrel, do you hear? an infernal scoundrel, sir!'

"'I do; but it's news to me,' replied the other quietly.

"'News, you scoundrel! do you call it news?'

"'Entirely so.'

"'You needn't think to carry it off so quietly. I say, you're an infernal scoundrel, and I'll prove it.'

"'I beg you will not; I shouldn't like to be proved a scoundrel,' replied the other, smiling with the most provoking indifference.

"'No, I dare say you wouldn't. But answer me directly—did you, or did you not say, in the presence of certain ladies of my acquaintance, that I was a mere—'

"'Calf? O, no, sir; the truth is not to be spoken at all times.'

"'The truth! Do you presume to call me a calf, sir?'

"'O, no, sir; I call you—nothing,' replied the stranger, just as cool and as pleasant as a morning in spring.

"'It's well you do; for if you had presumed to call me—'

"'A man, I should have been grossly mistaken.'

"'Do you mean to say I am not a man, sir?'

"'That depends upon circumstances.'

"'What circumstances?' demanded the other fiercely.

"'If I should be called as a witness in a court of justice, I should be bound to speak the truth.'

"'And you would say I was not a man, hey? Do you see this cow-skin?'

"'Yes; and I have seen it with surprise ever since you came up,' replied the stranger, calmly, at the same time handing me his rifle to take care of.

"'With surprise!' exclaimed the politician, who saw that his antagonist had voluntarily disarmed himself. 'Why, did you suppose that I was such a coward that I dare not use the article when I thought it was demanded?'

"'Shall I tell you what I thought?'

"'Do, if you dare.'

"'I thought to myself what use has a calf for a cow-skin?' He turned to me, and said: 'I had forgot, Colonel, shall I trouble you to take care of this also?' Saying which he drew a long hunting knife from his belt, and placed it in my hand. He then resumed his careless attitude against the sign-post.

"'You distinctly call me a calf, then?'

" 'If you insist upon it, you may.'

" 'You hear, gentlemen,' said he, speaking to the by-standers. 'Do you hear the insult? What shall I do with the scoundrel?'

" 'Dress him, dress him!' exclaimed twenty voices, with shouts and laughter.

" 'That I'll do at once!' Then, turning to the stranger, he cried out fiercely: 'Come one step this way, you rascal, and I'll flog you within an inch of your, life.'

" 'I've no occasion.'

" 'You're a coward.'

" 'Not on your word.'

" 'I'll prove it by flogging you out of your skin.'

" 'I doubt it.'

WASHING THE STIFFENING OUT OF A BOASTER

" 'I am a liar, then, am I?'

" 'Just as you please.'

" 'Do you hear that, gentlemen?'

" 'Ay, we hear,' was the unanimous response. 'You can't avoid dressing him now.'

" 'O, heavens! grant me patience! I shall fly out of my skin.'

" 'It will be so much the better for your pocket; calf-skins are in good demand.'

" 'I shall burst.'

" 'Not here in the street, I beg of you. It would be disgusting.'

" 'Gentlemen, can I any longer avoid flogging him?'

" 'Not if you are able,' was the reply. 'Go at him.'

"Thus provoked, thus stirred up and enraged, the fierce politician went like lightning at his provoking antagonist. But before he could strike a blow he found himself disarmed of his cow-skin, and lying on his back under the spout of a neighboring pump, whither the young man had carried him to cool his rage, and before he could recover from his astonishment at such an unexpected handling, he was as wet as a thrice drowned rat, from the cataracts of water which his laughing antagonist had liberally pumped upon him. His courage, by this time, had fairly oozed out; and he declared, as he arose and went dripping away from the pump, that he would never again trust to quiet appearances, and that the devil himself might, the next time, undertake to cow-skin such a cucumber-blood scoundrel for him. The bystanders laughed heartily. The politician now went in pursuit of his horse and his woman, taking his yellow boy with him; and the landlady declared that he richly deserved what he had got, even if he had been guilty of no other offense than the dirty imposition he had practiced on her.

"The stranger now came to me, and calling me by name, asked for his rifle and knife, which I returned to him. I expressed some astonishment at being known to him, and he said that he had heard of my being in the village, and had sought me out for the purpose of accompanying me to Texas. He told me that he was a bee-hunter; that he had traveled pretty much over that country in the way of his business, and that I would find him of considerable use in navigating through the ocean of prairies."

Crockett was delighted to secure the company of the bee-hunter, for he rightly judged him to be a man of great courage, strong friendships, and one to be relied on in any emergency. He was also glad to learn that the gambler had known the bee-hunter in other days, and to see their acquaintance renewed under such circumstances as now brought them into companionship. It was arranged the next day to take their departure together for Nacogdoches, one hundred and twenty miles west of Natchitoches, and as the country through which their route lay was familiar to the bee-hunter, he acted as guide, and a reliable and cheery companion he proved to be.

CHAPTER X

En Route for the Alamo

Soon after day-break the three adventurers set out upon their journey to join, as soon as possible, in the struggle then going on between Texas and Mexico. Their route, though known as the old Spanish road, was often so indistinct that it could only be followed by carefully noting the blazes on the trees, for the trail was entirely obliterated in places. The bee-hunter proved himself an invaluable guide, for he never once lost the way, and besides inspiring his companions with confidence cheered their spirits, and enlivened the otherwise tedious hours, by singing sweet songs, of which he knew a large and pleasing variety. His was the soul of a poet, and the throat of a nightingale, a rare and gracious combination for a traveler.

In due season the party arrived at Nacogdoches, where a stop of two days was made to secure fresh horses, and to allow the bee-hunter proper time and opportunity for visiting with his sweet-heart, a beautiful girl of eighteen, who was daughter of a tavern keeper in the place. While the poetic young hero was singing love songs to his sweet-heart, and the gambler was picking up an occasional dime from saloon loafers who had the curiosity to experiment at guessing where the pea could be found, Crockett was moving among the people haranguing them to join the Lone Star Standard and under it march to independence. Though he gained no recruits he made such a favorable impression that the citizens serenaded him, with bass-drum and fife, as at Little Rock.

Fresh mustang horses having been secured, and a supply of provisions put up in their saddle-bags, the three were ready to push on again for the fortress of Alamo, which was the American headquarters, or recruiting rendezvous. The parting between the bee-hunter and Katie, his sweet-heart, was very affecting. They had been lovers for several years and affianced for many months, his roving disposition alone having prevented their marriage sometime before, notwithstanding her youth. But great as was his love for the girl, it was not strong enough to curb his ambition for glory. He would go away and fight for Texas, win a name, and perhaps position, and then return to claim her as a hero's bride. He kissed her with a manifestation of great fervor, tried hard to keep back the tears, and, to conceal his emotion the better, sang in that sweet voice which no other could rival:

> "Saddled and bridled, and booted rode he,
> A plume in his helmet, a sword at his knee."

She had heard him sing the song many a time before, and the refrain now came back to her in such oppressive and prophetic cadence, that she lifted her voice in reply:

"But home came the saddle, all bloody to see,
And home came the steed, but home never came he."

No longer able to hide his grief the bee-hunter dashed off, followed by Crockett and the gamester and the shouts of many voices bidding them God-speed.

Through Haunts of the Wolf and Bear

For two hours or more the three rode on without exchanging a word, the reverie of the bee-hunter being too deep and sacred to intrude upon, but at length he broke the painful silence and tried to forget his grief by regaling his soul with its own music. Thus he began to sing, first plaintive and sweet, and then changed, as his despondency gradually vanished, to more cheerful ditties, until he had quite recovered himself. Some good-natured jokes were cracked and by evening all were in high spirits. On the following day their route lay through an immense cane-brake which was the haunt of almost countless wolves and bears, the trails of which were seen leading across the path in such number as to make the region appear like a checkerboard. Of this brake Crockett writes:

"Canebrakes are common in some parts of Texas. Our way led us through one of considerable extent. The frequent passage of men and horses had kept open a narrow path not wide enough for two mustangs to pass with convenience. The reeds, the same as are used in the Northern States as fishing rods, had grown to the height of about twenty feet, and were so slender, that having no support directly over the path, they drooped a little inward, and intermingled their tops, forming a complete covering overhead. We rode about a quarter of a mile along this singular arched avenue with the view of the sky completely shut out. The bee-hunter told me that the largest brake is that which lines the banks of Caney Creek, and is seventy miles in length, with scarcely a tree to be seen the whole distance. The reeds are eaten by cattle and horses in the winter when the prairies yield little or no other food."

Meeting with a Pirate

At night they found shelter at the house of a poor woman whose store of provisions was so scanty that she could offer them no other accommodation than a part of her floor to sleep on. This they were glad enough to accept, and make their supper off what had been brought, for emergencies, in their saddle-bags. While hobbling their horses they saw approaching two men on foot, with small packs, but heavy rifles and big knives. The bee-hunter knew them, and after shaking their hands with a certain show of respect, introduced them to Crockett and the gambler. Crockett thus describes their appearance:

"They were both armed with rifles and hunting-knives, and though I have been accustomed to the sight of men who have not stepped far over the line of civilization, I must say these were just about the roughest samples I had seen any where. One was a man of about fifty years old, tall and raw-boned. He was dressed in a sailor's round jacket, with a tarpaulin on his head. His whiskers nearly covered his face; his hair was coal black and long, and there was a deep scar across his forehead, and another on the back of his right hand. His companion, who was considerably younger, was bareheaded, and clad in a deer-skin dress made after our fashion. Though he was not much darker than the old man, I perceived that he was an Indian. They spoke friendly to the bee-hunter, for they both knew him, and said they were on their way to join the Texan forces, at that time near the San Antonio River. Though they had started without horses, they reckoned they would come across a couple before they went much farther. The right of ownership to horse flesh is not much regarded in Texas, for those that have been taken from the wild droves are soon after turned out to graze on the prairies, the owner having first branded them with his mark, and hobbled them by tying their fore feet together, which will enable another to capture them just as readily as himself."

The two men who had thus fallen into Crockett's company were quite as bad as their savage appearances indicated. The elder one had been a pirate and fought under the black flag of Lafitte, while the other was an Indian who had not hesitated at crimes quite as iniquitous. But their repulsive looks and base characters was somewhat atoned for by the circumstance that in their pack were several wild-turkey eggs and two fat jackrabbits, which they offered to share. Crockett and the bee-hunter promptly accepted this generous proffer as an appetizing addition to their own slender fare, but the gambler objected, and sat off in one corner with no disposition to associate, even at the board, with criminals of their ilk. Nevertheless, the rabbits and eggs were quickly cooked and spread upon a table for eating, and the gambler was invited to "set up." But again he emphatically refused, whereupon, as Crockett says, the old pirate remarked:

"'Stranger, you had better take a seat at the table, I think,' at the same time drawing a long hunting-knife from his belt, and laying it on the table. 'I think you had better take some supper with us,' he added, in a mild tone, but fixing his eye sternly upon Thimblerig. The conjurer first eyed the knife, and then the fierce whiskers of the pirate, and, unlike some politicians, he wasn't long in making up his mind what course to pursue, but he determined to vote as the pirate voted, and said: 'I second that motion, stranger,' at the same time seating himself on the bench beside me. The old man then commenced cutting up the meat, for which purpose he had drawn his hunting knife, though the gambler had thought it was for a different purpose; and being relieved from his fears everything passed off quite sociable."

Notwithstanding the fierce and criminal character of the new comers, Crockett and his party passed a comfortable night, and the next day continued on their journey, none the worse for their few hours association with a pirate. They rode on until towards noon, when they came to a small cluster of trees in the boundless prairies, under which they stopped to refresh themselves and rest their horses. Having built a fire and roasted some game killed on the way, they were making a spread on the grass preparatory to enjoying an *al fresco* or open air feast, when suddenly the bee-hunter made a rush for his horse, and without saying a word rode away at a mad pace towards the west until he had disappeared in the far distance from the astonished gaze of Crockett and the gambler. For a considerable time they were utterly at a loss to know what could have caused their companion to thus desert them, for they could hardly bring themselves to believe that he had lost his mind. At length the idea came into Crockett's head that there was some good reason for the bee-keeper's strange action which would be explained in due time, and he therefore resolved to patiently wait results.

A Hurricane of Buffalos

Again Crockett and the gamester renewed preparations for their noon repast, but before they had begun to eat, a strange sound fell on their ears, unlike anything they had ever before heard, and withal, so ominous as to immediately drive away their appetites. It was one of the most beautiful of summer days. There was not a cloud to be seen. The undulating prairie, waving with flowers, lay spread out before them, more beautiful under nature's bountiful adornings than the most artistic parterre, park or lawn which the hand of man ever reared. A gentle, cool breeze swept through the grove, fragrant and refreshing as if from Araby the blest. It was just one of those scenes and one of those hours in which all vestiges of the Fall seemed to have been obliterated, and Eden itself again appeared blooming in its pristine beauty.

Still those sounds, growing more and more distinct, were not sounds of peace, were not aeolian warblings; they were mutterings as of a rising tempest, and inspired awe and a sense of peril. Straining their eyes towards the far distant west, whence the sounds came, they soon saw an immense black cloud just emerging from the horizon and apparently very low down, sweeping the very surface of the prairie. This strange, menacing cloud was approaching with manifestly great rapidity. It was coming directly toward the grove where the travelers were sheltered. A cloud of dust accompanied the phenomenon, ever growing thicker and rising higher in the air.

"What can all that mean?" exclaimed Crockett, in evident alarm.

The juggler sprang to his feet, saying, "Burn my old shoes, if I know."

Even the mustangs, which were grazing near by, were frightened. They stopped eating, pricked up their ears, and gazed in terror upon the approaching danger. It was then supposed that the black cloud, with its muttered thunderings, must be one of those terrible tornadoes which occasionally swept the region, bearing down everything before it. The men all rushed for the protection of the mustangs. In the greatest haste they struck off their hobbles and led them into the grove for shelter.

The noise grew louder and louder, and they had scarcely brought the horses beneath the protection of the trees, when they perceived that it was an immense herd of buffaloes, of countless hundreds, dashing along with the speed of the wind, and bellowing and roaring in tones as appalling as if a band of demons were flying and shrieking in terror before some avenging arm.

The herd seemed to fill the horizon. Their numbers could not be counted. They were all driven by some common impulse of terror. In their headlong plunge those in front pressed on by the innumerable throng behind, it was manifest that no ordinary obstacle would in the slightest degree retard their rush. The spectacle was sublime and terrible. Had the travelers been upon the open plain, it seemed inevitable that

A HURRICANE OF BUFFALOES

they must have been trampled down and crushed out of every semblance of humanity by these thousands of hard hoofs.

But it so chanced that they were upon what is called a rolling prairie, with its graceful undulations and gentle eminences. It was one of these beautiful swells which the grove crowned with its luxuriance.

As the enormous herd came along with its rush and roar, like the bursting forth of a pent-up flood, the terrified mustangs were too much frightened to attempt to escape. They shivered in every nerve as if stricken by an ague.

An immense black bull led the band. He was a few feet in advance of all the rest. He came roaring along, his tail erect in the air: as a javelin, his head near the ground, and his stout, bony horns projected as if he were just ready to plunge upon his foe. Crockett writes:

"I never felt such a desire to have a crack at anything in all my life. He drew nigh the place where I was standing. I raised my beautiful Betsey to my shoulder and blazed away. He roared and suddenly stopped. Those that were near him did so like-wise. The commotion occasioned by the impetus of those in the rear was such that it was a miracle that some of them did not break their heads or necks. The black bull stood for a few moments pawing the ground after he was shot, then darted off around the cluster of trees, and made for the uplands of the prairies. The whole herd followed, sweeping by like a tornado. And I do say I never witnessed a sight more beautiful to the eye of a hunter in all my life."

The temptation to pursue them was too strong for Crockett to resist. For a moment he was himself bewildered, and stood gazing with astonishment upon the wondrous spectacle. Speedily he reloaded his rifle, sprang upon his horse, and set out in pursuit over the expanse of prairie as destitute of landmarks as the ocean. For two hours he followed the herd, heedless of the direction he was taken or giving a thought to anything save the sport ahead. His mustang, scarcely larger than a donkey, kept up bravely under the weight of its rider for a distance of twelve or more miles, when it showed signs of fatigue. Crockett would, no doubt, have passed on regardless of the spent condition of his little steed, had he not now discovered the futility of further pursuit, as the herd had gained on him steadily and was now beyond rifle-shot.

Lost on the Prairie

Reining up his mustang, after the game had escaped, Crockett looked about him for some sign that would enable him to retrace his way, but the hoofs of mustang and buffaloes had blended, nor was it possible to distinguish them in the hoof-marks that everywhere indented the loose soil, for he was in the great buffalo range, where

CROCKETT LOST ON THE PRAIRIE

thousands upon thousands roamed. Taking his direction by guess he rode on for an hour until he became so bewildered that it was impossible for him to proceed with confidence, and he began to feel the awful oppression that follows a reflection upon the thought of being lost on the boundless prairies, with no means of protection against the myriads of half-famished wolves that wander over the wilderness ready to break their fast upon a distracted traveler like himself. Being lost was quite enough to worry his mind beyond measure, but to this trouble was added a great anxiety for the gambler who had been left alone, and for the bee-hunter, who had apparently gone in pursuit of a phantom.

After pausing a considerable tine to reflect upon his situation, he started in search of a stream of water, reasoning very properly that if he could find a water-course, it would not only serve to refresh him, but by following it there was a likelihood of coming upon some settler's cabin, besides, he might be able to take refuge in the water if pursued by wolves. But he had not proceeded far, when he saw in the distance a large herd of animals bearing swiftly down towards him, which at first he believed to be buffaloes. As they came nearer, however, he discovered that it was a drove of wild horses. In a few minutes they had overtaken him and by their rapid pace and incessant whinnying so excited his own mustang that Crockett was unable to control him, and off he dashed with the herd. It was now a mad race, in which, despite the handicap of one hundred and fifty pounds, the little mustang held his own among the wild, free rovers for nearly half an hour, and did not drop behind until the Navasola River was reached, where he fell completely exhausted.

A Fight with a Mexican Lion

The drove plunged into the stream and bravely stemming its rushing waters, which were much swollen by recent rains, all reached the other side in safety. Crockett unsaddled his horse and tried in vain for a long while to revive him. Night was fast coming on, and he must now needs look about for some place in which to take refuge. On the river bank he perceived, a few rods away, a large tree that had been recently blown down, in the still thick and green branches of which he decided to conceal himself and pass the night. But as he approached and began scrambling upon the trunk, a fierce growl arrested his attention, and gave him plainly to understand that the place was already pre-empted. Crockett thus describes the terrible battle that followed:

"Looking about to see what sort of a bed-fellow I was likely to have, I discovered, not more than five or six paces from me, an enormous Mexican cougar, eyeing me as an epicure surveys the table before he selects his dish, for I have no doubt the cougar looked upon me as the subject of a future supper. Rays of light darted from his large eyes, he showed his teeth like a negro in hysterics, and he was crouching on his haunches ready for a spring; all of which convinced me that unless I was pretty quick upon the trigger, posterity would know little of the termination of my eventful career, and it would be far less glorious and useful than I intend to make it.

"One glance satisfied me that there was no time to be lost, as Pat thought when falling from a church steeple, and exclaimed, 'This would be mighty pleasant, now, if it would only last'—but there was no retreat either for me or the cougar, so I leveled my Betsey and blazed away. The report was followed by a furious growl (which is sometimes the case in Congress), and the next moment, when I expected to find the tarnal critter struggling with death, I beheld him shaking his head as if nothing more than a bee had stung him. The ball had struck him on the forehead and glanced off, doing no other injury than stunning him for an instant, and tearing off the skin, which tended to infuriate him the more. The cougar wasn't long in making up his mind what to do, nor was I neither; but he would have it all his own way, and vetoed my motion to back out. I had not retreated three steps before he sprang at me like a steamboat; I stepped aside, and as he lit upon the ground, I struck him violently with the barrel of my rifle, but he didn't mind that, but wheeled around and made at me again. The gun was now of no use, so I threw it away, and drew my hunting knife, for I knew we should come to close quarters before the fight would be over. This time he succeeded in fastening on my left arm, and was just beginning to amuse himself by tearing the flesh off with his fangs, when I ripped my knife into his side, and he let go his hold much to my satisfaction.

"He wheeled about and came at me with increased fury, occasioned by the smarting of his wounds. I now tried to blind him, knowing that if I succeeded he would become an easy prey; so as he approached me I watched my opportunity, and aimed a blow at his eyes with my knife, but unfortunately it struck him on the nose, and he paid no other attention to it than by a shake of the head and a low growl. He pressed me close, and as I was stepping backward my foot tripped in a vine, and I fell to the ground. He was down upon me like a night-hawk upon a June bug. He seized hold of the outer part of my right thigh, which afforded him considerable amusement; the hinder part of his body was towards my face; I grasped his tail with my left hand, and tickled his ribs with my hunting knife, which I held in my right. Still the critter wouldn't let go his hold; and as I found that he would lacerate my leg dreadfully, unless he was speedily shaken off, I tried to hurl him down the bank into the river, for our scuffle had already brought us to the edge of the bank. I stuck my knife into his

CROCKETT'S FIGHT WITH THE MEXICAN LION

side, and summoned all my strength to throw him over. He resisted, was desperate heavy; but at last I got him so far down the declivity that he lost his balance, and he rolled over and over till he landed on the margin of the river; but in his fall he dragged me along with him. Fortunately, I fell uppermost, and his neck presented a fair mark for my hunting knife. Without allowing myself time even to draw breath, I aimed one desperate blow at his neck, and the knife entered his gullet up to the handle, and reached his heart. He struggled for a few moments, and died. I have had many fights with bears, but that was mere child's play; this was the first fight I ever had with a cougar, and I hope it may be the last.

"I now returned to the tree-top to see if any one else would dispute my lodging; but now I could take peaceable and quiet possession. I parted some of the branches, and cut away others to make a bed in the opening; I then gathered a quantity of moss, which hung in festoons from the trees, which I spread on the litter, and over this I spread my horse blanket; and I had as comfortable a bed as a weary man need ask for. I now took another look at my mustang, and from all appearances he would not live until morning. I ate some of the cakes that little Kate of Nacogdoches had made for me, and then carried my saddle into my tree-top, and threw myself down upon my bed with no very pleasant reflections at the prospect before me.

"I was weary, and soon fell asleep, and did not awake until daybreak the next day. I felt somewhat stiff and sore from the wounds I had received in the conflict with the cougar; but I considered myself as having made a lucky escape. I looked over the bank, and as I saw the carcass of the cougar lying there, I thought that it was an even chance that we had not exchanged conditions; and I felt grateful that the fight had ended as it did."

An Adventure with Comanche Indians

Upon arising from his bed in the tree Crockett went at once to look for his horse, but to his surprise the animal was gone, leaving behind no evidence of regret at thus basely deserting his master. To one great trouble another much greater had thus been added, but Crockett had not forgotten the philosophy that had served him in former trials and he resolved to make the best of his really desperate situation. Having had neither dinner nor supper the preceding day, hunger was destroying his strength and must be appeased. Taking his rifle he went up the stream a short distance when he was so fortunate as to discover a flock of geese sitting on the shore, one of which he shot and soon had it roasting over a comfortable fire. Upon this he satisfied his well-whetted appetite, and was upon the point of taking up his journey on foot down the river, when a third surprise was given him. This time it was neither buffaloes nor wild horses, but a war party of one hundred Comanche Indians that had been attracted to Crockett's camp by seeing the smoke arising from his fire. Resistance or attempt at escape being useless, he submitted himself to whatever fate they chose to visit upon him. Several of the Indians could speak English and to these Crockett addressed himself, relating all that had befallen him since he left his comrade to go in pursuit of the buffaloes. He also showed them the dead cougar, and described the manner in which he had killed it. The Indians were so well pleased with him that instead of offering any indignity, expressed a desire to adopt him into their tribe, an honor which he respectfully declined and with excuses for his refusal so satisfactory that the chief gave him a horse, and offered to conduct him to the Colorado River.

This was a kindness that came as a veritable God-send to Crockett, and he was quick to embrace it. He put his saddle and bridle on the horse that had been given him, and set off with his Indian friends towards the Texas rendezvous at Bexar. After riding a few miles they saw a herd of wild horses grazing, and one of the Indians who had a lasso started in pursuit of them. The drove did not take alarm immediately, but permitted him to get within less than a hundred yards, when all but one of them dashed away and soon disappeared. The solitary animal that had refused to flee was directly lassoed, and being brought back to the party Crockett at once recognized it as his mustang that had, by apparent shamming, escaped the night before. Crockett expressed his astonishment that the horse allowed himself to be so easily taken, whereupon the chief explained that when wild mustangs are first captured with the lasso they are hurled so violently to the ground that they never forget the hard experience, and the very sight of a lasso frequently subdues them even after they have escaped and run wild for years.

Towards evening the party discovered a herd of buffaloes, which the Indians gave chase to, and offered Crockett one of the most interesting sights of his life, for they gave him an example of the manner in which they hunt this animal from horseback, with lance and bow and arrow, and showed an expertness in the handling of their horses really wonderful to see.

Finding the Gambler

After the hunt the party moved forward till they reached a crossing of the Colorado, when their attention was attracted to a column of smoke rising from a clump of trees, which the Indians at once investigated. Crockett and the chief crept towards the fire until they came in view of a camp, when to the former's astonishment he saw sitting on a log a solitary man amusing himself at the game of thimblerig while his coffee was simmering and the fire burning low. Crockett recognized in this lone gamester his comrade, the gambler, but to test his nerve he withdrew while the Indians rushed

THE BUFFALO CHASE

forward with tomahawks uplifted, and yelling only as Comanches can. The poor gambler was taken by complete surprise, and so frightened that he forgot his ruling passion and fell into that which he had never practiced before—praying. The test was complete, and to save him from an attack of hysterics Crockett now stepped forward and taking the gambler's hand quieted his fears and explained the situation, as also the reason of his long absence.

It now became the gambler's turn to relate his experience, which Crockett was equally anxious to hear, and he immediately proceeded with his story which was to the effect that after waiting a long while the return of his comrades the gambler was upon the point of retracing his steps for the States, and was already on his mustang for that purpose, when the bee-hunter most unexpectedly appeared before him well laden with a supply of golden honey, and explained his abrupt departure by saying that it was a bee he had followed to its goodly store.

"But where is the bee-hunter now?" eagerly asked Crockett.

"Oh," replied the gambler, "he is out hunting and will return presently with some game, for I heard the report of his gun about fifteen minutes ago not more than a mile down the river."

The Indians, being anxious to renew their journey, now bade Crockett adieu, but not until he had presented the chief with a large bowie-knife, which effectually cemented their friendship, as an Indian, especially in those days, prized nothing so highly as a large knife.

Soon after the Indians had taken their departure, the bee-hunter came to the camp with a big turkey slung over his shoulder, and was met by Crockett with open arms and hugs that showed his transport at the reunion.

While supper was being prepared, the neighing of a horse broke upon their ears and, as enemies were thicker than friends in that lawless region, the three seized their rifles and made ready for any adventure. Their fears were presently relieved, however, by the sight of two horsemen, one of whom Crockett quickly perceived was the old pirate and the other his Indian companion. They were cordially received and invited to partake of the supper that was now ready.

A Fight with Mexicans

When supper was finished, the bee-hunter entertained the party with several stirring war songs that fired them all with patriotic enthusiasm. In the conversation that followed the old pirate stated that he was on his way to the fortress of Alamo to join the Texas rangers, and would be glad to finish the remainder of the journey in such good company as that of his three new friends. Crockett was delighted with the proposition, for in such a country as Texas was at this time, infested with robbers, cut-throats, and every species of lawless characters, an increase of company was very acceptable, while the pirate's desire to join the Texas patriots inspired Crockett at once with a confidence in the outlaw that he had not felt before.

Early the following morning the five started for Bexar, with their spirits greatly stimulated by the songs of the bee-hunter. Nothing occurred to prevent their rapid progress until they were within twenty miles of Bexar (which is now called San Antonio), when an incident occurred which Crockett thus describes:

"We were in the open prairie, and beheld a band of about fifteen or twenty armed men approaching us at full speed. 'Look out for squalls,' said the old pirate, who had not spoken for an hour; 'they are a scouting party of Mexicans.' 'And are three or four times our number,' said Thimblerig. 'No matter,' replied the old man; 'they are convicts, jail birds, and cowardly ruffians, no doubt, who would tremble at a loud word as much as a mustang at the sight of a lasso. Let us spread ourselves, dismount, and trust to our arms.'

"We followed his orders, and stood beside our horses, which served to protect our persons, and awaited the approach of the enemy. When they perceived this movement of ours, they checked their speed, appeared to consult together for a few minutes, then spread their line, and came within rifle shot of us. The leader called out to us in Spanish, but as I did not understand him, I asked the old man what it was, who said he called upon us to surrender.

" 'There will be a brush with those blackguards,' continued the pirate. 'Now each of you single out your man for the first fire, and they are greater fools than I take them for if they give us a chance at a second. Colonel, as you are a good shot, just settle the business for that talking fellow with the red feather; he's worth any three of the party.'

" 'Surrender, or we fire,' shouted the fellow with the red feather, in Spanish.

" 'Fire, and be d——d,' returned the pirate, at the top of his voice, in plain English.

"And sure enough they took his advice, for the next minute we were saluted with a discharge of musketry, the report of which was so loud that we were convinced they all had fired. Before the smoke had cleared away we had each selected our man, fired, and I never did see such a scattering among their ranks as followed. We beheld several mustangs running wild without their riders over the prairie, and the balance of the company were already retreating at a more rapid gait than they approached. We hastily mounted, and commenced pursuit, which we kept up until we beheld the indepen-

THE BATTLE WITH THE MEXICAN BANDITS

dent flag flying from the battlements of the fortress of Alamo, our place of destination. The fugitives succeeded in evading our pursuit, and we rode up to the gates of the fortress, announced to the sentinel who we were, and the gates were thrown open, through which we entered amid shouts of welcome bestowed upon us by the patriots."

CHAPTER XI

At the Alamo

Following the arrival of Crockett at Bexar, a bacchanalian orgy was instituted by way of celebrating his enlistment in the Texas war for independence. While this drunken carousal reflects no credit upon the participants, it was characteristic of life in the far southwest, and is not, therefore, deserving of such severe condemnation as if the same scenes had been enacted in a more civilized community. Crockett thus humorously describes the convivial exhibition in which he acted a part:

"We had a little sort of convivial party last evening; just about a dozen of us set to work, most patriotically, to see whether we could not get rid of that curse of the land, whisky, and we made considerable progress; but my poor friend, Thimblerig, got sewed up just about as tight as the eyelet-hole in a lady's corset, and a little tighter, too, I reckon; for when he went to bed he called for a bootjack, which was brought to him, and he bent down on his hands and knees, and very gravely pulled off his hat with it, for the darned critter was so thoroughly swiped that he didn't know his head from his heels. But this wasn't all the folly he committed; he pulled off his coat and laid it on the bed, and then hung himself over the back of a chair; and I wish I may be shot if he didn't go to sleep in that position, thinking everything had been done according to Gunter's late scale. Seeing the poor fellow completely used up, I carried him to bed, though he did belong to the temperance society; and he knew nothing about what had occurred until I told him the next morning. The bee-hunter didn't join us in this blow out. Indeed, he will seldom drink more than just enough to prevent his being called a total abstinence man. But then he is the most jovial fellow for a water drinker I ever did see."

Less than two months before Crockett reached the place, or on December 10th, 1835, Bexar, which is now universally known as San Antonio, was captured from the Mexicans by the Texas patriots, the former being under the command of General Cos, a brother-in-law of Santa Anna, and the latter under General Burlison. The town, which then contained about twelve hundred inhabitants, was garrisoned by seventeen hundred Mexicans, while the attacking force numbered only two hundred and sixteen.

Notwithstanding the overwhelming odds against them, and the disadvantage of having to make the assault, the Texans bravely rushed to the attack, and though beaten back it was only to gain fresh impetus. For five days and nights the siege was kept up, with the Texans always gaining ground, until at length the Mexicans were driven to take refuge in the public square, or plaza, which they had walled up and prepared for a desperate resistance. But these defenses were soon battered down and the Texans swept over them as the Mexicans retreated to what had been a monastery, but which, being now converted into a fortress, was called the Castle of Alamo, which stood opposite the plaza. Though this building was secure against assault, General Cos found himself in danger of being starved out, and as his provisions were already expended, he raised a white flag and sent out his terms for capitulation. It is hardly necessary to say that the first draft was favorable to himself, but as there was not another round of ammunition left among the Texans, the terms were accepted. By them General Cos was given permission to retire within six days with his officers, on parole of honor, and to retain their side arms and private property. The public property, money, ammunition and arms of the fighting rank, however, were to be delivered over to General Burlison, of the Texan army, all of which stipulations were accepted and faithfully carried out.

The Brave Defenders of the Alamo

In this memorable siege the Mexicans are said to have lost three hundred men, while the Texans suffered a loss of only four men killed and twenty wounded. This remarkable victory, won with so few casualties to their own forces while administering such severe punishment to their enemies, inspired the Texans with such courage that they believed themselves almost invincible.

At the time Crockett joined the patriots the Alamo was garrisoned by less than two hundred men, under command of Colonel Travis, one of the bravest men that ever lifted a sword in defense of American liberty. He was ably supported by Colonel Bonham, and that most celebrated duelist and desperate fighter, Colonel Bowie. The two latter gentlemen were called "Colonel" out of courtesy, though had they survived the war their promotion would have been to positions higher than that by which they are designated in Texas annals. But these officers of such dash and daring were made of no better material than were their men, for every soldier within the ranks of the band that held the Alamo under the Texan star was a hero, with the courage of a Spartan and a fidelity to the trusts reposed in them like true knights in the wars of old.

The defeat sustained by General Cos enraged Santa Anna beyond measure and he immediately resolved to march against Bexar and to head the attack himself, for it was his boast that he would wreak a desperate vengeance upon the Texans and then sow their land with salt that it might never produce a green thing again. This resolve, nor his threats could intimidate the garrison, now so well schooled in fighting and with the laurels of victory yet fresh upon their brows.

Description of the Alamo

As the Alamo has since become one of the famous landmarks of San Antonio de Bexar, and still stands the monument of a bloody conflict not surpassed by that even of ancient Thermopylae, some account of it will be necessary to a proper understanding of the story of its heroic defense. It was first established as the Alamo Mission by the Franciscan Friars in 1718 and the cornerstone of the building was laid May 8, 1745. A volunteer who visited the fort soon after the battle sent the following description to the *Hesperian,* or *Western Monthly Magazine* published at Columbus, Ohio: "The Alamo, the grave of poor Crockett, he writes, stands on the east side of the river, on an eminence which commands the entire city. It is a quadrangular fort, including the third of an acre, with walls from eighteen to twenty feet in height, and no less than four or five feet in thickness. Within the limits of the fort is a large stone church now in ruins. On the east and west, parallel walls were constructed in the inside, fifteen feet from the outer walls. Beams were laid from one to the other a few feet from the top, and the space filled by beaten earth. Doors open through the inner wall to the space between the two, which was divided into a number of small rooms for the accommodation of the garrison."

It was on a gray, cold Sunday morning, the 6th of March, 1836, that 183 men (14 of whom were on the sick list and unable to take part in the battle) attempted to check the progress of five thousand troops of Mexico, commanded in person by Santa Anna, who from his previous success was deemed invincible in war. Had the bold attempt proved successful it would have formed one of the most brilliant achievements in modern warfare; but the awful conclusion of the tragedy has stamped it as a rash attempt. The disparity in numbers was so great as to render defeat and destruction morally certain. Col. Travis, who commanded during the siege, was ordered to fall back upon the main army under the command of General Houston. But a spirit of chivalry, of reckless daring, was stronger than the feeling of military subordination.

Massacre of a Squad of Texans

On the 25th of February, 1836, the post was attacked by the advance division of President Santa Anna's army, numbering 1,600 men who were repulsed with heavy loss. About the same time, Col. Johnson, with a party of 70 men, while reconnoitering to the west of San Patricio, was surrounded in the night by a large body of Mexican troops. In the morning an unconditional surrender was demanded which was refused; but an offer of surrender was made as prisoners of war, which was acceded to by the Mexicans. But no sooner had the Texans marched out of their quarters and stacked their arms, than a general fire was opened upon them by the whole Mexican force; the Texans attempted to escape, but only three of them succeeded, one of whom was Colonel Johnson.

Between the 25th of February and the 2d of March the Mexicans were employed in throwing up entrenchments around the Alamo, and bombarding the place. On the latter date Colonel Crockett wrote that two hundred shells had been thrown into the Alamo without injuring a man. On the day before, the garrison of the Alamo received a re-enforcement of thirty-two Texans from Gonzales, having forced their way through the enemy's lines, augmenting the number in the Alamo to 183 men, while that of the besieging force amounted to between 5,000 and 7,000. Santa Anna, who was a few days behind his advance, now reached the scene, and his presence was announced by a salute of cannon. The drama was soon to open with all its horrors. On the 4th of March a Mexican council of war was held and it was determined to carry the place by assault on the 6th at daylight. The following evening Col. Travis, having been apprised of the intention of Santa Anna, assembled his little band within the court of the Alamo, and first solemnly tracing a long line with the point of his sword, delivered a short address. He frankly admitted to his men that unless re-enforcements speed-ily reached them from the Texan army that there was at best only a desperate hope for their escape, as the place would be stormed in the morning by an overwhelming force. There were, he said, three courses to pursue. One was to surrender on the best terms that could be made and take their chances; the second was to undertake a retreat, and the third to remain and die like men for their country; as for himself the latter would be his course and he called upon all who chose to die with him to cross over the line he had drawn. Instantly the whole party, and without a remark being made, rushed over the line. Their choice was made. Even the brave Colonel Bowie (of bowie-knife fame) who was sick on his cot, called loudly for the boys to pick him up and carry him across the line, which was immediately done.

Attack on the Alamo

Before daylight next morning Santa Anna ordered the bugles sounded as the signal for the charge, and soon the Alamo was surrounded by the whole Mexican army. They rushed to the assault—the infantry being divided into two columns, and supported by cavalry—amid a deadly volley of cannon shot and musketry. The army made a simultaneous attack on the three sides of the fortress, but were hurled back by a withering fire which swept down nearly two hundred of the enemy and almost obstructed the passage of those behind. But the army soon reformed for another onset. The bugle again sounded the charge, and a second time the Mexicans rushed forward, but only to meet the same deadly flame that prevented them before from reaching the foot of the walls against which they sought to place their scaling ladders.

The Texans stood to their guns firing at close and long range, while during a short lull in the battle the Mexican bands were playing *the dequelo*, which signifies no quarter.

All this time three batteries, planted on a commanding hill in the rear of the town, were sending their shots against the fortress walls, making occasional breeches, but which were repaired before the enemy could turn them to advantage. But doomed as they appeared to be the patriots never thought of surrender and resolved to ask no quarter in any extremity. Many acts of wonderful valor were performed in this fierce and unequal struggle. It is related that during a short lull in the attack a Mexican was seen at a distance of two hundred yards from the fort busy in making some repairs, or perhaps constructing a battery. His person was completely exposed and he worked as one regardless of danger. In this situation he caught the eye of Crockett, who put a suitable charge into his rifle and taking his station on one of the angles of the fort, where he was exposed to every gun of the besiegers, let drive at the enemy. At the crack of his rifle the Mexican leaped into the air, shot directly through the heart, a victim to the intrepid hunter and no less skillful fighter.

The tragedy now hastened to a terrible conclusion. Such was the extent of the fort, that it required the incessant vigilance of all the besieged, at the different points of attack, to repel the assaults, which were generally made upon the three sides simultaneously. A third and final charge was now made by the Mexicans on the doomed fort. Santa Anna gave the signal for the onslaught to his buglers from a battery near the Commerce Street Bridge. General Castrillo, a brilliant officer, was in immediate command of the assaulting columns, while Santa Anna, in person, encouraged the Mexicans with assurances of victory.

This time the enemy reached the foot of the walls and succeeded in planting their ladders, up which they rushed in a tumultuous horde, and met the brave defenders, who with clubbed guns, not having time to reload them, fought until they fell in their bloody tracks, overwhelmed by sheer force of numbers. Then commenced the last struggle of the garrison. Colonel Travis was killed within the first hour of the storming of the garrison. He met his death like a true hero while standing on the wall cheering his men, having first met the assailants and run his sword through the body of General Monro, who led the storming party, the two fierce warriors expiring almost at the same moment locked together.

Death of Crockett

On the fall of Travis the command of the Texans devolved on Adjutant, Major J. J. Baugh, who was mortally wounded in the course of another hour, and was succeeded by Crockett, who likewise soon fell. He was found dead within the Alamo, in an angle made by two houses, lying on his back, a frown on his brow, a smile of scorn on his lips, his knife in his hand, a dead Mexican lying across his body, and twenty-two more lying pell-mell before him in the angle. Major Evans was shot while setting fire to the magazine, according to the order of Travis.

The fate of Col. Bowie is better known from a female servant who was so fortunate as to escape the general destruction. On the night of the attack he was confined to his cot, as previously stated, by sickness. When the Mexicans broke over the walls several of them rushed to his apartment, but were met at the door by the sick man, who had summoned strength to meet the invaders, and whose arm, nerved by desperation, was still able to wield the knife that bears his name. For a time he kept the assailants at bay, but when they at length crowded upon him nearly a dozen were dispatched before a ball crashed through his brain, when he fell upon the bloody heap he had made at the door.

The Massacre

At last the numbers of the patriots were so thinned that the few who remained, exhausted with long fighting, began to relax in their exertions, when the Mexicans rushed forward and surrounding them on all sides, butchered and cut them to pieces. But with all this bloody work before him, still the last man refused to cry for quarter, preferring to die with his comrades.

Total extermination succeeded the successful assault, and of all the persons in the place Mrs. Dickinson and her child, and a negro servant of Col. Travis were alone spared.

Half an hour after sunrise, the gallant spirits who had so bravely defended the post, and killed and wounded more than five times their own number, were sweltering in their own gore where they fell, and Santa Anna, surrounded by his life-guards, made his triumphant entry into the fort. As he entered the fortress, among the heaps of dead he discovered the body of Major Evans; with a savageness and cowardice which distinguished him he drew his dirk and planting his knee upon the dead man thrust it twice into the noble breast. General Cos was no less a barbarian, who sought his revenge in a most cowardly and inhuman act. Finding the servant of Col. Travis he compelled him to point out the body of his dead master; when with his sword he

THE MEXICAN ASSAULT ON THE ALAMO

mangled the face and limbs with the ferocity and feelings of a Comanche savage. The bodies of the valiant defenders were then stripped, thrown into a heap and burned.

Immediately after the capture, General Santa Anna sent Mrs. Dickinson and the servant to General Houston's camp, accompanied by a Mexican dispatch bearer, who carried a note from Santa Anna, offering the Texans general amnesty if they would lay down their arms and submit to his government. General Houston's reply was, "True, sir, you have succeeded in killing some of our brave men, but the Texans are not yet conquered."

The preceding account of the storming and capture of the Alamo is based upon information current throughout Texas, but that it contains many mistakes I can have no doubt. The circumstances were such as prevented any entirely authentic description, except we give reliance to the story as related by the Mexicans themselves; but even these could not tell us how all the brave Texans died. In many respects the battle and massacre resembled that in which Custer surrendered up his life on the Little Big Horn, when only a single friendly Indian was left to tell the harrowing details, and even his story is hardly worthy of complete reliance.

I have gathered from a new source an account of the scenes following the capture of the Alamo, which is of undoubted interest and historical value as well, since the particulars are related by one in whom those who know him place implicit confidence.

For the facts as here recorded I am indebted to Mr. W. P. Tuber, of Iola, Texas, who learned them from a Mexican fifer named Apolinario Saldigua, a boy only sixteen years of age, who was an eye-witness of the scenes he described. This boy was best known as Poleen, or Polin, an abbreviation of his Christian name, who related to Mr. Tuber the sad story substantially as follows:

Story of the Mexican Fifer

After the fort (the celebrated church of the Alamo at San Antonio) had been stormed and all of its defenders had been reported to have been slain, and when the Mexican assailants had been recalled from within the walls, Santa Anna, accompanied by his staff, entered the fortress. Polin, being a fifer, and therefore a privileged person, and possibly the more so on account of his tender age, by permission entered with them. He desired to see all that was to be seen; and for this purpose he kept himself near to his general-in-chief. Santa Anna had ordered that no corpses should be disturbed till after he had looked upon them all, and seen how every man had fallen. He had employed three or four citizens of San Antonio to enter with him, and to point out to him the bodies of several distinguished Texans.

The principal corpses that Santa Anna desired to see were those of Colonel W. Barrett Travis, Col. James Bowie, and another man, whose name Polin could not remember, but which, by his description, must have been Crockett

On entering the fort, the eyes of the conquerors were greeted by a scene which Polin could not well describe. The bodies of the Texans lay as they had fallen, and many of them were covered by those of Mexicans who had fallen upon them. The close of the struggle seemed to have been a hand-to-hand engagement, and the number of dead Mexicans exceeded that of the Texans. The ground was covered by the bodies of the slain. Santa Anna and suite for a time wandered from one apartment of the fortress to another, stepping over and upon the dead, and seemingly enjoying this scene of human butchery.

After a general reconnoitering of the premises, the dictator came upon the body of Col. Travis. After viewing the form and features for a few moments, Santa Anna thrust his sword through the dead man's body and turned away. He was then conducted to the remains of the man (Crockett) whose name Polin could not remember. This man lay with his face upward, and his body was covered by those of many Mexicans who had fallen upon him. His face was florid, like that of a living person, and he looked like a healthy man asleep. Santa Anna also viewed him for a few moments, thrust his sword through his breast, and turned away.

The one who had come to point out certain bodies made a long but unsuccessful search for that of Col. Bowie, and reported to Santa Anna that it could not be found.

Then a detail of Mexican soldiers came into the fort. They were commanded by two officers, a captain, and a junior officer whose title Polin could not explain, but whom I shall for convenience call the lieutenant. They were both quite young men, very fair, very handsome, and so nearly alike in complexion, form, size and features, that Polin judged them to be brothers, the captain being apparently a little older than the other. Polin did not remember to have seen them before, was confident that he never saw them afterward, and he did not learn their names.

After the entry of this detail, Santa Anna and his suite retired; but the two officers, with their men, remained within. The two kept themselves close together, side by side. Polin was desirous to know what was to be done, and remained with the detail, and to enable himself to see all that was to be seen, he kept near the two officers, never losing sight of them.

As soon as the dictator and suite had retired, the squad began to take up the dead Texans and to bring them together and lay them in a pile, but before thus depositing them the Mexicans rifled the pockets and, in many cases, stripped the bodies of all clothing.

The two officers took a stand about the center of the main area. The first corpse was brought and laid as the captain directed. This formed a nucleus for the pile. The bodies were brought successively, each by four men, and dropped near the captain's feet. In imitation of his general, the captain viewed the bodies of each Texan for a few moments, then thrust his sword through it, after which the mutilated corpse was cast upon the heap at another motion of the captain's sword.

When the Texans had all been thrown upon the pile, four soldiers walked around it, each carrying a can of camphene, that was poured upon the bodies for a funeral pyre. This process was continued until the bodies were thoroughly wetted. Then a match was cast upon the pile, and the combustible fluid instantly sent up a flame to an immense height.

While the fluid was being thrown upon the pile, four soldiers brought a cot, on which lay a sick man, and set it down by the captain, and one of them remarked: "Here, captain, is a man who is not dead." "Why is he not dead?" said the captain. "We found him in a room by himself," said the soldier. "He seems to be very sick and, I suppose, he was not able to fight, and was placed there by his companions, to be in a safe place and out of the way." ' The captain gave the sick man a searching look,

HEROIC DEATH OF CROCKETT

and said: "I think I have seen this man before." The lieutenant replied: "I think I have, too," and, stooping down, he examined his features closely. Then, raising himself up, he addressed the captain: "He is no other than the infamous Col. Bowie!"

The captain then also stooped, gazed intently on the sick man's face, assumed an erect position, and confirmed the conviction of the lieutenant.

The captain looked fiercely upon the sick man, and said: "How is it, Bowie, that you have been found hidden in a room by yourself; and have not died fighting, like your companions?" To which Bowie replied in good Castilian: "I should certainly have done so; but you see that I am sick, and cannot get off this cot." "Ah, Bowie," said the captain, you have come to a *fearful* end—and well do you deserve it. As an immigrant to Mexico you have taken an oath, before God, to support the Mexican Government; but now you are violating that oath by fighting against the very government which you have sworn to defend. But this perjury, common to all of your rebellious countrymen, is not your only offense. You have married a respectable Mexican lady and are fighting against her countrymen. Thus you have not only perjured yourself, but you have also betrayed your own family."

"I did," said Bowie, "take an oath to support the Constitution of Mexico; and in defense of that Constitution am I now fighting. You took the same oath, when you accepted your commission in the army; and you are now violating that oath, and betraying the trust of your countrymen, by fighting under a faithless tyrant for the destruction of that Constitution, and for the ruin of your people's liberties. The perjury and treachery are not *mine*, but *yours*."

A Horrible Recital

The captain indignantly ordered Bowie to shut his mouth. "I shall never shut my mouth for your like," said Bowie, "while I have a tongue to speak." "I will soon relieve you of that," said the captain.

Then he caused four of his minions to hold the sick man, while a fifth, with a sharp knife split his mouth, on each side, to the ramus of the jaw, then took hold of his tongue, drew as much of it as he could between the teeth, out of his mouth, cut it off and threw it upon the pile of dead men. Then, in obedience to a motion of the captain's sword, the four soldiers who held him, lifted the writhing body of the mutilated, bleeding, tortured invalid from his cot, and pitched him alive upon the funeral pile.

At that moment a match was touched to the bodies. The combustible fluid instantly sent up a flame to an amazing height. The sudden generation of a great heat drove all the soldiers back to the wall. The officers, pale as corpses, stood gazing at the immense column of fire, and trembling from head to foot, as if they would break asunder at every joint. Polin stood between them, and saw and heard the lieutenant whisper, in a faltering and broken articulation: "It takes him—up—to God."

Polin believed that the lieutenant alluded to the ascension, upon the wings of that flame, of Bowie's soul to that God who would surely award due vengeance to his fiendish murderers.

Not being able to fully comprehend the great combustibility of the camphene, Polin also believed that the sudden elevation of that great pillar of fire was an indication of God's hot displeasure toward those torturing murderers. He further believed that the two officers were of the same opinion, and thus he accounted for their great agitation. And he thought that the same idea pervaded the whole detail, as every man appeared to be greatly frightened.

For a time Polin stood amazed, expecting each moment that the earth would open a chasm through which every man in the fort would drop into perdition. Terrified by this conviction, he left the fort as speedily as possible.

On a subsequent day Polin entered the fort again. It was then cleansed, and it seemed to be a comfortable place. But in a conspicuous place, in the main area, he saw the one relic of the great victory—a pile of charred fragments of human bones.

CHAPTER XII

How the News Was Brought to the States

The fall of the Alamo, or "Bexar," as the tail end of the name of the town was then called, happened on the morning of the 6th day of March, 1836. With the telegraph facilities of the present day, the particulars would have been flashed to the farthest extremities of the States and across the continent of Europe to the most distant capitals before sundown. But at that time the news was twenty-three days in getting to New Orleans, and was a month before it reached New York. The schooner *Comanche* brought the first report of the slaughter *via* the Gulf from Texas, and it was first published in the New Orleans *Bulletin* on the 29th, or more than three weeks after the battle. On the same day the Louisiana *Gazette* had the news in the shape of a letter from Mr. Briscoe, from near the scene of the massacre, who sent the particulars by pony express to Natchitoches, where it was printed in the Red River *Herald*. From Natchitoches a passenger brought a copy on the steamer *Levant* to New Orleans. From New Orleans the letter was carried by sailing vessel around by ocean to New York, where, on the 16th of April, it was printed in Horace Greeley's *New Yorker*, so that the news was exactly forty days in getting before the New York readers. As a matter of curiosity the letter containing the fall of the Alamo is here given; it will be seen, when compared with the facts as subsequently molded into history, to be about as correct as the first bulletins of war news usually are:

Copy of First Dispatch

To Editor Red River Herald:

SIR—Bexar has fallen! Its garrison was only 187 strong, commanded by Lieut.-Col. W. Travis. After standing repeated attacks for two weeks, and an almost constant cannonade and bombarding during that time, the last attack was made on the morning of the 6th inst. by upwards of 2,000 men under the command of Santa Anna in person. They carried the place about sunrise, with the loss of 520 men killed, and about the same number wounded. After about an hour's fighting the whole garrison was put to death (save the sick and wounded and seven men who asked for quarter). All fought desperately until entirely cut down. The rest were coolly murdered. The brave and gallant Travis, to prevent his falling into the hands of the enemy, shot himself. Not an individual escaped, and the news is only known to us by a citizen of Bexar, who came to our army at Gonzales—but from the cessation of Travis' signal guns, there is no doubt of its truth. . . . Col. James Bowie and David Crockett are among the slain—the first was murdered in his bed, in which he had been confined by illness—the latter fell fighting like a tiger. The Mexican army is estimated at 8,000 men; it may be more or less.

A. BRISCOE

The same number of the paper, containing the above, has an editorial, by Mr. Greeley, on the startling news, which concludes as follows:

Greeley's Eulogy on Crockett

"There is one item of the disastrous intelligence from Bexar, which struck us with even more painful interest than was excited by the general disaster. We allude to the death of the intrepid and true-hearted Col. David Crockett, who had enrolled himself under the banner of the Texans from a sentiment of devotion to the cause of liberty, as pure and chivalrous as ever animated the human bosom. Whatever may have been the imputed eccentricities of the frank Tennesseean's political career, we believe he left no enemies on earth, and that many a noble heart will heave a sigh at the recollection of his manly virtues, his uncalculating honesty of purpose and independence of character, his simplicity and kindness of heart, and the generous gallantry which impelled him to seek an untimely, but glorious death beneath the swords of the Mexican enslavers. May the flowers of the far prairie cluster thickly and brightly above his mouldering ashes."

The Uprising to Avenge Crockett's Death

Everywhere the fall of the Alamo, and particularly the death of the gallant Crockett, was received with expressions of sorrow.

From the Rio Grande to the northern lakes, the fate of that heroic spirit was bewailed with unfeigned tokens of universal grief. From Tennessee and other Southern States volunteers proffered their services to avenge his fall, and even a company of seventy-four men, under Col. E. K. Stanley, sailed from New York for the Brazos and volunteered their services in the cause of Texan independence, stimulated to this action solely by their desire to avenge the death of Crockett. The Convention of Texas, then in session at Washington, the capital of the State, took a firm course on hearing of the barbarities committed by the more than savage conquerors of the Alamo, and of the death of Travis and Crockett, by ordering a draft of two-thirds of the population, and the confiscation of the property of all who refused to serve. Calvin Henderson, who was in the Convention Hall when the express arrived bringing the mournful intelligence that San Antonio de Bexar had at length fallen, sent out the following stirring dispatch: "Poor David Crockett was one of the garrison of San Antonio. His bravery was more than gallant. His example animated everybody. His death was worthy of himself. He certainly killed twenty-five of the enemy during the siege. Tell his friends to come *and avenge his death*."

There is no doubt that the heroic example of Crockett and his brave comrades roused hundreds to join General Houston, and nerved the arm of many a Texan to avenge their deaths. Santa Anna followed up his barbarous system of warfare and no quarter, until his utter rout at San Jacinto, when the poor devils of Mexicans would hold up their hands, cross themselves, and sing out, "Me no Alamo," but nothing could save them. The blood of our countrymen was too fresh in the memory of the Texans to let one Mexican escape, until worn down with pursuit and slaughter, they commenced making prisoners.

Character of Crockett

It is wonderful to look back and realize the hold that David Crockett had in the hearts and affections of the American people in his day. Before he entered Congress his reputation was only local. He was known among his constituents in Tennessee as the great "bar hunter," and stories were told of his conflicts with the wild "varmints" amid the cane-brakes, and his tussles with the catamounts and bears brought down by his trusty rifle from the branches of the girdled trees in the corn and cotton fields. Even the very negroes of the South, when they heard of his bravery in bear fights and skill in 'possum-hunting, would roll up their yellow eyes and say: "Him a hoss, dat Massa Crockett." It was not till he came to Washington that his reputation followed him. Stories were told of his hunting exploits, and his curt sayings were quoted and circulated all over the country. Such expressions attributed to him as "Be sure you're right, then go ahead," became a popular maxim, and is as firmly imbedded in the language as any of the sayings of John Randolph of Roanoke, or of any of the distinguished celebrities who were the colleagues in Congress of Col. Crockett. His renown crossed the Atlantic, where his unique character was drawn in glowing colors, and set forth as an original specimen of an American great man. Visitors at Washington had Crockett pointed out as one of the lions in Congress. A New York correspondent, among some pen and ink sketches of John Quincy Adams, "the old man eloquent," George McDuffie, who rolls out his words and bites them off; Burgess, "the bald eagle of the House"; Richard M. Johnson "the Tecumseh killer," and Edward Everett, "the accomplished scholar and fine writer," says of our "hunter statesman": "Crockett, there is a better Neptune and holds a steadier trident. And when a man can grin and fight, flag a steamboat, or whip his weight in wild-cats, what is the use of reading and writing. What singular samples of our vast country! Here sits a Tennesseean and there a Missourian, educated among buffaloes and nurtured in the forest—as intimate with the passes of the Rocky Mountains as the citizen with Broadway; who lives where hunters and trappers have vexed every hill, and who cares no more for a Pawnee than a professed beau for a bright plumed belle."

But Crockett, aside from his reputation as a hunter and quaint story-teller, won popularity from his honesty, integrity and frankness of manner. Natural and unaffected, his daily life was a protest against false pretension, affectation, pomposity, the conventionalism and artificial manners of the pampered votaries of fashionable life. Crockett needed none of these circumstances to bring his greatness to light His tour to Boston was a perfect ovation. His words, casually dropped, were gathered up and treasured as genuine mint-drops.

Gen. George P. Morris, in the New York *Mirror*, wrote of Crockett, "We know not how many ages the fame of this gentleman will last, but he certainly makes a 'pretty considerable noise' in his own times; and though he may not be so great a man as Lafayette, it cannot be denied that he is a great man in his way. 'He who is fated to rise in the world will do so, in spite of all obstacles,' says the old adage; we firmly believe in its truth, and that Mr. Crockett, if he were not born great, was foreordained to achieve greatness. No rudeness of language can disguise strong sense and shrewdness; and a 'demonstration,' as Bulwer says, 'will force its way through all perversions of grammar.' David Crockett is neither grammatical nor graceful—we cannot say that he possesses eloquence; but verily there is something, a certain *je ne sais quoi* in the man that makes people attentive whenever he opens his mouth. Honest Davy, who knows as little of Lindley Murray as he does of Horace, hears his name resound from one end of the Union to the other. His fame rolls on increasing, like an avalanche, and burying beneath its mass the names of all the minor worthies of the West. The hunter of Columbia River, in his loudest boasting, calls himself the best man in the world, after David Crockett." (The above extract was written in February, 1834, two years before Crockett's death.)

A short time before, some author, led by the love of money, gave to the public a spurious work which he called "The Life of David Crockett." David, very indignant, promptly denied its authenticity, and forthwith disabused the world by writing a true memoir of himself called "David Crockett's Own Book," from which I have taken the liberty to quote freely, believing it difficult, and to me impossible, to improve upon the original text.

In summing up the character of Davy Crockett I may, without exaggeration, pronounce him a prototype of all that is noble, courageous, honest and unselfish devotion to principle. Had he been at Troy at the historic siege Homer would have immortalized him in his heroic verse.

MONUMENT ERECTED TO THE HEROES OF THE ALAMO

Life of
Kit Carson

KIT CARSON

CHAPTER I

The Heroes That Prepared the Way
for Western Settlement

Under wise and courageous leaderships the great West has been reclaimed from the savage, and in the desperate dispute for permanent possession of that rich and vast region lying beyond the Alleghenies many heroes were developed, whose names and valorous deeds deserve perpetuation in the annals of American history. But justice in this respect has been so tardy that we have now to deplore the fact that a majority of the brave spirits who participated in the wars and hardships of Western settlement have not even received the small need of a mention in the history of our progress as a nation. To those thus unremembered I beg to pay the tribute of my hearty apprecia-tion and praise, and to lay the laurel of my country's gratitude upon their neglected graves. Though unmarked be their beds, we may hope that fairy fingers bedeck them with sweetest wildwood flowers, and that the chorus of nature makes ceaseless music above their sacred dust.

The practice has long obtained among all nations of bestowing personal praise upon particular leaders in every victory, and giving scanty thanks, in general expres-sions, to those who fight in the ranks. I am sorry that circumstances prevent me from departing from that rule, for I can in truth and sincerity say, that for all my comrades, humble as many of them have been, if measured by the official positions they held, I entertain a warmth of friendship quite as great as if they were the mightiest kings of earth and value their good opinions no less highly. But I am debarred the plea-sure which an extended description of their brave and noble deeds would afford me by reason of my lack of knowledge of particulars, and because the number of those worthy of this recognition is so large that the necessary space is not at my disposal. To overcome the embarrassment of this position, somewhat, I have therefore chosen to describe the lives of three representative characters best known in frontier history, whose careers coincide with as many distinct periods; to wit, that of the flint-lock, percussion-cap, and repeating rifle. In the life of Boone we have a history of that period corresponding with the age, so to speak, of the flint-lock rifle, from 1770 to 1820; Crockett lived in the secondary period, or when the percussion-cap rifle had superseded the unreliable pan-flashing weapon of the very early settlers, his active career beginning at the close of that of Boone's and ending, as we have seen, in a blaze of heroism, in 1836. Carson belonged to the tertiary epoch of Western settlement, when the frontier had been pushed across the plains to the shores of the beating sea, and during whose eventful career the repeating rifle was invented and first brought into use. He was the natural successor of Crockett, both in the order of chronological sequence and as a promoter of Western civilization. We have, therefore, in the history of these three men a description of the reclamation and development of a belt of our country west of the Alleghenies, and south of the Mason and Dixon Line, and incidentally, sketches of many of the brave men who helped to make the first trail across the continent.

Anomalous Character of Kit Carson

No character of which history gives any account presents more anomalous peculiarities than that of Kit Carson. His whole nature was enigmatic, for no two persons, however intimate they might have been with him, whether on the plains or in the councils of white men or Indians, could agree in their estimation of his traits of character. Like the Temple of Janus, he always presented two or more unlike sides, each so distinctly prominent that those about him were invariably diverse in their opinions respecting his disposition. He was, apparently, at once the polished gentleman and the rough plainsman; shrinking from and courting danger at the same time; an adviser and the reckless mad-cap of his companions; large in his own estimation, yet modest and most unpretentious among his associates; a lover of peace, though still the organizer of discord. In brief, he was unlike any person save himself alone, and had it been possible his spirit would certainly have abandoned its own castle, so as to present a perfect dissimilarity. These strange peculiarities will be partly seen in the following biographical sketch, which pretends to no other merit than that of a faithful portraiture, after a thorough consideration of all the available facts connected with his remarkable career.

Christopher (Kit) Carson's birth-place has been variously located, and all authors who have attempted to write the history of his adventures have usually prefaced their labors with an argument attempting to prove their respective claims, some asserting that he was born in Kentucky, others in Illinois and yet others claiming Missouri as his place of nativity. The opinion of the writer, gained from proofs adduced by Peters and Burdett, both of whom have been Carson's biographers, is, that his native place was Madison County, Kentucky, where he was born on the 24th of December, 1809. In the following year the family removed to what was then Upper Louisiana, but what is now Missouri, settling in a region of country which, at this time, is defined as Howard County.

Missouri in the Early Days

Gen. John C. Fremont, during his great exploring expedition through the West in the years 1843–44, employed Kit Carson as his chief guide, and in giving an exhaustive report of his travels and discoveries devoted much space to a description of the renowned hunter and his wonderful adventures. The General, in this report, claims that Carson was a native of Boonslick County, Missouri, but as there is no such county in that State the assertion furnishes the proof of its own error. It is very probable, however, that Gen. Fremont meant Boone County, which adjoins Howard, and as Missouri was not organized into counties until some time after Carson's birth, being ceded to the United States by France in 1804 and admitted as a State in 1821, the causes which led to such an error are manifest. Another important fact in this connection affords a still readier means for determining the cause of the error referred to, and also the reasons which induced a removal of Kit Carson's father to Missouri, which may be stated as follows:

Directly after the formation of the territorial government over Missouri, the great Salt Springs of Howard County, bearing the name of "Boonslick," in honor of Daniel Boone, the famous Kentucky woodsman, became the center of attraction to all emigrants seeking homes west of the Mississippi River. Although this section of the country was occupied by numerous bands of Indians, none of the tribes offered any hostility to the settlement of white men on their lands, but the continued encroachments and rapid settlement finally incited cupidity and numerous crimes were the consequence. These salt works were operated by Major James Morrison, and with such success that they became the means of a rapid building up of the new territory.

One of the first offices opened by the United States for the sale of lands west of the Mississippi was in the vicinity of Boonslick in the year 1818, when Illinois had just been admitted to the sisterhood of States. It was immediately thronged with purchasers of lands which the settlers, however, had already been cultivating. Some of these had located themselves on the public domain as soon as it had been purchased by the United States, and foregoing personal safety and the comforts of refined society, had plunged into the wilderness and carved out homes with their own hands. Among this number was the father of Kit Carson, who became possessed of a fine tract of land on Bonne Femme Creek.

In the year 1810, when the infant Kit came to Missouri, the territory contained a population of 20,845 souls, and but a single newspaper, the *Gazette*, which is still running as the *Missouri Republican*. The primitive condition of the wilderness in which the brave hunter was to be reared, and the causes which led to his adoption of a hunter's life, destined to be so replete with adventure, can thus be readily conceived. The numerous Indian wars which engaged the settlers during the years of 1811 to 1820 it is hardly appropriate to describe here, especially since the father of Kit Carson rarely participated, or if he did no record is available from which the circumstances may be gathered.

Kit Bound to Service as a Saddler

Kit Carson's father, like nearly all the early settlers of Missouri, was extremely poor, and was sorely put to it in procuring the means for support of his large family. He spent most of his time hunting, subsisting off the meat thus obtained and depending for clothing upon the proceeds of sale of peltries, which dependence was so precarious that his children were generally so illy clad during winter that their suffering from cold was acute. When Kit was therefore fifteen years of age his father called him from the pursuit most congenial to his adventurous spirit (hunting), and bound him as an apprentice to a saddler named Workman. At this employment Kit continued faithfully for two years, but not from a natural inclination for the dull monotony of his engagement, for he longed to escape to wider and freer fields, having no intention of ever following such a trade even should he finish his service. The desire to throw off his yoke of servitude grew on him to such an extent that at length he deserted his master and, with the hope of gratifying his ambitions, joined a band of traders that passed the place where he was working en route for Santa Fe, New Mexico. This incident, which was the turning point in his life, occurred in 1826, when he was seventeen years of age, the most impressionable period in a youth's life, and it is but natural that the scenes and experiences of this, his first trip to a strange region, should excite a desire for new adventures in the wild sections of the far Southwest.

Carson Amputates the Arm of
a Wounded Comrade

When the expedition had proceeded as far as the Arkansas River, one of the teamsters, while carelessly handling a rifle, discharged the weapon and received the bullet in his left arm, shattering the bone and producing such a wound that he nearly bled to death before the flow of blood could be stopped with the rude remedies and appliances at hand. The arm was bandaged, however, and the expedition continued on until the third day thereafter, when unmistakable signs of gangrene were noticeable while dressing the wound, and it became apparent that the man's life could only be saved by an amputation of the arm. But who among the party could perform such an operation? One after another of the older members declined to undertake such a responsible duty, when Kit, seeing the extreme urgency of prompt action, stepped forward and volunteered his services, though not without confessing his inexperience and reluctance at attempting such a grave task. Nevertheless, he acted upon the principle, which he now thoroughly comprehended, that in desperate situations heroic remedies must be employed. After a search among the effects of the traders, no other instruments could be found useful in the operation than a razor, handsaw and a king-bolt. But rude as were these instruments Carson did not hesitate to use them. With the razor he carefully cut the flesh above the fracture and then while four men held the sufferer, he sawed the arm off as he would a stick of wood. A copious hemorrhage followed the amputation, but Carson had provided against fatal results from this cause by heating the king-bolt to an intense heat, which he now applied as a cautery and thus speedily stopped the flow of blood. Unskillful as was the operation it was, nevertheless, a success, for the man recovered and afterwards served with Carson in several expeditions.

Carson's First Fight with Indians

After the arrival of the traders at Santa Fe Carson abandoned the party and went to Fernandez de Taos, where he became intimate with a mountaineer and remained during the following year, engaged chiefly in breaking wild horses, which, after being caught, were kept in haciendos until a rider could be secured to domesticate them. Being thrown with Mexicans exclusively, Kit applied himself earnestly to the acquirement of the Spanish language, in which, after a year of study, he became sufficiently conversant to fill the position of interpreter to a rich American merchant named Trammell, with whom he made a trip to El Paso and Chihuahua. Leaving this service a year afterward, Carson became teamster in an expedition fitted out by Robt. M. Knight, for a trip to the copper mines on the Gila River, but returning within a few months he again visited Taos.

Having saved a few dollars from the services in which he had been employed, Kit spent some months in Taos, and until an opportunity was offered him to join a band of forty trappers under Ewing Young. These trappers were organized into a well armed body in order to repel the attacks of Indians, who bitterly resisted the attempts of white men to trap beavers on the waters of the Gila or its tributaries.

The party proceeded directly to Salt River, one of the affluents of the Rio Gila, upon reaching which they were attacked by a body of Indians, but the engagement was short and decisive. The Indians were routed with severe loss, leaving eleven of their number dead on the ground, their flight being too hasty to permit of carrying the fallen ones with them. This was Carson's first Indian fight, but he displayed the rare presence of mind and cool decision of character which at once furnish the true index to the success of his subsequent adventures.

After trapping with much success on the Salt and San Francisco Rivers, the company broke camp and divided, one portion returning to Santa Fe and the other, eighteen in number, including Carson, started for the Sacramento Valley, California. In this dreary journey, rendered more difficult by the dry deserts through which the route lay, the party suffered greatly for want of both food and water. So reduced did they become before reaching their destination that, availing themselves of the last resource, they killed several of their horses, drinking the blood and consuming the flesh of the faithful animals. Reaching the beautiful valley of the Sacramento, after weeks of exhausting effort, they began trapping again for beaver, in which occupation they spent several months most profitably.

Battle Between Twelve Whites and a Hundred Indians

Shortly before the close of the trapping season a band of Digger Indians came upon the party during the night and succeeded in driving off nearly all their horses, fleeing with the animals to the mountains. The Mohave Indians at the mission of San Gabriel, with whom the trappers had been maintaining commercial intercourse, kindly loaned the party the necessary number of horses to pursue the dusky thieves. Carson, though scarcely twenty years of age, had nevertheless demonstrated his marvelous abilities as a fighter, and to him was entrusted the leadership of the expedition for the recovery of the

RECONNOITERING THE INDIANS' POSITION

STORMING THE CAMP

stolen horses. Accordingly, selecting eleven of his comrades, and leaving the remainder to protect the camp and peltries, he started after the marauding Indians without having the slightest idea of their number. But discovering the trail soon after, no doubt was left that the band comprised not less than one hundred savages. But this fact did not deter him in his previously formed resolution, for he advanced with all possible speed through valleys and over mountains until the fresh trail admonished him to move more cautiously. More than a hundred miles from the trappers' camp the red skins were discovered during a late hour in the afternoon, just as they were going into camp for the night.

Having located the Indians and taken careful note of the surroundings, the time had now come for an exhibition of Carson's abilities. Twelve men set over against a hundred furnished an inequality which could only be compensated by extraordinary cunning and complete surprise. Kit was fully equal to the occasion, and his comrades having perfect confidence in the dexterity and capacity of their leader were prompt in obedience to his orders.

Carson disposed his men in such a manner that, while they remained concealed from view, they could yet readily distinguish every movement of the Indians, ascertain the location of sentinels and the weak points in the camp. Maintaining this position, the party awaited the approach of midnight before making an attack, the wisdom of which decision was determined in the result. Their purpose was assisted by the pall of darkness which fell on the landscape, rendering objects almost invisible except by a concentration of vision and a previous knowledge of the position occupied by the object sought.

When the auspicious hour had arrived Carson led his men in a careful detour, until having approached to the position it was necessary to first reach, he made a dash, followed by the others, directly through the Indian camp, shooting into the tents as they sped by, and whooping with such vigor that the horse thieves evidently believed that they had been surprised by an entire tribe of native enemies. The direst confusion followed this sudden attack, and as the greatest advantage was now offered, Carson and his men rushed on to the corral, where they found the Indians' horses tethered. These they speedily released and then stampeded, affording the party means of escape during the confusion, for Carson's good judgment told him that after the first tremor of surprise had run through the camp his enemies would recover their scattered senses and not only give battle but follow hard in pursuit.

Directing his men to secure at least one extra horse, some time was spent chasing the flying ponies over the mountains, but the darkness prevented the party from capturing any of the stampeded animals until the following day when thirty head were secured, and the trappers then returned to their companions, who had been oppressed with grave fears for their safety, and hailed their return with many manifestations of joy.

Carson Forced to Flee from Santa Fe

Shortly after this event the trappers, still accompanied by Mr. Young as the leader, broke camp, and with an immense quantity of beaver skins returned to Santa Fe over the same route they had passed in going to the Sacramento and San Jose Valleys. These products of their labors they disposed of, and upon a division of the proceeds, each man in the party was given $500 as his share. In possession of so much money, Carson was unable to restrain his bent for indulging freely in the dissipations peculiar to Mexican towns, and during this period of hilarious intercourse with the rude natives he became involved in a desperate street brawl, which terminated by his flight after having killed one of his opponents.

Being forced to leave New Mexico, owing to the numerous threats made against his life, Carson proceeded toward Missouri, but meeting a party of trappers under James Fitzpatrick, he joined them in a journey to Utah. For a time the party trapped on the Platte, Sweet Water, Goose and Salmon Rivers, but with indifferent success; besides, the Blackfeet Indians gave them constant anxiety, as the tribe was a very numerous and hostile one, whose delight was in massacring the whites.

In the spring of 1830 Kit Carson and four others left Mr. Fitzpatrick's party and proceeded to New Park, on the headwaters of the Arkansas, where they continued trapping in the company of Captain John Yount and twenty others, until the return of spring the following year. While wintering in camp a band of sixty Crow Indians robbed the party of several horses, to recapture which Carson was dispatched with fifteen men after the robbers.

Taking up the trail, he followed the Indians until he found them entrenched behind a rude fortification of logs with the stolen horses tied within ten feet of their shelter. Carson gave his men no time to reflect on the rashness of his undertaking, but ordering an immediate charge, rushed upon the protected savages, nor did he stop until he had seized the horses and led them triumphantly away. In this attack three of Carson's men were killed, but they were brought away, while five of the Indians were slain, one of whom was scalped by Carson himself.

Shortly after this daring attack Carson and Captain Yount's men were surprised by a force of two hundred Crow Indians, and the fleetness of their horses alone saved them from a massacre. The attack having been made after due preparation by the Indians they possessed all the advantages, not only in numbers, but also in effective fighting. No other recourse was therefore left Capt. Yount's party but to retreat and trust to the fleetness of their horses for escape. The flight continued under a rain of arrows and bullets for nearly fifty miles, the Indians being determined to possess themselves of the scalps and property of the little band of whites. Several of the party were killed, but Carson received only a slight wound. Had all the Indians been armed with rifles not one of the men would have escaped, but being able to keep a considerable distance in advance of their pursuers, the range was too great for the effective use of arrows, the few rifles the Indians possessed doing all the execution.

CHAPTER II

A Rash Undertaking

Of the several expeditions in which Carson participated up to this time the last one described had proved the least satisfactory and led him to believe that trapping could be carried on more successfully if conducted by small parties than if pursued by a considerable company. The Indians were everywhere extremely hostile, their natural opposition to an invasion of their hunting and trapping grounds being increased by the large numbers of whites engaged in the pursuit. Carson therefore concluded that a small party of two or three might succeed better, by reason of being able to the more easily disguise their operations and escape the notice of the Indians. Accordingly he decided to begin trapping on his own account. He therefore settled with Captain

Yount, and early in the spring of 1832 packed up his possessions and prepared to brave the dangers of the forest alone. But before setting out two favorite comrades who had been connected with Yount's party expressed their desire to accompany him, which companionship Carson accepted. The three proceeded up the streams into Colorado—or what is now known as Colorado—where they found the braver more abundant, and there pursued their labors with considerable profit for nearly a year. Returning to Taos with their furs they sold out to much advantage, and immediately afterward Carson joined Capt. Lee in an expedition up Green River.

Capt. Lee's company consisted of thirty trappers under the direction of an old mountaineer named Robideau. This experienced trapper had engaged the services of a young California Indian as a guide and interpreter, such native assistant being rendered necessary by the hostile character of roving Indians which the trappers were constantly meeting.

In the following October, 1833, while the party was encamped on a tributary of Green River, and meeting with much success catching both beaver and otter, the young Indian guide contrived to clandestinely secure six of the best horses belonging to the company and made his escape. The theft was soon discovered, and Kit Carson, who had now become a renowned "thief-catcher," was deputed to recover the stolen animals.

The thieving redskin having had several hours the start, and Carson being little acquainted with the country, he procured the services of a Utah Indian to assist him in tracing the fugitive.

Killing an Indian at Long Range

The trail was not definitely determined until the second day after Kit and his companion had started out, but once they became certain of the discovery the speed at which their pursuit was conducted, after one hundred miles had been made, disabled the Utah Indian's horse so that he could proceed no further, and being unwilling to accompany Kit on foot, he returned again to the camp of his tribe. Carson, however, not to be deterred in his undertaking, pressed on alone and after a half-day's further ride discovered the thieving Indian riding one of the stolen horses and leading the five others. Almost at the same moment that Carson sighted the Indian the fugitive also saw his pursuer, and a fight to the death each realized was inevitable. The Indian, who carried a rifle and was regarded as an excellent shot, besides being possessed of the courage to make his skill in an encounter most effective, leaped from his horse and sought shelter. Kit fully comprehended the tactics of the Indian, and the distance being great between them he concluded to hazard a shot, knowing that

CARSON KILLS AN INDIAN THIEF AT LONG RANGE

he could reload before the Indian could reach him, especially since he was mounted. Therefore, stopping his horse, Kit drew a bead on the Indian as he was making for a tree, and fired. The aim was so perfect that the thief fell forward dead, with a bullet through his body. This shot was in a measure accidental, for the distance was fully three hundred yards, and the Indian being at the time in a brisk run, the aim was rendered more doubtful.

The six horses were recovered and returned to the camp after an absence of six days, and for his services Captain Lee and Robideau presented Carson with a large quantity of peltries, which made the incident one of great profit to him.

In the following year, 1834, Carson, in company with three excellent companions, concluded to spend a season trapping on the Laramie, a stream reputed to be fairly alive with beaver, otter and mink. The expectations of the party were fully realized a few weeks later, when they had pitched their tents on the banks of that clear, but sometimes doubtful river. In fact, during all of Carson's experience as a trapper, he never met with success equal to that which he found on the Laramie.

Thrilling Adventure with a Grizzly Bear

On one occasion, while he was acting as hunter during this most profitable season, to obtain a fresh supply of meat, he met with an adventure so full of peril that he never afterward entertained the least desire to be similarly situated. Game of every kind was very abundant, and within a mile of the camp he killed a large elk, but as he was

CARSON'S ADVENTURE WITH A GRIZZLY BEAR

proceeding to cut its throat, suddenly there appeared, coming toward him, a species of game for which he had not been hunting. A large grizzly bear, one of the most ferocious and dreadful denizens of North American forests, moved by hunger, resolved, apparently, to make the hunter its victim. Time was just now very precious to Kit, so that he made all possible use of his extremities in reaching the nearest tree, leaving his unloaded gun lying beside the animal he had just killed. The bear, not discovering the dead elk, made directly for Kit, who managed, but just how he was never able to tell, to ascend a goodly sized tree in time to save himself from the voracious maw of the terrible beast. But his perch appeared decidedly unsafe, as the bear would rear up almost to the limb on which he was seated, opening its mighty jaws and blowing hot gusts of air through teeth nearly as long as a man's finger. At every lunge it made Kit felt that the bear would surely reach him, which caused him to involuntarily hitch up his legs while all the flesh would crawl as though it were trying to get on top of his head. Grabbing about for something with which to defend himself, he twisted off a branch from the tree, and this he dexterously used in striking the nose of the grizzly whenever it reached up its head uncomfortably close. This so enraged the brute that it fell to gnawing the body of the tree, but being able to make but little impression, abandoned that and began growling with a fierceness which made Kit quake with the most direful anticipations.

The bear kept him a prisoner in the tree until nearly midnight, when it began to walk around the spot, gradually extending the circle until it at length scented the dead elk, upon which it speedily gorged itself, and then disappeared in the woods. Kit got down from his anxious seat speculating on the probabilities of the bear's return, and though every bone in his body seemed to be splitting from the strain to which he had been subjected, he nevertheless made excellent speed toward the camp. His comrades had become very much alarmed at his prolonged absence, and a safe return fully compensated them for their beaver supper, from which unsavory game they had been compelled to satisfy their hunger in the absence of more desirable meat.

Carson Wounded While Saving a Friend

After collecting several hundred valuable peltries, Carson and his companions went to Santa Fe, where the product of their season's trapping was disposed of satisfactorily. But Kit did not remain idle more than a few days, for he soon found opportunity of joining another party of fifty men bound for the Blackfeet country, on the Upper Missouri. The trip was a long and tedious one, and in the end proved not only unprofitable but disastrous to several of the men, including Kit himself, for they had struck a country in which none of them had ever been before, and to add to their other hardships they had penetrated a section held by a tribe of the most treacher-ous and cruel Indians on the frontier, which made eternal watchfulness the price of their safety.

Shortly after the encampment of the party on Big Snake River, a band of Blackfeet stampeded the horses of the whites and stole eighteen of their best ani-mals. Carson, to whom the whole company looked for needful assistance, at once proposed pursuit, and taking twenty of the best men in the expedition, set out after the thieves. A heavy snow covered the ground, which made the trail easy to follow until on the succeeding night, when another fall of snow began to rapidly obliter-ate the tracks. The pursuit was continued with all possible speed until the trail had become so nearly extinct that Kit and another experienced trailer named Markland had to leave their horses from time to time during the night and search for the tracks by the aid of small torches.

The party rode for a distance of seventy-five miles, the latter half of the journey being made through extraordinary difficulties, before they came in sight of the Indians. The thieving Blackfeet, numbering about forty warriors, discovered their pursuers, but instead of trying to escape, stopped and desired a parley with the trappers, which being consented to, some time was spent in speech-making and pipe-smoking. The Indians declared that they had no intention of wronging the whites, and had taken

CARSON WOUNDED WHILE TRYING TO SAVE A FRIEND

the horses because they thought the animals belonged to the Snake Indians, their enemies. But with all their protestations of friendship, they still refused to deliver up the stolen animals. An attempt was then made by the trappers to take their property by force, which brought on a fight as Kit had anticipated.

The Indians were armed chiefly with bows and arrows, but a few of them had rifles, which they had obtained at various trading posts. The Indians, therefore, while twice as many in number as the trappers, were not nearly so well armed, and the fighting advantages were about equal. Every man, red and white alike, sought the protection of trees and carried on the battle with all the cunning available. Carson and Markland were bosom companions and fought from adjacent shelters. It chanced that they were directly opposed by two swarthy warriors, each of whom was also armed with a rifle. As Kit sought opportunity to fire at his antagonist he discovered another Indian in the act of taking a deadly aim at Markland, who was unconscious of his own danger. Kit instantly turned his weapon on the Indian and shot him dead, thereby saving his comrade's life; but in this commendable act he came near sacrificing his own life, for the Indian he had been previously watching fired, the bullet striking Kit in the left shoulder, shattering the bone and making a terrible wound. The fight continued with unabated fury until nightfall, when the Indians drew off, taking their stolen property with them.

Carson was found by his companions lying in the snow perfectly conscious, but refusing to make any manifestation of the great suffering he was enduring. He had gathered his coat in a lump at the shoulder, trying to staunch the flow of blood which had saturated the clothing on his left side. The cold had at last stopped the ebbing life-current, but not until he was so weak that it became necessary to carry him back over the long route and through the deep snow to the trappers' camp. Three others of the party were killed and four wounded, but those that were injured were fortunately able to ride. It was a terrible journey to Kit, but he endured his sufferings with such fortitude that those who ministered to his needs could not comprehend how severe was the pain he felt.

Carson's Duel with a Big Frenchman

Upon their return to camp, Capt. Bridger took thirty men and started out again after the depredating Blackfeet, but though he beat the country for more than a week, he was unable to find the trail, and so returned without accomplishing anything.

Soon after this unfortunate incident in the season on Big Snake River, the party left that immediate section and camped on Green River, where they were joined by a large party of Frenchmen and Canadians who were trapping for the Hudson Bay Fur

Company. The camp, by these accessions, numbered about one hundred men, a force sufficient to afford some security against hostile Indians.

Carson was not long in establishing a most favorable reputation among the men, because, while some in the party knew how courageously he had always deported himself in moments of extreme peril, they all soon learned that under every circumstance he remained courteous and obliging, which won respect quite as quickly as his reputation for bravery.

Among the number of imported trappers was a large Frenchman named Shuman; a man particularly fond of bad whisky and who delighted in bullying his companions. He was rarely engaged in a fight himself, because his arrogant boasts had intimidated nearly all the men; but not content with his own autocratic domineering, he found pleasure in creating discord and embroiling comrades. On one occasion, while riding about the camp with gun in hand, Shuman, among other indiscriminate insults, began a tirade of abuse directed against the Americans, pronouncing them scullions and chicken-livered scoundrels, who merited nothing but thrashings with hickory withes for their cowardice and villainy. This unprovoked language aroused the spirit of Carson, who stepped forward toward the boasting Frenchman and said:

"I am an American, and no coward; but you are a vaporing bully, and to show you how Americans can punish liars, I'll fight you here in any manner your infamous heart may desire."

Shuman fairly boiled over with rage at this proposition from a man so far inferior to him in size; besides, he had never before had his privilege of abusing the men questioned. He therefore replied:

"If you want to be killed I have no objections to shooting you as I would a dog. Get on your horse and fight me, starting at one hundred yards and riding toward each other, firing as we come together. Come on, you pale-faced little scullion!"

Kit returned no answer to this arrogant acceptance of his challenge, but mounting his horse he prepared for the duel. The two first rode apart, each divining the purpose of the other, until a proper distance was reached, when they wheeled their horses as if entering a race course under stipulations,

CARSON'S DUEL WITH THE FRENCHMAN

and rushed toward each other. The entire camp was, of course, speedily apprised of the duel, and every trapper came out to witness the combat, the sympathies of the men being unanimously with Carson. Shuman was an excellent rifleman and had trained himself to fire from his running horse by shooting buffaloes, and he therefore felt confident of putting a bullet through the head of his adversary. Kit carried a pistol, but this was from choice, as he was an expert with that weapon. The two determined men rushed toward each other like knights of mediaeval chivalry, until within a few yards, when Shuman raised himself in his stirrups, and taking aim, fired. The bullet went so close to the mark that a lock of Kit's hair was seen to fall, cut from above his ear. But the aim, though good, had not dispatched a fatal messenger, and Shuman was compelled to take Kit's fire. The smoke from the Frenchman's rifle was still rolling away over his head when Carson presented his pistol almost as the heads of the two horses came together, and saluted his enemy. The ball struck Shuman in the hand, and passing upward in the arm, lodged near the elbow. Though not fatal, the wound was sufficient to thoroughly humble the desperado, and so change his disposition as to eliminate all braggadocio from his character.

At the Point of Starvation

Soon after this incident the party of trappers returned to New Mexico, and there Carson joined Capt. McCoy, who was outfitting for another expedition to the Yellowstone in the Blackfeet country. This party, consisting of a dozen men, upon arriving at the Yellowstone found no signs of either beaver or otter; so breaking camp, they set out to hunt a stream affording reasonable expectations for success. They continued to travel through a country supporting nothing but artemesia, which barely subsisted their horses, until all their provisions were exhausted and starvation seriously threatened the whole party.

Day after day went by and still neither game nor grass roots could be found until at length they were reduced to such dreadful extremities that to prevent death from starvation they bled their horses and drank the blood. Happily, when it was decided to kill one of the horses for its flesh, a body of Snake Indians appeared, from whom a fat pony was purchased and this the party killed and subsisted upon until they reached Ft. Hall.

After a rest of several days Carson, McCoy and the other members of the party equipped themselves for another trapping expedition, this time intending to plant their traps on Green River, but on arriving at that stream another party of nearly one hundred men was found who, meeting with no success, were preparing to leave for the headwaters of the Yellowstone, and if finding no game there had arranged to follow up to the Missouri River sources.

A consolidation was made between the two parties, who now selected Carson and Mr. Fontenelle as their leaders. This union of forces was made more as a precaution against the Blackfeet Indians, who were very numerous and vindictive in the Yellowstone country.

The winter, which was very severe, was passed among the Crow Indians, who were well provided with large lodges made of buffalo hides; some of these were twenty feet in diameter with an opening at the top which served as a chimney to permit the smoke from the fire inside to escape. But it was difficult to provide food for the trappers' horses, owing to a deep snow which covered the ground during the entire winter. It was necessary to feed their horses on bark stripped from cottonwood trees, and twigs of willow, a collection of which involved almost constant work.

Extraordinary Bravery of Carson in Saving a Fallen Comrade

When spring appeared the trappers started out to begin operations, but their first attempts were discovered by the Blackfeet, who, though greatly reduced in numbers by small-pox which had raged among them during the winter, were still a powerful tribe. Carson, with forty men, was attacked at their traps and it was only by the most desperate fighting that they saved themselves from annihilation. The Indians were kept in check until the trappers' ammunition was almost exhausted, when a retreat was made back toward the camp. During this movement a horse, bearing one of the trappers, stumbled and fell in such a manner that the rider was thrown with great violence, and for a time, rendered unconscious. Five Indians rushed rapidly forward on their horses to scalp the unlucky rider; seeing which Carson ran back to the aid of his prostrate comrade. He shot the foremost Indian and held the others at bay until he revived the trapper when the two retreated to a place of security, the Indians being too cowardly to push their advantage.

It was not long before the other trappers, who had gone off in a southeasterly direction to place their traps, hearing the firing, ran to the rescue of Carson's party. With a fresh supply of ammunition and re-enforced by sixty men, Carson turned on the Indians and the fight was renewed with great earnestness by both sides. The Indians were at last defeated with a loss of so many of their warriors that they beat a retreat and never afterward molested the victorious trappers.

After prosecuting their operations for two months a large number of peltries were secured and the expedition then broke camp and repaired to the trading post on Nend River, where the skins were sold at a large profit.

CARSON'S BRAVE RESCUE OF A COMRADE

Carson's next enterprise was in trapping for beaver on the streams flowing from the Rocky Mountains into Great Salt Lake. He took with him only a single companion, believing he could operate more successfully without being restricted by the limitations of a large party, as the Utah Indians regarded him with friendly feelings, but opposed the invasion of their territory by any considerable number of white men.

Carson's Terrible Fight with a Mountain Lion

It was while trapping in this section that he met with an adventure of a truly thrilling character. He was walking along the bank of a stream where many of his traps were set, while his companion was back in camp preparing supper. Carson had a large rifle with him, as was his custom, and seeing a turkey strutting along a few yards in

CARSON'S BATTLE WITH A MOUNTAIN LION

advance, was preparing to shoot it when his attention was directed to a pair of fierce eyes gleaming from out the roots of a great tree. It was scarcely twenty feet away, and a moment's inspection convinced him that he was in the presence of a powerful mountain lion. To retreat he knew would have invited the attack he felt was about to be made, so raising his rifle he fired, but there was such a profusion of snake-like roots surrounding the lion's body that his shot resulted only in an exasperating wound, as it struck the animal in the left shoulder. In the next instant the lion was upon him, roaring like its ancestral kith of African jungles. Carson had no other weapon now save the large knife he carried, and with this he defended himself most valiantly. But the sharp poniard-like claws of the ferocious beast penetrated his flesh and cut like a two-edged sword. Carson's shirt was ripped off him and while he slashed with his knife and thrust it to the hilt time and again into the lion's body, the infuriated animal still fought with such success that, weakened by the loss of so much blood, Carson was fairly on the point of yielding. But it is hard to give up life, and this universal human feeling impelled Kit to use his last energies in this terrible contest. Fortune at last favored him, for the lion also much exhausted, fell under one of Carson's blows and as it rolled on to its back with its dreadful fangs still fastened in the remnants of Kit's tattered shirt, a plunge of the knife deep into the animal's throat, severing its head almost from the body, terminated the battle in Carson's favor.

But the victory was purchased at a great expense, for the wounded trapper was so overcome by the lacerations of his flesh and sinews that he fainted and would undoubtedly have died had not his comrade in camp, alarmed at his long absence, instituted a search which resulted in the discovery of the bleeding and unconscious body of his companion lying beside the dead lion. Kit was carried back to the camp and given all the care that one true and anxious comrade can give another. This tender and excellent treatment renewed the life so near exhausted, and after a month of dangerous suspension between life and death, Carson began to recover rapidly, and in another month was able to renew his labors.

Carson's Marriage to an Indian Girl

After returning from his trapping expedition in Utah, which, despite his terrible fight with the mountain lion, had proved a profitable one, Carson returned to New Mexico and there made an engagement with Messrs. Bent and St. Vrain to hunt and supply the garrison at Bent's Fort with meat. It was during this occupation that he married an Indian girl belonging to the Comanche tribe. This union was severed ten months after by the singular devotion of the Indian wife, who learning of Carson's illness at Ft. Hall, immediately mounted a horse and rode the one hundred miles that separated her from him in twelve hours. This exertion, which was made within two weeks after she had given birth to a daughter, brought on a fever from which she died in a few days.

Carson sincerely mourned the loss of his young wife, who, though she was an Indian, possessed many noble qualities of heart, not the least being her soul-absorbing love for her husband. The little girl baby was well cared for by a Mexican family, and lived and grew under their kind treatment. Five years after the death of his wife Kit visited St. Louis, taking his child with him for the purpose of placing her in an educational institution, that she might have the advantage of excellent schooling and training. The little girl developed into a stately and beautiful woman, and when twenty years of age she married a gentleman in St. Louis named Boggs, who is at this time a resident of Los Animos, Colorado, where Kit Carson, Jr., also has his handsome residence.

CHAPTER III

Carson Engaged as Guide to the Fremont Expedition

When Carson arrived in St. Louis he was received with public demonstrations of delight and there were none too great or rich to pay him homage, as he had long been regarded as "The Monarch of the Plains."

At the time of this visit it chanced that Gen. John C. Fremont was in the city, organizing an expedition for exploring that part of the country lying between Missouri and the Rocky Mountains. Although this was his original intention, the General made the overland trip to California, and included in his report all the explorations along the entire route.

Gen. Fremont sent for Carson, as soon as the presence of the great trapper became known to him, and a long interview between the two resulted in the employment of Carson as chief guide to the expedition, which left St. Louis by steamer the 22d of May, 1842. The other members of the exploring party consisted of twenty-one men, principally Creoles, Charles Preuso, first assistant in the topographical survey, and Louis Maxwell, of Kaskaskia, Illinois, who was engaged as hunter.

The expedition disembarked from the steamer at the mouth of the Kaw River, and then struck across the broad prairies of Kansas on to the Platte River, for the exploration of which a large rubber boat was carried with them, which was very useful on several occasions. From the South Platte they followed the Oregon Trail past Fort Laramie and from thence on to the Rocky Mountains.

An Exciting Buffalo Hunt

Just before leaving the Platte the monotony of the journey was relieved by a grand buffalo hunt, which Gen. Fremont describes as follows:

"As we were riding quietly along the bank, a great herd of buffalo, some seven or eight hundred in number, came crowding up from the river, where they had been to drink, and commenced crossing the plain slowly, eating as they went. The wind was favorable; the coolness of the morning invited to exercise; the ground was apparently good, and the distance across the prairie (two or three miles) gave us a fine opportunity to charge them before they could get among the river hills. It was too fine a prospect for a chase to be lost; and halting for a few moments, the hunting horses were brought up and saddled and Kit Carson, Maxwell and I started together. The buffaloes were now somewhat less than half a mile distant, and we rode easily along until within about three hundred yards, when a sudden agitation, a wavering in the herd, and a galloping to and fro of some which were scattered along the skirts, gave us the intimation that we were discovered. We now started together at a hard gallop, riding steadily abreast of each other, and here the interest of the chase became so engrossingly intense that we were sensible to nothing else. We were closing upon them rapidly, and the front of the mass was already in rapid motion.

"A crowd of bulls, as usual, brought up the rear, and every now and then some of them faced about, and then dashed on after the herd, and then turned and looked again as if more than half inclined to stand and fight. In a few moments, however, during which we had been quickening our pace, the rout was universal, and we were going over the ground like a hurricane. When at about thirty yards, we gave the usual shout (the hunter's *pas de charge*) and broke into the herd. We entered on the side, the mass giving way in every direction in their heedless course. Many of the bulls, less active and less fleet than the cows, paying no attention to the ground, and occupied solely with the hunter, were precipitated to the earth with great force, rolling over and over with the violence of the shock, and hardly distinguishable in the dust. We separated on entering the herd, each singling out his own game.

"My horse was a trained hunter, famous in the West under the name of Provean, and with his eyes flashing, and the foam flying from his mouth, sprang on after the cow I was pursuing like a hungry tiger. In a few moments he brought me alongside of her, and rising in the stirrups, I fired at the distance of a yard, the ball entering at the termination of the long hair, and passing near the heart. She fell headlong at the report of the gun, and, checking my horse, I looked around for my companions.

"At a little distance Kit was on the ground engaged in tying his horse to the horns of a cow, which he was preparing to cut up. Among the scattered bands at some distance below I caught a glimpse of Maxwell, and while I was looking a light wreath of white smoke curled away from his gun, from which I was too far to hear the report. Nearer and between me and the hill was the body of the herd, and giving my horse the reins we dashed after them. A thick cloud of dust hung upon their rear which filled my mouth and eyes and nearly smothered me. In the midst of this I could see nothing and the buffaloes were not distinguishable until within thirty feet.

"They crowded together more densely still as I came upon them and rushed along in such a compact body that I could not obtain an entrance—the horse almost leaping upon them. In a few moments the mass divided to the right and left, the horns clattering with a noise above everything else, and my horse darted into the opening.

"Five or six bulls emerged on us as we dashed along the line, but were left far behind, and singling out a cow I gave her my fire, but struck too high. She gave a tremendous leap and scoured on swifter than before. I reined up my horse and the band swept on like a torrent and left the place quiet and clear. Our chase had led us into dangerous ground, a prairie-dog village, so thickly settled that there were three or four holes in every twenty yards square, occupying the whole bottom for nearly two miles in length."

While Gen. Fremont was making his second attack on the herd Carson left the buffalo which he had killed and partly cut up to pursue a large bull that came rushing by him alone. He chased the game for nearly a quarter of a mile, not being able to gain rapidly owing to the blown condition of his horse. Coming up at length to the side of the fleeing buffalo Carson fired, but at the same instant his horse stepped into a prairie-dog hole, going down and throwing Kit over his head fully fifteen feet. The bullet struck the buffalo low under the shoulder, which only served to so enrage him that the next moment the infuriated animal was pursuing Kit, who, fortunately not much hurt, was able to run toward the river. It was a race for life now, Carson using his nimble heels to the utmost of their capacity, accelerated very much by the thundering, bellowing bull bringing up the rear. For several minutes it was nip and tuck which should reach the Platte River first, but Kit got there by a scratch a little in advance. It was a big stream, and deep water under the bank, but heavens! it was paradise indeed compared with the hades plunging at his back, so Kit leaped into the water, trusting to providence that the bull would not follow. The trust was well placed for the bull did not continue the pursuit, but stood on the bank and shook his fists— head—vehemently at the struggling hunter, who preferred deep waves to the horns of a dilemma on shore.

Kit swam around for some time, carefully guarded by the bull, until his position was observed by Maxwell, who attacked the belligerent animal successfully with a No. 44 slug, and then Kit crawled out and—skinned the enemy.

Carson Acts as Guide to Fremont's Second Expedition

Carson continued with Fremont until the expedition reached Laramie, after Fremont's ascent to the summit of the loftiest peak in the Rocky Mountain range. Upon leaving the expedition Carson returned to New Mexico, where, in 1843, he contracted a second marriage, espousing a Mexican lady, with whom he lived happily for many years, and who gave him two children, a boy and a girl, the former, Kit Carson, Jr., reaching manhood, but the daughter died while young.

Carson engaged his services again to Bent & St. Vrain, for whom he hunted and acted as courier, until, learning that Fremont had started out on a second expedition of exploration, and was within two days' journey of Fort Bent, he decided to visit him. When Carson came into General—then Lieutenant —Fremont's presence, the latter, after greeting him with great warmth, said:

FREMONT HOISTING THE STARS AND STRIPES ON THE
HIGHEST PEAK OF THE ROCKIES

"Carson, you are the man, of all others, I am most delighted to see. If I had known your address I should certainly have communicated my desire to have you accompany me on the present expedition; but since I am so fortunate as to meet you at my camp, your services, I trust, will be given me."

Carson had not thought of accompanying Fremont, but being offered a good salary, he gave his consent. First returning to Fort Benton for a number of mules, which Fremont required, he came back to the rendezvous, after which, heading the cavalcade, the expedition moved westward for the Sacramento Valley.

On the 21st of August, 1844, the party of hardy adventurers reached Bear River, and descending that stream twenty miles, they came upon the Great Salt Lake, which Fremont, in company with Carson and two other members of the expedition, circumnavigated in their rubber boat. From this point the journey was continued until Nez Perce was reached, which was a trading post established by the Hudson Bay Fur Company in Northern California. This was the western limit of Fremont's journey, as at this point a connection was made with Commander Wilkes, who had completed the survey eastward from San Francisco.

After a rest of several days, Fremont sent Carson to the Dallas, with instructions to prepare a number of pack-saddles, blankets, provisions and other things needful for a long expedition during the winter, having determined to start back upon his return journey at once. Notwithstanding the fact that it was now almost midwinter, the bold explorer had decided to pass through a new section of country, thereby adding to his discoveries upon the return. He therefore chose a route which would take him, first, to Tlamath Lake, and from there by a southeast course to the Great Basin; thence to the Buenaventura River, and from thence to the Rocky Mountains at the headwaters of the Arkansas, and then strike Bent's Fort, from which place the government trail would be taken for St. Louis.

This projected route for the return journey, or at least a greater portion of it, was practically *terra incognita* to white men, and therefore concealed obstacles which put to the severest test man's powers of endurance.

The entire party consisted of twenty-five persons, comprising six distinct nationalities, several of them being under age, one of whom, a son of Hon. Thomas H. Benton, was only a lad. But provision having been made, the journey was begun about the latter part of December with light hearts and joyous anticipations. Two Indian guides were engaged at Vancouver's to conduct the party through to Tlamath Lake, which proved to be only a shallow basin containing a little water when the snows were melting during spring time. From this place they started for Mary's Lake without any guide save the compasses they carried. This journey brought them into a land of desolation, in which several perished from cold and starvation, their pack animals were lost, and progress was made only by carving a highway through snow often twenty feet in depth. But as Gen. Fremont has himself often graphically described the perils and terrible hardships of this expedition while searching for Mary's Lake and Buenaventura River, it is useless to repeat the incidents of the expedition here.

Fort Sutter was not reached until the 6th of March, at which time the horses belonging to the expedition had been reduced from sixty-seven to thirty-three, from which, and considering the men who died and were lost, the terrible, almost unparalleled sufferings of the men in this unfortunate expedition may be approximated by the reader. Those of the party who reached Sutter were so reduced by privations they had suffered on the dreary route that each man was little more than an animate skeleton of skin and bone, and their horses were so poor and weak that not one could bear the burden of a rider, so that they had to be led.

An abundant store of good provisions was set before the famished party that while proving a blessing to all was not without its dangers. The men had been so long without food that it was impossible to restrain their appetites even by warnings against filling their empty stomachs with strong meats. The men ate ravenously, and when the feasting was concluded two of the party became raving maniacs, from their inordinate indulgence. This necessitated a stay at the fort for a considerable time, for all were sick and the two most unfortunate required the closest watching for nearly two weeks before their reason was restored.

A Thrilling Incident on the Return Trip

Four days after Fremont's party had started from Fort Sutter, on their return, and while going into camp for the night, they were surprised by the sudden appearance of two men approaching over the crest of a hill evidently making for the camp. Such a sight, in a country so barren, and beset with so many dangers, was well calculated to excite wonder and Carson was immediately upon the alert to discover what new adventure was thus promised. The two strangers came on in great haste until they reached the camp, when exhausted by their exertions in running, they fell in a faint, and were unable for some time to utter a word. Their breath being at length recovered they related in a manner that showed their extreme agitation the particulars of a calamity that had befallen them on the day before. The two strangers proved to be Mexicans who had by rare good fortune made their escape from a band of Indians that had attacked and killed two of their companions and carried away as captives the wife and mother of the speakers. They implored the help of some of Fremont's men to aid them in recovering the women and horses that had been thus stolen.

Appeals, such as the Mexicans made, always found a ready response in Carson's heart and in a few minutes he was mounted and ready to enter upon a pursuit after the marauders. Another man of Fremont's party named Godey volunteered to accompany him and together they set out at once with one of the two Mexicans as guide. After traveling at great speed all night they came upon the Indian trail, but before they had followed it many miles the Mexican's horse

CAPTURE OF THE TWO MEXICAN WOMEN

gave out and he was left behind. Carson and Godey continued on in hot pursuit but, unable to come up with the Indians after a hard day's ride they went into camp on the second night to refresh themselves and their horses. Early the following morning they again mounted and pressed on, but before going a mile further they discovered smoke rising above the trees that lined a small ravine, which admonished them to pause and reconnoiter. Crawling carefully to the summit of a knoll which was covered with grass and a thick growth of artemisia, but which commanded a view of the ravine below, they discovered a band of thirty Indians making a breakfast off horse-flesh. Towards the right, about one hundred yards from the camp, were nearly forty horses, all picketed, and grazing in a close body. Carson and Godey now turned towards the horses, hoping to be able to draw the pickets and then stampede the animals, which would have left the Indians unmounted and no means for pursuit, thus placing them practically at Carson's mercy. But before the horses could be reached, a colt sprang out from a thicket where it had been concealed, and ran whinnying towards the herd. This alarmed the horses and in turn the Indians became apprised of the presence of some bold intruder. In another moment there was a commotion in the camp and every Indian seized his weapon and prepared to meet any danger. Carson and Godey were still in the grass but they knew their position must soon be discovered, in which event their fate could not long be averted. In moments of extreme peril, self-possession and the courage to act with decision are the surest aids to preservation. It was the possession of these traits of character that distinguished Carson in his long, adventurous and successful career as a plainsman and which secured his safety in the dangerous situation he now found himself. Understanding thoroughly the Indians' cowardice in the presence of a concealed enemy, Carson and his companion opened fire upon the excited savages, and with such excellent aim that two were instantly killed. As the great scout had foreseen, the Indians were so surprised at the sudden attack that they at once concluded the attacking party was only the advance guard of a large one which was about to surround them, and like a pack of scared coyotes they fled in such haste and terror that several of the horses and all of their camping outfit were abandoned.

When the Indians had made good their escape, Carson and Godey returned to their horses and then rode back to the camp where they witnessed a sight well calculated to excite a desire for vengeance. Beside a burning log were the bodies of two white men each pierced with a score of arrows and horribly mutilated, while ten yards away were the naked bodies of the two Mexican women, through each of which a large stake had been driven pinning them to the ground. That these horrible atrocities had been perpetrated on the victims while alive was evident from the look of agony that was on the face of each; nor were these cruelties all that the four unfortunates suffered before death came to their relief, for their persons had been subjected to indignities not to be described in print.

Carson and Godey interred the bodies as best they could and then taking the horses that had been abandoned, made their way back to the camp of their companions. The two Mexicans were there awaiting the result of the pursuit, and when they learned of the fearful fate that had befallen the women their grief was really pitiful to see. They refused every offer of assistance, or to accompany the expedition, but sat down beside the camp-fire where they were left by Fremont's party, giving expression to their sorrow in hysterical exclamations, nor did Carson ever afterwards hear anything concerning them, though it is more than probable that they perished from some of the many dangers that surrounded them.

CHAPTER IV

The War in California

Returning again to Taos after the second expedition disbanded, Carson cast about for several months in quest of some employment. Nothing better offering, in the spring of 1845 he entered into partnership with a man named Owen and started a sheep-ranch. The two were old acquaintances, having served together in both of Fremont's expeditions, and it is not strange to find that they were both much better content when following a life of wild adventure than in the calm tranquility and uneventful occupation they had now chosen. Therefore when Fremont projected a third expedition and again called for Carson's services, the sheep-ranch was disposed of at a reckless sacrifice and the two made all possible haste to join their old commander at Bent's Fort on the Upper Arkansas.

The journey of this last expedition lay through the same country over which they had passed previously, but while there was no lack of suffering on this trip the party experienced few trials to be compared with those met with before. After reaching Sutter's Fort the expedition recruited and marched toward Monterey, but were met en route by Gen. Castro at the head of four hundred Mexicans, who opposed Fremont's further progress and ordered his immediate return. Although Fremont had but forty men, each one had been tried in the crucible of hard experience and knew how to meet any opposition, so by skillful tactics they evaded Castro and moved on to Monterey, where there were a number of Americans ready to join them, appreciating the probabilities of a war between Mexico and the United States, which was then being prepared for.

Very soon after this the war tocsin was sounded, and Fremont, with Carson as his first lieutenant, was duly enlisted for the fray, in which they contested with commendable valor and made their power felt throughout California.

A Fierce Battle with Indians

The Mexicans, though overwhelming in numbers, hesitated to attack Fremont, knowing the mettle of his small force, and sought to accomplish the destruction of the whites by instigating the Apache Indians to attack them, who could marshal a large army of redoubtable warriors at ten days' notice, and were, as they are to-day, distinguished for their cruelty. So well did the Mexicans manage their Indian allies, that while Fremont was in quarters at Lawson's Post word reached him of the approach of a thousand Apaches all well armed and mounted, determined upon the destruction of every white man in California. Lawson's Post was not built with any view of offering resistance to an enemy; in fact, being located in a basin around which were towering hills, it presented an excellent target for an investing army. A council of war was therefore speedily held, at which it was decided to abandon the post and to march against the enemy, and if possible, fall upon the Indians when they were least expecting an attack. These tactics had often been employed with success by Carson, and Fremont now placed him in active command of the little force, though his rank was that of Lieutenant.

SURPRISING THE APACHE CAMP

The company proceeded nearly fifty miles before they discovered the position of the Indians, but their progress had been slow in order to save their animals from fatigue, appreciating the need of fresh horses should the enemy be met with by day and given time to make a charge. Fortune, however, favored the explorers for, by keeping two scouts a mile or more in advance, they found the Indians, at the close of a beautiful evening, going into camp, and so indifferent to their surroundings, least expecting an attack, that they had not thought it necessary to adopt any precautions against surprise.

Carson and Fremont disposed their men to the best possible advantage, after a careful view of the grounds, and about ten o'clock, when the camp was still in slumber, they surrounded the sleeping Indians and at a signal put spurs to their horses and dashed down upon the unsuspecting savages, yelling and firing, so that the camp was thrown into the utmost confusion, and before the Indians could discover the cause or rally, hundreds of them were shot down as they were crawling from their tents. It was a veritable riot of death in which bloody slaughter acted as master of ceremonies. Men fell like leaves in autumn, and even the squaws that had accompanied the war party could not be respected in the rain of bullets that rattled through the raided camp. So sudden and impetuous had been the charge, and so terrible was the execution that the Indians were panic-stricken and with only a faint show of resistance retreated in the wildest confusion, leaving their camp in possession of the brave invaders.

After this decisive victory, which Carson prophesied would prove a lesson that the Indians would be slow to forget, Fremont returned to Lawson's Post, where he renewed his outfit, and then departed northward, with the purpose of exploring and opening a route to the Wahlahmath settlements in Oregon.

Carson Detailed to Act as Dispatch Bearer

While the party was journeying northward they were surprised by the appearance of two white men, who, travel-stained and fatigued to the point of exhaustion, approached after giving signs that they wished to make a communication. When they drew near Fremont was rejoiced to find that the two were old *voyageurs* who had accompanied him on his first expedition. They quickly told their story, which was to the effect that they were part of a guard of six men conducting Lieutenant Gillespie, of the United States Marines, who had been sent from Washington for the Slope, with dispatches for Fremont. Hearing of his presence in that region these two had been sent forward to find him, and if their search proved successful, they were ordered to report back to the command as soon as possible. All this was good news for Fremont, who decided to immediately return with the two guards and ten picked men, of which Carson was one, and meet the Lieutenant, who was reported to be in sore distress for want of provisions.

Fremont's party, guided by the two *voyageurs*, journeyed back a distance of sixty miles, and was upon the point of giving the Lieutenant over for lost, as the Indians were very numerous and hostile in that region and would make short work of so small a party if able to surprise them, when he discovered Gillespie's camp in one of the mountain passes, where he had remained for three days awaiting succor, fearing to proceed further lest he should be unable to find so good a shelter again, and believing that the two men sent out would easily discover his position in a pass that was in the highway to California. In a letter written by Carson in June, 1847, and published in the Washington *Union*, the interview between Fremont and Gillespie, as well also some of the exciting incidents of the return trip are thus graphically described:

A Massacre by the Indians and Carson's Narrow Escape

"Mr. Gillespie had brought the Colonel letters from home—the first he had had since leaving the States the year before—and he was up, and kept a large fire burning until after midnight; the rest of us were tired out and all went to sleep. This was the only night in all our travels, except the one night on the island in the Salt Lake, that we failed to keep guard; and as the men were so tired, and we expected no attack now that we had sixteen in the party, the Colonel didn't like to ask it of them, but sat up late himself. Owens and I were sleeping together, and we were waked at the same time by the licks of the axe that killed our men. At first I didn't know it was that, but I called to Basil, who was on that side—'What's the matter there? What's that fuss about?'—he never answered, for he was dead then, poor fellow, and he never knew what killed him—his head had been cut open, in his sleep; the other groaned a little as he died. The Delawares (we had four with us) were sleeping at that fire, and they sprang up as the Tlamaths charged them. One of them caught up a gun, which was unloaded; but, although he could do no execution, he kept them at bay, fighting like a soldier, and didn't give up until he was shot full of arrows—three entering his heart; he died bravely. As soon as I had called out I saw it was Indians in the camp, and I and Owens together cried out 'Indians.' There were no orders given; things went on too fast, and the Colonel had men with him that didn't need to be told their duty. The Colonel and I, Maxwell, Owens, Godey and Stepp jumped together, we six, and ran to the assistance of our Delawares. I don't know who fired and who didn't, but I think it was Stepp's shot that killed the Tlamath chief, for it was at the crack of Stepp's gun that he fell. He had an English half-axe slung to his wrist by a cord, and there were forty arrows left in his quiver—the most beautiful and warlike arrows I ever saw. He must have been the bravest man among them, from the way he was armed and judg-

CARRYING AWAY THE BODY OF THE TLAMATH CHIEF

ing by his cap. When the Tlamaths saw him fall they ran; but we lay, every man with
his rifle cocked, until daylight, expecting another attack.

"In the morning we found by the tracks that from fifteen to twenty of the Tlamaths
had attacked us. They had killed three of our men and wounded one of the Delawares,
who scalped the chief, but they prevented his body from falling into our hands by
drawing it away on a travoi. Our dead men we carried on mules; but, after going about
ten miles, we found it impossible to get them any farther through the thick timber,
and finding a secret place, we buried them under logs and chunks, having no way to
dig a grave. It was only a few days before this fight that some of these same Indians
had come into our camp; and, although we had only meat for two days, and felt sure
that we should have to eat mules for ten or fifteen days to come, the Colonel divided
with them, and even had a mule unpacked to give them some tobacco and knives."

Carson's Revenge

The massacre so cruelly perpetrated by the Tlamath Indians aroused in Fremont's party an intense desire for vengeance, which they were not long in gratifying. By the dispatches which Gillespie had brought it was known that war had been declared with Mexico, and as the Indians were then acting as Mexican allies they were properly regarded as being enemies in a double sense, and fit subjects for extirpation if opportunity offered. On the day following the massacre just described Carson took ten men and passed around to the opposite side of Tlamath Lake, where, as he had expected, he found the Indian trail, and followed it until he came upon a village of fifty lodges. To his surprise, however, he found that very few warriors were in the camp, those engaged in the massacre evidently having not yet returned. Regarding his force, therefore, sufficiently strong for the enterprise, he ordered a charge upon the encampment, and rushed down upon the surprised Indians with whoop and yell that threw them into the greatest confusion. Three or four warriors returned the fire of Carson's party but without effect, and in a trice the camp was carried and its puny defenders sent flying in panic across the prairie, pursued by Carson's men and shot down with the same measure of mercy as that meted out to their murdered comrades.

When Carson grew tired of the pursuit and slaughter, he returned to the deserted village, and gathering into one pile all the tents and their contents, set fire to the whole and consumed every vestige of the camp.

Carson's Duel with an Indian

On the day following this rout of the Indians Fremont's party set out on a journey to the Sacramento Valley, where their services would most likely be needed in the war that had just been declared. Nothing of special interest occurred on this march until the fourth day, when a war party of Tlamath Indians rushed out upon the band of explorers from a cañon in which they had laid concealed, but though they charged with much valor Fremont's men were prepared for them, and after counter-charging dispersed the Indians with small loss. Although the main body made a precipitate retreat, one of the Indians boldly disputed the ground with all of Fremont's party. His bravery was so conspicuous that Carson would gladly have spared the warrior's life, so chivalric was his regard for the truly heroic, under whatever mask of nature it might be displayed. But the Indian disdained the offer of a truce, having apparently some mortal offense against the whites to avenge, and continued to advance and discharge his bow with marvelous precision. Seeing him so determined upon a contest Carson resolved to give him an equal chance for his life; bidding his comrades to retire a pace

Carson rode forward to engage the Indian in a duel, where arrow and rifle should be brought in conflict. Perceiving his enemy's intention the Indian sought the cover of a tree, from which protecting shelter he sent several arrows in dangerous proximity to his adversary, some of them lodging in his saddle. Without a sign of fear Carson continued to maneuver for some time until at length the Indian, in his daring, exposed a part of his body through which Carson quickly sent a bullet with unerring precision. Having killed his brave and dexterous enemy, Carson leaped from his horse and divested the body of its rich ornaments, including the bow and quiver still half filled with beautiful arrows headed with polished jade, and presented the fighting outfit to Lieutenant Gillespie, as a memento of the march through that dangerous country.

Hostilities Begun with the Mexicans

The party now resumed their journey without further interruption until they returned to Lawson's Post. Here they remained for a week and then moved down the Sacramento where they again went into camp to await developments and discover, if possible, the plans of the Mexicans. Another week of inaction passed, when Fremont decided to begin hostilities by an aggressive movement against the Mexican garrison at Sonoma. The place was accordingly attacked and carried after a brief contest, in which the losses on either side were inconsiderable. The victory, however, was an important one, since among the prisoners taken was General Vallejos, besides a considerable store of ammunition and three cannons. After the reduction of Sonoma Fremont rallied to his standard all the Americans of that section and marched against a force of eight hundred Mexicans sent out by General Castro from San Francisco, with the declared purpose of exterminating every American in California. Instead, however, of carrying this boastful enterprise into execution the Mexicans, upon learning of Fremont's advance, retreated with precipitation, and suffered themselves to be pursued for six days without once offering an engagement. Fremont followed at the flying heels of the enemy almost to Los Angeles, and then returned to Sonoma, which he garrisoned with a company of new recruits, after which he pushed on to Sutter's Fort where he left his prisoners and put the place in an excellent state of defense.

His operations against the Mexicans had been so successful that Americans from the several quarters of California joined him, augmenting his force to nearly one thousand men. At the head of this considerable army he set out to lay siege to Monterey, but upon arrival before that port he found his purpose had been anticipated by Commodore Sloat, who had taken the place several days before and before it had anchored the American squadron. Colonel Fremont made due report to Commodore Stockton, as his superior officer, of his operations against the

Mexicans, and made a tender of the standard he had adopted upon declaring the independence of California, after his capture of Sonoma. This flag, used only a few weeks, was composed of red and white, with the figure of a bear in the center, from whence it became known as the "Bear Flag." During its brief service as an emblem of California independence it inspired an enthusiasm that has rarely been equaled by any banner in all history.

CHAPTER V

Carson's Service as a Scout and Guide

Nearly all Fremont's force was now composed of hardy adventurers, who had drifted to California in early years, attracted either by the trade that had been created by the several missions that had been established along the coast, or by a roving desire such as leads men into every habitable section of the globe. But the character of these adventurers was of the quality that easily develops heroes, being inured to hardships and possessing stout hearts ready for any enterprise, and destitute of the effeminate element of fear. At the head of two hundred such men Fremont had no hesitancy in undertaking to drive his way into the enemy's country, and accordingly he set out resolved upon the capture of Los Angeles and the cowardly Castro, who had escaped him, as has just been described. Commodore Stockton promised to act in conjunction with Fremont so as to make a combined attack upon the place, but after all their preparations and lofty expectations of an exciting battle they were doomed to disappointment. By some means General Castro learned of the intended attack on Los Angeles, and though his force was double that which Fremont and Stockton were able to bring against him, he evacuated the place and suffered it to fall into the hands of his enemies without a struggle

California was now practically free from Mexican rule, the war having been so vigorously prosecuted by Fremont that his operations had hardly been disputed. He returned now to Monterey and was appointed Governor of California by Commodore Stockton, with headquarters at that place, where long before the capital had been established. The Commodore set sail for San Diego, and thus leaving Southern California unprotected, General Castro re-occupied Los Angeles.

In the meantime, Kit Carson, at the head of fifteen men, was sent on the long and perilous journey across the continent to Washington, with reports of the military operations of Stockton as commandant of the squadron and of Fremont as leader of the land forces. It was necessary that the trip should be made with all possible expedition, for which reason Carson was chosen to undertake it, as his knowledge of the country and peculiar fitness in a hundred ways pointed him out as the most competent man for such a dangerous duty.

The little party set out in good spirits and traveled without interruption until they reached the line of New Mexico, where they were intercepted by a large band of Apaches. Carson had been so long among these Indians that he spoke their language sufficiently well to make himself understood, and this accomplishment he now used to excellent advantage. Requesting, by signs, a parley, he met the chief and explained to him the peaceful motive of his journey, at the same time offering to barter some of the trinkets he brought along for such provisions as the Indians might be able to spare. So well did Carson ingratiate himself into the chief's favor that he not only secured immunity from molestation, but obtained a supply of buffalo meat of which his half-starved party stood sorely in need.

Meeting with General Kearney

The party now continued on their march, meeting with no further adventure until they reached the vicinity of Taos. As Carson's family lived in this place, his anxiety was greatly increased in the expectation of seeing his wife and children, from whom he had been a year separated. But when within about twenty miles of the town, which he expected to reach on the following day, Carson met an expedition under the command of General Stephen W. Kearney, who was hurrying to the aid of Fremont and Stockton, and bearing orders from the War Department at Washington. This expedition consisted of three hundred dragoons, well mounted, and ten wagons loaded with provisions for a sixty-five days' journey. To General Kearney Carson delivered one of his dispatches, which read as follows:

"The Pacific Squadron, in command of Commodore Stockton, has taken possession of California, and the American flag is now proudly streaming above the walls of Monterey, the capital of the country. Lieutenant-Colonel Fremont was on the Rio Sacramento when the squadron arrived off the coast, and was not present when the capital surrendered. Five men of war were anchored in the bay when the express left Monterey. The inhabitants submitted with a struggle. Colonel Fremont has been appointed Governor of California."

In addition to this dispatch were several sealed messages, the contents of which Carson did not himself know, and it was important that these should be transmitted with all possible celerity. But when Carson desired to resume his journey towards Washington General Kearney detained him and said: "Lieutenant, you have just passed over the route which we must pursue in order to reach California, and since you are so perfectly familiar with the trail and country as well, I should be very glad to have you return with us and act as guide."

To this request Carson replied by informing the General that he had pledged himself to see that the messages which he bore were promptly delivered to the proper officials in Washington, and that he would not neglect to fulfill that promise. General Kearney, unwilling to entrust himself to the dangers of the wilderness that lay between him and California without a competent guide, thus answered Carson's excuse for refusing to accompany him. Said he: "I will relieve you of all responsibility by entrusting the messages to a reliable person who will carry them safely and speedily, and in the event of their miscarriage I will assume all the blame." As Kearney had been promoted to the position of Brigadier-General, and thus outranked all land officers at that time in California, Carson considered his request and guarantee as equivalent to an order, and consented to pilot the expedition to California. In engaging to return he was forced to abandon the hope of a speedy meeting with his family, for the army was then on the march under orders to push forward as rapidly as possible, and delay was not permitted. This fact caused Carson much regret and came near deciding him to give up his expressed intention, and he would have done so but for the persistent persuasion of General Kearney. However, he did act as guide to the expedition and piloted it safely through to Monterey, while the dispatches he had been entrusted with were given to Fitzpatrick, Kearney's guide to Santa Fe, and by him were carried to Ft. Leavenworth, from whence they were transmitted to Washington by the regular mails.

A Terrible Situation and How Carson Relieved It

When Kearney reached California, in December, he found that all the advantages which the Americans had gained during the preceding summer had been lost by neglect to garrison the places that had been captured, or to take any means for keeping the Mexicans without the territorial boundary. Los Angeles and all Lower California had been re-occupied, while the Mexicans were in force almost as far north as Sonoma. Hostilities were therefore renewed after Kearney had taken command of all the land forces within California and issued his orders for an advance. Fremont quickly responded to the call and took the field with a company of fifty men, of which Carson acted as first lieutenant. They promptly marched south and began maneuvering in the vicinity of San Diego, which was, of all the southern ports, the only one now held by the Americans. Having just penetrated the country, after a long absence, they were not informed of the strength of the Mexicans in that region, and before they became aware of any threatened danger, or the proximity of any considerable force of the enemy, they suddenly found themselves surrounded by a large army and their

ATTACKED BY APACHES AND MEXICANS

retreat completely cut off. The Americans managed, however, to reach a clump of timber, where they hastily entrenched themselves and resisted the attack that soon followed until all hope of escape from utter annihilation seemed exhausted. For six hours the brave little band fought with coolness but desperation, in which time they had killed of the enemy more than double their own number. Their several assaults having been repulsed with great loss, the Mexicans and a war party of Apache allies settled down to a siege, first investing the Americans with an almost solid cordon of soldiers, and hoping to starve them out, or by some strategy induce them to attempt a retreat.

When night approached, fully appreciating their desperate situation, Carson addressed the men, declaring that the only conceivable means for their escape lay in the possibility of communicating with the forces at San Diego and securing their assistance. But this plan seemed anything but feasible, as the Mexicans had established a complete cordon around the American squad and any attempt to break through the lines would certainly be detected. After counseling with the men for some time on the hopelessness of their situation, Carson volunteered to make an attempt at establishing communication with San Diego, and in this effort Lieutenant Beale offered to accompany him. The two therefore started out at midnight, and crawling on their hands and knees, they approached the first line of guards without detection. Their shoes were then removed to prevent noise, and again they resumed their perilous progress, over rocks and through briars, each step lacerating their feet, and the breaking of each twig exciting the gravest fears of discovery. But the outlying posts were passed, and then they made all possible haste for San Diego, which was reached shortly after daylight. The sufferings of this journey were so acute that Lieutenant Beale was for several days deranged from the effects and did not recover his usual physical health until two years had elapsed. Carson's feet were so badly torn and bruised that for a time amputation seemed necessary, and he was unable to walk again for nearly two months. But the object of their mission was accomplished, Commodore Stockton sending relief forward, which arrived barely in time to save the Americans from massacre.

Recapture of Los Angeles

The United States forces at San Diego were not in condition to again take the field until a number of weeks had elapsed, when a command of six hundred men was organized for the purpose of again capturing Los Angeles, where the Mexican forces were concentrated. General Kearney and Commodore Stockton, operating in conjunction, after a two days march arrived within fifteen miles of the town, near where the Mexican army, to the number of seven hundred, had established themselves strongly upon a hill beside their camp, and between whom and the Americans flowed a stream of water.

General Kearney ordered two pieces of artillery planted where they would rake the position of the Mexicans, which soon forced them to break up their camp; the Americans then marched into the town, but only to find it destitute of any military control, as the Mexican army had gone northward to meet Col. Fremont, who had left Monterey with a force of four hundred Americans to come to Los Angeles.

The purpose of the Mexicans in abandoning Los Angeles and departing northward to meet Fremont was not a hostile one, for realizing now the futility of further efforts to subjugate the Americans in California, and conceiving a bitter personal hatred to General Kearney, to avoid falling captive to him they determined to give the honor, whatever it might be, to Col. Fremont, for whom, even as enemies, they entertained much respect. Accordingly, the Mexican army of seven hundred men met Fremont some distance north of Los Angeles, and to him surrendered themselves as prisoners of war. This act was the virtual closing of hostilities, and the whole country in dispute, that had long been under Mexican authority, came into possession of the United States as conquered territory.

The following dispatch was sent by Gen. Kearney to the War Department, in which it will be seen that he did not withhold the meed of credit from Fremont, but on the other hand was so generous as to award him a full measure of praise:

"This morning Lieutenant-Colonel Fremont, of the regiment of mounted riflemen, reached here with four hundred volunteers from Sacramento; the enemy capitulated with him yesterday near San Fernando, agreeing to lay down their arms; we have now the prospect of having peace and quietness in this country, which I hope may not be interrupted again."

Fremont's Wild Cohort

We have thus briefly followed some of the more important events in the California war in which Carson acted a conspicuous part. But while these were few, they are sufficient to prove his indomitable will and heroic character, as well also the confidence, so worthily bestowed, reposed in him by Fremont, Kearney, and his humbler comrades. When Fremont penetrated the vast western wilderness, though acting as a government officer, his equipment for the three expeditions undertaken was meager, and more like that of hardy trappers who brave the perils of mountain forests, unexplored regions and almost limitless prairies, than an officer outfitted by a rich government to explore a large portion of its domain. But in some respects, and notably so in the composition of the party that accompanied him, these seeming obstacles to success proved in the end his greatest advantages. His baggage being limited, there was less liability to interruption, and relying largely for his provisions upon the game that abounded throughout the wild West, his men became inured to hardships, and more ready to engage in any adventure that required physical endurance or great daring. Relying, also, upon volunteers for the service required, naturally it was only the brave and hardy that would engage with him; men who had already spent a portion of their lives in the primeval solitudes of the trackless wilderness, of mountains, cañon, woods and plains, or who, impelled by an inherent love of wild adventure, sought this means to gratify their longings. A description of the heroic cohort that followed Fremont is thus given by Mr. Walpole, who was an officer on a British war ship that was lying at anchor in the bay of Monterey when the capital was taken by Commodore Stockton:

"During our stay in Monterey Captain Fremont and his party arrived. They naturally excited curiosity. Here were true trappers, the class that produced the heroes of Fennimore Cooper's best works. These men had passed years in the wilds, living upon their own resources; they were a curious set. A vast cloud of dust appeared first, and thence in long file emerged this wildest wild party. Fremont rode ahead, a spare, active looking man, with such an eye! He was dressed in a blouse and leggings, and wore a felt hat. After him came five Delaware Indians, who were his body-guard, and have been with him through all his wanderings; they had charge of two baggage horses. The rest, many of them blacker than the Indians, rode two and two, the rifle held by one hand across the pommel of the saddle. Thirty-nine of them are his regular men, the rest are loafers picked up lately; his original men are principally backwoods-men, from the State of Tennessee and the banks of the upper waters of the Missouri. He has one or two with him who enjoy a high reputation in the prairies. Kit Carson is as well known there as "the Duke" is in Europe. The dress of these men was prin-cipally a long loose coat of deer skin, tied with thongs in front; trousers of the same, of their own manufacture, which, when wet through, they take off, scrape well inside with a knife, and put on as soon as dry; the saddles were of various fashions, though these and a large drove of horses, and a brass field-gun, were things they had picked up about California. They are allowed no liquor, tea and sugar only; this, no doubt, has much to do with their good conduct; and the discipline, too, is very strict. They were marched up to an open space on the hills near the town, near some large fires, and there took up their quarters, in messes of six or seven, in the open air. The Indians lay beside their leader. One man, a doctor, six feet high, was an odd-looking fellow. May I never come under his hands!"

CHAPTER VI

Carson's Fourth Overland Journey

Carson remained in California from December, 1847, until March following, sta-tioned latterly at a post called Bridge Creek, which was some fifteen miles from Los Angeles. Peace having been concluded; or, rather, hostilities having entirely ceased, a party of twenty of Fremont's men was detailed to convey the accumulated letters and messages to Washington. The party was placed under the command of Lieutenant Geo. D. Brewerton, and Carson was chosen to act as guide, a position he accepted with much pleasure as the route over which they would have to travel was by way of Taos, and the trip would therefore give him an opportunity of seeing his family from whom he had now so long been separated.

Preparations for the journey being completed the caravan of pack animals and mounted men started forth presenting a curious sight, as everything about the party betokened a primitive, not to say a wild, appearance. All the animals used were mules, which were caparisoned with saddles, bridles and packs peculiar to the early Mexican civilization, and of patterns that can be found among no other people.

Nothing of interest occurred on the journey until the party were eight days out from their starting point, when they met a Mexican *cabelledo*, or caravan, of two hundred greasers, driving a large herd of mules and horses, the product of their trading with South California Indians, which they were taking back with them to Santa Fe. This company was even more grotesque in appearance than the party that Carson was guiding, and in some respects bore a striking resemblance, as we imagine, to the Arabian caravans that cross equatorial Africa with a horde of fresh captive slaves. The Mexicans were dressed in an inconceivable variety of costumes, ranging from the richly embroidered jacket usually worn by wealthy Californians in those days, with its bell-shaped silver buttons, to the scanty habiliments of the skin-clad Indian. Their *cabelledo* contained not only horses and mules but stray burros destined to pack wood across the mountains of New Mexico. Their line of march extended over a mile. It would have been quite easy to capture the whole outfit, as many of them had no arms, being only provided with the long bow and arrows usually carried by New Mexican herdsmen. Others were armed with old English muskets condemned long ago as unserviceable, while many carried old dragoon sabers, dull, rusty, and perfectly worthless even at close quarters. Carson and his party spent the night with this motley crowd, and in passing through their camp were still more struck with their singular customs. Their pack saddles and bales were taken off at night and carefully piled, so as to not only protect them from damp, but to form a sort of barricade, in case of attack, for the owner. From one side to the other of these little piles a blanket was stretched, under which the trader lay stretched, smoking his cigaretto, while his servant prepared his coffee and "atole."

Precautions Used in Passing Through a Hostile Country

Not long after leaving this caravan the party had the satisfaction of finding quantities of clear and tempting water that oozed from the rocks into small pools which had not been muddied by the feet of dirty men and animals. As they moved on, they found that the only living creatures which inhabit the desert, except the prowling Digger Indians, were small rabbits which burrow in the ground, lizards in great quantities, and a small but very venomous description of rattlesnake. The daily routine of life in the desert has a sort of terrible sameness in it; they rode from fifteen to fifty miles a day according to the distance from water. Occasionally, after a long drive, they halted for twenty-four hours, to recruit their stock on the scanty grass. Among the men there was but little talking, and less joking and laughing even round the camp-fire. The gloomy wastes, the scanty food and hard travel, together with a consciousness of continued perils, all tended to repress the animal spirits. Carson, while traveling, scarcely spoke. His keen eye was continually examining the country, and his whole manner

DIGGER INDIAN BOYS RACING

was that of a man deeply impressed with a sense of responsibility. They ate but twice a day and their food was so coarse and scanty that it was not a pleasure, but a necessity. At night every care was taken to prevent surprise. In an Indian country, a mule is the best sentry. They discover, either by their keen sense of smell or of vision the vicinity of the lurking savage long before the mountaineer, experienced as he is, can see him. If thus alarmed, the mule shows its uneasiness by snorting and extending the head and ears toward the object of suspicion.

During this journey Lieut. Brewerton says he often watched with great curiosity Carson's preparation for the night. "A braver man," says the Lieutenant, "than Kit perhaps never lived; in fact I doubt if he ever knew what fear was, but with all this he exercised great caution. While arranging his bed, his saddle, which he always used as a pillow, was disposed in such a manner as to form a barricade for his head; his pistols, half cocked, were laid above it, and his trusty rifle reposed beneath his blanket by his side, where it was not only ready for instant use, but perfectly protected from the damp. Except now and then to light his pipe, you never caught Kit exposing himself to the full glare of the camp-fire. He knew too well the treacherous character of the tribes among whom he was now traveling; he had seen men killed at night by a concealed foe, who, veiled in darkness, stood in perfect security, while he shot down the mountaineer, clearly seen by the fire-light. 'No, no, boys,' Kit would say, 'hang round the fire if you will, it may do for you, if you like it, but I don't want to have a Digger slip an arrow into me when I can't see him.' "

In crossing the desert it is often necessary to march long distances without water. These dry stretches are called by the Mexicans "*jornados*"; one of these which they were about to enter was sometimes called the "*Jornado del Muerto*" (the journey of death) the distance from one water hole to another being not less than eighty miles, and on account of the animals it was highly important it should be traveled at once. To accomplish this, a start was made about three o'clock one afternoon and the other side of the *jornado* was reached late in the morning of the following day, the greater part of the distance being gone over by moonlight. None can forget the impressions left on the mind by such a night's journey. Sometimes the trail leads over large basins of deep sand, where the tramplings of the mules' feet give forth no sound; this, added to the almost terrible silence that always reigns in the solitudes of the desert, renders the transit more like the passage of some airy spectacle where the actors are shadows instead of men. Scattered along the route were seen numerous remains of animals and horses which at some former period had dropped down and died by the wayside. The frequent recurrence of these bleaching bones and skulls were familiar scenes to Carson, and the old hunters of the party. The Pau-Eutaw, or Digger Indians (so-called from the roots which they dig from the ground and on which they depend for a greater portion of their miserable existence) began to make their appearance shortly after the party had crossed the great *jornado*. They then had a genuine Indian alarm in camp thus described by the Lieutenant:

An Alarm in Camp

"Our camp was pitched on the borders of a little stream, where a few scanty patches of grass afforded some refreshment to our tired beasts; and our party with few exceptions, besides the watchful horseguard, were stretched upon the ground resting wearily after the long night's ride. Carson, who was lying beside me, suddenly raised himself upon his elbow, and turning to me asked: 'Do you see those Indians?' at the same time pointing to the crest of one of the gravelly, bluff-like hills with which we were surrounded. After a careful examination I was obliged to reply in the negative. 'Well,' said Kit, 'I saw an Indian's head there just now, and there are a party of at least a dozen or more or I am much mistaken.' Scarcely were the words out of his mouth, when a savage rose to his full height, as if he had grown from the rocks which fringed the hill top; this fellow commenced yelling in a strange, guttural tongue, at the same time gesticulating violently with his hands. This he intended as a declaration of friendship; and Kit answered him in his own language: 'Tigabu! Tigabu!' (friend, friend). After a little delay, and an evident consultation with his people, the old Digger (for such he proved to be) came at first rapidly and then more slowly towards us, descending the steep hillside with an agility astonishing in so aged a being. Carson advanced a short distance to meet him, and again renewed his assurance of our friendship; but it was not until the old man had been presented with some trifling gifts that he seemed fully at his ease and then yelled to his companions to join him. This they did with evident caution, coming into our camp two or three at a time, until they numbered upwards of a dozen. The old man had evidently been sent as a sort of forlorn hope to fall a victim should we be inclined to hostility."

Carson's party were arranging themselves on the ground in a circle, for the purpose of smoking and having a talk "*à la* Indian," when a new party, with a large drove of horses and mules made their appearance. These new comers proved to be a small band of Americans who were driving their cattle into the Utah country with a view of trading with that tribe of Indians. The owner of the animals and leader of the party was a Mr. Walker, an old acquaintance of Carson's from Missouri. After securing his *cabelledo*, and making a camp in the vicinity, Walker joined the party and the interrupted council was resumed. The pipe having finally gone the rounds, Kit explained as much of his route and future intentions as he thought necessary, and concluded by charging divers murders and outrages upon the tribe to which the visitors belonged. The Diggers answered to the effect that there were bad Indians living among the hills, but as for themselves, they were perfectly innocent, never did anything wrong in their lives, liked the whites and Carson in particular, and wound up by diplomatically hinting that a present of a horse or some such trifle would not be unacceptable as an evidence of esteem.

Disgusting Habits of the Digger Indians

These Digger Indians, says Lieut. Brewerton, are the most degraded and miserable beings who inhabit this continent; their bag-like covering is of the very scantiest description, their food revolting. Some of them brought lizards with them into camp and ate them raw; or with no further preparation than jerking off the reptile's tail. The hair of these savages is long, reaching nearly to their middle, and almost as coarse as the mane of a mule. Their faces are perfectly devoid of any intellectual expression, save the eye, which is exceedingly keen. Both in manners and appearances they have

DIGGER INDIAN WOMEN

a strong similarity to a wild beast, and while walking they turn the head from left to right quickly in the manner of a prairie wolf. In voracity they bear a greater resemblance to the anaconda than any human being. Five or six of these Indians will sit around a dead horse and eat until nothing but the bones remain. The arms of this degraded people consists of a bow of uncommon strength and arrows headed with flint; these last they are said to poison with rattlesnake's venom and an extract distilled from some plant known only to themselves.

Shortly after Carson's departure from this encampment they perceived smoke rising from prominent hills in the vicinity. These fires were repeated at various points along their route, showing that the Diggers were signaling the passage of strangers through their country. The following day parties of these Indians showed themselves upon the crests of inaccessible hills and seemed unwilling to come within gun shot; nor was it until they had gone two days' journey from their camp that a few of the Diggers mustered courage to visit them; and when they did so Carson concluded to retain one of their number, a young warrior, as a hostage for their good behavior.

Some time during the night the captive's companions on the hills set up a most dismal howling. This disturbance Carson finally quieted by replying in the Pau-Eutaw tongue, aided by the assurances of the prisoner, who yelled back to his friends an answer to the effect that he was still alive and unharmed. The night passed quietly away and in the morning the hostage was allowed to depart with a few trifling presents.

A Frightful Spectacle

At the Archilette, a well known camping ground in the desert, they passed a day and a night. This dreary spot obtained a notoriety from having been the scene of one of Carson's exploits enacted April 24th, 1844. On the day preceding this date a small party of traders under the leadership of Andreas Fuentes, a Mexican, was attacked by one hundred Indians who pounced on the camp at night, charging, shouting and discharging flights of arrows. The principal object of the Indians was to get possession of the horses, to accomplish which they immediately surrounded the herd and tried to stampede them, but Fuentes and his men drove several of the animals over and through the assailants in spite of their arrows, and, abandoning the rest to their fate, hurried the horses off at full speed across the plains. Knowing that they would be pursued, without making any halt, except to shift their saddles to other horses, they drove them on about sixty miles, and left them to rest and recruit at a watering place called Agua de Tomaso, and then hurried to meet the Spanish caravan, which they knew was in the vicinity, and which they found at Fremont's camp, the two parties having met on the previous night. After traveling about twenty-five miles, Fremont arrived at the Agua de Tomaso—the spring where the horses had been left—but as he expected, the animals were gone, having been found and driven off by the Indians. Carson and Godey volunteered to accompany Fuentes in pursuit of the thieves, and, well mounted, the three set out on the trail. The next afternoon Fremont was greeted with a war-whoop, such as Indians make when returning from a victorious enterprise, and soon Carson and Godey appeared, driving before them Fuentes's stolen horses. Two bloody scalps dangled from their guns, indicating they had overtaken the Indians as well as the horses.

Fremont gives a detailed account of the exploit from the lips of Carson, in which he says the three pursuers struck the Indian trail and followed it through a narrow defile by moonlight until midnight when, afraid of losing the trail owing to the darkness that succeeded the setting moon, they tied up their horses, struck no fire, and lay down to sleep in silence. At daylight they resumed the pursuit and at sunrise discovered the horses. Immediately dismounting, they crept cautiously to a rising ground, from the crest of which they perceived the Indian lodges close by but the movement of the captive horses discovered them to the Indians. Giving the war-whoop, the three brave men instantly charged into camp, taking the Indians so completely by surprise that only a few arrows were discharged at the invaders, one of which cut through Godey's shirt collar, barely missing his neck. Two Indians were killed, and the rest fled with great precipitation, not even halting to carry away the two dead bodies with them. A third Indian also fell, so badly wounded that he appeared as dead, but while Carson was scalping the three the wounded Indian recovered consciousness and sprang to his feet, the blood streaming from his skinned head, and uttered a hideous howl. An old squaw, possibly his mother, stopped and looked back from the mountain side she was climbing, threatening and lamenting. The stout hearts of the men, appalled by the frightful spectacle, did what humanity required, and quickly put an end to the agonies of the gory savage. Carson and his companion were now masters of the camp. They found preparations made for a great feast. Several of the best horses had been butchered, skinned and sliced up, and large earthen vessels were on the fire boiling and stewing the horse-beef. Fearing that the Indians might rally after discovering that their assailants were only three, as against nearly fifty of their own party, Carson speedily gathered the fifteen horses and drove them with all possible speed back to the camp of Fremont, when they were turned over to Fuentes.

Carson and Godey had ridden about one hundred miles in pursuit of the Indians, recaptured the horses and returned to camp in less than thirty hours. Fremont observes of this exploit: "The time and place, object and numbers considered, the expedition of Carson and Godey may be placed among the boldest acts of disinterested kindness which the annals of Western adventure, so full of daring deeds, can present. Two men in a savage desert, pursue day and night an unknown body of Indians, into the defiles of an unknown mountain—attack them on sight without counting numbers—and defeat them in an instant, and for what? To punish the robbers of the desert, and to avenge the wrongs of Mexicans whom they did not know."

Some of the foregoing details were narrated to Lieut. Brewerton by Carson, one of the principal actors in the affair, while encamped on the ground where it took place.

The Bleaching Bones of a Murdered Party

The adventures of Carson and his party in the desert were terminated at the *Las Vegas de Santa Clara* where they were once more cheered with the sight of green grass and pure sweet water. Their journey then led them past Little Salt Lake and along the foot of the Wahsatch Mountains, whose summits were covered with snow many feet in depth. In traversing one of these gorges they came suddenly upon ten human remains, which lay scattered here and there bleached by the elements. The bones had been

RELICS OF THE MASSACRE

dragged by hungry wolves along a space of some yards in extent. It was concluded that these mournful relics were the remains of some unfortunate party of whites who had been cut off by Indians. One of the skeletons which lay alone and separated from the rest, appeared, from the arrow heads and bullets yet marking the tree which guarded it, to have belonged to an individual of the party who had fought from this shelter until overcome by numbers. It was afterwards learned that the bones belonged to a party of Americans from Arkansas, who had been surprised by hostile Indians while resting at noon, and instantly killed, with the exception of one of their number, who snatched up his rifle, retreated to the nearest cover, and there fought with all the energy of despair, killing several of the savages before being dispatched by the arrows of his assailants.

Wreck of the Raft

No further incident of note occurred until the party reached Grand River, which had become much swollen by melting snows, and was now become an angry stream. The only possible way of effecting a crossing was by means of a raft, which the men quickly fell to work constructing. Several large trees were felled and being cut into desirable lengths were rolled into the water and secured together by means of riatas. Upon this raft the mails and provisions, including guns, ammunition and riding saddles were placed and preparations made to pole it across. The stream, however, proved much too deep for any pole to reach bottom, whereupon it was proposed that some of the best swimmers should undertake to make a passage carrying across with them a rope made fast to the raft. Carson was one of five who swam the stream, but when he had crossed, the rope became detached from the raft and another passage had to be made, though the stream was nearly one thousand feet wide. After repeated failures and an accident, by which Lieutenant Brewerton came near being drowned, the raft was finally got over, but in landing it was dashed against some drift wood and broken asunder, letting all the provisions into the water. The mail was recovered, but six guns, three saddles, and considerable ammunition was lost. The horses were driven into the stream, before the raft was started, and following the lead of a bell-mare made the passage in safety, apparently enjoying the swim.

The journey thenceforth was not interrupted, except at Green River, where the party passed through an experience very similar to that which befell them in crossing the Grand, though with less loss. Several bands of Indians were met, but they offered

CARSON RESCUING THE LIEUTENANT

little opposition, being readily placated by Carson who spoke their tongue with fluency and was thus able to explain his peaceful mission.

Taos was at length reached, and Carson now realized the long anticipated joy of meeting his family, from whom he had been separated and heard nothing for more than a year. Lieutenant Brewerton became his guest for a week and speaks in the highest terms of the generous hospitality of Carson and of the gentle and charming manners of his Spanish wife. At Taos the mail that had been brought by the party from California was entrusted to a company of cavalry that carried it through to Leavenworth, from which it was transmitted by the usual conveyance.

Carson Proceeds to Washington and Is Lionized

Carson had been in Taos only a short while when he received news that his appointment as Lieutenant, by President Polk, had not been confirmed by the Senate owing to some objection being raised by a party whose name Carson was never able to learn, nor could the object of his opposition ever be ascertained. The tardy recognition of his services, and particularly the insult which the rejection of his nomination implied, worried and angered the sensitive nature of Carson, until he concluded to proceed to Washington and personally determine the extent and cause of the opposition that had been made to his appointment. This determination was reached after a serious reflection on his wrongs, but not until he received an engagement to guide a party of ten men to Ft. Leavenworth, the regular route being at the time so invested with hostile Comanches as to make travel over it, except in large and well-armed parties, exceedingly dangerous. For this reason Carson piloted his party northward to the Platte, and thence by Fort Kearney over an untrodden way, but succeeded in reaching Leavenworth in due season and without encountering any dangers or serious difficulties.

Carson proceeded to St. Louis by steamer and on his arrival there was received by U. S. Senator Thomas Benton who induced him to stop over a few days and be presented to the prominent people of the city. His presence being soon known a large number of St. Louisans, both ladies and gentlemen, called on him at Col. Benton's house, and manifested their admiration in many ways, the ladies generally by fairly embowering him with bouquets and the gentlemen presenting more substantial tokens of their regard. All these tender attentions, while gratifying in one sense were very embarrassing to Carson whose diffidence in society and repugnance to adulation of any kind, caused him to make his stay in St. Louis shorter than it would probably have been under more quiet circumstances.

From St. Louis Carson went directly to Washington, and his coming being heralded in advance, a delegation headed by Mrs. Fremont met him at the depot and composed a distinguished escort to accompany him to a hotel selected for his accommodation. In Washington the attention bestowed upon him was even more ostentatious than that which he received in St. Louis. He was presented to the President and Cabinet officials who accorded him a recognition and regard equal to that which a powerful potentate might receive. The Senate being then in session he visited that body and was presented to both branches of Congress. Under the excitement occasioned by his visit the Senate took up the matter of his appointment, action having been suspended to await the report of a committee to whom the nomination had been referred. This committee now reported favorably, and on a vote the Senate unanimously confirmed his appointment.

After a week's stay in Washington Carson grew tired of the festivities and flattering attentions to which he was continually subjected and returned to Taos, arriving home almost simultaneously with the return to that post of General Fremont, whom he had the pleasure of entertaining for several days. In fact, when Fremont reached Taos he was in too feeble a condition to move further without recuperating, as he had passed through a period of unparalleled suffering, entailed by incompetent guides, who, not being familiar with the country, had led him out of the way and left him lost for several weeks in the mountains, unable to get out on account of snow blocking the passes. A record of this return journey from California appears in General Fremont's report of his last operations on the Pacific Slope, and composes a chapter thrilling for its sadness, with descriptions of suffering that will wring a tear of pity from any reader.

CHAPTER VII

Carson Again Called from a Quiet Pursuit

Upon Carson's return to Taos he decided to settle down again in the quiet and promising pursuit of sheep-raising, and was joined in this resolution by his old friend Maxwell. The two formed a copartnership, and by uniting their means purchased a thousand head of sheep with which they started a ranch fifty miles east of Taos, in a beautiful valley to which the Indians had given the name *Rayedo*. No spot in all New Mexico is so delightfully situated, or so advantageous for the purposes to which it was now to be devoted. A perennial mountain stream cleaves the valley, which ensures a permanently rich pasturage, while abruptly rising mountains afford shelter from the destructive blizzards that occasionally visit that region. Here in this wondrously favored valley Carson and Maxwell not only began the raising of sheep but also built several *adobe* houses and soon had established a flourishing settlement which still remains, though small in population.

In the congenial pursuit now adopted Carson was not long permitted to continue, for his reputation was now co-extensive with the nation, and he was almost constantly being called to participate in some expedition against marauding Indians or to act as guide to parties of traders, many of which were always traveling through the country buying up horses and peltries. Though at this time there was a considerable population of whites in New Mexico the Indians had not as yet been sufficiently punished to compel them to observe the treaties they had made, and depredations by prowling bands were common.

Indian Outrages

Very soon after Carson's settlement in Rayedo Valley a party of Apaches made a raid through northern New Mexico, murdering defenseless people, running off horses, and plundering every home they were able to desolate. Near Santa Fe they made an attack on the house of a merchant named White, and before assistance could be summoned, broke down the door and rushing in killed the merchant and his son, though not until the two had slain three of their foes. The other Indians now seized the women and children of the violated home and carried them away captives, making off in the direction of the Las Vegas Mountains. News of these outrages spread rapidly and it was determined to administer a lesson to the perpetrators that would not soon be forgotten. Rayedo was more than one hundred miles northeast of the region where the atrocities were committed, but so great was Carson's reputation as an Indian fighter that the party of New Mexicans organized to hunt down the murderers, sent for him and would not move until he responded to their summons. For some reason even after Carson had joined the party, he was not called to act as leader, that responsible position being given to a Frenchman named Leroux. But this neglect to accord to him the leadership gave no affront to Carson, who, at the distress call was always ready to answer to the best of his abilities in whatever way circumstances or exigencies might dictate.

The party set out for the mountains immediately after Carson joined them and pushed forward with all possible haste on the trail with the hope of rescuing the captive women and children, but so much time had already been lost that the pursuit promised to end in disappointment. Four days after the murder of Mr. White, however, the New Mexicans found the object of their search. The Indians were already within their mountain fastnesses and well prepared to resist attack from ten times the number that had given pursuit, but without considering disadvantages Carson gave a shout and dashed after the savages, expecting of course to be re-enforced by his followers; but instead of the party making a simultaneous charge they all

APACHES' ATTACK AND MURDER OF THE WHITE FAMILY

fell back, a fact which Carson did not discover until he had advanced so far alone that escape seemed impossible. An admirable horseman, and cool-headed under all circumstances, he turned, as the Indians charged on him, and throwing himself on the off-side of his horse rode back at the top of his speed towards the others of his party who had made a stand in anticipation of an attack. Had the Indians possessed modern fire-arms Carson would no doubt have fallen a victim to his over confidence in his followers, but fortune always favored him and in this instance spared his life, though no less than six arrows struck his horse, and a bullet passed through his suspended coat-tail.

Being indifferently armed, the Indians did not long follow up the pursuit but paused upon discovering the squad of horsemen, and soon retired again to a rocky apex from whence they could watch every movement of the whites. Carson was furiously mad at the apathy, not to say cowardice, of the men whom he had accompanied, but he was too anxious for the concern of the captives to manifest his feelings. After exhorting the men upon their duty and the avowed purpose that had enlisted his services, he induced them to make a charge on the Indians, which was accomplished in dashing style, and so bravely that the savages broke and fled without scarcely an effort to defend themselves, five of the number having been killed. But though the charge was successful it was made too late to save the captives, for anticipating the result of an attack the Indians had murdered the women and their children. Pursuit was given but, owing to the rocky and mountainous region, was necessarily slow, and as the Indians scattered they soon managed to escape; the New Mexicans were therefore compelled to return with no other trophies of their victory than five scalps and the bodies of the murdered women and children.

A HAIR-BREADTH ESCAPE

Another Fight with the Indians

In the following winter a band of twenty Apaches made a descent upon a corral of government horses near Rayedo that were in charge of ten dragoons stationed at that point to guard the settlers against the Indians. This small party afforded so little real protection that the Apaches only became bolder in committing their depredations, apparently believing that the government was unable to provide a stronger force of soldiers. The Indians accordingly dashed into the corral at night and stampeding the dozen horses within, ran them off and were more than twenty miles away before the theft was discovered. On the following morning the dragoons reported their loss to Carson, and requested him to accompany them in pursuit, which he promptly complied with by enlisting three of his neighbors and providing the entire party with horses. The trail was easily found and followed for two days, at the end of which time the horses ridden by four of the dragoons gave out and thus compelled them to stop. The others kept on, however, and overtook the Indians on an open prairie where all the conditions for a good fight were offered, barring the disparity in numbers, for there were only ten white men against twenty Indians. Carson was made the leader now, and with characteristic dash and chivalric courage he ordered a charge. The Indians might have easily escaped, for their horses were comparatively fresh, or by making a stand could no doubt have repelled their assailants, for all were well armed, but instead of offering battle they only strove to effect an escape with the stolen property to the adjacent hills, in which they partially succeeded, though six of their number were killed and all the horses except four were recaptured.

In the following year Carson and a company of six men rescued Messrs. Brevoort and Weatherhead, two traders from St. Louis, with a large train of goods, from a party of twelve desperadoes, who accompanied the train and had planned to murder the traders and appropriate their effects. Their plot was revealed by one of their number who had deserted, and Carson learning the particulars boldly headed a rescuing party. By swift riding he overtook the caravan in a mountain pass and disputed its passage under the pretense of a desire to deliver a communication to the two men whose lives had been plotted against. The desperadoes, suspecting nothing, offered no opposition, and when Brevoort and Weatherhead were told of the plot they were at once put on their guard. Everything was secretly managed by Carson and with such adroitness that he got the leader, a fellow named Fox, in his power before any suspicions of his real purpose were discovered. At a signal Carson's company drew their rifles on the would-be murderers, and compelled them to continue their journey, but Fox was detained and escorted to Taos, where he was delivered over to the proper authorities, but he soon after dug through the adobe walls of his prison and managed to escape.

Carson Again Resumes Trapping

The reputation and disposition of Carson to aid the weak and assist in punishing crime became so well known that in the hostile and lawless country he had selected for his home, his services were in almost constant demand though little to his profit. In sheep raising he had been only fairly prosperous, but would probably have been contented but for the affrays he was brought into in assisting others, which served to keep aflame his natural love for adventure; nor was this feeling diminished by the counsel of his partner. Maxwell, whose disposition was very similar. Finally, in 1853, to justify his longing for new enterprises in more exciting fields he proposed to his partner a resumption of their old occupation of trapping which he thought might be prosecuted profitably on the South Platte. The suggestion met with ready approval, and the two soon organized a company of eighteen choice spirits and set out for the appointed grounds, well provisioned and prepared for a year's hunt. Reaching the stream after a journey of nearly three weeks they were rejoiced to find beaver signs abundant and after making their camp were not disappointed in their expectations. No trapping had been done on these waters for many years, and beavers had become so numerous that the hunt was wonderfully successful. The party continued trapping down the river, and thence on the streams in New and Old Parks, in each

CARSON'S CAMP ON THE SOUTH PLATTE

place taking many hundred beaver skins until they could find no means for conveying any more.

With their valuable stock of furs they returned to Rayedo and thence to Taos where the skins were sold at a very large profit, making Carson richer than he had ever been before. Soon after this gainful enterprise he took his eldest daughter to St. Louis and placed her in a Catholic seminary, resolved to give her the advantages of an excellent education, a determination that was only defeated by her untimely death.

While in St. Louis, Carson was proffered the hospitality of several prominent citizens who would have been glad to make a public display of their regard for him, but all these attentions he declined with the excuse that urgent business required his immediate return to New Mexico. His stay in St. Louis was, therefore, limited to a single day, for city life or the adulation of admiring people had no charms for him, nor could he find contentment in the crowded but civil walks of life where even elbow-room is farmed out at a high rental. Returning to New Mexico, he again joined forces with Maxwell, for whom he conceived the affection of a brother, and the two bought up several thousand head of sheep which they drove to the California market, going by way of Fort Laramie and Salt Lake in order to avoid hostile Indians that were then pillaging the settlements in Arizona. They reached California without disaster and disposed of their flocks but with such small advantage that Carson had no desire to repeat the experiment. He spent some time in California visiting the old towns he had known in earlier days, as well as those that had sprung up since his last visit, and in the spring of 1854 he returned to Taos where he received the unexpected information that he had been appointed Indian Agent for New Mexico. This recognition of his services in the reclamation of the Southwest was so gratifying that he immediately sent to Washington his acceptance of the office, and entered at once upon the discharge of his duties, a position he held for several years and filled to the eminent satisfaction of both the government and its wards.

CHAPTER VIII

Carson's Career from 1862 to 1866

Generally—and without pretense to a complete or even invariably authentic history, because the facts are not always accessible, and tradition has largely taken the place of verified statements—I have, in the preceding chapters traced Carson in his adventurous career as Indian fighter, scout and guide of exploring expeditions. We are now to contemplate him in charge of an independent military command. Already his name was known from the Yellowstone to the Spanish peaks, and from the Missouri to the Pacific as "Kit Carson, the daring scout," and the fame of his exploits was as wide as the extent of the Union itself.

In 1862 he was entrusted with an important command against some of the turbulent and thieving Indian tribes of New Mexico and Arizona, in which, it will be seen, he displayed great tactical skill, and knowledge of the Indian mode of warfare, which earned for himself much glory and the approval of his superior in command and the government at Washington.

As no connected account of this portion of Carson's life has heretofore been written it became necessary therefore to dig it out from the departmental reports, and more especially from the report of the Joint Special Committee upon the "Condition of the Indian Tribes."

Early in 1862, following the raid of the Confederate General Sibley, from Texas into New Mexico, the Indians of that territory knowing that the attention of the Federal troops could not for the time be turned towards them, commenced robbing the inhabitants of their stock, and killed and scalped a great number of people. These marauding bands consisted principally of the Navajos on the western side and the Mescalero Apaches on the eastern side of the settlement. Both of these powerful tribes began their depredations at the same time.

Many outrages were committed and the settlements were left impoverished. In the neighborhood of Fort Stanton they were entirely abandoned. Men, women, and children, terror stricken, were forced to flee from their homes to escape the swift bullet and arrow, the gleaming scalping-knife and the torch of the stealthy foe.

General James H. Carleton, the department commander, headquarters at Santa Fe, resolved to punish and subdue these hostile tribes. For this purpose he gave the command of the first regiment New Mexican volunteers (cavalry) to Colonel Carson, and ordered him to move immediately with five companies to reoccupy Fort Stanton. The Lieutenant-Colonel, J. Francisco Chaves, with four mounted companies of the same regiment, was dispatched to the Navajo country, to establish Fort Wingate on the Gallo. The Governor of New Mexico also called out some militia to serve in the Navajo country and Col. West, commanding the District of Arizona, was ordered to co-operate with Carson's forces against the enemy. One division was sent to proceed by way of Dog Cañon and operate to the eastward of that noted haunt of the Mescaleros. At the same time Captain Roberts was directed to start from Franklin, Texas, proceeding by the Wacco Janks, and thence northward to cut off all Apaches found in that direction. He was to hold no council or "talks" with the Indians but to slay the warriors whenever found; the women and children, however, were to be made prisoners.

Battle with the Mescaleros

With these forces co-operating with him, Carson soon brought the Mescaleros to terms. His first aggressive movement was to make a dash into their country and in one small affair killed Jose Largo and Manuelita, two of the principal chiefs, and nine warriors. The pursuit was so swift that a large number were captured and with their women and children sent to the fort.

Of course, all know the custom of the nomadic, roving tribes has been, up to the present time, to divide up and flee into the recesses of the mountains, until they bring up, perhaps, in the territory of Old Mexico, far from their original abode. In this mode of warfare they elude the vigilance of their pursuers and place at naught the best laid plans for their destruction. The only show of success is to suddenly surprise them in their camps of skin lodges, or meet them in organized bodies when the superior discipline of the whites is generally successful in overcoming largely superior numbers. Colonel Carson's campaign against the Mescaleros lasted till the middle of January, when they were completely subdued. He brought in to Fort Sumner three hundred and fifty of that tribe. These comprised all that were left alive of those Indians except a few who either ran off into Mexico or joined the Gila Apaches. The expedition into the Gila country, in carrying out the plan of campaign, proved also quite successful. The principal chief, Mangus Colorado, considered the worst Indian within our territories, and one who was the cause of more murders and of more torturings and burnings at the stake than all others together, was killed. In another battle a few days after over twenty of his followers were slain. The war against the Gila Apaches continued until spring. Colonel Carson kept out strong detachments scouting all the time about the Sacramento and Blanco Mountains. In one of these Maj. Morrison, with Capt. Pfeiffer's company, from Fort Stanton to Fort McRae, at San Nicolas Spring came upon a wounded Mexican, who belonged to Martin Lyon's train from Soccoro, Texas. The train had been attacked by Indians and nearly all the party killed, he being wounded in three places and left for dead. Major Morrison, with Lieutenant Bargie and eighteen men went in pursuit, reaching the salt marshes at daybreak, where they found ten wagons stripped of everything portable, and within the circuit of three miles seven dead bodies of Mexicans, dreadfully mutilated and filled with arrows. Halting only long enough to bury the dead, they then followed the trail of the Indians towards the Sacramento Mountains and the Sierra Blanca until noon, when they met a party of Mexicans who had heard of the massacre from a member of the unfortunate party who had escaped and had started out to punish the perpetrators.

The Indians had at this time twenty hours the start and were hidden in the recesses of the Sierra Blanca. Major Morrison had therefore to return to San Nicolas Spring, having traveled one hundred and fifty miles without accomplishing the prime object of his pursuit, but he surprised another hostile party and killed forty-five of their number.

Expedition Against the Navajos

The main bands of the Mescaleros having been broken up, Colonel Carson was ordered to send an expedition against the Navajos. He employed one hundred Ute Indians as guides and auxiliaries. General Carleton urged the importance of time. "Make every string draw," said he to Carson. "Much is expected of you, both here and in Washington."

August 20th, Carson set out with his command for the Navajo country from Fort Canby, while Major Willis, with two companies from Fort Wingate, marched

IN THE CAÑON DE CHELLY

out to co-operate with him. Another force was ordered to guard a pass of the Jemez Mountains known as El Valle Grand, to prevent stock being driven through that noted thoroughfare. Still another force was pelted at Cebola Springs, west of Limitar, and some smaller detachments were employed in scouting the country east of the Rio Grande from Forts Bascom, Sumner and Stanton, and from Albuquerque and Los Pinos.

In spite of these precautions, small parties of Navajos and Apaches, invariably well mounted, were ranging about the country, robbing and committing depredations. So bold had these marauding parties become that a trail of two hundred Navajos going south was seen by a gentleman after Carson's command had passed. The trail was fresh, as seen near Laguna. The Navajos, about the same time, run off eight thousand sheep from Beguin Valley, near Fort Union. The mountains in the Navajo country were difficult of penetration by troops, the Indians being scattered over a country several hundred miles in extent. There are cañons thirty miles in length, with walls a thousand feet high, and at times have been so well guarded that it had been found extremely dangerous for even a large army to force a passage through them. In the main cañon, de Chelly, previous expeditions had been frustrated. Col. Sumner, in the fall of 1851, penetrated the Cañon de Chelly with several hundred men and two pieces of artillery. He got into the defile some eight or ten miles, but was compelled lo retreat out of it at night. General Canby also undertook to enter the canon, but was forced to back out of it the next morning. The Indians that occupy these haunts have regular fortifications, averaging from one to two hundred feet in height, pierced with port-holes for firing. No small arms can reach them and artillery cannot be used against such defenses.

A Wonderful Campaign

With a knowledge of the exact situation of the theater of war, Colonel Carson concerted his measures so ably and judiciously that he effected his object without any serious loss of men or bloodshed. Without exposing his forces to the danger of having their brains dashed out by rocks hurled down on them from towering precipices, he adopted the starving out process. Regarding the cañons as impregnable, he waited till about the 6th of January, after a heavy snowfall, having first destroyed the crops and every means for the enemy's subsistence, and then laid siege to the Indians with the intention of starving them out of their fastnesses.

He continued active operations, however, and while holding the Indians within their defenses, occasionally fell upon an exposed party. As the expeditionary force waded through the deep snow the following were the more notable happenings in the

Cañon de Chelly. On the 8th instant, one warrior was killed by the Colonel's escort. On the 12th, Sergeant Andres Herrera, with fifty men, who was sent out the previous night, returned, bringing into camp two men, two women and two children, prisoners, and one hundred and thirty head of sheep and goats, and reported that his men had killed eleven and wounded five Indians. On the 14th, Captain Pfeiffer and party, who had been sent out from Fort Canby, some five days in advance, to operate in the east opening of the cañon, came into camp and reported having passed through the cañon without a single casualty to his command. He killed three Indians and brought in nineteen prisoners. On the 15th instant sixty Indians arrived in camp and surrendered themselves as prisoners. On the same day a party under command of Captain Joseph Berney killed two Indians and captured four. One hundred and ten Indians surrendered to Captain Carey's command while on its return march to Fort Canby. Result of this expedition: Indians killed, twenty-three; wounded, five; prisoners, thirty-four taken in battle; voluntarily surrendered, two hundred, and two hundred sheep and goats captured. It took three hundred men most of one day to destroy a field of corn. In the main Cañon de Chelly 3,000 peach trees were destroyed by the troops. The consequence of this destruction of crops and fruit trees was to render the country a desolation, so as to force the Navajos to abandon their homes and come in. The first batch of Navajo prisoners was conducted to Santa Fe, and thence they were sent to the Bosque Redondo, on the Lower Pecos, a reservation of some forty square miles in extent, voted by the Legislature of New Mexico and intended to be set apart as the homes of the Mescalero Apaches and the Navajos. Some of the captured chiefs, with Jesus, the interpreter, were sent back to the Navajos' country to let others know what treatment they received and what kind of a place they were expected to move to. Numbers embraced the offer held out and forsook their country without offering further opposition. But with those determined to remain numerous skirmishes and fights took place. A sharp battle was fought within thirty-five miles of Fort Sumner, with 130 Navajo Indians, on the open plains. Twelve Navajos were left dead on the field. Two Apache chiefs, Cadella and Blanco, distinguished themselves as allies on the side of Carson's troops against the Navajos in this fight. Only the year before they themselves had been captured on the war-path.

Carson Specially Complimented

Colonel Carson was highly complimented by the commander of the department for his success in marching his command through the deep snows in the dead of winter and making a passage of the celebrated Cañon de Chelly, the great stronghold of the Navajo tribe, and for his success in killing and capturing large numbers of the enemy, besides forcing them, by his system of warfare, to eventually come in and sur-render themselves. In his report of operations to Washington General Carleton says: "This is the first time any troops, whether when the country belonged to Mexico, or since we acquired it, have been able to pass through the Cañon de Chelly, which for its great depth, its length, its perpendicular walls and its labyrinthine character, has been regarded by eminent geologists as the most remarkable of any fissure (for such it is held to be) upon the face of the globe. It has been the great fortress of the tribe since time out of mind. To this point they fled when pressed by our troops. Colonel Washington, Colonel Sumner, and many other commanders have made an attempt to go through it, but had to retrace their steps. It was reserved for Colonel Carson to be the first to succeed; and I respectfully request that the government will favorably notice that officer, and give him a substantial reward for this crowning act in a long life spent in various capacities, in the service of his country, in fighting the savages among the fastnesses of the Rocky Mountains."

Submission of the Navajos

This expedition of Colonel Carson was fruitful of the most perfect success. The Navajos from time to time, though not without numerous brisk skirmishes and many fatalities to both sides, finally unconditionally surrendered and were given new homes on the Bosque Redondo, their numbers amounting in all to about seven thousand persons.

Thus Colonel Carson, by multiplying as much as possible the points of attack, and although no great battle was fought, still the persistent pounding away of small parties, acting simultaneously over a large space, destroyed a great many hostile Indians and harassed the survivors until they became thoroughly broken up and sub-dued. In looking back to the result, it has been well said by General Carleton that "the exodus of a whole people from the land of their fathers was not only a touching, but an interesting sight. The Navajos fought us gallantly for years, they defended their mountains and their stupendous cañons with a heroism which any people might be proud to emulate. At length they had to abandon their beautiful country, their homes, their associations and the bones of their kindred to the insatiable progress of the white race." After the larger portion had surrendered, Colonel Carson was ordered to come in from the Navajo country and proceed to the Bosque Redondo to give the Indians the counsel they were so much in need of, how to start their farm and to commence their new mode of life. This, from his long experience of Indian life, no man was bet-ter capable of performing.

While Carson was engaged in this work, his regiment was still active in hurrying up the reluctant Navajos.

Carson Recommends the Reservation System

In July, Lieutenant Abeyta, while en route with twenty-six Navajos and seven Apache Indian prisoners, came upon a party of Navajos at Fish Spring, numbering three hundred and seventy-five warriors coming in to surrender themselves and go to the reservation. They had in their possession three hundred horses, sixteen mules, one thousand and eighty-five sheep and three hundred and fifty goats. August 1, twelve hundred and nine Navajos and twelve Apaches left Los Pinos for the Bosque Redondo. These Indians had in their possession three hundred and fifty-seven horses, nineteen mules and two thousand and five sheep and goats. This is but a sample of this Indian hegira, caused by military pressure and without much fighting, carrying out the system inaugurated by Carson. Having campaigned against them eight months, finding them scattered over a country several hundred miles in extent, Carson considered the reservation system as the only one to be adopted for them. In his testimony before Doolittle's committee he told the members if the Navajos "were sent back to their own country to-morrow it would not be a month before hostilities would commence again." A part of the Navajos, he said, were wealthy and wished to live in peace; but the poorer classes were in the majority and they have no chiefs who can control them. He knew that even before the acquisition of New Mexico there had always existed a hereditary warfare between the Navajos and the Mexicans. Forays were made into each other's country and stock, women and children stolen. Since the acquisition the same state has existed. We would hardly get back from fighting and making peace with them before they would be at war again. In this connection, it may be added, though somewhat in anticipation of the order of time, that the Navajos at length became discontented and longed to go back to their old country, so unhappy had they become, and on representations to that effect made at Washington, the Indian Peace Commission, in the spring of 1868, sent two of their number, Gen. Sherman and Col. Tappan, to visit the Navajos and report the condition of the tribe. They did so and recommended that they be sent back to their former homes, some four hundred miles from the Bosque Redondo, which was accordingly done.

War with the Kiowas

But the services of Col. Carson were again needed in the field, to crush and put a stop to the depredations of marauding bands of Cheyennes, Kiowas and Comanches on the plains. Early in the spring of 1865 he was ordered, with three companies, to proceed from Fort Union, New Mexico, to Cedar Bluffs or Cold Spring, on the Cimarron route, to the States and there establish a fortified camp. The object in

CARSON'S GREAT FIGHT WITH THE KIOWAS

establishing a post at that dangerous part of the route was in order to give protection to trains passing to and from the States. The Indians on the plains had for some time been harassing government trains and citizens going out with supplies. An expedition was therefore planned by Col. Carson to punish the Indians. The Kiowas had been the most hostile, committing numerous murders as well as capturing and spoiling government trains, and against these Carson first directed his forces. He soon found an opportunity to strike a blow on the enemy's camp near the adobe fort on the Canadian River in Texas. Carson's force consisted of the first cavalry, New Mexico volunteers. The command numbered fourteen commissioned officers, three hundred and twenty-one enlisted men and seventy-five friendly Indians. With these he attacked the Kiowa village of about one hundred and fifty lodges. The fight was a severe one and lasted from half past eight in the morning till sun down. The Indians, with more than ordinary intrepidity and boldness, made repeated stands against the fierce onslaughts of Carson's brave cavalrymen, but were at last forced to give way and were hewn down as they stubbornly retreated. The Kiowas suffered a loss of sixty killed and wounded. In this fight only two privates were killed and Corporal Newman and nine privates, with four Utes, were wounded. The command destroyed one hundred and fifty lodges of the best manufacture, a large amount of dried meats, berries, buffalo robes, powder, cooking utensils, etc., also a buggy and spring wagon, the property of Sierrito, or Little Mountain, the Kiowa chief.

Col. Carson, in his report of the battle, states that he found powder and lead in the Kiowa camp, which had been furnished, no doubt, by unscrupulous Mexican traders. The gallant Carson was thanked in general orders for the handsome manner in which he met so formidable an enemy and defeated him. "This brilliant affair," remarked the General in command to Carson, "adds another green leaf to the laurel wreath which you have so nobly won in the service of your country."

Carson Brings the Great Tribes into Council

Owing to his great knowledge of the Indians, and what was desired of them on the part of the government, he was in August 1865 appointed by Secretary Stanton, at the request of the Congressional Committee, special commissioner, with power to hold

GREAT MEDICINE DANCE HELD AT THE GRAND COUNCIL
This dance was witnessed by Carson at the Great Council, when a treaty of peace was made with the several tribes, as described in the foregoing pages. The dance is one of endurance, but differs from the sun, or torture dance, in that the participants move about in a circumscribed circle with their eyes fixed upon a small totem, or image, and continue their movements, without food or drink, until the Medicine Chief concludes the ceremony. It frequently happens that one or more of the dancers fall dead from sheer exhaustion.

councils and make preliminary arrangements with the Comanches, Kiowas, Cheyennes and Arapahoes, for holding a conference with the peace commissioners with the view of settling all differences. Carson was given an escort by General Carleton, and the latter requested him to look over the country passed through with an eye to the selection of a suitable site for the establishing of a ten-company post with six companies of cavalry, which it was found necessary to build in the country occupied by the Kiowas and Comanches during winter.

In this hazardous mission Carson passed over the country between Taos and Fort Union, New Mexico, and Fort Lyon, Colorado. At the latter post he found time to write a very excellent letter to the Congressional Committee, in answer to their interrogatories concerning Indian affairs. He was opposed to the old idea of forcing the Indians westward, as since the discovery of the California gold-fields civilization had encircled them with its chain of progress. Each year sees the chain drawing rapidly closer around the hunting ground of the red men of the prairie. "As," said Carson, "humanity shuddered at the picture of their extermination, I favor placing them on reservations, under wise rules, enforced by military power." As a result of Carson's mission among the plains Indians, and his recommendation as to their treatment, may be traced the assembling of the great council at Medicine Lodge Creek, a year or two later, and the adoption of the reservation system, as approved by the Indian Peace Commissioners.

The Last Days of Carson

After the close of the rebellion and removal of the Navajos to appointed reservations Carson continued to fill the position of Indian agent, with credit to the government and perfect satisfaction to the Indians. In January, 1868, he was called to Washington to give evidence and advice in a matter of dispute between the government and Apaches, and was accompanied on the trip by a deputation from that tribe. His coming was heralded in advance and several trades bodies in cities along his route besought of him the favor of a short visit, many of which urgent invitations he accepted. His journey was more like a triumphal tour of some proclaimed hero fresh from the field of decisive battle, for everywhere along his route flags were flung to the breeze and cities put on a holiday attire as a token of the admiration generally felt for his character as a man and heroism as an Indian fighter.

Carson returned from Washington some time in March in good health and highly elated over the adoption of pacificatory measures he had proposed for settling disputes that had arisen over the removal of the Apaches to their present reservation. But in the hour of quiet content and satisfaction with attained ambition, a stronger foe than he had ever met in battle appeared before Carson to oppose his further progress, though it could not wrest from his brow the laurel that a grateful country had placed there. The angel of death stole upon him with the stealth of a burglar, and with scarce a warning struck him down in the very flush of health and vigorous manhood. On the 23d of May, 1868, during a visit to his son at Ft. Lyons, Colorado, while in the act of mounting his horse an artery in his neck was ruptured, from the effects of which he died in a few moments.

In Carson's death the country lost its most distinguished representative of the intrepid race of mountaineers, and its most noted trapper, guide, pioneer and Indian fighter. As a frontiersman, in all honorable characteristics, he had no superiors, if indeed his equal ever lived. His reputation is not tainted with the moral stains that cloud the names of so many Western men who marched in the van of civilization, for he was neither a murderer nor a brawler, but always a gentleman where gentleness was permissible and courageous in defense of the weak, bold in maintenance of the right, faithful to every trust, true to his friends, magnanimous under all circumstances, and as quick to forgive an injury as to avenge a brutal insult. The world can ill afford to lose so good a man.

Autobiography
of Buffalo Bill

HON. W. F. CODY (BUFFALO BILL)

CHAPTER I

Incidents of My Childhood

After describing the stirring incidents in the lives of America's most renowned pioneers, Boone, Crockett and Carson, it is with some feeling of embarrassment and trepidation that I trench so far upon the borders of apparent vanity as to classify myself with such distinguished characters in the great work of redeeming to civilization the territory lying west of the Mississippi Valley. Nor would I make so bold a display of self-complacency or venture to obtrude myself so prominently before the world's audience, where critics are more prompt to cavil than my readers may be disposed to applaud, but for the fact that many requests have been made for the story of my life written by my own hand, that the public may discover the truth and falsehood of the numerous exploits that have been attributed to me. While this may not be a sufficient excuse for this autobiography, it appears so to me, and I therefore set myself to the far from pleasing task of describing the vicissitudes of my somewhat eventful life, which have been strangely mixed with the ingredients of opposing circumstance and happy fortune.

I made my debut upon the stage of life February 26th, 1845. The scene of this extremely important event, to me, was a little log cabin situated in the backwoods of Scott County, Iowa, where opportunities were few and society was in a state of embryo, as the settling up of that State was just then beginning. My father, Isaac, and mother, Mary Ann, were honest folks, but their possessions comprehended scarcely anything more than good characters and eight children, of which latter I was fourth in rank. I was christened William Frederick, which name I have never discarded, though more than once in my life I would have found it convenient, and decidedly to my comfort, to be known, for the time being at least, as some other fellow.

If in early youth I was different from other boys it was because I was without example and not from any inherent distinguishing characteristics. Playmates I had none, save among my brothers, and of these there were only two, one of whom was too young to appreciate my ambitions and the other too old to indulge my fancies. Accordingly, we were forced to the rather unsatisfactory compromise of each brother playing by himself, a condition very harmful in the raising of a large family.

My father did not make a successful farmer, and when I was five years of age he abandoned the log cabin of my nativity and moved the family to a little village fifteen miles north of Davenport, on the Mississippi River, named LeClair. A year before this removal he became so seriously affected by the California fever that he resolved to emigrate to that exciting climate of gold, flowers, oranges, sweet odors and fighting whisky. A party was organized, an outfit provided and a start was made, but after proceeding some fifty miles on the way they all thought it best to change their former determination before increasing the distance from home, and carried this idea so far and successfully that every one in the party returned to their respective habitations.

At LeClair I was sent to a school where, by diligence and fairly good conduct I managed to familiarize myself with the alphabet, but further progress was arrested by a suddenly developed love for skiff-riding on the Mississippi, which occupied so much of my time thereafter that really I found no convenient opportunity for further attendance at school, though neither my father nor mother had the slightest idea of my new found, self-imposed employment, much to my satisfaction, let me add. When I was thrown in the society of other boys I was not slow to follow their example, and I take to myself no special credit for my conduct as a town-boy; for, like the majority, I foraged among neighboring orchards and melon patches, rode horses when I was able to catch them grazing on the commons, trapped innocent birds, and sometimes tied the exposed clothes of my comrades while they were in swimming and least suspicious of my designs or acts. I would not like to admit any greater crimes, though anything may be implied in the confession that I was quite as bad, though no worse, than the ordinary every-day boy who goes barefoot, wears a brimless hat, one suspender and a mischievous smile.

Removal to Kansas

Shortly after my father's removal to LeClair he became a stage-driver on the line between Davenport and Chicago, but he had not followed this occupation long when he was chosen a justice of the peace, and soon after was elected to the Legislature, positions which reflected honor rather than material profit. He was a very popular man and I may with justice also add that he possessed considerable ability for the meager opportunities he had received. But he was a natural pioneer and his longing for new fields of adventure led him away from the place where his popularity was rapidly extending, and to the wilds of what was then the far West. Following the bent of his inclination, in the spring of 1852 he disposed of a small farm he owned at Walnut Grove, and packing his possessions in one carriage and three wagons he started with his family for the territory of Kansas. Father had a brother, Elijah, living at that time at Weston, Jackson County, Missouri, near the Kansas line, and as he was a well-to-do merchant of the place, father concluded to stop with him awhile until he could decide upon a desirable location in the territory. The overland trip was an uneventful one, save as it gave me an opportunity for seeing a large stretch of uninhabited wilderness, and the meeting of several rough characters on the route of which we stood in no small dread, and afforded me my first sight of a negro. When within twenty miles of Weston we asked permission to stop at a farm-house owned by a widow lady, but owing to the feeling of insecurity excited by frequent acts of pillage and outrage committed by a bad class of emigrants, our request was refused until, by chance, my father mentioned his brother's name, when a conversation was begun that resulted in a hospitable welcome from the widow, whose name was Burnes, and who was well acquainted with my uncle Elijah. We stopped at the farm-house a day and were regaled with many good things, among which was *wheat-bread,* something that I had not before eaten nor ever heard of, as corn-dodger had always been the chief staff of our frugal lives.

On the following day father and mother drove over to Weston in the carriage and in the evening returned with Elijah, who was very glad to see us and who took us to his home in Weston where we remained for some time. Father did not tarry long, but crossed over into Kansas, on a prospecting tour, hoping to find a place in which to settle his family. He visited the Kickapoo agency in Leavenworth County and soon after established a trading post at Salt Creek Valley, within four miles of the agency. Having thus entered into business, he settled his family on a farm belonging to Elijah, three miles from Weston, intending that we should remain here until the territory was opened up for settlement.

Boyhood Days in Kansas

At this time Kansas was occupied by numerous tribes of Indians who were settled on reservations, and through the territory ran the great highway to California and Salt Lake City. In addition to the thousands of gold-seekers who were passing through Kansas by way of Ft. Leavenworth, there were as many more Mormons on their hegira from Illinois to found a new temple in which to propagate their doctrines. This extensive travel made the business of trade on the route a most profitable one. But with the caravans were those fractious elements of adventurous pioneering, and here I first saw the typical Westerner, with white sombrero, buckskin clothes, long hair, moccasined feet and a belt full of murderous bowies and long pistols. But instead of these *outré* peculiarities impressing me with feelings of trepidation, they inspired me with an ambition to become a daring plainsman. The rare and skillful feats of horsemanship which I daily witnessed bred in me a desire to excel the most expert; and when, at seven years of age my father gave me a pony, the full measure of my happiness had ripened, like Jonah's gourd, in a night. Thenceforth my occupation was horseback riding, in which pleasurable employment I made myself useful in performing necessary journeys in father's interest.

In anticipation of the early passage of what was known as the "Enabling Act of Kansas Territory," which was then pending before Congress, my father, in the fall of 1853, took his family from the farm of his brother and settled them at the post in Kansas, where he at once set about erecting suitable log buildings. In the succeeding winter the act was passed which opened up the territory for settlement, and father immediately pre-empted the claim on which he was living.

During the summer of this year we lived in our little log house, and father continued to trade with the Indians, who became very friendly; hardly a day passed without a social visit from them. I spent a great deal of time with the Indian boys, who taught me how to shoot with the bow and arrow, at which I became quite expert. I also took part in all their sports, and learned to talk the Kickapoo language to some extent.

Father desired to express his friendship for these Indians, and accordingly arranged a grand barbecue for them. He invited them all to be present on a certain day, which they were; he then presented them with two fat beeves, to be killed and cooked in the various Indian styles. Mother made several large boilers full of coffee, which she gave to them, together with sugar and bread. There were about two hundred Indians in attendance at the feast, and they all enjoyed and appreciated it. In the evening they had one of their grand fantastic war dances, which greatly amused me, it being the first sight of the kind I had ever witnessed.

My Uncle Elijah and quite a large number of gentlemen and ladies came over from Weston to attend the entertainment. The Indians returned to their homes well satisfied.

My uncle at that time owned a trading post at Silver Lake, in the Pottawattamie country, on the Kansas River, and he arranged an excursion to that place. Among the party were

STAKING OUT CLAIMS

several ladies from Weston, and father, mother and myself. Mr. McMeekan, my uncle's superintendent, who had come to Weston for supplies, conducted the party to the post.

The trip across the prairies was a delightful one and we remained at the post several days. Father and one or two of the men went out to Fort Riley to view the country, and upon their return my uncle entertained the Pottawattamie Indians with a barbecue similar to the one given by father to the Kickapoos.

During the latter part of the summer father filled a hay contract at Fort Leavenworth. I passed much of my time among the campers, and spent days and days in riding over the country with Mr. William Russell, who was engaged in the freighting business and who seemed to take a considerable interest in me. In this way I became acquainted with many wagon-masters, hunters and teamsters, and learned a great deal about the business of handling cattle and mules.

It was an excellent school for me, and I acquired a great deal of practical knowledge, which afterwards I found to be of invaluable service, for it was not long before I became employed by Majors & Russell, remaining with them in different capacities for several years.

The winter of 1853–54 was spent by father at our little prairie home in cutting house logs and fence rails, which he intended to use on his farm, as soon as the bill for the opening of the territory should pass. This bill, which was called the "Enabling Act of Kansas Territory," was passed in April, 1854, and as before stated father immediately pre-empted the claim on which we were living.

The summer of that year was an exciting period in the history of the new territory. Thousands and thousands of people, seeking new homes, flocked thither, a large number of the emigrants coming over from adjoining States. The Missourians, some of them, would come laden with bottles of whisky, and after drinking the liquor would drive the bottles into the ground to mark their land claims, not waiting to put up any buildings.

Warfare on the Border

Every reader of American history is familiar with the disorders which followed close upon the heels of the "Enabling Act." Pending its passage the western boundary of Missouri was ablaze with the camp-fires of intending settlers. Thousands of families were sheltered under the canvas of their ox wagons, impatiently awaiting the signal from the Nation announcing the opening of the territorial doors to the brawny immigrants, and when the news was heralded the waiting host poured over the boundary line and fairly deluged the new public domain.

In this rapid settlement of the territory a most perplexing question arose, which was contested with such virulence that a warfare was inaugurated which became a stain upon the nation's escutcheon, and was not abated until the Missouri and Kansas borders became drunk with blood. Nearly all those who came from Missouri were intent upon extending slavery into the territory, whilst those who emigrated from Illinois, Iowa and Indiana and sought homes in the new domain were equally determined that the cursed hydra-head of slavery should never be reared in their midst. Over this question the border warfare began, and its fierceness can only find comparison in the inquisitorial persecutions of the fifteenth century. Men were shot down in their homes, around their firesides, in the furrows behind the plow—everywhere. Widows and orphans multiplied, the arm of industry was palsied, while the incendiary torch lit up the prairie heavens, feeding on blighted homes and trailing along in the path of granaries and store-houses. Mobs of murder-loving men, drunk with fury, and with hearts set on desolation, day and night descended upon unguarded households, and tearing away husbands and brothers from the loving arms of wives and sisters, left their bodies dangling from the shade trees of their unhappy homes, or shot them down where their blood might sear the eyes of helpless, agonized relatives. Anguish sat on every threshold, pity had no abiding-place, and for four years the besom of destruction, with all its pestilential influences, blighted the prairies and rendered every heart on the border sad and despondent.

The Stabbing of My Father

In this war of vengeance the Cody family did not escape a full measure of affliction. Near the Salt Creek trading post was another store, kept by a Missourian named Rively, around which a considerable settlement had been made, which became the rendezvous of many different elements, and particularly of pro-slavery men, who enjoyed Rively's sympathies. In the summer of 1854, and within a few months after the "Enabling Act" was passed, a very large meeting was held at the popular rendezvous and father being present was pressed to address the crowd on the slavery question, he being regarded as favorably disposed to making Kansas a slave territory, owing to the fact that his brother, Elijah, was a Missourian.

After much urging he at length spoke substantially as follows:

"GENTLEMEN: You have called upon me for a speech, and I have accepted your invitation rather against my will, as my views may not accord with the sentiments of a majority of this assembly. My remarks will therefore be brief and to the point. The question before us to-day is, shall the territory of Kansas admit slavery, and hereafter, upon her admission, shall she be a slave State? The question of slavery is itself a broad

MURDEROUS ATTACK UPON MY FATHER

one, which will not permit of discussion at length in this place. I apprehend that your motive in calling upon me is to have me express my sentiments in regard to the introduction of slavery into Kansas. I shall gratify your wishes in that respect. I was one of the pioneers of the State of Iowa, and aided in its settlement when it was a territory, and helped to organize it as a State.

"Gentlemen, I voted that it should be a *white* State—that negroes, whether free or slave, should never be allowed to locate within its limits; and, gentlemen, I say to you now, and I say it boldly, that I propose to exert all my power in making Kansas the same kind of a State as Iowa. I believe in letting slavery remain as it now exists, and I shall always oppose its further extension. These are my sentiments, gentlemen, and let me tell you—"

He never finished this sentence, or his speech. His expressions were anything but acceptable to the rough-looking crowd, whose ire had been gradually rising to fever heat, and at this point they hooted and hissed him, and shouted, "You black Abolitionist, shut up!" "Get down from that box!" "Kill him!" "Shoot him!" and so on. Father, however, maintained his position on the dry goods box, notwithstanding the excitement and numerous invitations to step down, until a hot-headed pro-slavery man, who was in the employ of my Uncle Elijah, crowded up and said: "Get off that box, you black Abolitionist, or I'll pull you off."

Father paid but little attention to him, and attempted to resume his speech, intending doubtless to explain his position and endeavor to somewhat pacify the angry crowd. But the fellow jumped up on the box, and pulling out a huge bowie knife, stabbed father twice, who reeled and fell to the ground. The man sprang after him, and would have ended his life then and there, had not some of the better men in the crowd interfered in time to prevent him from carrying out his murderous intention.

The excitement was intense, and another assault would probably have been made on my father, had not Rively hurriedly carried him to his home. There was no doctor within any reasonable distance, and father at once requested that he be conveyed in the carriage to his brother Elijah's house in Weston. My mother and a driver accordingly went there with him, where his wounds were dressed. He remained in Weston several weeks before he was able to stir about again, but he never fully recovered from the wounds, which eventually proved the cause of his death.

My uncle of course at once discharged the ruffian from his employ. The man afterwards became a noted desperado, and was quite conspicuous in the Kansas war.

Father's Escape from an Armed Mob

My father's indiscreet speech at Rively's brought upon our family all of the misfortunes and difficulties which from that time on befell us. As soon as he was able to attend to his business again, the Missourians began to harass him in every possible way, and kept it up with hardly a moment's cessation. Kickapoo City, as it was called, a small town that had sprung into existence seven miles up the river from Fort Leavenworth, became the hot-bed of the pro-slavery doctrine and the headquarters of its advocates. Here was really the beginning of the Kansas troubles. My father, who had shed the first blood in the cause of the freedom of Kansas, was notified, upon his return to his trading post, to leave the territory, and he was threatened with death by hanging or shooting, if he dared to remain.

One night a body of armed men, mounted on horses, rode up to our house and surrounded it. Knowing what they had come for, and seeing that there would be but little chance for him in an encounter with them, father determined to make his escape by a little stratagem. Hastily disguising himself in mother's bonnet and shawl, he boldly walked out of the house and proceeded towards the corn-field. The darkness proved a great protection, as the horsemen, between whom he passed, were unable to detect him in his disguise; supposing him to be a woman, they neither halted him nor followed him, and he passed safely on into the corn-field, where he concealed himself.

The horsemen soon dismounted and inquired for father; mother very truthfully told them that he was away. They were not satisfied with her statement, however, and they at once made a thorough search of the house. They raved and swore when they could not find him, and threatened him with death whenever they should catch him. I am sure if they had captured him that night they would have killed him. They carried off nearly everything of value in the house and about the premises; then going to the pasture, they drove off all the horses; my pony, Prince, afterward succeeded in breaking away from them and came back home. Father lay secreted in the corn-field for three days, as there were men in the vicinity who were watching for him all the time; he finally made his escape, and reached Fort Leavenworth in safety, whither the pro-slavery men did not dare to follow him.

While he was staying at Fort Leavenworth he heard that Jim Lane, Captain Cleveland and Captain Chandler were on their way from Indiana to Kansas with a body of Free State men, between two and three hundred strong. They were to cross the Missouri River near Doniphan, between Leavenworth and Nebraska City, their destination being Lawrence. Father determined to join them, and took passage on a steamboat which was going up the river. Having reached the place of crossing, he made himself known to the leaders of the party, by whom he was most cordially received.

The pro-slavery men, hearing of the approach of the Free State party, resolved to drive them out of the territory. The two parties met at Hickory Point, where a severe battle was fought, several being killed; the victory resulted in favor of the Free State men, who passed on to Lawrence without much further opposition. My father finally left them, and seeing that he could no longer live at home, went to Grasshopper Falls, thirty-five miles west of Leavenworth; there he began the erection of a saw-mill.

While he was thus engaged we learned from one of our hired workmen at home, that the pro-slavery men had laid another plan to kill him, and were on their way to Grasshopper Falls to carry out their intention. Mother at once started me off on Prince (my pony) to warn father of the coming danger. When I had gone about seven miles I suddenly came upon a party of men who were camped at the crossing of Stranger Creek, As I passed along I heard one of them, who recognized me, saying, "That's the son of the old Abolitionist we are after"; and the next moment I was commanded to halt.

Instead of stopping I instantly started my pony on a run, and on looking back I saw that I was being pursued by three or four of the party, who had mounted their horses, no doubt supposing that they could easily capture me. It was very fortunate that I had heard the remark about my being "the son of the Abolitionist," for then I

TO SAVE MY FATHER'S LIFE

knew in an instant that they were *en route* to Grasshopper Falls to murder my father. I at once saw the importance of my escaping and warning father in time. It was a matter of life or death to him. So I urged Prince to his utmost speed, feeling that upon him and myself depended a human life—a life that was dearer to me than that of any other man in the world. I led my pursuers a lively chase for four or five miles; finally, when they saw they could not catch me, they returned to their camp. I kept straight on to Grasshopper Falls, arriving there in ample time to inform father of the approach of his old enemies. That same night he and I rode to Lawrence, which had become the headquarters of the Free State men. There he met Jim Lane and several other leading characters, who were then organizing what was known as the Lecompton Legislature. Father was elected a member of that body, and took an active part in organizing the first Legislature of Kansas, under Governor Reeder, who, by the way, was a Free State man and a great friend of father's.

About this time agents were being sent to the East to induce emigrants to locate in Kansas, and father was sent as one of these agents to Ohio. After the Legislature had been organized at Lawrence, he departed for Ohio and was absent several months. A few days after he had gone, I started for home by the way of Fort Leavenworth, accompanied by two men, who were going to the fort on business. As we were crossing a stream called Little Stranger, we were fired upon by some unknown party;

one of my companions, whose name has escaped my memory, was killed. The other man and myself put spurs to our horses and made a dash for our lives. We succeeded in making our escape, though a farewell shot or two was sent after us. At Fort Leavenworth I parted company with my companion, and reached home without any further adventure.

My mother and sisters, who had not heard of my father or myself since I had been sent to warn him of his danger, had become very anxious and uneasy about us, and were uncertain as to whether we were dead or alive. I received a warm welcome home, and as I entered the house, mother seemed to read from the expression of my countenance that father was safe; of course the very first question she asked was as to his whereabouts, and in reply I handed her a long letter from him which explained everything. Mother blessed me again and again for having saved his life.

While father was absent in Ohio, we were almost daily visited by some of the pro-slavery men, who helped themselves to anything they saw fit, and frequently compelled my mother and sisters to cook for them, and to otherwise submit to a great deal of bad treatment. Hardly a day passed without some of them inquiring "where the old man was," saying they would kill him on sight. Thus we passed the summer of 1855, remaining at our home notwithstanding the unpleasant surroundings, as mother had made up her mind not to be driven out of the country. My uncle and other friends advised her to leave Kansas and move to Missouri, because they did not consider our lives safe, as we lived so near the headquarters of the pro-slavery men, who had sworn vengeance upon father.

Nothing, however, could persuade mother to change her determination. She said that the pro-slavery men had taken everything except the little home, and she proposed to remain there as long as she lived, happen what might. Our only friends in Salt Creek Valley were two families; one named Lawrence, the other Hathaway, and the peaceable Indians, who occasionally visited us. My uncle, living in Missouri and being somewhat in fear of the pro-slavery men, could not assist us much, beyond expressing his sympathy and sending us provisions.

In the winter of 1854–55 father returned from Ohio, but as soon as his old enemies learned that he was with us, they again compelled him to leave. He proceeded to Lawrence, and there spent the winter in attending the Lecompton Legislature. The remainder of the year he passed mostly at Grasshopper Falls, where he completed his saw-mill. He occasionally visited home under cover of the night, and in the most secret manner; virtually carrying his life in his hand.

In the spring of this year (1855) a pro-slavery party came to our house to search for father; not finding him, they departed, taking with them my pony, Prince. I shall never forget the man who stole that pony. He afterwards rose from the low level of a horse thief to the high dignity of a justice of the peace, and I think still lives at Kickapoo. The loss of my faithful pony nearly broke my heart and bankrupted me in business, as I had nothing to ride.

Engagement with the Great Overland Freighters

One day, soon afterwards, I met my old friend, Mr. Russell, to whom I related all my troubles, and his generous heart was touched by my story. "Billy, my boy," said he, "cheer up, and come to Leavenworth, and I'll employ you. I'll give you twenty-five dollars a month to herd cattle."

I accepted the offer, and heartily thanking him, hurried home to obtain mother's consent. She refused to let me go, and all my pleading was in vain. Young as I was—being then only in my tenth year, my ideas and knowledge of the world, however, being far in advance of my age—I determined to run away from home. Mr. Russell's offer of twenty-five dollars a month was a temptation which I could not resist. The remuneration for my services seemed very large to me, and I accordingly stole away and walked to Leavenworth.

Mr. Badger, one of Mr. Russell's superintendents, immediately sent me out, mounted on a little gray mule, to herd cattle. I worked at this for two months, and then came into Leavenworth. I had not been home during all this time, but mother had learned from Mr. Russell where I was, and she no longer felt uneasy, as he had

THE BULL-WHACKER

advised her to let me remain in his employ. He assured her that I was all right, and said that when the herd came in he would allow me to make a visit home.

Upon my arrival in Leavenworth with the herd of cattle, Mr. Russell instructed his book-keeper, Mr. Byers, to pay me my wages, amounting to fifty dollars. Byers gave me the sum all in half-dollar pieces. I put the bright silver coins into a sack, which I tied to my mule, and started home, thinking myself a *millionaire*. This money I gave to mother, who had already forgiven me for running away.

Thus began my service for the firm of Russell & Majors, afterwards Russell, Majors & Waddell, with whom I spent seven years of my life in different capacities— such as cavallard-driver, wagon-master, pony express rider and driver. I continued to work for Mr. Russell during the rest of the summer of 1855, and in the winter of 1855–56 I attended school.

Father, who still continued to secretly visit home, was anxious to have his children receive as much education as possible, under the adverse circumstances surrounding us, and he employed a teacher, Miss Jennie Lyons, to come to our house and teach. My mother was well educated—more so than my father—and it used to worry her a great deal because her children could not receive better educational advantages. However, the little school at home got along exceedingly well, and we all made rapid advances in our studies, as Miss Lyons was an excellent teacher. She afterwards married a gentleman named Hook, who became the first mayor of Cheyenne, where she now lives.

A Mob Outwitted

The Kansas troubles reached their highest pitch in the spring of 1856, and our family continued to be harassed as much as ever by our old enemies. I cannot now recollect one-half of the serious difficulties that we had to encounter; but I very distinctly remember one incident well worth relating. I came home one night on a visit from Leavenworth, being accompanied by a fellow-herder—a young man. During the night we heard a noise outside of the house, and soon the dogs began barking loudly. We looked out to ascertain the cause of the disturbance, and saw that the house was surrounded by a party of men. Mother had become accustomed to such occurrences, and on this occasion she seemed to be master of the situation from the start. Opening a window, she coolly sang out, in a firm tone of voice: "Who are you? What do you want here?"

"We are after that old Abolition husband of yours," was the answer from one of the crowd.

"He is not in the house and has not been here for a long time," said my mother.

"That's a lie! We know he is in the house and we are bound to have him," said the spokesman of the party.

I afterwards learned they had mistaken the herder, who had ridden home with me, for my father, for whom they had been watching.

"My husband is not at home," emphatically repeated my heroic mother—for if there ever was a heroine she certainly was one—"but the house is full of armed men," continued she, "and I'll give you just two minutes to get out of the yard; if you are not out by the end of that time I shall order them to fire on you."

She withdrew from the window for a few moments and hurriedly instructed the herder to call aloud certain names—any that he might think of—just as if the house were full of men to whom he was giving orders. He followed her directions to the very letter. He could not have done it any better had he rehearsed the act a dozen times.

The party outside heard him, as it was intended they should, and they supposed that my mother really had quite a force at her command. While this little by-play was being enacted, she stepped to the open window again and said—

"John Green, you and your friends had better go away or the men will surely fire on you."

At this point the herder, myself and my sisters commenced stamping on the floor in imitation of a squad of soldiers, and the herder issued his orders in a loud voice to his imaginary troops, who were apparently approaching the window preparatory to firing a volley at the enemy. This little stratagem proved eminently successful. The cowardly villains began retreating, and then my mother fired an old gun into the air which greatly accelerated their speed, causing them to break and run. They soon disappeared from view in the darkness.

The next morning we accidentally discovered that they had intended to blow up the house. Upon going into the cellar which had been left open on one side, we found two kegs of powder together with a fuse secreted there. It only required a lighted match to have sent us into eternity. My mother's presence of mind, which had never yet deserted her in any trying situation, had saved our lives.

Another Attempt to Assassinate My Father

Shortly after this affair I came home again on a visit and found father there sick with fever and confined to his bed. One day my old enemy rode up to the house on my pony Prince, which he had stolen from me.

"What is your business here to-day?" asked mother.

"I am looking for the old man," he replied. "I am going to search the house, and if I find him I am going to kill him. Here, you girls," said he, addressing my sisters, "get me some dinner, and get it quick, too, for I am as hungry as a wolf."

"Very well; pray be seated, and we'll get you something to eat," said one of my sisters, without exhibiting the least sign of fear.

He sat down, and while they were preparing a dinner for him, he took out a big knife and sharpened it on a whetstone, repeating his threat of searching the house and killing my father.

I had witnessed the whole proceeding and heard the threats, and I determined that the man should never go upstairs where father was lying in bed unable to rise. Taking a double-barreled pistol, which I had recently bought, I went to the head of the stairs, cocked the weapon, and waited for the ruffian to come up, determined that the moment he set foot on the steps I would kill him. I was relieved, however, from the stern necessity, as he did not make his appearance.

The brute was considerably intoxicated when he came to the house, and the longer he sat still the more his brain became muddled with liquor, and he actually forgot what he had come there for. After he had eaten his dinner, he mounted his horse and rode off, and it was a fortunate thing for him that he did.

Father soon recovered and returned to Grasshopper Falls, while I resumed my cattle herding.

CHAPTER II

My First Love Affair

Common school advantages were denied us in the early settlement of Kansas, and to provide a means for educating the few boys and girls in the neighborhood of my home, a subscription school was started in a small log-cabin that was built on the bank of a creek that ran near our house. My mother took great interest in this school and at her persuasion I returned home and became enrolled as a pupil, where I made satisfactory progress until the evil circumstance of a love affair suddenly blasted my prospects for acquiring an education.

Like all school-boys, I had a sweetheart with whom I was "dead in love"—in a juvenile way. Her name was Mary Hyatt. Of course I had a rival, Stephen Gobel, a boy about three years my senior—the "bully" of the school. He was terribly jealous, and sought in every way to revenge himself upon me for having won the childish affections of sweet little Mary.

The boys of the school used to build play-houses or arbors among the trees and bushes for their sweethearts. I had built a play-house for Mary, when Steve, as we called him, leveled it to the ground. We immediately had a very lively fight, in which I got badly beaten. The teacher heard of our quarrel and whipped us both. This made matters worse than ever, as I had received two thrashings to Steve's one; I smothered my angry feelings as much as possible under the humiliating circumstances, and during the afternoon recess built another play-house, thinking that Gobel would not dare to destroy a second one; but I was mistaken, for he pushed the whole structure over at the first opportunity. I came up to him just as he finished the job, and said:

"Steve Gobel, the next time you do that, I'll hurt you." And I meant it too; but he laughed and called me names.

At recess, next morning, I began the construction of still another play-house, and when I had it about two-thirds finished, Steve slyly sneaked up to the spot and tipped the whole thing over. I jumped for him with the quickness of a cat and clutching him by the throat for a moment I had the advantage of him. But he was too strong for me, and soon had me on the ground and was beating me severely. While away from home I had some way come into possession of a very small pocket dagger, which I had carried about with me in its sheath, using it in place of a knife. During the struggle this fell from my pocket, and my hand by accident rested upon it as it lay upon the ground. Exasperated beyond measure at Steve's persistence in destroying my play-houses, and smarting under his blows, I forgot myself for the moment, grasped the dagger and unthinkingly thrust it into Steve's thigh. Had it been larger it would probably have injured him severely; as it was, it made a small wound, sufficient to cause the blood to flow freely and Steve to cry out in affright: "I am killed! O, I am killed!"

The school children all rushed to the spot and were terrified at the scene. "What's the matter?" asked one. "Bill Cody has killed Steve Gobel," replied another.

TWO TO ONE

The uproar reached the teacher's ear, and I now saw him approaching, with vengeance in his eye and a big club in his hand. I knew that he was coming to interview *me*. I was dreadfully frightened at what I had done, and undecided whether to run away or to remain and take the consequences; but the sight of that flag-staff in the school teacher's hand was too much for me. I no longer hesitated, but started off like a deer. The teacher followed in hot pursuit, but soon became convinced that he could not catch me, and gave up the chase. I kept on running, until I reached one of Russell, Major & Waddell's freight trains which I had noticed going over the hill for the West. Fortunately for me I knew the wagon-master, John Willis, and as soon as I recovered my breath I told him what had happened.

"Served him right, Billy!" said he, "and what's more, we'll go over and clean out the teacher."

"Oh no; don't do that," said I, for I was afraid that I might fall into the hands of the wounded boy's friends, who I knew would soon be looking for me.

"Well, Billy, come along with me; I am bound for Fort Kearney; the trip will take me forty days. I want you for a cavallard-driver."

"All right," I replied, "but I must go home and tell mother about it, and get some clothes."

"Well, then, to-night after we make our camp, I'll go back with you."

Pursued by the Wounded Boy's Father

The affray broke up the school for the rest of the day as the excitement was too much for the children. Late in the afternoon, after the train had moved on some considerable distance, I saw Steve's father, his brother Frank, and one of the neighbors rapidly approaching.

"Mr. Willis, there comes old Gobel, with Frank and somebody else, and they are after me—what am I going to do?" I asked.

"Let 'em come," said he, "they can't take you if I've got anything to say about it, and I rather think I have. Get into one of the wagons—keep quiet and lay low. I'll manage this little job. Don't you fret a bit about it."

I obeyed his orders and felt much easier.

Old Gobel, Frank and the neighbor soon came up and inquired for me.

"He's around here somewhere," said Mr. Willis.

"We want him," said Gobel; "he stabbed my son a little while ago, and I want to arrest him."

"Well, you can't get him; that settles it; so you needn't waste any of your time around here," said Willis.

Gobel continued to talk for a few minutes, but getting no greater satisfaction, the trio returned home.

When night came, Willis accompanied me on horseback to my home. Mother, who had anxiously searched for me everywhere—being afraid that something had befallen me at the hands of the Gobels—was delighted to see me, notwithstanding the difficulty in which I had become involved. I at once told her that at present I was afraid to remain at home, and had accordingly made up my mind to absent myself for a few weeks or months—at least until the excitement should die out. Mr. Willis said to her that he would take me to Fort Kearney with him, and see that I was properly cared for, and would bring me back safely in forty days.

Mother at first seriously objected to my going on this trip, fearing I would fall into the hands of Indians. Her fears, however, were soon overcome, and she concluded to let me go. She fixed me up a big bundle of clothing and gave me a quilt. Kissing her and my sisters a fond farewell, I started off on my first trip across the plains, with a light heart too, notwithstanding my trouble of a few hours before.

The trip proved a most enjoyable one to me, although no incidents worthy of note occurred on the way. On my return from Fort Kearney I was paid off the same as the rest of the employees. The remainder of the summer and fall I spent in herding cattle and working for Russell, Majors & Waddell.

I finally ventured home—not without some fear, however, of the Gobel family—and was delighted to learn that during my absence mother had had an interview with Mr. Gobel, and having settled the difficulty with him, the two families had become friends again, and I may state, incidentally, that they ever remained so. I have since often met Stephen Gobel, and we have had many a laugh together over our love affair and the affray at the school-house. Mary Hyatt, the innocent cause of the whole difficulty, is now married and living in Chicago. Thus ended my first love scrape.

In the winter of 1856–57 my father, in company with a man named J. C. Boles, went to Cleveland, Ohio, and organized a colony of about thirty families, whom they brought to Kansas and located on the Grasshopper. Several of these families still reside there.

It was during this winter that father, after his return from Cleveland, caught a severe cold. This, in connection with the wound he had received at Rively's—from which he had never entirely recovered—affected him seriously, and in April, 1857, he died at home from kidney disease.

This sad event left my mother and the family in poor circumstances, and I determined to follow the plains for a livelihood for them and myself. I had no difficulty in obtaining work under my old employers, and in May, 1857, I started for Salt Lake City with a herd of beef cattle, in charge of Frank and Bill McCarthy, for General

Albert Sidney Johnston's army, which was then being sent across the plains to fight the Mormons.

My First Fight with Indians

Nothing occurred to interrupt our journey until we reached Plum Creek, on the South Platte River, thirty-five miles west of Old Fort Kearney. We had made a morning drive and had camped for dinner. The wagon-masters and a majority of the men had gone to sleep under the mess wagons; the cattle were being guarded by three men, and the cook was preparing dinner. No one had any idea that Indians were anywhere near us. The first warning we had that they were infesting that part of the country was the firing of shots and the whoops and yells from a party of them, who, catching us napping, gave us a most unwelcome surprise. All the men jumped to their feet and seized their guns. They saw with astonishment the cattle running in every direction, they having been stampeded by the Indians, who had shot and killed the three men who were on day-herd duty, and the red devils were now charging down upon the rest of us.

I then thought of mother's fears of my falling into the hands of the Indians, and I had about made up my mind that such was to be my fate; but when I saw how coolly and determinedly the McCarthy brothers were conducting themselves and giving orders to the little band, I became convinced that we would "stand the Indians off," as the saying is. Our men were all well armed with Colt's revolvers and Mississippi yagers, which last carried a bullet, and two buckshots.

The McCarthy boys, at the proper moment, gave orders to fire upon the advancing enemy. The volley checked them, although they returned the compliment, and shot one of our party through the leg. Frank McCarthy then sang out, "Boys, make a break for the slough yonder, and we can then have the bank for a breast-work."

We made a run for the slough which was only a short distance off, and succeeded in safely reaching it, bringing with us the wounded man. The bank proved to be a very effective breast-work, affording us good protection. We had been there but a short time when Frank McCarthy, seeing that the longer we were corralled the worse it would be for us, said:

"Well, boys, we'll try to make our way back to Fort Kearney by wading in the river and keeping the bank for a breast-work."

We all agreed that this was the best plan, and we accordingly proceeded down the river several miles in this way, managing to keep the Indians at a safe distance with our guns, until the slough made a junction with the main Platte River. From there down we found the river at times quite deep, and in order to carry the wounded man along with us, we constructed a raft of poles for his accommodation, and in this way he was transported.

Occasionally the water would be too deep for us to wade, and we were obliged to put our weapons on the raft and swim. The Indians followed us pretty close, and were continually watching for an opportunity to get a good range and give us a raking fire. Covering ourselves by keeping well under the bank, we pushed ahead as rapidly as possible, and made pretty good progress, the night finding us still on the way and our enemies yet on our track.

How I Killed My First Indian

I being the youngest and smallest of the party, became somewhat tired, and without noticing it I had fallen behind the others for some little distance. It was about ten o'clock and we were keeping very quiet and hugging close to the bank, when I happened to look up to the moon-lit sky and saw the plumed head of an Indian peeping over the bank. Instead of hurrying ahead and alarming the men in a quiet way, I instantly aimed my gun at his head and fired. The report rang out sharp and loud on the night air, and was immediately followed by an Indian whoop, and the next moment about six feet of dead Indian came tumbling into the river. I was not only overcome with astonishment, but was badly scared, as I could hardly realize what I had done. I expected to see the whole force of Indians come down upon us. While I was standing thus bewildered, the men, who had heard the shot and the war-whoop and had seen the Indian take a tumble, came rushing back.

"Who fired that shot?" cried Frank McCarthy.

"I did," replied I, rather proudly, as my confidence returned and I saw the men coming up.

"Yes, and little Billy has killed an Indian stone-dead—too dead to skin," said one of the men, who had approached nearer than the rest, and had almost stumbled upon the corpse. From that time forward I became a hero and an Indian killer. This was, of course, the first Indian I had ever shot, and as I was not then more than eleven years of age, my exploit created quite a sensation.

The other Indians, upon learning what had happened to their "advance guard," set up a terrible howling, and fired several volleys at us, but without doing any injury, as we were so well protected by the bank. We resumed our journey down the river, and traveled all night long. Just before daylight, Frank McCarthy crawled out over the bank and discovered that we were only five miles from Fort Kearney, which post we reached in safety in about two hours—shortly after *reveille*—bringing the wounded man with us. It was indeed a relief to us all to feel that once more I was safe, after such a dangerous initiation.

KILLING MY FIRST INDIAN

Frank McCarthy immediately reported to the commanding officer and informed him of all that had happened. The commandant at once ordered a company of cavalry and one of infantry to proceed to Plum Creek on a forced march—taking a howitzer with them—to endeavor to recapture the cattle from the Indians.

The firm of Russell, Majors & Waddell had a division agent at Kearney, and this agent mounted us on mules so that we could accompany the troops. On reaching the place where the Indians had surprised us, we found the bodies of the three men whom they had killed and scalped, and literally cut into pieces. We of course buried the remains. We caught but few of the cattle; the most of them having been driven off and stampeded with the buffaloes, there being numerous immense herds of the latter in that section of the country at the time. The Indians' trail was discovered running south towards the Republican River, and the troops followed it to the head of Plum Creek, and there abandoned it, returning to Fort Kearney without having seen a single redskin.

The company's agent, seeing that there was no further use for us in that vicinity—as we had lost our cattle and mules—sent us back to Fort Leavenworth. The company, it is proper to state, did not have to stand the loss of the expedition, as the government held itself responsible for such depredations by the Indians.

On the day that I got into Leavenworth, sometime in July, I was interviewed for the first time in my life by a newspaper reporter, and the next morning I found my name in print as "the youngest Indian slayer on the plains." I am candid enough to admit that I felt very much elated over this notoriety. Again and again I read with eager interest the long and sensational account of our adventure. My exploit was related in a very graphic manner, and for a long time afterwards I was considerable of a hero. The reporter who had thus set me up, as I then thought, on the highest pinnacle of fame, was John Hutchinson, and I felt very grateful to him. He now lives in Wichita, Kansas.

On the Road to Salt Lake

In the following summer Russell, Majors & Waddell entered upon a contract with the government for transporting supplies for General Albert Sidney Johnston's army that was sent against the Mormons. A large number of teams and teamsters were required for this purpose, and as the route was considered a dangerous one, men were not easily engaged for the service, though the pay was forty dollars per month in gold. An old wagon-master named Lew Simpson, one of the best that ever commanded a bull-train, was upon the point of starting with about ten wagons for the company, direct for Salt Lake, and as he had known me for some time as an ambitious youth, requested me to accompany him as an extra hand. My duties would be light, and in fact I would have nothing to do, unless some one of the drivers should become sick, in which case I would be required to take his place. But even more seductive than this inducement was the promise that I should be provided with a mule of my own to ride, and be subject to the orders of no one save Simpson himself.

The offer was made in such a manner that I became at once wild to go, but my mother interposed an emphatic objection and urged me to abandon so reckless a desire. She reminded me that in addition to the fact that the trip would possibly occupy a year, the journey was one of extreme peril, beset as it was by Mormon

ON THE OVERLAND TRAIL

assassins and treacherous Indians, and begged me to accept the lesson of my last experience and narrow escape as a providential warning. But to her pleadings and remonstrances I returned the answer that I had determined to follow the plains as an occupation, and while I appreciated her advice and desired greatly to honor her commands, yet I could not forego my determination to accompany the train.

Seeing that it was impossible to keep me at home, she reluctantly gave her consent, but not until she had called upon Mr. Russell and Mr. Simpson in regard to the matter, and had obtained from the latter gentleman his promise that I should be well taken care of, if we had to winter in the mountains. She did not like the appearance of Simpson, and upon inquiry she learned, to her dismay, that he was a desperate character, and that on nearly every trip he had made across the plains he had killed some one. Such a man, she thought, was not a fit master or companion for her son, and she was very anxious to have me go with some other wagon-master; but I still insisted upon remaining with Simpson.

"Madam, I can assure you that Lew Simpson is one of the most reliable wagon-masters on the plains," said Mr. Russell, "and he has taken a great fancy to Billy. If your boy is bound to go, he can go with no better man. No one will dare to impose on him while he is with Lew Simpson, whom I will instruct to take good care of the boy. Upon reaching Fort Laramie, Billy can, if he wishes, exchange places with some fresh man coming back on a returning train, and thus come home without making the whole trip."

This seemed to satisfy mother, and then she had a long talk with Simpson himself, imploring him not to forget his promise to take good care of her precious boy. He promised everything that she asked. Thus, after much trouble, I became one of the members of Simpson's train. Before taking our departure, I arranged with Russell, Majors & Waddell that when my pay fell due it should be paid over to mother.

Description of the Bull-Train Outfit

As a matter of interest to the general reader, it may be well in this connection to give a brief description of a freight train. The wagons used in those days by Russell, Majors & Waddell were known as the "J. Murphy wagons," made at St. Louis specially for the plains business. They were very large and were strongly built, being capable of carrying seven thousand pounds of freight each. The wagon-boxes were very commodious—being about as large as the rooms of an ordinary house—and were covered with two heavy canvas sheets to protect the merchandise from the rain. These wagons were generally sent out from Leavenworth, each loaded with six thousand pounds of freight, and each drawn by several yokes of oxen in charge of one driver. A train consisted of twenty-five wagons, all in charge of one man, who was known as the wagon-master. The second man in command was the assistant wagon-master; then came the "extra hand," next the night herder; and lastly, the cavallard-driver, whose duty it was to drive the lame and loose cattle. There were thirty-one men all told in a train. The men did their own cooking, being divided into messes of seven. One man cooked, another brought wood and water, another stood guard, and so on, each having some duty to perform while getting meals. All were heavily armed with Colt's pistols and Mississippi yagers, and every one always had his weapons handy so as to be prepared for any emergency.

The wagon-master, in the language of the plains, was called the "bull-wagon boss"; the teamsters were known as "bull-whackers;" and the whole train was denominated a "bull-outfit.' Everything at that time was called an "outfit." The men of the plains were always full of droll humor and exciting stories of their own experiences, and many an hour I spent in listening to the recitals of thrilling adventures and hair-breadth escapes.

The Trail

The trail to Salt Lake ran through Kansas northwestwardly, crossing the Big Blue River, then over the Big and Little Sandy, coming into Nebraska near the Big Sandy. The next stream of any importance was the Little Blue, along which the trail ran for sixty miles; then crossed a range of sand-hills, and struck the Platte River ten miles below old Fort Kearney; thence the course lay up the South Platte to the old Ash Hollow Crossing, thence eighteen miles across to the North Platte, near the mouth of the Blue Water, where General Harney had his great battle in 1855 with the Sioux and Cheyenne Indians. From this point the North Platte was followed, passing Court House Rock, Chimney Rock and Scott's Bluffs, and then on to Fort Laramie, where the Laramie River was crossed. Still following the North Platte for some considerable distance, the trail crossed the river at old Richard's Bridge, and followed it up to the celebrated Red Buttes, crossing the Willow Creeks to the Sweet Water, passing the great Independence Rock and the Devil's Gate, up to the Three Crossings of the Sweet Water, thence past the Cold Springs, where, three feet under the sod, on the hottest day of summer, ice can be found; thence to the Hot Springs and the Rocky Ridge, and through the Rocky Mountains and Echo Cañon, and thence on to the great Salt Lake Valley.

In order to take care of the business which then offered, the freight for transportation being almost exclusively government provisions, Russell, Majors & Waddell operated 6,250 wagons, for the hauling of which they used 75,000 oxen, and gave employment to 8,000 men; the capital invested by these three freighters was nearly $2,000,000. In their operations, involving such an immense sum of money, and employing a class of laborers incomparably reckless, some very stringent rules were adopted by the firm, to which all their employees were made to subscribe.

In this code of discipline was the following obligation: "I, —— do hereby solemnly swear, before the Great and Living God, that during my engagement, and while I am in the employ of Russell, Majors & Waddell, that I will under no circumstances use profane language; that I will drink no intoxicating liquors of any kind; that I will not quarrel or fight with any other employee of the firm and that in every respect I will conduct myself honestly, be faithful to my duties, and so direct all my acts as will win the confidence and esteem of my employers, so help me God."

This oath was the creation of Mr. Majors, who was a very pious and rigid disciplinarian; he tried hard to enforce it, but how great was his failure it is needless to say. It would have been equally profitable had the old gentleman read the riot act to a herd of stampeded buffaloes. And he believes it himself now.

A Buffalo Stampede

Nothing transpired on the trip to delay or give us any trouble whatever, until the train struck the South Platte River. One day we camped on the same ground where the Indians had surprised the cattle herd in charge of the McCarthy brothers. It was with difficulty that we discovered any traces of anybody ever having camped there before, the only landmark being the single grave, now covered with grass, in which we had buried the three men who had been killed. The country was alive with buffaloes. Vast herds of these monarchs of the plains were roaming all around us, and we laid over one day for a grand hunt. Besides killing quite a number of buffaloes and having a day of rare sport, we captured ten or twelve head of cattle, they being a portion of the herd which had been stampeded by the Indians two months before. The next day we pulled out of camp, and the train was strung out to a considerable length along the road which ran near the foot of the sand-hills, two miles from the river. Between the road and the river we saw a large herd of buffaloes grazing quietly, they having been down to the stream for a drink.

Just at this time we observed a party of returning Californians coming from the west. They, too, noticed the buffalo herd, and in another moment they were dashing

THE BUFFALO STAMPEDE

down upon them, urging their steeds to the greatest speed. The buffalo herd stampeded at once and broke down the hills; so hotly were they pursued by the hunters that about five hundred of them rushed through our train pell-mell, frightening both men and oxen. Some of the wagons were turned clear round, and many of the terrified oxen attempted to run to the hills, with the heavy wagons attached to them. Others turned around so short that they broke the wagon tongues off. Nearly all the teams got entangled in their gearing, and became wild and unruly, so that the perplexed drivers were unable to manage them.

The buffaloes, the cattle and the drivers were soon running in every direction, and the excitement upset nearly everybody and everything. Many of the cattle broke their yokes and stampeded. One big buffalo bull became entangled in one of the heavy wagon-chains, and it is a fact that in his desperate efforts to free himself he not only actually snapped the strong chain in two, but broke the ox-yoke to which it was attached, and the last seen of him he was running towards the hills with it hanging from his horns. A dozen other equally remarkable incidents happened during the short time that the frantic buffaloes were playing havoc with our train, and when they got through and left us our outfit was badly crippled and scattered. This caused us to go into camp and spend a day in replacing the broken tongues and repairing other damages, and gathering up our scattered ox-teams.

Captured by Danites

The next day we rolled out of camp and proceeded on our way towards the setting sun. Everything ran along smoothly with us from that point until we came within about eighteen miles of Green River, in the Rocky Mountains—where we camped at noon. At this place we had to drive our cattle about a mile and a half to a creek to water them. Simpson, his assistant George Woods and myself, accompanied by the usual number of guards, drove the cattle over to the creek, and while on our way back to camp we suddenly observed a party of twenty horsemen rapidly approaching us. We were not yet in view of our wagons, as a rise of ground intervened, and therefore we could not signal the train-men in case of any unexpected danger befalling us. We had no suspicion, however, that we were about to be trapped, as the strangers were white men. When they had come up to us, one of the party, who evidently was the leader, rode out in front and said:

"How are you, Mr. Simpson?"

"You've got the best of me, sir," said Simpson, who did not know him.

"Well, I rather think I have," coolly replied the stranger, whose words conveyed a double meaning, as we soon learned. We had all come to a halt by this time and the strange horsemen had surrounded us. They were all armed with double-barreled shot guns, rifles and revolvers. We also were armed with revolvers, but we had had no idea of danger, and these men, much to our surprise, had "got the drop" on us and had covered us with their weapons, so that we were completely at their mercy. The whole movement of corralling us was done so quietly and quickly that it was accomplished before we knew it.

"I'll trouble you for your six shooters, gentlemen," now said the leader.

"I'll give 'em to you in a way you don't want," replied Simpson.

The next moment three guns were leveled at Simpson. "If you make a move you're a dead man," said the leader.

Simpson saw that he was taken at a great disadvantage, and thinking it advisable not to risk the lives of the party by any rash act on his part, he said: "I see now that you have the best of me, but who are you, anyhow?"

"I am Joe Smith," was the reply.

"What! the leader of the Danites?" asked Simpson.

"You are correct," said Smith, for he it was.

"Yes," said Simpson, "I know you now; you are a spying scoundrel."

Simpson had good reason for calling him this and applying to him a much more opprobrious epithet, for only a short time before this, Joe Smith had visited our train in the disguise of a teamster, and had remained with us two days. He suddenly disappeared, no one knowing where he had gone or why he had come among us. But it was all explained to us now that he had returned with his Mormon Danites. After they had disarmed us, Simpson asked, "Well, Smith, what are you going to do with us?"

"Ride back with us and I'll soon show you," said Smith.

Destruction of the Train by Mormons

We had no idea of the surprise which awaited us. As we came upon the top of the ridge, from which we could view our camp, we were astonished to see the remainder of the train-men disarmed and stationed in a group and surrounded by another squad of Danites, while other Mormons were searching our wagons for such articles as they wanted.

"How is this?" inquired Simpson. "How did you surprise my camp without a struggle? I can't understand it."

"Easily enough," said Smith; "your men were all asleep under the wagons, except the cooks, who saw us coming and took us for returning Californians or emigrants, and paid no attention to us until we rode up and surrounded your train. With our arms covering the men, we woke them up, and told them all they had to do was to walk out and drop their pistols—which they saw was the best thing they could do under circumstances over which they had no control—and you can just bet they did it."

"And what do you propose to do with us now?" asked Simpson.

"I intend to burn your train," said he; "you are loaded with supplies and ammunition for Sidney Johnston, and as I have no way to convey the stuff to my own people, I'll see that it does not reach the United States troops."

"Are you going to turn us adrift here?" asked Simpson, who was anxious to learn what was to become of himself and his men.

"No; I am hardly so bad as that. I'll give you enough provisions to last you until you can reach Fort Bridger," replied Smith; "and as soon as your cooks can get the stuff out of the wagons, you can start."

"On foot?" was the laconic inquiry of Simpson.

"Yes, sir," was the equally short reply.

"Smith, that's too rough on us men. Put yourself in our place and see how you would like it," said Simpson; "you can well afford to give us at least one wagon and six yokes of oxen to convey us and our clothing and provisions to Fort Bridger. You're a brute if you don't do this."

"Well," said Smith, after consulting a minute or two with some of his company, "I'll do that much for you."

The cattle and the wagon were brought up according to his orders, and the clothing and provisions were loaded on.

"Now you can go," said Smith, after everything had been arranged.

"Joe Smith, I think you are a mean coward to set us afloat in a hostile country without giving us our arms," said Simpson, who had once before asked for the weapons, and had had his request denied.

Smith, after further consultation with his comrades, said: "Simpson, you are too brave a man to be turned adrift here without any means of defense. You shall have your revolvers and guns." Our weapons were accordingly handed over to Simpson, and we at once started for Fort Bridger, knowing that it would be useless to attempt the recapture of our train.

When we had traveled about two miles we saw the smoke arising from our old camp. The Mormons after taking what goods they wanted and could carry off, had set fire to the wagons, many of which were loaded with bacon, lard, hard-tack, and other provisions, which made a very hot, fierce fire, and the smoke to roll up in dense clouds. Some of the wagons were loaded with ammunition, and it was not long before loud explosions followed in rapid succession. We waited and witnessed the burning of the train, and then pushed on to Fort Bridger. Arriving at this post, we learned that two other trains had been captured and destroyed in the same way, by the Mormons. This made seventy-five wagon loads, or 450,000 pounds of supplies, mostly provisions, which never reached General Johnston's command to which they had been consigned.

On the Point of Starvation

After reaching the fort, it being far in November, we decided to spend the winter there with about four hundred other employees of Russell, Majors & Waddell, rather than attempt a return, which would have exposed us to many dangers and the severity of the rapidly approaching winter. During this period of hibernation, however, the larders of the commissary became so depleted that we were placed on one-quarter rations, and at length, as a final resort, the poor, dreadfully emaciated mules and oxen were killed to afford sustenance for our famishing party.

Fort Bridger being located in a prairie, all fuel there used had to be carried for a distance of nearly two miles, and after our mules and oxen were butchered we had no other recourse than to carry the wood on our backs or haul it on sleds, a very tedious and laborious alternative.

Starvation was beginning to lurk about the post when spring approached, and but for the timely arrival of a westward-bound train loaded with provisions for Johnston's army some of our party must certainly have fallen victims to deadly hunger.

The winter finally passed away, and early in the spring, as soon as we could travel, the civil employees of the government, with the teamsters and freighters, started for the Missouri River, the Johnston expedition having been abandoned.

On the way down we stopped at Fort Laramie, and there met a supply train bound westward. Of course we all had a square meal once more, consisting of hard tack, bacon, coffee and beans. I can honestly say that I thought it was the best meal I had ever eaten; at least I relished it more than any other, and I think the rest of the party did the same.

On leaving Fort Laramie, Simpson was made brigade wagon-master, and was put in charge of two large trains, with about four hundred extra men, who were bound for Fort Leavenworth. When we came to Ash Hollow, instead of taking the usual trail over to the South Platte, Simpson concluded to follow the North Platte down to its junction with the South Platte. The two trains were traveling about fifteen miles apart, when one morning while Simpson was with the rear train, he told his assistant wagon-master, George Wood and myself to saddle up our mules, as he wanted us to go with him and overtake the head train.

Attacked by Indians

We started off at about eleven o'clock, and had ridden about seven miles, when—while we were on a big plateau, back of Cedar Bluffs—we suddenly discovered a band of Indians coming out of the head of a ravine, half a mile distant, and charging down upon us at full speed. I thought that our end had come this time. Simpson, however, was equal to the occasion, for with wonderful promptness he jumped from his jaded mule and in a trice shot his own animal and ours also and ordered us to assist him to jerk their bodies into a triangle. This being quickly done we got inside the barricade of mule flesh and were prepared to receive the Indians. We were each armed with a Mississippi yager and two revolvers, and as the Indians came swooping down on our improvised fort we opened fire with such good effect that three fell dead to the first volley. This caused them to retreat out of range, as with two exceptions they were armed with bows and arrows and therefore to approach near enough to do execution

HOLDING THE FORT

would expose at least several of them to certain death. Seeing that they could not take our little fortification, or drive us from it, they circled around several times, shooting their arrows at us. One of these struck George Wood in the left shoulder, inflicting only a slight wound, however, and several lodged in the bodies of the dead mules; otherwise they did us no harm. The Indians finally galloped off to a safe distance, where our bullets could not reach them, and seemed to be holding a council. This was a lucky move for us, for it gave us an opportunity to reload our guns and pistols, and prepare for the next charge of the enemy. During the brief cessation of hostilities, Simpson extracted the arrow from Wood's shoulder, and put an immense quid of tobacco on the wound. Wood was then ready for business again.

The Indians did not give us a very long rest, for with another desperate charge, as if to ride over us, they came dashing towards the mule barricade. We gave them a hot reception from our yagers and revolvers. They could not stand or understand the rapidly repeating fire of the revolver, and we checked them again. They circled around once more and gave us a few parting shots as they rode off, leaving behind them another dead Indian and a horse.

For two hours afterwards they did not seem to be doing anything but holding a council. We made good use of this time by digging up the ground inside the barricade with our knives and throwing the loose earth around and over the mules, and we soon had a very respectable fortification. We were not troubled any more that day, but during the night the cunning rascals tried to burn us out by setting fire to the prairie. The buffalo grass was so short that the fire did not trouble us much, but the smoke concealed the Indians from our view, and they thought that they could approach close to us without being seen. We were aware of this and kept a sharp look-out, being prepared all the time to receive them. They finally abandoned the idea of surprising us.

A Timely Rescue

Next morning, bright and early, they gave us one more grand charge and again we "stood them off." They then rode away half a mile or so and formed a circle around us. Each man dismounted and sat down, as if to wait and starve us out. They had evidently seen the advance train pass on the morning of the previous day, and believed that we belonged to that outfit and were trying to overtake it; they had no idea that another train was on its way after us.

Our hopes of escape from this unpleasant and perilous situation now depended upon the arrival of the rear train, and when we saw that the Indians were going to besiege us instead of renewing their attacks, we felt rather confident of receiving timely assistance. We had expected that the train would be along late in the afternoon of the previous day, and as the morning wore away we were somewhat anxious and uneasy at its non-arrival.

At last, about ten o'clock, we began to hear in the distance the loud and sharp reports of the big bull-whips, which were handled with great dexterity by the teamsters, and cracked like rifle shots. These were as welcome sounds to us as were the notes of the bag-pipes to the besieged garrison at Lucknow, when the re-enforcements were coming up and the pipers were heard playing, "The Campbells Are Coming." In a few moments we saw the lead or head wagon coming slowly over the ridge, which had concealed the train from our view, and soon the whole outfit made its appearance. The Indians observed the approaching train and assembling in a group they held a short consultation. They then charged upon us once more, for the last time, and as they turned and dashed away over the prairie we sent our farewell shots rattling after them. The teamsters, seeing the Indians and hearing the shots, came rushing forward to our assistance, but by the time they reached us the red-skins had almost disappeared from view. The teamsters eagerly asked us a hundred questions concerning our fight, admired our fort and praised our pluck. Simpson's remarkable presence of mind in planning the defense was the general topic of conversation among all the men.

When the teams came up we obtained some water and bandages with which to dress Wood's wound, which had become quite inflamed and painful, and we then put him into one of the wagons. Simpson and myself obtained a remount, bade good-bye to our dead mules which had served us so well, and after collecting the ornaments and other plunder from the dead Indians, we left their bodies and bones to bleach on the prairie. The train moved on again and we had no other adventures except several exciting buffalo hunts on the South Platte, near Plum Creek.

We arrived at Fort Leavenworth about the middle of July 1858, when I immediately visited home. I found mother in very poor health, as she was suffering from asthma. My oldest sister, Martha, had, during my absence, been married to John Crane, and was living at Leavenworth.

Engage in Trapping

I had been home only about a month, after returning from Fort Bridger, when I again started out with another train, going this time as assistant wagon-master under Buck Bomer. We went safely through to Fort Laramie, which was our destination, and from there we were ordered to take a load of supplies to a new post called Fort Wallace, which was being established at Cheyenne Pass. We made this trip and got back to Fort Laramie about November 1st. I then quit the employ of Russell, Majors & Waddell, and joined a party of trappers who were sent out by the post trader, Mr. Ward, to trap on the streams of the Chugwater and Laramie for beaver, otter, and other fur animals, and also to poison wolves for their pelts. We were out two months, but as the expedition did not prove very profitable, and was rather dangerous on account of the Indians, we abandoned the enterprise and came into Fort Laramie in the latter part of December.

Being anxious to return to the Missouri River, I joined with two others, named Scott and Charley, who were also desirous of going East on a visit, bought three ponies and a pack-mule, and we started out together. We made rapid progress on our journey, and nothing worthy of note happened until one afternoon, along the banks of the Little Blue River, we spied a band of Indians hunting on the opposite side of the stream, three miles away. We did not escape their notice, and they gave us a lively chase for two hours, but they could find no good crossing, and as evening came on we finally got away from them.

We traveled until late in the night, when upon discovering a low, deep ravine which we thought would make a comfortable and safe camping-place, we stopped for a rest. In searching for a good place to make our beds, I found a hole, and called to my companions that I had found a fine place for a nest. One of the party was to stand guard while the others slept. Scott took the first watch, while Charley and I prepared our beds.

A Horrible Discovery

While clearing out the place we felt something rough, but as it was dark we could not make out what it was. At any rate we concluded that it was bones or sticks of wood; we thought perhaps it might be the bones of some animal which had fallen in there and died. These bones, for such they really proved to be, we pushed one side and then we lay down. But Charley, being an inveterate smoker, could not resist the temptation of indulging in a smoke before going to sleep. So he sat up and struck a match to light his old pipe. Our subterranean bed-chamber was thus illuminated for a moment or two; I sprang to my feet in an instant for a ghastly and horrifying sight was revealed to us. Eight or ten human skeletons lay scattered upon the ground!

The light of the match died out, but we had seen enough to convince us that we were in a large grave, into which, perhaps, some unfortunate emigrants, who had been killed by the Indians, had been thrown; or, probably, seeking refuge there, they had been corralled and then killed on the spot. If such were the cave they had met the fate of thousands of others, whose friends have never heard of them since they left their Eastern homes to seek their fortunes in the far West. However, we did not care to investigate this mystery any further, but we hustled out of that chamber of death and informed Scott of our discovery. Most of the plainsmen are very superstitious, and we were no exception to the general rule. We surely thought that this incident was an evil omen, and that we would be killed if we remained there any longer.

"Let us dig out of here quicker than we can say Jack Robinson," said Scott; and we began to "dig out" at once. We saddled our animals and hurriedly pushed forward through the darkness, traveling several miles before we again went into camp. Next morning it was snowing fiercely, but we proceeded as best we could, and that night we succeeded in reaching Oak Grove ranch which had been built during the summer. We here obtained comfortable accommodations and plenty to eat and drink—especially the latter.

Scott and Charley were great lovers and consumers of "tanglefoot" and they soon got gloriously drunk, keeping it up for three days, during which time they gambled with the ranchmen, who got away with all their money; but little they cared for that, as they had their spree. They finally sobered up, and we resumed our journey, urging our jaded animals as much as they could stand, until we struck Marysville on the Big Blue. From this place to Leavenworth we secured first-rate accommodations along the road, as the country had become pretty well settled.

It was in February, 1859, that I got home. As there was now a good school in the neighborhood, taught by Mr. Devinny, my mother wished me to attend it, and I did so for two months and a half—the longest period of schooling that I ever received at any

A HORRIFYING DISCOVERY

one time in my life. As soon as the spring came and the grass began growing, I became uneasy and discontented, and again longed for the free and open life of the plains.

Off for Pike's Peak

The Pike's Peak gold excitement was then at its height, and everybody was rushing to the new gold diggings. I caught the gold fever myself, and joined a party bound for the new town of Auraria on Cherry Creek, afterwards called Denver, in honor of the then Governor of Kansas. On arriving at Auraria we pushed on to the gold streams in the mountains, passing up through Golden Grate and over Guy Hill, and thence on to Black Hawk. We prospected for two months, but as none of us knew anything about mining we met with very poor success, and therefore concluded that prospecting for gold was not our forte. We accordingly abandoned the enterprise and turned our faces eastward once more.

When we struck the Platte River, the happy thought of constructing a small raft—which would float us clear to the Missouri and thence down to Leavenworth—entered our heads, and we accordingly carried out the plan. Upon the completion of the raft, we stocked it with provisions and "set sail" down the stream. It was a light craft and a jolly crew, and all was smooth sailing for four or five days.

When we got near old Julesburg we met with a serious mishap. Our raft ran into an eddy, and quick as lightning went to pieces, throwing us all into the stream, which was so deep that we had to swim ashore. We lost everything we had, which greatly discouraged us, and we thereupon abandoned the idea of rafting it any further. We then walked over to Julesburg, which was only a few miles distant. This ranch, which became a somewhat famous spot, had been established by "Old Jules," a Frenchman, who was afterwards killed by the notorious Alf. Slade.

A Pony Express Rider

The great pony express, about which so much has been said and written, was at that time just being started. The line was being stocked with horses and put into good running condition. At Julesburg I met Mr. George Chrisman, the leading wagon-master of Russell, Majors & Waddell, who had always been a good friend to me. He had bought out "Old Jules," and was then the owner of Julesburg ranch, and the agent of the pony express line. He hired me at once as a pony express rider, but as I was so young he thought I was not able to stand the fierce riding which was required of the messengers. He knew, however, that I had been raised in the saddle—that I felt more at home there than in any other place—and as he saw that I was confident that I could stand the racket, and could ride as far and endure it as well as some of the old riders, he gave me a short route of forty-five miles, with the stations fifteen miles apart, and three changes of horses. I was required to make fifteen miles an hour, including the changes of horses. I was fortunate in getting well broken animals, and being so light, I easily made my forty-five miles on time on my first trip out, and ever afterwards.

I wrote to mother and told her how well I liked the exciting life of a pony express rider. She replied, and begged of me to give it up, as it would surely kill me. She was right about this, as fifteen miles an hour on horseback would, in a short time, shake any man "all to pieces"; and there were but very few, if any, riders who could stand it for any great length of time. Nevertheless, I stuck to it for two months, and then, upon receiving a letter informing me that my mother was very sick, I gave it up and went back to the old home in Salt Creek Valley.

CHAPTER III

Accidents and Escapes

My restless, roaming spirit would not allow me to remain at home very long, and in November, after the recovery of my mother, I went up the Republican River and its tributaries on a trapping expedition in company with Dave Harrington. Our outfit consisted of one wagon and a yoke of oxen for the transportation of provisions, traps and other necessaries. We began trapping near Junction City, Kansas, and then proceeded up the Republican River to the mouth of Prairie Dog Creek, where we found plenty of beavers.

Having seen no signs of Indians thus far, we felt comparatively safe. We were catching a large number of beavers and were prospering finely, when one of our oxen, having become rather poor, slipped and fell upon the ice, dislocating his hip, so that we had to shoot him to end his misery. This left us without a team; but we cared little for that, however, as we had made up our minds to remain there till spring, but it was decided that one of us should go to the nearest settlement and get a yoke of oxen with which to haul our wagon into some place of safety where we could leave it.

We would probably have pulled through the winter all right had it not been for a very serious accident which befell me just at that time. Spying a herd of elk, we started in pursuit of them, and creeping up towards them as slyly as possible, while going around the bend of a sharp bluff or bank of the creek I slipped and broke my leg just above the ankle. Notwithstanding the great pain I was suffering, Harrington could not help laughing when I urged him to shoot me, as he had the ox, and thus end my misery. He told me to "brace up," and that he would bring me out "allright." "I am not much of a surgeon," said he, " but I can fix that leg of yours, even if I haven't got a diploma."

He succeeded in getting me back to camp, which was only a few yards from the creek, and then he set the fracture as well as he knew how and made me as comfortable as was possible under the circumstances. We then discussed the situation, which, to say the least, looked pretty blue. Knowing that, owing to our mishaps, we could not do anything more that winter, and as I dreaded the idea of lying there on my back with a broken leg for weeks, and perhaps months, I prevailed upon Harrington to go to the nearest settlement—about one hundred and twenty-five miles distant—to obtain a yoke of cattle and then come back for me.

This he consented to do; but before leaving he gathered plenty of wood, and as the ground was covered with snow, I would have no difficulty in getting water if I had a fire. There was plenty of fresh meat and other provisions in the "dug-out," so that I had no fears of starvation. The "dug-out," which we had built immediately after we had determined to remain there all winter, was a cozy hole in the ground, covered with poles, grass and sod, with a fire-place in one end.

Harrington thought it would take him twenty days or more to make the round trip; but being well provided for—for this length of time—I urged him to go at once. Bidding me good-bye, he started on foot. After his departure, each day, as it came and went, seemed to grow longer to me as I lay there helpless and alone. I made a note of each day, so as to know the time when I might expect him back.

A Desperate Situation

On the twelfth day after Harrington had left me I was awakened from a sound sleep by some one touching me upon the shoulder. I looked up and was astonished to see an Indian warrior standing at my side. His face was hideously daubed with paint which told me more forcibly than words could have done that he was on the war-path. He spoke to me in broken English and Sioux mixed, and I understood him to ask what I was doing there, and how many there were with me.

By this time the little dug-out was nearly filled with other Indians, who had been peeping in at the door, and I could hear voices of still more outside as well as the stamping of horses. I began to think that my time had come, as the saying is, when into the cabin stepped an elderly Indian, whom I readily recognized as old Rain-in-the-Face, a Sioux chief from the vicinity of Fort Laramie. I rose up as well as I could and showed him my broken leg. I told him where I had seen him, and asked him if he remembered me. He replied that he knew me well, and that I used to come to his lodge at Fort Laramie to visit him. I then managed to make him understand that I was there alone and having broken my leg, I had sent my partner off for a team to take me away. I asked him if his young men intended to kill me, and he answered that was what they had proposed to do, but he would see what they had to say.

The Indians then talked among themselves for a few minutes, and upon the conclusion of the consultation, old Rain-in-the-Face turned to me and gave me to understand that as I was yet a "papoose," or a very young man, they would not take my life. But one of his men who had no fire-arms wanted my gun and pistol. I implored old Rain-in-the-Face to be allowed to keep the weapons, or at least one of them, as I needed something with which to keep the wolves away. He replied that as his young men were out on the war-path, he had induced them to spare my life; but he could not prevent them from taking whatever else they wanted.

They unsaddled their horses as if to remain there for some time, and sure enough they stayed the remainder of the day and all night. They built a fire in the dug-out and cooked a lot of my provisions, helping themselves to everything as if they owned it.

CHIEF RAIN-IN-THE-FACE SAVES MY LIFE

However, they were polite enough to give me some of the food after they had cooked it. It was a sumptuous feast that they had, and they seemed to relish it as if it were the best layout they had had for many a long day. They took all my sugar and coffee, and left me only some meat and a small quantity of flour, a little salt and some baking-powder. They also robbed me of such cooking utensils as they wished; then bidding me good-bye, early in the morning, they mounted their ponies and rode off to the south, evidently bent on some murdering and thieving expedition.

I was glad enough to see them leave, as my life had undoubtedly hung by a thread during their presence. I am confident that had it not been for my youth and the timely recognition and interference of old Rain-in-the-Face they would have killed me without any hesitation or ceremony.

The second day after the Indians left it began snowing, and for three long and weary days the snow continued to fall thick and fast. It blocked the door-way and covered the dug-out to the depth of several feet, so that I became a snow-bound prisoner. My wood was mostly under the snow, and it was with great difficulty that I could get enough to start a fire with. My prospects were gloomy indeed. I had just faced death at the hands of the Indians, and now I was in danger of losing my life from starvation and cold. I knew that the heavy snow would surely delay Harrington on his return; and I feared that he might have perished in the storm, or that some other accident might have befallen him. Perhaps some wandering band of Indians had surprised and killed him.

I was continually thinking of all these possibilities, and I must say that my outlook seemed desperate. At last the twentieth day arrived—the day on which Harrington was to return—and I counted the hours from morning till night, but the day passed away with no signs of Harrington. The wolves made the night hideous with their howls; they gathered around the dug-out; ran over the roof; and pawed and scratched as if trying to get in.

Several days and nights thus wore away, the monotony all the time becoming greater, until at last it became almost unendurable. Some days I would go without any fire at all, and eat raw frozen meat and melt snow in my mouth for water. I became almost convinced; that Harrington had been caught in the storm and had been buried under the snow, or was lost. Many a time during that dreary period of uncertainty I made up my mind that if I ever got out of that place alive I would abandon the plains and the life of a trapper forever. I had nearly given up all hopes of leaving the dug-out alive.

A Joyous Meeting

It was on the twenty-ninth day, while I was lying thus despondently thinking and wondering, that I heard the cheerful sound of Harrington's voice as he came slowly up the creek, yelling, "whoa! haw!" to his cattle. A criminal on the scaffold, with the noose around his neck, the trap about to be sprung, and receiving a pardon just at the last moment, thus giving him a new lease of life, could not have been more grateful than I was at that time. It was useless for me to try to force the door open, as the snow had completely blockaded it, and I therefore anxiously awaited Harrington's arrival.

"Hello! Billy!" he sang out in a loud voice as he came up, he evidently being uncertain as to my being alive.

"All right, Dave," was my reply.

"Well, old boy, you're alive, are you?" said he.

"Yes; and that's about all. I've had a tough siege of it since you've been away, and I came pretty nearly passing in my chips. I began to think you never would get here, as I was afraid you had been snowed under," said I.

He soon cleared away the snow from the entrance and opening the door he came in. I don't think there ever was a more welcome visitor than he was. I remember that I was so glad to see him that I put my arms around his neck and hugged him for five minutes; never shall I forget faithful Dave Harrington.

"Well, Billy, my boy, I hardly expected to see you alive again," said Harrington, as soon as I had given him an opportunity to draw his breath; "I had a terrible trip of it, and I didn't think I ever would get through. I was caught in the snowstorm, and was laid up for three days. The cattle wandered away, and I came within an ace of losing them altogether. When I got started again the snow was so deep that it prevented me from making much headway. But as I had left you here I was bound to come through, or die in the attempt."

Again I flung my arms around Dave's neck and gave him a hug that would have done honor to a grizzly bear. My gratitude was thus much more forcibly expressed than it could have been by words. Harrington understood this, and seemed to appreciate it. The tears of joy rolled down my cheeks, and it was impossible for me to restrain them. When my life had been threatened by the Indians I had not felt half so miserable as when I lay in the dug-out thinking I was destined to die a slow death by starvation and cold. The Indians would have made short work of it, and would have given me little or no time to think of my fate.

I questioned Harrington as to his trip, and learned all the details. He had passed through hardships which but few men could have endured. Noble fellow, that he was. He had risked his own life to save mine.

After he had finished his story, every word of which I had listened to with eager interest, I related to him my own experiences, in which he became no less interested. He expressed great astonishment that the Indians had not killed me, and he considered it one of the luckiest and most remarkable escapes he had ever heard of. It amused me, however, to see him get very angry when I told him that they had taken my gun and pistol and had used up our provisions. "But never mind, Billy," said he, "we can stand it till the snow goes off, which will not be long, and then we will pull our wagon back to the settlements."

The Return and Death of Harrington

A few days afterwards Harrington gathered up our traps, and cleaned the snow out of the wagon. Covering it with the sheet which we had used in the dug-out, he made a comfortable bed inside, and helped me into it. We had been quite successful in trapping, having caught three hundred beavers and one hundred otters, the skins of which Harrington loaded on the wagon. We then pulled out for the settlements, making good headway, as the snow had nearly disappeared, having been blown or melted away, so that we had no difficulty in finding a road. On the eighth day out we came to a farmer's house, or ranch, on the Republican River, where we stopped and rested for two days, and then went on to the ranch where Harrington had obtained the yoke of cattle. We gave the owner of the team twenty-five beaver skins, equal to $60, for the use of the cattle, and he let us have them until we reached Junction City, sending his boy with us to bring them back.

At Junction City we sold our wagon and furs and went with a government mule train to Leavenworth—arriving there in March, 1860. I was just able to get around on crutches when I got into Leavenworth, and it was several months after that before I entirely recovered the use of my leg.

During the winter I had often talked to Harrington about my mother and sisters, and had invited him to go home with me in the spring. I now renewed the invitation, which he accepted, and accompanied me home. When I related to mother my adventures and told her how Harrington had saved my life, she thanked him again and again. I never saw a more grateful woman than she was. She asked him to always make his home with us, as she never could reward him sufficiently for what he had done for her darling boy, as she called me. Harrington concluded to remain with us through the summer and farm mother's land. But alas! the uncertainty of life. The coming of death when least expected was strikingly illustrated in his case. During the latter part of April he went to a nursery for some trees, and while coming home late at night he caught a severe cold and was taken seriously sick, with lung fever. Mother did everything in her power for him. She could not have done more had he been her own son, but notwithstanding her motherly care and attention, and the skill of a physician from Leavenworth, he rapidly grew worse. It seemed hard, indeed, to think that a great strong man like Harrington, who had braved the storms and endured the other hardships of the plains all winter long, should, during the warm and beautiful days of spring, when surrounded by friends and the comforts of a good home, be fatally stricken down. But such was his fate. He died one week from the day on which he was taken sick. We all mourned his loss as we would that of a loved son or brother, as he was one of the truest, bravest, and best of friends. Amid sorrow and tears we laid him away to rest in a picturesque spot on Pilot Knob. His death cast a gloom over our household, and it was a long time before it was entirely dispelled. I felt very lonely without Harrington, and I soon wished for a change of scene again.

CHAPTER IV

Adventures on the Overland Road

As the warm days of summer approached I longed for the cool air of the mountains; and to the mountains I determined to go. After engaging a man to take care of the farm, I proceeded to Leavenworth and there met my old wagon-master and friend, Lewis Simpson, who was fitting out a train at Atchison and loading it with supplies for the Overland Stage Company, of which Mr. Russell, my old employer, was one of the proprietors. Simpson was going with this train to Fort Laramie and points further west.

"Come along with me, Billy," said he, "I'll give you a good lay-out. I want you with me."

"I don't know that I would like to go so far west as that again," I replied, "but I do want to ride the pony express once more; there's some life in that."

"Yes, that's so; but it will soon shake the life out of you," said he. "However, if that's what you've got your mind set on, you had better come to Atchison with me and see Mr. Russell, who I'm pretty certain will give you a situation."

I replied that I would do that. I then went home and informed mother of my intention, and as her health was very poor I had great difficulty in obtaining her consent. I finally convinced her that as I was of no use on the farm, it would be better and more profitable for me to return to the plains. So after giving her all the money I had earned by trapping, I bade her good-bye and set out for Atchison.

I met Mr. Russell there and asked him for employment as a pony express-rider; he gave me a letter to Mr. Slade, who was then the stage agent for the division extending from Julesburg to Rocky Ridge. Slade had his headquarters at Horseshoe Station, thirty-six miles west of Fort Laramie, and I made the trip thither in company with Simpson and his train.

Almost the very first person I saw after dismounting from my horse was Slade. I walked up to him and presented Mr. Russell's letter, which he hastily opened and read. With a sweeping glance of his eye he took my measure from head to foot, and then said:

"My boy, you are too young for a pony express-rider. It takes men for that business."

"I rode two months last year on Bill Trotter's division, sir, and filled the bill then; and I think I am better able to ride now," said I.

"What! are you the boy that was riding there, and was called the youngest rider on the road?"

"I am the same boy," I replied, confident that everything was now all right for me.

"I have heard of you before. You are a year or so older now, and I think you can stand it. I'll give you a trial anyhow and if you weaken you can come back to Horse Shoe Station and tend stock."

That ended our first interview. The next day he assigned me to duty on the road from Red Buttes on the North Platte, to the Three Crossings of the Sweetwater—a distance of seventy-six miles—and I began riding at once. It was a long piece of road, but I was equal to the undertaking; and soon afterwards had an opportunity to exhibit my power of endurance as a pony express-rider.

One day when I galloped into Three Crossings, my home station, I found that the rider who was expected to take the trip out on my arrival, had gotten into a drunken row the night before and been killed. This left that division without a rider and as it was very difficult to engage men for the service in that uninhabited region, the superintendent requested me to make the trip until another rider could be secured. The distance to the next station, Rocky Ridge, was eighty-five miles and through a very bad and dangerous country, but the emergency was great and I concluded to try it. I therefore started promptly from Three Crossings without more than a moment's rest and pushed on with usual rapidity, entering every relay station on time and accomplishing the round trip of three hundred and twenty-two miles back to Red Buttes without a single mishap and on time. This stands on the records as being the longest pony express journey ever made.

Pursued by Indians

A week after making this trip, and while passing over the route again, I was jumped by a band of Sioux Indians who dashed out from a sand ravine nine miles west of Horse Creek. They were armed with pistols and gave me a close call with several bullets, but it fortunately happened that I was mounted on the fleetest horse belonging to the Express Company, and one that was possessed of remarkable endurance. Being cut off from retreat back to Horseshoe, I put spurs to my horse, and lying flat on his back, kept straight for Sweetwater, the next station, which I reached without accident, having distanced my pursuers. Upon reaching that place, however, I found a sorry condition of affairs, as the Indians had made a raid on the station the morning of my adventure with them, and after killing the stock-tender had driven off all the horses, so that I was unable to get a remount. I therefore continued onto Ploutz's Station— twelve miles further—thus making twenty-four miles straight run with one horse. I told the people at Ploutz's what had happened at Sweetwater Bridge, and with a fresh horse went on and finished the trip without any further adventure.

Attack on a Stage Coach

About the middle of September the Indians became very troublesome on the line of the stage road along the Sweetwater. Between Split Rock and Three Crossings they robbed a stage, killed the driver and two passengers, and badly wounded Lieut. Flowers, the assistant division agent. The red-skinned thieves also drove off the stock from the different stations, and were continually lying in wait for the passing stages and pony express riders, so that we had to take many desperate chances in running the gauntlet.

The Indians had now become so bad and had stolen so much stock that it was decided to stop the pony express for at least six weeks, and to run the stages only occasionally during that period; in fact, it would have been almost impossible to have continued the enterprise much longer without restocking the line.

While we were thus nearly all lying idle, a party was organized to go out and search for stolen stock. This party was composed of stage-drivers, express-riders, stock-tenders, and ranchmen—forty of them altogether—and they were well-armed and well-mounted. They were mostly men who had undergone all kinds of hardships and braved every danger, and they were ready and anxious to "tackle" any number

A RACE FOR LIFE

of Indians. Wild Bill (who had been driving stage on the road and had recently come down to our division) was elected captain of the company.

It was supposed that the stolen stock had been taken to the head of Powder River and vicinity, and the party, of which I was a member, started out for that section in high hopes of success.

Twenty miles out from Sweetwater Bridge, at the head of Horse Creek, we found an Indian trail running north towards Powder River, and we could see by the tracks that most of the horses had been recently shod and were undoubtedly our stolen stage-stock. Pushing rapidly forward, we followed this trail to Powder River; thence down this stream to within about forty miles of the spot where old Fort Reno now stands. Here the trail took a more westerly course along the foot of the mountains, leading eventually to Crazy Woman's Fork—a tributary of Powder River. At this point we discovered that the party whom we were trailing had been joined by another band of Indians, and, judging from the fresh appearance of the trail, the united body could not have left this spot more than twenty-four hours before.

A Charge Through the Indian Camp

Being aware that we were now in the heart of the hostile country and might at any moment find more Indians than we had "lost," we advanced with more caution than usual and kept a sharp lookout. As we were approaching Clear Creek, another tributary of Powder River, we discovered Indians on the opposite side of the creek, some three miles distant; at least we saw horses grazing which was a sure sign that there were Indians there.

The Indians thinking themselves in comparative safety—never before having been followed so far into their own country by white men—had neglected to put out any scouts. They had no idea that there were any white men in that part of the country. We got the lay of their camp, and then held a council to consider and mature a plan for capturing it. We knew full well that the Indians would outnumber us at least three to one, and perhaps more. Upon the advice and suggestion of Wild Bill, it was finally decided that we should wait until it was nearly dark, and then, after creeping as close to them as possible, make a dash through their camp, open a general fire on them, and then stampede the horses.

This plan, at the proper time, was most successfully executed. The dash upon the enemy was a complete surprise to them. They were so overcome with astonishment that they did not know what to make of it. We could not have astounded them any more had we dropped down into their camp from the clouds. They did not recover from the surprise of this sudden charge until after we had ridden pell-mell through their camp and got away with our own horses as well as theirs. We at once circled the horses around towards the south, and after getting them on the south side of Clear Creek, some twenty of our men—just as the darkness was coming on—rode back and gave the Indians a few parting shots. We then took up our line of march for Sweetwater Bridge, where we arrived four days afterwards with all our own horses and about one hundred captured Indian ponies.

A General Drunk but Only One Murder

The expedition had proved a grand success, and the event was celebrated in the usual manner—by a grand spree. The only store at Sweetwater Bridge did a rushing business for several days. The returned stock-hunters drank and gambled and fought. The Indian ponies, which had been distributed among the captors, passed from hand to hand at almost every deal of the cards. There seemed to be no limit to the rioting and carousing; revelry reigned supreme. On the third day of the orgy, Slade, who had heard the news, came up to the bridge and took a hand in the "fun," as it was called. To add some variation and excitement to the occasion, Slade got into a quarrel with a stage-driver and shot him, killing him almost instantly.

The "boys" became so elated as well as "elevated" over their success against the Indians that most of them were in favor of going back and cleaning out the whole Indian race. One old driver especially, Dan Smith, was eager to open a war on all the hostile nations, and had the drinking been continued another week he certainly would have undertaken the job, single-handed and alone. The spree finally came to an end; the men sobered down and abandoned the idea of again invading the hostile country. The recovered horses were replaced on the road and the stages and pony express again began running on time.

Slade, having taken a great fancy to me, said: "Billy, I want you to come down to my headquarters, and I'll make you a sort of supernumerary rider, and send you out only when it is necessary."

A Hunt for Bear

I accepted the offer and went with him down to Horseshoe, where I had a comparatively easy time of it. I had always been fond of hunting, and I now had a good opportunity to gratify my ambition in that direction, as I had plenty of spare time on my hands. In this connection I will relate one of my bear-hunting adventures. One day, when I had nothing else to do, I saddled up an extra pony express horse, and arming myself with a good rifle and pair of revolvers, struck out for the foot-hills of Laramie

Peak for a bear-hunt. Riding carelessly along, and breathing the cool and bracing autumn air which came down from the mountains, I felt as only a man can feel who is roaming over the prairies of the far West, well armed and mounted on a fleet and gallant steed. The perfect freedom which he enjoys is in itself a refreshing stimulant to the mind as well as to the body.

Such indeed were my feelings on this beautiful day as I rode up the valley of the Horseshoe. Occasionally I scared up a flock of sage-hens or a jack-rabbit. Antelopes and deer were almost always in sight in any direction, but as they were not the kind of game I was after on that day I passed them by and kept on towards the higher mountains. The further I rode the rougher and wilder became the country, and I knew that I was approaching the haunts of the bear. I did not discover any, however, although I saw plenty of tracks in the snow.

About two o'clock in the afternoon, my horse having become tired, and myself being rather weary, I shot a sage-hen and, dismounting, I unsaddled my horse and tied him to a small tree, where he could easily feed on the mountain grass. I then built a little fire, and broiling the chicken and seasoning it with salt and pepper, which I had obtained from my saddle-bags, I soon sat down to a "genuine square meal," which I greatly relished.

After resting for a couple of hours, I remounted and resumed my upward trip to the mountain, having made up my mind to camp out that night rather than go back without a bear, which my friends knew I had gone out for. As the days were growing short, night soon came on, and I looked around for a suitable camping place. While thus engaged, I scared up a flock of sage-hens, two of which I shot, intending to have one for supper and the other for breakfast.

By this time it was becoming quite dark, and I rode down to one of the little mountain streams, where I found an open place in the timber suitable for a camp. I dismounted, and after unsaddling my horse and hitching him to a tree, I prepared to start a fire. Just then I was startled by hearing a horse whinnying further up the stream. It was quite a surprise to me, and I immediately ran to my animal to keep him from answering, as horses usually do in such cases. I thought that the strange horse might belong to some roaming band of Indians, as I knew of no white men being in that portion of the country at that time. I was certain that the owner of the strange horse could not be far distant, and I was very anxious to find out who my neighbor was, before letting him know that I was in his vicinity. I therefore re-saddled my horse, and leaving him tied so that I could easily reach him I took my gun and started out on a scouting expedition up the stream. I had gone about four hundred yards when, in a bend of the stream, I discovered ten or fifteen horses grazing.

A Robber's Haunt Discovered

On the opposite side of the creek, a light was shining high up the mountain bank. Approaching the mysterious spot as cautiously as possible, and when within a few yards of the light—which I discovered came from a dug-out in the mountain side—I heard voices, and soon I was able to distinguish the words, as they proved to be in my own language. Then I knew that the occupants of the dug-out, whence the voices proceeded, were white men. Thinking that they might be a party of trappers, I boldly walked up to the door and knocked for admission. The voices instantly ceased, and for a moment a death-like silence reigned inside. Then there seemed to follow a kind of hurried whispering—a sort of consultation—and then some one called out:

"Who's there?"

"A friend and a white man," I replied.

The door opened, and a big, ugly-looking fellow stepped forth and said:

"Come in."

I accepted the invitation with some degree of fear and hesitation, which I endeavored to conceal, as I saw that it was too late to back out, and that it would never do to weaken at that point, whether they were friends or foes. Upon entering the dug-out my eyes fell upon eight as rough and villainous looking men as I ever saw in my life. Two of them I instantly recognized as teamsters who had been driving in Lew Simpson's train, a few months before, and had been discharged.

They were charged with the murdering and robbing of a ranchman; and having stolen his horses it was supposed that they had left the country. I gave them no signs of recognition however, deeming it advisable to let them remain in ignorance as to who I was. It was a hard crowd, and I concluded that the sooner I could get away from them the better it would be for me. I felt confident that they were a band of horse thieves.

"Where are you going, young man; and who's with you?" asked one of the men who appeared to be the leader of the gang.

"I am entirely alone. I left Horseshoe Station this morning for a bear-hunt, and not finding any bears, I had determined to camp out for the night and wait till morning," said I; "and just as I was going into camp, a few hundred yards down the creek I heard one of your horses whinnying, and then I came to your camp."

I was thus explicit in my statement in order, if possible, to satisfy the cut-throats that I was not spying upon them, but that my intrusion was entirely accidental.

"Where's your horse? " demanded the boss thief.

"I left him down the creek," I answered.

In a Tight Place

They proposed going after the horse, but I thought that that would never do, as it would leave me without any means of escape, and I accordingly said, in hopes to throw them off the track, "Captain, I'll leave my gun here and go down and get my horse, and come back and stay all night."

I said this in as cheerful and as careless a manner as possible, so as not to arouse their suspicions in any way or lead them to think that I was aware of their true character. I hated to part with my gun, but my suggestion of leaving it was a part of the plan of escape which I had arranged. If they have the gun, thought I, they will surely believe that I intend to come back. But this little game did not work at all, as one of the desperadoes spoke up and said:

"Jim and I will go down with you after your horse, and you can leave your gun here all the same, as you'll not need it."

"All right," I replied, for I could certainly have said nothing else. It became evident to me that it would be better to trust myself with two men than with the whole party. It was apparent from this time on I would have to be on the alert for some good opportunity to give them the slip.

"Come along," said one of them, and together we went down the creek, and soon came to the spot where my horse was tied. One of the men unhitched the animal and said: "I'll lead the horse."

"Very well," said I, "I've got a couple of sage-hens here. Lead on."

I picked up the sage-hens, which I had killed a few hours before, and followed the man who was leading the horse, while his companion brought up the rear. The nearer we approached the dug-out the more I dreaded the idea of going back among the villainous cut-throats. My first plan of escape having failed, I now determined upon another. I had both of my revolvers with me, the thieves not having thought it necessary to search me. It was now quite dark, and I purposely dropped one of the sage-hens, and asked the man behind me to pick it up. While he was hunting for it on the ground, I quickly pulled out one of my Colt's revolvers and struck him a tremendous blow on the back of the head, knocking him senseless to the ground. I then instantly wheeled around, and saw that the man ahead, who was only a few feet distant, had heard the blow and had turned to see what was the matter, his hand upon his revolver. We faced each other at about the same instant, but before he could fire, as he tried to do, I shot him dead in his tracks. Then jumping on my horse, I rode down the creek as fast as possible, through the darkness and over the rough ground and rocks.

The other outlaws in the dug-out, having heard the shot which I had fired, knew there was trouble, and they all came rushing down the creek. I suppose by the time they reached the man whom I had knocked down, that he had recovered and hurriedly told them of what had happened. They did not stay with the man whom I had shot, but came on in hot pursuit of me. They were not mounted, and were making better time down the rough mountain than I was on horseback. From time to time I heard them gradually gaining on me.

At last they had come so near that I saw that I must abandon my horse. So I jumped to the ground, and gave him a hard slap with the butt of one of my revolvers, which started him on down the valley, while I scrambled up the mountain side. I had not ascended more than forty feet when I heard my pursuers coming closer and closer; I quickly hid behind a large pine tree, and in a few moments they all rushed by me, being led on by the rattling footsteps of my horse, which they heard ahead of them. Soon they began firing in the direction of the horse, as they no doubt supposed I was still seated on his back. As soon as they had passed me I climbed further up the steep mountain, and knowing that I had given them the slip, and feeling certain I could keep out of their way, I at once struck out for Horseshoe Station, which was twenty-five miles distant. I had hard traveling at first but upon reaching lower and

A HEROIC REMEDY FOR A DESPERATE SITUATION

better ground I made good headway, walking all night and getting into the station just before daylight—foot-sore, weary, and generally played out.

I immediately waked up the men of the station and told them of my adventure. Slade himself happened to be there, and he at once organized a party to go out in pursuit of the horse thieves. Shortly after daylight twenty well armed stage-drivers, stock-tenders and ranchmen were galloping in the direction of the dug-out. Of course I went along with the party, notwithstanding I was very tired and had had hardly any rest at all. We had a brisk ride, and arrived in the immediate vicinity of the thieves' rendezvous at about ten o'clock in the morning. We approached the dug-out cautiously, but upon getting in close proximity to it we could discover no horses in sight. We could see the door of the dug-out standing wide open, and we then marched up to the place. No one was inside and the general appearance of everything indicated that the place had been deserted—that the birds had flown. Such, indeed, proved to be the case.

We found a new-made grave, where they had evidently buried the man whom I had shot. We made a thorough search of the whole vicinity, and finally found their trail going southeast in the direction of Denver. As it would have been useless to follow them, we rode back to the station; and thus ended my eventful bear-hunt. We had no more trouble for some time from horse thieves after that.

During the winter of 1860 and the spring of 1861 I remained at Horseshoe, occasionally riding pony express and taking care of stock, but meeting with no adventure worthy to be recorded.

CHAPTER V

An Inglorious Service

Following the breaking out of the great Civil War in 1861, a general desertion of stage-drivers and express riders took place, a majority of whom were natural rovers, and always looking out for change of employment. I was not an exception, and as it had now been nearly a year since I saw my mother, while reports of her ill health frequently reached me, I decided to pay her a visit, and at the same time determine, if government service promised better pay and more excitement than I had been getting out of my engagement with the express company, to join the army. In pursuance of this resolve I went to Leavenworth, which was at that time an important outfitting post for the West and Southwest.

While in the city one day I met several of the old, as well as the young men, who had been members of the Free State party all through the Kansas troubles, and who had, like our family, lost everything at the hands of the Missourians. They now thought a good opportunity offered to retaliate and get even with their persecutors, as they were all considered to be Secessionists. That they were all Secessionists, however, was not true, as all of them did not sympathize with the South. But the Free State men, myself among them, took it for granted that as Missouri was a slave state the inhabitants must all be Secessionists, and therefore our enemies. A man by the name of Chandler proposed that we organize an independent company for the purpose of invading Missouri and making war on its people on our own responsibility. He at once went about it in a very quiet way, and succeeded in inducing twenty-five men to join him in the hazardous enterprise. Having a longing and revengeful desire to retaliate upon the Missourians for the brutal manner in which they had treated and robbed my family, I became a member of Chandler's company. His plan was that we should leave our homes in parties of not more than two or three together, and meet at a certain point near Westport, Missouri, on a fixed day. His instructions were carried out, and we assembled at the rendezvous at the appointed time. Chandler had been there some days before us and, thoroughly disguised, had been looking around the country for the whereabouts of all the best horses. He directed us to secretly visit certain farms and collect all the horses possible, and bring them together the next night. This we did, and upon reassembling it was found that nearly every man had two horses. We immediately struck out for the Kansas line, which we crossed at the Indian ferry on the Kansas River, above Wyandotte, and as soon as we had set foot upon Kansas soil we separated with the understanding that we were to meet one week from that day at Leavenworth.

Some of the parties boldly took their confiscated horses into Leavenworth, while others rode them to their homes. This action may look to the reader like horse-stealing, and some people might not hesitate to call it by that name; but Chandler plausibly maintained that we were only getting back our own, or the equivalent, from the Missourians, and as the government was waging war against the South, it was perfectly square and honest, and we had a good right to do it. So we didn't let our consciences trouble us very much.

We continued to make similar raids upon the Missourians off and on during the summer, and occasionally we had running fights with them; none of the skirmishes, however, amounting to much. The government officials hearing of our operations, put detectives upon our track, and several of the party were arrested. My mother, upon learning that I was engaged in this business, told me it was neither honor-able nor right, and she would not for a moment countenance any such proceedings. Consequently I abandoned the jay-hawking enterprise, for such it really was.

After abandoning the enterprise of crippling the Confederacy by appropriating the horses of non-combatants, I went to Leavenworth, where I met my old friend,

Wild Bill, who was on the point of departing for Rolla, Mo., to assume the position of wagon-master of a government train. At his request to join him as an assistant I cheerfully accompanied him to Rolla, where we loaded a number of wagons with government freight and drove them to Springfield.

Busted at a Horse-Race

On our return to Rolla we heard a great deal of talk about the approaching fall races at St. Louis, and Wild Bill having brought a fast running horse from the mountains, determined to take him to that city and match him against some of the high-flyers there; and down to St. Louis we went with this running horse, placing our hopes very high on him.

Wild Bill had no difficulty in making up a race for him. All the money that he and I had we put up on the mountain runner, and as we thought we had a sure thing, we also bet the horse against $250. I rode the horse myself, but nevertheless, our sure thing, like many another sure thing, proved a total failure, and we came out of that race minus the horse and every dollar we had in the world.

Before the race it had been "make or break" with us, and we got "broke." We were "busted" in the largest city we had ever been in, and it is no exaggeration to say that we felt mighty blue.

On the morning after the race we went to the military headquarters, where Bill succeeded in securing an engagement for himself as a government scout, but I being so young failed in obtaining similar employment. Wild Bill, however, raised some money, by borrowing it from a friend, and then buying me a steamboat ticket he sent me back to Leavenworth, while he went to Springfield, which place he made his headquarters while scouting in Southeastern Missouri.

A Duel in the Street

One night, after he had returned from a scouting expedition, he took a hand in a game of poker, and in the course of the play he became involved in a quarrel with Dave Tutt, a professional gambler, about a watch which he had won from Tutt, but who would not give it up.

Bill told him he had won it fairly, and that he proposed to have it; furthermore, he declared his intention of carrying the watch across the street next morning to military headquarters, at which place he had to report at nine o'clock. To which boast Tutt replied that he would himself carry the watch across the street at nine o'clock, and no other man would do it.

"If you make the attempt one of us will have to die at the hour named," was the answer Bill returned, and then walked carelessly away.

A challenge to a duel had virtually been given and accepted, and everybody knew that the two men meant business. At nine o'clock the next morning, Tutt started to cross the street. Wild Bill, who was standing on the opposite side, told him to stop. At that moment Tutt, who was carrying his revolver in his hand, fired at Bill but missed him. Bill quickly pulled out his revolver and returned the fire, hitting Tutt squarely in the forehead and killing him instantly.

Quite a number of Tutt's friends were standing in the vicinity, having assembled to witness the duel, and Bill, as soon as Tutt fell to the ground, turned to them and asked if any one of them wanted to take it up for Tutt; if so, he would accommodate any of them then and there. But none of them cared to stand in front of Wild Bill to be shot at by him. Nothing of course was ever done to Bill for the killing of Tutt.

WILD BILL'S DUEL WITH DAVE TUTT

CHAPTER VI

How I Became a Soldier

Early in the fall of 1861 I made a trip to Fort Larned, Kansas, carrying military dispatches, and in the winter I accompanied George Long through the country, and assisted him in buying horses for the government.

The next spring, 1862, an expedition against the Indians was organized, consisting of a volunteer regiment, the Ninth Kansas under Colonel Clark. This expedition, which I had joined in the capacity of guide and scout, proceeded to the Kiowa and Comanche country, on the Arkansas River, along which stream we scouted all summer between Fort Lyon and Fort Larned, on the old Santa Fe trail. We had several engagements with the Indians, but they were of no great importance.

In the winter of 1862, I became one of the "Red Legged Scouts"—a company of scouts commanded by Captain Tuff. Among its members were some of the most noted Kansas Rangers, such as Red Clark, the St. Clair brothers, Jack Harvey, an old pony express-rider named Johnny Fry, and many other well-known frontiersmen. Our field of operations was confined mostly to the Arkansas country and Southwestern Missouri. We had many a lively skirmish with the bushwhackers and Younger brothers, and when we were not hunting them, we were generally employed in carrying dispatches between Forts Dodge, Gibson, Leavenworth and other posts. Whenever we were in Leavenworth we had a very festive time. We usually attended all the balls in full force, and "ran things" to suit ourselves. Thus I passed the winter of 1862 and the spring of 1863.

Subsequently I engaged to conduct a small train to Denver for some merchants, and on reaching that place in September, I received a letter stating that my mother was not expected to live. I hastened home, and found her dangerously ill. She grew gradually worse, and at last, on the 22d of November, 1863, she died. Thus passed away a loving and affectionate mother and a noble, brave, good and loyal woman.

Previous to this sad event my sister Julia had been married to a gentleman named J. A. Goodman, and they now came to reside at our house and take charge of the children, as my mother had desired that they should not be separated. Mr. Goodman became the guardian of the minor children.

With the Jay-Hawkers

I soon left the home now rendered gloomy by the absence of her whom I had so tenderly loved and going to Leavenworth I entered upon a dissolute and reckless life—to my shame be it said—and associated with gamblers, drunkards, and bad characters generally. I continued my dissipation about two months, and was becoming a very "hard case." About this time the Seventh Kansas regiment, known as "Jennison's Jayhawkers," returned from the war, and re-enlisted and re-organized as veterans. Among them I met quite a number of my old comrades and neighbors, who tried to induce me to enlist and go South with them. I had no idea of doing anything of the kind; but one day, after having been under the influence of bad whisky, I awoke to find myself a soldier in the Seventh Kansas. I did not remember how or when I had enlisted, but I saw I was in for it, and that it would not do for me to endeavor to back out.

In the spring of 1864 the regiment was ordered to Tennessee, and we got into Memphis just about the time that General Sturgis was so badly whipped by General Forrest. General A. J. Smith re-organized the army to operate against Forrest, and after marching to Tupelo, Mississippi, we had an engagement with him and defeated him. This kind of fighting was all new to me, being entirely different from any in which I had ever before engaged. I soon became a non-commissioned officer, and was put on detached service as a scout.

After skirmishing around the country with the rest of the army for some little time, our regiment returned to Memphis, but was immediately ordered to Cape Giradeau, in Missouri, as a Confederate force under General Price was then raiding that State. The command of which my regiment was a part hurried to the front to intercept Price, and our first fight with him occurred at Pilot Knob. From that time for nearly six weeks we fought or skirmished every day.

A Singular Meeting with Wild Bill

I was still acting as a scout, when one day I rode ahead of the command, some considerable distance, to pick up all possible information concerning Price's movements. I was dressed in gray clothes, or Missouri jeans, and on riding up to a farm house and entering I saw a man, also dressed in gray costume, sitting at a table eating bread and milk. He looked up as I entered, and startled me by saying:

"You little rascal, what are you doing in those 'secesh' clothes?" Judge of my surprise when I recognized in the stranger my old friend and partner, Wild Bill, disguised as a Confederate officer.

WILD BILL

"I ask you the same question, sir," said I, without the least hesitation.

"Hush! sit down and have some bread and milk, and we'll talk it all over afterwards," said he.

I accepted the invitation and partook of the refreshments. Wild Bill paid the woman of the house, and we went out to the gate where my horse was standing.

"Billy, my boy," said he, "I am mighty glad to see you. I haven't seen or heard of you since we got busted on that St. Louis horse race."

"What are you doing here?" I asked.

"I am a scout under General McNiel. For the last few days I have been with General Marmaduke's division of Price's army, in disguise as a Southern officer from Texas, as you see me now," said he.

"That's exactly the kind of business that I am out on to-day," said I; "and I want to get some information concerning Price's movements."

"I'll give you all that I have"; and he then went on and told me all that he knew regarding Price's intentions, and the number and condition of his men. He then asked about my mother, and when he learned that she was dead he was greatly surprised and grieved; he thought a great deal of her, for she had treated him almost as one of her own children. He finally took out a package, which he had concealed about his person, and handing it to me he said:

"Here are some letters which I want you to give to General McNeil."

"All right," said I as I took them," but where will I meet you again?"

"Never mind that," he replied; "I am getting so much valuable information that I propose to stay a little while longer in this disguise." Thereupon we shook hands and parted.

It is not necessary to say much concerning Price's raid in general, as that event is a matter of recorded history. I am only relating the incidents in which I was personally interested either as one of the actors or as an observer.

A Pleasant Little Episode

Another interesting, and I may say exciting, episode happened to me a day or two after my unexpected meeting with Wild Bill. I was riding with the advance guard of our army, and wishing a drink of water, I stopped at a farm house. There were no men about the premises, and no one excepting a very fine and intellectual looking lady and her two daughters. They seemed to be almost frightened to death at seeing me—a "yank"—appear before them. I quieted their fears somewhat and the mother then asked me how far back the army was. When I told her it would be along shortly, she expressed her fears that they would take everything on the premises. They set me out a lunch and treated me very kindly, so that I really began to sympathize with them; for I knew that the soldiers would ransack their house and confiscate everything they could lay their hands on. At last I resolved to do what I could to protect them.

After the generals and the staff officers had passed by, I took it upon myself to be a sentry over the house. When the command came along some of the men rushed up with the intention of entering the place and carrying off all the desirable plunder possible, and then tearing and breaking everything to pieces, as they usually did along the line of march.

"Halt!" I shouted; "I have been placed here by the commanding officer as a guard over this house, and no man must enter it." This stopped the first squad; and seeing that my plan was a success, I remained at my post during the passage of the entire command and kept out all intruders.

It seemed as if the ladies could not thank me sufficiently for the protection I had afforded them. They were perfectly aware of the fact that I had acted without orders and entirely on my own responsibility, and therefore they felt the more grateful. They urgently invited me to remain a little while longer and partake of an excellent dinner which they said they were preparing for me. I was pretty hungry about that time, as our rations had been rather slim of late, and a good dinner was a temptation I could not withstand, especially as it was served up by such elegant ladies. While I was eating the meal I was most agreeably entertained by the young ladies, and before I finished it the last of the rear-guard was at least two miles beyond the house.

Suddenly three men entered the room, and I looked up and saw three double-barreled shot-guns leveled straight at me. Before I could speak, however, the mother and her daughters sprang between the men and me.

"Father! Boys! Lower your guns! You must not shoot this man," and similar exclamations were uttered by all three. The guns were lowered and then the men, who were the father and brothers of the young ladies, were informed of what I had done for them. It appeared that they had been concealed in the woods near by while the army was passing, and on coming into the house and finding a Yankee there, they determined to shoot him. Upon learning the facts, the old man extended his hand to me, saying:

"I would not harm a hair of your head for the world; but it is best that you stay here no longer, as your command is some distance in advance now, and you might be cut off by bushwhackers before reaching it."

Bidding them all good-bye, and with many thanks from the mother and daughters, I mounted my horse and soon overtook the column, happy in the thought that I had done a good deed, and with no regrets that I had saved from pillage and destruction the home and property of a Confederate and his family.

Our command kept crowding against Price and his army until they were pushed into the vicinity of Kansas City, where their further advance was checked by United States troops from Kansas; and then was begun their memorable and extraordinary retreat back into Kansas.

A Wonderful Escape

While both armies were drawn up in skirmish line near Fort Scott, Kansas, two men on horseback were seen rapidly leaving the Confederate lines, and suddenly they made a dash towards us. Instantly quick volleys were discharged from the Confederates, who also began a pursuit, and some five hundred shots were fired at the flying men. It was evident that they were trying to reach our lines, but when within about a quarter of a mile of us, one of them fell from his horse to rise no more. He had been fatally shot. His companion galloped on unhurt, and seven companies of our regiment charged out and met him, and checked his pursuers. The fugitive was dressed in Confederate uniform, and as he rode into our lines I recognized him as Wild Bill, the Union scout. He immediately sought Generals Pleasanton and McNiel, with whom he held a consultation. He told them that although Price made a bold showing on the front, by bringing all his men into view, yet he was really a great deal weaker than the appearance of his lines would indicate; and that he was then trying to cross a difficult stream four miles from Fort Scott.

It was late in the afternoon, but General Pleasanton immediately ordered an advance, and we charged in full force upon the rear of Price's army, and drove it before us for two hours.

If Wild Bill could have made his successful dash into our lines earlier in the day, the attack would have been made sooner, and greater results might have been expected. The Confederates had suspected him of being a spy for two or three days, and had watched him too closely to allow an opportunity to get away from them sooner. His unfortunate companion who had been shot, was a scout from Springfield, Missouri, whose name I cannot now remember.

From this time on, Wild Bill and myself continued to scout together until Price's army was driven south of the Arkansas River and the pursuit abandoned.

CHAPTER VII

Courtship and Marriage

Camp-life and fighting guerrillas is not a very desirable occupation, and even scouting in the service is not so agreeable as making love to pretty girls; appreciating this fact, after nearly four years of hardships along the advance, I was very much pleased with the change when in the winter of 1864–65 I was permitted to spend a time at military headquarters in St. Louis on detached service. It was while I was in this pleasing situation that I became acquainted with a young lady named Louisa Frederici, whom I greatly admired and in whose charming society I spent many a pleasant hour.

The war closing in 1865, I was discharged, and after a brief visit at Leavenworth I returned to St. Louis, having made up my mind to capture the heart of Miss Frederici, whom I now adored above any other young lady that I had ever seen. Her lovely face, her gentle disposition and her graceful manners, won my admiration and love; and I was not slow in declaring my sentiments to her. The result was that I obtained her consent to marry me in the near future, and when I bade her good-bye I considered myself one of the happiest of men.

OVERLAND STAGE COACH

Meantime I drove a string of horses from Leavenworth to Fort Kearney, where I met my old friend Bill Trotter, who was then division stage agent. He employed me at once to drive stage between Kearney and Plum Creek, the road running near the spot where I had my first Indian fight with the McCarthy brothers, and where I killed my first Indian, nearly nine years before. I drove stage over this route until February, 1866, and while bounding over the cold, dreary road day after day, my thoughts turned continually towards my promised bride, until I at last determined to abandon staging forever, and marry and settle down. Immediately after coming to this conclusion, I went to St. Louis, where I was most cordially received by my sweetheart; it was arranged between us that our wedding should take place on the 6th day of March following.

At last the day arrived and the wedding ceremony was performed at the residence of the bride's parents, in the presence of a large number of invited friends, whose hearty congratulations we received. I was certainly to be congratulated, for I had become possessed of a lovely and noble woman, and as I gazed upon her as she stood beside me arrayed in her wedding costume, I indeed felt proud of her; and from that time to this I have always thought that I made a most fortunate choice for a life partner.

Bridal Trip on a Missouri Steamer

An hour after the ceremony we—my bride and myself—were on board of a Missouri river steamboat, bound for our new home in Kansas. My wife's parents had accompanied us to the boat, and had bidden us a fond farewell and a God-speed on our journey.

During the trip up the river several very amusing, yet awkward, incidents occurred, some of which I cannot resist relating. There happened to be on board the boat an excursion party from Lexington, Missouri, and those comprising it seemed to shun me, for some reason which at the time I could not account for. They would point at me, and quietly talk among themselves, and eye me very closely. Their actions seemed very strange to me. After the boat had proceeded some little distance, I made the acquaintance of several families from Indiana, who were *en route* to Kansas. A gentleman, who seemed to be the leader of these colonists said to me, "The people of this excursion party don't seem to have any great love for you."

"What does it mean?" I asked; "what are they saying? It's all a mystery to me."

"They say that you are one of the Kansas Jay-hawkers, and one of Jennison's house burners," replied the gentleman.

"I am from Kansas—that's true; and was a soldier and a scout in the Union army," said I; "and I was in Kansas during the border ruffian war of 1856. Perhaps these people know who I am, and that explains their hard looks." I had a lengthy conversation with this gentleman—for such he seemed to be—and entertained him with several chapters of the history of the early Kansas troubles, and told him the experiences of my own family.

In the evening the Lexington folks got up a dance, but neither the Indiana people, my wife or myself were invited to join them. My new-found friend thereupon came to me and said: "Mr. Cody, let us have a dance of our own."

"Very well," was my reply.

"We have some musicians along with us, so we can have plenty of music," remarked the gentleman.

"Good enough!" said I, "and I will hire the negro barber to play the violin for us. He is a good fiddler, as I heard him playing only a little while ago." The result was that we soon organized a good string band and had a splendid dance, keeping it up as long as the Lexington party did theirs.

A Close Call

The second day out from St. Louis the boat stopped to wood-up at a wild looking landing. Suddenly twenty horsemen were seen galloping up through the timber, and as they came nearer the boat they fired on the negro deck-hands, against whom they seemed to have a special grudge, and who were engaged in throwing wood on board. The negroes all quickly jumped on the boat and pulled in the gang-plank, and the captain had only just time to get the steamer out into the stream before the bush-whackers—for such they proved to be—appeared on the bank.

"Where is the black Abolition jay-hawker?" shouted the leader. "Show him to us, and we'll shoot him," yelled another. But as the boat had got well out in the river by this time they could not board us, and the captain ordering a full head of steam, pulled out and left them.

I afterwards ascertained that some of the Missourians, who were with the excursion party, were bushwhackers themselves, and had telegraphed to their friends from some previous landing that I was on board, telling them to come to the landing which we had just left and take me off. Had the villains captured me they would have undoubtedly put an end to my career, and the public would never have had the pleasure of being bored by this autobiography.

I noticed that my wife felt grieved over the manner in which these people had treated me. Just married, she was going into a new country, and seeing how her husband was regarded, how he had been shunned, and how his life had been threatened, I was afraid she might come to the conclusion too soon that she had wedded a "hard customer." So when the boat landed at Kansas City I telegraphed to some of my friends in Leavenworth that I would arrive there in the evening. My object was to have my acquaintances give me a reception, so that my wife could see that I really did have some friends and was not so bad a man as the bushwhackers tried to make out.

Just as I expected, when the boat reached Leavenworth I found a general round-up of friends at the landing to receive us. There were about sixty gentlemen and ladies. They had a band of music with them and we were given a fine serenade. Taking carriages, we all drove to South Leavenworth to the home of my sister Eliza, who had married George Myers, and there we were given a very handsome reception. All this cheered up my wife, who concluded that I was not a desperado after all.

Keeping a Hotel

Having promised my wife that I would abandon the plains, I rented a hotel in Salt Creek Valley—the same house, by the way, which my mother had formerly kept, but which was then owned by Dr. J. J. Crook, late surgeon of the 7th Kansas. This hotel I called the Golden Rule House, and I kept it until the next September. People generally said I made a good landlord, and knew how to run a hotel—a business qualification which, it is said, is possessed by comparatively few men. But it proved too tame employment for me, and again I sighed for the freedom of the plains. Believing that I could make more money out West on the frontier than I could at Salt Creek Valley, I sold out the Golden Rule House and started alone for Saline, Kansas, which was then the end of the track of the Kansas Pacific railway, which was at that time being built across the plains. On my way I stopped at Junction City, where I again met my old friend Wild Bill, who was scouting for the government, his headquarters being at Fort Ellsworth, afterwards called Fort Harker. He told me that they needed more scouts at this post, and I accordingly accompanied him to that fort, where I had no difficulty in obtaining employment.

During the winter of 1866–67, I scouted between Fort Ellsworth and Fort Fletcher. In the spring of 1867 I was at Fort Fletcher, when General Custer came out to go on an Indian expedition with General Hancock. I remained at this post until it was drowned out by the heavy floods of Big Creek, on which it was located; the water rose about the fortifications and rendered the place unfit for occupancy; so the government abandoned the fort and moved the troops and supplies to a new post—which had been named Fort Hays—located further west, on the south fork of Big Creek. It was while scouting in the vicinity of Fort Hays that I had my first ride with the dashing and gallant Custer, who had come up to the post from Fort Ellsworth with an escort of only ten men. He wanted a guide to pilot him to Fort Larned, a distance of sixty-five miles across the country.

Acting as Guide to Custer

I was ordered by the commanding officer to guide General Custer to his desired destination, and I soon received word from the General that he would start out in the morning with the intention of making the trip in one day. Early in the morning, after a good night's rest, I was on hand, mounted on my large mouse-colored mule—an animal of great endurance—and ready for the journey; when the General saw me he said:

"Cody, I want to travel fast and go through as quickly as possible, and I don't think that mule of yours is fast enough to suit me."

"General, never mind the mule," said I, "he'll get there as soon as your horses. That mule is a good one," as I knew that the animal was better than most horses.

"Very well; go ahead, then," said he, though he looked as if he thought I would delay the party on the road.

For the first fifteen miles, until we came to the Smoky Hill River, which

GEN. GEO. A. CUSTER

we were to cross, I could hardly keep the mule in advance of the General, who rode a frisky, impatient and ambitious thoroughbred steed; in fact, the whole party was finely mounted. The General repeatedly told me that the mule was "no good" and that I ought to have had a good horse. But after crossing the river, and striking the sand-hills, I began letting my mule out a little, and putting the "persuaders" to him. He was soon out-traveling the horses, and by the time we had made about half the distance to Fort Larned, I occasionally had to wait for the General or some of his party, as their horses were beginning to show signs of fatigue.

"General, how about this mule, anyhow?" I asked at last.

"Cody, you have a better vehicle than I thought you had," was his reply.

From that time on to Fort Larned I had no trouble in keeping ahead of the party. We rode into the fort at four o'clock in the afternoon with about half the escort only, the rest having lagged far behind.

A Fight with the Indians

General Custer thanked me for having brought him straight across the country without any trail, and said that if I were not engaged as post-scout at Fort Hays he would like to have me accompany him as one of his scouts during the summer; and he added that whenever I was out of employment, if I would come to him he would find something for me to do. This was the beginning of my acquaintance with General Custer, whom I always admired as a man and as an officer.

A few days after my return to Fort Hays, the Indians made a raid on the Kansas Pacific railroad, killing five or six men and running off about one hundred horses and mules. The news was brought to the commanding officer, who immediately ordered Major Arms, of the Tenth Cavalry—which, by the way, was a negro regiment—with his company and one mountain howitzer, to go in pursuit of the redskins, and I was sent along with the expedition as scout and guide. On the second day out we suddenly discovered, on the opposite side of the Saline River, about a mile distant, a large body of Indians, who were charging down upon us. Major Arms, placing the cannon on a little knoll, limbered it up and left twenty men to guard it; and then, with the rest of the command, he crossed the river to meet the Indians.

Just as he had got the men over the stream we heard a terrific yelling and shouting in our rear, and looking back to the knoll where the cannon had been stationed, we saw the negroes, who had been left there to guard the gun, flying toward us, being pursued by about one hundred Indians, while another large party of the latter were dancing around the captured cannon, as if they had secured a trophy that

A DASHING CHARGE BY THE INDIANS

was dangerous for them to handle. Major Arms soon turned his attention towards the Indians and with a sharp charge drove them from the gun and recaptured it, but not until the carriage was broken and the gun rendered useless. The fight became hotter when the Indians were re-enforced by another large war party, that now came back at us in fine style. In this charge five of our men were killed and many more wounded, among the latter being Major Arms himself. The colored troops became fear-stricken and it was almost impossible to prevent a panic. In this sorry condition, and the danger of our position becoming a perilous one if the unequal contest was continued, Major Arms ordered a retreat, which was obeyed with singular spirit and alacrity. The Indians pursued us for a while, but darkness soon came on and under its protecting mantle we managed to escape, and to reach Fort Hays at daylight the following morning in an exhausted condition.

During our absence on this expedition the cholera broke out at the post, from which terrible disease five or six soldiers died daily, but the colored troops had so much less dread of cholera than they had of Indians that there was no dearth of nurses for the sick, as every negro at the post became a volunteer minister to the cholera patients.

CHAPTER VIII

A Millionaire in Prospective

Soon after returning to Fort Hays I was sent with dispatches to Fort Harker. After delivering the messages I visited the town of Ellsworth, about three miles west of Fort Harker, and there I met a man named William Rose, a contractor on the Kansas Pacific railroad, who had a contract for grading near Fort Hays. His stock had been stolen by the Indians, and his visit to Ellsworth was to buy more.

During the course of our conversation, Mr. Rose incidentally remarked that he had some idea of laying out a town on the west side of Big Creek, about one mile from the fort, where the railroad was to cross. He asked my opinion of the contemplated enterprise, and I told him that I thought it was "a big thing." He then proposed taking me as a partner in the scheme, and suggested that after we got the town laid out and thrown open to the public, we should establish a store and saloon there.

Thinking it would be a grand thing to be half-owner of a town, I at once accepted his proposition. We bought a stock of such articles as are usually found in a frontier store, and transported them to the place on Big Creek where we were to found our town. We hired a railroad engineer to survey the site and stake it off into lots; and we gave the new town the ancient and historical name of Rome. As a "starter," we donated lots to any one who would build on them, but reserved the corner lots and others which were best located for ourselves. These reserved lots we valued at fifty dollars each.

A Howl from Rome

Our modern Rome, like all mushroom towns along the line of a new railroad, sprang up as if by magic, and in less than one month we had two hundred frame and log houses, three or four stores, several saloons, and one good hotel. Rome was looming up, and Rose and I already considered ourselves millionaires, and thought we "had the world by the tail." But one day a fine looking gentleman, calling himself Dr. W. E. Webb, appeared in town, and dropping into our store introduced himself in a very pleasant way:

"Gentlemen, you've got a very flourishing little town here. Wouldn't you like to have a partner in your enterprise?"

"No, thank you," said I, " we have too good a thing here to whack up with anybody."

My partner agreed with me, but the conversation was continued, and at last the stranger said:

"Gentlemen, I am the agent or prospector of the Kansas Pacific railroad, and my business is to locate towns for the company along the line."

"We think we have the only suitable town-site in this immediate locality," said Mr. Rose, "and as a town is already started, we have saved the company considerable expense."

"You know as well as I do," said Dr. Webb, "that the company expects to make money by selling lands and town lots; and as you are not disposed to give the company a show, or share with me, I shall probably have to start another town near you. Competition is the life of trade, you know."

"Start your town, if you want to. We've got the 'bulge' on you, and can hold it," said I, somewhat provoked at his threat.

But we acted too independently and too indiscreetly for our own good. Dr. Webb, the very next day after his interview with us, began hauling material to a spot about one mile east of us, where he staked out a new town, which he called Hays City. He took great pains to circulate in our town the story that the railroad company would locate their round-houses and machine shops at Hays City, and that it was to be *the* town and a splendid business center. A ruinous stampede from our place was the result. People who had built in Rome came to the conclusion that they had settled in the wrong place; they began pulling down their buildings and

A HOWL FROM ROME

moving them over to Hays City, and in less than three days our once flourishing city had dwindled down to the little store which Rose and I had built.

It was on a bright summer morning that we sat on a pine box in front of our crib, moodily viewing the demolition of the last building. Three days before we had considered ourselves millionaires; on that morning we looked around and saw that we were reduced to the ragged edge of poverty. Our sanguine expectations of realizing immense fortunes were dashed to the ground and we felt pretty blue. The new town of Hays had swallowed Rome entirely. Mr. Rose facetiously remarked that he felt like "the last rose of summer," with all his lovely companions faded and gone, and *he* left blooming alone. I told him I was still there, staunch and true, but he replied that that didn't help the matter much. Thus ends the brief history of the "Rise, Decline and Fall" of Modern Rome.

It having become evident to me that there was very little hope of Rome ever regaining its former splendor and prosperity, I sent my wife and daughter Arta—who had been born at Leavenworth in the latter part of December, 1866—to St. Louis on a visit. They had been living with me for some little time in the rear part of our "store."

At this time Mr. Rose and myself had a contract under Schumacher, Miller & Co., constructors of the Kansas Pacific, for grading five miles of track westward from Big Creek, and running through the site of Rome. Notwithstanding we had been deserted, we had some small hope that they would not be able to get water at the new town, and that the people would all soon move back to Rome, as we really had the best location. We determined, therefore to go on with our grading contract, and wait for something better to turn up. It was indeed hard for us, who had been millionaires, to come down to the level of common railroad contractors—but we had to do it all the same.

We visited the new town of Hays almost daily, to see how it was progressing, and in a short time we became much better acquainted with Dr. Webb, who had reduced us from our late independent to our present dependent position. We found him a perfect gentlemen—a whole-souled, genial-hearted fellow, whom everybody liked and respected. Nearly every day "Doc" and I would take a ride over the prairie together and hunt buffalo.

A Little Sport with the Hostiles

On one occasion, having ventured about ten miles from the town, we spied a band of Indians not over two miles distant, who were endeavoring to get between us and the town, and thus cut us off. I was mounted on my celebrated horse Brigham, the fleetest steed I ever owned. On several subsequent occasions he saved my life, and he was the horse that I rode when I killed sixty-nine buffaloes in one day. Dr. Webb was riding a beautiful thoroughbred bay, which he had brought with him from the East. Having such splendid horses, we laughed at the idea of a band of Indians overtaking us on a square run, no matter how well they might be mounted, but not caring to be cut off by them, we ran our steeds about three miles towards home, thus getting between the braves and the town. The Indians were then about three-quarters of a mile distant, and we stopped and waved our hats at them, and fired some shots at long range. There were thirteen in the party, and as they were getting pretty close to us, we struck out for Hays. They came on in pursuit and sent several scattering shots after us, but we easily left them behind. They finally turned and rode off towards the Saline River.

The Doctor thought this glorious sport, and panted to organize a party to go in pursuit of them, but I induced him to give up this idea, although he did so rather reluctantly. The Doctor soon became quite an expert hunter, and before he had remained on the prairie a year there were but few men in the country who could kill more buffaloes on a hunt than he.

Being aware that Rose and myself felt rather down-hearted over our deserted village, the Doctor one day said that, as he had made the proprietors of Rome "howl," he would give us two lots each in Hays, and did so. We finally came to the conclusion that our old town was dead beyond redemption or revival, and we thereupon devoted our undivided attention to our railroad contract. One day we were pushed for horses to work on our scrapers—so I hitched up Brigham, to see how he would work. He was not much used to that kind of labor, and I was about giving up the idea of making a work-horse of him, when one of the men called to me that there were some buffaloes coming over the hill. As there had been no buffaloes seen anywhere in the vicinity of the camp for several days, we had become rather short of meat. I immediately told one of our men to hitch his horses to a wagon and follow me, as I was going out after the herd, and we would bring back some fresh meat for supper. I had no saddle, as mine had been left at the camp a mile distant, so taking the harness from Brigham, I mounted him bareback and started out after the game, being armed with my celebrated buffalo-killer, "Lucretia Borgia"—a newly-improved breech-loading needle gun, which I had obtained from the government.

Brigham to the Front

While I was riding toward the buffaloes I observed five horsemen coming out from the fort, who had evidently seen the buffaloes from the post, and were going out for a chase. They proved to be some newly-arrived officers in that part of the country, and when they came up closer, I could see by the shoulder straps that the senior officer was a captain, while the others were lieutenants.

"Hello! my friend," sang out the Captain, "I see you are after the same game we are."

"Yes, sir; I saw those buffaloes coming over the hill, and as we were about out of fresh meat I thought I would go and get some," said I.

They scanned my cheap-looking outfit pretty closely, and as my horse was not very prepossessing in appearance, having on only a blind bridle, and otherwise looking like a work-horse, they evidently considered me a green hand at hunting.

"Do you expect to catch those buffaloes on that Gothic steed?" laughingly asked the captain.

"I hope so, by pushing on the reins hard enough," was my reply.

"You'll never catch them in the world, my fine fellow," said the captain. "It requires a fast horse to overtake the animals on these prairies."

"Does it?" asked I, as if I didn't know it.

"Yes; but come along with us as we are going to kill them more for pleasure than anything else. All we want are the tongues and a piece of tender-loin, and you may have all that is left," said the generous man.

"I am much obliged to you, Captain, and will follow you," I replied.

There were eleven buffaloes in the herd and they were not more than a mile from us. The officers dashed ahead as if they had a sure thing on killing them all before I could come up with them; but I had noticed that the herd was making towards the creek for water, and as I knew buffalo nature, I was perfectly aware that it would be difficult to turn them from their direct course. Thereupon, I started towards the creek to head them off, while the officers came up in the rear and gave chase.

A Pretty Buffalo Drive

The buffaloes came rushing past me not a hundred yards distant, with the officers about three hundred yards in the rear. "Now," thought I, is the time to "get my work in," as they say; and I pulled the blind-bridle from my horse, who knew as well as I did that we were out for buffaloes—as he was a trained hunter. The moment the bridle was off, he started at the top of his speed, running in ahead of the officers, and with a few jumps he brought me alongside of the rear buffalo. Raising old "Lucretia Borgia" to my shoulder, I fired, and killed the animal at the first shot. My horse then carried me alongside the next one, not ten feet away, and I dropped him at the next fire.

As soon as one buffalo would fall, Brigham would take me so close to the next that I could almost touch it with my gun. In this manner I killed the eleven buffaloes with twelve shots; and, as the last animal dropped, my horse stopped. I jumped to the ground, knowing that he would not leave me—it must be remembered that I had been riding him without bridle, reins or saddle—and turning around as the party of astonished officers rode up, I said to them:

"Now, gentlemen, allow me to present to you all the tongues and tender-loins you wish from these buffaloes."

Captain Graham, for such I soon learned was his name, replied: "Well, I never saw the like before. Who under the sun are you, anyhow?"

"My name is Cody," said I.

One of the lieutenants, Thompson by name, who had met me at Fort Harker, then recognized me, and said: "Why, that is Bill Cody, our old scout." He then introduced me to the other officers, who were Captain Graham of the Tenth Cavalry, and Lieutenants Reed, Emmick and Ezekiel.

Captain Graham, who was considerable of a horseman, greatly admired Brigham, and said: "That horse of yours has running points."

"Yes, sir; he has not only got the points, he is a runner and knows how to use the points," said I.

"So I noticed," said the captain.

ACCEPT THE TONGUES AND TENDER-LOINS

They all finally dismounted, and we continued chatting for some little time upon the different subjects of horses, buffaloes, Indians and hunting. They felt a little sore at not getting a single shot at the buffaloes, but the way I had killed them had, they said, amply repaid them for their disappointment. They had read of such feats in books, but this was the first time they had ever seen anything of the kind with their own eyes. It was the first time, also, that they had ever witnessed or heard of a white man running buffaloes on horseback without a saddle or a bridle.

I told them that Brigham knew nearly as much about the business as I did, and if I had twenty bridles they would have been of no use to me, as he understood everything, and all that he expected of me was to do the shooting. It is a fact, that Brigham would stop if a buffalo did not fall at the first fire, so as to give me a second chance, but if I did not kill the buffalo then, he would go on, as if to say, "You are no good, and I will not fool away my time by giving you more than two shots." Brigham was the best horse I ever owned or saw for buffalo chasing.

Our conversation was interrupted in a little while by the arrival of the wagon which I had ordered out; I loaded the hindquarters of the youngest buffaloes on it, and then cut out the tongues and tender-loins, and presented them to the officers, after which I rode towards the fort with them, while the wagon returned to camp.

Captain Graham told me that he expected to be stationed at Fort Hays during the summer, and would probably be sent out on a scouting expedition, and in case he was he would like to have me accompany him as scout and guide. I replied that notwithstanding I was very busy with my railroad contract I would go with him if he was ordered out. I then left the officers and returned to our camp.

In Pursuit of Indians

That very night the Indians unexpectedly made a raid on the horses, and ran off five or six of our very best work-teams, leaving us in a very crippled condition. At daylight I jumped on old Brigham and rode to Fort Hays, where I reported the affair to the commanding officer; Captain Graham and Lieutenant Emmick were at once ordered out with their company of one hundred colored troops, to pursue the Indians and recover our stock if possible. In an hour we were under way. The darkies had never been in an Indian fight and were anxious to catch the band we were after and "Sweep de red debels from off de face of de yearth." Captain Graham was a brave, dashing officer, eager to make a record for himself, and it was with difficulty that I could trail fast enough to keep out of the way of the impatient soldiers. Every few moments Captain Graham would ride up to see if the trail was freshening and how soon we should be likely to overtake the thieves.

At last we reached the Saline River, where we found the Indians had only stopped to feed and water the animals, and had then pushed on towards the Solomon. After crossing the Saline they made no effort to conceal their trail, thinking they would not be pursued beyond that point—consequently we were able to make excellent time. We reached the Solomon before sunset, and came to a halt; we surmised that if the Indians were camped on this river, that they had no suspicion of our being in the neighborhood. I advised Captain Graham to remain with the company where it was, while I went ahead on a scout to find the Indians, if they were in the vicinity.

After riding some distance down the ravine that led to the river, I left my horse at the foot of a hill; then, creeping to the top, I looked cautiously over the summit upon the Solomon below. I at once discovered in plain view, not a mile away, a herd of horses grazing, our lost ones among them; very shortly I made out the Indian camp, noted its lay, and how we could best approach it. Reporting to Captain Graham, whose eyes fairly danced with delight at the prospect of surprising and whipping the red-skins, we concluded to wait until the moon rose, then get into the timber so as to approach the Indians as closely as possible without being discovered, and finally to make a sudden dash into their camp and clean them out. We had everything "cut and dried," as we thought, but alas! just as we were nearing the point where we were to take the open ground and make our charge, one of the colored gentlemen became so excited that he fired off his gun. We immediately commenced the charge, but the firing of the gun and the noise of our rush through the crackling timber alarmed the Indians, who at once sprang to their horses and were away from us before we reached their late camp. Captain Graham called out, "Follow me, boys!" which we did for a while, but in the darkness the Indians made good their escape. The bugle then gave the recall, but some of the darkies did not get back until morning, having, in their fright, allowed their horses to run away with them whithersoever it suited the animals' pleasure to go.

We followed the trail the next day for awhile, but as it became evident that it would be a long chase to overtake the enemy, and as we had rations only for the day, we commenced the return. Captain Graham was bitterly disappointed in not being able to get the fight when it seemed so near at one time. He roundly cursed the "nigger" who fired the gun, and as a punishment for his carelessness, he was compelled to walk all the way back to Fort Hays.

How I Received the Title of Buffalo Bill

The construction of the Kansas Pacific railroad was pushed forward with great rapidity, and when track-laying began it was only a very short time before the road was ready for construction trains as far west as the heart of the buffalo country. Twelve hundred men were employed in the work, and as the Indians were very troublesome it became difficult to obtain sufficient fresh meat to feed such an army of workmen. This embarrassment was at length overcome by the construction company engaging hunters to kill buffaloes, the flesh of which is equal to the best corn-fed beef.

Having heard of my experience and success as a buffalo hunter, Messrs. Goddard Brothers, who had the contract for boarding the employees of the road, met me in Hays City one day and made me a good offer to become their hunter, and I at once entered into a contract with them. They said that they would require about twelve buffaloes per day; that would be twenty-four hams, as we took only the hind-quarters and hump of each buffalo. As this was to be dangerous work, on account of the Indians, who were riding all over that section of the country, and as I would be obliged to go from five to ten miles from the road each day to hunt the buffaloes, accompanied by only one man with a light wagon for the transportation of the meat, I of course demanded a large salary. They could afford to remunerate me well, because the meat would not cost them anything.

They agreed to give me five hundred dollars per month, provided I furnished them all the fresh meat required.

Leaving my partner, Rose, to complete our grading contract, I immediately began my career as a buffalo hunter for the Kansas Pacific railroad, and it was not long before I acquired considerable notoriety. It was at this time that the very appropriate name of "Buffalo Bill" was conferred upon me by the road-hands. It has stuck to me ever since, and I have never been ashamed of it.

During my engagement as hunter for the company—a period of less than eighteen months—I killed 4,280 buffaloes; and I had many exciting adventures with the Indians, as well as hair-breadth escapes, some of which are well worth relating.

A Race for My Scalp

One day in the spring of 1868 I mounted Brigham and started for Smoky Hill River. After galloping about twenty miles I reached the top of a small hill overlooking the valley of that beautiful stream. As I was gazing on the landscape, I suddenly saw a band of about thirty Indians nearly half a mile distant; I knew by the way they jumped on their horses that they had seen me as soon as I came into sight.

The only chance I had for my life was to make a run for it, and I immediately wheeled and started back towards the railroad. Brigham seemed to understand what was up, and he struck out as if he comprehended that it was to be a run for life. He crossed a ravine in a few jumps, and on reaching a ridge beyond I drew rein, looked back and saw the Indians coming for me at full speed and evidently well mounted.

I would have had little or no fear of being overtaken if Brigham had been fresh; but as he was not, I felt uncertain as to how he would stand a long chase.

My pursuers seemed to be gaining on me a little, and I let Brigham shoot ahead again; when we had run about three miles further, some eight or nine of the Indians were not over two hundred yards behind, and five or six of these seemed to be shortening the gap at every jump. Brigham now exerted himself more than ever, and for the next three or four miles he got "right down to business," and did some of the prettiest running I ever saw. But the Indians were about as well mounted as I was, and one of their horses in particular—a spotted animal—was gaining on me all the time. Nearly all the other horses were strung out behind for a distance of two miles, but still chasing after me.

A Great Shot

The Indian who was riding the spotted horse was armed with rifle, and would occasionally send a bullet whistling along, sometimes striking the ground ahead of me. I saw that this fellow must be checked, or a stray bullet from his gun might hit me or

CHECKING A HOT PURSUIT

my horse; so, suddenly stopping Brigham and quickly wheeling him around, I raised old "Lucretia" to my shoulder, took deliberate aim at the Indian and his horse, hoping to hit one or the other, and fired. He was not over eighty yards away from me at this time, and at the crack of my rifle down went his horse. Not waiting to see if he recovered, I turned Brigham, and in a moment we were again fairly flying towards our destination; we had urgent business about that time, and were in a hurry to get there.

The other Indians had gained on us while I was engaged shooting at their leader, and they sent several shots whizzing past me, but fortunately none of them hit the intended mark. To return their compliment I occasionally wheeled myself in the saddle and fired back at them, and one of my shots broke the leg of one of their horses, which left its rider *hors (e) de combat*, as the French would say.

Only seven or eight Indians now remained in dangerous proximity to me, and as their horses were beginning to lag somewhat, I checked my faithful old steed a little, to allow him an opportunity to draw an extra breath or two. I had determined, if it should come to the worst, to drop into a buffalo wallow, where I could stand the Indians off for a while; but I was not compelled to do this, as Brigham carried me through most nobly.

Sauce for the Gander

The chase was kept up until we came within three miles of the end of the railroad track, where two companies of soldiers were stationed for the purpose of protecting the workmen from the Indians. One of the outposts saw the Indians chasing me across the prairie and gave the alarm. In a few minutes I saw, greatly to my delight, men coming on foot, and cavalrymen too came galloping to my rescue as soon as they could mount their horses. When the Indians observed this, they turned and ran in the direction from which they had come. In a very few minutes I was met by some of the infantrymen and trackmen, and jumping to the ground and pulling the blanket and saddle off of Brigham, I told them what he had done for me; they at once took him in charge, led him around, and rubbed him down so vigorously that I thought they would rub him to death.

Captain Nolan, of the Tenth Cavalry, now came up with forty of his men, and upon learning what had happened he determined to pursue the Indians. He kindly offered me one of the cavalry horses, and after putting my own saddle and bridle on the animal, we started out after the flying Indians, who only a few minutes before had been making it so uncomfortably lively for me. Our horses were all fresh and of excellent stock, and we soon began shortening the distance between ourselves and the redskins. Before they had gone five miles we overtook and killed eight of their number.

The others succeeded in making their escape. On coming up to the place where I had killed the first horse—the spotted one—on my "home run," I found that my bullet had struck him in the forehead and killed him instantly. He was a noble animal, and ought to have been engaged in better business.

When we got back to camp I found old Brigham grazing quietly and contentedly on the grass. He looked up at me as if to ask if we had got away with any of those fellows who had chased us. I believe he read the answer in my eyes.

Run to Cover by Indians

Another very exciting hunting adventure of mine which deserves a place in these reminiscences occurred near Saline River. My companion at the time was a man called Scotty, a butcher, who generally accompanied me on these hunting expeditions to cut up the buffaloes and load the meat into a light wagon which he brought to carry it in. He was a brave little fellow and a most excellent shot. I had killed some fifteen buffaloes and we had started for home with a wagon-load of meat. When within about eight miles of our destination we suddenly ran on to a party of at least thirty Indians who came riding out of the head of a ravine.

On this occasion I was mounted on a most excellent horse belonging to the railroad company and could easily have made my escape; but of course I could not leave Scotty, who was driving a pair of mules hitched to the wagon. To think was to act in those days; and as Scotty and I had often talked over a plan of defense in case we were ever surprised by Indians, we instantly proceeded to carry it out. We jumped to the ground, unhitched the mules quicker than it had ever been done before, and tied them and my horse to the wagon. We threw the buffalo hams upon the ground and piled them around the wheels in such a shape as to form a breast-work. All this was done in a shorter time than it takes to tell it; and then, with our extra box of ammunition and three or four extra revolvers, which we always carried along with us, we crept under the wagon and were fully prepared to give our visitors the warmest kind of a reception.

The Indians came on pell-mell, but when they were within one hundred yards of us we opened such a sudden and galling fire upon them that they held up and began to circle around the wagon instead of riding up to take tea with us. They however charged back and forth upon us several times and their shots killed the two mules and my horse; but we gave it to them right and left and had the satisfaction of seeing three of them fall to the ground not more than fifty yards away. On perceiving how well we were fortified and protected by our breast-work of hams, they probably came to the conclusion that it would be a difficult undertaking to dislodge us, for they drew off and gave us a rest, but only a short one.

Sending Up a Signal for Help

This was the kind of fighting we had been expecting for a long time, as we knew that sooner or later we would be "jumped" by Indians while we were out buffalo hunting. I had an understanding with the officers who commanded the troops at the end of the track, that in case their pickets should at any time notice a smoke in the direction of our hunting ground they were to give the alarm, so that assistance might be sent to us, for the smoke was to indicate that we were in danger.

I now resolved to signal to the troops in the manner agreed on and at the first opportunity set fire to the grass on the windward side of the wagon. The fire spread over the prairie at a rapid rate, causing a dense smoke which I knew would be seen at the camp. The Indians did not seem to understand this strategic movement. They got off from their horses and from behind a bank or knoll again and peppered away at us; but we were well fortified, and whenever they showed their heads we let them know that we could shoot as well as they.

After we had been cooped up in our little fort for about an hour, we discovered cavalry coming toward us at full gallop over the prairie. Our signal of distress had

A SIGNAL OF DISTRESS

proved a success. The Indians saw the soldiers at about the same time that we did, and thinking that it would not be healthy for them to remain much longer in that vicinity, they mounted their horses and disappeared down the cañons of the creek. When the soldiers came up we had the satisfaction of showing them five *"good"* Indians—that is dead ones. Two hours later we pulled into camp with our load of meat, which was found to be all right, except that it had a few bullets and arrows sticking in it.

CHAPTER IX

Champion Buffalo Killer

Pretty soon after the adventures mentioned in the preceding chapter, I had my celebrated buffalo hunt with Billy Comstock, a noted scout, guide and interpreter, who was then chief of scouts at Fort Wallace, Kansas. Comstock had the reputation, for a long time, of being a most successful buffalo hunter, and the officers in particular, who had seen him kill buffaloes, were very desirous of backing him in a match against me. It was accordingly arranged that I should shoot him a buffalo-killing match, and the preliminaries were easily and satisfactorily agreed upon. We were to hunt one day of eight hours, beginning at eight o'clock in the morning, and closing at four o'clock in the afternoon. The wager was five hundred dollars a side, and the man who should kill the greater number of buffaloes from on horseback was to be declared the winner.

The hunt took place about twenty miles east of Sheridan, and as it had been pretty well advertised and noised abroad, a large crowd witnessed the interesting and exciting scene. An excursion party, mostly from St. Louis, consisting of about a hundred gentlemen and ladies, came out on a special train to view the sport, and among the number was my wife, with little baby Arta, who had come to remain with me for a while.

The buffaloes were quite plenty, and it was agreed that we should go into the same herd at the same time and "make a run," as we called it, each one killing as many as possible. A referee was to follow each of us on horseback when we entered the herd, and count the buffaloes killed by each man. The St. Louis excursionists, as well as the other spectators, rode out to the vicinity of the hunting grounds in wagons and on horseback, keeping well out of sight of the buffaloes, so as not to frighten them, until the time came for us to dash into the herd—when they were to come up as near as they pleased and witness the chase.

We were fortunate in the first run in getting good ground. Comstock was mounted on one of his favorite horses, while I rode old Brigham. I felt confident that I had the advantage of Comstock in two things: first, I had the best buffalo horse that ever made a track; and second, I was using what was known at that time as the needle-gun, a breech-loading Springfield rifle—caliber 50—it was my favorite old "Lucretia," which has already been introduced to the notice of the reader; while Comstock was armed with a Henry rifle, and although he could fire a few shots quicker than I could, yet I was pretty certain that it did not carry powder and lead enough to do execution equal to my caliber 50.

A Dash into the Herd

At last the time came to begin the match. Comstock and I dashed into a herd, followed by the referees. The buffaloes separated; Comstock took the left bunch and I the right. My great *forte* in killing buffaloes from horseback was to get them circling by riding my horse at the head of the herd, shooting the leaders, thus crowding their followers to the left, till they would finally circle round and round.

THE GREAT BUFFALO-KILLING MATCH

On this morning the buffaloes were very accommodating, and I soon had them running in a beautiful circle, when I dropped them thick and fast, until I had killed thirty-eight; which finished my run. Comstock began shooting at the rear of the herd which he was chasing, and they kept straight on. He succeeded, however, in killing twenty-three, but they were scattered over a distance of three miles, while mine lay close together. I had "nursed" my buffaloes, as a billiard-player does the balls when he makes a big run.

After the result of the first run had been duly announced, our St. Louis excursion friends—who had approached to the place where we had stopped—set out a lot of champagne, which they had brought with them, and which proved a good drink on a Kansas prairie, and a buffalo hunter was a good man to get away with it.

While taking a short rest, we suddenly spied another herd of buffaloes coming toward us. It was only a small drove, and we at once prepared to give the animals a lively reception. They proved to be a herd of cows and calves—which, by the way, are quicker in their movements than the bulls. We charged in among them, and I concluded my run with a score of eighteen, while Comstock killed fourteen. The score now stood fifty-six to thirty-seven, in my favor.

An Exhibition for the Ladies

Again the excursion party approached, and once more the champagne was tapped. After we had eaten a lunch which was spread for us, we resumed the hunt. Striking out for a distance of three miles, we came up close to another herd. As I was so far ahead of my competitor in the number killed, I thought I could afford to give an extra exhibition of my skill. I had told the ladies that I would, on the next run, ride my horse without saddle or bridle. This had raised the excitement to fever heat among the excursionists, and I remember one fair lady who endeavored to prevail upon me not to attempt it.

"That's nothing at all," said I; "I have done it many a time, and old Brigham knows as well as I what I am doing, and sometimes a great deal better."

So, leaving my saddle and bridle with the wagons, we rode to the windward of the buffaloes, as usual, and when within a few hundred yards of them we dashed into the herd. I soon had thirteen laid out on the ground, the last one of which I had driven down close to the wagons, where the ladies were. It frightened some of the tender creatures to see the buffalo coming at full speed directly toward them; but when he had got within fifty yards of one of the wagons, I shot him dead in his tracks. This made my sixty-ninth buffalo, and finished my third and last run, Comstock having killed forty-six.

DEATH OF BILLY COMSTOCK

As it was now late in the afternoon, Comstock and his backers gave up the idea that he could beat me, and thereupon the referees declared me the winner of the match, as well as the champion buffalo-hunter of the plains.*

On our way back to camp, we took with us some of the choice meat and finest heads. In this connection it will not be out of place to state that during the time I was hunting for the Kansas Pacific, I always brought into camp the best buffalo heads, and turned them over to the company, who found a very good use for them. They had them mounted in the best possible manner, and sent them to all the principal cities and railroad centers in the country, having them placed in prominent positions at the leading hotels, depots, and other public buildings, as a sort of trade-mark, or advertisement, of the Kansas Pacific railroad; and to-day they attract the attention of

---

* Poor Billy Comstock was afterwards treacherously murdered by the Indians. He and Sharpe Grover visited a village of Indians, supposed to be peaceably inclined, near Big Spring Station, in Western Kansas; and after spending several hours with the red-skins in friendly conversation, they prepared to depart, having declined an invitation to pass the night there. It appears that Comstock's beautiful white-handled revolver had attracted the attention of the Indians, who overtook him and his companion when they had gone about half a mile. After surrounding the two men they suddenly attacked them. They felled, scalped and robbed Comstock; but Grover, although severely wounded, made his escape, owing to the fleetness of the excellent horse which he was riding. This sad event occurred August 27, 1868.

---

the traveler almost everywhere. Whenever I am traveling over the country and see one of these trade-marks, I feel pretty certain that I was the cause of the death of the old fellow whose body it once ornamented, and many a wild and exciting hunt is thus called to mind.

The end of the track finally reached Sheridan, in the month of May, 1868, and as the road was not to be built any farther just then, my services as a hunter were not any longer required. At this time there was a general Indian war raging all along the Western borders. General Sheridan had taken up his headquarters at Fort Hays, in order to be in the field to superintend the campaign in person. As scouts and guides were in great demand, I concluded once more to take up my old avocation of scouting and guiding for the army.

Brigham and I Part Company

Having no suitable place in which to leave my old and faithful buffalo-hunter Brigham, and not wishing to kill him by scouting, I determined to dispose of him. I was very reluctant to part with him, but I consoled myself with the thought that he would not be likely to receive harder usage in other hands than he had in mine. I had several good offers to sell him; but at the suggestion of some gentlemen in Sheridan, all of whom were anxious to obtain possession of the horse, I put him up at a raffle, in order to give them all an equal chance of becoming the owner of the famous steed. There were ten chances at thirty dollars each, and they were all quickly taken.

Old Brigham was won by a gentleman—Mr. Ike Bonham—who took him to Wyandotte, Kansas, where he soon added new laurels to his already brilliant record. Although I am getting ahead of my story, I must now follow Brigham for a while. A grand tournament came off four miles from Wyandotte, and Brigham took part in it. As has already been stated, his appearance was not very prepossessing, and nobody suspected him of being anything but the most ordinary kind of a plug. The friends of the rider laughed at him for being mounted on such a dizzy-looking steed. When the exercises—which were of a very tame character, being more for style than speed—were over, and just as the crowd was about to return to the city, a purse of $250 was made up, to be given to the horse that could first reach Wyandotte, four miles distant. The arrangement was carried out, and Brigham was entered as one of the contestants for the purse. Everybody laughed at Mr. Bonham when it became known that he was to ride that poky-looking plug against the five thoroughbreds which were to take part in the race.

When all the preliminaries had been arranged, the signal was given, and off went the horses for Wyandotte. For the first half-mile several of the horses led Brigham, but on the second mile he began passing them one after another, and on the third mile he was in advance of them all, and was showing them the road at a lively rate. On the fourth mile his rider let him out, and arrived at the hotel—the home-station—in Wyandotte a long way ahead of his fastest competitor.

Everybody was surprised as well as disgusted, that such a homely "critter" should be the winner. Brigham, of course, had already acquired a wide reputation, and his name and exploits had often appeared in the newspapers, and when it was learned that this "critter" was none other than the identical buffalo-hunting Brigham, nearly the whole crowd admitted that they had heard of him before, and had they known him in the first place they certainly would have ruled him out.

But to return to the thread of my narrative, from which I have wandered. Having received the appointment of guide and scout, and having been ordered to report at Fort Larned, then commanded by Captain Dangerfield Parker, I saw it was necessary to take my family—who had remained with me at Sheridan after the buffalo-hunting match—to Leavenworth and there leave them. This I did at once, and after providing them with a comfortable little home I returned and reported for duty at Fort Larned.

CHAPTER X

Acting as Special Scout

Nearly all the scouts operating in Western Kansas, at the time of which I write, made their principal headquarters at Fort Larned, and were commanded by Dick Curtis, an old guide, frontiersman and Indian interpreter. When I first visited the place in the line of duty there were some three hundred lodges of Kiowas and Comanche Indians camped near the fort. These Indians had not as yet gone upon the war-path, but were restless and discontented, and their leading chiefs, Satanta, Lone Wolf, Kicking Bird, Satank, Sittamore, and other noted warriors, were rather saucy. The post at the time was garrisoned by only two companies of infantry and one of cavalry.

General Hazen, who was at the post, was endeavoring to pacify the Indians and keep them from going on the war-path. I was appointed as his special scout, and one morning he notified me that he was going to Fort Harker and wished me to accompany him as far Fort Zarah, thirty miles distant. The General usually traveled in an ambulance, but this trip he was to make in a six-mule wagon, under the escort of a squad of twenty infantry-men.

So, early one morning in August, we started, arriving safely at Fort Zarah at twelve o'clock. General Hazen thought it unnecessary that we should go farther, and he proceeded on his way to Fort Harker without an escort, leaving instructions that we should return to Fort Larned the next day.

After the General had gone I went to the sergeant in command of the squad and told him that I was going back that very afternoon instead of waiting until the next morning; and I accordingly saddled up my mule and set out for Fort Larned. I proceeded uninterruptedly until I got about half-way between the two posts, when at Pawnee Rock I was suddenly "jumped" by about forty Indians, who came dashing up to me, extending their hands and saying, "How! How!" They were some of the Indians who had been hanging around Fort Larned in the morning. I saw they had on their war paint, and were evidently now out on the war-path.

Captured by Indians

My first impulse was to shake hands with them, as they seemed so desirous of it. I accordingly reached out my hand to one of them, who grasped it with a tight grip, and jerked me violently forward; another pulled my mule by the bridle, and in a moment I was completely surrounded. Before I could do anything at all, they had seized my

CAPTURED BY THE INDIANS

revolvers from the holsters, and I received a blow on the head from a tomahawk which nearly rendered me senseless. My gun, which was lying across the saddle, was snatched from its place, and finally the Indian who had hold of the bridle started off towards the Arkansas River, leading the mule, which was being lashed by the other Indians who were following. The savages were all singing, yelling and whooping, as only Indians can do, when they are having their little game all their own way. While looking towards the river I saw, on the opposite side, an immense village moving down along the bank, and then I became convinced that the Indians had left the post and were now starting out on the war-path. My captors crossed the stream with me, and as we waded through the shallow water they continued to lash the mule and myself. Finally they brought me before an important looking body of Indians, who proved to be chiefs and principal warriors. I soon recognized old Satanta among them, as well as others whom I knew and I supposed it was all over with me.

The Indians were jabbering away so rapidly among themselves that I could not understand what they were saying. Satanta at last asked me where I had been; and as good luck would have it, a happy thought struck me: I told him I had been after a herd of cattle or "whoa-haws," as they called them. It so happened that the Indians had been out of meat for several weeks, as the large herd of cattle which had been promised them had not yet arrived, although expected by them.

A Clever Ruse Secures My Escape

The moment I mentioned that I had been searching for the "whoa-haws," old Satanta began questioning me in a very eager manner. He asked me where the cattle were, and I replied that they were back only a few miles, and that I had been sent by General Hazen to inform him that the cattle were coming, and that they were intended for his people. This seemed to please the old rascal, who also wanted to know if there were any soldiers with the herd, and my reply was that there were. Thereupon the chiefs held a consultation, and presently Satanta asked me if General Hazen had really said that they should have the cattle. I replied in the affirmative, and added that I had been directed to bring the cattle to them. I followed this up with a very dignified inquiry, asking why his young men had treated me so. The old wretch intimated that it was only "a freak of the boys"; that the young men wanted to see if I was brave; in fact, they had only meant to test my bravery, and that the whole thing was a joke.

The veteran liar was now beating me at my own game of lying; but I was very glad of it, as it was in my favor. I did not let him suspect that I doubted his veracity, but I remarked that it was a rough way to treat friends. He immediately ordered his young men to give me back my arms and scolded them for what they had done. Of course, the sly old dog was now playing it very fine, as he was anxious to get possession of the cattle, with which he believed "there was a heap of soldiers coming." He had concluded it was not best to fight the soldiers if he could get the cattle peaceably.

Another council was held by the chiefs and in a few minutes old Satanta came and asked me if I would go over and bring the cattle down to the opposite side of the river, so that they could get them. I replied: 'Of course; that's my instruction from General Hazen."

Satanta said I must not feel angry at his young men, for they had only been acting in fun. He then inquired if I wished any of his men to accompany me to the cattle herd. I replied that it would be better for me to go alone, and then the soldiers could keep right on to Fort Larned, while I could drive the herd down on the bottom. So, wheeling my mule around, I was soon re-crossing the river, leaving old Satanta in the firm belief that I had told him a straight story and was going for the cattle which only existed in my imagination.

I hardly knew what to do, but thought that if I could get the river between the Indians and myself I would have a good three-quarters of a mile the start of them, and could then make a run for Fort Larned, as my mule was a good one.

Stretching My Mule

Thus far my cattle story had panned out all right; but just as I reached the opposite bank of the river I looked behind and saw that ten or fifteen Indians who had begun to suspect something crooked were following me. The moment that my mule secured a good foothold on the bank I urged him into a gentle lope towards the place where, according to my statement, the cattle were to be brought. Upon reaching a little ridge and riding down the other side out of view, I turned my mule and headed him westward for Fort Larned. I let him out for all that he was worth, and when I came out on a little rise of ground I looked back and saw the Indian village in plain sight. My pursuers were now on the ridge which I had passed over and were looking for me in every direction.

Presently they spied me, and seeing that I was running away they struck out in swift pursuit, and in a few minutes it became painfully evident that they were gaining on me. They kept up the chase as far as Ash Creek, six miles from Fort Larned. I still led them half a mile, as their horses had not gained much during the last half of the race. My mule seemed to have gotten his second wind, and as I was on the old road I played the whip and spurs on him without much cessation. The Indians likewise urged their steeds to the utmost.

Finally, upon reaching the dividing ridge between Ash Creek and Pawnee Fork, I saw Fort Larned only four miles away. It was now sundown and I heard the evening gun at the fort. The troops of the little garrison little dreamed that there was a man flying for his life from the Indians and trying to reach the post. The Indians were once more gaining on me, and when I crossed the Pawnee Fork, two miles from the post, two or three of them were only a quarter of a mile behind me. Just as I had gained the opposite bank of the stream I was overjoyed to see some soldiers in a government wagon only a short distance off. I yelled at the top of my voice and, riding up to them, told them that the Indians were after me.

Ambushing the Pursuers

Denver Jim, a well known scout, asked how many there were, and upon my informing him that there were about a dozen, he said: "Let's drive the wagon into the trees, and we'll lay for 'em." The team was hurriedly driven in among the trees and low box-elder bushes, and there secreted.

We did not have to wait long for the Indians, who came dashing up, lashing their horses, which were panting and blowing. We let two of them pass by, but we opened a lively fire on the next three or four, killing two at the first crack. The others following, discovered that they had run into an ambush, and whirling off into the brush they turned and ran back in the direction whence they had come. The two who had passed heard the firing and made their escape. We scalped the two that we had killed, and appropriated their arms and equipments; and then catching their horses, we made our way into the post. The soldiers had heard us firing, and as we were approaching the fort the drums were being beaten, and the buglers were sounding the call to fall in. The officers thought that Satanta and his Indians were coming in to capture the fort.

It seems that on the morning of that day, two hours after General Hazen had taken his departure, old Satanta drove into the post in an ambulance, which he had received some months before as a present from the government. He appeared to be angry and bent on mischief. In an interview with Captain Parker, the commanding officer, he asked why General Hazen had left the post without supplying the beef cattle which he had promised him. The Captain told him that the cattle were surely on the road, but he could not explain why they were detained.

The interview proved to be a stormy one, and Satanta made numerous threats, saying that if he wished, he could capture the whole post with his warriors. Captain Parker, who was a brave man, gave Satanta to understand that he was reckoning beyond his powers, and would find it a more difficult undertaking than he had any idea of, as they were prepared for him at any moment. The interview finally terminated, and Satanta angrily left the officer's presence. Going over to the sutler's store, he sold his ambulance to Mr. Tappan the post-trader, and with a portion of the proceeds he secretly managed to secure some whisky from some bad men around the fort. There are always to be found about every frontier post some men who will sell whisky to the Indians at any time and under any circumstances, notwithstanding it is a flagrant violation of both civil and military regulations.

Satanta mounted his horse, and taking the whisky with him he rode rapidly away and proceeded straight to his village. He had not been gone over an hour, when he returned to the vicinity of the post accompanied by his warriors who came in from every direction, to the number of seven or eight hundred. It was evident that the irate old rascal was "on his ear," so to speak, and it looked as if he intended to carry out his threat of capturing the fort. The garrison at once turned out and prepared to receive the red-skins, who, when within half a mile, circled around the fort and fired numerous shots into it, instead of trying to take it by assault.

Going on the War-Path

While this circular movement was going on, it was observed that the Indian village in the distance was packing up, preparatory to leaving, and it was soon under way. The mounted warriors remained behind some little time, to give their families an opportunity to get away, as they feared that the troops might possibly in some manner intercept them. Finally, they encircled the post several times, fired some farewell rounds, and then galloped away over the prairie to overtake their fast departing village. On their way thither, they surprised and killed a party of wood-choppers down on the Pawnee Fork, as well as some herders who were guarding beef cattle; some seven or eight men in all were killed, and it was evident that the Indians meant business.

The soldiers with the wagon—whom I had met at the crossing of the Pawnee Fork—had been out for the bodies of the men. Under the circumstances it was no wonder that the garrison, upon hearing the reports of our guns when we fired upon the party whom we ambushed, should have thought the Indians were coming back to give them another "turn."

We found that all was excitement at the post; double guards bad been put on duty, and Captain Parker had all the scouts at his headquarters. He was endeavoring to get some one to take some important dispatches to General Sheridan at Fort Hays. I reported to him at once, and stated where I met the Indians and how I had escaped from them.

"You were very fortunate, Cody, in thinking of that cattle story; but for that little game your hair would now be an ornament to a Kiowa's lodge," said he.

Just then Dick Curtis spoke up and said: "Cody, the Captain is anxious to send some dispatches to General Sheridan, at Fort Hays, and none of the scouts here seem to be very willing to undertake the trip. They say they are not well enough acquainted with the country to find the way at night."

A Terrible Duty

As a storm was coming up it was quite dark, and the scouts feared that they would lose the way; besides, it was a dangerous ride, as a large party of Indians were known to be camped on Walnut creek, on the direct road to Fort Hays. It was evident that Curtis was trying to induce me to volunteer, so I made some evasive answer to him for I did not care to volunteer after my long day's ride. But Curtis did not let the matter drop. Said he:

"I wish, Bill, that you were not so tired by your chase of today, for you know the country better than the rest of the boys, and I am certain that you could go through."

"As far as the ride to Fort Hays is concerned, that alone would matter but little to me," I said, "but it is a risky piece of work just now, as the country is full of hostile Indians; still, if no other scout is willing to volunteer, I will chance it. I'll go, provided I am furnished with a good horse. I am tired of being chased on a government mule by Indians." At this Captain Nolan, who had been listening to our conversation, said:

"Bill, you may have the best horse in my company. You can take your choice if you will carry these dispatches. Although it is against regulations to dismount an enlisted man, I have no hesitancy in such a case of urgent necessity as this is, in telling you that you may have any horse you may wish."

"Captain, your first sergeant has a splendid horse, and that's the one I want. If he'll let me ride that horse, I'll be ready to start in one hour, storm or no storm," said I.

"Good enough, Bill; you shall have the horse; but are you sure you can find your way on such a dark night as this?"

"I have hunted on nearly every acre of ground between here and Fort Hays, and I can almost keep my route by the bones of the dead buffaloes," I confidently replied.

"Never fear, Captain, about Cody not finding the way; he is as good in the dark as he is in the daylight," said Curtis.

Off in the Dark

An orderly was sent for the horse, and the animal was soon brought up, although the sergeant "kicked" a little against letting him go. After eating a lunch and filling a canteen with brandy, I went to headquarters and put my own saddle and bridle on the horse I was to ride. I then got the dispatches, and by ten o'clock was on the road to Fort Hays, which was sixty-five miles distant across the country.

AN ACCIDENT IN THE DARK

It was dark as pitch, but this I rather liked, as there was little probability of any of the red-skins seeing me unless I stumbled upon them accidentally. My greatest danger was that my horse might run into a hole and fall down, and in this way get away from me. To avoid any such accident, I tied one end of my rawhide lariat to the bridle and the other end to my belt. I didn't propose to be left on foot alone out on the prairie.

It was, indeed, a wise precaution that I had taken, for within the next three miles the horse, sure enough, stepped into a prairie-dog's hole, and down he went, throwing me clear over his head. Springing to his feet, before I could catch hold of the bridle, he galloped away into the darkness; but when he reached the full length of the lariat, he found that he was not so loose as he believed. I brought him up standing, and after finding my gun, which had dropped to the ground, I went up to him and in a moment was in the saddle again, and went on my way rejoicing, keeping straight on my course until I came to the ravines leading into Walnut Creek, twenty-five miles from Fort Larned, where the country became rougher, requiring me to travel slower and more carefully, as I feared the horse might fall over the bank, it being difficult to see anything five feet ahead. As a good horse is not very apt to jump over a bank, if left to guide himself, I let mine pick his own way. I was now proceeding as quietly as possible, for I was in the vicinity of a band of Indians who had recently camped in that locality. I thought that I had passed somewhat above the spot, having made a little circuit to the west with that intention; but as bad luck would have it this time, when I came up near the creek I suddenly rode in among a herd of horses. The animals became frightened and ran off in every direction.

Stumbling onto a Hornets' Nest

I knew at once that I was among Indian horses, and had walked into the wrong pew; so without waiting to apologize, I backed out as quickly as possible. At this moment a dog, not fifty yards away, set up a howl, and then I heard some Indians engaged in conversation—they were guarding the horses, and had been sleeping. Hearing my horse's retreating footsteps towards the hills, and thus becoming aware that there had been an enemy in their camp, they mounted their steeds and started for me.

I urged my horse to his full speed, taking the chances of his falling into holes, and guided him up the creek bottom. The Indians followed me as fast as they could by the noise I made, but I soon distanced them, and then crossed the creek.

When I had traveled several miles in a straight course, as I supposed, I took out my compass and by the light of a match saw that I was bearing two points to the east of north. At once changing my course to the direct route, I pushed rapidly on through the darkness towards Smoky Hill River. At about three o'clock in the morning I began traveling more cautiously, as I was afraid of running into another band of Indians. Occasionally I scared up a herd of buffaloes, or antelopes, or coyotes, or deer, which would frighten my horse for a moment, but with the exception of these slight alarms I got along all right.

After crossing Smoky Hill River, I felt comparatively safe as this was the last stream I had to pass. Riding on to the northward I struck the old Santa Fe trail, ten miles from Fort Hays, just at break of day.

My horse did not seem much fatigued, and being anxious to make good time and get as near the post as possible before it was fairly daylight, as there might be bands of Indians camped along Big Creek, I urged him forward as fast as he could go. As I had not "lost" any Indians, I was not now anxious to make their acquaintance, and shortly after *reveille* rode into the post. I proceeded directly to General Sheridan's headquarters, and was met at the door by Colonel Moore, *aid-de-camp* on General Sheridan's staff, who asked me on what business I had come.

"I have dispatches for General Sheridan, and my instructions from Captain Parker, commanding Fort Larned, are that they shall be delivered to the General as soon as possible," said I.

Colonel Moore invited me into one of the offices, and said he would hand the dispatches to the General as soon as he got up.

"I prefer to give these dispatches to General Sheridan myself, and at once," was my reply.

The General, who was sleeping in the same building, hearing our voices, called out, "Send the man in with the dispatches." I was ushered into the General's presence, and as we had met before he recognized me and said: "Hello, Cody, is that you?"

"Yes, sir; I have some dispatches here for you, from Captain Parker," said I, as I handed the package over to him.

He hurriedly read them, and said they were important; and then he asked me all about General Hazen and where he had gone, and about the breaking out of the Kiowas and Comanches. I gave him all the information that I possessed, and related the events and adventures of the previous day and night.

An Interview with Sheridan

"Bill!," said he, "you must have had a pretty lively ride. You certainly had a close call when you ran into the Indians on Walnut Creek. That was a good joke that you played on old Satanta. I suppose you're pretty tired after your long journey?"

"I am rather weary, General, that's a fact, as I have been in the saddle since yesterday morning"; was my reply, "but my horse is more tired than I am, and needs attention fully as much if not more," I added. Thereupon the General called an orderly and gave instructions to have my animal well taken care of, and then he said, "Cody, come in and have some breakfast with me."

"No, thank you, General," said I, "Hays City is only a mile from here, and I prefer riding over there, as I know about every one in the town, and want to see some of my friends."

AN EARLY CALL ON SHERIDAN

"Very well; do as you please, and come to the post afterwards as I want to see you," said he.

Bidding him good-morning, and telling him that I would return in a few hours, I rode over to Hays City, and at the Perry House I met many of my old friends who were of course all glad to see me. I took some refreshments and a two hours' nap, and afterward returned to Fort Hays, as I was requested.

As I rode up to the headquarters I noticed several scouts in a little group, evidently engaged in conversation on some important matter. Upon inquiry I learned that General Sheridan had informed them that he was desirous of sending a dispatch to Fort Dodge, a distance of ninety-five miles.

The Indians had recently killed two or three men while they were carrying dispatches between Fort Hays and Fort Dodge, and on this account none of the scouts seemed at all anxious to volunteer, although a reward of several hundred dollars was offered to any one who would carry the dispatches. They had learned of my experiences of the previous day, and asked me if I did not think it would be a dangerous trip. I gave it as my opinion that a man might possibly go through without seeing an Indian, bat that the chances were ten to one that he would have an exceedingly lively run and a hard time before he reached his destination, if he ever got there at all.

A Long Ride

Leaving the scouts to decide among themselves as to who was to go, I reported to General Sheridan, who also informed me that he wished some one to carry dispatches to Fort Dodge. While we were talking, his chief of scouts, Dick Parr, entered and stated that none of the scouts had yet volunteered. Upon hearing this I got my "brave" up a little, and said: "General, if there is no one ready to volunteer, I'll carry your dispatches myself."

"I had not thought of asking you to do this duty, Cody, as you are already pretty hard worked. But it is really important that these dispatches should go through,'" said the General.

"Well, if you don't get a courier by four o'clock this afternoon, I'll be ready for business at that time. All I want is a fresh horse," said I; "meantime I'll take a little more rest."

It was not much of a rest, however, that I got, for I went over to Hays City again and had "a time with the boys." I came back to the post at the appointed hour, and finding that no one had volunteered, I reported to General Sheridan. He had selected an excellent horse for me, and on handing me the dispatches, he said: "You can start as soon as you wish—the sooner the better; and good luck go with you, my boy."

In about an hour afterwards I was on the road, and just before dark I crossed Smoky Hill River. I had not yet urged my horse much, as I was saving his strength for the latter end of the route, and for any run that I might have to make in case the "wildboys " should "jump" me. So far I had not seen a sign of Indians, and as evening came on I felt comparatively safe.

I had no adventures worth relating during the night, and just before daylight I found myself approaching Saw-log Crossing, on the Pawnee Fork, having then ridden about seventy miles. A company of colored cavalry, commanded by Major Cox, was stationed at this point, and I approached their camp cautiously, for fear that the pickets might fire upon me—as the darkey soldiers were liable to shoot first and cry

READY FOR BUSINESS

"halt" afterwards. When within hearing distance I yelled out at the top of my voice, and was answered by one of the pickets. I told him not to shoot, as I was a scout from Fort Hays; and then, calling the sergeant of the guard, I went up to the vidette of the post, who readily recognized me. I entered the camp and proceeded to the tent of Major Cox, to whom I handed a letter from General Sheridan requesting him to give me a fresh horse. He at once complied with the request. After I had slept an hour and had eaten a lunch, I again jumped into the saddle, and before sunrise I was once more on the road. It was twenty-five miles to Fort Dodge, and I arrived there between nine and ten o'clock, without having seen a single Indian.

After delivering the dispatches to the commanding officer, I met Johnny Austin, chief of scouts at this post, who was an old friend of mine. Upon his invitation I took a nap at his house, and when I awoke, fresh for business once more, he informed me that the Indians had been all around the post for the past two or three days, running off cattle and horses, and occasionally killing a stray man. It was a wonder to him that I had met with none of the red-skins on the way there. The Indians, he said, were also very thick on the Arkansas River, between Fort Dodge and Fort Larned, and making considerable trouble. Fort Dodge was located sixty-five miles west of Fort Larned, the latter post being on the Pawnee Fork, about five miles from its junction with the Arkansas River.

A Dangerous Undertaking

The commanding officer at Fort Dodge was anxious to send some dispatches to Fort Larned, but the scouts, like those at Fort Hays, were rather backward about volunteering, as it was considered a very dangerous undertaking to make the trip. As Fort Larned was my post, and as I wanted to go there anyhow, I said to Austin that I would carry the dispatches, and if any of the boys wished to go along, I would like to have them for company's sake. Austin reported my offer to the commanding officer, who sent for me and said he would be happy to have me take his dispatches, if I could stand the trip on top of all that I had already done. "All I want is a good fresh horse, sir," said I.

"I am sorry to say that we haven't a decent horse here, but we have a reliable and honest government mule, if that will do you," said the officer. "Trot out your mule," said I, "that's good enough for me. I am ready at any time, sir."

The mule was forthcoming, and at dark I pulled out for Fort Larned, and proceeded uninterruptedly to Coon Creek, thirty miles out from Dodge. I had left the main wagon road some distance to the south, and had traveled parallel with it, thinking this to be a safer course, as the Indians might be lying in wait on the main road for dispatch bearers and scouts.

At Coon Creek I dismounted and led the mule by the bridle down to the water, where I took a drink, using my hat for a dipper. While I was engaged in getting the water, the mule jerked loose and struck out down the creek. I followed him in hopes that he would catch his foot in the bridle-rein and stop, but this he seemed to have no idea of doing. He was making straight for the wagon road, and I did not know what minute he might run into a band of Indians. He finally got on the road, but instead of going back toward Fort Dodge, as I naturally expected he would do, he turned eastward toward Fort Larned, and kept up a little jog trot just ahead of me, but would not let me come up to him, although I tried it again and again, I had my gun in my hand, and several times I was strongly tempted to shoot him, and would probably have done so had it not been for fear of bringing Indians down upon me, and besides he was carrying the saddle for me. So I trudged on after the obstinate "critter," and if there ever was a government mule that deserved and received a good round cursing it was that one. I had neglected the precaution of tying one end of my lariat to his bit and the other to my belt, as I had done a few nights before, and I blamed myself for this gross piece of negligence.

A Provoking Mule

Mile after mile I kept on after that mule, and every once in a while I indulged in strong language respecting the whole mule fraternity. From Coon Creek to Fort Larned

PLAGUED BY A MULE

it was thirty-five miles, and I finally concluded that my prospects were good for "hoofing" the whole distance. We—that is to say, the confounded mule and myself—were making pretty good time. There was nothing to hold the mule, and I was all the time trying to catch him—which urged him on. I made every step count, for I wanted to reach Fort Larned before daylight, in order to avoid if possible the Indians, to whom it would have been "pie" to have caught me there on foot.

The mule stuck to the road and kept on for Larned, and I did the same thing. Just as day was beginning to break, we—that is the mule and myself—found ourselves on a hill looking down into the valley of the Pawnee Fork, in which Fort Larned was located, only four miles away; and when the morning gun belched forth we were within half a mile of the post.

"Now," said I, "Mr. Mule, it is my turn," and raising my gun to my shoulder, in "dead earnest" this time, I blazed away, hitting the animal in the hip. Throwing a second cartridge into the gun, I let him have another shot, and I continued to pour the lead into him until I had him completely laid out. Like the great majority of government mules, he was a tough one to kill, and he clung to life with all the tenaciousness of his obstinate nature. He was, without doubt, the toughest and meanest mule I ever saw, and he died hard.

The troops, hearing the reports of the gun, came rushing out to see what was the matter. They found that the mule had passed in his chips, and when they learned the cause they all agreed that I had served him just right. Taking the saddle and bridle from the dead body, I proceeded into the post and delivered the dispatches to Captain

Parker. I then went over to Dick Curtis's house, which was headquarters for the scouts, and there put in several hours of solid sleep.

During the day General Hazen returned from Fort Harker and he also had some important dispatches to send to General Sheridan. I was feeling quite elated over my big ride; and seeing that I was getting the best of the other scouts in regard to making a record, I volunteered to carry General Hazen's dispatches to Fort Hays. The General accepted my services, although he thought it was unnecessary for me to kill myself. I told him that I had business at Fort Hays, and wished to go there anyway, and it would make no difference to the other scouts, for none of them appeared willing to undertake the trip.

Accordingly, that night I left Fort Larned on an excellent horse, and next morning at daylight found myself once more in General Sheridan's headquarters at Fort Hays. The General was surprised to see me, and still more so when I told him of the time I had made in riding to Fort Dodge, and that I had taken dispatches from Fort Dodge to Fort Larned; and when, in addition to this, I mentioned my journey of the night previous, General Sheridan thought my ride from post to post, taken as a whole, was a remarkable one, and he said that he did not know of its equal. I can safely say that I have never heard of its being beaten in a country infested with hostile Indians.

To recapitulate: I had ridden from Fort Larned to Fort Zarah (a distance of sixty-five miles) and back in twelve hours, including the time when I was taken across the Arkansas by the Indians. In the succeeding twelve hours I had gone from Fort Larned to Fort Hays, a distance of sixty-five miles. In the next twenty-four hours I had gone from Fort Hays to Fort Dodge, a distance of ninety-five miles. The following night I had traveled from Fort Dodge thirty miles on muleback and thirty-five miles on foot to Fort Larned; and the next night sixty-five miles more to Fort Hays. Altogether I had ridden (and walked) 355 miles in fifty-eight riding hours, or an average of over six miles an hour. Of course, this may not be regarded as very fast riding, but taking into consideration the fact that it was mostly done in the night and over a wild country, with no roads to follow, and that I had to be continually on the look-out for Indians it was thought at the time to be a big ride, as well as a most dangerous one.

CHAPTER XI

My Appointment as Chief of Scouts

General Sheridan highly complimented me for what I had done and informed me that I need not report back to General Hazen, as he had more important work for me to do. He told me that the Fifth Cavalry—one of the finest regiments in the army—was on its way to the Department of the Missouri, and that he was going to send it on an expedition against the Dog Soldier Indians, who were infesting the Republican River region.

"Cody," continued he, "I have decided to appoint you as guide and chief of scouts with the command. How does that suit you?"

"First-rate, General, and I thank you for the honor," I replied, as gracefully as I knew how.

The Dog Soldier Indians were a band of Cheyennes and unruly, turbulent members of other tribes, who would not enter into any treaty, or keep a treaty if they made one, and who had always refused to go upon a reservation. They were a warlike body of well-built, daring and restless braves, and were determined to hold possession of the country in the vicinity of the Republican and Solomon Rivers. They were called "Dog Soldiers" because they were principally Cheyennes—a name derived from the French *chien*, a dog.

Scouting

On the third day of October the Fifth Cavalry arrived at Fort Hays, and I at once began making the acquaintance of the different officers of the regiment. I was introduced by General Sheridan to Colonel William Royal, who was in command of the regiment. He was a gallant officer and an agreeable and pleasant gentleman. He was afterwards stationed at Omaha as Inspector-General in the Department of the Platte. I also became acquainted with Major W. H. Brown, Major Walker, Captain Sweetman, Quartermaster E. M. Hays, and in fact all the officers of the regiment.

General Sheridan, being anxious to punish the Indians who had lately fought General Forsyth, did not give the regiment much of a rest, and accordingly on the 5th of October it began its march for the Beaver Creek country. The first night we camped on the south fork of Big Creek, four miles west of Hays City. By this time I had become pretty well acquainted with Major Brown and Captain Sweetman, who invited me to mess with them on this expedition, and a jolly mess we had. There were other scouts in the command besides myself and I particularly remember Tom Renahan, Hank Fields and a character called "Nosey" on account of his long nose.

On the morning of the 6th we pulled out to the north, and during the day I was very favorably struck with the appearance of the regiment. It was a beautiful command and when strung out on the prairie with a train of seventy-five six-mule-wagons, ambulances and pack-mules, I felt very proud of my position as guide and chief of scouts of such a warlike expedition.

Just as we were about to go into camp on the Saline River that night, we ran on to a band of about fifteen Indians, who, seeing us, dashed across the creek, followed

GOVERNMENT MULE TEAM

by some bullets which we sent after them; but as the small band proved to be a scouting party, we pursued them only a mile or two, when our attention was directed to a herd of buffaloes, which we immediately pursued and killed ten or fifteen for the command.

The next day we marched thirty miles, and late in the afternoon we went into camp on the south fork of the Solomon. At this encampment Colonel Royal asked me to go out and kill some buffaloes for the boys.

"All right, Colonel, send along a wagon or two to bring in the meat," I said.

"I am not in the habit of sending out my wagons until I know that there is something to be hauled in; kill your buffaloes first and then I'll send out the wagons," was the Colonel's reply. I said no more, but went out on a hunt, and after a short absence returned and asked the Colonel to send his wagons over the hill for the half dozen buffaloes I had killed.

Bringing Live Buffaloes into Camp

The following afternoon he again requested me to go out and get some fresh buffalo meat. I didn't ask him for any wagons this time, but rode out some distance, and coming up with a small herd, I managed to get seven of them headed straight for the encampment, and instead of shooting them just then, I ran them at full speed right into the camp, and then killed them all, one after the other in rapid succession. Colonel Royal witnessed the whole proceeding, which puzzled him somewhat, as he could see

BRINGING LIVE MEAT INTO CAMP

no reason why I had not killed them on the prairie. He came up rather angrily, and demanded an explanation. "I can't allow any such business as this, Cody," said he, "what do you mean by it?"

"I didn't care about asking for any wagons this time, Colonel; so I thought I would make the buffaloes furnish their own transportation," was my reply. The Colonel saw the point in a moment, and had no more to say on the subject.

No Indians had been seen in the vicinity during the day and Colonel Royal having carefully posted his pickets, supposed everything was serene for the night. But before morning we were aroused from our slumbers by hearing shots fired, and immediately afterwards one of the mounted pickets came galloping into camp, saying that there were Indians close at hand. The companies all fell into line, and were soon prepared and anxious to give the red-skins battle; but as the men were yet new in the Indian country a great many of them were considerably excited. No Indians, however, made their appearance, and upon going to the picket-post where the picket said he'd seen them none could be found, nor could any traces of them be discovered. The sentinel—who was an Irishman—insisted that there certainly had been red-skins there.

A Scared Irishman

"But you must be mistaken," said Colonel Royal.

"Upon me sowl, Colonel, I'm not; as shure ez me name's Pat Maloney, one of thim rid divils hit me on the head wid a club, so he did," said Pat; and so, when morning came, the mystery was further investigated and was easily solved. Elk tracks were found in the vicinity and it was undoubtedly a herd of elks that had frightened Pat; as he had turned to run, he had gone under a limb of a tree, against which he hit his head, and supposed he had been struck by a club in the hands of an Indian. It was hard to convince Pat however, of the truth.

A three days' uninteresting march brought us to Beaver Creek where we camped and from which point scouting parties were sent out in different directions. Neither of these, however, discovering Indians they all returned to camp about the same time, finding it in a state of great excitement, it having been attacked a few hours previous by a party of Indians, who had succeeded in killing two men and in making off with sixty horses belonging to Co. H.

That evening the command started on the trail of these Indian horse thieves; Major Brown with two companies and three days rations pushing ahead in advance of the main command. Being unsuccessful, however, in overtaking the Indians, and getting nearly out of provisions—it being our eighteenth day out—the entire command marched towards the nearest railroad point, and camped on the Saline River, distant three miles from Buffalo Tank. While waiting for supplies we received a new commanding officer, Brevet Major-General E. A. Carr, who was the senior major of the regiment, and who ranked Colonel Royal. He brought with him the now celebrated Forsyth scouts, who were commanded by Lieutenant Pepoon, a regular-army officer.

"INDIANS, UPON ME SOWL."

It was also while waiting in this camp that Major Brown received a new lieutenant to fill a vacancy in his company. On the day that this officer was to arrive, Major Brown had his private ambulance brought out, and invited me to accompany him to the railroad station to meet his lieutenant, whose name was A. B. Bache. He proved to be a fine gentleman, and a brave, dashing officer. On the way to the depot Major Brown had said, "Now, Cody, when we come back we'll give Bache a lively ride and shake him up a little."

A Lively Shaking Up

Major Brown was a jolly good fellow, but sometimes he would get "a little off," and as this was one of his "off days" he was bound to amuse himself in some original and mischievous way. Reaching the depot just as the train came in, we easily found the Lieutenant, and giving him the back seat in the ambulance we were soon headed for camp.

Pretty soon Major Brown took the reins from his driver, and at once began whipping the mules. After getting them into a lively gallop he pulled out his revolver and fired several shots. The road was terribly rough and the night was so dark that we could hardly see where we were going. It was a wonderful piece of luck that we were not tipped over and our necks broken. Finally Bache said, good-humoredly:

"Is this the way you break in all your Lieutenants, Major?"

"Oh, no; I don't do this as a regular thing, but it's the way we frequently ride in this country," said the Major; "just keep your seat, Mr. Bache, and we'll take you through on time." The Major appropriated the reply of the old California stage-driver, Hank Monk, to Horace Greeley.

We were now rattling down a steep hill at full speed, and just as we reached the bottom, the front wheels struck a deep ditch over which the mules had jumped. We were all brought up standing by the sudden stoppage of the ambulance. Major Brown and myself were nearly pitched out on the wheels, while the Lieutenant came flying headlong from the back seat to the front of the vehicle.

"Take a back seat, Lieutenant," coolly said Major Brown.

"Major, I have just left that seat," said Bache.

We soon lifted the wagon out of the ditch, and then resumed our drive, running into camp under full headway, and creating considerable amusement. Every one recognized the ambulance and knew at once that Major Brown and I were out on a "lark," and therefore there was not much said about our exploit. Halting with a grand flourish in front of his tent, Major Brown jumped out in his most gallant style and politely asked his lieutenant in. A very pleasant evening was spent there, quite a number of the officers calling to make the acquaintance of the new officer, who entertained the visitors with an amusing account of the ride from the depot.

Next morning at an early hour, the command started out on a hunt for Indians. General Carr having a pretty good idea where he would be most likely to find them, directed me to guide him by the nearest route to Elephant Rock on Beaver Creek.

In Search of Indians

Upon arriving at the south fork of the Beaver on the second day's march, we discovered a large, fresh Indian trail which we hurriedly followed for a distance of eight miles, when suddenly we saw on the bluffs ahead of us, quite a large number of Indians.

General Carr ordered Lieutenant Pepoon's scouts and Company M to the front. This company was commanded by Lieutenant Schinosky, a Frenchman by birth and a reckless dare-devil by nature, who was anxious to have a hair-lifting match. Having advanced his company nearly a mile ahead of the main command, about four hundred Indians suddenly charged down upon him and gave him a lively little fight, until he was supported by our full force.

The Indians kept increasing in numbers all the while until it was estimated that we were fighting from eight hundred to one thousand of them. The engagement became quite general, and several were killed and wounded on each side. The Indians were evidently fighting to give their families and village a chance to get away. We had undoubtedly surprised them with a larger force than they had expected to see in that part of the country. We fought them until dark, all the time driving them before us. At night they annoyed us considerably by firing down into our camp from the higher hills, and several times the command was ordered out to dislodge them from their position and drive them back.

After having returned from one of these little sallies, Major Brown, Captain Sweetman, Lieutenant Bache and myself were taking supper together, when "whang!" came a bullet into Lieutenant Bache's plate, breaking a hole through it. The bullet came from the gun of one of the Indians, who had returned to the high bluff overlooking our camp. Major Brown declared it was a crack shot, because it broke the plate. We finished our supper without having any more such close calls.

At daylight next morning we struck out on the trail, and soon came to the spot where the Indians had camped the day before. We could see that their village was a very large one, consisting of about five hundred lodges; and we pushed forward rapidly from this point on the tail which ran back toward Prairie Dog Creek.

About two o'clock we came in sight of the retreating village, and soon the warriors turned back to give us battle. They set fire to the prairie grass in front of us,

A CRACK SHOT

and on all sides, in order to delay us as much as possible. We kept up a running fight for the remainder of the afternoon, and the Indians repeatedly attempted to lead us off the track of their flying village, but their trail was easily followed, as they were continually dropping tepee poles, camp kettles, robes, furs and all heavy articles belonging to them. They were evidently scattering, and it finally became difficult for us to keep on the main trail. When darkness set in, we went into camp, it being useless to try to follow the Indians after nightfall.

Next morning we were again on the trail, which led north and back towards Beaver Creek, which stream it crossed within a few miles of the spot where we had first discovered the Indians, they having made nearly a complete circle, in hopes of misleading us. Late in the afternoon, we again saw them going over a hill far ahead of us, and towards evening the main body of warriors came back and fought us once more; but we continued to drive them until darkness set in, when we camped for the night.

The Indians soon scattered in every direction, but we followed the main trail to the Republican River, where we made a cut-off, and then went north towards the Platte River. We found, however, that the Indians by traveling night and day had got a long start, and the General concluded that it was useless to follow them any further, as we had pushed them so hard, and given them such a scare that they would leave the Republican country and go north across the Union Pacific railroad. Most of the Indians, as he had predicted, did cross the Platte River, near Ogalalla, on the Union Pacific, and thence continued northward.

That night we returned to the Republican River and camped in a grove of cotton-woods, which I named Carr's Grove, in honor of the commanding officer.

Out in a Dry Country

The General told me that the next day's march would be towards the head-waters of the Beaver, and he asked me the distance. I replied that it was about twenty-five miles, and he said he would make it the next day. Getting an early start in the morning, we struck out across the prairie, my position as guide being ahead of the advance guard. About two o'clock General Carr overtook me, and asked how far I supposed it was to water. I thought it was about eight miles, although we could see no sign or indication of any stream in our front.

"Pepoon's scouts say you are going in the wrong direction," said the General, "and in the way you are bearing it will be fifteen miles before you can strike any of the branches of the Beaver; and that when you do, you will find no water, for the Beavers are dry at this time of the year at that point."

"General, I think the scouts are mistaken," said I, "for the Beaver has more water near its head than it has below; and at the place where we will strike the stream we will find immense beaver dams, large enough and strong enough to cross the whole command, if you wish."

"Well, Cody, go ahead," said he, "I'll leave it to you, but remember that I don't want a dry camp."

"No danger of that," said I, and then I rode on, leaving him to return to the command. As I had predicted, we found water seven or eight miles further on, where we came upon a beautiful little stream—a tributary of the Beaver—hidden in the hills. We had no difficulty in selecting a good halting place, and obtaining fresh spring water and excellent grass. The General, upon learning from me that the stream—which was only eight or nine miles long—had no name, took out his map and located it, and named it Cody's Creek, which name it still bears.

Surprised by Indians

We pulled out early next morning for the Beaver, and when we were approaching the stream I rode on ahead of the advance guard, in order to find a crossing. Just as I turned a bend of the creek "bang!" went a shot, and down went my horse—myself with him. I disentangled myself, and jumped behind the dead body. Looking in the direction whence the shot had come I saw two Indians, and at once turned my gun loose on them, but in the excitement of the moment I missed my aim. They fired two or three more shots, and I returned the compliment, wounding one of their horses.

On the opposite side of the creek, going over the hill, I observed a few lodges moving rapidly away, and also some mounted warriors, who could see me, and who kept blazing away with their guns. The two Indians who had fired at me and had killed my horse were retreating across the creek on a beaver-dam. I sent a few shots after them to accelerate their speed, and also fired at the ones on the other side of the stream. I was undecided as to whether it was best to run back to the command on foot or hold my position. I knew that within a few minutes the troops would come up, and I therefore decided to hold my position. The Indians, seeing that I was alone, turned and charged down the hill, and were about to re-cross the creek to corral me, when the advance guard of the command put in an appearance on the ridge, and dashed forward to my rescue. The red-skins whirled and made off.

When General Carr came up, he ordered Company I to go in pursuit of the band. I accompanied Lieutenant Brady, who commanded, and we had a running fight with the Indians, lasting several hours. We captured several head of their horses and most of their lodges. At night we returned to the command, which by this time had crossed the creek on the beaver-dam.

FLIGHT OF THE INDIANS

We scouted for several days along the river, and had two or three lively skirmishes. Finally our supplies began to run low, and General Carr gave orders to return to Fort Wallace, which we reached three days afterwards, and where we remained several days. While the regiment was waiting here for orders, I spent most of the time in hunting buffaloes, and one day, while I was out with a small party, we were "jumped" by about fifty Indians. We had a severe fight for at least an hour, when we succeeded in driving the enemy. They lost four of their warriors, and probably concluded that we were a hard crowd. I had some excellent marksmen with me, and they did some fine work, sending the bullets thick and fast where they would do the most good. Two or three of our horses had been hit, and one man had been wounded; we were ready and willing to stay with the red-skins as long as they wished—but they finally gave it up, however, as a bad job, and rode off. We finished our hunt, and went back to the post loaded down with buffalo meat, and received the compliment of the General for our little fight.

CHAPTER XII

A Hard Winter's Campaign

Very soon after our fight on Beaver Creek, Gen. Carr received orders from Gen. Sheridan for a winter's campaign in the Canadian River country, instructing him to proceed at once to Fort Lyon, Colorado, and there to fit out for the expedition. Leaving Fort Wallace in November, 1868, we arrived at Fort Lyon in the latter part of the month without special incident, and at once began our preparations for invading the enemy's country.

General Penrose had left this post three weeks previously with a command of some three hundred men. He had taken no wagons with him and his supply train was composed only of pack mules. General Carr was ordered to follow with supplies on his trail and overtake him as soon as possible. I was particularly anxious to catch up with Penrose's command, as my old friend, Wild Bill, was among his scouts. We followed the trail very easily for the first three days, and then we were caught in Freeze-Out Canyon by a fearful snow storm, which compelled us to go into camp for a day. The ground now being covered with snow, we found that it would be impossible to follow Penrose's trail any further, especially as he had left no sign to indicate the direction he was going. General Carr sent for me and said that as it was very important that we should not lose the trail, he wished that I would take some scouts with me, and while the command remained in camp, push on as far as possible and see if I could not discover some traces of Penrose or where he had camped at any time.

Accompanied by four men I started out in the blinding snow storm, taking a southerly direction. We rode twenty-four miles, and upon reaching a tributary of the Cimarron, we scouted up and down the stream for a few miles and finally found one of Penrose's old camps. It was now late in the afternoon, and as the command would come up the next day, it was not necessary for all of us to return with the information to General Carr. So riding down into a sheltered place in a bend of the creek, we built a fire and broiled some venison from a deer which we had shot during the day, and after eating a substantial meal I left the four men there, while I returned to bring up the troops.

It was eleven o'clock at night when I got back to the camp. A light was still burning in the General's tent, he having remained awake, anxiously awaiting my return. He was glad to see me, and was overjoyed at the information I brought, for he had great fears concerning the safety of General Penrose. He roused up his cook and ordered him to get me a good hot supper, all of which I greatly appreciated. I passed the night in the General's tent, and next morning rose refreshed and prepared for a big day's work.

A Rough March

The command took up its march next day for the Cimarron, and had a hard tramp of it on account of the snow having drifted to a great depth in many of the ravines, and in some places the teamsters had to shovel their way through. We arrived at the Cimarron at sundown, and went into a nice warm camp. Upon looking around next morning, we found that Penrose, having been unencumbered by wagons, had kept on the west side of the Cimarron, and the country was so rough that it was impossible for us to stay on his trail with our wagons; but knowing that he would certainly follow down the river, General Carr concluded to take the best wagon route along the stream, which I discovered to be on the east side. Before we could make any headway with our wagon train we had to leave the river and get out on the divide. We were very fortunate that day in finding a splendid road for some distance, until we were all at once brought up standing on a high table-land, overlooking a beautiful winding creek that lay far below us in the valley. The question that troubled us was how we were to get the wagons down. We were now in the foot-hills of the Rattoon Mountains, and the bluff we were on was very steep.

"Cody, we're in a nice fix now," said General Carr.

"Oh, that's nothing," was my reply.

"But you can never take the train down," said he.

"Never you mind the train, General. You say you are looking for a good camp. How does that beautiful spot down in the valley suit you?" I asked him.

"That will do. I can easily descend with the cavalry, but how to get the wagons down there is a puzzler to me," said he.

"By the time you've located your camp, your wagons shall be there," said I.

"All right, Cody, I'll leave it to you, as you seem to want to be boss," he replied pleasantly. He at once ordered the command to dismount and lead the horses down the mountain-side. The wagon train was a mile in the rear, and when it came up, one of the drivers asked: "How are we going down there?"

"Run down, slide down or fall down—any way to get down," said I.

"We never can do it; it's too steep; the wagons will run over the mules," said another wagon-master.

"I guess not; the mules have got to keep out of the way," was my reply.

I told Wilson, the chief wagon-master, to bring on his mess-wagon, which was at the head of the train, and I would try the experiment at least. Wilson drove the team and wagon to the brink of the hill, and following my directions he brought out some extra chains with which we locked both wheels on each side, and then rough-locked them. We now started the wagon down the hill. The wheel-horses—or rather the wheel-mules—were good on the hold-back, and we got along finely until we nearly reached the bottom, when the wagon crowded the mules so hard that they started on a run and galloped down into the valley and to the place where General Carr had located his camp. Three other wagons immediately followed in the same way, and in half an hour every wagon was in camp, without the least accident having occurred. It was indeed an exciting sight to see the six-mule teams come straight down the mountain and finally break into a full run. At times it looked as if the wagons would turn a somersault and land on the mules.

This proved to be a lucky march for us, as far as gaining on Penrose was concerned, for the route he had taken on the west side of the stream turned out to be a bad one, and we went with our immense wagon-train as far in one day as Penrose had in seven. His command had marched on to a plateau or high table-land so steep that not even a pack-mule could descend it, and he was obliged to retrace his steps a long ways, thus losing three days' time, as we afterwards learned.

A Turkey Hunt with Clubs

While in this camp we had a lively turkey hunt. The trees along the banks of the stream were literally alive with wild turkeys, and after unsaddling the horses between two and three hundred soldiers surrounded a grove of timber and had a grand turkey round-up, killing four or five hundred of the birds, with guns, clubs and stones. Of course, we had turkey in every style after this hunt—roast turkey, boiled turkey, fried turkey, "turkey on toast," and so on; and we appropriately called this place Camp Turkey.

From this point on, for several days, we had no trouble in following Penrose's trail, which led us in a southeasterly direction towards the Canadian River. No Indians were seen nor any signs of them found. One day, while riding in advance of the command, down San Francisco Creek, I heard some one calling my name from a little bunch of willow brush on the opposite bank, and, upon looking closely at the spot, I saw a negro.

"Sakes alive! Massa Bill, am dat you?" asked the man, whom I recognized as one of the colored soldiers of the Tenth Cavalry.

I next heard him say to some one in the brush: "Come out o' heah. Dar's Massa Buffalo Bill." Then he sang out: "Massa Bill, is you got any hawd tack?"

"Nary a hard tack; but the wagons will be along presently and then you can get all you want," said I.

"Dat's de best news I'se heerd foah sixteen long days, Massa Bill," said he.

"Where's your command? Where's General Penrose?' I asked.

"I dunno," said the darkey; "we got lost and we been a starvin' eber since."

By this time two other negroes had emerged from their place of concealment. They had deserted Penrose's command—which was out of rations and nearly in a starving condition—and were trying to make their way back to Fort Lyon. General Carr concluded, from what they could tell him, that General Penrose was somewhere on Palladora Creek; but we could not learn anything definite from the starved "mokes," for they knew not where they were themselves.

Rescue of a Starving Command

Having learned that General Penrose's troops were in such bad shape, General Carr ordered Major Brown to start out the next morning with two companies of cavalry and fifty pack-mules loaded with provisions, and to make all possible speed to reach and relieve the suffering soldiers. I accompanied this detachment, and on the third day out we found the half-famished soldiers camped on the Palladora. The camp presented a pitiful sight, indeed. For over two weeks the men had had only quarter rations and were now nearly starved to death. Over two hundred horses and mules were lying dead, having died from fatigue and starvation. General Penrose, fearing that General Carr would not find him, had sent back a company of the Seventh Cavalry to Fort Lyon for supplies; but no word as yet had been heard from them. The rations which Major Brown brought to the command came none too soon and were the means of saving many lives.

DISCOVERY OF PENROSE'S STARVING COMMAND

About the first man I saw after reaching the camp was my old, true and tried friend, Wild Bill. That night we had a jolly reunion around the camp-fires.

General Carr, upon arriving with his force, took command of all the troops, he being the senior officer and ranking General Penrose. After selecting a good camp, he unloaded the wagons and sent them back to Fort Lyon for fresh supplies. He then picked out five hundred of the best men and horses, and, taking his pack-train with him, he started south for the Canadian River, distant about forty miles, leaving the rest of the troops at the supply camp.

Successful Raid on a Beer Train

I was ordered to accompany this expedition. We struck the south fork of the Canadian River, or Rio Colorado, at a point a few miles above the old *adobe* walls, which at one time had composed a fort, and was the place where Kit Carson once had a big Indian fight. We were now within twelve miles of a new supply depot, called Camp Evans, which had been established for the Third Cavalry and Evans's Expedition from New Mexico. The scouts who had brought in this information also reported that they expected the arrival at Camp Evans of a bull-train from New Mexico with a large quantity of beer for the soldiers. This news was grateful to Wild Bill and myself, and we determined to lie low for that beer outfit. That very evening it came along, and the beer that was destined for the soldiers at Camp Evans never reached its destination. It went straight down the thirsty throats of General Carr's command. It appears that the Mexicans living near Fort Union had manufactured the beer, and were taking it through to Camp Evans to sell to the troops, but it struck a lively market without going so far. It was sold to our boys in pint cups, and as the weather was very cold we warmed the beer by putting the ends of our picket-pins heated red hot into the cups. The result was one of the biggest beer jollifications I ever had the misfortune to attend.

One evening General Carr summoned me to his tent, and said he wished to send some scouts with dispatches to Camp Supply, which were to be forwarded from there to Sheridan. He ordered me to call the scouts together at once at his headquarters, and select the men who were to go. I asked him if I should not go myself, but he replied that he wished me to remain with the command, as he could not spare me. The distance to Camp Supply was about two hundred miles, and owing to the very cold weather it was anything but a pleasant trip. Consequently none of the scouts were anxious to undertake it. It was finally settled, however, that Wild Bill, a half-breed called Little Geary, and three other scouts should carry the dispatches, and they accordingly took their departure next day, with instructions to return to the command as soon as possible.

For several days we scouted along the Canadian River, but found no signs of Indians. General Carr then went back to his camp, and soon afterwards our wagon train came in from Fort Lyon with a fresh load of provisions. Our animals being in poor condition, we remained in different camps along San Francisco Creek and the north fork of the Canadian until Wild Bill and his scouts returned from Camp Supply.

A Free Fight Among the Scouts

Among the scouts of Penrose's command were fifteen Mexicans, and between them and the American scouts there had existed a feud; when General Carr took command of the expeditions—uniting it with his own—and I was made chief of all the scouts, this feud grew more intense, and the Mexicans often threatened to clean us out; but they postponed the undertaking from time to time, until one day, while we were all at the sutler's store, the long-expected fight took place, and resulted in the Mexicans getting severely beaten.

General Carr upon hearing of the row, sent for Wild Bill and myself, he having concluded, from the various statements which had been made to him, that we were the instigators of the affair. But after listening to what we had to say, he thought that the Mexicans were as much to blame as we were.

It is not to be denied that Wild Bill and myself had been partaking too freely of "tangle-foot" that evening; and General Carr said to me: "Cody, there are plenty of antelopes in the country, and you can do some hunting for the camp while we stay here."

"All right, General, I'll do it."

After that I put in my time hunting, and with splendid success, killing from fifteen to twenty antelopes a day, which kept the men well supplied with fresh meat.

At length, our horses and mules having become sufficiently recruited to travel, we returned to Fort Lyon, arriving there in March, 1869, where the command was to rest and recruit for thirty days, before proceeding to the Department of the Platte, whither it had been ordered.

CHAPTER XIII

I Am Accused of Selling Government Property

Upon my return to Fort Lyon General Carr granted me a leave of absence of one month which I improved by paying a visit to my family which was at this time in St. Louis. The nearest railroad station to Fort Lyon was Sheridan, fully one hundred and forty miles distant, and as I had no conveyance of my own, General Carr instructed Captain Hays, our quartermaster, to give me the use of a horse to make the necessary journey. When I received the horse it was with instructions to leave the animal in the quartermaster's corral at Fort Wallace until my return, but instead of so doing I placed the horse in the care of an old friend named Perry, who was a hotel-keeper in Sheridan.

After a twenty days' absence in St. Louis, pleasantly spent with my family, I returned to Sheridan, and there learned that my horse had been seized by the government. It seems that the quartermaster's agent at Sheridan had reported to General Bankhead, commanding Fort Wallace, and to Captain Laufer, the quartermaster, that

I had left the country and had sold a government horse and mule to Mr. Perry, and of course Captain Laufer took possession of the animals and threatened to have Perry arrested for buying government property. Perry explained to him the facts in the case and said that I would return in a few days; but the Captain would pay no attention to his statements.

I immediately went over to the office of the quartermaster's agent, and had Perry point him out to me. I at once laid hold of him, and in a short time had treated him to just such a thrashing as his contemptible lie deserved. He then mounted a horse, rode to Fort Wallace, and reported me to General Bankhead and Captain Laufer, and obtained a guard to return with and protect him.

The next morning I secured a horse from Perry, and proceeding to Fort Wallace demanded my horse and mule from General Bankhead, on the ground that they were Quartermaster Hays's property and belonged to General Carr's command and that I had obtained permission to ride them to Sheridan and back. General Bankhead in a gruff manner ordered me out of his office and off the reservation, saying that if I didn't take a hurried departure he would have me forcibly put out. I told him to do it and be hanged; I might have used a stronger expression, and upon second thought, I believe I did. I next interviewed Captain Laufer and demanded of him also the horse and mule, as I was responsible for them to Quartermaster Hays. Captain Laufer intimated that I was a liar and that I had disposed of the animals. Hot words ensued between us, and he too ordered me to leave the post. I replied that General Bankhead had commanded me to do the same thing, but that I had not yet gone; and that I did not propose to obey any orders of an inferior officer.

Seeing that it was of no use to make any further effort to get possession of the animals I rode back to Sheridan, and just as I reached there I met the quartermaster's agent coming out from supper, with his head tied up. It occurred to me that he had not received more than one-half of the punishment justly due him, and that now would be a good time to give him the balance—so I carried the idea into immediate execution. After finishing the job in good style, I informed him that he could not stay in that town while I remained there, and convinced him that Sheridan was not large enough to hold us both at the same time; he accordingly left the place and again went to Fort Wallace, this time reporting to General Bankhead that I had driven him away, and had threatened to kill him.

Arrested and Thrown into the Guard-House

That night while sleeping at the Perry House, I was awakened by a tap on the shoulder and upon looking up I was considerably surprised to see the room filled with armed negroes who had their guns all pointed at me. The first words I heard came from the sergeant, who said:

"Now look a-heah, Massa Bill, ef you makes a move we'll blow you off de farm, shuah!" Just then Captain Ezekiel entered and ordered the soldiers to stand back.

"Captain, what does this mean?" I asked.

"I am sorry, Bill, but I have been ordered by General Bankhead to arrest you and bring you to Fort Wallace," said he.

"That's all right," said I, "but you could have made the arrest alone, without having brought the whole Thirty-Eighth Infantry with you."

"I know that, Bill," replied the Captain, "but as you've not been in very good humor for the last day or two, I didn't know how you would act."

I hastily dressed, and accompanied Captain Ezekiel to Fort Wallace, arriving there at two o'clock in the morning.

"Bill, I am really sorry," said Captain Ezekiel, as we alighted, "but I have orders to place you in the guard-house, and I must perform my duty."

"Very well, Captain; I don't blame you a bit," said I; and into the guard-house I went as a prisoner for the first and only time in my life. The sergeant of the guard— who was an old friend of mine, belonging to Captain Graham's company, which was stationed there at the time—did not put me into a cell, but kindly allowed me to stay in his room and occupy his bed, and in a few minutes I was snoring away as if nothing unusual had occurred.

Shortly after *reveille* Captain Graham called to see me. He thought it was a shame for me to be in the guard-house, and said that he would interview General Bankhead in my behalf as soon as he got up. The Captain had a nice breakfast prepared for me, and then departed. At guard-mount I was not sent for, contrary to my expectations, and thereupon I had word conveyed to Captain Graham, who was officer of the day, that I wanted to see General Bankhead. The Captain informed me that the General absolutely refused to hold any conversation whatever with me.

At this time there was no telegraph line between Fort Wallace and Fort Lyon, and therefore it was impossible for me to telegraph to General Carr, and I determined to send a dispatch direct to General Sheridan. I accordingly wrote out a long telegram informing him of my difficulty, and had it taken to the telegraph office for transmission; but the operator, instead of sending it at once as he should have done, showed it to General Bankhead, who tore it up, and instructed the operator not to pay any attention to what I might say, as he was running that post. Thinking it very strange that I received no answer during the day I went to the telegraph office, accompanied by a guard, and learned from the operator what he had done.

A Dispute over a Telegram

"See here, my young friend," said I, "this is a public telegraph line, and I want my telegram sent, or there'll be trouble."

I re-wrote my dispatch and handed it to him, accompanied with the money to pay for the transmission, saying, as I did so: "Young man, I wish that telegram sent direct to Chicago. You know it is your duty to send it, and it must go."

He knew very well that he was compelled to transmit the message, but before doing so he called on General Bankhead and informed him of what I had said, and told him that he would certainly have to send it, for if he didn't he might lose his position. The General, seeing that the telegram would have to go, summoned me to his headquarters, and the first thing he said, after I got into his presence was:

"If I let you go, sir, will you leave the post at once and not bother my agent at Sheridan again?"

"No, sir," I replied, "I'll do nothing of the kind. I'll remain in the guard-house until I receive an answer from General Sheridan."

"If I give you the horse and mule will you proceed at once to Fort Lyon?"

"No, sir; I have some bills to settle at Sheridan and some other business to transact," replied I.

"Well, sir; will you at least agree not to interfere any further with the quartermaster's agent at Sheridan?"

"I shall not bother him any more, sir, as I have had all I want from him," was my answer.

General Bankhead thereupon sent for Captain Laufer and ordered him to turn the horse and mule over to me. In a few minutes more I was on my way to Sheridan, and after settling my business there, I proceeded to Fort Lyon, arriving two days afterwards. I related my adventures to General Carr, Major Brown, and other officers, who were greatly amused thereby.

In Pursuit of Horse Thieves

"I'm glad you've come, Bill," said General Carr, "as I have been wanting you for the last two weeks. While we have been at this post several valuable animals, as well as a large number of government horses and mules have been stolen, and we think the thieves are still in the vicinity of the fort, but as yet we have been unable to discover their rendezvous. I have had a party out for the last few days in the neighborhood of old Fort Lyon, and they have found fresh tracks down there and seem to think that the stock is concealed somewhere in the timber, along the Arkansas River. Bill Green, one of the scouts who is just up from there, can perhaps tell you something more about the matter."

Green, who had been summoned, said that he had discovered fresh trails before striking the heavy timber opposite old Fort Lyon, but that in the tall grass he could not follow them. He had marked the place where he had last seen fresh mule tracks, so that he could find it again.

"Now, Cody, you're just the person we want," said the General.

"Very well, I'll get a fresh mount, and to-morrow I'll go down and see what I can discover," said I.

"You had better take two men besides Green, and a pack mule with eight or ten days' rations," suggested the General, "so that if you find the trail you can follow it up, as I am very anxious to get back this stolen property. The scoundrels have taken one of my private horses and also Lieutenant Forbush's favorite little black race mule."

Next morning I started out after the horse thieves, being accompanied by Green, Jack Farley and another scout. The mule track, marked by Green, was easily found, and with very little difficulty I followed it for about two miles into the timber and came upon a place where, as I could plainly see from numerous signs, quite a number of head of stock had been tied among the trees and kept for several days. This was evidently the spot where the thieves had been hiding their stolen stock until they had accumulated quite a herd. From this point it was difficult to trail them, as they had taken the stolen animals out of the timber one by one and in different directions, thus showing that they were experts at the business and experienced frontiersmen, for no Indian could have exhibited more cunning in covering up a trail than did they.

I abandoned the idea of following their trail in this immediate locality, so calling my men together, I told them that we would ride out for about five miles and make a complete circuit about the place, and in this way we would certainly find the trail on which they had moved out. While making the circuit we discovered the tracks of twelve animals—four mules and eight horses—in the edge of some sand-hills, and from this point we had no trouble in trailing them down the Arkansas River, which they had crossed at Sand Creek, and then had gone up the latter stream, in the direction of Denver, to which place they were undoubtedly bound. When nearing Denver their trail became so obscure that we at last lost it; but by inquiring of the settlers along the road which they had taken, we occasionally heard of them.

The Thieves Run Down

When within four miles of Denver—this was on a Thursday—we learned that the horse thieves had passed there two days before. I came to the conclusion they would attempt to dispose of the animals at Denver, and being aware that Saturday was the great auction day there, I thought it best to remain where we were, at a hotel, and not go into the city until that day. It certainly would not have been advisable for me to have gone into Denver meantime, because I was well known there, and if the thieves had learned of my presence in the city they would at once have suspected my business.

Early Saturday morning we rode into town and stabled our horses at the Elephant Corral. I secured a room from Ed. Chase, overlooking the corral, and then took up my post of observation. I did not have long to wait, for a man whom I readily recognized as one of our old packers, rode into the corral mounted upon Lieutenant Forbush's racing mule, and leading another government mule, which I also identified. It had been recently branded, and over the "U. S." was a plain "D. B." I waited for the man's companion to put in an appearance, but he did not come, and my conclusion was that he was secreted outside of the city with the rest of the animals.

Presently the black mule belonging to Forbush was put up at auction. Now, thought I, is the time to do my work. So, walking through the crowd, who were bidding for the mule, I approached the man who had offered him for sale. He recognized me and endeavored to escape, but I seized him by the shoulder, saying: "I guess, my friend, that you'll have to go with me. If you make any resistance, I'll shoot you on the spot." He was armed with a pair of pistols, which I took away from him. Then informing the auctioneer that I was a United States detective, and showing him—as well as an inquisitive officer—my commission as such, I told him to stop the sale, as the mule was stolen property, and that I had arrested the thief, whose name was Williams.

Farley and Green, who were near at hand, now came forward, and together we took the prisoner and the mules three miles down the Platte River; there, in a thick bunch of timber, we all dismounted and made preparations to hang Williams from a limb, if he did not tell us where his partner was. At first he denied knowing anything about any partner, or any other stock; but when he saw that we were in earnest, and would hang him at the end of the given time—five minutes—unless he " squealed," he told us that his "pal" was at an unoccupied house three miles further down the river.

We immediately proceeded to the spot indicated, and as we came within sight of the house we saw our stock grazing near by. Just as we rode up to the door, another one of our old packers, whom I recognized as Bill Bevins, stepped to the front and I covered him instantly with my rifle before he could draw his revolver. I ordered him to throw up his hands, and he obeyed the command. Green then disarmed him and brought him out. We looked through the house and found their saddles, pack-saddles, blankets, overcoats, lariats and two Henry rifles, which we took possession of. The horses and mules we tied in a bunch, and with the whole outfit we returned to

Denver, where we lodged Williams and Bevins in jail, in charge of my friend, Sheriff Edward Cook. The next day we took them out, and tying each one on a mule we struck out on our return trip to Fort Lyon.

Escape of Bevins

At the hotel outside the city, where we had stopped on Thursday and Friday, we were joined by our man with the pack-mule. That night we camped on Cherry Creek, seventeen miles from Denver. The weather—it being in April—was cold and stormy, but we found a warm and cozy camping place in a bend of the creek. We made our beds in a row, with our feet towards the fire. The prisoners so far had appeared very docile, and had made no attempt to escape, and therefore I did not think it necessary to hobble them. We made them sleep on the inside, and it was so arranged that some one of us should be on guard all the time.

At about one o'clock in the night it began snowing, while I was watching. Shortly before three o'clock, Jack Farley, who was then on guard, and sitting on the foot of the bed, with his back to the prisoners, was kicked clear into the fire by Williams, and the next moment Bevins, who had got hold of his shoes—which I had thought were out of his reach—sprang up a jumped over the fire, and started on a run. I sent a shot after him as soon as I awoke sufficiently to comprehend what was taking place. Williams attempted to follow him, and as he did so I whirled around and knocked him down with my revolver. Farley by this time had gathered himself out of the fire, and Green had started after Bevins, firing at him on the run; but the prisoner made his escape into the brush. In his flight, unfortunately for him, and luckily for us, he dropped one of his shoes.

Leaving Williams in the charge of Farley and "Long Doc," as we called the man with the pack-mule, Green and myself struck out after Bevins as fast as possible. We heard him breaking through the brush, but knowing that it would be useless to follow him on foot, we went back to the camp and saddled up two of the fastest horses, and at daylight we struck out on his trail, which was plainly visible in the snow. He had got an hour and a half the start of us. His tracks led us in the direction of the mountains and the South Platte River, and, as the country through which he was passing was covered with prickly pears, we knew that he could not escape stepping on them with his one bare foot, and hence we were likely to overtake him in a short time. We could see, however, from the long jumps that he was taking that he was making excellent time, but we frequently noticed, after we had gone some distance, that the prickly pears and stones along his route were cutting his bare foot, as nearly every track of it was spotted with blood.

An Extraordinary Run for Liberty

We had run our horses some twelve miles when we saw Bevins crossing a ridge about two miles ahead. Urging our horses up to their utmost speed, we reached the ridge

A HORSE THIEF THAT WAS GAME

just as he was descending the divide towards the South Platte, which stream was very deep and swift at this point. It became evident that if he should cross it ahead of us, he would have a good chance of making his escape. So pushing our steeds as fast as possible, we rapidly gained on him, and when within a hundred yards of him I cried to him to halt or I would shoot. Knowing I was a good shot, he stopped, and coolly sitting down waited till we came up.

"Bevins, you've given us a good run," said I.

"Yes," said he, "and if I had had fifteen minutes more of a start, and got across the Platte, I would have laughed at the idea of your ever catching me."

Bevins's run was the most remarkable feat of the kind ever known either of a white man, or an Indian. A man who could run bare-footed in the snow eighteen miles through a prickly pear patch, was certainly a "tough one," and that's the kind of a person Bill Bevins was. Upon looking at his bleeding foot I really felt sorry for him. He asked me for my knife, and I gave him my sharp-pointed bowie, with which he dug the prickly pear briars out of his foot. I considered him as "game" a man as I had ever met.

"Bevins, I have got to take you back," said I, "but as you can't walk with that foot, you can ride my horse and I'll foot it."

We accordingly started back for our camp, with Bevins on my horse, which was led either by Green or myself, as we alternately rode the other horse. We kept a close watch on Bevins, for we had ample proof that he needed watching. His wounded foot must have pained him terribly but not a word of complaint escaped him. On arriving at the camp we found Williams bound as we had left him and he seemed sorry that we had captured Bevins.

A Successful Break in the Dark

After breakfasting we resumed our journey, and nothing worthy of note again occurred until we reached the Arkansas River, where we found a vacant cabin and at once took possession of it for the night. There was no likelihood of Bevins again trying to escape, for his foot had swollen to an enormous size and was useless. Believing that Williams could not escape from the cabin, we unbound him. We then went to sleep, leaving Long Doc on guard, the cabin being comfortably warmed and well lighted by the fire. It was a dark, stormy night—so dark that you could hardly see your hand before you. At about ten o'clock Williams asked Long Doc to allow him to step to the door for a moment.

Long Doc, who had his revolver in his hand, did not think it necessary to wake us up, and believing that he could take care of the prisoner, he granted his request. Williams thereupon walked to the outer edge of the door, while Long Doc, revolver in hand, was watching him from the inside. Suddenly Williams made a spring to the

ROBBING A
STAGE COACH

right, and before Doc could even raise his revolver, he had dodged around the house. Doc jumped after him, and fired just as he turned a corner, the report bringing us all to our feet, and in an instant we knew what had happened. I at once covered Bevins with my revolver, but as I saw that he could hardly stir, and was making no demonstration, I lowered the weapon. Just then Doc came in swearing "a blue streak," and announced that Williams had escaped. There was nothing for us to do except to gather our horses close to the cabin and stand guard over them for the rest of the night, to prevent the possibility of Williams sneaking up and stealing one of them. That was the last I ever saw or heard of Williams.

Breaking Up of the Gang

We finally got back to Fort Lyon with Bevins, and General Carr, to whom I immediately reported, complimented us highly on the success of our trip, notwithstanding we had lost one prisoner. The next day we took Bevins to Boggs's ranch on Picket Wire

Creek, and there turned him over to the civil authorities, who put him in a log jail to await his trial. He was never tried, however, for he soon made his escape, as I expected he would. I heard no more of him until 1872, when I learned that he was skirmishing around on Laramie plains at his old tricks. He sent word by the gentleman from whom I gained this information, that if he ever met me again he would kill me on sight. He was finally arrested and convicted for robbery, and was confined in the prison at Laramie City. Again he made his escape, and soon afterwards he organized a desperate gang of outlaws who infested the country north of the Union Pacific railroad, and when the stages began to run between Cheyenne and Deadwood, in the Black Hills, they robbed the coaches and passengers, frequently making large hauls of plunder. They kept this up for some time, till finally most of the gang were caught, tried, convicted and sent to the penitentiary for a number of years. Bill Bevins and nearly all of his gang are now confined in the Nebraska State prison, to which they were transferred from Wyoming.

CHAPTER XIV

A Military Expedition

A day or two after my return to Fort Lyon, the Fifth Cavalry were ordered to the Department of the Platte, and took up their line of march for Fort McPherson, Nebraska. We laid over one day at Fort Wallace, to get supplies, and while there I had occasion to pass General Bankhead's headquarters. His orderly called to me and said the General wished to see me. As I entered the General's office he extended his hand and said: "I hope you have no hard feelings toward me, Cody, for having you arrested when you were here. I have just had a talk with General Carr and Quartermaster Hays and they informed me that you had their permission to ride the horse and mule, and if you had stated this fact to me there would have been no trouble about the matter whatever."

"That is all right, General," said I; "I will think no more of it. But I don't believe that your quartermaster's agent will ever again circulate false stories about me."

"No," said the General; "he has not yet recovered from the beating that you gave him."

From Fort Wallace we moved down to Sheridan, where the command halted for us to lay in a supply of forage which was stored there. I was still messing with Major Brown, with whom I went into the village to purchase a supply of provisions for our mess; but unfortunately we were in too jolly a mood to fool away money on "grub." We bought several articles, however, and put them into the ambulance and sent them back to the camp with our cook. The Major and myself did not return until *reveille* next morning. Soon afterwards the General sounded "boots and saddles," and presently the regiment was on its way to McPherson.

It was very late before we went into camp that night and we were tired and hungry. Just as Major Brown was having his tent put up his cook came to us and asked where the provisions were that we had bought the day before.

"Why, did we not give them to you—did you not bring them to camp in the ambulance?" asked Major Brown.

"No, sir; it was only a five-gallon demijohn of whisky, a five-gallon demijohn of brandy, and two cases of Old Tom-Cat gin," said the cook.

"The mischief!" I exclaimed; "didn't we spend any money on grub at all?"

"No, sir," replied the cook.

"Well, that will do for the present," said Major Brown.

It seems that our minds had evidently been running on a different subject than provisions while we were loitering in Sheridan, and we found ourselves, with a two hundred and fifty mile march ahead of us, without anything more inviting than ordinary army rations.

At this juncture Captain Denny came up and the Major apologized for not being able to invite him to take supper with us; but we did the next best thing, and asked him to take a drink. He remarked that that was what he was looking for, and when he learned of our being out of commissary supplies and that we had bought nothing except whisky, brandy and gin, he said, joyously:

"Boys, as we have an abundance, you can eat with us and we will drink with you."

It was a satisfactory arrangement, and from that time forward we traded our liquids for their solids. When the rest of the officers heard of what Brown and I had done they all sent us invitations to dine with them at any time. We returned the compliment by inviting them to drink with us whenever they were dry. Although I would not advise anybody to follow our example, yet it is a fact that we got more provisions for our whisky than the same money, which we paid for the liquor, would have bought, so after all it proved a very profitable investment.

A Big Indian Trail

On reaching the north fork of the Beaver and riding down the valley towards the stream, I suddenly discovered a large fresh Indian trail. On examination I found it to be scattered all over the valley on both sides of the creek, as if a very large village had recently passed down that way. Judging from the size of the trail, I thought there could not be less than four hundred lodges, or between twenty-five hundred and three thousand warriors, women and children in the band. I galloped back to the command, distant about three miles, and reported the news to General Carr, who halted the regiment, and, after consulting a few minutes, ordered me to select a ravine, or as low ground as possible, so that he could keep the troops out of sight until we could strike the creek.

We went into camp on the Beaver, and the General ordered Lieutenant Ward to take twelve men and myself and follow up the trail for several miles, and find out how fast the Indians were traveling. I was soon convinced, by the many camps they had made, that they were traveling slowly, and hunting as they journeyed. We went down the Beaver on this scout about twelve miles, keeping our horses well concealed under the banks of the creek, so as not to be discovered.

At this point, Lieutenant Ward and myself, leaving our horses behind us, crawled to the top of a high knoll, where we could have a good view for some miles distant down the stream. We peeped over the summit of the hill, and not over three miles away we could see a whole Indian village in plain sight, and thousands of ponies grazing around on the prairie. Looking over to our left on the opposite side of the creek, we observed two or three parties of Indians coming in, loaded down with buffalo meat.

"This is no place for us, Lieutenant," said I; "I think we have important business at the camp to attend to as soon as possible."

"I agree with you," said he, "and the quicker we get there the better it will be for us."

We quickly descended the hill and joined the men below. Lieutenant Ward hurriedly wrote a note to General Carr, and handing it to a corporal, ordered him to make all possible haste back to the command and deliver the message. The man started off on a gallop, and Lieutenant Ward said: "We will march slowly back until we meet the troops, as I think the General will soon be here, for he will start immediately upon receiving my note."

Attack on the Courier

In a few minutes we heard two or three shots in the direction in which our dispatch courier had gone, and soon after we saw him come running around the bend of the creek, pursued by four or five Indians. The Lieutenant, with his squad of soldiers and myself, at once charged upon them, when they turned and ran across the stream.

"This will not do," said Lieutenant Ward, "the whole Indian village will now know that soldiers are near by."

"Lieutenant, give me that note, and I will take it to the General," said I.

He gladly handed me the dispatch, and spurring my horse I dashed up the creek. After having ridden a short distance, I observed another party of Indians also going

ATTACK ON A COURIER

to the village with meat; but instead of waiting for them to fire upon me, I gave them a shot at long range. Seeing one man firing at them so boldly, it surprised them, and they did not know what to make of it. While they were thus considering, I got between them and our camp. By this time they had recovered from their surprise, and, cutting their buffalo meat loose from their horses, they came after me at the top of their speed; but as their steeds were tired out, it did not take me long to leave them far in the rear.

I reached the command in less than an hour, delivered the dispatch to General Carr, and informed him of what I had seen. He instantly had the bugler sound "boots and saddles," and all the troops—with the exception of two companies which we left to guard the train—were soon galloping in the direction of the Indian camp.

A Lieutenant in Sharp Quarters

We had ridden about three miles when we met Lieutenant Ward, who was coming slowly towards us. He reported that he had run into a party of Indian buffalo hunters, and had killed one of the number, and had had one of his horses wounded. We immediately pushed forward and after marching about five miles came within sight of hundreds of mounted Indians advancing up the creek to meet us. They formed a complete line in front of us. General Carr, being desirous of striking their village, ordered the troops to charge, break through their line, and keep straight on. This movement would, no doubt, have been successfully accomplished had it not been for the rattlebrained and dare-devil French Lieutenant Schinosky, commanding Company B, who, misunderstanding General Carr's orders, charged upon some Indians at the left, while the rest of the command dashed through the enemy's line, and was keeping straight on, when it was observed that Schinosky and his company were surrounded by four or five hundred red-skins. The General, to save the company, was obliged to sound a halt and charge back to the rescue. The company, during this short fight, had several men and quite a number of horses killed.

All this took up valuable time, and night was coming on. The Indians were fighting desperately to keep us from reaching their village, which being informed by couriers of what was taking place, was packing up and getting away. During that afternoon it was all we could do to hold our own in fighting the mounted warriors, who were in our front and contesting every inch of the ground. The General had left word for our wagon train to follow up with its escort of two companies, but as it had not made its appearance he entertained some fears that it had been surrounded, and to prevent the possible loss of the supply train we had to go back and look for it. About 9 o'clock that evening we found it, and went into camp for the night.

CHARGING BACK TO THE RESCUE

Early the next day we broke camp and passed down the creek but there was not an Indian to be seen. They had all disappeared and gone on with their village. Two miles further we came to where a village had been located, and here we found nearly everything belonging or pertaining to an Indian camp, which had been left in the great hurry to get away. These articles were all gathered up and burned. We then pushed out on the trail as fast as possible. It led us to the northeast towards the Republican; but as the Indians had a night the start of us we entertained but little hope of overtaking them that day. Upon reaching the Republican in the afternoon the General called a halt, and as the trail was running more to the east, he concluded to send his wagon train on to Fort McPherson by the most direct route, while he would follow on the trail of the red-skins.

Next morning at daylight we again pulled out and were evidently gaining rapidly on the Indians for we could occasionally see them in the distance. About 11 o'clock that day while Major Babcock was ahead of the main command with his company, and while we were crossing a deep ravine, we were surprised by about three hundred warriors who commenced a lively fire upon us. Galloping out of the ravine on to the rough prairie the men dismounted and returned the fire. We soon succeeded in driving the enemy before us, and were so close upon them at one time that they aban-

THE MEN DISMOUNTED AND RETURNED THE FIRE

doned and threw away nearly all their lodges and camp equipages, and everything that had any considerable weight. They left behind them their played-out houses, and for miles we could see Indian furniture strewn along in every direction. The trail became divided, and the Indians scattered in small bodies, all over the prairie. As night was approaching and our horses were about giving out, a halt was called. A company was detailed to collect all the Indian horses running loose over the country, and to burn the other Indian property.

The command being nearly out of rations I was sent to the nearest point, Old Fort Kearney, about sixty miles distant for supplies.

Re-Enforced by the Pawnee Scouts

Shortly after we reached Fort McPherson, which continued to be the headquarters of the Fifth Cavalry for some time, we fitted out for a new expedition to the Republican River country, and were re-enforced by three companies of the celebrated Pawnee Indian scouts, commanded by Major Frank North: his officers being Captain Lute North, brother of the Major, Captain Cushing, his brother-in-law, Captain Morse, and Lieutenants Beecher, Matthews and Kislandberry. General Carr recommended at this time to General Augur, who was in command of the Department, that I be made chief of scouts in the Department of the Platte, and informed me that in this position I would receive higher wages than I had been getting in the Department of the Missouri. This appointment I had not asked for.

I made the acquaintance of Major Frank North and I found him and his officers perfect gentlemen, and we were all good friends from the very start. The Pawnee scouts had made quite a reputation for themselves as they had performed brave and valuable services in fighting against the Sioux, whose bitter enemies they were; being thoroughly acquainted with the Republican and Beaver country, I was glad that they were to be with the expedition, and my expectation of the aid they would render was not disappointed.

During our stay at Fort McPherson I made the acquaintance of Lieutenant George P. Belden, known as the "White Chief," whose life was written by Colonel Brisbin, U. S. army. I found him to be an intelligent, dashing fellow, a splendid rider and an excellent shot. An hour after our introduction he challenged me for a rifle match, the preliminaries of which were soon arranged. We were to shoot ten shots each for fifty dollars, at two hundred yards, off hand. Belden was to use a Henry rifle, while I was to shoot my old "Lucretia." This match I won and then Belden proposed to shoot a one hundred yard match, as I was shooting over his distance. In this match Belden was victorious. We were now even, and we stopped right there.

A Comical Sight

While we were at this post General Augur and several of his officers, and also Thomas Duncan, Brevet Brigadier and Lieutenant-Colonel of the Fifth Cavalry, paid us a visit for the purpose of reviewing the command. The regiment turned out in fine style and showed themselves to be well drilled soldiers, thoroughly understanding military tactics. The Pawnee scouts were also reviewed and it was very amusing to see them in their full regulation uniform. They had been furnished a regular cavalry uniform and on this parade some of them had their heavy overcoats on, others their large black hats, with all the brass accoutrements attached; some of them were minus pantaloons and only wore a breech-clout. Others wore regulation pantaloons but no shirts and were bare headed; others again had the seat of the pantaloons cut out, leaving only leggins; some of them wore brass spurs, though without boots or moccasins; but for all this they seemed to understand the drill remarkably well for Indians. The commands, of course, were given to them in their own language by Major North, who could talk it as well as any full-blooded Pawnee. The Indians were well mounted and felt proud and elated because they had been made United States soldiers. Major North had for years complete power over these Indians and could do more with them than any man living. That evening after the parade was over the officers and quite a number of ladies visited a grand Indian dance given by the Pawnees, and of all the Indians I have seen their dances excel those of any other tribe.

Battle Between the Sioux and Pawnees

Next day the command started; when encamped, several days after, on the Republican River near the mouth of the Beaver, we heard the whoops of Indians, followed by shots in the vicinity of the mule herd, which had been taken down to water. One of the herders came dashing into camp with an arrow sticking into him. My horse was close at hand, and, mounting him bare-back, I at once dashed off after the mule herd, which had been stampeded. I supposed certainly that I would be the first man on the ground, but I was mistaken, however, for the Pawnee Indians, unlike regular soldiers, had not waited to receive orders from their officers, but had jumped on their ponies without bridles or saddles, and placing ropes in their mouths, had dashed off in the direction whence the shots had come, and had got there ahead of me. It proved to be a party of about fifty Sioux, who had endeavored to stampede our mules, and it took them by surprise to see their inveterate enemies—the Pawnees—coming at full gallop towards them. They were not aware that the Pawnees were with the command, and as they knew that it would take regular soldiers some time to turn out, they thought they would have ample opportunity to secure the herd before the troops could give chase.

We had a running fight of fifteen miles and several of the enemy were killed. During this chase I was mounted on an excellent horse, which Colonel Royal had picked out for me, and for the first mile or two I was in advance of the Pawnees. Presently a Pawnee shot by me like an arrow and I could not help admiring the horse that he was riding. Seeing that he possessed rare running qualities, I determined if possible to get possession of the animal in some way. It was a large buckskin or yellow horse, and I took a careful view of him so that I would know him when I returned to camp.

After the chase was over I rode up to Major North and inquired about the buckskin horse.

"Oh, yes," said the Major, "that is one of our favorite steeds."

"What chance is there to trade for him?' I asked.

"It is a government horse," said he, "and the Indian who is riding him is very much attached to the animal."

PAWNEE BUFFALO HUNTERS

"I have fallen in love with the horse myself," said I, "and I would like to know if you have any objections to my trading for him if I can arrange it satisfactorily with the Indian?"

He replied: "None whatever, and I will help you to do it; you can give the Indian another horse in his place."

A few days after this, I persuaded the Indian, by making him several presents, to trade horses with me, and in this way I became the owner of the buckskin steed, not as my own property, however, but as a government horse that I could ride. I gave him the name of "Buckskin Joe" and he proved to be a second Brigham. That horse I rode on and off during the summers of 1869, 1870, 1871 and 1872, and he was the horse that the Grand Duke Alexis rode on his buffalo hunt. In the winter of 1872, after I had left Fort McPherson, Buckskin Joe was condemned and sold at public sale, and was bought by Dave Perry, at North Platte, who in 1877 presented him to me, and I owned him until his death in 1879.

The command scouted several days up the Beaver and Prairie Dog Rivers, occasionally having running fights with way parties of Indians, but did not succeed in getting them into a general battle. At the end of twenty days we found ourselves back on the Republican.

The Indians Think Better of Me

Hitherto the Pawnees had not taken much interest in me, but while at this camp I gained their respect and admiration by showing them how I killed buffaloes. Although the Pawnees were excellent buffalo killers, for Indians, I have never seen one of them who could kill more than four or five in one run. A number of them generally surround the herd and then dash in upon them, and in this way each one kills from one to four buffaloes. I had gone out in company with Major North and some of the officers, and saw them make a "surround." Twenty of the Pawnees circled a herd and succeeded in killing only thirty-two.

While they were cutting up the animals another herd appeared in sight. The Indians were preparing to surround it, when I asked Major North to keep them back and let me show them what I could do. He accordingly informed the Indians of my wish and they readily consented to let me have the opportunity. I had learned that Buckskin Joe was an excellent buffalo horse, and felt confident that I would astonish the natives; galloping in among the buffaloes, I certainly did so by killing thirty-six in less than a half-mile run. At nearly every shot I killed a buffalo, stringing the dead animals out on the prairie, not over fifty feet apart. This manner of killing was greatly admired by the Indians who called me a big chief, and from that time on I stood high in their estimation.

CHAPTER XV

A Desperate Fight

On leaving camp, the command took a westward coarse up the Republican, and Major North with two companies of his Pawnees and two or three companies of cavalry, under the command of Colonel Royal, made a scout to the north of the river. Shortly after we had gone into camp, on the Black Tail Deer Fork, we observed a band of Indians coming over the prairie at full gallop, singing and yelling and waving their lances and long poles. At first we supposed them to be Sioux, and all was excitement for a few moments. We noticed, however, that our Pawnee Indians made no hostile demonstrations or preparations toward going out to fight them, but began swinging and yelling themselves. Captain Lute North stepped up to General Carr and said: "General, those are our men who are coming, and they have had a fight. That is the way they act when they come back from a battle and have taken any scalps."

The Pawnees came into camp on the run. Captain North calling to one of them—a sergeant—soon found out that they had run across a party of Sioux who were following a large Indian trail. These Indians had evidently been in a fight, for two or three of them had been wounded and they were conveying the injured persons on *travoix*. The Pawnees had "jumped" them and had killed three or four after a sharp fight, in which much ammunition was expended.

Next morning the command, at an early hour, started out to take up this Indian trail which they followed for two days as rapidly as possible; it becoming evident from the many campfires which we passed that we were gaining on the Indians. Wherever they had encamped we found the print of a woman's shoe, and we concluded that they had with them some white captive. This made us all the more anxious to overtake them, and General Carr accordingly selected all his best horses, which could stand a hard run, and gave orders for the wagon train to follow as fast as possible, while he pushed ahead on a forced march. At the same time

GENERAL E. A. CARR

I was ordered to pick out five or six of the best Pawnees, and go on in advance of the command, keeping ten or twelve miles ahead on the trail, so that when we overtook the Indians we could find out the location of their camp, and send word to the troops before they came in sight, thus affording ample time to arrange a plan for the capture of the village.

After having gone about ten miles in advance of the regiment, we began to move very cautiously, as we were now evidently nearing the Indians. We looked carefully over the summits of the hills before exposing ourselves to plain view, and at last we discovered the village, encamped in the sand-hills south of the South Platte River at Summit Springs. Here I left the Pawnee scouts to keep watch, while I went back and informed General Carr that the Indians were in sight.

The General at once ordered his men to tighten their saddles and otherwise prepare for action. Soon all was excitement among the officers and soldiers, every one being anxious to charge the village. I now changed my horse for old Buckskin Joe, who had been led for me thus far, and was comparatively fresh. Acting on my suggestion, the General made a circuit to the north, believing that if the Indians had their scouts out, they would naturally be watching in the direction whence they had come. When we had passed the Indians and were between them and the Platte River, we turned toward the left and started toward the village.

By this maneuver we had avoided discovery by the Sioux scouts, and we were confident of giving them a complete surprise. Keeping the command wholly out of sight, until we were within a mile of the Indians, the General halted the advance guard until all closed up, and then issued an order that, when he sounded the charge, the whole command was to rush into the village.

A Charge Through the Indian Village

As we halted on the top of the hill overlooking the camp of the unsuspecting Indians, General Carr called out to his bugler: "Sound the charge!" The bugler for a moment became intensely excited, and actually forgot the notes. The General again sang out: "Sound the charge!" and yet the bugler was unable to obey the command. Quartermaster Hays—who had obtained permission to accompany the expedition— was riding near the General, and comprehending the dilemma of the man, rushed up to him, jerked the bugle from his hands and sounded the charge himself in clear and distinct notes. As the troops rushed forward, he threw the bugle away, then drawing his pistols, was among the first men that entered the village.

The Indians had just driven up their horses and were preparing to make a move of the camp, when they saw the soldiers coming down upon them. A great many of

A MAGNIFICENT CHARGE

them succeeded in jumping upon their ponies, and leaving everything behind them, advanced out of the village and prepared to meet the charge; but upon second thought they quickly concluded that it was useless to try to check us, and those who were mounted rapidly rode away, while the others on foot fled for safety to the neighboring hills. We went through their village, shooting right and left at everything we saw. The Pawnees, the regular soldiers and officers were all mixed up together, and the Sioux were flying in every direction.

The pursuit continued until darkness made it impossible to longer follow the Indians, who had scattered and were leading off in every direction like a brood of young quails. The expedition went into camp along the South Platte, much exhausted by so long a chase, and though very tired, every trooper seemed anxious for the morrow.

It was nearly sunrise when "boots and saddles" was sounded, breakfast having been disposed of at break of day. The command started in a most seasonable time, but finding that the trail was all broken up, it was deemed advisable to separate into companies, each to follow a different trail.

The company which I headed struck out toward the Northwest over a route indicating the march of about one hundred Indians, and followed this for nearly two days. At a short bend of the Platte a new trail was discovered leading into the one the company was following, and at this point it was evident that a junction had been made. Further along evidences of a reunion of the entire village increased, and now it began to appear that further pursuit would be somewhat hazardous, owing to the largely increased force of Indians. But there were plenty of brave men in the company and nearly all were anxious to meet the Indians, however great their numbers might be. This anxiety was appeased on the third day, when a party of about six hundred Sioux was discovered riding in close ranks near the Platte. The discovery was mutual and there was immediate preparation for battle on both sides. Owing to the overwhelming force of the Indians, extreme caution became necessary, and instead of advancing boldly the soldiers sought advantageous ground. Seeing this, the Indians became convinced that there had been a division in Gen. Carr's command and that the company before them was a fragmentary part of the expedition; they therefore assumed the aggressive, charging us until we were compelled to retire to a ravine and act on the defensive. The attack was made with such caution that the soldiers fell back without undue haste, and had ample opportunity to secure their horses in the natural pit, which was a ravine that during wet seasons formed a branch of the Platte.

Corralled by Hostiles

After circling about the soldiers with the view of measuring their full strength, the Indians, comprehending how small was the number, made a desperate charge from two sides, getting so near us that several of the soldiers were badly wounded by arrows. But the Indians were received with such withering fire that they fell back in confusion, leaving twenty of their warriors on the ground. Another charge resulted like the first, with heavy loss to the red-skins, which so discouraged them that they drew off and held a long council. After discussing the situation among themselves for more than an hour they separated, one body making off as though they intended to leave, but I understood their motions too well to allow the soldiers to be deceived.

The Indians that remained again began to ride in a circle around us, but maintained a safe distance, out of rifle range. Seeing an especially well mounted Indian riding at the head of a squad, passing around in the same circle more than a dozen times, I decided to take my chances for dismounting the chief (as he proved to be) and to accomplish this purpose I crawled on my hands and knees three hundred yards up the ravine, stopping at a point which I considered would be in range of the Indian when he should again make the circuit. My judgment proved correct, for soon the Indian was seen loping his pony through the grass, and as he slackened speed to cross the ravine, I rose up and fired, the aim being so well taken that the chief tumbled

THE KILLING OF CHIEF TALL BULL

to the ground while his horse, after running a few hundred yards, approached the soldiers, one of whom ran out and caught hold of the long lariat attached to the bridle, and thus secured the animal. When I returned to the company, all of whom had witnessed my feat of killing an Indian at a range of fully four hundred yards, by general consent the horse of my victim was given to me.

This Indian whom I killed proved to be Tall Bull, one of the most cunning and able chiefs the Sioux ever had, and his death so affected the Indians that they at once retreated without further attempt to dislodge us.

Some days after this occurrence Gen. Carr's command was brought together again, and had an engagement with the Sioux, in which more than three hundred warriors and a large number of ponies were captured, together with several hundred squaws, among the latter being Tall Bull's widow, who told with pathetic interest how the Prairie Chief* had killed her husband. But instead of being moved with hatred against me, as most civilized women would have been under like circumstances, she regarded me with special favor, and esteemed it quite an honor that her husband, a great warrior himself, should have met his death at my hands.

My Meeting with Ned Buntline

The expedition having succeeded in thoroughly dispersing and punishing the Sioux, Gen. Carr went into barracks at Fort Sedgwick, but we had not remained long in quarters before reports of fresh outbreaks reached us and we had therefore to remain in constant expectation of orders for moving.

One day, while we were lying at Fort Sedgwick, General Carr received a telegram from Fort McPherson stating that the Indians had made a dash on the Union Pacific railroad, derailing a freight train, from which they captured several bolts of calico and other dry goods, and had killed several section-men, besides running off some stock near O'Fallon's Station; also that an expedition was going out from Fort McPherson to catch and punish the red-skins if possible. The General ordered me to accompany the expedition, and accordingly that night I proceeded by rail to McPherson Station, and from thence rode on horseback to the fort. Two companies, under command of Major Brown, had been ordered out, and next morning, just as we were about to start, Major Brown said to me:

"By the way, Cody, we are going to have quite an important character with us as a guest on this scout. It's old Ned Buntline, the novelist."

Just then I noticed a gentleman, who was rather stoutly built, and who wore a blue military coat, on the left breast of which were pinned about twenty gold medals and badges of secret societies. He walked a little lame as he approached us, and I at once concluded that he was Ned Buntline.

"He has a good mark to shoot at on the left breast," said I to Major Brown, "but he looks like a soldier." As he came up. Major Brown said:

"Cody, allow me to introduce you to Colonel E. B. C. Judson, otherwise known as Ned Buntline."

"Colonel Judson, I am glad to meet you," said I; "the Major tells me that you are to accompany us on the scout."

"Yes, my boy, so I am," said he; "I was to deliver a temperance lecture to-night, but no lectures for me when there is a prospect for a fight. The Major has kindly offered me a horse, but I don't know how I'll stand the ride, for I haven't done any

---

* For many years I was known among all Northern Indians as the Prairie Chief.

RIOTING WITH SPOILS TAKEN FROM A FREIGHT TRAIN

riding lately; but when I was a young man I spent several years among the fur companies of the Northwest, and was a good rider and an excellent shot."

"The Major has given you a fine horse, and you'll soon find yourself at home in
the saddle," said I.

The command soon pulled out for the South Platte River, which was very wide
and high, owing to recent mountain rains, and in crossing it we had to swim our
horses in some places. Buntline was the first man across. We reached O'Fallon's at
eleven o'clock, and in a short time I succeeded in finding the Indian trail; the party
seemed to be a small one, which had come up from the south. We followed their track
to the North Platte, but as they had a start of two days. Major Brown abandoned
the pursuit, and returned to Fort McPherson, while I went back to Fort Sedgwick,
accompanied by Buntline.

During this short scout, Buntline had asked me a great many questions, and he
was determined to go out on the next expedition with me, providing he could obtain
permission from the commanding officer. I introduced him to the officers—excepting
those he already knew—and invited him to become my guest while he remained at the
post, and gave him my pony Powder Face to ride.

THE LAST OF THE BUFFALOES—GATHERING THE BONES

Horse Racing in the Hostile Country

By this time I had learned that my horse Tall Bull was a remarkably fast runner, and therefore when Lieutenant Mason, who was quite a sport and owned a racer, challenged me to a race, I immediately accepted it. We were to run our horses a single dash of half a mile for one hundred dollars a side. Several of the officers, and also Reub. Wood, the post-trader, bantered me for side bets, and I took them all until I had put up my last cent on Tall Bull.

The ground was measured off, the judges were selected, and all other preliminaries were arranged. We rode our horses ourselves, and coming up to the score nicely we let them go. I saw from the start that it would be mere play to beat the Lieutenant's horse, and therefore I held Tall Bull in check, so that none could see how fast he really could run. I easily won the race, and pocketed a snug little sum of money. Of course everybody was now talking horse. Major North remarked that if Tall Bull could beat the Pawnees' fast horse, I could break his whole command.

The next day the troops were paid off, the Pawnees with the rest, and for two or three days they did nothing but run horse-races, as all the recently captured horses had to be tested to find out the swiftest among them. Finally the Pawnees wanted to run their favorite horse against Tall Bull, and I accordingly arranged a race with them. They raised three hundred dollars and bet it on their horse, while of course I backed Tall Bull with an equal amount, and in addition took numerous side bets. The race was a single dash of a mile, and Tall Bull won it without any difficulty. I was ahead on this race about seven hundred dollars, and the horse was fast getting a reputation. Heretofore nobody would bet on him, but now he had plenty of backers.

The Trick of Powder Face

I also made a run for my pony Powder Face against a fast pony belonging to Captain Lute North. I selected a small boy living at the post to ride Powder Face, while an Indian boy was to ride the other pony. The Pawnees as usual wanted to bet on their pony, but as I had not fully ascertained the running qualities of Powder Face, I did not care about risking very much money on him. Had I known him as well then as I did afterwards I would have backed him for every dollar I had, for he proved to be one of the swiftest ponies I ever saw, and had evidently been kept as a racer.

The race was to be four hundred yards, and when I led the pony over the track he seemed to understand what he was there for. North and I finally put the riders on, and it was all I could do to hold the fiery little animal after the boy became seated on his back. He jumped around and made such quick movements, that the boy was not at all confident of being able to stay on him. The order to start was at last given by the judges, and as I brought Powder Face up to the score and the word "go" was given, he jumped away so quickly that he left his rider sitting on the ground; notwithstanding, he ran through and won the race without him. It was an easy victory, and after that I could get up no more races. Thus passed the time while we were at Fort Sedgwick.

General Carr having obtained a leave of absence Colonel Royal was given the command of an expedition that was ordered to go out after the Indians, and in a few days—after having rested a couple of weeks—we set out for the Republican, having learned that there were plenty of Indians in that section of the country. At Frenchman's Fork we discovered an Indian village, but did not surprise it, for its people had noticed us approaching, and were retreating when we reached their camping place. We chased them down the stream, and they finally turned to the left, went north and crossed the South Platte River five miles above Ogalalla. We pushed rapidly after them, following them across the North Platte and on through the sand-hills towards the Niobrara, but as they were making much better time than we, the pursuit was abandoned.

An Interesting Indian Tradition

While we were in the sand-hills, scouting the Niobrara country, the Pawnee Indians brought into camp, one night, some very large bones, one of which a surgeon of the expedition pronounced to be the thigh bone of a human being. The Indians claimed that the bones they had found were those of a person belonging to a race of people who a long time ago lived in this country: That there was once a race of men on the earth whose size was about three times that of an ordinary man, and they were so swift and powerful that they could run alongside of a buffalo, and taking the animal in one arm could tear off a leg and eat the meat as they walked. These giants denied the existence of a Great Spirit, and when they heard the thunder or saw the lightning they laughed at it and said they were greater than either. This so displeased the Great Spirit that he caused a great rain storm to come, and the water kept rising higher and higher so that it drove those proud and conceited giants from the low grounds to the hills, and thence to the mountains, but at last even the mountain tops were submerged, and then those mammoth men were all drowned. After the flood had subsided, the Great Spirit came to the conclusion that he had made man too large and powerful, and that he would therefore correct the mistake by creating a race of men of smaller size and less strength. This is the reason, say the Indians, that modern men are small and not like the giants of old, and they claim that this story is a matter of Indian history, which has been handed down among them from time immemorial.

As we had no wagons with us at the time this large and heavy bone was found, we were obliged to leave it.

CHAPTER XVI

Some Pleasing Novelties

Remaining at Fort Sedgwick during the winter, early in the following spring I returned to Fort McPherson under orders to report to Major-General Emory, of the Fifth Cavalry, who had been appointed commandant of the district of the Republican, with headquarters at that post.

As the command had been continually in the field, it was generally thought that we were to have a long rest; and it looked as if this post was to be my home and headquarters for some time to come. I accordingly sent to St. Louis for my wife and daughter to join me there. General Emory promised to build a house for me, but before the building was completed my family arrived.

During the fall of 1869 there were two or three scouting expeditions sent out; but nothing of very great importance was accomplished by them. I found Fort McPherson to be a lively and pleasant post to be stationed at, especially as there was plenty of game in the vicinity, and within a day's ride there were large herds of deer, antelope and elk.

ANTELOPE CHASING

During the winter of 1869-70 I spent a great deal of time in pursuit of game, and during the season we had two hunting parties of Englishmen there; one party being that of Mr. Flynn, and the other that of George Boyd Houghton, of London—the well-known caricaturist. Among the amusements which I arranged for the party's entertainment were several horse races, in which, however, Tall Bull and Powder Face were invariably the winners, much to my profit. Tall Bull by this time had such a reputation as a running horse, that it was difficult to make a race for him. I therefore had recourse to a novel proposition in order to run him against a horse in Captain Spaulding's company of the Second Cavalry.

This race was an interesting affair. I made a bet that Tall Bull would beat the Second Cavalry horse around a one mile track, and that during the time he was running, I would jump off and on the horse eight times. I rode the horse bareback, seized his mane with my left hand, rested my right on his withers, and while he was going at full speed, I jumped to the ground, and sprang again upon his back, eight times in succession. Such feats I had seen performed in the circus and I had practiced considerably at it with Tall Bull, so that I was certain of winning the race in the manner agreed upon.

In Pursuit of Indian Horse Thieves

Early one morning, in the spring of 1870, the Indians, who had approached during the night, stole some twenty-one head of horses from Mr. John Burke—a government contractor—Ben Gallagher and Jack Waite. They also ran off some horses from the post, among the number being my pony Powder Face. The commandant at once ordered out Lieutenant Thomas with Company I of the Fifth Cavalry, and directed me to accompany them as trailer. We discovered the trail after some little difficulty, as the Indians were continually trying to hide it, and followed it sixty miles, when darkness set in.

We were now within about four miles of Red Widow Creek and I felt confident the Indians would camp that night in that vicinity. Advising Lieutenant Thomas to halt his company and "lay low" I proceeded on to the creek, where moving around cautiously, I suddenly discovered horses feeding in a bend of the stream on the opposite side. I hurried back to the troops with the information, and Lieutenant Thomas moved his company to the bank of the creek, with the intention of remaining there until daylight, and then, if possible, surprise the Indians.

Just at break of day we mounted our horses, and after riding a short distance we ascended a slight elevation, when, not over one hundred yards distant, we looked down into the Indian camp. The Indians, preparing to make an early start, had driven up their horses and were in the act of mounting, when they saw us charging down upon them. In a moment they sprang upon their ponies and dashed away. Had it not been for the creek, which lay between us and them, we would have got them before they could have mounted their horses; but as it was rather miry, we were unexpectedly delayed. The Indians fired some shots at us while we were crossing, but as soon as we got over we went for them in hot pursuit. A few of the red-skins had not had time to mount and had started on foot down the creek towards the brush. One of these was killed.

Two Indians Bagged at a Single Shot

A number of our soldiers, who had been detailed before the charge to gather up any of the Indian horses that might be stampeded, succeeded in capturing thirty-two. I hurriedly looked over them to see if Powder Face was among them; but he was not there. Starting in pursuit of the fugitives I finally espied an Indian mounted on my favorite, dashing away and leading all the others. We continued the chase for two or three miles, overtaking a couple who were mounted on one horse. Coming up behind them I fired my rifle, when about thirty feet distant; the ball passed through the backs of both, and they fell headlong to the ground; but I made no stop however just then, for I had my eye on the gentleman who was riding Powder Face. It seemed to be fun for him to run away from us, and run away he did, for the last I saw of him was when he went over a divide, about three miles away. I bade him adieu. On my way back to the Indian camp I stopped and secured the war bonnets and accoutrements of the pair I had killed, and at the same time gently "raised their hair."

A GORY TROPHY OF VICTORY

We were feeling rather tired and hungry, as we had started out on the trail thirty-six hours before without a breakfast or taking any food with us; but not a murmur or complaint was heard among the men. In the abandoned Indian camp, however, we found enough dried buffalo meat to give us all a meal, and after remaining there for two hours, to rest our animals, we started on our return to Fort McPherson, where we arrived at night, having traveled 130 miles in two days.

This being the first fight Lieutenant Thomas had ever commanded in, he felt highly elated over his success, and hoped that his name would be mentioned in the special orders for gallantry; sure enough, when we returned both he, myself and the whole command received complimentary mention in a special order. This he certainly deserved for he was a brave, energetic, dashing little officer. The war bonnets which I had captured I turned over to General Carr, with the request that he present them to General Augur, whose daughters were visiting at the post at the time.

A Tough Officer

Shortly after this, another expedition was organized at Fort McPherson for the Republican River country. It was commanded by General Duncan, who was a jolly, blustering old fellow, and the officers who knew him well said that we would have a good time, as he was very fond of hunting. He was a good fighter, and one of the officers said that an Indian bullet never could hurt him, as he had been shot in the head with a cannon ball which had not injured him in the least; another said the ball glanced off and killed one of the toughest mules in the army.

The Pawnee scouts, who had been mustered out of service during the winter of 1869 and '70 we reorganized to accompany this expedition. I was glad of this, as I had become quite attached to one of the officers, Major North, and to many of the

Indians. The only white scout we had at the post, besides myself at that time, was John Y. Nelson, whose Indian name was Sha-Cha-Cha-Opoyeo,* which interpreted means Red-Willow-Fill-the-Pipe. This man is a character in his way; he has a Sioux squaw for a wife, and consequently a half-breed family.

We started out from the post with the regimental band playing the lively air of "The Girl I Left Behind Me." We made but a short march that day, and camped at night at the head of Fox Creek. Next morning General Duncan sent me word by his orderly that I was to bring up my gun and shoot at a mark with him; but I can assure the reader that I did not feel much like shooting anything except myself, for on the night before I had returned to Fort McPherson and spent several hours in interviewing the sutler's store in company with Major Brown. I looked around for my gun and found that I had left it behind. The last I could remember about it was that I had it at the sutler's store. I informed Major Brown of my loss, who said that I was a nice scout to start out without a gun. I replied that that was not the worst of it, as General Duncan had sent for me to shoot a match with him, and I did not know what to do; for if the old gentleman discovered my predicament, he would very likely severely reprimand me.

"Well, Cody," said he, "the best you can do is to make some excuse, and then go and borrow a gun from some of the men, and tell the General that you lent yours to some man to go hunting with to-day. While we are waiting here, I will send back to the post and get your rifle for you." I succeeded in obtaining a gun from John Nelson, and then marching up to the General's headquarters I shot the desired match with him, which resulted in his favor.

This was the first scout the Pawnees had been out on under command of General Duncan, and in stationing his guards around the camp he posted them in a manner entirely different from that of General Carr and Colonel Royal, as he insisted that the different posts should call out the hour of the night thus:

The Pawnee Indian on Guard Duty

"Post No. 1, nine o'clock, all is well! Post No. 2, nine o'clock, all is well!" etc.

The Pawnees, who had their regular turns at standing upon guard, were ordered to call the hour the same as the white soldiers. This was very difficult for them to do, as there were but few of them who could express themselves in English. Major North explained to them that when the man on post next to them should call out the hour, they must call it also as nearly like him as possible. It was very amusing to hear them do this. They would try to remember what the other man had said on the post next to

---

*Who is still shooting Indians from the top of the old Deadwood stage coach in the Wild West show.

them. For instance, a white soldier would call out: "Post No. 1, half-past nine o'clock, all is well!" The Indian standing next to him knew that he was bound to say something in English, and he would sing out something like the following:

"Poss number half pass five cents—go to ——! I don't care!"

This system was really so ridiculous and amusing that the General had to give it up, and the order was accordingly countermanded.

Nothing of any great interest occurred on this march, until one day, while proceeding up Prairie Dog Creek,* Major North and myself went out in advance of the command several miles and killed a number of buffaloes. Night was approaching, and I began to look around for a suitable camping ground for the command. Major North dismounted from his horse and was resting, while I rode down to the stream to see if there was plenty of grass in the vicinity. I found an excellent camping spot, and returning to Major North told him that I would ride over the hill a little way, so that the advance guard could see me. This I did, and when the advance came in sight I dismounted and laid down upon the grass to rest.

A Red Hot Situation

Suddenly I heard three or four shots, and in a few moments Major North came dashing up towards me, pursued by eight or ten Indians. I instantly sprang into my saddle, and fired a few shots at the Indians, who by this time had all come in sight, to the number of fifty. We turned our horses and ran, the bullets flying after us thick and fast—my whip being shot from my hand and daylight being put through the crown of my hat. We were in close quarters, when suddenly Lieutenant Valkmar came galloping up to our relief with several soldiers, and the Indians seeing them whirled and retreated. As soon as Major North got in sight of his Pawnees, he began riding in a circle. This was a sign to them that there were hostile Indians in front, and in a moment the Pawnees broke ranks pell-mell and, with Major North at their head, started for the flying warriors. The rest of the command pushed rapidly forward also, and chased the enemy for three or four miles, killing three of them.

But this was a wrong move on our part, as their village was on Prairie Dog Creek, while they led us in a different direction; one Indian only kept straight on up the creek—a messenger to the village. Some of the command who had followed him, stirred up the village and accelerated its departure. We finally got back to the main force, and then learned that we had made a great mistake. Now commenced another stern chase.

---

* Near the lonely camp where I had so long been laid up with a broken leg, when trapping years before with Dave Harrington.

FINDING THE REMAINS OF THE BUCK PARTY

The second day that we had been following these Indians we came upon an old squaw, whom they had left on the prairie to die. Her people had built for her a little shade or lodge, and had given her some provisions, sufficient to last her on her trip to the Happy Hunting grounds. This the Indians often do when pursued by an enemy, and one of their number becomes too old and feeble to travel any longer. This squaw was recognized by John Nelson who said she was a relative of his wife. From her we learned that the flying Indians were known as Pawnee-Killer's band, and that they had lately killed Buck's surveying party, consisting of eight or nine men; the massacre having occurred a few days before on Beaver Creek. We knew that they had had a fight with the surveyors, as we found quite a number of surveying instruments, which had been left in the abandoned camp. We drove these Indians across the Platte River and then returned to Fort McPherson, bringing the old squaw with us; from there she was sent to the Spotted Tail agency.

During my absence, my wife had given birth to a son, and he was several weeks old when I returned. No name had yet been given to him and I selected that of Elmo Judson, in honor of Ned Buntline; but this the officers and scouts objected to. Major Brown proposed that we should call him Kit Carson, and it was finally settled that that should be his name.

During the summer we made one or two more scouts and had a few skirmishes with the Indians: but nothing of any great importance transpired. In the fall of 1870, while I was a witness in a court-martial at Fort D. A. Russell I woke up one morning and found that I was dead broke—this is not an unusual occurrence to a frontiersman, or an author I may add, especially when he is endeavoring to kill time—and to raise necessary funds I sold my race-horse Tall Bull to Lieutenant Mason, who had long wanted him.

In the winter of 1870 and 1871 I first met George Watts Garland, an English gentleman, and a great hunter, whom I had the pleasure of guiding on several hunts and with whom I spent some weeks. During the winter I also took several parties out on the Loupe River country hunting and trapping. Although I was still chief of scouts I did not have much to do, as the Indiana were comparatively quiet, thus giving me plenty of time for sporting.

In the spring of 1871 several short scouting expeditions were sent out from Fort McPherson, but all with minor results.

Appointed Justice of the Peace

About this time General Emory was considerably annoyed by petty offenses committed in the vicinity of the post, and as there was no justice of the peace in the neighborhood, he was anxious to have such an officer there to attend to the civilians; one day he remarked to me that I would make an excellent justice.

"General, you compliment me rather too highly, for I don't know any more about law than a government mule does about book-keeping," said I.

"That doesn't make any difference," said he, "for I know that you will make a good 'Squire." He accordingly had the county commissioners appoint me to the office of justice of the peace, and I soon received my commission.

One morning a man came rushing up to my house and stated that he wanted to get out a writ of replevin, to recover possession of a horse which a stranger was taking out of the country. I had no blank forms, and had not yet received the statutes of Nebraska to copy from, so I asked the man:

"Where is the fellow who has got your horse?"

"He is going up the road, and is about two miles way," replied he.

"Very well," said I, "I will get the writ ready in a minute or two." I saddled up my horse, and then taking my old reliable gun, "Lucretia," I said to the man: "That's the best writ of replevin that I can think of; come along, and we'll get that horse, or know the reason why." We soon overtook the stranger, who was driving a herd of horses, and as we came up to him, I said: "Hello, sir; I am an officer, and have an attachment for that horse," and at the same time I pointed out the animal.

"Well, sir, what are you going to do about it?" he inquired.

"I propose to take you and the horse back to the post," said I.

"You can take the horse," said he, "but I haven't the time to return with you."

"You'll have to take the time, or pay the cost here and now," said I.

"How much are the costs?"

"Twenty dollars."

"Here's your money," said he, as he handed me the green-backs.

I then gave him a little friendly advice and told him that he was released from custody. He went on his way a wiser and a poorer man, while the owner of the horse and myself returned to the fort. I pocketed the twenty dollars, of course. Some people might think it was not a square way of doing business, but I didn't know any better just then. I had several little cases of this kind, and I became better posted on the law in the course of time, being assisted by Lieutenant Burr Reilly, of the Fifth Cavalry, who had been educated for a lawyer.

Performing a Marriage Ceremony

One evening I was called upon to perform a marriage ceremony. The bridegroom was one of the sergeants of the post. I had "braced up" for the occasion by imbibing rather freely of stimulants, and when I arrived at the house with a copy of the Statutes of Nebraska, which I had recently received, I felt somewhat confused. Whether my bewilderment was owing to the importance of the occasion and the large assembly, or to the effect of Louis Woodin's "tanglefoot," I cannot now distinctly remember—but my suspicions have always been that it was due to the latter cause. I looked carefully through the statutes to find the marriage ceremony, but my efforts were unsuccessful. Finally the time came for the knot to be tied. I told the couple to stand up and then I said to the bridegroom: "Do you take this woman to be your lawful wedded wife, to support and love her through life?"

"I do," was the reply.

Then addressing myself to the bride, I said: "Do you take this man to be your lawful wedded husband through life, to love, honor and obey him?"

"I do," was her response.

"Then join hands," said I to both of them; "I now pronounce you to be man and wife, and whomsoever God and Buffalo Bill have joined together let no man put asunder. May you live long and prosper. Amen."

This concluded the interesting ceremony, which was followed by the usual festivities on such occasions. I was highly complimented for the elegant and eloquent manner in which I had tied the matrimonial knot.

PERFORMING A MARRIAGE CEREMONY

During the summer of 1871, Professor Marsh, of Yale College, came out to McPherson with a large party of students to have a hunt and to look for fossils. Professor Marsh had heard of the big bone which had been found by the Pawnees in the Niobrara country, and he intended to look for that as well as other bones. He accordingly secured the services of Major F. North and the Pawnees as an escort. I was also to accompany the bone hunters, and would have done so had it not been for the fact that just at that time I was ordered out with a small scouting party to go after some Indians.

A Run for Our Lives

The day before the Professor arrived at the fort I had been out hunting on the north side of the North Platte River, near Pawnee Springs, with several companions, when we were suddenly attacked by Indians, who wounded one of our number, John Weister. We stood the Indians off for a little while, and Weister got even with them by killing one of their party. The Indians, however, outnumbered us, and at last we were forced to make a run for our lives. In this we succeeded and reached the fort in safety. The General wanted to have the Indians pursued and said he could not spare me to accompany Professor Marsh.

However, I had the opportunity to make the acquaintance of the eminent Professor, whom I found to be not only a well-posted person, but a very entertaining gentleman. He gave me a geological history of the country, told me in what section fossils were to be found, and otherwise entertained me with several scientific yarns, some of which seemed too complicated and too mysterious to be believed by an ordinary man like myself; but it was all clear to him. I rode out with him several miles, as he was starting on his bone-hunting expedition, and I greatly enjoyed the trip. His party had been provided with government transportation and his students were all mounted on government horses. As we rode along he delivered a scientific lecture and he convinced me that he knew what he was talking about. I finally bade him good-bye and returned to the post. While the fossil-hunters were out on their expedition we had several lively little skirmishes with the Indians. After having been absent some little time Professor Marsh and his party came back with their wagons loaded down with all kinds of bones and the Professor was in his glory. He had evidently struck a bone-yard, and "gad!"* wasn't he happy! But they had failed to find the big bone which the Pawnees had unearthed the year before.

CHAPTER XVII

Helping to Entertain a Distinguished Party

Post McPherson was in the center of a fine game country, in which buffalo were particularly plentiful, and though fairly surrounded by hostile Indians, it offered so many attractions for sportsmen that several hunting parties braved the dangers for the pleasure of buffalo-chasing. In September, 1871, General Sheridan brought a number of friends out to the post for a grand hunt, coming by way of North Platte in a special car, and thence by government wagons to the fort, which was only eighteen miles from that station.

The party consisted of General Sheridan, Lawrence E. Jerome, James Gordon Bennett, of the New York *Herald*; Leonard W. Jerome, Carroll Livingston, Major J. G. Hecksher, General Fitzhugh, General H. E. Davies, Captain M. Edward Rogers, Colonel J. Schuyler Crosby, Samuel Johnson, General Anson Stager, of the Western

---

*A favorite expression of the Professor's.

Union Telegraph Company; Charles Wilson, editor of the Chicago *Evening Journal*; General Rucker, Quartermaster-General, and Dr. Asch—the two last named being of General Sheridan's staff. They were met at the station by General Emory and Major Brown, with a cavalry company as escort and a sufficient number of vehicles to carry the distinguished visitors and their baggage.

A brisk drive of less than two hours over a hard and smooth road brought them to the fort, where they found the garrison, consisting of five companies of the Fifth Cavalry, under the command of General Carr, out on parade awaiting their arrival. The band played some martial music, and the cavalry passed very handsomely in review before General Sheridan. The guests were then most hospitably received, and assigned to comfortable quarters.

Lieutenant Hayes, the quartermaster of the expedition, arranged everything for the comfort of the party. One hundred cavalry under command of Major Brown were detailed as an escort. A train of sixteen wagons was provided to carry the baggage, supplies, and forage for the trip; and, besides these, there were three four-horse ambulances in which the guns were carried, and in which members of the party who became weary of the saddle might ride and rest. At General Sheridan's request I was to accompany the expedition; he introduced me to all his friends, and gave me a good send-off.

During the afternoon and evening the gentlemen were all entertained at the post in a variety of ways, including dinner and supper parties, and music and dancing; at a late hour they retired to rest in their tents at the camp which they occupied outside the post—named Camp Rucker, in honor of General Rucker.

Putting On a Little Style for the Occasion

At five o'clock next morning a cavalry bugle sounded the *reveille*, and soon all were astir in the camp, preparatory to pulling out for the first day's march. I rose fresh and eager for the trip, and as it was a nobby and high-toned outfit which I was to accompany, I determined to put on a little style myself. So I dressed in a new suit of light buckskin, trimmed along the seams with fringes of the same material; and I put on a crimson shirt handsomely ornamented on the bosom, while on my head I wore a broad *sombrero*. Then mounting a snowy white horse—a gallant stepper—I rode down from the fort to the camp, rifle in hand. I felt first-rate that morning, and looked well.

The expedition was soon under way. Our road for ten miles wound through a wooded ravine called Cottonwood Cañon, intersecting the high ground, or divide, as it is called, between the Platte and Republican Rivers. Upon emerging from the cañon we found ourselves upon the plains. First in the line rode General Sheridan, followed by his guests, and then the orderlies. Then came the ambulances, in one of which were carried five greyhounds, brought along to course the antelope and rabbit. With the ambulances marched a pair of Indian ponies belonging to Lieutenant Hayes—captured during some Indian fight—and harnessed to a light wagon, which General Sheridan occasionally used. These little horses, but thirteen hands high, showed more vigor and endurance than any other of the animals we had with us. Following the ambulances came the main body of the escort and the supply wagons.

We marched seventeen miles the first day, and went into camp on Fox Creek, a tributary of the Republican. No hunting had as yet been done; but I informed the gentlemen of the party that we would strike the buffalo country the next day. A hundred or more questions were then asked me by this one and that one, and the whole evening was spent principally in buffalo talk, sandwiched with stories of the plains—both of war and of the chase. Several of the party, who were good vocalists, gave us some excellent music. We closed the evening by christening the camp, naming it Camp Brown, in honor of the gallant officer in command of the escort.

At three o'clock next morning the bugle called us to an early start. We had breakfast at half-past four, and at six were in the saddle. All were eager to see and shoot the buffaloes, which I assured them we would certainly meet during the day. After marching five miles, the advance guard, of which I had the command, discovered six buffaloes grazing at a distance of about two miles from us. We returned to the hunters with this information, and they at once consulted with me as to the best way to attack the "enemy."

An Attack on the Buffalos

Acting upon my suggestions, Fitzhugh, Crosby, Lawrence Jerome, Livingston, Hecksher and Rogers, accompanied by myself as guide, rode through a convenient cañon to a point beyond the buffaloes, so that we were to the windward of the animals. The rest of the party made a detour of nearly five miles, keeping behind the crest of a hill. We charged down upon the buffaloes at full gallop, and just then the other party emerged from their concealment and witnessed the exciting chase. The buffaloes started off in a line, single file. Fitzhugh, after a lively gallop, led us all and soon came alongside the rear buffalo, at which he fired. The animal faltered, and then with another shot Fitzhugh brought him to the ground. Crosby dashed by him and leveled another of the herd, while Livingston dropped a third. Those who were not directly engaged in the hunt now came up and congratulated the men upon their success, and Fitzhugh was at once hailed as the winner of the buffalo-cup, while all sympathized with Hecksher, whose chance had been the best at the start, but who lost by reason of his horse falling and rolling over him.

The hunt being over, the column moved forward on its march, passing through a prairie-dog town, several miles in extent. These animals are found throughout the plains, living together in a sort of society; their numberless burrows in their "towns" adjoin each other, so that great care is necessary in riding through these places, as the ground is so undermined as often to fall in under the weight of a horse. Around the entrance to their holes the ground is piled up almost a foot high; on these little elevations the prairie-dogs sit upon their hind legs, chattering to each other and observing whatever passes on the plains. They will permit a person to approach quite near, but when they have viewed him closely, they dive into their dens with wonderful quickness. They are difficult to kill, and if hit generally succeed in crawling underground before they can be captured. Rattlesnakes and small owls are generally found in great numbers in the prairie-dog towns, and live in the same holes with the dogs on friendly terms. A few of the prairie dogs were killed, and were found to be very palatable eating.

A short distance beyond the dog town we discovered a settlement of five white men, who proved to be the Clifford brothers, Arthur Huff, Dick Seymour and John Nelson—the latter already referred to in these pages. Each of them had a squaw wife and numerous half-breed children, living in tents of buffalo skins. They owned a herd of horses and mules and a few cattle, and had cultivated a small piece of land. Their principal occupation was hunting, and they had a large number of buffalo hides, which they had tanned in the Indian manner.

Upon reaching Pleasant Valley, on Medicine Creek, our party divided into two detachments—one hunting along the bank of the stream for elk or deer, and the other remaining with the main body of the escort. The elk hunters met with no success whatever, but the others ran across plenty of buffaloes, and nearly everybody killed one or more before the day was over. Lawrence Jerome made an excellent shot; while riding in an ambulance he killed a buffalo which attempted to cross the line of march. About four o'clock P.M., we arrived at Mitchell's Fork of the Medicine, having traveled thirty-five miles during that day, and there we went into camp—calling it Camp Jack Hayes, in honor of Lieutenant Hayes.

On the next morning, the 25th, we moved out of camp at eight o'clock. The party was very successful through the day in securing game, Hecksher, Fitzhugh, Livingston and Lieutenant Hayes, and in fact all, doing good shooting.

Lawrence Jerome persuaded me to let him ride Buckskin Joe, the best buffalo horse in the whole outfit, and on his back he did wonders among the buffaloes. Leonard Jerome, Bennett and Rogers also were very successful in buffalo hunting. Our camp of this night was named Camp Asch to commemorate our surgeon, Dr. Asch. The evening was pleasantly spent around the camp-fires in relating the adventures of the day.

Leonard Jerome's Predicament

Upon crossing the Republican River on the morning of the 26th, we came upon an immense number of buffaloes scattered over the country in every direction, as far as the eye could reach, and all had an opportunity to do as much hunting as they wished. The wagons and troops moved slowly along in the direction of the next camp, while the hunters went off separately, or by twos and threes, in different directions, and all were rewarded with abundant success. Lawrence Jerome, however, had his career suddenly checked. He had dismounted to make a steady and careful shot, and thoughtlessly let go of the bridle. The buffalo failing to take a tumble, as he ought to have done, started off at a lively gait, followed by Buckskin Joe, the horse being determined to do some hunting on his own account; the last seen of him, he was a little ahead of the buffalo, and gaining slightly, leaving his late rider to his own reflections and the prospect of a tramp; his desolate condition was soon discovered and another horse, warranted not to run under any provocation, was sent to him. It may be stated here that three days afterwards, as I subsequently learned, Buckskin Joe, all saddled and bridled, turned up at Fort McPherson.

We pitched our tents for the night in a charming spot on the bank of Beaver Creek. The game was so abundant that we remained there one day. This stopping place was called Camp Cody, in honor of the reader's humble servant. The next day was spent in hunting jack-rabbits, coyotes, elks, antelopes and wild turkeys, and in the afternoon we sat down to the finest dinner ever spread on the plains.

Charged with a Heinous Offense

In the evening a court-martial was held, at which I presided as chief justice. We tried one of the gentlemen for aiding and abetting in the loss of a government horse, and for having something to do with the mysterious disappearance of a Colt's pistol. He was charged also with snoring in a manner that was regarded as fiendish, and with committing a variety of other less offenses too numerous to mention.

The accused made a feeble defense as to the pistol, and claimed that instead of losing a government horse, the fact was that the horse had lost him. His statements were all regarded as "too thin," and finally failing to prove good character, he confessed all, and threw himself upon the mercy of the court. The culprit was Lawrence Jerome.

As chief justice I delivered the opinion of the court, which my modesty does not prevent me from saying was done in an able and dignified manner; as an act of clemency I suspended judgment for the time being, remarking that while the camp-fire held out to burn, the vilest sinner might return; and in hope of the accused's amendment, I would defer pronouncing sentence. The trial afforded us considerable amusement, and gave me a splendid opportunity to display the legal knowledge which I had acquired while acting as justice of the peace at Fort McPherson.

On the morning of the 28th the command crossed the South Beaver, distant nine miles from Camp Cody, and then striking a fair road we made a rapid march until we reached our camp on Short Nose or Prairie Dog Creek, about 2 P.M., after having made twenty-four miles. The remainder of the afternoon was spent in hunting buffaloes and turkeys. Camp Stager was the name given to this place, in honor of General Stager, of the Western Union Telegraph Company.

Still Pursuing the Enemy

The next day we made a march of twenty-four miles, and then halted at about 1 P.M. on the North Solomon River. This day we killed three buffaloes, two antelopes, two raccoons, and three teal ducks. Near our camp, which we named Camp Leonard Jerome, was a beaver dam some six feet high and twenty yards wide; it was near the junction of two streams, and formed a pond of at least four acres.

On the 30th we traveled twenty-five miles, and during the march nine turkeys, two rabbits, and three or four buffaloes were killed. We went into camp on the bank of the south fork of the Solomon River, and called the place Camp Sam Johnson. We were now but forty-five miles from Fort Hays, the point at which General Sheridan and his guests expected to strike the Kansas Pacific Railway and thence return home. That evening I volunteered to ride to Fort Hays and meet the party next day bringing with me all the letters that might be at the post. Taking the best horse in the command I started out, expecting to make the trip in about four hours.

The next morning the command got an early start and traveled thirty miles to Saline River, where they made their last camp on the plains. As some of the party were attacking a herd of buffaloes, I rode in from Fort Hays and got into the middle of the herd, and killed a buffalo or two before the hunters observed me. I brought a large number of letters, which proved welcome reading matter.

Camp-Fire Chats

In the evening we gathered around the camp-fire for the last time. The duty of naming the camp, which was called Camp Davies, having been duly performed, we all united in making that night the pleasantest of all that we had spent together. We had eloquent speeches, songs, and interesting anecdotes. I was called upon, and entertained the gentlemen with some lively Indian stories.

The excursionists reached Fort Hays, distant fifteen miles, on the morning of October 2d, where we pitched our tents for the last time, and named the camp in honor of Mr. Hecksher. That same afternoon General Sheridan and his guests took the train for the East, after bidding Major Brown, Lieutenant Hayes and myself a hearty good-bye, and expressing themselves as greatly pleased with their hunt, and the manner in which they had been escorted and guided.

It will be proper and fair to state here that General Davies afterwards wrote an interesting account of this hunt and published it in a neat volume of sixty-eight pages, under the title of "Ten Days on the Plains." I would have inserted the volume bodily in this book, were it not for the fact that the General has spoken in a rather too complimentary manner of me. However, I have taken the liberty in this chapter to condense from the little volume, and in some places I have used the identical language of General Davies without quoting the same; in fact, to do the General justice, I ought to close this chapter with several lines of quotation marks to be pretty generally distributed by the reader throughout my account of our ten days' hunt.

Soon after the departure of General Sheridan's party, we returned to Fort McPherson and found General Carr about to start out on a twenty days' scout, not so much for the purpose of finding Indians, but more for the object of taking some friends on a hunt. His guests were a couple of Englishmen—whose names I cannot now remember—and Mr. McCarthy, of Syracuse, New York, who was a relative of General Emory. The command consisted of three companies of the Fifth Cavalry, one company of Pawnee Indians, and twenty-five wagons. Of course I was called on to accompany the expedition.

A Little Joke on McCarthy

One day, after we had been out from the post for some little time, I was hunting on Deer Creek, in company with Mr. McCarthy, about eight miles from the command. I had been wishing for several days to play a joke on him, and had arranged a plan with Captain Lute North to carry it into execution. I had informed North at about what time we would be on Deer Creek, and it was agreed that he should appear in the vicinity with some of his Pawnees, who were to throw their blankets around them, and come dashing down upon us, firing and whooping in true Indian style, while he was to either conceal or disguise himself. This program was faithfully and completely carried out. I had been talking about Indians to McCarthy, and he had become considerably excited, when just as we turned a bend of the creek, we saw not half a mile from us about twenty Indians, who instantly started for us on a gallop, firing their guns and yelling at the top of their voices.

AROUND THE CAMP-FIRE

"McCarthy, shall we dismount and fight, or run?" said I.

He didn't wait to reply, but wheeling his horse, started at full speed down the creek, losing his hat and dropping his gun; away he went, never once looking back to see if he was being pursued. I tried to stop him by yelling at him and saying that it was all right, as the Indians were Pawnees. Unfortunately he did not hear me, but kept straight on, not stopping his horse until he reached the camp.

I knew that he would tell General Carr that the Indians had jumped him, and that the General would soon start out with the troops. So as quick as the Pawnees rode up to me I told them to remain there while I went after my friend. I rode after him as fast as possible, but he had arrived at the command some time before me and when I got there the General had, as I had suspected he would do, ordered out two companies of cavalry to go in pursuit of the Indians. I told the General that the Indians were only some Pawnees, who had been out hunting and that they had merely played a joke upon us. I forgot to inform him that I had put up the trick, but as he was always fond

NO TIME FOR LOOKING BACK

of a good joke himself, he did not get very angry. I had picked up McCarthy's hat and gun which I returned to him, and it was some time afterwards before he discovered who was at the bottom of the affair.

Remains of the Murdered Buck Party

When we returned to Fort McPherson we found there Mr. Royal Buck, whose father had been killed with his entire party by Pawnee Killer's band of Indians on the Beaver Creek. He had a letter from the commanding officer of the department requesting that he be furnished with an escort to go in search of the remains of his father and the party. Two companies of cavalry were sent with him and I accompanied them as a guide. As the old squaw, which we had captured, and of which mention is made in a previous chapter, could not exactly tell us the place on Beaver Creek where the party had been killed, we searched the country over for two days and discovered no signs of the murdered men. At last, however, our efforts were rewarded with success. We found pieces of their wagons and among other things an old letter or two which Mr. Buck recognized as his father's handwriting. We then discovered some of the remains, which we buried; but nothing further. It was now getting late in the fall and we accordingly returned to Fort McPherson.

A short time after this the Fifth Cavalry was ordered to Arizona, a not very desirable country to soldier in. I had become greatly attached to the officers of the regiment, having been continually with them for over three years, and had about made up my mind to accompany them, when a letter was received from General Sheridan instructing the commanding officer "not to take Cody" with him, and saying that I was to remain in my old position. In a few days the command left for its destination, taking the cars at McPherson Station, where I bade my old friends adieu. During the next few weeks I had but little to do, as the post was garrisoned by infantry, awaiting the arrival of the Third Cavalry.

Hunting with a Grand Duke

About the first of January, 1872, General Forsyth and Dr. Asch, of Sheridan's staff came out to Fort McPherson to make preparations for a big buffalo hunt for the Grand Duke Alexis, of Russia; and as this was to be no ordinary affair, these officers had been sent by General Sheridan to have all the necessary arrangements perfected by the time the Grand Duke should arrive. They learned from me that there were plenty of buffaloes in the vicinity, and especially on the Red Willow, sixty miles distant. They said they would like to go over on the Red Willow and pick out a suitable place for the camp; they also inquired the location of the camp of Spotted Tail, chief of the Sioux Indians. Spotted Tail had permission from the Government to hunt the buffalo with his people during the winter, in the Republican River country. It was my opinion that they were located somewhere on the Frenchman's Fork, about one hundred and fifty miles from Fort McPherson.

General Sheridan's commissioner informed me that he wished me to visit Spotted Tail's camp, and induce about one hundred of the leading warriors and chiefs to come to the point where it should be decided to locate the Alexis hunting camp, and to be there by the time the Grand Duke should arrive, so that he could see a body of American Indians and observe the manner in which they killed buffaloes. The Indians would also be called upon to give a grand war dance in honor of the distinguished visitor.

Next morning General Forsyth and Dr. Asch, accompanied by Captain Hays, who had been left at Fort McPherson in charge of the Fifth Cavalry horses, taking an ambulance and a light wagon, to carry their tents and provisions sufficient to last them two or three days, started, under my guidance, with a small escort, for Red Willow Creek, arriving there at night. The next day we selected a pleasant camping place on a little knoll in the valley of the Red Willow. General Forsyth and his party returned to the post the next day while I left for Spotted Tail's camp.

The weather was very cold and I found my journey by no means a pleasant one as I was obliged to camp out with only my saddle-blankets; and besides, there was more or less danger from the Indians themselves; for, although Spotted Tail himself was friendly, I was afraid I might have difficulty in getting into his camp. I was liable at any moment to run into a party of his young men who might be out hunting, and as I had many enemies among the Sioux, I would be running considerable risk in meeting them.

A Visit to Spotted Tail

At the end of the first day I camped on Stinking Water, a tributary of the Frenchman's Fork, where I built a little fire in the timber; but it was so very cold I was not able to sleep much. Getting an early start in the morning I followed up the Frenchman's Fork and late in the afternoon I could see, from the fresh horse tracks and from the dead buffaloes lying here and there, recently killed, that I was nearing Spotted Tail's camp. I rode on for a few miles further, and then hiding my horse in a low ravine, I crawled up a high hill, where I obtained a good view of the country. I could see for four or five miles up the creek, and got sight of a village and of two or three hundred ponies in its vicinity. I waited until night came and then I succeeded in riding into the Indian camp unobserved.

I had seen Spotted Tail's camp when he came from the North and I knew the kind of lodge he was living in. As I entered the village I wrapped a blanket around

CHIEF SPOTTED TAIL

my head so that the Indians could not tell whether I was a white or a red man. In this way I rode around until I found Spotted Tail's lodge. Dismounting from my horse I opened his tent door and looking in, saw the old chief lying on some robes. I spoke to him and he recognized me at once and invited me to enter. Inside the lodge I found a white man, an old frontiersman, Todd Randall, who was Spotted Tail's agent and who had lived a great many years with the Indians. He understood their language perfectly and did all the interpreting for Spotted Tail. Through him I readily communicated with the chief and informed him of my errand. I told him that the warriors and chiefs would greatly please General Sheridan if they would meet him about ten sleeps at the old Government crossing of the Red Willow. I further informed him that there was a great chief from across the water who was coming there to visit him.

Spotted Tail replied that he would be very glad to go; that the next morning he would call his people together and select those who would accompany him. I told Spotted Tail how I had entered his camp. He replied that I had acted wisely; that although his people were friendly, yet some of his young men had a grudge against me, and I might have had difficulty with them had I met them away from the village. He directed his squaw to get me something to eat, and ordered that my horse be taken care of and upon his invitation I spent the remainder of the night in his lodge.

They Wanted to Lift My Hair

Next morning the chiefs and warriors assembled according to orders, and to them was stated the object of my visit. They were asked: "Do you know who this man is?"

"Yes, we know him well," replied one, "that is Pa-he-haska," (that being my name among the Sioux, which translated means "Long-Hair") "that is our old enemy"; a great many of the Indians, who were with Spotted Tail at this time, had been driven out of the Republican country.

"That is he," said Spotted Tail. "I want all my people to be kind to him and treat him as my friend."

I noticed that several of them were looking daggers at me. They appeared as if they wished to raise my hair then and there. Spotted Tail motioned and I followed him into his lodge, and thereupon the Indians dispersed. Having the assurance of Spotted Tail that none of the young men would follow me I started back for the Red Willow, arriving the second night.

There I found Captain Egan with a company of the second Cavalry and a wagon train loaded with tents, grain, provisions, etc. The men were leveling off the ground and were making preparations to put up large wall tents for the Grand Duke Alexis and his *suite* and for General Sheridan, his staff and other officers, and invited guests of the party. Proceeding to Fort McPherson I reported what had been done. Thereupon Quartermaster Hays selected from the five or six hundred horses in his charge seventy-five of the very best, which were sent to the Red Willow, to be used by Alexis and his party at the coming hunt. In a day or two a large supply of provisions, liquors, etc., arrived from Chicago, together with bedding and furniture for the tents; all of which were sent over to Camp Alexis.

Arrival of the Grand Duke

At last, on the morning of the 12th of January, 1872, the Grand Duke and party arrived at North Platte by special train, in charge of a Mr. Francis Thompson.

THE GRAND DUKE, ALEXIS

Captain Hays and myself, with five or six ambulances, fifteen or twenty extra saddle horses and a company of cavalry under Captain Egan, were at the depot in time to receive them. Presently General Sheridan and a large, fine looking young man, whom we at once concluded to be the Grand Duke, came out of the cars and approached us. General Sheridan at once introduced me to the Grand Duke as Buffalo Bill, for he it was, and said that I was to take charge of him and show him how to kill buffalo.

In less than half an hour the whole party were dashing away towards the south, across the South Platte and towards the Medicine, upon reaching which point we halted for a change of horses and a lunch. Resuming our ride we reached Camp Alexis in the afternoon. General Sheridan was well pleased with the arrangements that had been made and was delighted to find that Spotted Tail and his Indians had arrived on time. They were objects of great curiosity to the Grand Duke, who spent considerable time in looking at them, and watching their exhibitions of horsemanship, sham fights, etc. That evening the Indians gave the grand war dance, which I had arranged for.

Giving Duke Alexis the Cue

General Custer, who was one of the hunting party, carried on a mild flirtation with one of Spotted Tail's daughters, who had accompanied her father thither, and it was noticed also that the Duke Alexis paid considerable attention to another handsome red-skin maiden. The night passed pleasantly, and all retired with great expectations of having a most enjoyable and successful buffalo hunt. The Duke Alexis asked me a great many questions as to how we shot buffaloes, and what kind of a gun or pistol we used, and if he was going to have a good horse. I told him that he was going to have my celebrated buffalo horse Buckskin Joe, and when we went into a buffalo herd all he would have to do was to sit on the horse's back and fire away.

At nine o'clock next morning we were all in our saddles and in a few minutes were galloping over the prairies in search of a buffalo herd. We had not gone far before we observed a herd some distance ahead of us crossing our way; after that we proceeded cautiously, so as to keep out of sight until we were ready to make a charge.

In a moment the Duke became very much excited and anxious to charge directly toward the buffaloes, but I restrained him for a time until getting around to windward and keeping behind the sand-hills the herd was gradually approached.

"Now," said I, "is your time; you must ride as fast as your horse will go, and don't shoot until you get a good opportunity."

Away we went, tearing down the hill and throwing up a sandstorm in the rear, leaving the Duke's retinue far behind. When within a hundred yards of the fleeing

THE GRAND DUKE KILLING HIS FIRST BUFFALO

buffaloes the Duke fired, but unfortunately missed, being unused to shooting from a running horse.

I now rode up close beside him and advised him not to fire until he could ride directly upon the flank of a buffalo, as the sport was most in the chase. We dashed off together and ran our horses on either flank of a large bull, against the side of which the Duke thrust his gun and fired a fatal shot. He was very much elated at his success, taking off his cap and waving it vehemently, at the same time shouting to those who were fully a mile in the rear. When his retinue came up there were congratulations and every one drank to his good health with overflowing glasses of champagne. The hide of the dead buffalo was carefully removed and dressed, and the royal traveler in his journeyings over the world has no doubt often rested himself upon this trophy of his skill (?) on the plains of America.

An encampment was now made, as the party was quite fatigued, and the evening passed with song and story. On the following day, by request of Spotted Tail, the Grand Duke hunted for a while beside "Two Lance," a celebrated chief, who claimed he could send an arrow entirely through the body of the largest buffalo. This feat seemed so incredulous that there was a general denial of his ability to perform it; nevertheless, the

TWO LANCE SHOOTING AN ARROW THROUGH A BUFFALO

Grand Duke and also several others who accompanied the chief, witnessed, with profound astonishment, an accomplishment of the feat, and the arrow that passed through the buffalo was given to the Duke as a memento of Two Lance's skill and power. On the same day of this performance the Grand Duke killed a buffalo at a distance of one hundred paces with a heavy navy revolver. The shot was a marvelous—scratch.

When the Grand Duke was satisfied with the sport, orders were given for the return to the railroad. The conveyance provided for the Grand Duke and General Sheridan was a heavy double-seated open carriage, or rather an Irish dog-cart, and it was drawn by six spirited cavalry horses which were not much used to the harness. The driver was Bill Reed, an old overland stage driver and wagon-master; on our way in, the Grand Duke frequently expressed his admiration of the skillful manner in which Reed handled the reins. General Sheridan informed the Duke that I also had been a stage driver in the Rocky Mountains, and thereupon His Royal Highness expressed a desire to see me drive. I was in advance at the time, and General Sheridan sang out to me:

"Cody, get in here and show the Duke how you can drive. Mr. Reed will exchange places with you and ride your horse."

"All right, General," said I, and in a few moments I had the reins and we were rattling away over the prairie. When we were approaching Medicine Creek, General Sheridan said: "Shake 'em up a little Bill, and give us some old-time stage-driving."

Giving the Duke a Shaking Up

I gave the horses a crack or two of the whip, and they started off at a very rapid gait. They had a light load to pull, and kept increasing their speed at every jump, and I found it difficult to hold them. They fairly flew over the ground, and at last we reached a steep hill, or divide, which led down into the valley of the Medicine. There was no brake on the wagon, and the horses were not much on the hold back. I saw that it would be impossible to stop them. All I could do was to keep them straight in the track and let them go it down the hill, for three miles, which distance, I believe, was made in about six minutes. Every once in a while the hind wheels would strike a rut and take a bound, and not touch the ground again for fifteen or twenty feet The Duke and the General were kept rather busy in holding their positions on the seats, and when they saw that I was keeping the horses straight in the road, they seemed to enjoy the dash which we were making. I was unable to stop the team until they ran into the camp where we were to obtain a fresh relay, and there I succeeded in checking them. The Grand Duke said he didn't want any more of that kind of driving, as he preferred to go a little slower.

On arriving at the railroad, the Duke invited me into his car, and made me some valuable presents, at the same time giving me a cordial invitation to visit him, if ever

SHAKING UP THE GRAND DUKE

I should come to his country. At the same time General Sheridan took occasion to remind me of an invitation to visit New York which I had received from some of the gentlemen who accompanied the General on the hunt from Fort McPherson to Hays City, in September of the previous year. Said he: "You will never have a better opportunity to accept that invitation than now. I have had a talk with General Ord concerning you, and he will give you leave of absence whenever you are ready to start. Write a letter to General Stager, of Chicago, that you are now prepared to accept the invitation, and he will send you a pass." Thanking the General for his kindness, I then bade him and the Grand Duke good-bye, and soon their train was out of sight.

CHAPTER XVIII

Scouting in a Swallow-Tail Outfit

General Ord, commanding the Department of the Platte at the time, and who had been out on the Alexis hunt, had some business to attend to at Fort McPherson, and I accepted his invitation to ride over to the post with him in an ambulance. On the way thither he asked me how I would like to have an officer's commission in the regular army. He said that General Sheridan and himself had had some conversation about the matter, and if I wanted a commission, one could easily be procured for me. I thanked General Ord for his kindness, and said that although an officer's commission in the regular army was a tempting prize, yet I preferred to remain in the position I was then holding. He concluded by stating that if at any time I should wish a commission, all that I would have to do to secure it would be to inform him of my desire.

Having determined to visit New York, I acted upon General Sheridan's suggestion and wrote to General Stager, from whom in a few days I received my railroad passes. Obtaining thirty days' leave of absence from the department, I struck out for the East. On arriving in Chicago, in February, 1872, I was met at the depot by Colonel M. V. Sheridan, who said that his brother, the General, had not yet returned, but had sent word that I was to be his and the Colonel's guest, at their house, while I remained in Chicago.

I spent two or three days very pleasantly in the great city of the West, meeting several gentlemen who had been out on the Sheridan hunt in September: General Stager, Colonel Wilson, editor of the *Journal*; Mr. Sam Johnson, General Rucker and others, by all of whom I was most cordially received and well entertained. I was introduced to quite a number of the best people of the city, and was invited to several "swell" dinners. I also accompanied General Sheridan—who meantime had returned to the city—to a ball at Riverside, an aristocratic suburb. On this occasion I became so embarrassed that it was more difficult for me to face the throng of beautiful ladies, than it would have been to confront a hundred hostile Indians. This was my first trip to the East, and I had not yet become accustomed to being stared at. And besides this, the hundreds of questions which I was called upon to answer further embarrassed and perplexed me.

According to the route laid out for me by General Stager, I was to stop at Niagara Falls, Buffalo and Rochester on my way to New York, and he provided me with all the necessary railroad passes. Just as I was about to leave Chicago I met Professor Henry A. Ward, of Rochester, for whom during the previous year or two I had collected a large number of specimens of wild animals. He was on his way to Rochester, and kindly volunteered to act as my guide until we reached that point. We spent one day in viewing the wonders of Niagara, and I stopped one day at Rochester and was shown the beauties of that handsome city by Professor Ward, and I had the honor of receiving an invitation to dine with the Mayor.

A Guest of the Union Club

On arriving at New York I was met at the depot by Mr. J. G. Hecksher, who had been appointed as "a committee of one" to escort me to the Union Club, where James

SCOUTING AMONG THE CIVILIANS

Gordon Bennett, Leonard W. Jerome and others were to give me an informal reception, and where I was to make my headquarters during my visit to the great metropolis. I had an elegant dinner at the club rooms, with the gentlemen who had been out on the September hunt, and other members of the club.

After dinner, in company with Mr. Hecksher—who acted as my guide—I started out on the trail of my friend, Ned Buntline, whom we found at the Brevoort Place Hotel. He was delighted to see me, and insisted on my becoming his guest. He would listen to no excuses, and on introducing me to Messrs. Overton & Blair, proprietors of the Brevoort, they also gave me a pressing invitation to make my home at their house.

I finally compromised the matter by agreeing to divide my time between the Union Club, the Brevoort House, and Ned Buntline's headquarters.

The next few days I spent in viewing the sights of New York, everything being new and startling, convincing me that as yet I had seen but a small portion of the world. I received numerous dinner invitations, as well as invitations to visit different places of amusement and interest; but as they came in so thick and fast, I soon became badly demoralized and confused. I found I had accepted invitations to dine at half a dozen or more houses on the same day and at the same hour. James Gordon Bennett had prepared a dinner for me, at which quite a large number of his friends were to be present, but owing to my confusion, arising from the many other invitations I had received, I forgot all about it and dined elsewhere. This was "a bad break," but I did not learn of my mistake until next day, when at the Union Club House several gentlemen, among them Lawrence Jerome, inquired "where in the world I had been," and why I had not put in an appearance at Bennett's dinner. They said that Bennett had taken great pains to give me a splendid reception, that the party had waited till nine o'clock for me and that my non-arrival caused considerable disappointment. I apologized as well as I could by saying that I had been out on a scout and had got lost and had forgotten all about the dinner, and expressed my regret for the disappointment I had created by my forgetfulness. August Belmont, the banker, being near, said: "Never mind, gentlemen, I'll give Cody a dinner at my house."

"Thank you, sir," said I; "I see you are determined that I shall not run short of rations while I am in the city. I'll be there, sure." Both Mr. Jerome and Mr. Hecksher told me that I must not disappoint Mr. Belmont, for his dinners were splendid affairs. I made a note of the date, and at the appointed time I was promptly at Mr. Belmont's mansion, where I spent a very enjoyable evening.

Mr. Bennett, who was among the guests, having forgiven my carelessness, invited me to accompany him to the Liederkranz masked ball, which was to take place in a few evenings and would be a grand spectacle. Together we attended the ball and during the evening I was well entertained. The dancers kept on their masks until midnight, and the merry and motley throng presented a brilliant scene, moving gracefully beneath the bright gas-light to inspiriting music. To me it was a novel and entertaining sight, and in many respects reminded me greatly of an Indian war-dance.

Acting upon the suggestion of Mr. Bennett, I had dressed myself in my buckskin suit, and I naturally attracted considerable attention; especially when I took part in the dancing and exhibited some of my backwoods steps, which, although not as graceful as some, were a great deal more emphatic. But when I undertook to do artistic dancing, I found I was decidedly out of place in that crowd, and I accordingly withdrew from the floor.

I occasionally passed an evening at Niblo's Garden, viewing the many beauties of "The Black Crook," which was then having its long run, under the management of Jarrett & Palmer, whose acquaintance I had made, and who extended to me the freedom of the theater.

My Alter Ego on the Stage

Ned Buntline and Fred Maeder had dramatized one of the stories which the former had written about me for the *New York Weekly*. The drama was called "Buffalo Bill, the King of Border Men." While I was in New York it was produced at the Bowery Theater; J. B. Studley, an excellent actor, appearing in the character of "Buffalo Bill," and Mrs. W. G. Jones, a fine actress, taking the part of my sister, a leading *rôle*. I was curious to see how I would look when represented by some one else, and of course I was present on the opening night, a private box having been reserved for me. The theater was packed, every seat being occupied as well as all standing-room. The drama was played smoothly and created a great deal of enthusiasm.

The audience, upon learning that the real "Buffalo Bill" was present, gave several cheers between the acts, and I was called on to come out on the stage and make a speech. Mr. Freleigh, the manager, insisted that I should comply with the request, and that I should be introduced to Mr. Studley. I finally consented, and the next moment. I found myself standing behind the footlights and in front of an audience for the first time in my life. I looked up, then down, then on each side, and everywhere I saw a sea of human faces, and thousands of eyes all staring at me. I confess that I felt very much embarrassed—never more so in my life—and I knew not what to say. I made a desperate effort, and a few words escaped me, but what they were I could not for the life of me tell, nor could any one else in the house. My utterances were inaudible even to the leader of the orchestra, Mr. Dean, who was sitting only a few feet in front of me. Bowing to the audience, I beat a hasty retreat into one of the cañons of the stage. I never felt more relieved in my life than when I got out of the view of that immense crowd.

My First Appearance on the Stage

That evening Mr. Freleigh offered to give me five hundred dollars a week to play the part of "Buffalo Bill" myself. I thought that he was certainly joking, especially as he had witnessed my awkward performance; but when he assured me that he was in earnest, I told him that it would be useless for me to attempt anything of the kind, for I never could talk to a crowd of people like that, even if it was to save my neck, and that he might as well try to make an actor out of a government mule. I thanked him for the generous offer, which I had to decline owing to a lack of confidence in myself; or as some people might express it, I didn't have the requisite cheek to undertake a thing of that sort. The play of "Buffalo Bill" had a very successful run of six or eight weeks, and was afterwards produced in all the principal cities of the country, everywhere being received with genuine enthusiasm.

I had been in New York about twenty days when General Sheridan arrived in the city. I met him soon after he got into town. In answer to a question how I was enjoying myself, I replied that I had struck the best camp I had ever seen, and if he didn't have any objections I would like to have my leave of absence extended about ten days. This he willingly did, and then informed me that my services would soon be required at Fort McPherson, as there was to be an expedition sent out from that point.

At Westchester, Pennsylvania, I had some relatives living whom I had never seen, and now being so near, I determined to make them a visit. Upon mentioning the matter to Buntline, he suggested that we should together take a trip to Philadelphia, and thence run out to Westchester. Accordingly the next day found us in the "City of Brotherly Love," and in a few hours we arrived at the home of my uncle, General Henry R. Guss, the proprietor of the Green Tree Hotel, who gave us a cordial reception.

Inviting us into the parlor, my uncle brought in the members of his family, among them an elderly lady, who was my grandmother, as he informed me. He told me that my Aunt Eliza, his first wife, was dead, and that he had married a second time; Lizzie Guss, my cousin, I thought was the most beautiful girl I had ever seen. They were all very anxious to have us remain several days, but as I had some business to attend to in New York, I was obliged to return that day. Assuring them, however, that I would visit them again soon, I bade them adieu, and with Buntline took the train for New York.

The time soon arrived for my departure for the West; so packing up my traps I started for home, and on the way thither I spent a day with my Westchester relatives, who did everything in their power to entertain me during my brief stay with them.

CHAPTER XIX

Again on the Indian Trail

Upon reaching Fort McPherson, I found that the Third Cavalry, commanded by General Reynolds, had arrived from Arizona, in which Territory they had been on duty for some time, and where they had acquired quite a reputation on account of their Indian fighting qualities. Shortly after my return, a small party of Indians made

INDIAN HIDING HIS TRAIL

a dash on McPherson Station, about five miles from the fort, killing two or three men and running off quite a large number of horses. Captain Meinhold and Lieutenant Lawson with their company were ordered out to pursue and punish the Indians if possible. I was the guide of the expedition and had an assistant, T. B. Omohundro, better known as "Texas Jack," and who was a scout at the post.

Finding the trail, I followed it for two days, although it was difficult trailing because the red-skins had taken every possible precaution to conceal their tracks. On the second day Captain Meinhold went into camp on the south fork of the Loupe, at a point where the trail was badly scattered. Six men were detailed to accompany me on a scout in search of the camp of the fugitives. We had gone but a short distance when we discovered Indians camped, not more than a mile away, with horses grazing near by. They were only a small party, and I determined to charge upon them with my six men, rather than return to the command, because I feared they would see us as we went back and then they would get away from us entirely. I asked the men if they were willing to attempt it, and they replied that they would follow me wherever I would lead them. That was the kind of spirit that pleased me, and we immediately moved forward on the enemy, getting as close to them as possible without being seen.

I finally gave the signal to charge, and we dashed into the little camp with a yell. Five Indians sprang out of a willow tepee, and greeted us with a volley, and we returned the fire. I was riding Buckskin Joe, who with a few jumps brought me up to the tepee, followed by my men. We nearly ran over the Indians who were endeavoring to reach their horses on the opposite side of the creek. Just as one was jumping the narrow stream a bullet from my old "Lucretia" overtook him. He never reached the other bank, but dropped dead in the water. Those of the Indians who were guarding the horses, seeing what was going on at the camp, came rushing to the rescue of their friends. I now counted thirteen braves, but as we had already disposed of two, we had only eleven to take care of. The odds were nearly two to one against us.

A Sharp Fight—Wounded

While the Indian re-enforcements were approaching the camp I jumped the creek with Buckskin Joe to meet them, expecting our party would follow me; but as they could not induce their horses to make the leap, I was the only one who got over. I ordered the sergeant to dismount his men, leaving one to hold the horses, and come over with the rest and help me drive the Indians off. Before they could do this, two mounted warriors closed in on me and were shooting at short range. I returned their fire and had the satisfaction of seeing one of them fall from his horse. At this moment I felt blood trickling down my forehead, and hastily running my hand through my hair I discovered that I had received a scalp wound. The Indian, who had shot me, was not more than ten yards away, and when he saw his partner tumble from his saddle he turned to run.

By this time the soldiers had crossed the creek to assist me, and were blazing away at the other Indians. Urging Buckskin Joe forward, I was soon alongside of the

RAISING MYSELF IN THE STIRRUPS I SHOT HIM THROUGH THE HEAD

chap who had wounded me, when raising myself in the stirrups I shot him through the head.

The reports of our guns had been heard by Captain Meinhold, who at once started with his company up the creek to our aid, and when the remaining Indians, whom we were still fighting, saw these re-enforcements coming, they whirled their horses and fled; as their steeds were quite fresh they made their escape. However, we killed six out of the thirteen Indians, and captured most of their stolen stock. Our loss was one man killed, and another—myself—slightly wounded. One of our horses was killed, and Buckskin Joe was wounded, but I didn't discover the fact until some time afterwards, as he had been shot in the breast and showed no signs of having received a scratch of any kind. Securing the scalps of the dead Indians and other trophies we returned to the fort.

I made several other scouts during the summer with different officers of the Third Cavalry, one being with Maj. Alick Moore, a good officer, with whom I was out for thirty days. Another long one was with Major Curtis, with whom I followed some Indians from the South Platte River to Fort Randall on the Missouri River, in Dakota, on which trip the command ran out of rations and for fifteen days subsisted entirely upon the game we killed.

Hunting with an Earl

In the fall of 1872 the Earl of Dunraven and Dr. Kingsley, with several friends, came to Fort McPherson with a letter from General Sheridan, asking me to accompany them on an elk hunt. I did so, and afterwards spent several weeks in hunting with the

Earl of Dunraven, who was a thorough sportsman and an excellent hunter. It was while I was out with the Earl that a Chicago party—friends of General Sheridan—arrived at Fort McPherson for the purpose of going out on a hunt also. They, too, had a letter from the General requesting me to go with them. The Earl had not yet finished his hunt, but as I had been out with him for several weeks, and he had by this time learned where to find plenty of elks and other game, I concluded to leave him and accompany the Chicago party. I informed him of my intention and gave him my reasons for going, at the same time telling him I would send him one of my scouts, Texas Jack, who was a good hunter, and would be glad to accompany him. The Earl seemed to be somewhat offended at this, and I don't think he has ever forgiven me for "going back on him." Let that be as it may, he found Texas Jack a splendid hunter and guide, and Jack was his guide on several hunts afterwards.

Among the gentlemen who composed the Chicago party were E. P. Green—son-in-law of Remington, the rifle manufacturer—Alexander Sample, Mr. Milligan, of the firm of Heath & Milligan, of Chicago, and several others, whose names I do not now remember. Mr. Milligan was a man full of life, and was continually "boiling over with fun." He was a regular velocipede, so to speak, and was here, there, and everywhere. He was exceedingly desirous of having an Indian fight on the trip, not that he was naturally a blood-thirsty man, but just for variety he wanted a little "Indian pie." He was in every respect the life of the party, during the entire time that we were out. One day while he was hunting with Sample and myself we came in sight of a band of thirty mounted Indians.

"Milligan, here's what you've been wanting for some time," said I, "for yonder is a war party of Indians and no mistake; and they'll come for us, you bet."

"I don't believe this is one of my fighting days," replied Milligan, "and it occurs to me that I have urgent business at the camp."

A Party Which Milligan Refused to Attend

Our camp was five or six miles distant on the Dismal River, and our escort consisted of a company of cavalry commanded by Captain Russell. The soldiers were in camp, and Milligan thought that Captain Russell ought to be at once notified of the appearance of these Indians. Knowing that we could reach the camp in safety, for we were well mounted, I continued to have considerable amusement at Milligan's expense, who finally said:

"Cody, what's making my hat raise up so. I can hardly keep it on my head."

Sample, who was as cool as a cucumber, said to Milligan: "There must be something wrong with your hair. It must be trying to get on end."

"It's all very fine for you fellows to stand here and talk," replied Milligan, "but I am not doing justice to my family by remaining. Sample, I think we are a couple of old fools to have come out here, and I never would have done so if it had not been for you."

By this time the Indians had discovered us and were holding a consultation, and Milligan turned his horse in the direction of the camp. I never believed that he was half as scared as he seemed to be, but that he was merely pretending so that we could enjoy our joke. However, we did not wait any longer, but rode into camp and notified Captain Russell, who immediately started with his company to pursue the band. While we were riding along with the company Milligan said to Sample: "Now, Alick, let them come on. We may yet go back to Chicago covered with glory."

We struck the trail going north, but as we had not come out on a scout for Indians, we concluded not to follow them; although Milligan was now very anxious to proceed and clean them out. The hunt came to an end in a day or two, and we escorted the visiting sportsmen to North Platte, where they took the train for Chicago. Before their departure they extended to me a very cordial invitation to come to their city on a visit, promising that I should be well taken care of.

Roping a Buffalo

Soon after this I had the pleasure of guiding a party of gentlemen from Omaha on a buffalo hunt. Among the number were Judge Dundy, Colonel Watson B. Smith, and U. S. District Attorney Neville. We left Fort McPherson in good trim. I was greatly amused at the "style" of Mr. Neville, who wore a stove-pipe hat and a swallow-tail coat, which made up a very comical rig for a buffalo hunter. As we galloped over the prairie, he jammed his hat down over his ears to keep it from being shaken off his head, and in order to stick to his horse, he clung to the pommel of his saddle. He was not much of a rider, and he went bouncing up and down, with his swallow-tails flopping in the air. The sight I shall never forget, for it was enough to make a "horse laugh," and I actually believe old Buckskin Joe did laugh.

However, we had a splendid hunt, and on the second day I lariated, or roped, a big buffalo bull and tied him to a tree—a feat which I had often performed, and which the gentlemen requested me to do on this occasion for their benefit, as they had heard of my skill with the lariat. I captured several other buffaloes in the same way. The gentlemen returned to Omaha well pleased with their hunt.

In the fall of the year 1872, a convention was held at Grand Island, when some of my friends made me their candidate to represent the Twenty-sixth District in the Legislature of Nebraska; but as I had always been a Democrat and the State was largely Republican, I had no idea of being elected. In fact I cared very little about it, and therefore made no effort whatever to secure an election. However, I was elected and that is the way in which I acquired my title of Honorable.

CHAPTER XX

An Actor

During the summer and fall of 1872, I received numerous letters from Ned Buntline, urging me to come East and go upon the stage to represent my own character. "There's money in it," he wrote, "and you will prove a big card, as your character is a novelty on the stage." At times I almost determined to make the venture; but the recollection of that night when I stood on the stage of the Bowery Theater and was unable to utter a word above a whisper, would cause me to stop and think and become irresolute. I feared that I would be a total failure, and wrote Buntline to that effect. But he insisted that I would soon get over all that embarrassment, and become accustomed to the stage, so that I would think no more of appearing before five thousand people than I would before half a dozen. He proposed to organize a good company, and wished me to meet him in Chicago, where the opening performance would be given.

I remained undecided as to what I ought to do. The officers at the fort, as well as my family and friends to whom I had mentioned the matter, laughed at the idea of my ever becoming an actor. That I, an old scout who had never seen more than twenty or thirty theatrical performances in my life, should think of going upon the stage, was ridiculous in the extreme—so they all said.

A few days after my election to the Legislature a happy event occurred in my family circle, in the birth of a daughter whom we named Ora; about the same time I received another letter from Buntline, in which he requested me to appear on the stage for a few months as an experiment; and he said that if I made a failure or did not like the business, I could easily return to my old life.

My two sisters who had been living with us had married—Nellie, to A. C. Jester, a cattle man, and May, to Ed. Bradford, a railroad engineer—and consequently left us; and my wife had been wishing for a long time to visit her parents in St. Louis. Taking these and other things into consideration I finally resolved to resign my seat in the Legislature and try my luck behind the footlights. I informed General Reynolds of my determination, telling him at the same time that at the end of the month, November, I would resign my position under him. The General regretted to hear this, and advised me not to take the step, for I was leaving a comfortable little home, where I was sure of making a good living for my family; while, on the other hand, I was embarking upon a sea of uncertainty. Having once made up my mind, however, nothing could change it.

Arranging the Preliminaries

While I was selling my horses and other effects, preparatory to leaving the fort, one of my brother scouts, Texas Jack, said he would like to accompany me. Now as Jack had also appeared as the hero in one of Ned Buntline's stories, I thought that he would make as good a "star" as myself, and it was accordingly arranged that Jack should go with me. On our way east we stopped in Omaha a day or two to visit General Augur and other officers, and also the gentlemen who were out on the Judge Dundy Hunt. Judge Dundy and his friends gave a dinner party in my honor at the leading restaurant and entertained me very handsomely during my stay in the city.

TEXAS JACK (J. B. OMOHUNDRO)

At Omaha I parted with my family, who went to St. Louis, while Jack and myself proceeded to Chicago. Ned Buntline and Mr. Milligan, having been apprised of our coming by a telegram, met us at the depot. Mr. Milligan accompanied us to the Sherman house, where he had made arrangements for us to be his guests while we remained in the city. I didn't see much of Buntline that evening, as he hurried off to deliver a temperance lecture in one of the public halls. The next day we met him by appointment, and the first thing he said, was:

"Boys, are you ready for business?"

"I can't answer that," replied I, "for we don't know what we are going to do."

"It's all arranged," said he, "and you'll have no trouble whatever. Come with me. We'll go and see Nixon, manager of the Amphitheater. That's the place where we are to play. We'll open there next Monday night." Jack and myself accordingly accompanied him to Manager Nixon's office without saying a word, as we didn't know what to say.

"Here we are, Mr. Nixon," said Buntline; "here are the stars for you. Here are the boys; and they are a fine pair to draw to. Now, Nixon, I am prepared for business."

Nixon and Buntline had evidently had a talk about the terms of our engagement. Buntline, it seems, was to furnish the company, the drama, and the pictorial printing, and was to receive sixty per cent. of the gross receipts for his share; while Nixon was to furnish the theater, the *attaches*, the orchestra, and the local printing, and receive forty per cent. of the gross receipts.

Now, Here's a How D'do

"I am ready for you, Buntline. Have you got your company yet?" asked Nixon.

"No, sir; but there are plenty of idle theatrical people in town, and I can raise a company in two hours," was his reply.

"You haven't much time to spare, if you open on Monday night," said Nixon. "If you will allow me to look at your drama, to see what kind of people you want, I'll assist you in organizing your company."

"I have not yet written the drama," said Buntline.

"What the deuce do you mean? This is Wednesday, and you propose to open on next Monday night. The idea is ridiculous. Here you are at this late hour without a company and without a drama. This will never do, Buntline. I shall have to break my contract with you, for you can't possibly write a drama, cast it, and rehearse it properly for Monday night. Furthermore, you have no pictorial printing as yet. These two gentlemen, whom you have with you, have never been on the stage, and they certainly must have time to study their parts. It is preposterous to think of opening on Monday night, and I'll cancel the engagement."

This little speech was delivered in rather an excited manner by Mr. Nixon. Buntline said that he would write the drama that day and also select his company and have them at the theater for rehearsal next morning. Nixon laughed at him, and said there was no use of trying to undertake anything of the kind in so short a time—it was utterly impossible to do it. Buntline, whose ire was rising, said to Nixon: "What rent will you ask for your theater for next week? "

"Six hundred dollars," was the reply.

"Well, sir, I'll take your theater for next week at that price, and here is half the amount in advance," said Buntline, as he threw down three hundred dollars on the stand. Nixon took the money, gave a receipt for it, and had nothing more to say.

"Now, come with me boys," said Buntline, and away we went to the hotel. Buntline immediately obtained a supply of pens, ink and paper, and then engaged all the hotel clerks as penmen. In less than an hour after he had rented the theater, he was dashing off page after page of his proposed drama—the work being done in his room at the hotel. He then set his clerks at copying for him, and at the end of four hours he jumped up from the table, and enthusiastically shouted; "Hurrah for 'The Scouts of the Plains!' That's the name of the play. The work is done. Hurrah!"

The parts were then copied off separately by the clerks, and handing us our respective portions Buntline said: "Now, boys, go to work, and do your level best to have this dead-letter perfect for the rehearsal, which takes place to-morrow morning at ten o'clock prompt. I want to show Nixon that we'll be ready on time."

I looked at my part and then at Jack; and Jack looked at his part and then at me. Then we looked at each other, and then at Buntline. We did not know what to make of the man.

"How long will it take to commit your part to memory, Bill?" asked Jack.

"About six months, as near as I can calculate. How long will it take you?" answered I.

STUDYING THE PARTS

"It will take me about that length of time to learn the first line," said Jack. Nevertheless we went to our room and commenced studying. I thought it was the hardest work I had ever done.

"This is dry business," finally remarked Jack.

"That's just what it is," I answered; "jerk the bell, Jack." The bell-boy soon appeared. We ordered refreshments; after partaking thereof we resumed our task. We studied hard for an hour or two, but finally gave it up as a bad job, although we had succeeded in committing a small portion to memory. Buntline now came into the room and said: "Boys, how are you getting along?"

"I guess we'll have to go back on this studying business as it isn't our *forte*," said I.

"Don't weaken now, Bill; you'll come out on the top of the heap yet. Let me hear you recite your part," said Buntline. I began "spouting" what I had learned, but was interrupted by Buntline: "Tut! tut! you're not saying it right. You must stop at the cue."

"Cue! What the mischief do you mean by the cue? I never saw any cue except in a billiard room," said I. Buntline thereupon explained it to me, as well as to Jack, who was ignorant as myself concerning the "cue" business.

"Jack, I think we had better back out and go to hunting again," said I.

The Tide Taken at the Flood

"See here, boys; it won't do to go back on me at this stage of the game. Stick to it, and it may be the turning point in your lives and lead you on to fortune and to fame."

"A fortune is what we are after, and we'll at least give the wheel a turn or two to see what luck we have," said I. This satisfied Buntline, but we didn't study any more after he left us. The next morning we appeared at rehearsal and were introduced to the company. The first rehearsal was hardly a success; and the succeeding ones were not much better. The stage manager did his best to teach Jack and myself what to do, but when Monday night came we didn't know much more about it than when we began.

The clock struck seven, and then we put on our buckskin suits, which were the costumes we were to appear in. The theater was being rapidly filled, and it was evident that we were going to make our *début* before a packed house. As the minutes passed by, Jack and I became more and more nervous. We occasionally looked through the holes in the curtain, and saw that the people were continuing to crowd into the theater; our nervousness increased to an uncomfortable degree.

When at length the curtain arose, our courage had returned, so that we thought we could face the immense crowd; yet when the time came for us to go on, we were

BEHIND THE FOOTLIGHTS

rather slow in making our appearance. As we stepped forth we were received with a storm of applause, which we acknowledged with a bow.

Buntline, who was taking the part of "Cale Durg," appeared, and gave me the "cue" to speak "my little piece," but for the life of me I could not remember a single word. Buntline saw I was "stuck," and a happy thought occurred to him. He said, as if it were in the play:

A Little Funny Business

"Where have you been, Bill? What has kept you so long?"

Just then my eye happened to fall on Mr. Milligan, who was surrounded by his friends, the newspaper reporters, and several military officers, all of whom had heard of his hunt and "Indian fight"—he being a very popular man, and widely known in Chicago. So I said:

"I have been out on a hunt with Milligan."

This proved to be a big hit. The audience cheered and applauded, which gave me greater confidence in my ability to get through the performance all right. Buntline, who was a very versatile man, saw that it would be a good plan to follow this up and said: "Well, Bill, tell us all about the hunt." I thereupon proceeded to relate in detail the particulars of the affair. I succeeded in making it rather funny, and I was frequently interrupted by rounds of applause. Whenever I began to "weaken," Buntline would give me a fresh start, by asking some question. In this way I took up fifteen minutes, without once speaking a word of my part; nor did I speak a word of it during the whole evening. The prompter, who was standing between the wings, attempted to prompt me, but it did no good; for while I was on the stage I "chipped in" anything I thought of.

The "Scouts of the Plains" was an Indian drama, of course; and there were between forty and fifty "supers" dressed as Indians. In the fight with them, Jack and I were at home. We blazed away at each other with blank cartridges; and when the scene ended in a hand-to-hand encounter—a general knock-down and drag-out—the way Jack and I killed Indians was "a caution." We would kill them all off in one act, but they would come up again ready for business in the next. Finally the curtain dropped, the play was ended, and I congratulated Jack and myself on having made such a brilliant and successful *début*. There was no backing out after that.

Criticisms of the Press

The next morning there appeared in the Chicago papers some funny criticisms on our first performance. The papers gave us a better send-off than I expected, for they did not criticize us as actors. The Chicago *Times* said that if Buntline had actually spent four hours in writing that play, it was difficult for any one to see what he had been doing all the time. Buntline, as "Cale Durg," was killed in the second act, after a long temperance speech; and the *Inter-Ocean* said that it was to be regretted that he had not been killed in the first act. The company, however, was very good, and M'dlle. Morlacchi, as "Pale Dove," particularly fine; while Miss Cafarno "spouted" a poem of some seven hundred and three verses, more or less, of which the reader will be glad to know that I only recall the words "I was born in March."

Our engagement proved a decided success financially, if not artistically. Nixon was greatly surprised at the result, and at the end of the week he induced Buntline to take him in as a partner in the company.

The next week we played at DeBar's Opera House, in St. Louis, doing an immense business. The following week we were at Cincinnati, where the theater was so crowded every night that hundreds were unable to obtain admission. We met with equal success all over the country. Theatrical managers, upon hearing of this new and novel combination, which was drawing such tremendous houses, were all anxious to secure us; and we received offers of engagements at all the leading theaters. We played one week at the Boston Theater, and the gross receipts amounted to $16,200. We also appeared at Niblo's Garden, New York, the theater being crowded to its utmost capacity every night of the engagement. At the Arch Street Theater, Philadelphia, it was the same way. There was not a single city where we did not have crowded houses.

We closed our tour on the 16th of June, 1873, at Port Jervis, New York, and when I counted up my share of the profits I found that I was only about $6,000 ahead. I was somewhat disappointed, for, judging from our large business, I certainly had expected a greater sum.

Texas Jack and myself longed for a hunt on the Western prairies once more; and on meeting in New York a party of gentlemen who were desirous of going with us, we all started westward, and after a pleasant trip arrived at Fort McPherson.

Lively Experiences of Wild Bill

Texas Jack and I spent several weeks hunting in the western part of Nebraska, and after this pleasant recreation we went to New York and organized a theatrical company for the season of 1873–74. Among the people we engaged for our next tour was Wild Bill, whose name, we knew, would be a drawing card. Bill did not think well of our enterprise on account of our unfamiliarity with the stage, but a large salary forced him to forego his diffidence before the public, and he accordingly made his *début* as an actor. He remained with us during a greater part of the season,

WILD BILL'S IMPROMPTU PERFORMANCE

much to our advantage, and would have continued but for a demoralizing habit that compelled us to part with him. The habit to which I refer was that of firing blank cartridges at the legs of the supers, often burning them severely and at times almost bringing our performance to a ridiculous close. I remonstrated with him time and again, but all to no purpose, and at last, worn out with expostulations, I reluctantly told him he must either quit shooting the supers or leave the company. Without making any reply he retired to the dressing room and there changing his clothes he elbowed his way out through the audience, leaving word with the stage-carpenter that I could go to thunder with my show. I met him later in the evening and tried to persuade him to remain with me, but to no avail, and finding him determined Jack and I paid him his wages and gave him an extra purse of $1,000, with which he bade us good-bye.

The next I heard of Wild Bill was as a star at the head of a would-be rival organization that soon went to pieces. Bill left the troupe under the belief that it had disbanded, but he directly after learned that the company had reorganized and were presenting the same play with an actor personating him. When Bill ascertained this fact he sent a letter to the manager demanding that the name of Wild Bill be stricken from the advertisements, but no attention was paid to his objections. Determined to stop the bogus exhibition Bill went to a town where the company was announced to appear and, purchasing a ticket, took a seat near the orchestra, ready for business. When the bogus character at length appeared Bill jumped over the footlights and seizing his personator, threw him through one of the scenes, and then knocked down the manager, who was dressed in the disguise of an Indian, and kicked him over the lights and onto the fellow who was blowing a big horn in the orchestra. The excitement broke up the performance and Bill was arrested, but was let off with a fine of three dollars, which he cheerfully paid for so happy a privilege, after which he went West and participated in several adventures of a thrilling character, a description of which, however, does not properly belong here.

A Hunt with Mr. Medley

Jack and I played a very successful season, closing at Boston on the 13th of May, 1874. Business called me to New York, and while attending to several matters preparatory to returning to the West, I met an English gentleman, Thomas P. Medley, of London, who had come to America for a hunt on the plains. He had often heard of me and was anxious to engage me as his guide and companion, and he offered to pay the liberal salary of one thousand dollars a month while I was with him. He was a very wealthy man, as I learned upon inquiry, and was a relative of Mr. Lord, of the firm of Lord & Taylor, of New York. Of course I accepted his offer.

When we reached the hunting ground in Nebraska, he informed me, somewhat to my surprise, that he did not want to go out as Alexis did, with carriages, servants, and other luxuries, but that he wished to rough it just as I would do—to sleep on the ground in the open air, and kill and cook his own meat. We started out from North Platte, and spent several weeks in hunting all over the country.

Mr. Medley proved to be a very agreeable gentleman and an excellent hunter. While in camp he busied himself carrying wood and water, attending to the fire, and preparing and cooking the meals, never asking me to do a thing. He did not perform these menial services to save expenses, but because he wanted to do as the other hunters in the party were doing. After spending as much time as he wished, we returned to the railroad, and he took the train for the East. Everything that was required on this hunt was paid for in a most liberal manner by Mr. Medley, who also gave the members of the party several handsome presents.

About this time an expedition consisting of seven companies of cavalry and two companies of infantry, to be commanded by Colonel Mills of the Third Cavalry, was being organized to scout the Powder River and Big Horn country, and I was

WHY THE BUFFALO QUICKLY DISAPPEARED

employed as guide for the command. Proceeding to Rawlins, Wyoming, we "outfitted," and other guides were engaged—among them Tom Sun and Bony Ernest, two noted Rocky mountain scouts. We there left the railroad, and passing through the Seminole range of the Rocky Mountains we established our supply camp at the foot of Independence Rock on the Sweet Water. I was now on my old familiar stamping ground, and it seemed like home to me. Fifteen years before, I had ridden the pony express and driven the overland stages through this region, and the command was going into the same section of country where Wild Bill's expedition of stage-drivers and express-riders had recaptured from the Indians a large number of stolen stage-horses, as previously related.

Leaving the infantry to guard the supply camp, Colonel Mills struck out for the north with the seven companies of cavalry, and in a few days surprised Little Wolf's band of Arapahoes and drove them into the agencies. We then scouted the Powder River, Crazy Woman's Fork, and Clear Fork, and then pushed westward through the mountains to the Wind River. After having been out for a month or two we were ordered to return.

I immediately went East and organized another dramatic company for the season of 1874–75, Texas Jack being absent in the Yellowstone country hunting with the Earl of Dunraven. I played my company in all the principal cities of the country, doing a good business wherever I went. The summer of 1875 I spent at Rochester with my family.

Death of My Only Little Boy

For the season of 1875–76, Texas Jack and I reorganized our old combination, and made a very successful tour. While we were playing at Springfield, Massachusetts, April 20th and 21st, 1876, a telegram was handed me just as I was going on the stage. I opened it and found it to be from Colonel G. W. Torrence, of Rochester, an intimate friend of the family, who stated that my little boy Kit was dangerously ill with the scarlet fever. This was indeed sad news, for little Kit had always been my greatest pride. I sent for John Burke, our business manager, and showing him the telegram, told him that I would play the first act, and making a proper excuse to the audience, I would then take the nine o'clock train that same evening for Rochester, leaving him to play out my part. This I did, and at ten o'clock the next morning I arrived in Rochester, and was met at the depot by my intimate friend Moses Kerngood who at once drove me to my home. I found my little boy unable to speak but he seemed to recognize me and putting his little arms around my neck he tried to kiss me. We did everything in our power to save him, but it was of no avail. The Lord claimed his own, and that evening at six o'clock my beloved little Kit died in my arms. We laid him away to rest in the beautiful cemetery of Mount Hope amid sorrow and tears.

CHAPTER XXI

Scouting with the Fifth Cavalry

We closed our theatrical season earlier than usual in the spring of 1876, because I was anxious to take part in the Sioux war which was then breaking out. Colonel Mills had written me several letters saying that General Crook was anxious to have me accompany his command, and I promised to do so, intending to overtake him in the Powder River country. But when I arrived at Chicago, on my way west, I learned that my old regiment, the gallant Fifth Cavalry, was on its way back from Arizona to join General Crook, and that my old commander, General Carr, was in command. He had written to military headquarters at Chicago to learn my whereabouts, as he wished to secure me as his guide and chief of scouts. I then gave up the idea of overtaking General Crook, and hastening on to Cheyenne, where the Fifth Cavalry had already arrived, I was met at the depot by Lieutenant King, adjutant of the regiment, he having been sent down from Fort D. A. Russell for that purpose by General Carr, who had learned by a telegram from military headquarters at Chicago that I was on the way. I accompanied the lieutenant on horseback to the camp, and as we rode, one of the boys shouted,

SIOUX INDIANS DESTROYING
THE TELEGRAPH LINE

"Here's Buffalo Bill!" Soon after there came three hearty cheers from the regiment. Officers and men were all glad to see me, and I was equally delighted to meet them once more. The General at once appointed me his guide and chief of scouts.

The next morning the command pulled out for Fort Laramie, and on reaching the post we found General Sheridan there, accompanied by General Frye and General Forsyth, *en route* to Red Cloud agency. As the command was to remain here a few days, I accompanied General Sheridan to Red Cloud and back, taking a company of cavalry as escort.

The Indians having recently committed a great many depredations on the Union Pacific railroad, destroying telegraph lines, and also on the Black Hills road running off stock, the Fifth Cavalry was sent out to scout the country between the Indian agencies and the hills. The command operated on the south fork of the Cheyenne and at the foot of the Black Hills for about two weeks, having several small engagements with roving bands of Indians during the time. General Wesley Merritt—who had lately received his promotion to the Colonelcy of the Fifth Cavalry—now came out and took control of the regiment. I was sorry that the command was taken from General Carr, because under him it had made its fighting reputation. However, upon becoming acquainted with General Merritt, I found him to be an excellent officer.

Report of the Custer Massacre and Causes Leading Thereto

The regiment, by continued scouting, soon drove the Indians out of that section of the country, as we supposed, and we had started on our way back to Fort Laramie, when a scout arrived at the camp and reported the massacre of General Custer and his band of heroes on the Little Big Horn, on the 25th of June, 1876; and he also brought orders to General Merritt to proceed at once to Fort Fetterman and join General Crook in the Big Horn county.

The extraordinary and sorrowful interest attaching to the destruction of Custer and his brave followers, felt by the whole civilized world, prompts me to give herewith a brief description of the causes leading thereto, and some of the details of that horrible sacrifice which so melts the heart to pity.

When the Black Hills gold fever first broke out in 1874, a rush of miners into that country resulted in much trouble, as the Indians always regarded that region with jealous interest, and resisted all encroachments of white men. Instead of the Government adhering to the treaty of 1868 and restraining white men from going into the Hills, Gen. Custer was sent out, in 1874, to intimidate the Sioux. The unrighteous spirit of this order the General wisely disregarded, but proceeded to Prospect Valley, and from there he pushed on to the valley of the Little Missouri. Custer expected to find good grazing ground in this valley, suitable for a camp which he intended to pitch there for several days, and reconnoiter, but the country was comparatively barren and the march was therefore continued to the Belle Fourche valley, where excellent grazing, water, and plenty of wood was found.

Crossing the Fourche the expedition was now among the outlying ranges of the Hills, where a camp was made and some reconnoitering done; but finding no Indians, Gen. Custer continued his march, skirting the Black Hills and passing through a country which he described as beautiful beyond description, abounding with a most luxurious vegetation, cool, crystal streams, a profusion of gaudy, sweet smelling flowers, and plenty of game.

Proceeding down this lovely valley, which he appropriately named Floral Park, an Indian camp-fire, recently abandoned, was discovered, and fearing a collision unless pains were taken to prevent it, Custer halted and sent out his chief scout, Bloody Knife, with twenty friendly Indian allies to trail the departed Sioux. They had gone but a short distance when, as Custer himself relates: "Two of Bloody Knife's young men came galloping back and informed me that they had discovered five Indian lodges a few miles down the valley, and that Bloody Knife, as directed, had concealed his party in a wooded ravine, where they awaited further orders. Taking E company with me, which was afterward reinforced by the remainder of the scouts and Col. Hart's company, I proceeded to the ravine where Bloody Knife and his party lay concealed, and from the crest beyond obtained a full view of the five Indian lodges, about which a considerable number of ponies were grazing. I was enabled to place my command still nearer to the lodges undiscovered. I then dispatched Agard, the interpreter, with a flag of truce, accompanied by ten of our Sioux scouts, to acquaint the occupants of the lodges that we were friendly disposed and desired to communicate with them. To prevent either treachery or flight on their part, I galloped the remaining portion of my advance and surrounded the lodges. This was accomplished almost before they were aware of our presence. I then entered the little village and shook hands with its occupants, assuring them through the interpreter, that they had no cause to fear, as we were not there to molest them, etc."

Finding there was no disposition on the part of Gen. Custer to harm them, the Indians dispatched a courier to their principal village, requesting the warriors to be present at a council with the whites. This council was held on the following day, but though Custer dispensed coffee, sugar, bacon and other presents to the Indians, his advice to them regarding the occupation of their country by miners was treated with indifference, for which, he observes in his official report, "I cannot blame the poor savages."

Miners in the Black Hills

During the summer of 1875 Gen. Crook made several trips into the Black Hills to drive out the miners and maintain the government's faith, but while he made many arrests there was no punishment and the whole proceeding became farcical. In August of the same year Custer City was laid out and two weeks later it contained a population of six hundred souls. These Gen. Crook drove out, but as he marched from the place others swarmed in and the population was immediately renewed.

It was this inability, or real indisposition, of the government to enforce the terms of the treaty of 1868 that led to the bitter war with Sitting Bull and which terminated so disastrously on the 25th of June, 1876.

It is a notorious fact that the Sioux Indians, for four years immediately preceding the Custer massacre, were regularly supplied with the most improved fire-arms and ammunition by the agencies at Brule, Grand River, Standing Rock, Fort Berthold, Cheyenne and Fort Peck. Even during the campaign of 1876, in the months of May, June and July, just before and after Custer and his band of heroes rode down into the valley of death, these fighting Indians received eleven hundred and twenty Winchester and Remington rifles and 413,000 rounds of patent ammunition, besides large quantities of loose powder, lead and primers, while during the summer of 1875 they received several thousand stand of arms and more than a million rounds of ammunition. With this generous provision there is no cause for wonder that the Sioux were able to resist the government and attract to their aid all the dissatisfied Cheyennes and other Indians in the Northwest.

Besides a perfect fighting equipment, all the Indians recognized in Sitting Bull the elements of a great warrior, one whose superior, perhaps, has never been known among any tribe; he combined all the strategic cunning of Tecumseh with the cruel, uncompromising hatred of Black Kettle, while his leadership was far superior to both. Having decided to precipitate a terrible war, he chose his position with consummate judgment, selecting a central vantage point surrounded by what is known as the "bad lands," and then kept his supply source open by an assumed friendship with the Canadian French. This he was the better able to accomplish, since some years before he had professed conversion to Christianity under the preaching of Father Desmet and maintained a show of great friendship for the Canadians.

War Declared Against the Sioux

War against the Sioux having been declared, brought about by the combined causes of Black Hill outrages and Sitting Bull's threatening attitude, it was decided to send out three separate expeditions, one of which should move from the north, under Gen. Terry, from Fort Lincoln; another from the east, under Gen. Gibbon, from Fort Ellis, and another from the south, under Gen. Crook, from Fort Fetterman; these movements were to be simultaneous, and a junction was expected to be formed near the headwaters of the Yellowstone River.

For some cause, which I will refrain from discussing, the commands did not start at the same time. Gen. Crook did not leave Fetterman until March 1st, with seven hundred men and forty days' supply. The command was entrusted to Col. Reynolds, of the Third Cavalry, accompanied by Gen. Crook, the department commander. Nothing was heard of this expedition until the 22d following, when Gen. Crook forwarded from Ft. Reno a brief account of his battle on Powder River. The result of this fight, which lasted five hours, was the destruction of Crazy Horse's village of one hundred and five lodges; or that is the way the dispatch read, though many assert that

THE SUN, OR TORTURE DANCE

Among the curious ceremonies practiced by some of the Northwest Indians, particularly the Sioux tribe, is the Sun Dance, which, however, is very rarely performed. Once in a great while some of the more courageous, to show their bravery and endurance, inflict upon themselves such tortures as are shown in the illustration, in which condition they remain sometimes for days, and until either completely prostrated, or the flesh is torn out.

the battle resulted in little else than a series of remarkable blunders which suffered the Indians to make good their escape, losing only a small quantity of their property.

One serious trouble arose out of the Powder River fight, which was found in an assertion made by Gen. Crook, or at least attributed to him, that his expedition had proved that instead of there being 15,000 or 20,000 hostile Indians in the Black Hills and Big Horn county, that the total number would not exceed 2,000. It was upon this estimation that the expeditions were prepared.

The Terry column, which was commanded by Gen. Custer, consisted of twelve companies of the Seventh Cavalry, and three companies of the Sixth and Seventeenth Infantry, with four Gatling guns, and a detachment of Indian scouts. This force comprised twenty-eight officers and seven hundred and forty-seven men, of the Seventh Cavalry, eight officers and one hundred and thirty-five men of the Sixth and Seventeenth Infantry, two officers and thirty-two men in charge of the Gatling battery, and forty-five enlisted Indian scouts, a grand total of thirty-eight officers and nine hundred and fifty-nine men, including scouts.

The combined forces of Crook, Gibbon, Terry and Custer, did not exceed twenty-seven hundred men, while opposed to them were fully 17,000 Indians, all of whom were provided with the latest and most improved patterns of repeating rifles.

On the 16th of June Gen. Crook started for the Rosebud, on which stream it was reported that Sitting Bull and Crazy Horse were stationed; about the same time a party of Crow Indians, who were operating with Gen. Crook, returned from a scout and reported that Gen. Gibbon, who was on Tongue River, had been attacked by Sitting Bull, who had captured several horses. Crook pushed on rapidly toward the Rosebud, leaving his train behind and mounting his infantry on mules. What were deemed accurate reports, stated that Sitting Bull was still on the Rosebud, only sixty miles from the point where Gen. Crook camped on the night of the 15th of June. The command traveled forty miles on the sixteenth, and when within twenty miles of the Sioux principal position, instead of pushing on, Gen. Crook went into camp.

Attacked by Sitting Bull

The next morning he was much surprised at finding himself attacked by Sitting Bull, who swooped down on him with the first streaks of coming dawn, and a heavy battle followed. Gen. Crook, who had camped in a basin surrounded on all sides by high hills, soon found his position so dangerous that it must be changed at all hazards. The advance was therefore sounded with Noyes's battalion occupying a position on the right, Mills on the right center, Chambers in the center, and the Indian allies on the left. Mills and Noyes charged the enemy in magnificent style, breaking the line and striking the rear. The fight continued hot and furious until 2 P.M., when a gallant charge of Col. Royall, who was in reserve, supported by the Indian allies, caused the Sioux to draw off to their village, six miles distant, while Gen. Crook went into camp, where he remained inactive for two days.

In the meantime, as the official report recites: "Generals Terry and Gibbon communicated with each other June 1st, near the junction of the Tongue and Yellowstone rivers, and learned that a heavy force of Indians had concentrated on the opposite bank of the Yellowstone, but eighteen miles distant. For fourteen days the Indian pickets had confronted Gibbon's videttes."

Gen. Gibbon reported to Gen. Terry that the cavalry had thoroughly scouted the Yellowstone as far as the mouth of the Big Horn, and no Indians had crossed it. It was now certain that they were not prepared for them, and on the Powder, Tongue, Rosebud, Little Horn and Big Horn Rivers, Gen. Terry at once commenced feeling for them. Major Reno, of the Seventh Cavalry, with six companies of that regiment, was sent up Powder River one hundred and fifty miles, to the mouth of Little Powder to look for the Indians, and, if possible to communicate with General Crook. He reached the mouth of the Little Powder in five days, but saw no Indians, and could hear nothing of Crook. As he returned, he found on the Rosebud a very large Indian

THE LAST ONE OF CUSTER'S BRAVE BAND

trail, about nine days old, and followed it a short distance, when he turned about up Tongue River, and reported to Gen. Terry what he had seen. It was now known that no Indians were on either Tongue or Little Powder Rivers, and the net had narrowed down to Rosebud, Little Horn and Big Horn Rivers.

Gen. Terry, who had been waiting with Custer and the steamer *Far West*, at the mouth of Tongue River, for Reno's report, as soon as he heard it, ordered Custer to march up the south bank to a point opposite Gen. Gibbon, who was encamped on the north bank of the Yellowstone. Accordingly Terry, on board the steamer *Far West*, pushed up the Yellowstone, keeping abreast of Gen. Custer's column.

Gen. Gibbon was found in camp quietly awaiting developments. A consultation was had with Gens. Gibbon and Custer, and then Gen. Terry definitely fixed upon the plan of action. It was believed the Indians were at the head of the Rosebud, or over on the Little Horn, a dividing ridge only fifteen miles wide separating the two streams. It was announced by Gen. Terry that Gen. Custer's column "would strike the blow."

At the time that a junction was formed between Gibbon and Terry, Gen. Crook was about one hundred miles from them, while Sitting Bull's forces were between the commands. Crook, after his battle, fell back to the head of Tongue River. The Powder, Tongue, Rosebud and Big Horn Rivers all flow northwest, and empty into the Yellowstone; as Sitting Bull was between the headwaters of the Rosebud and Big Horn, the main tributary of the latter being known as the Little Big Horn, a sufficient knowledge of the topography of the country is thus afforded by which to definitely locate Sitting Bull and his force.

Having now ascertained the position of the enemy, or reasoned out the probable position, Gen. Terry sent a dispatch to Gen. Sheridan, as follows: "No Indians have been met with as yet, but traces of a large and recent camp have been discovered twenty or thirty miles up the Rosebud. Gibbon's column will move this morning on the north side of the Yellowstone, for the mouth of the Big Horn, where it will be ferried across by the supply steamer, and whence it will proceed to the mouth of the Little Horn, and so on. Custer will go up the Rosebud tomorrow with his whole regiment, and thence to the headwaters of the Little Horn, thence down that stream."

Following this report came an order, signed by E. W. Smith, Captain of the Eighteenth Infantry, Acting Assistant Adjutant-General, directing General Custer to follow the Indian trail discovered, pushing the Indians from one side, while Gen. Gibbon pursued them from an opposite direction. As no instructions were given as to the rate each division should travel, Custer, noted for his quick, energetic movements, made ninety miles the first three days, and, discovering the Indians in large numbers, divided his command into three divisions, one of which he placed under Major Reno, another under Major Benteen, and led the other himself.

Custer Strikes the Indians

As Custer made a detour to enter the village, Reno struck a large body of Indians, who, after retreating nearly three miles, turned on the troops and ran them pell mell across Grassy Creek into the woods. Reno over-estimated the strength of his enemies and thought he was being surrounded. Benteen came up to the support of Reno, but he too took fright and got out of his position without striking the enemy.

While Reno and Benteen were trying to keep open a way for their retreat, Custer charged on the village, first sending a courier, Trumpeter Martin, to Reno and Benteen with the following dispatch: "Big village; be quick; send on the packs." This order was too plain to be misconstrued. It clearly meant that he had discovered the village, which he intended attacking at once; to hurry forward to his support and bring up the packs, ambulances, etc. But instead of obeying orders, Reno and Benteen stood aloof, fearful lest they should endanger their position, while the brave Custer and his squad of noble heroes rushed down like a terrible avalanche upon the Indian village. In a moment, fateful incident, the Indians came swarming about that heroic band until the very earth seemed to open and let loose the elements of

CUSTER'S LAST SHOT

volcanic fury, or like a riot of the fiends of Erebus, blazing with the hot sulfur of their impious dominion. Down from the hillside, up through the valleys, that dreadful torrent of Indian cruelty and massacre poured around the little squad to swallow it up with one grand swoop of fire. But Custer was there at the head, like Spartacus fighting the legions about him, tall, graceful, brave as a lion at bay, and with thunderbolts in his hands. His brave followers formed a hollow square, and met the rush, and roar, and fury of the demons. Bravely they breasted that battle shock, bravely stood up and faced the leaden hail, nor quailed when looking into the blazing muzzles of five thousand deadly rifles.

Hoping Against Hope

Brushing away the powder grimes that had settled in his face, Custer looked over the boiling sea of fury around him, peering through the smoke for some signs of Reno and Benteen, but seeing none yet thinking of the aid which must soon come, with cheering words to his comrades, he renewed the battle, fighting still like a Hercules and piling heaps of victims around his very feet.

Hour after hour passed and yet no friendly sign of Reno's coming; nothing to be seen saving the battle smoke, streaks of fire splitting through the misty clouds, blood flowing in rivulets under tramping feet, dying comrades, and Indians swarming about him, rending the air with their demoniacal "hi-yi-yip-yah—yah-hi-yah."

The Massacre

The fight continued with unabated fury until late in the afternoon; men had sunk down beside their gallant leader until there was but a handful left, only a dozen, bleeding from many wounds and hot carbines in their stiffening hands. The day is almost done, when look! heaven now defend him! the charm of his life is broken, for Custer has fallen; a bullet cleaves a pathway through his side, and as he falters another strikes his noble breast. Like a strong oak stricken by the lightning's bolt, shivering the mighty trunk and bending its withering branches down close to the earth, so fell Custer; but like the reacting branches, he rises partly up again, and striking out like a fatally wounded giant lays three more Indians dead and breaks his mighty sword on the musket of a fourth; then, with useless blade and empty pistol falls back the victim of a dozen wounds. He is the last to succumb to death, and dies, too, with the glory of accomplished duty on his conscience and the benediction of a grateful country on his head. The place where fell these noblest of God's heroes is sacred ground, and though it be the Golgotha of a nation's mistakes it is bathed with precious blood, rich with the germs of heroic inheritance.

I have avoided attaching blame to any one, using only the facts that have been furnished me of how Custer came to attack the Sioux village and how and why he died.

When the news of the terrible massacre was learned, soldiers everywhere made a pilgrimage to the sacred place, and friendly hands reared a monument on that distant

THE FINDING OF CUSTER'S BODY

spot commemorative of the heroism of Custer and his men; collected together all the bones and relics of the battle and piled them up in pyramidal form, where they stand in sunshine and storm, overlooking the Little Big Horn.

Soon after the news of Custer s massacre reached us preparations were immediately made to avenge his death. The whole Cheyenne and Sioux tribes were in revolt and a lively, if not very dangerous, campaign was in prospective.

After the Murderers of Custer

Two days before receipt of the news of the massacre, Colonel Stanton, who was with the Fifth Cavalry, had been sent to Red Cloud agency and on the evening of the receipt of news of the Custer fight a scout arrived in our camp with a message from the Colonel informing General Merritt that eight hundred Cheyenne warriors had that day left Red Cloud agency to join Sitting Bull's hostile forces in the Big Horn country.

Notwithstanding the instructions to proceed immediately to join General Crook by the way of Fort Fetterman, Colonel Merritt took the responsibility of endeavoring to intercept the Cheyennes, and as the sequel shows he performed a very important service.

INDIANS RUNNING OFF STOCK

He selected five hundred men and horses, and in two hours we were making a forced march back to Hat, or War Bonnet Creek—the intention being to reach the main Indian trail running to the north across that creek before the Cheyennes could get there. We arrived there the next night, and at daylight the following morning, July 17th, 1876, I went out on a scout, and found that the Indians had not yet crossed the creek. On my way back to the command I discovered a large party of Indians, which proved to be the Cheyennes, coming up from the south, and I hurried to the camp with this important information.

The cavalrymen quietly mounted their horses, and were ordered to remain out of sight, while General Merritt, accompanied by two or three aides and myself, went out on a little tour of observation to a neighboring hill, from the summit of which we saw that the Indians were approaching almost directly towards us. Presently fifteen or twenty of them dashed off to the west in the direction from which we had come the night before; and upon closer observation with our field glasses, we discovered two mounted soldiers, evidently carrying dispatches for us, pushing forward on our trail.

My Duel with Yellow Hand

The Indians were evidently endeavoring to intercept these two men, and General Merritt feared that they would accomplish their object. He did not think it advisable to send out any soldiers to the assistance of the couriers, for fear they would show to the Indians that there were troops in the vicinity who were waiting for them. I finally suggested that the best plan was to wait until the couriers came closer to the command, and then just as the Indians were about to charge, to let me take the scouts and cut them off from the main body of the Cheyennes, who were coming over the divide.

"All right, Cody," said the General, "if you can do that, go ahead."

I rushed back to the command, jumped on my horse, picked out fifteen men, and returned with them to the point of observation. I told General Merritt to give us the word to start out at the proper time, and presently he sang out:

"Go in now, Cody, and be quick about it. They are going to charge on the couriers."

The two messengers were not over four hundred yards from us, and the Indians were only about two hundred yards behind them. We instantly dashed over the bluffs, and advanced on a gallop towards the Indians. A running fight lasted several minutes, during which we drove the enemy some little distance and killed three of their number. The rest of them rode off towards the main body, which had come into plain sight, and halted, upon seeing the skirmish that was going on. We were about half a mile from General Merritt, and the Indians whom we were chasing suddenly turned upon us, and another lively skirmish took place. One of the Indians, who was handsomely decorated with all the ornaments usually worn by a war chief when engaged in a fight, sang out to me, in his own tongue: "I know you, Pa-he-haska; if you want to fight, come ahead and fight me."

The chief was riding his horse back and forth in front of his men, as if to banter me, and I concluded to accept the challenge. I galloped towards him for fifty yards and he advanced towards me about the same distance, both of us riding at full speed, and then, when we were only about thirty yards apart, I raised my rifle and fired; his horse fell to the ground, having been killed by my bullet. Almost at the same instant my own horse went down, he having stepped into a gopher hole. The fall did not hurt me much, and I instantly sprang to my feet. The Indian had also recovered himself, and we were now both on foot, and not more than twenty paces apart. We fired at each other simultaneously. My usual luck did not desert me on this occasion, for his bullet missed me, while mine struck him in the breast. He reeled and fell, but before he had fairly touched the ground I was upon him, knife in hand, and had driven the keen-edged weapon to its hilt in his heart. Jerking his war-bonnet off, I scientifically scalped him in about five seconds.

THE DUEL WITH YELLOW HAND

A Moment of Great Danger

The whole affair from beginning to end occupied but little time, and the Indians, seeing that I was some little distance from my company, now came charging down upon me from a hill, in hopes of cutting me off. General Merritt had witnessed the duel, and realizing the danger I was in, ordered Colonel Mason with Company K to hurry to my rescue. The order came none too soon, for had it been given one minute later I would have had not less than two hundred Indians upon me. As the soldiers came up I swung the Indian chieftain's top-knot and bonnet in the air, and shouted:

"The first scalp for Custer."

General Merritt, seeing that he could not now ambush the Indians, ordered the whole regiment to charge upon them. They made a stubborn resistance for a little while, but it was of no use for any eight hundred, or even sixteen hundred Indians to try and check a charge of the gallant old Fifth Cavalry, and they soon came to that conclusion and began a running retreat towards Red Cloud agency. For thirty-five miles we drove them, pushing them so hard that they were obliged to abandon their loose horses, their camp equipage and everything else. We drove them into the agency, and followed in ourselves, notwithstanding the possibility of our having to encounter the thousands of Indians at that point. We were uncertain whether or not the other agency Indians had determined to follow the example of the Cheyennes: strike out upon the war-path; but that made no difference with the Fifth Cavalry, for they would have fought them all if necessary. It was dark when we rode into the agency, where we found thousands of Indians collected together; but they manifested no disposition to fight.

While at the agency I learned the name of the Indian chief whom I had killed in the morning; it was Yellow Hand, a son of old Cut-nose—a leading chief of the Cheyennes. Cut-nose having learned that I had killed his son sent a white interpreter to me with a message to the effect that he would give me four mules if I would turn over to him Yellow Hand's war-bonnet, guns, pistols, ornaments, and other paraphernalia which I had captured. I sent back word to the old gentleman that it would give me pleasure to accommodate him, but I could not do it this time.

Again in Pursuit of the Sioux

The next morning we started to join General Crook, who was camped near the foot of Cloud Peak in the Big Horn Mountains, awaiting the arrival of the Fifth Cavalry, before proceeding against the Sioux, who were somewhere near the head of the Little Big Horn—as his scouts informed him. We made rapid marches and reached General Crook's camp on Goose Creek about the 3d of August.

THE FIRST SCALP FOR CUSTER

At this camp I met many old friends, among whom was Colonel Royall, who had received his promotion to the Lieutenant-Colonelcy of the Third Cavalry. He introduced me to General Crook, whom I had never met before, but of whom I had often heard. He also introduced me to the General's chief guide, Frank Grouard, a half breed, who had lived six years with Sitting Bull, and knew the country thoroughly.

We remained in this camp only one day, and then the whole troop pulled out for the Tongue River, leaving our wagons behind, but taking with us a large pack train. We marched down the Tongue River for two days, thence in a westerly direction over to the Rosebud, where we struck the main Indian trail, leading down this stream. From the size of the trail, which appeared to be about four days old, we estimated that there must have been in the neighborhood of seven thousand Indians in the war party.

For two or three days we pushed on, but we did not seem to gain much on the Indians, as they were evidently making about the same marches that we were. On the fourth or fifth morning of our pursuit, I rode ahead of the command about ten miles, and mounting a hill I scanned the country far and wide with my field glass, and discovered an immense column of dust rising about ten miles further down the creek, and soon I noticed a body of men marching towards me, that at first I believed to be the Indians of whom we were in pursuit; but subsequently they proved to be General Terry's command. I sent back word to that effect to General Crook, by a scout who had accompanied me, but after he had departed I observed a band of Indians on the opposite side of the creek, and also another party directly in front of me. This led me to believe that I had made a mistake. But shortly afterwards my attention was attracted by the appearance of a body of soldiers, who were forming into a skirmish line, and then I became convinced that it was General Terry's command after all, and that the red-skins whom I had seen were some of his friendly Indian scouts, who had mistaken me for a Sioux, and fled back to their command terribly excited, shouting, "The Sioux are coming!"

A Little Dust Causes Much Excitement

General Terry at once came to the post, and ordered the Seventh Cavalry to form line of battle across the Rosebud; he also ordered up his artillery and had them prepare for action, doubtless dreading another "Custer massacre." I afterwards learned the Indian had seen the dust raised by General Crook's forces, and had reported that the Sioux were coming.

These maneuvers I witnessed from my position with considerable amusement, thinking the command must be badly demoralized, when one man could cause a whole army to form line of battle and prepare for action. Having enjoyed the situation to my heart's content, I galloped down towards the skirmish line, waving my hat and when within about one hundred yards of the troops, Colonel Weir, of the Seventh Cavalry, galloped out and met me. He recognized me at once, and accompanied me inside the line; then he sang out, "Boys, here's Buffalo Bill. Some of you old soldiers know him; give him a cheer!" Thereupon the regiment gave three rousing cheers, and it was followed up all along the line.

Colonel Weir presented me to General Terry, and in answer to his question I informed him that the alarm of Indians which had been given was a false one, as the dust seen by his scouts was caused by General Crook's troops. General Terry thereupon rode forward to meet General Crook, and I accompanied him at his request.

That night both commands went into camp on the Rosebud. General Terry had his wagon train with him, and everything to make life comfortable on an Indian campaign. He had large wall tents and portable beds to sleep in, and commodious hospital tents for dining-rooms. His camp looked very comfortable and attractive, and presented a great contrast to that of General Crook, who had for his headquarters only one small fly tent; and whose cooking utensils consisted of a quart cup—in which he made his coffee himself—and a stick upon which he broiled his bacon. When I compared the two camps, I came to the conclusion that General Crook was an Indian fighter; for it was evident that he had learned that, to follow and fight Indians, a body of men must travel lightly and not be detained by a wagon train or heavy luggage of any kind.

That evening General Terry ordered General Mills to take his regiment, the Fifth Infantry, and return by a forced march to the Yellowstone, and proceed down the river by steamboat to the mouth of Powder River, to intercept the Indians, in case they attempted to cross the Yellowstone. General Miles made a forced march that night of thirty-five miles, which was splendid traveling for an infantry regiment through a mountainous country.

Generals Crook and Terry spent that evening and the next day in council, and on the following morning both commands moved out on the Indian trail. Although General Terry was the senior officer, he did not assume command of both expeditions, but left General Crook in command of his own troops, although they operated together. We crossed the Tongue River to Powder River, and proceeded down the latter stream to a point twenty miles from its junction with the Yellowstone, where the Indian trail turned to the southeast in the direction of the Black Hills. The two commands now being nearly out of supplies, the trail was abandoned, and the troops kept on down Powder River to its confluence with the Yellowstone, and remained there several days. Here we met General Mills, who reported that no Indians had as yet crossed the Yellowstone. Several steamboats soon arrived with a large quantity of supplies, and once more the "Boys in Blue " were made happy.

CHAPTER XXII

Dangerous Work

One evening while we were in camp on the Yellowstone at the mouth of Powder River, I was informed that the commanding officers had selected Louis Richard, a half breed and myself to accompany General Mills on a scouting expedition on the steamer *Far West*, down the Yellowstone as far as Glendive Creek. We were to ride

SCOUTING ON A STEAMBOAT

on the pilot house and keep a sharp lookout on both sides of the river for Indian trails that might have crossed the stream. The idea of scouting on a steamboat was indeed a novel one to me, and I anticipated a pleasant trip.

At daylight next morning we reported on board the steamer to General Mills, who had with him four or five companies of his regiment. We were somewhat surprised when he asked us where our horses were, as we had not supposed that horses would be needed if the scouting was to be done on the steamer. He said we might need them before we got back, and thereupon we had the animals brought onboard. In a few minutes we were booming down the river at the rate of about twenty miles an hour.

The steamer *Far West* was commanded by Captain Grant Marsh, whom I found to be an interesting character. I had often heard of him, for he was and is yet one of the best known river captains in the country. He it was who, with his steamer the *Far West*, transported the wounded men from the battle of the Little Big Horn to Fort Abraham Lincoln on the Missouri River, and on that trip he made the fastest steamboat time on record. He was a skillful and experienced pilot, handling his boat with remarkable dexterity.

While Richard and myself were at our stations on the pilot house, the steamer with a full head of steam went flying past islands, around bends over sand-bars, at a rate that was exhilarating. Presently I thought I could see the horses grazing in a distant bend of the river and I reported the fact to General Mills, who asked Captain Marsh if he could land the boat near a large tree which he pointed out to him. "Yes, sir; I can land her there, and make her climb the tree if necessary," said he.

On reaching the spot designated, General Mills ordered two companies ashore, while Richard and myself were instructed to take our horses off the boat and push out as rapidly as possible to see if there were Indians in the vicinity. While we were getting ashore, Captain Marsh remarked that if there was only a good heavy dew on the grass he would shoot the steamer ashore and take us on the scout without the trouble of leaving the boat.

It was a false alarm, however, as the objects we had seen proved to be Indian graves. Quite a large number of braves who had probably been killed in some battle, were laid on scaffolds, according to the Indian custom, and some of their clothing had been torn loose from the bodies by the wolves and was waving in the air.

On arriving at Glendive Creek we found that Colonel Rice and his company of the Fifth Infantry who had been sent there by General Mills, had built quite a good little fort with their trowel-bayonets—a weapon which Colonel Rice was the inventor of, and which is, by the way, a very useful implement of war, as it can be used for a shovel in throwing up entrenchments and can be profitably utilized in several other ways. On the day previous to our arrival, Colonel Rice had a fight with a party of Indians, and had killed two or three of them at long range with his Rodman cannon.

A Ride Through the Bad Lands

The *Far West* was to remain at Glendive over night, and General Mills wished to send dispatches back to General Terry at once. At his request I took the dispatches and rode seventy-five miles that night through the bad lands of the Yellowstone, and reached General Terry's camp next morning, after having nearly broken my neck a dozen times or more.

There being but little prospect of any more fighting, I determined to go East as soon as possible to organize a new "Dramatic Combination," and have a new drama written for me based upon the Sioux war. This I knew would be a paying investment as the Sioux campaign had excited considerable interest. So I started down the river on the steamer Yellowstone *en route* to Fort Beauford. On the same morning Generals

INDIAN RAIDERS ON THE LINE OF THE U. P. R. R.

Terry and Crook pulled out for Powder River, to take up the old Indian trail which we had recently left.

The steamer had proceeded down the stream about twenty miles when it was met by another boat on its way up the river, having on board General Whistler and some fresh troops for General Terry's command. Both boats landed, and almost the first person I met was my old friend and partner, Texas Jack, who had been sent out as a dispatch carrier for the New York *Herald*.

General Whistler, upon learning that General Terry had left the Yellowstone, asked me to carry to him some important dispatches from General Sheridan, and although I objected, he insisted upon my performing this duty, saying that it would only detain me a few hours longer; as an extra inducement he offered me the use of his own thorough-bred horse, which was on the boat. I finally consented to go, and was soon speeding over the rough and hilly country towards Powder River, and I delivered the dispatches to General Terry the same evening. General Whistler's horse, although a good animal was not used to such hard riding, and was far more exhausted by the journey than I was.

After I had taken a lunch, General Terry asked me if I would carry some dispatches back to General Whistler, and I replied that I would. Captain Smith, General Terry's aid-de-camp, offered me his horse for the trip, and it proved to be an excellent animal; for I rode him that same night forty miles over the bad lands in four hours, and reached General Whistler's steamboat at one o'clock. During my absence the Indians had made their appearance on the different hills in the vicinity, and the troops from the boat had had several skirmishes with them. When General Whistler had finished reading the dispatches, he said: "Cody, I want to send information to General Terry concerning the Indians who have been skirmishing around here all day. I have been trying all the evening long to induce some one to carry my dispatches to him, but no one seems willing to undertake the trip, and I have got to fall back on you. It is asking a great deal, I know, as you have just ridden eighty miles; but it is a case of necessity, and if you'll go Cody, I'll see that you are well paid for it."

"Never mind about the pay," said I, "but get your dispatches ready and I'll start at once."

A Terrible Journey

In a few minutes he handed me the package and, mounting the same horse which I had ridden from General Terry's camp, I struck out for my destination. It was two o'clock in the morning when I left the boat, and at eight o'clock I rode into General Terry's camp, just as he was about to march—having made one hundred and twenty miles in twenty-two hours.

General Terry, after reading the dispatches, halted his command and then rode on and overtook General Crook, with whom he held a council; the result was that Crook's command moved on in the direction which they had been pursuing, while Terry's forces marched back to the Yellowstone and crossed the river on steamboats. At the urgent request of General Terry I accompanied the command on a scout in the direction of the dry fork of the Missouri, where it was expected we would strike some Indians.

The first march out from the Yellowstone was made in the night, as we wished to get into the hills without being discovered by the Sioux scouts. After marching three days, a little to the east of north, we reached the buffalo range and discovered fresh signs of Indians, who had evidently been killing buffaloes. General Terry now called on me to carry dispatches to Colonel Rice, who was still camped at the mouth of Glendive Creek, on the Yellowstone—distant about eighty miles from us.

Night had set in with a storm and a drizzling rain was falling when, at ten o'clock, I started on this ride through a section of country with which I was entirely unacquainted. I traveled through the darkness a distance of about thirty-five miles, and at daylight I rode into a secluded spot at the head of a ravine where stood a bunch of ash trees and there I concluded to remain till night, for I considered it a dangerous undertaking to cross the wide prairies in broad daylight—especially as my horse was a poor one. I accordingly unsaddled my animal and ate a hearty breakfast of bacon and hard tack which I had stored in the saddle-pockets; then, after taking a smoke, I lay down to sleep, with my saddle for a pillow. In a few minutes I was in the land of dreams.

Lying Low

After sleeping some time—I can't tell how long—I was suddenly awakened by a roaring, rumbling sound. I instantly seized my gun, sprang to my horse and hurriedly secreted him in the brush. Then I climbed up the steep side of the bank and cautiously looked over the summit; in the distance I saw a large herd of buffalos which were being chased and fired at by twenty or thirty Indians. Occasionally a buffalo would drop out of the herd, but the Indians kept on until they had killed ten or fifteen. They then turned back and began to cut up their game.

I saddled my horse and tied him to a small tree where I could reach him conveniently in case the Indians should discover me by finding my trail and following it. I then crawled carefully back to the summit of the bluff, and in a concealed position watched the Indians for two hours, during which time they were occupied in cutting

WATCHING THE HOSTILES

up the buffaloes and packing the meat on their ponies. When they had finished this work they rode off in the direction whence they had come and on the line which I had proposed to travel. It appeared evident to me that their camp was located somewhere between me and Glendive Creek, but I had no idea of abandoning the trip on that account.

I waited till nightfall before resuming my journey, and then I bore off to the east for several miles, and by making a semicircle to avoid the Indians, I got back on my original course, and then pushed on rapidly to Colonel Rice's camp, which I reached just at daylight.

Colonel Rice had been fighting Indians almost every day since he had been encamped at this point, and he was very anxious to notify General Terry of the fact. Of course I was requested to carry his dispatches. After remaining at Glendive a single day I started back to find General Terry, and on the third day I overhauled him at the head of Deer Creek while on his way to Colonel Rice's camp. He was not, however, going in the right direction, but bearing too far to the east, and I so informed him. He then asked me to guide the command and I did so.

On arriving at Glendive I bade good-bye to the General and his officers and took passage on the steamer *Far West*, which was on her way down the Missouri. At Bismarck I left the steamer, and proceeded by rail to Rochester, New York, where I met my family. Mr. J. Clinton Hall, manager of the Rochester Opera House, was very anxious to have me play an engagement at his theater, so I agreed to open the season with him as soon as I had got my drama written; and I did so, meeting with an enthusiastic reception.

My new drama was arranged for the stage by J. V. Arlington, the actor. It was a five-act play, without head or tail, and it made no difference at which act we commenced the performance. Before we had finished the season several newspaper critics, I have been told, went crazy in trying to follow the plot. It afforded us, however, ample opportunity to give a noisy, rattling, gunpowder entertainment, and to present a succession of scenes in the late Indian war, all of which seemed to give general satisfaction.

Return to the Mimic Stage

From Rochester I went to New York and played a very successful engagement at the Grand Opera House under the management of Messrs. Poole and Donnelly. Thence my route took me to all the principal cities in the Eastern, Western and Middle States, and I everywhere met with crowded houses. I then went to the Pacific Coast, against the advice of friends who gave it as their opinion that my style of plays would not take very well in California. I opened for an engagement of two weeks at the Bush Street

Theater, in San Francisco, in a season when the theatrical business was dull and Ben DeBar and the Lingards were playing there to empty seats. I expected to play to a slim audience on the opening night, but instead of that I had a fourteen hundred dollar house. Such was my success that I continued my engagement for five weeks, and the theater was crowded at every performance. Upon leaving San Francisco I made a circuit of the interior towns and closed the season at Virginia City, Nevada.

Some time previously I had made arrangements to go into the cattle business in company with my old friend, Major Frank North, and while I was in California he had built our ranches on the south fork of the Dismal River, sixty-five miles north of North Platte, in Nebraska. Proceeding to Ogalalla, the headquarters of the Texas cattle drovers, I found Major North there awaiting me, and together we bought, branded and drove to our ranches our first installment of cattle. This occupied us during the remainder of the summer.

Leaving the cattle in charge of Major North, I visited Red Cloud Agency early in the fall, and secured some Sioux Indians to accompany me on my theatrical tour of 1877–78. Taking my family and the Indians with me, I went directly to Rochester. There I left my oldest daughter, Arta, at a young ladies' seminary, while my wife and youngest child traveled with me during the season.

I opened at the Bowery Theater, New York, September 3d, 1877, with a new border drama entitled, "May Cody, or Lost and Won," from the pen of Major A. S. Burt, of the United States army. It was founded on the incidents of the "Mountain Meadow Massacre," and life among the Mormons. It was the best drama I had yet produced, and proved a grand success both financially and artistically. The season of 1877–78 was the most profitable one I had ever had.

In February, 1878, my wife became tired of traveling, and proceeded to North Platte, Nebraska, where, on our farm adjoining the town, she personally superintended the erection of a comfortable family residence, and had it all completed when I reached there, early in May. In this house we are now living, and we hope to make it our home for many years to come.

On a Round-Up

After my arrival at North Platte, I found that the ranchmen, or cattlemen, had organized a regular annual "round-up," to take place in the spring of the year.

The word "round-up" is derived from the fact that during the winter months the cattle become scattered over a vast tract of land, and the ranchmen assemble together in the spring to sort out and each secure his own stock. They form a large circle, often of a circumference of two hundred miles, and drive the cattle toward a

ON THE ROUND-UP

common center, where, all stock being branded, each owner can readily separate his own from the general herd, and then he drives them to his own ranch.

In this cattle driving business is exhibited some most magnificent horsemanship, for the "cow-boys," as they are called, are invariably skillful and fearless horsemen—in fact only a most expert rider could be a cow-boy, as it requires the greatest dexterity and daring in the saddle to cut a wild steer out of the herd. Major North was awaiting me, upon my arrival at North Platte, having with him our own horses and men. Other cattle owners, such as Keith and Barton, Coe and Carter, Jack Pratt, the Walker brothers, Guy and Sim Lang, Arnold and Ritchie and a great many others with their outfits, were assembled and were ready to start on the round-up.

As there is nothing but hard work on these round-ups, having to be in the saddle all day, and standing guard over the cattle at night, rain or shine, I could not possibly find out where the fun came in that North had promised me. But it was an exciting life, and the days sped rapidly by; in six weeks we found ourselves at own ranch on Dismal River, the round-up having proved a great success, as we had found all our cattle and driven them home. This work being over, I proposed to spend a few weeks with my family at North Platte, for the purpose of making their better acquaintance, for my long and continued absence from home made me a comparative stranger under my own roof. One great source of pleasure to me was that my wife was delighted with the home I had given her amid the prairies of the far West. Soon after my arrival, my sisters, Nellie and May, came to make us a visit, and a delightful time we had during their stay. When they left us I accompanied them to their home in Denver, Colorado, where I passed several days visiting old friends and scenes. Proceeding thence to Ogallala I purchased from Bill Phant, an extensive cattle drover from Texas, a herd of cattle, which I drove to my ranch on the Dismal River, after which I bade my partner and the boys good-bye, and started for the Indian Territory to procure Indians for my Dramatic Combination for the season of 1878–79.

Putting Real Indians on the Stage

Having secured my Indian actors, and along with them Mr. C. A. Burgess, a government interpreter, and Ed. A. Burgess, known as the "Boy Chief of the Pawnees," I started for Baltimore, where I organized my combination, and which was the largest troupe I had had yet on the road, opening in that city at the Opera House, under the management of Hon. John T. Ford, and then started on a southern tour, playing in Washington, Richmond and as far south as Savannah, Georgia, where we were brought to a sudden halt, owing to the yellow fever which was then cruelly raging in the beautiful cities of the "Land of the cotton and the cane."

The Wild West
in England

THE WILD WEST IN ENGLAND

 When the season of 1882–83 closed I found myself richer by several thousand dollars than I had ever been before, having done a splendid business at every place where my performance was given in that year. Immense success and comparative wealth, attained in the profession of showman, stimulated me to greater exertion and largely increased my ambition for public favor.

Accordingly, I conceived the idea of organizing a large company of Indians, cow-boys, Mexican vaqueros, famous riders and expert lasso throwers, with accessories of stage coach, emigrant wagons, bucking horses and a herd of buffaloes, with which to give a realistic entertainment of wild life on the plains. To accomplish this purpose, which in many respects was a really herculean undertaking, I sent agents to various points in the far West to engage Indians from several different tribes, and then set about the more difficult enterprise of capturing a herd of buffaloes. After several months of patient work I secured the services of nearly fifty cow-boys and Mexicans skilled in lasso-throwing and famous as daring riders, but when these were engaged, and several buffaloes, elk and mountain sheep were obtained, I found all the difficulties had not yet been overcome, for such exhibitions as I had prepared to give could only be shown in large open-air enclosures, and these were not always to be rented, while those that I found suitable were often inaccessible by such popular conveyances as street cars. The expenses of such a show as I had determined to give were so great that a very large crowd must be drawn to every exhibition or a financial failure would be certain; hence I soon found that my ambitious conception, instead of bringing me fortune, was more likely to end in disaster. But having gone so far in the matter I determined to see the end whatever it might be.

In the spring of 1883 (May 17th) I opened the Wild West Show at the fair grounds in Omaha, and played to very large crowds, the weather fortunately proving propitious. We played our next engagement at Springfield, Ill., and thence in all the large cities, to the seaboard. The enterprise was not a complete financial success during the first season, though everywhere our performances were attended by immense audiences.

Nate Salsbury Joins Me as a Partner

Though I had made no money at the end of the first year, the profit came to me in the way of valuable experience and I was in no wise discouraged. Flattering offers were made me by circus organizations to go on the road as an adjunct to their exhibitions, but I refused them all, determined to win success with my prairie Wild West Show or go down in complete failure. The very large patronage I received during my first season convinced me that if I could form a partnership with some one capable of attending to the management and business details that the enterprise would prove a magnificent success, a belief which I am glad to say was speedily realized.

My career on the stage threw me in contact with a great many leading stars, and I came to have an acquaintanceship with nearly all my contemporary American actors. Among those with whom I became most intimate was Nate Salsbury, a comedian whose equal I do not believe graces the stage of either America or England to-day. Aside from his popularity and wealth, acquired in legitimate comedy, I knew him to be a reliable friend, and withal endowed with a rare business sagacity that gave him the reputation of being one of the very best, as well as successful, managers in the show business. Knowing his character as such, I approached him with a proposition to join me as an equal partner, in putting the Wild West entertainment again on the road. The result of my overtures was the formation of a partnership that still continues, and under the new management and partnership of Cody & Salsbury, the Wild West has won all its glory.

NATE SALSBURY

The reader will pardon a digression from the general scope of this autobiography for the probably more interesting, though all too brief, allusion to the career of my esteemed partner, who has won success in life by struggles quite as difficult and trying as any through which I have passed.

Nate (Nathan) Salsbury was born in Freeport, Ill., in 1846, when his parents were in such humble circumstances that his early training was all in the direction of "digging sand and sawing wood." As there was little to bind his affections to the home of his nativity, when the war broke out Nate joined the Fifteenth Illinois, with which he remained, as a private in the ranks, sixteen months. In 1863 he again enlisted and participated in a dozen battles and was wounded three times. His career as an active participant was terminated by his capture and incarceration in Andersonville prison, where he remained subjected to all the horrors of that dreadful pen for a period of seven months. Being at length exchanged he returned home and entered the law office of Judge Beck, now Chief Justice of Colorado, with the idea of becoming a lawyer. A few months of office study and attendance at commercial school only served to impress him with the idea that the profession would still have a fairly large membership even though his name were not added to the list. Abandoning his former expectations he went to school for a time and in the class exhibitions and amateur theatricals of his town developed a desire to go on the stage.

The first experience Nate had in search of a crown for his greatest ambition was far from a pleasant one. Having saved up less than a score of dollars he went to Grand Rapids, Mich., and there made application of the Opera House managers, Johnson, Oates & Hayden, for a situation. Mr. Oates asked him his line of business to which Nate modestly replied, "Oh, anything." "Well," said Oates, "what salary do you expect?" "Oh, anything," was the equally prompt response. Seeing that the applicant had evidently not yet passed the threshold of the profession. Oates said to him, in an indifferent manner, "I will give you twelve dollars a week and you'll be d——d lucky if you get a cent." He didn't; but he entered the profession, which was the next best thing.

From Grand Rapids Nate went to Detroit, where he remained three months without advancing himself either financially or professionally. Somewhat discouraged he returned to his Illinois home, but only to stay a few months, when his restless ambition prompted him to try his fortune in the East. Accordingly he went to Baltimore, and thence to Boston, where he secured a situation at the Boston Museum with a salary of twelve dollars per week. Here his talent was soon discovered by the management, who raised his salary to twenty-eight dollars per week. Others also saw the budding genius of Nate and after playing a season at the Museum he accepted the position of leading heavy man at Hooley's theater in Chicago.

His progress thenceforward was rapid, as his popularity grew apace and his salary rose with every new engagement. But there was too much originality in the man to permit of him remaining a member of a stock company, so at the conclusion of his second season at Hooley's he conceived and constructed a comedy entertainment, with eight people in the cast, to which he gave the title of "The Troubadours." For twelve years this organization, as originally formed, with very slight changes, continued on the road and played repeatedly in all the largest cities with splendid success.

SITTING BULL

Following "The Troubadours," Nate wrote another comedy, called "Patchwork," which had a run of eighteen months, and then he brought out his most successful comedy, "The Brook," which he wrote entire in eight hours, and at a single sitting. This piece he played continuously for five years, making a large amount of money and pleasing millions of people, until he joined me and took the active management of the Wild West Show, which compelled him to withdraw from the stage.

A Bigger Show Put On the Road

Immediately upon forming a partnership with Salsbury we set about increasing the company and preparing to greatly enlarge the exhibition. Nearly one hundred Indians, from several tribes, were engaged, among the number being the world famous Chief Sitting Bull, and several other Sioux that had distinguished themselves in the Custer massacre. Besides these we secured the services of many noted plainsmen, such as Buck Taylor, the great rider, lasso thrower and King of the Cowboys; Utah Frank; John Nelson, and a score of other well-known characters. We also captured a herd of elk, a dozen buffaloes and some bears with which to illustrate the chase.

The Show Is Dumped into the Mississippi

Our vastly enlarged and reorganized company gave daily exhibitions in all the large cities to enormous crowds during the summer of 1884, and in the fall we started for New Orleans to spend the winter exhibiting at the Exposition Grounds. We accordingly chartered a steamer to transport our property and troupe to the Crescent City. Nothing of moment transpired on the trip until we were a few miles above Memphis, when our boat collided with another and was so badly damaged that she sank in less than an hour. In this accident we lost all our personal effects, including wagons, camp equipage, arms, ammunition, donkeys, buffaloes and one elk. We managed, however, to save our horses, Deadwood coach, band wagon, and—ourselves. The loss thus entailed was about $20,000.

As soon as I could reach Memphis with the remnant I sent a telegram to Salsbury, who was with the Troubadours at Denver, as follows: "Outfit at bottom of the river, what do you advise?" As I learned afterwards, Salsbury was just on the point of going upon the stage to sing a song when my rueful telegram was handed him. The news hit him hard, but in no wise disconcerted him; stepping to the speaking tube connecting with the orchestra he shouted to the leader, "Play that symphony again and a little louder, I want to think a minute." As the music struck up he wrote out the following message: "Go to New Orleans, reorganize and open on your date," which I received and promptly complied with his instructions.

In eight days I had added to the nucleus that had been saved a herd of buffalo and elk, and all the necessary wagons and other properties, completing the equipment so thoroughly that the show in many respects was better prepared than at the time of the accident—and we opened on our date.

A Season in New York

The New Orleans exposition did not prove the success that many of its promoters anticipated and the expectations of Mr. Salsbury and myself were alike disappointed, for at the end of the winter we counted our losses at about $60,000.

The following summer we played at Staten Island, on the magnificent grounds of Mr. Erastus Wiman, and met with such splendid success that our losses at New Orleans were speedily retrieved. So well satisfied were we with New York that we leased Madison Square Garden for the winter of 1886–87 and gave our exhibition there for the first time in a covered space. We gave two performances every day during the entire winter and nearly always played to crowded houses, though the seating capacity of the place was about 15,000.

An Ambitious but Hazardous Undertaking

The immortal bard has well said, "ambition grows with what it feeds on." So with Salsbury and I, our unexampled success throughout America with the Wild West show excited our ambition to conquer other nations than our own. Though the idea of transplanting our exhibition, for a time, to England had frequently occurred to us, the importance of such an undertaking was enlarged and brought us to a more favorable consideration of the project by repeated suggestions from prominent persons of America, and particularly by urgent invitations extended by distinguished Englishmen. While inclined to the enterprise we gave much thought to the enormous expense involved in such a step and might not have decided so soon to try the rather hazardous experiment but for an opportunity that promised to largely increase our chances of success.

Several leading gentlemen of the United States conceived the idea of holding an American Exhibition in the heart of London and to this end a company was organized that pushed the project to a successful issue, aided as they were by several prominent residents of the English capital. When the enterprise had progressed so far as to give flattering promise of an opening at the time fixed upon, a proposition was made to Mr. Salsbury and myself, by the president and directors of the company, to take our

RED SHIRT KILLNG HIS RIVAL

show to London and play the season of six months as an adjunct of the American Exhibition, the proposition being a percentage of the gate receipts.

After a mature consideration of the offer we accepted it and immediately set about enlarging our organization and preparing for a departure for England.

A great deal of preliminary work was necessary, but we set manfully about the task of securing the services of a hundred Indians, representative types of the Sioux, Cheyenne, Kiowa, Pawnee and Ogalallas tribes, and succeeded in getting the required number, none of whom had ever been off their reservations prior to joining my show. Among the prominent chiefs thus engaged was Red Shirt, a redoubtable warrior and second only in influence to Sitting Bull himself. A short while before his engagement with us he had quelled an uprising among his people, instigated by a pretender to the chieftainship of the tribe, by invading the pretender's camp with only two of his followers and shooting the leader dead before the eyes of his affrighted wife. This fearless act had served to elevate him very much in the eyes of his people, who thereafter accepted him as a leader. When, therefore, he decided to join the Wild West show, under the flattering offers I made him, his influence aided us very much in procuring our complement of Indians, not only from his own tribe, but from others as well.

Seeking New Worlds to Conquer

Our arrangements having at length been completed, by collecting together a company of more than two hundred men and animals, consisting of Indians, cowboys (including the celebrated Cowboy band), Mexican wild riders, celebrated rifle shots, buffaloes, Texas steers, burros, bronchos, racing horses, elk, bears, and an immense amount of camp paraphernalia, such as tents, wagons, stage coach, etc., we chartered the steamship *State of Nebraska*, of the State line, Capt. Braes, and were ready to set sail to a country that I had long wished to visit—the Motherland. Accordingly, on Thursday, March 31st, 1887, we set sail from New York, the piers crowded with thousands of our good friends who came down to wave their adieux and to wish us a pleasant voyage. Our departure was an occasion I shall never forget, for as the ship drew away from the pier such cheers went up as I never before heard, while our Cowboy band played "The Girl I left Behind Me" in a manner that suggested more reality than empty sentiment in the familiar air. Salsbury and I, and my daughter Arta, waved our hats in sad farewells and stood upon the deck watching the still cheering crowd until they faded in the distance, and we were out upon the deep, for the first time in my life.

The Indians' Fears Are Excited

Before starting on the trip several of the Indians expressed grave fears that if they trusted themselves to the great waters a horrible death would soon overtake them, and at the last moment it required all our arts of persuasion to induce them to go on board.

OUR DEPARTURE FOR ENGLAND

Red Shirt explained that these fears were caused by a belief prevalent among many tribes of Indians, that if a red man attempted to cross the ocean, soon after beginning his journey he would be seized of a malady that would first prostrate the victim and then slowly consume his flesh, day after day, until at length the very skin itself would drop from his bones, leaving nothing but the skeleton and this even could never find burial. This gruesome belief was repeated by chiefs of the several tribes to the Indians who had joined me, so that there is little reason for wonder, that with all our assurances, the poor unlearned children of a nature run riot by neglect, should hesitate to submit themselves to such an experiment.

On the day following our departure from New York the Indians began to grow weary and their stomachs, like my own, became both treacherous and rebellious. Their fears were now so greatly intensified that even Red Shirt, the bravest of his people, looked anxiously towards the hereafter, and began to feel his flesh to see if it were really diminishing. The seal of hopelessness stamped upon the faces of the Indians aroused my pity, and though sick as a cow with hollow-horn myself, I used my utmost endeavors to cheer them up and relieve their forebodings. But for two days nearly the whole company was too sick for any other active service than feeding the fishes, in which I am not proud to say that I performed more than an ordinary share. On the third day, however, we all began to mend so far that I called the Indians together in the main saloon and gave them a Sunday address, as did also Red Shirt, who was now recovered from his anxiety about the future.

After the third day at sea we had an entertainment every afternoon, in which Mr. Salsbury, as singer and comedian, took the leading part, to the intense delight of all on board. On the seventh day a storm came up that raged so fiercely that for a time the ship had to lay to, and during which our stock suffered greatly, but we gave them such good care, and had such excellent luck as well, that none of our animals, save one horse, died on the trip.

"Off Gravesend"

At last as we cast anchor off Gravesend a tug boat approaching attracted the entire company on deck, for we were expecting to meet our advance manager, Jno. M. Burke, with general instructions as to our landing, etc. It turned out, however, to be a government boat loaded with custom-house and quarantine officials, under whom we were to pass the usual inspection. Another official accompanied them, with whom arrangements had been made for the passage of our arms, as a restriction was placed upon the landing of our ammunition, of which we had brought a large quantity, the English government regulations requiring that it be unloaded and turned over to the arsenal authorities, in whose charge it was kept during our stay in London, we drawing on them daily for our supply as needed. I feel in duty bound to acknowledge here that the English government, through its different officials, extended to us every kind of courtesy, privileges and general facilities that materially assisted in rendering pleasant the last few hours of a remarkable voyage. The bovines and buffalo that were a part of our outfit were inspected, and a special permit granted us to take them to the Albert dock, the place of our debarkation, and after holding them in quarantine there for a few days they were allowed to join us in camp.

Recent disastrous outbreaks of rinderpest, foot and mouth disease, and other ills that bovine flesh is heir to, necessitate the law being very strict as regards importation of cattle, all foreign beasts being required to be killed within twenty-four hours after their arrival.

Some Anxious Reflections

During this delay time was given me for reflection and gradually as my eyes wandered over the crowded waterway with its myriads of crafts of every description, from the quaint channel fishing-boat to the mammoth East India trader and ocean steamers, topped by the flags of all nations and hailing from every accessible part of the known world, carrying the productions of every clime and laden with every commodity, I thought of the magnitude of the enterprise I was engaged in and wondered what its results would be.

The freight I had brought with me across the broad Atlantic was such a strange and curious one that I naturally wondered whether, after all the trouble, time and expense it had cost me, this pioneer cargo of Nebraska goods would be marketable. In fact, it would take a much more facile pen than mine to portray the thick crowding thoughts that scurried through my brain. Standing on the deck of a ship, called the *State of Nebraska*, whose arrival had evidently been watched for with great curiosity, as the number of yachts, tug boats and other crafts which surrounded us attested, my memory wandered back to the days of my youth, when in search of the necessaries of existence and braving the dangers of the then vast wild plains, a section of which comprised the then unsettled territory of Nebraska. I contrasted that epoch of my life, its lonely duties and its hardships, and all its complex history, as the home and battle-ground of a savage foe, with its present great prosperity and its standing as the empire State of the central West. A certain feeling of pride came over me when I thought of the good ship on whose deck I stood, and that her cargo consisted of early pioneers and rude, rough riders from that section, and of the wild horses of the same district, buffalo, deer, elk and antelope—the king game of the prairie—together with over one hundred representatives of that savage foe that had been compelled to submit to a conquering civilization and were now accompanying me in friendship, loyalty and peace, five thousand miles from their homes, braving the dangers of the to them great unknown sea, now no longer a tradition, but a reality—all of us combined in an exhibition intended to prove to the center of old world civilization that the vast region of the United States was finally and effectively settled by the English-speaking race.

Our Reception in England

This train of thought was interrupted by the sight of a tug with the starry banner flying from her peak bearing down upon us, and a tumultuous waving of handkerchiefs on board, evoking shouts and cheers from all our company.

As the tug came nearer, strains of "The Star Spangled Banner," rendered by a band on her deck, fell upon our ears, and immediately our own Cowboy band responded with "Yankee Doodle," creating a general tumult on our ship as the word was passed from bow to stern that friends were near. Once alongside, the company on board the tug proved to be the directors of the American Exhibition, with Lord Ronald Gower heading a distinguished committee accompanied by Maj. Burke and representatives of the leading journals, who made us feel at last that our sea voyage was ended.

First Impressions of London

After the usual introductions, greetings and reception of instructions, I accompanied the committee on shore at Gravesend, where quite an ovation was given us amid cries of "Welcome to old England" and "three cheers for Bill," which gave pleasing evidence of the public interest that had been awakened in our coming.

A special train of saloon carriages was waiting to convey us to London and we soon left the quaint old Kentish town behind us, and in an hour we arrived at Victoria station. The high road-bed of the railroad, which runs level with the chimney tops, was a novel sight, as we scurried along through what seemed to be an endless sea of habitation, and I have scarcely yet found out where Gravesend finishes and London commences, so dense is the population of the suburbs off the "boss village" of the British Isles, and so numerous the small towns through which we passed. The impression created by the grand Victoria station, by the underground railroad, the strange sights and busy scenes of the "West End," the hustle and the bustle of a first evening view of mighty London, would alone make a chapter.

My first opinion of the streets was that they were sufficiently lively and noisy to have alarmed all the dogs in every Indian village in the Platte country, from the Missouri River to the headwaters of the Platte, in its most primitive days.

A short trip on the somewhat dark and sulfurous underground railroad brought us to West Kensington, a quiet section of the West End, the station of which had been already connected by special bridges, then nearly completed, with the grounds as yet unknown to London, but destined to become the scene of several months' continuous triumphs. Entering the headquarters of the exhibition we found a bounteous repast set and a generous welcome accorded as. The heartiness of my reception, combined with the natural sense of relief after such a journey and the general indications of success, proved a happy relaxation of the nervous strain to which I had been subjected for several weeks. Speeches, toasts and well wishes, etc., accompanied the spirited and spirituous celebration of the occasion. My genial hosts' capacity for the liquid refreshments would have made me envy them in the '60s, and led me to suspect that there might be accomplishments in England in which even western pioneers are excelled.

Preparing the Exhibition Grounds

After brief social converse, and a tranquilizing smoke, we made a casual visit to the grounds, where the preparations for the stabling, the arena and the grand stand, with busy hundreds of workmen hastening their completions by night by the aid of *lucigen* lights and bon-fires, presented an animated scene, and a display of energy rarely witnessed in connection with an amusement enterprise. These operations were dealing with the expenditure of $125,000, including the fencing in of an arena more than a third of a mile in circumference, flanked by a grand stand filled with seats and boxes, estimated to accommodate 20,000 persons. Sheltered stands for 10,000 more were also being erected; it being understood that room for 40,000 spectators in all should be provided at each performance. For the Indian encampment a large hill had been thrown up by spare labor, and this was already decorated by a grove of newly planted trees. The stables for horses, mules and mustangs, and the corrals for buffaloes, antelope, elk, etc., were all in simultaneous course of construction. Everything so far impressed me very favorably and I began to feel that if we did not command success we would, with our advantages of location, surroundings and novelty and realism, at least deserve it.

The interest evinced by the British workmen in my presence detracting somewhat from their attention to business, caused us to retire after a brief inspection. This same curiosity however was as a straw indicating which way the wind blew. I was now, for the first time, introduced in its own habitat to that world-famed vehicle, the London hansom cab. In one of them I was whirled through the West End, past the famous Hyde Park, through Piccadilly, around Leicester and Trafalgar Squares, to that central resort and theatrical hub of this vast community, the Strand. This narrow street, in its relation to the great city, reminded me of one of the contracted passes in the "Rockies," to which traffic had been naturally attracted, and usage had made a necessity. The density of its foot traffic, the thronging herd of omnibuses, the twisting, wriggling, shouting, whip-cracking cabbies, seemed like Broadway squeezed narrower, and I realized at once the utility and necessity of the two-wheeled curio in which I was whirled through the bewildering mingle of Strand traffic. With but one or two hub-bumps we were soon landed at the magnificent hotel Metropole, in Northumberland avenue, where I met many American gentlemen from different cities, who recognized me on sight and gave me hearty greeting. I retired early, determined to retrace my steps to Gravesend at daylight and ascend the Thames on board the *Nebraska* as my great anxiety was the successful debarkation.

Steaming up the Thames

Steaming up on an early tide, which at its flood I now felt certain would lead on to fortune, and with flags flying, we entered amid a perfect ovation the great port of London. The short trip made on that bright morning was one of great pleasure to all on board. The ship's officers pointed out the many sites of historical interest, as we steamed past them, such as the Old Tillbury Fort, facing Gravesend, erected by Henry the Eighth, and memorable as the place where Queen Elizabeth reviewed her troops after the destruction of the Spanish Armada. Woolwich and its mighty arsenals and gun factories; Greenwich with its grand old Naval College, now used as a free hospital for *sick seamen of all nations*, in front of which stands the obelisk erected to the dauntless explorer, Billot, at the back of it the emerald hills of the Old Park, topped by the observatory which supplies the correct time—all of these engaged our attention in turn. As we moved slowly up the tideway, the huge fleets of seagoing vessels became more crowded; forests of masts and spars stretching away seemingly in illimitable perspective, while on our starboard side the extensive docks in an endless series spoke of the majesty of commerce and the overflowing glories of what Englishmen only call "The Port of London." This magnificent revelation reminded me of a remark made by an English gentleman on the street, who said, "we may not be very large geographically, but we are gigantic commercially."

My attention was especially attracted by a movable crane in the center of one great basin taking up a car containing 20 tons of coal and emptying it in the hole of a ship in a few seconds.

Establishing Our Camp—A Queer Scene

With the assistance of our horsemen, each looking after his own horse, we were unloaded with a rapidity that astonished even the old dock hands and officials. Through the courtesy of the custom-house people, there was hardly a moment's delay in the process of debarkation, but although landed in London, we were still twelve miles from our future camp. So, quickly loading our entire outfit on three trains we were very speedily delivered at the Midland railway depot, almost adjoining our grounds, and by four o'clock that afternoon the horses were in the stables, watered, fed, and bedded, camp equipage and bedding distributed; our own regular camp cooks were hastening a meal; tents were going up, stoves being erected, tables spread and set in the open air; tepees rapidly erected, and by 6 o'clock a perfect canvas city had sprung up in the heart of West-End London. The halliards of the flag staff raised the starry banner to the breeze, and as the Cowboy band rendered our national air a storm of shouts and cheers went up from the thousands that lined the walls, streets and house-tops of the surrounding neighborhoods. This was very gratifying, and in answer to these hearty plaudits we gave them "God Save the Queen," and so The Wild West and Bill Cody, of Nebraska, U. S. A., "was at home in camp in London." The first domestic episode (our camp-meal being necessarily eaten in full view of our kindly neighbors, the large dining tents not yet being up), was as novel to them, from our variegated and motley population of Indians, cowboys, scouts, Mexicans, etc., and eminently practical method of "grubbing," as the supply of fresh beef, mutton, corn-bread, ham, etc., *l'Americaine* was grateful to our seafaring palates. The meal was finished by seven o'clock, and by 9 P.M. the little camp was almost as complete as if it had been there for months, and its tired occupants, men, women and children, were reposing more snugly and peacefully than they had done in many weeks.

American Methods of Doing Business
Excite Favorable Surprise

Trivial as these details may appear at first sight, the rapidity with which we had transported our stuff from dock to depot, and depot to grounds, and made our camp as above related, had an immense effect. The number of notable visitors present, representatives of the press and the well-to-do people of the neighborhood, expressed surprise and astonishment, and communicated the same feeling to the whole of London. It was generally remarked, "By St. George, the Yankees mean business." As we had several days before the opening there were plenty of opportunities given me to receive the many distinguished persons who called, and whom I afterwards found so friendly and hospitable. Mr. Henry Irving, who had witnessed our performance at Staten Island, and who had kindly assisted in the most generous manner to pave the way for our success, was among the first to offer his kindly offices and lent us a strength of public, professional, personal, and social influence that to me was almost invaluable. He had already, long before our arrival, spoken of us in the kindest terms to a representative of the *Era*, the principal dramatic organ of London; and I may here take the liberty of quoting a portion of his highly sympathetic remarks:

Henry Irving's Generous Praise

"I saw an entertainment in New York the like of which I had never seen before, which impressed me immensely. It is coming to London, and will be exhibited somewhere near Earl's Court, on the grounds of the forthcoming American Exhibition. It is an entertainment in which the whole of the most interesting episodes of life on the extreme frontier of civilization in America are represented with the most graphic vividness and scrupulosity of detail. You may form some idea of the scale upon which the scene is played when I say that when I saw it the stage extended over five acres. You have real cowboys, with bucking horses, real buffaloes, and great hordes of cows, which are lassoed and stampeded in the most realistic fashion imaginable. Then there are real Indians, who execute attacks upon coaches driven at full speed. No one can exaggerate the extreme excitement and 'go' of the whole performance. However well it may be rehearsed—and the greatest care is taken that it shall go properly—it is impossible to avoid a considerable share of the impromptu and the unforeseen. For you may rehearse with buffaloes as much as you like, but no one can say in what way they will stampede when they are suddenly turned loose in the open. No one can say how the ox has to be lassoed, or in what way the guns have to be fired when the border fight comes on. The excitement is immense, and I venture to predict that when it comes to London it will take the town by storm."

A writer in the same journal had published the following lively description of our doings at Erastina, Staten Island. I place this article here as an evidence of the good-natured way in which the English press had prepared the public mind for our comings, and a partial explanation of the avidity with which our opening day was looked for:

A Wild West Performance

"In the grove of Erastina, is the Wild West encampment, adjoining the exhibition grounds. It is not unlike a military camp, with its headquarters under canvas, and its grouped tepees savagely ornamented with scalps and feathers. The picturesque Indian

OUR FIRST EVENING PERFORMANCE—BY THE ELECTRIC LIGHT—IN LONDON

children playing under the trees, the uncouth, extemporized comfort and the prevailing air of organization give it a novel interest. There are no restrictions upon visitors, who are allowed to enter the tents, chuck the Indian babies under the chin, watch the squaws at work, and interview the patriarchal chief who sits grim and stoical on his blanket. Of the exhibition on the grounds (and the proprietors will not allow you to call it a performance), especially at night when lit by the electric lights, the wild beauty of it is an entirely new element in our arena sports. When I saw it there were by gate record 12,000 people on the stands, which you will understand is the population of a goodly town. A stentorian voice in front of the grand stand makes the announcements, and as he does so, the bands make their entry from the extreme end of the grounds, dashing up to the stand, a third of a mile, at a whirlwind pace. As an exhibition of equestrianism nothing in the world can equal this. Pawnees, Sioux, Cut Off Band, Ogalallas, cowboys, make this dash in groups, successively, and pull up in a growing array before the stand 200 strong. Such daredevil riding was never seen among Cossacks, Tartars, Arabs. All the picturesque horsemanship of the famous Bedouins sinks to child's play before these reckless Mamelukes of the plains. When the American cowboys sweep like a tornado up the track, forty or fifty strong, every man swinging his hat and every pony at his utmost speed, a roar of wonder and delight breaks from the thousands, and the men reach the grand stand in a cloud, welcomed by a thunderburst. Col. Cody, the far-famed Buffalo Bill, comes last. I don't know that anybody ever described Buffalo Bill on a horse. I am inclined to think nobody can. Ainsworth's description of Dick Turpin's ride stood for many years as the finest thing of its kind, and then young Winthrop in his clever story of 'John Brent' excelled it in his ride to the Suggernell Springs. Either one of these men, given a month and a safe publisher, might have wrought Buffalo Bill upon paper. He is the complete restoration of the Centaur. No one that I ever saw so adequately fulfills to the eye all the conditions of picturesque beauty, absolute grace, and perfect identity with his animal. If an artist or a riding master had wanted to mold a living ideal of romantic equestrianship, containing in outline and action the men of Harry of Navarre, the Americanism of Custer, the automatic majesty of the Indian, and the untutored cussedness of the cowboy, he would have measured Buffalo Bill in the saddle. Motion swings into music with him. He is the only man I ever saw who rides as if he couldn't help it and the sculptor and the soldier had jointly come together in his act. It is well worth a visit to Erastina to see that vast parterre of people break into white handkerchiefs, like a calm sea suddenly whipped to foam, as this man dashes up to the grand stand. How encumbered, and uncouth and wooden are the best of the red braves beside the martial leadership of this long-limbed pale-face! There they are, drawn up in platoon front. No circus can approximate its actuality. Look down the line. Every man has a record of daring, and there, shaking her long hair, is Georgie Duffle, the Colorado girl. A word of command, the line breaks. Away they go with shouts and yells. In an instant the grounds are covered with the vanishing hoofs. Feathers and war-paint glimmer in the mad swirl and they are gone in the distance. It is impossible to escape the thrill of this intense action. The enthusiasm of the multitude goes with them. All the abeyant savagery in the blood and bones comes to the surface, and men and women shout together. An impression prevailed among some of the spectators that these wild bucking horses are trained after the manner of circus horses. Nothing can be further from the truth, as I had occasion to learn after staying at the camp for two or three days and making their acquaintance. They are simply wild horses spoiled in the breaking. There is one black mare they call Dynamite that is, without exception, the wickedest animal I ever saw. You are to understand that when a man attempts to mount her she jumps into the air, and turning a back somersault, falls upon her back with her heels upward. To escape being crushed to death is to employ the marvelous celerity and dexterity that a cowboy alone exhibits. The other day a cowboy undertook to ride this animal. It was necessary for four men to hold her and she had to be blindfolded before he could get on her, and then, letting out a scream like a woman in pain, she made a headlong dash and plunged with all her force into a fence, turning completely over head first and apparently falling upon the rider. A cry of horror rose from the spectators. But the rest of the exhibition went on. Poor Jim was dragged out, bleeding and maimed, and led away. What was the astonishment of the multitude, when the other refractory animals had had their sport, to see Dynamite again led out and the cowboy, limping and pale, came forward to make another attempt to ride her. 'No, no,' cried the spectators, 'take her away.' But the indomitable cowboy only smiled grimly and gave them to understand that in the cowboys' code a man who fails to ride his animal might as well retire from business. It was do or die. For fifteen minutes the fight went on between man and beast. Animal strength against pluck and intelligence. I never saw a multitude brought to such intense interest. It was the gladiatorial contest revived. The infuriated beast shook off the men who held her like insects. She leapt into the air with a scream and fell on her back. She laid down and groveled. But the cowboy got upon her back by some superhuman skill, and then he was master. As he punished the animal mercilessly and swung his hat triumphantly, the concourse of people stood up and cheered long and loud."

Helpful Influence from Distinguished Persons

Not only England's greatest actor living but his old friend the genial Jno. L. Toole, Miss Ellen Terry, Mr. Justin McCarthy, M. P., Minister Phelps, Consul-General Gov. Thos. Waller, Deputy Consul Moffat (to whom we are greatly indebted for assistance rendered us in landing), Mr. Henry Labouchere, Miss Mary Anderson, Mrs. Brown-Potter, Mr. Chas. Wyndham, and in fact all of the prominent members of the theatrical profession, and the literati in general, seemed to take an immense and friendly interest in our enterprise. Lord Ronald Gower, Sir Cundiffe Owen, Lord Henry Pagett, Lord Charles Beresford, the Grand Duke Michael of Russia, who was an early jubilee visitor, Lady Monckton, Sir Francis Knollys, private secretary to the Prince of Wales, Colonel Clark, Colonel Montague, Lady Alice Bective, whom the Indians presently named "The sunshine of the camp," Lord Strathmore, Lord Windsor, Lady Randolph Churchill, Mrs. J. W. Mackay, a host of distinguished American residents of London and hundreds of other prominent personages, visited the camp and stables before the regular opening, and by their expressions of friendship and good-will gave us the greatest encouragement for the future. It thus became increasingly evident to me that we had struck a responsive chord in the heart of all Londoners. The sight of the Indians, cowboys, American girls, and Mexicans living in their primitive simplicity, was very attractive to them, while the innate English love of horsemanship and feats of skill presaged an appreciative community which I must say from the first to last never disappointed us. In fact, it may be said we commenced business with a strong predisposition of all Englishmen to be pleased with us if we gave the public anything at all

WAR DANCES

A LITTLE INTERNATIONAL FLIRTATION — BUCKING PONIES — WHITE FAWN (SIOUX SQUAW) AND PAPOOSE — REARING HORSE — *John Drisdale*

approaching the surprising novelty of brilliant realism they had been led to expect. The press were generous to us to an extent possibly never before known. Its columns were teeming daily with information about us, so eulogistic that I almost feared we would not come up to expectations. Twenty-five scrap books filled to repletion with such notices now adorn my library and as a sample I insert these few, of varied form, to show how the subject of the day was variously treated. The *London Illustrated News* of April 16, in connection with a two page illustration and four columns of descriptive matter, is drawn upon for the following extract:

How the Press Treated Me

"It is certainly a novel idea for one nation to give an Exhibition devoted exclusively to its own frontier history or the story enacted by genuine characters of the dangers and hardships of its settlement upon the soil of another country three thousand miles away. Yet this is exactly what the Americans will do this year in London, and it is an idea worthy of that thorough-going and enterprising people. We frankly and gladly allow that there is a natural and sentimental view of the design which will go far to obtain for it a hearty welcome in England. The progress of the United States, now the largest community of the English race on the face of the earth, though not in political union with Great Britain, yet intimately connected with us by social sympathies, by a common language and literature, by ancestral traditions and many centuries of a common history, by much remaining similarity of civil institutions, laws, morals and manners, by the same forms of religions, by the same attachment to the principles of order and freedom, and by the mutual interchange of benefits in a vast commerce and in the materials and sustenance of their staple industries, is a proper subject of congratulation; for the popular mind, in the United Kingdom, does not regard, and will never be taught to regard, what are styled 'Imperial' interests—those of mere political dominion—as equally valuable with the habits and ideas and domestic life of the aggregate of human families belonging to our own race. The greater numerical "proportion of these, already exceeding sixty millions, are inhabitants of the great American Republic, while the English-speaking subjects of Queen Victoria number a little above forty-five millions, including those in Canada and Australasia and scattered among the colonial dependencies of this realm. It would be unnatural to deny ourselves the indulgence of a just gratification in seeing what men of our own blood, men of our own mind and disposition, in all essential respects, though tempered and sharpened by more stimulating conditions, with some wider opportunities for exertion, have achieved, in raising a wonderful fabric of modern civilization, and bringing it to the highest prosperity, across the whole breadth of the Western Continent, from the Atlantic to the Pacific Ocean. We feel sure that this sentiment will prevail in the hearts of hundreds of thousands of visitors to Buffalo Bill's American camp, about to be opened at the West End of London; and we take it kindly of the great kindred people of the United States, that they now send such a magnificent representation to the Motherland, determined to take some part in celebrating the Jubilee of her Majesty the Queen, who is the political representative of the people of Great Britain and Ireland."

The tone of this article strikes the same chord, I may say, as the whole of the comments of the English press. It divested the Wild West of its attributes as an entertainment simply, and treated our visit as an event of first class international importance, and a link between the affections of the two kindred nations, such as had never before been forged. Following it came a very flattering description of the site of our operations:

"A large covered bridge, crossing the railway, leads eastward to the grounds near Earl's Court Station, where will be located 'Buffalo Bill's' Wild West Exhibition. The preparations for the reception of this unique entertainment have been very extensive; they were made under the supervision of Major J. M.. Burke, the general manager of the 'Wild West.' The track is over one-third of a mile in circumference, and within this is the arena. It is flanked by a grand stand filled with seats and boxes, which will accommodate twenty thousand persons. Standing room under shelter is provided for over ten thousand more, and this, with the spectators in the open, will give a good view of the entertainment to about forty thousand people. A large hill has been thrown up of earth and rocks; and on this, amidst a grove of newly-planted trees, will

SCENES IN THE WILD WEST SHOW

be the encampment of the Indians, the 'cowboys,' and scouts. At the other side of the grounds are extensive stables for the broncho horses and mules, and a corral for the buffaloes, antelopes, elk, and other wild animals. This remarkable exhibition, the 'Wild West,' has created a furor in America, and the reason is easy to understand. It is not a circus, nor indeed is it acting at all, in a theatrical sense; but an exact reproduction of daily scenes in frontier life, as experienced and enacted by the very people who now form the 'Wild West' company. It comprises Indian life, 'cowboy life,' Indian fighting, and burning Indian villages, lassoing and breaking in wild horses, shooting, feats of strength, and border athletic games and sports. It could only be possible for such a remarkable undertaking to be carried out by a remarkable man: and the Hon. W. F. Cody, known as 'Buffalo Bill,' guide, scout, hunter, trapper, Indian fighter, and legislator, *is* a remarkable man. He is a perfect horseman, an unerring shot, a man of magnificent presence and physique, ignorant of the meaning of fear or fatigue; his life is a history of hairbreadth escapes, and deeds of daring, generosity, and self-sacrifice, which compare very favorably with the chivalric actions of romance, and he has been not inappropriately designated the 'Bayard of the Plains.' "

It may seem a little egotistical to present this last sentence to the reader's notice, but as I am free to confess pleasure at the generous allusion to my country and myself, I feel the reader will forgive me, if the result to him or her should be the sinking of any fragment of thoughtless prejudice and the building up of a feeling of reciprocal appreciation. Personally, I feel of course, that I was simply the accidental opportunity for the expression of latent kindly feeling from the sons of our ancestors—political countrymen. The journals seemed to vie with each other in varied expressions of cordial welcome, which took the form of lengthy eulogy, pictorial and editorial description, comic and poetic effusions, as *vide* the following excerpts. Here speaks the *Referee*:

The Poetic Muse Is Evoked

Buffalo Bill

South Kensington's lustre is waning,
   The Westminster fun's getting stale;
The star of the Battenbergs' setting,
   The Parnellite comet grows pale.
The Crawford-Dilke scandal's forgotten.
   The Law Court sensations are nil;
Society needs a new tonic,—
   So come along, Buffalo Bill

We hear that the cowboys are wonders.
   And do what no rough-rider dare.
So wherever the "pitch" is in London
   Its wild horses *will* drag us there.
O, fancy the scene of excitement!
   O, fancy five acres of thrill,
The cowboys and Injuns and horses
   And the far-famed Buffalo Bill!

They say he's a darling, a hero,
   A truly magnificent man,
With hair that falls over his shoulders,
   And a face that's a picture to scan;
And then he's so strong and so daring,
   Yet gentle and nice with it still—
Only fancy if all the young ladies
   Go mashed upon Buffalo Bill!

The world is a wearisome desert.
   The life that we live is a bore;
The cheek of the apple is rosy.
   But the canker-worm hides in the core.
Our hearts have a void that is aching —
   That void, then, O, hasten to fill
With your mustangs and Injuns and
   cowboys
   And yourself, O great Buffalo Bill!

Punch appeared with your humble servant pictured as a centaur, with bull-whip and revolver, and the annexed stanzas:

The Coming Centaur

Midst cheering tremendous,
O'er valley and hill—
A marvel stupendous
Of courage and skill—
He's quickly advancing,
With singing and dancing
That Centaur Heroic called Buffalo Bill.

With horsemanship daring
Our sight will be blest;
All the town will be staring
At sports of the West.
His American cowboys
Will kick up a row boys,
Such as London will witness with
rapturous zest.

Soon he'll cross the Atlantic,
In quest of new game.
With horses half frantic
And riders the same:
A novel sensation
He'll make in this nation—
So cheers half a hundred for Buffalo Bill!

This Centaur Heroic
Would gladden a Stoic,
So droll is his humor, so curious his skill.
We'll got something sunny
And fresh for our money—
Hip! hip! hip! hooray! then, for Buffalo Bill.

Visit of Mr. Gladstone—Private View by the Grand Old Man

We were yet in the throes of our extensive preparations, and the backward English spring was getting in its work with a saddening, soddering supply of surplus fresh water, when I received intimation that the ex-Premier, the Right Hon. W. E. Gladstone, M. P., intended to honor the Wild West with a preliminary call. This visit was fixed for the 25th of April, and although worried almost to death with the exertions connected with "rounding up," I determined to make the veteran states-man's call as pleasant as possible, although, as the track was not completed, a full show could not be given. Shortly after one o'clock P.M. he arrived at Earl's Court with Mrs. Gladstone, and entered the grounds in company with the Marquis of Lorne (husband of the Princess Louise), attended by Lord Ronald Gower, Mr. Waller (Consul General of the United States), and a distinguished party, escorted by Nate Salsbury. The Cowboy band welcomed the visitors with the strains of "Yankee

Doodle," and I presently had the pleasure of shaking hands with and introducing Mr. and Mrs. Gladstone to the denizens of our encampment. The fine old statesman, looking like intellect personified, glanced around him with an amused expression as the savage Indians came flocking out with their characteristic cries of "ugh, ugh" and engaged at once in conversation with Red Shirt. I explained to the gallant Sioux warrior that Mr. Gladstone was one of the great white chiefs of England, and they were soon on excellent terms. The ex-Premier puzzled him exceedingly, however, by inquiring, through our interpreter, if he thought the Englishman looked enough like the Americans to make him think they were kinsmen and brothers. Red Shirt set us all laughing by replying that "he wasn't quite sure about that." It was clear that the red man hadn't studied the art of compliment to any great extent, but the incident passed off good humoredly enough and the party left the camp for the grand stand. Their astonishment, when the Indians in full war paint, riding their swift horses, dashed into the arena from an ambuscade, knew do bounds, and the enthusiasm grew, as placing myself at the head of the whole body, I wheeled them into line for a general salute. Then the lasso, our feats of shooting, and the bucking horses were introduced, and it was a real treat to see the evergreen ex-Premier enjoying himself like a veritable schoolboy, as the American cowboys tackled the incorrigible bucking horses, sometimes cheering the animal, sometimes the man. At the finish he assured me he could have conceived nothing more interesting or amusing. A luncheon followed in the exhibition building at which I sat beside Mrs. Gladstone. The Grand Old Man spoke in warm and affecting terms of the instrumental good work we had come to do. He proposed "success to the Wild West Show" in a brilliant little speech which aroused the enthusiasm of all present. He was highly complimentary to America and dwelt upon the great deeds of its western pioneers in a glowing peroration, and on subsequent occasions, when we met, his demeanor was such that I could quite understand the fascination he exercises over the masses of his countrymen. His is a singularly attractive personality and his voice is either a balm to comfort or a living sword, two-edged and fire tipped, for the oratorical combat as occasion may demand. Consul-General Thos. Waller responded effusively and I began to feel that I was really becoming a factor, in my humble way, in the great task of cementing an international good feeling.

A Hard-Worked Lion of the Season

Then commenced a long series of invitations to breakfasts, dinners, luncheons, and midnight lay-outs, garden parties and all the other attentions by which London society delights to honor what it is pleased to call the distinguished foreigner. I began to

SCENES IN THE AMPHITHEATER

feel that life is indeed sometimes too short to contain all the gayety that people would fain compress into its narrow limits. A reference to my diary shows that amongst other receptions I visited and was made an honorary member of most of the best clubs. Notably the Reform Club, where I met the Prince of Wales, the Duke of Cambridge, and a coterie of prominent gentlemen. Then came a civic lunch at the Mansion House with the Lord Mayor and Lady Mayoress; a dinner at the Beaufort Club, where that fine sportsman, the Duke of Beaufort, took the chair; and a memorable evening at the Savage Club, with Mr. Wilson Barrett (just back from America) presiding, and an attendance comprising such great spirits as Mr. Henry Irving, John L. Toole, and all that is great in literary, artistic and histrionic London; at the United Arts Club I was entertained by the Duke of Teck; and at the St. George's Club, by Lord Bruce, Lord Woolmex, Lord Lymington, Mr. Christopher Sykes, Mr. Herbert Gladstone and others; subsequently I dined at Mr. Irving's, Lady McGregor's, Lady Tenterden's, Mrs. Chas. Matthews (widow of the great actor), Mrs. J. W. Mackay's, Lord Randolph and

Lady Churchill's, Edmund Yates's, and at Great Marlow; also with Mrs. Courtland Palmer, U. S. Minister Phelps, and again at the Savage Club with Gov. Thos. Waller. Then came invites from Mrs. J. Tandell Phillips, the Hon. Cecil and Mrs. Donovan, Mr. and Mrs. Brandon; from Chas. Wyndham, at the Criterion; from Mr. Lawson, of the *Daily Telegraph,* to meet the Duke of Cambridge. I was dined also at Lady Monckton's, Mr. and Mrs. Oscar Wilde's; the Burlingham Club, Mme. Minnie Hauk de Wartegg's, Lady Ardelsun's, Miss Mary Anderson's, an enthusiastic Wild Wester, Emma Nevada Palmer's, and at Mrs. Brown Potter's, who was very active in personal interest. I visited Mr. Henry Labouchere on the occasion when Mr. and Mrs. Labouchere gave their grand garden production of "A Midsummer Night's Dream." Then I remember riding in great style with Lord Chas. Beresford in the Coaching Club parade in Hyde Park, and received an invitation to a mount with the Hon. Artillery Co. of London (the oldest volunteer in the kingdom), in the parade in honor of Her Majesty's the Queen's birthday. This last, business prevented my accepting. These are but a few among the many social courtesies extended to me, all of which I shall forever appreciate and remember with the greatest pleasure. But I must say that, considering my pre-occupation with our preliminary arrangements, and the social demands made upon my time, it is now a wonder to myself how I succeeded in forming so good an exhibition at the opening day. It should be remembered that the Indians were all new from the Pine Ridge Agency, and had never seen the exhibition, and that a hundred of the ponies came direct from the plains of Texas and had never been ridden or shot over.

Visit of the Prince and Princess of Wales

Amidst all of this fashionable hurly-burly, I was extremely gratified to receive the following letter:

> Marlborough House,
> Pall Mall, S. W., 26 April, 1887
>
> DEAR SIR: I am desired by the Prince of Wales to thank you for your invitation. His Royal Highness is anxious I should see you with reference to it. Perhaps, therefore, you would kindly make it convenient to call at Marlborough House.
>
> Would it suit you to call at 11:30 or 5 o'clock, either to morrow (Wednesday) or Thursday? I am, dear sir.
>
> Yours faithfully,
> (Signed) FRANCIS KNOLLYS
> Private Secretary

This resulted in an arrangement to give a special performance for H. R. H. the Prince and Princess of Wales, although everything was still incomplete, the track unfinished, spoiled by rainy weather and the hauling on of vast timbers. The ground was in unspeakably bad condition.

The Prince of Wales being busily occupied in arranging matters for the Queen's Jubilee, had but limited latitude as regard to time. But for all this I determined to pull through, as the Wild West always suited me the more raw and wild it was. I retired the night previous to the visit fatigued to be sure, but with a hunter's pleasant reflections after striking a country where water is plenty and grazing good, two circumstances that always bring the weary pioneer renewed confidence and repose.

A Private Entertainment for the Prince of Wales

The entertainment was of course to be an exclusive one, confined entirely to the royal party, as it yet wanted several days to an opening date. I had got the royal box handsomely rigged out with American and English flags, and my object was to make use of the occasion as a further rehearsal of the whole entertainment. The party that was conducted into our precincts was a strong one numerically as well as in point of exalted rank: The Prince and Princess of Wales, with their three daughters, Princesses Louise, Victoria and Maud, led the way; then came the Princess Louise and her husband, the Marquis of Lorne; the Duke of Cambridge; H. S. H. of Teck and his son;

the Comtesse de Paris; the Crown Prince of Denmark; followed by Lady Suffield and Miss Knollys, Lady Cole, Colonel Clarke, Lord Edward Somerset and other high placed attendants on the assembled royalties. The Prince of Wales introduced me to the Princess, and introductions to the other exalted personages followed, in which Nate Salsbury and Major John Burke were included. His Royal Highness is under the medium height and rather inclined to corpulency. In manners mixed with that indescribable high bearing which comes from constant association with state ceremonial, he is just the *beau ideal* of a plain-spoken, pleasant, kindly gentleman. He takes the universal homage as a matter of course; but never acts as though he would exact it. I had the pleasure of meeting him many times subsequently, and found less pride in him than I have experienced in third-rate civic officials elsewhere. Before I left London he presented me with a very handsome diamond copy of his crest—the three ostrich feathers—mounted in gems and gold as a breast-pin. But of that more anon. The Princess of Wales is a quiet, self-possessed, gentle lady, much given to innocent merriment, and still speaking English with a slightly-clipped foreign accent. My knowledge of the state of the arena and the nervous feeling inseparable from a first performance made me anything but comfortable as I conducted my guests in their boxes, and left them in charge of Major Burke and Mr. Frank Richmond, who had the task of explaining the various acts in the performance. However, we were in for it and were bound to pull through, and my fears of a mishap were dispelled from the moment the Prince gave the signal, and the Indians, yelling like fiends, galloped out from their ambuscade and swept round the enclosure like a whirlwind. The effect was instantaneous and electric. The Prince rose from his seat and leaned eagerly over the front of the box, and the whole party seemed thrilled at the spectacle. "Cody," I said to myself, "you have fetched 'em!" From that moment we were right—right from the word "Go." Everybody was in capital form—myself included—and the whole thing went off grandly. Our lady shots, on being presented at the finish, committed the small solecism of offering to shake hands with the Princess; for be it known that feminine royalty offers the hand back uppermost, which the person presented is expected to reverently lift with the finger tips and to salute with the lips. However, the Princess got over the difficulty by taking their proffered hands and shaking them heartily.

Then came an inspection of Indian camp, and a talk between the Prince and Red Shirt. His Royal Highness expressed through the interpreter his great delight at what he had seen, and the Princess personally offered him a welcome to England. "Tell the Great Chief's wife," said Red Shirt with much dignity, "that it gladdens my heart to hear her words of welcome." The Royal party *cottoned* greatly to John Nelson's half-breed papoose, and while the ladies of the suite were petting the baby the Prince honored my headquarters tent with a visit and seemed much interested in

AN INTRODUCTION TO THE PRINCE AND PRINCESS OF WALES

the gold-mounted sword presented to me by the generals of the United States Army with whom I have served in the boisterous years that are never to return.

The Prince of Wales is an earnest sportsman and a bold rider to hounds. That I knew, but I was a little surprised when, in spite of the muddy state of the ground, he and his party determined to make an inspection of the stables where our 200 broncho horses and other animals were quartered. I never felt prouder of the military method that pervades our equine arrangements than during this visit, which was sprung upon me quite as a surprise. All was in apple-pie order and everybody seemed exceedingly pleased. He quite won my heart by demanding the full, true and particular history of Old Charlie, now in his twenty-first year, who carried me through so much arduous work in the plains, and who once bore me over a flight of 100 miles in nine hours and forty minutes when chased by hostile Indians. Charlie may not have felt the compliment, but I appreciated it keenly.

And so at seven o'clock our royal visit and our first full performance in England terminated by the prince presenting the contents of his cigarette case to Red Shirt. The rehearsal had been a triumphant success and we had earned the approval of the first gentleman in the land. It may be imagined how heartily Nate Salsbury, Major Burke, and I congratulated each other on this auspicious issue of a big occasion.

A walk round the principal streets of London at this time would have shown how by anticipation the Wild West had "caught on" to the popular imagination. The windows of the London bookseller were full of editions of Fennimore Cooper's novels, "The Path-Finder," "The Deer Stalker," "The Last of the Mohicans," "Leather Stocking," and in short, all that series of delightful romances which have placed the name of the American novelist on the same level with that of Sir Walter Scott. It was a real revival of trade for the booksellers, who sold thousands of volumes of Cooper where twenty years before they had sold them in dozens. I am convinced—and I say it in no boastful spirit, but as a plain statement of fact—that our visit to England has set the population of the British Islands reading, thinking, and talking about their American kinsmen to an extent before unprecedented. They are beginning to know more of the mighty nation beyond the Atlantic and consequently to esteem us better than at any time within the limits of modern history. I am proud of my small share in this desirable state of things, which will be a source of comfort to me to my dying day.

Our Opening Performance

A glorious change in the weather. Sunny skies and balmy breezes ushered in the morning of May 9, and the stars and stripes fluttered and glittered above us in the warm, soft air as if rejoicing in the good fortune that was to come. The happy omen was realized in the shape of a bumper attendance. The moment the doors were opened there was a great rush of the populace, and our money-takers had all their work cut out, "with both hands," to relieve the bustling perspiring crowd of the harmless necessary shillings that flowed in silver streams into our coffers. It was a thoroughly representative audience, fashionable and otherwise, in which all ranks were included; and if I had felt slightly nervous in the presence of royalty, I experienced a sensation of real stage fright on gazing at the vast sea of faces that confronted us from every available quarter when we made our first bow to the British public. A cutting from an influential London paper may be allowed to describe the scene:

The Wild West Show

"As we took our places in one of the little boxes which edge the arena in the grounds of the American Exhibition where Buffalo Bill's Wild West Show is given, we could not help being struck with the effectiveness of the scene before us. The size of the enclosure was one element of the impressiveness of the *coup d'œil* and this was cleverly increased by the picturesque scenery which enclosed half of the circle. At the edge of the ash-covered circle in the center were drawn up on parade the whole strength of the Wild West company. There were the various tribes of Indians in their war-paint and feathers, the Mexicans, the ladies, and the cowboys, and a fine array they made, with the chiefs of each tribe, the renowned Sergeant Bates, the equally celebrated Buffalo Bill, the stalwart Buck Taylor, and others who were introduced by Mr. Frank Richmond who, from the top of an elevated platform, described the show as it proceeded. The post of lecturer is no sinecure when such a vast area has to be filled by the voice of the speaker; but Mr. Richmond made every sentence distinctly heard, and the interesting information conveyed by him in a mellow and decidedly audible voice was one of the most agreeable features of the performance. Few, perhaps, of the audience would have remembered, without the notification of the lecturer, the history of the pony express, one of the most romantic in the annals of intercommunication, or have enjoyed fully the exposition by one of the leading cow-boys of the way in which the mails were carried. The emigrant train, which next wended its way across the arena with its teams of oxen and mules, its ancient wagons, and their burden of families and household goods, to be attacked by a tribe of redskins, who were soon repulsed by the ever ready cow-boys, was an equally interesting resurrection of a method of peopling the soil practiced even now in the remoter regions of the West, though the redskins, we believe, are pretty well confined nowadays to the Indian territory, and are reduced to, at least, an outward 'friendliness.' The next sensation was created by Miss Lillian Smith, 'the California girl,' whose forte is shooting at a swinging target.

BUCK TAYLOR RIDING AN ERUPTIVE MUSTANG

She complicated her feats by adding all kinds of difficulties to her aim, and her crown-ing achievements of smashing a glass ball made to revolve horizontally at great speed and clearing off ball after ball on the target just mentioned to the number of twenty were really marvelous. The part of the entertainment most novel to Londoners was undoubtedly the riding of the 'bucking' horses. As Mr. Richmond explained, no cru-elty is used to make these animals 'buck.' It is simply 'a way they've got.' The horses are saddled *coram publico*, and the ingenious maneuvers by means of which this is accomplished were extremely interesting to observe. Some escaped altogether from their masters, and had to be pursued and lassoed; others had to be thrown down in order that they might be mounted. When the cowboys were in the saddle came the tug of war. There were various degrees of violence in the leaps and springs of the animals, but the mildest of them would have thrown even a moderately good rider to the ground in a moment. The 'ugliest' of the lot seemed to be that bestridden at the conclusion of this part of the show by Antonio Esquival, but those mounted by Jim Kidd, Buck Taylor, Dick Johnson, Mitchell, and Webb were all 'customers' of the 'awkwardest' description, and showed what a rebellious demon there is in a half-broken horse who has lost his fear of man. There was enmity, savage or sullen, in every attitude and in every movement of these creatures. The bucking horses should be seen by everyone in London who takes an interest in the 'noble animal.' The attack on the Deadwood stage coach, which is a celebrated item of the show, was a very effective spectacle, and in this, as in an attack on a settler's homestead, there was a great amount of powder burnt. Mustang Jack performed the startling feat of clearing a horse sixteen hands high, having previously covered thirteen feet with a standing leap. He is, without doubt, an extraordinary jumper. Buffalo Bill's specialty is shooting whilst riding at full gallop, and he does this to wonderful perfection. He is accompanied by an Indian, bearing a basket full of glass balls, which he throws high into the air, and Mr. Cody smashes each with unerring aim whilst both horses are going at a hard gallop. The buffalo hunt was immensely realistic. There was also some interesting feats, riding by two ladies and several short races between them, and also between Indian boys mounted on mustang ponies. Summing up the Wild West show from an English and theatrical point of view, we should say that it is certain to draw thousands from its remarkably novel nature. We would also suggest for consideration the advantage of the introduction of a little scalping. Why should not the Indians overcome a party of scouts, and 'raise their hair?' Wigs and scalps are not very expensive, and carmine is decidedly cheap. But it will be a long time before public curiosity will be glutted, and until then 'Buffalo Bill' may be content to 'let her rip,' and regard with complacency the golden stream that is flowing with such a mighty current into the treasury of the Wild West Show."

Interest Without Bloody Accessories

The drawback to the exploiting of this ingenious idea is that a display of sham scalping would by no means satisfy gentlemen of this reporter's gory turn of mind. Nothing but a real massacre, with genuine blood flowing and a comfortable array of corpses for view would suffice to glut some people's appetite for a nice, thrilling sensation. Perhaps if the gentleman had ever seen the horrors of actual warfare with red Indians he would not be so zealous for realism. However, he meant well, and his pen was but one amongst the hundreds wielded by English journalists who shed ink in kindly praise of our endeavors to amuse and instruct the London public. Another critic, he of the *Sporting Life*, concludes a whimsical notice in laudatory terms thus:

"The opening of the Wild West Show was one of the most signal successes of recent years. Such a vast concourse of the cream—or it may be as well to say the *crème de la creme*—of society is seldom seen at any performance. The number of chariots waiting at the gates outnumbered those of Pharaoh, and the phalanx of footmen constituted quite a small army. There is much in the Wild West show to please. There is novelty of incident, wonderful tone, color, dexterous horsemanship, and a breezy independence of manner, which latter quality, by the way, is not entirely confined to the *dramatis personæ*. It is new, it is brilliant, it is startling, it will 'go!'"

Visit of Queen Victoria

"By command of Her Majesty, the Queen"—it must be understood, that the Queen never requests, desires, or invites, even her own Prime Minister to her own dinner-table, but "commands" invariably—a special performance was given by the Wild West, the understanding being that Her Majesty and suite would take a private view of the performance. The Queen, ever since the death of her husband, nearly thirty years ago, has cherished an invincible objection to appearing before great assemblages of her subjects. She visits her Parliament seldom; the theaters never. Her latest knowledge of her greatest actors and actresses has been gained from private performances at Windsor, whither they have been "commanded" to entertain her, and that at very infrequent intervals. But as with Mahomet and the mountain, the Wild West was altogether too colossal to take to Windsor, and so the Queen came to the Wild West—an honor of which I was the more deeply sensible on account of its unique and unexampled character. I am bound to say that the whole troupe, myself included, felt highly complimented; the public would hardly believe it, and if bets had been made at the clubs, the odds on a rank outsider in the Derby would have been nothing to the amount that would have been bet that it was a Yankee hoax. Her Majesty would arrive, I was informed, at five o'clock, and would require to see everything in an hour. A soldier is frequently ordered to accomplish the impossible—I had been tolerably used to that sort of thing, and have knocked the impossible stiff and cold on more than one occasion; but this was a poser. We would do our best and acquit ourselves like men and women; and that was all that could be said about it. We erected a dais for Her Majesty and had a box specially constructed, draped with crimson velvet and decorated with orchids, leaving plenty of accommodation for the attendant notables. All was made as bright and cheerful as possible, and these preparations completed we waited, very much in frame of mind like a lot of school boys attending an examination.

Her Majesty Salutes the American Flag

With royal punctuality the sovereign lady and her suite rolled up in their carriages, drove round the arena in state, and dismounted at the entrance to the box. The august company included, besides her Majesty, their Royal Highnesses Prince and Princess Henry of Battenberg, the Marquis of Lore, the Dowager Duchess of Athole and the Hon. Ethel Cadogan, Sir Henry and Lady Ponsonby, General Lynedoch Gardiner, Colonel Sir Henry Ewart, Lord Ronald Gower and a collection of uniformed celebrities and brilliantly attired fair ladies who formed a veritable parterre of living flowers around the temporary throne. During our introduction a very notable incident occurred, sufficient to send the blood surging through every American's veins at Niagara speed. As usual in our entertainment, the American flag, carried by a graceful, well-mounted horseman, was introduced, with the statement that it was

SALUTING HER MAJESTY, QUEEN VICTORIA

"an emblem of peace and friendship to all the world." As the standard-bearer waved the proud emblem above his head, Her Majesty rose from her seat and bowed deeply and impressively towards the banner. The whole court party rose, the ladies bowed, the generals present saluted, and the English noblemen took off their hats. Then—we couldn't help it—but there arose such a genuine heart-stirring American yell from our company as seemed to shake the sky. It was a great event. For the first time in history, since the Declaration of Independence, a sovereign of Great Britain had saluted the star spangled banner, and that banner was carried by a member of Buffalo Bill's Wild West! All present were constrained to feel that here was an outward and visible sign of the extinction of that mutual prejudice, sometimes almost amounting to race hatred, that has severed the two nations from the times of Washington and George the Third to the present day. We felt that the hatchet was buried at last and the Wild West had been at the funeral.

Presented to the Queen

Under the stimulus of the Queen's presence, the performance was admirably given. The whole company seemed infected with a determination to excel themselves. Personally I missed not a single shot; the young ladies excelled themselves in the same line; the charges on the Indians were delivered with a terrific *vim*; and the very bucking horses seemed to buck like steam-engines under the influence of that half minute of excitement. But perhaps this last may have been fancy. Better than all, the Queen not only abandoned her original intention of remaining to see only the first acts, but saw the whole thing through, and wound up with a "command" that Buffalo Bill should be presented to her. Her compliments, deliberate and unmeasured, modesty forbids me to repeat.

A kindly little lady, not five feet in height, but every inch a gracious queen. I had the pleasure of presenting Miss Lilian Smith, the mechanism of whose Winchester repeater was explained to Her Majesty, who takes a remarkable interest in fire-arms. Young California spoke up gracefully and like a little woman. Then Nate Salsbury was commanded to the presence and introduced, and took his blushing honors with all the grace of the polished American gentleman he is. Next came Red Shirt, gorgeous in his war-paint and most splendiferous feather trappings. His proud bearing seemed to fetch the royal party immensely. And when he quietly declared that "he had come a long way to see Her Majesty, and felt glad," and strolled abruptly away with dignity spread all over him three inches thick, the Queen smiled appreciatively, as who should say, "I know a real Duke when I see him." Finally two squaws were summoned, and came racing across the arena, their little brown papooses slung behind them. Upon these royalty, unbending, "rained gracious influence." The papooses were handed up for inspection, and behaved themselves nicely while Her Majesty petted them. And so the Queen's visit came to an end, with a last command, expressed through Sir Henry Ponsonby, that a record of all she had seen should be sent on to Windsor. A great occasion, of which the mental photograph will long remain with me.

Statesmen at the Wild West

Of the statesmen and men otherwise eminent who visited the Wild West in these bright summer days—it was a wonderful summer for England—a partial list will be found elsewhere. One of the earliest was John Bright, to whose honored name no Englishman ever thinks of tacking the "Mister." The People's Tribune met with an unfortunate accident on entering the show, reminding one of William the Conqueror's when he made that awkward stumble on Hasting's beach, to the dismay of his followers, who thought it a bad omen, and rose exclaiming: "Lo, here have I already seized two handfuls of this English earth; let us go on, my bully boys, and rope in the remainder." That was distinctly clever. John Bright tripped over the rubber mat at my tent portal, and arose, grasping, not the English earth, but the end of his nose, which was bleeding. I was truly distressed at this awkward fall occurring to the venerated leader, and made him as comfortable as possible in my tent until he had got over the shock. Major Burke stood by with much heroism and a bottle of eau-de-cologne and bathed the afflicted spot until the illustrious patient felt all right and able to go to his seat. The news of the accident had spread through the auditorium, and when the "old man eloquent" made his appearance in his box, smiling and quite chipper again, the packed audience gave him three mighty cheers that made him laugh some more.

Lord Randolph Churchill had heard of the incident, and it was quite amusing to see him look at that mat next time he came to the show, gather his muscles together, and deliberately leap over it. A born humorist is his lordship, affectionately dubbed "Little Randy" by the conservative democracy, principally because *Mr. Punch* delights in depicting him as a whipper-snapper. After all he is not a short man, either in stature or in intellectual "change." He is a right smart politician and one of the pleasantest of the many pleasant English gentlemen it has been my good fortune to meet.

A Rib-Roast Breakfast, à la Indian, to Gen. Cameron

While receiving generous attention from the most prominent people of England, I was by no means neglected by my own countrymen, many of whom were frequent visitors to the Wild West Show and who otherwise added, by their presence and influence, much to the popularity of the show and myself as well. Hon. James G. Blaine, accompanied by his family, spent several hours with me in my tent and was a frequent visitor to the show. So, also, was Hon. Joseph Pulitzer, Chauncy M. De Pew, Lawrence Jerome, Murat Halstead, General Hawley, Simon Cameron, and many other distinguished Americans. So many prominent Americans of my acquaintance were in London at the time, that Mr. Salsbury and I decided to give several of our countrymen a novel entertainment that would serve the double purpose of regaling their appetites while affording an illustration of the wild habits of many Indian tribes. In pursuance of our resolve we invited Gen. Simon Cameron as the specially honored guest of the occasion, and about one hundred other Americans, including in the list all of those named above, to a Rib-roast Breakfast, which was to be prepared by the Indians after the manner of their cooking when in their native habitat.

At nine o'clock in the morning all the invited guests responded to the summons and came to our large dining tent that was gorgeously festooned and decorated for the occasion. Before the tent a fire had been made, around which grouped a number of Indian cooks. A hole had been dug in the ground and in this a great bed of coals was now made, over which was set a wooden tripod from which was suspended several ribs of beef. An Indian noted for his skill as a rib-roaster attended to the cooking by gently

THE INDIAN DANCE BEFORE MY GUESTS

moving the meat over the hot coals for nearly half an hour, when it was removed to the quarters and there jointed ready to be served. The guests were much interested in the process of cooking and were equally anxious to sample the product of Indian culinary art. Several long tables, *à la* barbecue style, were set upon which the *menu* was spread consisting of ribs of beef, Indian style, grubstakes, salmon, roast beef, roast mutton, ham, tongue, stewed chicken, lobster salad, American hominy and milk, corn, potatoes, cocoanut pie, apple pie, Wild West pudding, American pop corn and peanuts.

The whole of the Indian tribes in camp breakfasted with the visitors, squatting on straw at the end of the long dining tent. Each "brave" had a sharp white stake in front of him, on which he impaled his portion of rib when not gnawing it from his fingers. Some dozen ribs were cooked and eaten in this primitive fashion, civilized and savage methods of eating confronting each other. The thoroughly typical breakfast over, excellent speeches, chiefly of a humorous nature, were made by the honored guest, Gen. Cameron, and Chauncy M. De Pew, Mr. Lawrence Jerome, Murat Halsted, General Joe. Hawley, Justin McCarthy, M. P., Red Shirt, Mr. Salsbury and myself. After the speeches an Indian dance was given, and the guests finally withdrew sometime after noon, while a majority availed themselves of an invitation to witness the Wild West entertainment.

The Prince of Wales and His Royal Flush

Business continued to boom splendidly, and yet another excitement was in store for us. There came to Earl's Court, carried by a royal equerry, a further command from her Majesty conveying the royal pleasure that on the 20th of June a special morning exhibition of the Wild West should be given to the kingly and princely guests of Queen Victoria on the occasion of her Jubilee. This was the third entertainment given to royalty in private, and surely never before since the world commenced has such a gathering honored a public entertainment. Caesar and his captive monarchs, the Field of the Cloth of Gold—nothing in history can compare with that gathering of the mighty ones of the earth which honored our entertainment. The Queen was to treat them to a display of quite another kind in Westminster Abbey the following day; but the Wild West was beforehand with her Majesty as will be seen. I was getting fairly hardened to royalty by this time; I had exhibited before it; I had met it at private parties and at club-houses; and I had seen it in its best aspects, honoring and honored by communion with that other royalty of brains which holds high court in England as everywhere. But this was to be a knock-down in the royalty line—a regular wholesale consignment—a pack of cards all pictures and waited on by the brightest, best and bravest and most beautiful that all Europe and a good part of Asia could produce. The gathering of personages consisted of the King of Denmark, the King of Saxony, the King and Queen of the Belgians, and the King of Greece, the Crown Prince of Austria, the Prince and Princess of Saxe-Meiningen, the Crown Prince and Princess of Germany, the Crown Prince of Sweden and Norway, the Princess Victoria of Prussia, the Duke of Sparta, the Grand Duke Michael of Russia, Prince George of Greece, Prince Louis of Baden and last, but not least, the Prince and Princess of Wales with their family, besides a great host of lords and ladies innumerable.

Our good old Dead wood coach, "baptized in fire and blood" so repeatedly on the plains, had the honor of carrying on its time-honored timbers four kings and the Prince of Wales that day, during the attack of the red-skins. Said His Royal Highness to me, when the show was over:

"Colonel, you never held four kings like these before."

"I've held four kings," said I, "but four kings and the Prince of Wales makes a royal flush, such as no man ever held before."

I suppose my old poker-playing experiences were instinctively in the ascendant and prompted the retort. The Prince took it, and went off with that hair-trigger laugh of his that is so well known to his intimates. To their European majesties the joke was somewhat recondite, and I almost pitied the Prince as he tried to explain it in three languages to his wondering but obtuse auditors. They don't play poker yet at

GIVING ROYALTY A SPIN DURING AN ATTACK BY INDIANS

the continental courts, and come to think of it, the game *does* want a deal of learning before you get the hang of it properly. I hope their majesties enjoyed that ride, but the Indians put in their shooting with a lot of energy, and somehow the crowned heads appeared to be glad when it was over.

The Prince Presents Me with A Diamond Pin

The appended letter of thanks from Marlborough House after this interesting gathering will probably be of as much interest to my readers as it was to myself:

> Marlborough House,
> Pall Mall, S.W.

DEAR SIR:—Lieut.-General Sir Dighton Probyn, Comptroller and Treasurer of the Prince of Wales' household, presents his compliments to Colonel Cody and is directed by his Royal Highness to forward him the accompanying pin as a souvenir of the performance of the Wild West, which Colonel Cody gave before the Prince and Princess of Wales, the Kings of Denmark, Belgium, Greece and Saxony and other royal guests on Monday last, to all of whom, the Prince desires Sir Dighton Probyn to say, the entertainment gave great satisfaction.

LONDON, JUNE 22d, 1887

A further souvenir, which I shall ever highly prize, took the form of the pin already referred to—the Prince of Wales's feathers worked in diamonds, with the motto "Ich dien" ("I serve") beneath. The story of how this crest and motto were wrested from the King of Bohemia at Cressy by the Black Prince, son of Edward II, of England, will, perhaps, be familiar to my youthful readers.

The Princess Rides in the Deadwood Coach

The Prince and Princess and their sons and daughters were frequent visitors during our stay in London. On one occasion her Royal Highness determined to try the novel sensation of a ride in the old stage, and sent me an intimation of her desire. I went to the royal box to mention the exact time at which the coach would start, and found that her royal lord and master had weighty objections to any such proceeding. He may not have liked it over well himself, and seemed a little nervous. But "when a lady will, she will, and there's an end on't," as the old proverb says, and so the gentle Alexandra was booked for inside passage, and took it smilingly. Her spouse seemed much relieved when we delivered her up safe and sound after her exciting expedition;

for herself she seemed highly delighted, and thanked me effusively for the novel pleasure she had experienced.

The Princess's liking for the entertainment seemed to grow upon acquaintance.
I received one day a startling intimation to the effect that the Princess would that evening visit the show *incognita*. For a royal lady whose face is as well known in London
as that of Big Ben at Westminster this seemed considerably cool. Our manager, whose
duty it was to receive her, declared himself in a "middling tight fix." The hour came,
and with it the willful lady, and the Major assisted her from
her private carriage into the lobby.

"Your Royal Highness will not desire to use your
own box, perhaps?" he said.

"No, sir; your band will play the national anthem, and
then I am in plain view, you see, discovered. Is it not?"

This was charmingly said, in her pretty unidiomatic
English, but the gallant manager rubbed his chin.

"Has your Royal Highness a desire for any particular position?" he asked.

"Certainly, yes. Put me immediately amongst the people. I
like the people."

Then the manager "struck a bright idea." It was an off-night
for the newspaper men and the commodious press box was sacred
from intrusion. Into the press box accordingly he ushered the royal
lady and her attendant. The performance had hardly commenced
when—horror of horrors!—in came a triplet of hardy press men and
a lady. To the manager and myself alone of all our company was the
secret of the Princess's visit known. Consequently the attendants
ushered the new-comers into their usual seats without question and
closed the door behind them.

Presently to the manager "dancing on thorns," came one of the
newspaper boys: "Say, partner, will you mind saying who are our
companions? I really never saw such a likeness in all my life to—"

"I know what you are going to say," said the manager; "the resemblance really *is*
rather striking. But come along; I'll introduce you."

The thing had to be bluffed out somehow; and in due course the press men were
formally introduced to "Colonel and Mrs. Jones, friends of mine from Texas," by the
imperturbable manager, who believes in taking the bull by the horns.

The Princess took the joke with becoming gravity, although her companion
seemed horribly disturbed. She confessed afterwards that it was one of the pleasan-

PIN
PRESENTED
ME BY THE
PRINCE OF
WALES

test and funniest evenings she had ever spent in her life. As to the manager he was in a cold perspiration until he had steered his onerous charge through the departing crowd of sight-seers and seen her comfortably seated in her carriage. His attempt at a murmured apology was cut short by a silvery laugh, as the Princess remarked the "evening has been most enjoyable and the adventure one grand success," and so, as the Frenchmen say, "the incident closed itself."

Close of the London Season

And so amidst innumerable social junketings, feastings, and courtly functions which now seem like the glistening pageant of a fairy dream thrown suddenly athwart the memories of my war-like, rough-and-tumble earlier career, our London experiences drew to a successful close. We had been making "barrels of money"; but it had been hard work for all hands, doubly and trebly hard for me, living the life of a hard-working member of the company; responsible master of our singularly complicated gathering of wild spirits from the several regions of half-civilized America, north, west, and south, and greatest if pleasantest toil of all, the fêted guest of all that was rich and frivolous, royal and talented, great and Bohemian in that mighty mixed congeries of many-shaded humanity, London society. I wonder as I write how much of me is flesh and blood, and how much steel and leather, that I should have endured the strain without breaking down. A man wants hardening for a life on the plains; but he wants to be tanned and tempered, hammered and welded into adamant to stand the tension of such a life as mine during that summer season. We had all the elements of success, a continuity of delightful weather, unknown in England for thirty years before our coming; an appreciative community, the help of hundreds of kind friends in the press and in society, to whom my gratitude is and ever will be inexpressible; and lastly, a really first-rate entertainment that awoke a strongly sympathetic response in the generous public sentiment of the British nation. With one more extract I conclude this eventful epoch of our history. It is from the "Thunderer" of Printing-house square; the great *Times* itself, and will serve to fitly round off my story of our magnificent reception in the metropolis of Britain, with its 100 square miles of bricks and mortar, and its population of 5,000,000 souls (asserted). It was printed on Nov. 1, the day after our final triumphant performance:

"The Wild West Exhibition, which has attracted all the town to West Brompton for the last few months, was brought yesterday to an appropriate and dignified close. A meeting of representative Englishmen and Americans was held, under the presidency of Lord Lorne, in support of the movement for establishing a Court of Arbitration for the settlement of disputes between this country and the United States. At first sight it might seem to be a far cry from the Wild West to an International Court. Yet the connection is not really very remote. Exhibitions of American products and of a few scenes from the wilder phases of American life certainly tend in some degree at least to bring America nearer to England. They are partly cause and partly effect. They are the effect of increased and increasing intercourse between the two countries, and they tend to promote a still more intimate understanding. The two things, the Exhibition and the Wild West Show, have supplemented each other. Those who went to be amused often stayed to be instructed. It must be acknowledged that the show was the attraction which made the fortune of the Exhibition. Without Colonel Cody, his cowboys, and his Indians, it is conceivable that the Exhibition might have reproduced the Wild West in one feature at any rate—namely, its solitude—with rare fidelity. But the Wild West was irresistible. Colonel Cody, much to the astonishment of some of his more superfine compatriots, suddenly found himself the hero of the London season. Notwithstanding his daily engagements and his punctual fulfillment of them, he found time to go everywhere, to see everything, and to be seen by all the world. All London contributed to his triumph, and now the close of his show is selected as the occasion for promoting a great international movement with Mr. Bright, Lord Granville, Lord Wolseley, and Lord Lorne for its sponsors. Colonel Cody can achieve no greater triumph than this, even if he some day realizes the design attributed to him of running the Wild West Show within the classic precincts of the Coliseum at Rome."

To which last suggestion, all I have to reply is that if the Coliseum at Rome possessed the requisite accommodation for an enterprise of the magnitude of the Wild West more unlikely things might well happen than a visit by our combination to the city of the Seven Hills. Columbus was a Genoese, and there would be no irreverence to antiquity in presenting his Italian fellow-countrymen with a few phases in the history of that gigantic New World which he was the first to bring to the knowledge of the old.

Our Tour in "The Provinces"

A brief but successful occupancy of the Aston Lower Grounds, Birmingham, followed almost immediately upon our London triumphs. Birmingham, the headquarters of the British gun-making industry, the fancy metal trades and of innumerable branches of the lighter hardware crafts, together with its numerous surrounding towns responded nobly to our invitation. The news of our reception in London had gone before us, and we met with a prodigious welcome from the screw-makers, the teapot turners and the manufacturers of artificial jewelry and "Brummagem goods" in general. But with the drifting season there were signs that the weather was breaking. It was manifest that the Wild West must get under cover in winter quarters, and a mightier center than Birmingham was extending its arms to us farther north.

Manchester, with its surrounding net work of a hundred smaller but yet important towns—"Cottonopolis," as it is endearingly called by its denizens—was issuing pressing invitations. This powerful district resembles nothing so much as a still greater London, split and separated by the explosion of a bombshell. A population of some six million toilers in mine and mill, divided into communities of from 10,000 to 100,000 or so, yet linked to the great center by a spider's web of railways—such was the object of our next and perhaps most gigantic effort of all.

A Visit to Italy

During the period of preparation for opening the Wild West exhibition in Manchester, I took advantage of the spare time that was offered, and with my daughter, Arta, spent a well-earned vacation of two weeks in Italy. I say well-earned because from the day of opening our show in London until the close of our engagement in that city I had not missed a single one of the three hundred performances given, notwithstanding the unexampled social courtesies that I was compelled to observe, which kept me occupied nearly eighteen hours out of every twenty-four. At one time it had been the ambition of Mr. Salsbury and myself to give a Wild West exhibition in the ancient Coliseum of Rome, but an examination of the ruins and surroundings speedily convinced me that to make the attempt would be a vaulting ambition overleaping itself, and the idea was abandoned. I made a rather hasty tour of the more important cities of Italy, but can hardly admit that the trip was an enjoyable one on account of a constant realization of the necessity of my presence with the show, and the hurried manner in which I was compelled to make my visit. Accordingly, I returned to Manchester and helped prepare for opening the winter season there.

The English winter, if not subject to such intense frosts and other rigors as are known to the American climate, is yet an extremely trying season. Variety, it is said, is charming, but he must be an optimist indeed, who can be charmed with the mixture of weather which favored us during our stay in the great northern center. Rain, fog, frost, drizzle, snow and searching east wind followed each other in fantastic succession, not one of them staying long enough to assert itself as the prevalent weather, but giving us a very choice assortment of samples. We had prepared for this state of things, however. The Manchester race-course, which, by the way, is situated in the adjoining borough of Salford, on the banks of the inky ditch known as the Irwell, is made on a magnificent stretch of green sward easily accessible from all parts of the district. At the race meetings which occur several times in the course of each year, it is not uncommon for 80,000 or 100,000 persons to assemble on this tract of land. Here, then, I decided to pitch our tents and go into winter quarters. In the short space of two months the largest theater ever seen in the world was erected by an enterprising firm of Manchester builders, together with a commodious building attached to it for the accommodation of the troop, whose tents and tepees were erected under its shelter, the whole of the structures being comfortably heated by steam and illuminated by the electric light. One great advantage of the race-course was the large and splendidly appointed range of stables, generally used for the accommodation of the horses of the English turf, which were placed at our disposal. The buildings in which Ormonde, Ben. d'Or, Robert the Devil, and a thousand other world-famed equine wonders had taken their rest and refreshment, were now appropriated to the comfort of our bronchos, mustangs and other four-footed coadjutors. Of the vast theater itself, and the novel style of entertainment which I had the pleasure of introducing to the hard-working millions and the cotton and iron princes of the North of England, no more vivid picture can be presented than that drawn by the reporter of the *Sunday Chronicle*, a paper of enormous influence in the wide area whose people we intended to attract. I may premise that the splendid scenery used upon our mammoth stage was from the brush of Mr. Matt. Morgan, an English artist whose name is familiar to Americans. The scenes, which cost us $40,000, were from nature, and enabled us to combine the painted full effects of a gigantic stage display with the free movement of our 250 horsemen upon the open plain. Says the reporter:

A Description of the Show

"A vast amphitheater, shaped somewhat like a horseshoe magnet, with giant proscenium stretched across its poles; an enormous stage, constructed without flooring, the scenery and set pieces of which are let down upon the bare earth; a drama, dealing with a period of five hundred years, in which nearly three hundred men and women, and as many horses, buffaloes, and other four-footed creatures take part, performed in great measure immediately under the eyes of the spectators, on a huge plain level with the stage and drifting into a perspective upon it—such is a general description of the performance which was given for the first time yesterday afternoon by Colonel Cody and his magnificent troupe. The theater, brilliantly lighted and well warmed throughout, is like nothing else ever constructed in this country. The seats, accommodating nearly ten thousand persons, are ranged in tiers, from the pew-like private boxes in front to a height of forty feet or so; and the distance from the extreme end of the auditorium to the back of the stage is so great that a horseman galloping across the whole area diminishes by natural perspective until the spectator is fairly cheated into the idea that the journey is to be prolonged until the rider vanishes in the pictured horizon. The illusion, indeed, is so well managed and complete, the boundless plains and swelling prairies are so vividly counterfeited, that it is difficult to resist the belief that we are really gazing over an immense expanse of country from some hillside in the far West. The pictures, from the brush of the talented Matt. Morgan, are singularly beautiful in themselves, and it only needs the constantly varying groups of living men and animals in front of them to complete the charm.

"In arranging the latest development of their exhibition, Messrs. Cody and Salsbury have undertaken no trifling task. Besides the displays of horsemanship and feats of shooting with which the notices of their doings in London have familiarized the public, they have determined to present the story of the development of the American Continent from primeval times until the present day. It is a play without a plot and without dialogue, unless the clever and humorous lecture of Mr. Frank Richmond, the 'orator' of the establishment, can be called such. This gentleman occupies a lofty pulpit to the left of the proscenium, and it says much for the acoustic properties of the gigantic building that his voice can be heard so distinctly as it is. The drama, however, has no lack of coherence, and the interest of the spectators is unflaggingly sustained throughout the long succession of exciting scenes from the introduction to the close.

"By the plan adopted the entertainment is divided into 'episodes,' of which the first, after the preliminary of a general personal introduction of the troupe, is the Forest Primeval, in which

> The murmuring pines and the hemlocks
> Bearded with moss, and in garments green,
> Indistinct in the twilight,
> Stand like Druids of old.

It is midnight, and wild animals lie scattered about in their lairs. With the opening dawn we make the acquaintance of the Red Indian as he used to be before the white man crowded him out of his possessions. At sunrise—a beautifully stage-managed effect—we have the meeting of two Indian tribes, who execute a friendly dance to a quaint barbaric measure. Then comes a courier with notice of the approach of a hostile tribe intent upon massacre and the collection of scalps. The attack is delivered with terrific vigor, and the battle that ensues is an unequalled picture of savage warfare.

"The Second Episode deals with the landing of the Pilgrim Fathers from the Mayflower on Plymouth Rock, with which the era of civilization is held to commence. Here, again, the scenery is remarkably fine, and the characters in the tableau are

COWBOY LASSOING AN INDIAN

characteristically dressed in the short capes, steeple-crowned hats, and sad-colored Puritan raiment of religious England in their day. From this, amidst appropriate music from Mr. Sweeny's Cowboy Band, the scene changes to Episode No. 8, the rescue from death of that heroic bearer of an honored name, John Smith, by that beauteous Indian princess, Pocahontas. Now ensues a most interesting delineation of Indian manners and customs, from the wedding to the war dance, by the whole of the Indian forces, under the command of Red Shirt himself.

"With the Fourth Episode we reach more stirring scenes. The picture, composed of innumerable front sets and a most lovely background, by Matt Morgan represents the prairie, with a drinking pool, or 'lick,' in the foreground, to which the wild buffaloes come to slake their thirst. In pursuit of the great game comes Buffalo Bill himself, on his famous horse, Old Charlie, who has covered one hundred miles in less than ten hours, conducting an emigrant train of white folks, with wagons, horsemen, women, and children, and all the accessories of a march across the wilderness. In the gathering twilight they camp around the pool, the fires are lit, and a clever performance of the 'Virginia horseback reel' takes place. Subsequently, with the gathering darkness, the camp sinks into slumber, and for awhile all is still. Then comes a piece of stage managing, which more nearly approaches the terrible than anything ever yet attempted in this country. A red streak upon the horizon gives warning that some unwonted danger is approaching the sleeping folks; the glow broadens and deepens, and seems to creep gradually over the pictured miles of open country, until the slumbering people are roused with the appalling intelligence that the prairie is on fire. The conflagration approaches nearer and nearer, until the whole landscape appears one lurid mass of incandescence, and the roaring flames leap down upon the foreground with wild fury, threatening all concerned with a horrible death. The men endeavor to stamp out the conflagration with their rugs and blankets, and in the midst of the horror there swoops upon them a maddened rush of wild animals, flying from the fire, and a 'stampede' ensues in all its terrors. This scene, which reflects the highest credit upon the stage management, is one of the grandest ever placed before the public, and fairly baffles description.

"Next ensues some cowboy and Mexican vaquero business with bucking horses, throwing the lasso, in which that handsome cavalier and King of the Cowboys, Buck Taylor, figures conspicuously; and we get some extraordinary feats in shooting by Johnny Baker, the Cowboy Kid, all of which is very novel and amusing. And so we arrive at the Fifth Episode, the scene of which is a cattle ranch in the Wild West, with a real log hut and all appropriate surroundings. The settlers, after an interesting representation of camp life in the wilds, are attacked by Indians, and a fierce battle ensues, which is waged with varying fortunes until it ends in the rescue of the besieged party by a band of whites, and the flight of the Redskins. An interlude is occupied by some fancy rifle shooting by Miss Lillian Smith, 'the California girl,' and then we come to another grand historical tableau in the Sixth Episode, wherein is set out the routine of a military camp on the frontier. The unfortunate General Custer, occupying with his regiment a stockade or log fort, receives intimation of the discovery of a camp of hostile Indians by his scouts. 'Boots and saddle' is sounded, and the troops move off to the second scene, which is the camp of Sitting Bull and his braves on the Little Big Horn River. The ambush and subsequent massacre of the whole of the gallant band of white men is presented with vivid realism, and the battle-field by night, which closes the episode, develops in its fan horrors what has been fitly called 'the reddest page of savage history.'

"A brilliant display of shooting on foot and on horseback by Buffalo Bill himself is now given in the arena, and the magical promptitude with which glass balls and other small objects are shattered before his never-erring aim while riding at full speed must be seen to be believed. In this remarkable exhibition, as in the other shooting performances, the iron fireproof curtain is made to do duty as a background or target, and the whole performance may be warranted to take the conceit out of any ordinary marksman. It is nothing less than marvellous.

LASSOING HORSES IN THE WILD WEST SHOW

"The Seventh Episode, which marks a still later period of frontier life, is per-haps the most exciting and picturesque of the whole entertainment. The first scene is a mining camp, 'Deadwood City,' in the Black Hills, with the 'Wild West Tavern' in the foreground, and we are treated *seriatim* to the incidents of a miners' holiday, with a shooting match, the arrival of the pony express, and a frontier duel, with its characteristic ending of 'another man for breakfast.' Then comes the departure of the Deadwood Coach, and the scene changes to a 'canyon' or rocky pass in the hills. The Deadwood Coach with its freight of passengers, guards and 'shotgun messengers,' is fallen upon in the canyon by Indians, and a stubborn battle occurs, in which the pas-sengers are likely to succumb, when they are rescued by the sudden appearance of Buffalo Bill and his Cowboy cavalry.

"It will be seen that there is no lack of exciting business in all this, and the con-sumption of gunpowder is enormous. The members of the company go at their work with appalling zest, and their picturesque mingling of spirited horses, quaint cos-tumes and warlike impedimenta, in all the wild confusion of a frontier melee, is bril-liantly effective. In the third scene of this episode we return to the mountain village, in which the climax of scenic effect is reached by the production of a genuine cyclone. Powerful wind-making machinery has been put down for this purpose, and a blast is delivered upon the stage strong enough to rend the log cabins to pieces, and scatter their fragments, together with wagons, camp furniture, and even human beings from one side of the stage to the other. The howling of the tornado and the disastrous effect of its resistless current are realistically presented. How it is done is, of course, a stage secret, but there is no gainsaying the magnificent completeness with which the hurricane gets in its work and reduces the camp of the little mining community to chaos. This brings the performance to an effective close."

The Crowd at Our Opening Performance

As a "send-off" to the new departure we had invited the whole of the beauty, rank and fashion of Manchester and the surrounding towns to a gratis performance of this program two days before our opening date. The mayors, town councils, corporation officials, prominent merchants and manufacturers, bishops and clergy of all denominations, and an able-bodied horde of pressmen came down in their thousands. From Liverpool across country through Leeds and York to Hull and Newcastle, and from Carlisle as far south as Birmingham, everybody of consequence was present, and the immense building was filled to its utmost capacity. The notice above quoted will show that all had reason to be pleased, and the story they had to tell of the marvelous things to be witnessed at the Wild West spread with lightning rapidity through every town from which they had gathered together. The consequence was that from our opening day it was often difficult to cope with the throngs who presented themselves at afternoon and evening performances, alike to feast their eyes upon the dangers and the glories of America's development. Despite the dreary winter weather, or perhaps because of it, the well-lighted, well-warmed "Temple of Buffalo Bill and Thespis," as somebody called it, was the constant resort of pleasure-seeking throngs.

Amongst other demands upon our seating space came scores of requisitions from the heads of schools and charitable institutions, which are thickly scattered through the mining, weaving and spinning towns of Bolton, Bury, Rochdale, Oldham, Stalybridge and a hundred more, as well as those in Manchester and Salford. "What is the lowest price at which you can allow us to give our little waifs a treat?" was the burden of I don't know how many letters. My invariable reply was "Let us know your numbers and come on Wednesday afternoon, which is the only time when we are not over-crowded, and we will fix you up for nothing at all, if we have to turn money away for you." I lay claim to no credit for generosity in this particular, for each invitation of the kind increased our popularity to a surprising extent, and it was only a further example of the good policy of "casting your bread upon the waters." Amongst these juvenile visitors were the 100 inmates of Chetham's College, a Manchester charitable institution dating back to the times of Henry VI, the boys of which are still quartered in the fine old Gothic building erected during the Wars of the Roses, over a hundred years before Columbus turned his vessel's prow to the westward and steered for nowhere in particular, to the great horror of the Old World navigators of his time.

During our stay in Cottonopolis I found the same ungrudging and overwhelming social hospitality that had tried my physical powers so severely in the capital. "Thrones, powers, dominions," and dynastic royalty are of course conspicuous by their absence from this vast manufacturing, money-making heart of Northern activity. But that sublimer royalty of commerce, of invention of fire and steel, of ever-flying shuttle and spindle here holds high state, and its entertainments are princely in scope and hearty in their hospitality. They have a pride of their own, too, these coal and cotton lords and self-made millionaires. The man himself and the great things he has done for humanity are held in more esteem than long descent or the glamours of inherited wealth. I found here, in fact, a closer resemblance to the natural dignity of the American citizen than I had experienced elsewhere in England. My invitation list would occupy more space than I can afford.

Presented with a Rifle

One event, amongst my endeavors to make some return for this unbounded stream of hospitality, caused a considerable sensation in the district, from its novelty. It had been determined by the artistic, dramatic, and literary gentlemen of Manchester to make me a public presentation of a magnificent rifle, decked in flowers and gaily adorned with ribbons, and the event having got wind in London, the *elite* of the metropolitan *literati*, headed by Sir Somers Vine and including representatives of all the great American journals, secured a special train and ran up to Manchester, some hundred strong, to grace the ceremony with their presence. The happy thought struck me of inviting the whole crowd of local celebrities and London visitors to what for them would be an entirely original lay-out. This was a camp dinner, with fried oysters, Boston pork and beans, Maryland chicken, and other American dishes, and a real Indian "rib-roast" as the *piece de resistance.*

The presentation, which took place in the arena, being over, the banquet was held in the race-course pavilion. The Mayor of Salford and a number of civic dignitaries from both Manchester and the neighboring borough graced the table with their presence; United Stales Consul Moffat of London honored me with his company and Consul Hale of Manchester—a gentleman held in high and well deserved respect by the whole of the rich and powerful community amongst whom he resides and labors—made the speech of the evening. Nate Salsbury, as the vice-chairman, simply excelled himself; and the comments of the English guests upon the novel and to them outlandish fare they were consuming were highly amusing to us of the American party. I have reason to believe that the corn-cake, hominy, and other American fixings, were a complete revelation to them. The rib-roast, served in tin platters and eaten in the fingers, without knives or forks, was a source of huge wonderment. I reckon that English men never toasted the American flag more heartily, and for a week afterwards the press of the country was dilating on the strange and savage doings at the Wild West camp. A newspaper genius of Manchester, who seems to have studied his Longfellow to some purpose, gushed into blank verse with the following epic, entitled:

The Rib-Roast of Pa-He-Haska

Mr. Editor.—
Should you ask me whence this poem.
Whence this yarn of tangled meaning,
With its odor of Havana,
And its marks of Mumm's best vintage
Staining every side of copy,
Staining text and staining margin—
I should answer, I should tell you:
From the festive board of William,
From the feast of Pa-he-haska,
Long-haired lord of many cowboys—
Buffalo Bill, the mighty hunter
From across the Gitche-Gumee
("Herring-pond" is what *we* call it).
When he fed the London Pressmen
On the Muskoday, the meadow
On the Manchester big Racecourse.
★ ★ ★ ★ ★ ★ ★ ★ ★
In the lodges of the Turfites,
There we gathered in the evening.
In the gloaming, O my darling!
When the *matinee* was over.

Many chieftains came from London,
Many from the heap big village,
Pioneered by stout Tom Burnside,

At the top end of the table
Sat the noble Pa-he-haska—
Buffalo Bill in all his glory!
Mighty Moffat, London Consul
And the puissant Mayor of Salford
Sachem of the model borough,
With his elders grave in council
(Not too grave when flows the grape-juice),
Flanked the chieftain on his right hand,
Fed like men well used to camp life,
Used to all a Hunter's manners!

On his left was Hale, the Consul,
From his eagle eyes out flashing
Uncle Sam's reflected glory!
In the vice-chair sat Nathaniel—
"Nate" they call him in the programmes,
Star-tongued Salsbury, William's partner,
Wary wielder of straight language.
Stalwart John of Arizona—
Major Burke, sun-browned and war-scarred,
Like Ke-neu, the great war-eagle
Hovered round about the table—
Kept the laughing wine-cup flowing.
Unk-ta-hee, the god of water
Didn't have a look-in at us!

With his waist of grand dimensions—
Equatorial enlargement—
On some cheeks the Pressman's totem
Oza-wa-beek, or the brass-mark,
Glowed, as round the board they gathered,
While the Manchester contingent,
Merry drivers of the goose-quill—
Of the quills of Wa-be-wawa—
Mingled with their Cockney brothers,
Mingled, too, with many Yankees
From across the Gitche-Gumee—
Uncle Sam's ink-slinging nephews.

If but distantly related
Yet in universal kinship
Held by bonds of gratis luncheon.

* * * * * * * *

Hominy and picalilli,
Went their way to bright Po-ne-mah.
To the Land of the Hereafter.

All the while a rhythmic plashing—
Mu-way-aush-ka, sound of sea waves!—
Pop of corks, and clink of glasses,
Told the dark-eyed Pa-he-haska—
Told the stalwart Colonel Cody
That his guests were not neglectful:
They could stand it long as he could,
Possibly might stand it longer!

* * * * * * * *

Shall I tell you of the speeches,
Of the pow-wow and palaver?
How the Mayor pledg'd Buffalo William,
How the Consul praised his valor,
Told how in the fight he'd met him,
On the field of death—of Pau-guk?

And the store of food outlandish
Disappeared before the Pressmen:
Dish by dish in swift destruction
Melted in the purple distance.
Bean soup first and then fried oysters;
Ribs of Pez-he-kee, the bison,
Served on plates of tin and garnished
With the sweet corn, the Mon-da-min—
Eaten in true savage fashion;
Knife and fork alike forbidden—
Gnaw the bone and suck your fingers.
That's the way to cop the flavor—
Of the noble redskin's rib-roast.

Pork and beans, that's Boston's glory.
Buck wheat cakes and thick molasses
Looming through the pale Puk-wana—
Through the clouds of much tobacco?

* * * * * * * *

No; I'll spare my paleface kinsmen
All the pain of that recital,
Just as I'd not rather dwell on
Certain subsequent proceedings;
Or our feelings in the morning,
When the med'cine men, the Me-das,
Gave us physic antibilious
So that we might keep our end up,
Keep our end up, and look sober.

* * * * * * * *

Gone are all those London persons.
Swept they southward, wild and boozy,
Like the cloud-wrack of a tempest,
Like the withered leaves of autumn
Scattered by Wild West tornado;
And their Shaw-shaws, their big swallows,

How Nate Salsbury's health, twice toasted,
Made him feel done brown on both sides.
How Red Shirt, the fighting chieftain,
Spoke in paragraphic Choctaw,
Telling us, as 'twas translated,
That he loved his pale-face brothers
Better than he loved his dinner,
And would meet us up in heaven—
In the Land of bright Po-ne-mah?—
(Red Shirt doesn't seem to know us,
Has not seen us paint the town red!)—
How the Pressmen all responded
"Ugh!" which means in English "Rather!"
How we pledged the noble chieftain
Till we saw two Red Shirts looming—

Now mop up the damp in Fleet-street,
Mop up all superfluous moisture.

Buffalo William still is with us,
So's Buck Taylor, so is Red Shirt,
And the Major's convalescing
Bet your life, he's still on deck here!
Still the Wild West Show is booming.
Booming just as it deserves to,
If I say the thing that is not,
Call me Ya-goo, call me liar!

But whene'er that feed's repeated,
Call me Early, Major darling,
Call me not too late for dinner!

English Love of Sport Illustrated

Good Friday came at last in the midst of our flood-tide of success, and I determined to devote the afternoon of the general holiday to a change of program. By the courtesy of the directors we secured the use of the Manchester race-track for a series of open-air horse races and athletic sports by the members of the company, red and white, including hurdle-races, bare-backed horsemanship, and so forth. The hold we had gained upon the popular appreciation, and the eagerness with which an Englishman starts at the mere mention of a horse-race were never more thoroughly evidenced. The day was ushered in with gloom and weeping skies, and our hearts sank within us as we realized that Jupiter Pluvius was sticking to us worse than a brother and had turned on a special watering-pot for the occasion. The downpour increased as the morning wore on, and at three o'clock, the hour for commencement, the weather was simply poisonous. Both Major Burke and I were in despair, but presently we had reason to rub our eyes, and our feelings of depression gave way to astonishment. From all parts, in carriages, omnibuses, horse-cars, and on foot a huge concourse of sport-loving Britons, braving the fury of the elements, commenced to pour in upon us and in a short time our money-takers, at the six entrances to the race-ground, were wrestling for dear life with the eager throngs who fought for admission. A total attendance of nearly 30,000 was recorded, and as a reward for their fortitude the weather presently cleared up and kept fine during the progress of the sports. Again we had to register a success, and the day of our first *al fresco* entertainment in Manchester is marked with a white stone in the records of the camp.

Amongst the many pleasant memories of our stay in Manchester, I shall especially cherish the hospitality extended to me by the Freemasons, who muster very strongly in the district, and at whose lodges I was frequently an honored guest. A mark of especial honor from this occult and powerful body was a public presentation of a magnificent gold watch, in the name of the Freemasons of England, by Worshipful Master ——, after a performance of the Wild West. Amongst the troops of friends whom I have made in the old country, I am delighted to record that I am now and forever solid with the great and generous body of English Masons, whose Grand Master is the Prince of Wales himself.

With such little amenities our labors were enlivened and our sojourn in the smoky city made very pleasant to us. We found that each week our friendships were extending and the kindly people began to regard us more and more as their neighbors and the Wild West as an established institution amongst them. But our engagements in the land of the Stars and Stripes were fixed and unalterable as the laws of the Medes and Persians; and though the opening of bright spring weather was bringing an extraordinary pressure of business upon us, it was necessary to tear ourselves away.

Honored by the Mayor of Salford

Our season in Manchester was a grand success in every way, during which I had made so many pleasant acquaintances among the citizens that notwithstanding my longing for home and America, it was with many painful feelings that we prepared to take our departure. A few days before taking leave of the scene of our magnificent triumphs I received the following letter from the Mayor of Salford:

MANCHESTER, March 9th, 1888

DEAR SIR:—It may interest you to know that I have named three streets on the New Barnes estate, on the north side of the Race-course, as follows: Cody street; Buffalo street; and Bill street, and plans for their construction will be submitted to the Salford corporation shortly.

These names will perpetuate the names of yourself and your show after your departure from Salford.

Yours truly,

Joshua Bury

The Hon. W. F. Cody,

Wild West Show, Salford

All the Manchester papers contained, on the 19th of April, generous notices of the action of Mayor Bury in thus perpetuating my memory among the good people of his populous district. As a sample of the press comments I extract the following from the Manchester *Courier:*

BUFFALO BILL'S ROAD, SALFORD.—Adjoining the Wild West Show at New Barnes, and between there and the cemetery, the contractor for the Ship Canal is busy converting acres of low-lying, and in some places swampy, land into good building land by placing thereon the "spoil" obtained from the big Salford dock. Within the next decade great changes in the district are manifestly impending. Long streets and broad must be formed, one of the leading and main of which is to be appropriately named Buffalo Bill's road. When completed in the near future, it will be a lengthy, broad, and busy avenue for traffic from the Ship Canal banks near Mode Wheel, into Salford. The road will commence at a point near where the buffalo, elk, etc., are at present housed, on the west side of the Wild West Show, and will extend along the boundary of the Race-course, in a due south-westerly direction, for nearly 1,000 yards. The local perpetuation of the name of Buffalo Bill and of his remarkable entertainment is thus ensured. It is expected that the Hon. W. F. Cody (Buffalo Bill) will perambulate the site of the intended road previous to his departure for New York at the beginning of next month.

A Magnificent Ovation

On Monday evening May 1st, we gave the last indoor representation, in the presence of a vast and one of the most enthusiastic audiences I ever appeared before; bouquets were presented to various members of the company and when I appeared I met with one of the warmest receptions of my life: bouquets were thrown, handed and carried into the arena to me while the vast audience cheered, waved hats, umbrellas and handkerchiefs, jumped upon their feet, and in fact the scene was very suggestive of a pandemonium. It was fully five minutes before the noise subsided sufficiently to enable us to proceed with the performance.

Every act went with a rush and a cheer, and was received by cries of "bravo," "well done," etc. At the close of the exhibition calls were made for Red Shirt and myself, in response to which I thanked my patrons and assured them that the recollection of that evening's display of kindness would ever be fresh in my memory. Cries of "bravo Bill" and the singing of "For he's a jolly good fellow" by the entire audience brought the demonstration to a close.

On Tuesday afternoon I was given a benefit by the race-course people, on which occasion I concluded to give our outdoor performance on the race-course and despite the unfavorable weather the turn-stiles showed that nearly 50,000 people had paid admission to the grounds. This audience, like the one in the building the previous evening, was also very enthusiastic and the people seemed to vie with each other in showering applause upon the various acts and features.

A Race for $2,500

Our Wild West performances in Manchester were now at a close but having two or three days to spare I concluded to accept a challenge made some days previously by Mr. B. Goodall, a noted horse breeder of Altrincham, for an international ten-mile race between his English thoroughbreds and my American bronchos, for £500 a side. The riders were J. Latham for Goodall and Tony Esquivel for me, and the conditions were that each rider should change horses without assistance at the completion of each half mile. The afternoon was fine with the exception of one fierce though fleeting rain storm. At five minutes to three o'clock thirteen of our bronchos, saddled with heavy cow-boy saddles, were brought into the enclosure and about ten minutes later nine English thoroughbreds made their appearance. The men mounted their first horses at 3:20 and got away well, Latham at once taking the lead. The Englishman effected his first change with an advantage but on the next occasion he lost this and Tony went to the front. Latham, however, gained a little for some succeeding minutes. There was no question of the speed of his horses, but Tony was more adroit in changing, and before many laps were over he led the Englishman by a good two furlongs. Then for a time Tony lost ground but Latham never succeeded in overhauling him and he passed the post 300 yards ahead, having made the remarkable time of twenty-one minutes. Wild enthusiasm was manifested throughout the race by the 20,000 spectators and at the termination of their arduous task both victorious Tony and defeated Latham were loudly cheered.

An Enthusiastic Farewell

On Friday morning May 4th, at 11 A.M., amid the cheers, well wishes and hand shaking of the vast crowd who had gathered to see us depart, we pulled slowly out of the Windsor Bridge station of the Lancashire and Yorkshire Railway en route by special passenger train for Hull, where after giving our farewell English performance we were to embark for home. The time of the arrival of our train at the various stations had become generally known, and all along the entire route we were met by vast crowds who cheered and wished us God speed. Upon our arrival at Hull the crowd was so large that it was necessary to send for a squad of police to enable us to make our way through them from the station to the conveyances. On Saturday afternoon, May 5th, we gave our farewell performance in England, at Hull, before an enormous crowd and that evening at 9 o'clock our entire effects were aboard the good ship *Persian Monarch* which, under the command of the brave, gallant and courteous Captain Bristow, was to leave her moorings at 3 A.M. the next morning for New York. We had chartered the ship for this trip and had everything to ourselves, and all evening the vast crowds who lined the docks cheered, sang songs and wished us *bon voyage*. A great many even remained until our departure and went wild with excitement when they saw us as a company leave their shores perhaps for ever.

A Pathetic Incident at Sea

The homeward voyage was marked with one very distressing and pathetic incident to me in the loss of my favorite horse Charlie, that I had ridden for fifteen years in sun-shine and in storm, in days of adversity as well as of prosperity, and to whose fleetness of foot I owed my life on more than one occasion when pursued by Indians. He stood the voyage very well, apparently, until May 14th, and even on the morning of that day when I visited him he seemed to be as well as usual.

A few minutes after leaving him, however, a groom ran to me and told me he had a chill. We did everything we could for him, but it was useless. He had lung fever, and after three days' illness he died. We could almost understand each other, and I felt very deeply. The sailors stitched him up in canvas and he lay all day Thursday, the 17th, on deck, covered with the American flag. At 8 o'clock in the evening we dropped the body, properly weighted, into the ocean. I did think of bringing him on here and burying him in his native soil, but finally concluded not to do so.

Our Arrival in New York Harbor

We arrived off New York harbor some time during the night of the 19th and by day-light of the 20th steamed up toward Staten Island, where we were to debark. The reception accorded us is thus graphically described by the New York *World*:

"The harbor has probably never known a more picturesque scene than was wit-nessed yesterday morning, when the Persian Monarch steamed up from Quarantine, with Buffalo Bill standing on the captain's bridge, his tall and striking figure clearly outlined and his long hair waving in the wind, with the gaily painted and blanketed Indians leaning over the ship's rail, with the flags of all nations fluttering from the masts and connecting cables, and the band playing 'Yankee Doodle' with a vim and enthusiasm which faintly indicated the joy felt by everybody connected with the Wild West exhibition, including the musicians, over the sight of home. The stolid Indians had lost their stolidity, and the white men on board declared that from the time the rising sun had enabled the redskins to discover America, or that part of it known as Staten Island, unwonted bustle and excitement had reigned supreme.

"Cut Meat, American Bear, Flat Iron, Tall Horse, Kills Plenty and scores more of chiefs, braves and squaws hugged the ship's side and watched every movement of the accompanying tugs until the great vessel was towed up alongside the long wharf at Tompkinsville, and the huzzas of two thousand small boys and the noisy excitement of what seemed to be Staten Island's entire population. And it was a great day for Staten Island. So far as is known the Persian Monarch is the first great ocean steamer which has ever landed there, and this, taken in connection with the unusual nature of her passengers and her cargo, furnished abundant reason for the greatest possible commotion, excitement and disturbance whereof Mr. Wiman's small kingdom is capable.

"All the teamsters for miles around had been engaged to carry the outfit of the exhibition and of the exhibitors across the island to Erastina, and the wharf was in consequence a confused commingling of express wagons, butcher carts, carpenter's wagons and other kinds of vehicles, with horses attached generally on their haunches, in response to the excited demands of vociferous drivers. If this scene needed any further animation it was provided by the small boys dodging imminent death, and scores of pretty girls in their Sunday best, scurrying away from out the reach of the horses' indiscriminate hoofs.

"The landing was at last effected, and Buffalo Bill, with his daughter and Major Burke, the general manager of the Wild West, Col. Ochiltree, George Trimble Davidson and several reporters, came up to the city on the tugboat Charles Stickney. Nate Salsbury, Col. Cody's partner, remained on the island and during the day the Indians and cowboys, with their tents, the Indian ponies and bucking horses, the Deadwood coach and emigrant wagons and all the paraphernalia of the show were transferred to Erastina."

"I cannot describe my joy upon stepping again on the shore of beloved America. Though I had received such honors while abroad as few persons have been favored with, and scored a triumph, both socially and professionally, that may well excite my pride, yet "there is no place like home," nor is there a flag like the old flag.

With the happiness of returning to my own country again came a double portion of joy in meeting with so many old friends whose arms opened to welcome me. But of the particular pleasures of these glad meetings it does not become me to speak now, since the space at my disposal is already exhausted.

The following letter, which I received from General Sherman, will serve to show the influence of the Wild West Exhibitions in London, in forging closer ties of friendship, binding the mother country to her brawny and intellectual offspring, our own beloved America. In this letter the General concurs in the sentiments expressed in the